Visual Basic® 6 Master Reference

Visual Basic® 6
Master Reference

Clayton Walnum

IDG Books Worldwide, Inc.

An International Data Group Company

Foster City, CA ■ Chicago, IL ■ Indianapolis, IN ■ New York, NY

Visual Basic® 6 Master Reference

Published by
IDG Books Worldwide, Inc.
An International Data Group Company
919 E. Hillsdale Blvd., Suite 400
Foster City, CA 94404
www.idgbooks.com (IDG Books Worldwide Web site)

Library of Congress Catalog Card Number: 98-75530

ISBN: 0-7645-3253-7

Printed in the United States of America

10 9 8 7 6 5 4 3 2 1

1P/QU/QS/ZZ/FC

Distributed in the United States by IDG Books Worldwide, Inc.

Distributed by Macmillan Canada for Canada; by Transworld Publishers Limited in the United Kingdom; by IDG Norge Books for Norway; by IDG Sweden Books for Sweden; by Woodslane Pty. Ltd. for Australia; by Woodslane (NZ) Ltd. for New Zealand; by Addison Wesley Longman Singapore Pte Ltd. for Singapore, Malaysia, Thailand, Indonesia, and Korea; by Norma Comunicaciones S.A. for Colombia; by Intersoft for South Africa; by International Thomson Publishing for Germany, Austria, and Switzerland; by Toppan Company Ltd. for Japan; by Distribuidora Cuspide for Argentina; by Livraria Cultura for Brazil; by Ediciencia S.A. for Ecuador; by Ediciones ZETA S.C.R. Ltda. for Peru; by WS Computer Publishing Corporation, Inc., for the Philippines; by Unalis Corporation for Taiwan; by Contemporanea de Ediciones for Venezuela; by Computer Book & Magazine Store for Puerto Rico; by Express Computer Distributors for the Caribbean and West Indies. Authorized Sales Agent: Anthony Rudkin Associates for the Middle East and North Africa.

For general information on IDG Books Worldwide's books in the U.S., please call our Consumer Customer Service department at 800-762-2974. For reseller information, including discounts and premium sales, please call our Reseller Customer Service department at 800-434-3422.

For information on where to purchase IDG Books Worldwide's books outside the U.S., please contact our International Sales department at 317-596-5530 or fax 317-596-5692.

For consumer information on foreign language translations, please contact our Customer Service department at 800-434-3422, fax 317-596-5692, or e-mail rights@idgbooks.com.

For information on licensing foreign or domestic rights, please phone +1-650-655-3109.

For sales inquiries and special prices for bulk quantities, please contact our Sales department at 650-655-3200 or write to the address above.

For information on using IDG Books Worldwide's books in the classroom or for ordering examination copies, please contact our Educational Sales department at 800-434-2086 or fax 317-596-5499.

For press review copies, author interviews, or other publicity information, please contact our Public Relations department at 650-655-3000 or fax 650-655-3299.

For authorization to photocopy items for corporate, personal, or educational use, please contact Copyright Clearance Center, 222 Rosewood Drive, Danvers, MA 01923, or fax 978-750-4470.

is a trademark under exclusive license to IDG Books Worldwide, Inc., from International Data Group, Inc.

ABOUT IDG BOOKS WORLDWIDE

Welcome to the world of IDG Books Worldwide.

IDG Books Worldwide, Inc., is a subsidiary of International Data Group, the world's largest publisher of computer-related information and the leading global provider of information services on information technology. IDG was founded more than 30 years ago by Patrick J. McGovern and now employs more than 9,000 people worldwide. IDG publishes more than 290 computer publications in over 75 countries. More than 90 million people read one or more IDG publications each month.

Launched in 1990, IDG Books Worldwide is today the #1 publisher of best-selling computer books in the United States. We are proud to have received eight awards from the Computer Press Association in recognition of editorial excellence and three from Computer Currents' First Annual Readers' Choice Awards. Our best-selling ...For Dummies® series has more than 50 million copies in print with translations in 31 languages. IDG Books Worldwide, through a joint venture with IDG's Hi-Tech Beijing, became the first U.S. publisher to publish a computer book in the People's Republic of China. In record time, IDG Books Worldwide has become the first choice for millions of readers around the world who want to learn how to better manage their businesses.

Our mission is simple: Every one of our books is designed to bring extra value and skill-building instructions to the reader. Our books are written by experts who understand and care about our readers. The knowledge base of our editorial staff comes from years of experience in publishing, education, and journalism — experience we use to produce books to carry us into the new millennium. In short, we care about books, so we attract the best people. We devote special attention to details such as audience, interior design, use of icons, and illustrations. And because we use an efficient process of authoring, editing, and desktop publishing our books electronically, we can spend more time ensuring superior content and less time on the technicalities of making books.

You can count on our commitment to deliver high-quality books at competitive prices on topics you want to read about. At IDG Books Worldwide, we continue in the IDG tradition of delivering quality for more than 30 years. You'll find no better book on a subject than one from IDG Books Worldwide.

John Kilcullen
Chairman and CEO
IDG Books Worldwide, Inc.

Steven Berkowitz
President and Publisher
IDG Books Worldwide, Inc.

Eighth Annual Computer Press Awards 1992

Ninth Annual Computer Press Awards 1993

Tenth Annual Computer Press Awards 1994

Eleventh Annual Computer Press Awards 1995

IDG is the world's leading IT media, research and exposition company. Founded, in 1964, IDG had 1997 revenues of $2.05 billion and has more than 9,000 employees worldwide. IDG offers the widest range of media options that reach IT buyers in 75 countries representing 95% of worldwide IT spending. IDG's diverse product and services portfolio spans six key areas including print publishing, online publishing, expositions and conferences, market research, education and training, and global marketing services. More than 90 million people read one or more of IDG's 290 magazines and newspapers, including IDG's leading global brands — Computerworld, PC World, Network World, Macworld and the Channel World family of publications. IDG Books Worldwide is one of the fastest-growing computer book publishers in the world, with more than 700 titles in 36 languages. The "...For Dummies®" series alone has more than 50 million copies in print. IDG offers online users the largest network of technology-specific Web sites around the world through IDG.net (http://www.idg.net), which comprises more than 225 targeted Web sites in 55 countries worldwide. International Data Corporation (IDC) is the world's largest provider of information technology data, analysis and consulting, with research centers in over 41 countries and more than 400 research analysts worldwide. IDG World Expo is a leading producer of more than 168 globally branded conferences and expositions in 35 countries including E3 (Electronic Entertainment Expo), Macworld Expo, ComNet, Windows World Expo, ICE (Internet Commerce Expo), Agenda, DEMO, and Spotlight. IDG's training subsidiary, ExecuTrain, is the world's largest computer training company, with more than 230 locations worldwide and 785 training courses. IDG Marketing Services helps industry-leading IT companies build international brand recognition by developing global integrated marketing programs via IDG's print, online and exposition products worldwide. Further information about the company can be found at www.idg.com. 10/8/98

Credits

Acquisitions Editor
Greg Croy

Development Editors
Denise Santoro
Terri Varveris

Technical Editor
Greg Guntle

Copy Editors
Eric Hahn
Michael D. Welch

Project Coordinator
Susan Parini

Book Designer
Kurt Krames

Graphics and Production Specialists
Mario Amador
Stephanie Hollier
E. A. Pauw
Dina F Quan

Graphic Technicians
Linda Marousek
Hector Mendosa

Quality Control Specialists
Mick Arellano
Mark Schumann

Proofreader
York Production Services

About the Author

Clayton Walnum started programming computers in 1982 when he traded in an IBM Selectric typewriter to buy an Atari 400 computer (16K of RAM!). Clay soon learned to combine his interest in writing with his newly acquired programming skills and started selling programs and articles to computer magazines. In 1985, Clay was hired as a technical editor by *ANALOG Computing*, a nationally distributed computer magazine; before leaving the magazine business in 1989 to become a freelance writer, he had worked his way up to executive editor. He has since acquired a degree in computer science and written over 30 books (translated into many languages) covering everything from computer gaming to 3D graphics programming. He's also written hundreds of magazine articles and software reviews, as well as countless programs. Clay's most recent book from IDG Books Worldwide is *Windows 98 Programming Secrets*. His other books include *AFC Black Book, Special Edition Using MFC and ATL, Java By Example,* and the award-winning *Building Windows 95 Applications with Visual Basic*. Clay's biggest disappointment in life is that he wasn't one of the Beatles. To compensate, he writes and records rock music in his home studio. You can reach Clay at his home page, which you'll find at http://www.claytonwalnum.com.

To Lynn

Preface

Visual Basic may be the most-used programming language in the world. The reason for its success is obvious: Visual Basic makes Windows programming so easy that just about anyone can sit down and create a simple program within a few hours. Of course, once you get past the basics, there's still a ton of stuff to learn. One of Visual Basic's strongest selling points is that you can use it to put together simple programs quickly—as well as write very sophisticated applications, if you're willing to dedicate the study time.

Of course, programmers, no matter how experienced, cannot possibly keep in their heads all the information they need to program Windows applications. (You could also try to fit the Atlantic Ocean into a drinking glass.) That's the role of *Visual Basic 6 Master Reference*. Using this book, you can quickly find the answers to most questions without having to dig through multiple volumes filled with information you'll probably never use. *Visual Basic 6 Master Reference*, in fact, provides all the information you need to build a fully logo-compliant Windows 98 application.

Who Should Use This Book

This book is not a Visual Basic tutorial. To understand the information presented here, you must already have at least a basic understanding of Visual Basic. If you're new to Visual Basic, you should pick up a good general Visual Basic programming book, such as Wallace Wang's *Visual Basic 6 For Windows For Dummies* (IDG Books Worldwide). Once you've worked through a book such as that, *Visual Basic 6 Master Reference* can be your main reference guide.

What This Book Covers

When my editors and I began to outline the contents of this book, we expected to be able to cover the entire Visual Basic 6 language and most of its controls and objects. (Okay, you can stop laughing now.) However, as you may have guessed, we soon discovered that such an undertaking would require a book twice this size while burying the reader under hundreds of pages of esoteric information.

So we started with the core language and worked our way up, adding material until we reached the maximum size book we thought would be reasonable yet still cover the most important elements of the Visual Basic language. As it turned out, we managed to include enough information to cover everything you need to know to program a fully logo-compliant Windows 98 application.

What exactly does this mean? A logo-compliant application is an application that includes all the features required by Microsoft to take best advantage of the Windows 98 operating system. An application that meets these requirements can obtain the "Designed for Windows 98" logo from Microsoft for use on its product packaging. The actual logo requirements are beyond the scope of this book, but you can find them on Microsoft's online MSDN (Microsoft Developer Network) at http://msdn.microsoft.com/developer/.

Specifically, the reference books covers the following elements of the Visual Basic language:

- The core language and keywords.
- All standard Visual Basic statements and functions.
- The intrinsic controls, such as CommandButton, TextBox, and PictureBox.
- The Windows 98 common ActiveX controls, such as Toolbar, TreeView, ListView, Animation, and Slider.
- The Windows 98 mail controls, MAPISession and MAPIMessages.
- Standard Visual Basic objects, such as App, Clipboard, File, Font, and Printer, as well as all objects (such as Band and ColumnHeader) associated with the covered controls.
- The Windows 98 common dialog boxes, including the Color, Font, Open, Save As, and Printer dialog boxes.
- All properties, methods, and events associated with the covered controls and objects.
- Visual Basic concepts, such as Event, Procedure, MaskRegion, and Twips.

This book does not cover the many additional controls (such as DataGrid, MonthView, MSChart, and WinSock) supplied with some editions of Visual Basic, as well as all events, methods, properties, and objects associated with these additional controls. Moreover, this book does not cover any controls, objects, properties, events, or methods used in Visual Basic database programming.

How This Book Is Organized

All the contents of this book, regardless of the topic, are arranged in alphabetical order. No matter what you're looking for — a property description, the use of a function, the methods of an object or control — you need look in only one place, rather than having to search through several manuals. For example, if you want to know what a TreeView control does, look it up in the *T*s. If you want to know what the `TabStyle` property is, also look in the *T*s. It doesn't matter that TreeView is a control and `TabStyle` is a property.

Note, however, that some entries may have several versions. For example, the property `Text` has three entries, each associated with a different control and a slightly different use. So, if you were looking for the `Text` property of a TextBox control, you'd need to find the entry "Text—TextBox." (This book also has "Text—ComboBox" and "Text—ListBox" entries.)

A note on alphabetization. This book's entries are alphabetized letter by letter, ignoring spaces and most punctuation, rather than word by word. This means that the entry for "Option Base" comes before "OptionButton," which comes before "Option Compare" (if the book had used the word-by-word scheme, "OptionButton" would have come *after* "Option Compare"). The only exception to the letter-by-letter alphabetization scheme is that sets of similar entries that include a dash are grouped. For example, all the "Add—" entries (such as "Add—ButtonMenus Collection" and "Add—Buttons Collection" through to "Add—Tabs Collection") are alphabetized as a single group. As a result, the entry for "AddItem" doesn't interrupt the "Add—" entries, and "Add—Tabs Collection" is not moved to follow "Address ResolveUI." Keep this alphabetization scheme in mind as you search for entries. To help you find what you're looking for, the top of each left-hand and right-hand page lists that page's first or last entry, respectively.

Understanding the Program Listings

Most of the entries in this book feature a short code excerpt that shows how to use the particular element of the language. Some entries, however, feature full (albeit short) programs that enable you to see the specific Visual Basic items in action. The source code for the main form of the program appears in the book, and the complete program appears on the book's CD-ROM.

More specifically, whenever you see a form's program listing in the book, you can find the complete program on the book's CD-ROM. If you're looking over this book as you sit in your favorite comfy chair (you know the one), you can just look over the printed program listing to see what's happening. If, however, you're perched in front of your computer, you can load the program from the CD-ROM and run it.

Like the entries in the book, the programs are ordered alphabetically on the CD-ROM. For example, if you want to find the demo program for the `GetFirstVisible` method, you look in the *G* folder for the GetFirstVisible folder. To run the program from the CD-ROM, find the project file (the file with the .vbp file-name extension) and double-click it. This action will load the program into Visual Basic with the current directory set to the program's directory, enabling the program to find any additional data file it may need to run.

System Requirements

The system and software requirements for the programs in this book are the same as the requirements for Visual Basic 6 running under Windows 95 or later. These minimum requirements are listed below:

- IBM-compatible with a 66 MHz 486DX processor (Pentium processor recommended)
- Microsoft Windows 95 or later
- 16MB RAM (24MB recommended)
- Hard disk
- CD-ROM drive
- VGA or better graphics (Super VGA recommended)
- Mouse
- Visual Basic 6

In Closing

A huge amount of effort went into making this book as accurate as possible. However, the rules of this universe forbid such an immense task to be free of all errors. For this reason, I ask you not only to forgive any errors and oversights, but also to notify me of any such discoveries. Your help will is greatly appreciated. You can reach me at my home page located at `http://www.claytonwalnum.com`.

Acknowledgments

I would like to thank the many people who helped move this book from my head to the bookshelf. Special thanks go to Greg Croy for handing me this project, Denise Santoro and Terri Varveris for keeping things rolling and ensuring that the text made sense, Eric Hahn and Michael Welch for polishing the text, and Greg Guntle for verifying the technical accuracy of this book. As always, thanks go to my family: Lynn, Christopher, Justin, Stephen, and Caitlynn.

Contents

AccessKeyPress

Event

Visual Basic sends a UserControl control an `AccessKeyPress` event when the user selects a control access key, including Enter and Esc.

Objects with an AccessKeyPress Event

UserControl

Example

A program can respond to an `AccessKeyPress` event by implementing the control's `AccessKeyPress` event procedure. The following code segment shows how a UserControl control defines an `AccessKeyPress` event procedure. The procedure's single parameter, `KeyAscii`, provides the ASCII value of the pressed access key.

```
Sub UserControl_AccessKeyPress(KeyAscii As Integer)
    ' Respond to the AccessKeyPress event here.
End Sub
```

CROSS-REFERENCE
For more information, see UserControl.

AccessKeys

Property

The `AccessKeys` property represents a string that contains hotkeys for an ActiveX control based on the UserControl object. The hotkeys enable the user to move the focus to a control by pressing Alt in conjunction with one of the control's access keys. You can get or set the `AccessKeys` property through a reference to the control object. UserControl is the base object for user-created ActiveX controls.

Objects with an AccessKeys Property

UserControl

Syntax

```
control.AccessKeys = string1
```

or

```
string2 = control.AccessKeys
```

- *control* — A reference to a UserControl object.
- *string1* — A string that contains the access-key characters.
- *string2* — The variable that will receive the string, returned by the property, that contains the access-key characters.

Example 1

In this example, a user-created ActiveX control sets its access keys in its `Initialize` method. When an application displays an instance of this control, the user will be able to use the letters *X*, *Y*, or *Z* as the control's hotkeys.

```
Private Sub UserControl_Initialize()
    ' Set the control's access keys.
    UserControl.AccessKeys = "XYZ"
End Sub
```

Example 2

Here, the control obtains the value of its `AccessKeys` property.

```
Dim vntString
vntString = UserControl.AccessKeys
```

 CROSS-REFERENCE
For more information, see UserControl.

ACStatus

Property

The `ACStatus` property represents the current status of the system's AC power. The property can be one of three values:

0   AC power is off

1   AC power is on

255   Status of AC power is not known

You can get the `AccessKeys` property's value through a reference to a SysInfo control, which provides valuable information about the system.

Objects with an ACStatus Property

SysInfo

Syntax

```
value = sysinfo.ACStatus
```

- *sysinfo*—A reference to an instance of the SysInfo control.
- *value*—A variable that will receive the return value of 0, 1, or 255.

Example

The following lines retrieve the status of the system's AC power and display the result in a message box. The `SysInfo1` object is an instance of the SysInfo control that the programmer added to the application.

```
Dim intACStatus As Integer

intACStatus = SysInfo1.ACStatus
If intACStatus = 0 Then
    MsgBox "AC power off"
ElseIf intACStatus = 1 Then
    MsgBox "AC power on"
Else
    MsgBox "AC power status unknown"
End If
```

CROSS-REFERENCE
For more information, see SysInfo.

Action — CommonDialog

Property

The `Action` property for the CommonDialog control determines the type of common dialog box that the program will display. The property can be one of the seven values shown in Table A-1.

Table A-1 Possible Values for the Action Property

Value	Description
1	Open dialog box
2	Save As dialog box
3	Color dialog box
4	Font dialog box
5	Printer dialog box
6	Windows Help

Setting the `Action` property automatically displays the associated common dialog box.

Syntax

```
dialog.Action = value1
```

or

```
value2 = dialog.Action
```

- *dialog* — A reference to an instance of the CommonDialog control.
- *value1* — An integer from 1 to 6, representing the type of dialog box to display.
- *value2* — A variable that will receive the returned integer from 1 to 6, representing the type of dialog box to display.

Example

The following lines of code display a Color dialog box when the user clicks a button. The `dlgCommonDialog1` object is an instance of the CommonDialog control and `btnCommand1` is an instance of the CommandButton control. Figure A-1 shows the dialog box displayed by the code segment.

```
Private Sub btnCommand1_Click()
    ' Display the Color dialog box.
    dlgCommonDialog1.Action = 3
End Sub
```

Figure A-1 The Color dialog box is one of the six common dialog boxes.

CROSS-REFERENCE
For other ways to display common dialog boxes, see the ShowColor, ShowFont, ShowHelp, ShowOpen, ShowPrinter, and ShowSave methods.

Action — MAPIMessages

Property

The `Action` property for the MAPIMessages control determines what action the control will take. The property can be one of the 15 values shown in Table A-2.

Table A-2 Possible Values for the Action Property

Value	Description
ATTACHMENT_DELETE	Delete a message attachment
MESSAGE_COMPOSE	Compose message
MESSAGE_COPY	Copy message
MESSAGE_DELETE	Delete message
MESSAGE_FETCH	Fetch message
MESSAGE_FORWARD	Forward message
MESSAGE_REPLY	Reply to message
MESSAGE_REPLYALL	Reply to all messages
MESSAGE_RESOLVENAME	Finds recipient's name
MESSAGE_SAVEMSG	Save message
MESSAGE_SEND	Send message
MESSAGE_SENDDLG	Send message
MESSAGE_SHOWADBOOK	Show the Address Book
MESSAGE_SHOWDETAILS	Show message details
RECIPIENT_DELETE	Delete a message recipient

Setting the Action property automatically invokes the MAPIMessages control. Note that the Action property is included in Visual Basic 6.0 only for backward compatibility with earlier versions. You should not use the Action property in new programs. Instead, call one of the new methods: Compose, Copy, Delete, Fetch, Forward, Reply, ReplyAll, ResolveName, Save, Send, or Show.

Syntax

    MAPIMessages.Action = value

- *MAPIMessages* — A reference to an instance of the MAPIMessages control.
- *value* — One of the predefined constants shown in Table A-2.

CROSS-REFERENCE
For other ways to manipulate the MAPIMessages control, see the Compose, Copy, Delete, Fetch, Forward, Reply, ReplyAll, ResolveName, Save, Send, and Show methods.

a

b

c

Action — MAPISession

Property

The `Action` property for the MAPISession control determines what action the control will take. The property can be one of the two values shown in Table A-3.

Table A-3 Possible Values for the Action Property

Value	Description
mapSignOff	Signs off the mail account
mapSignOn	Signs on to the mail account

Setting the `Action` property automatically invokes the MAPISession control. Note that the `Action` property is included in Visual Basic 6.0 only for backward compatibility with earlier versions. You should not use the `Action` property in new programs. Instead, call one of the new methods, `SignOn` or `SignOff`.

Syntax

```
MAPISession.Action = value
```

- *MAPISession* — A reference to an instance of the MAPISession control.
- *value* — One of the predefined constants shown in Table A-3.

CROSS-REFERENCE

For other ways to manipulate the MAPISession control, see the SignOn and SignOff methods.

Action — OLE Container

Property

The `Action` property for the OLE container control determines what action the control will take. The property can be one of the fourteen values shown in Table A-4.

Table A-4 Possible Values for the Action Property

Value	Description
0	Create an embedded item
1	Create a linked item
4	Copy an item to the Clipboard
5	Copy the Clipboard to the control
6	Updates the control's data
7	Executes an OLE verb
9	Closes an OLE item
10	Deletes an OLE item
11	Saves an OLE item
12	Loads a saved OLE item
14	Displays the Insert Object dialog
15	Displays the Paste Special dialog
17	Updates an item's verb list
18	Saves the item in an OLE 1.0 file

Note that the `Action` property is included in Visual Basic 6.0 only for backward compatibility with earlier versions. You should not use the `Action` property in new programs. Instead, call one of the new methods: `Close`, `Copy`, `CreateEmbed`, `CreateLink`, `Delete`, `DoVerb`, `FetchVerbs`, `InsertObjDlg`, `Paste`, `PasteSpecialDlg`, `ReadFromFile`, `SaveToFile`, `SaveToOle1File`, or `Update`.

Syntax

`OLEControl.Action = value`

- *OLEControl* — A reference to an instance of the OLE container control.
- *value* — One of the values shown in Table A-4.

CROSS-REFERENCE
For other ways to manipulate the OLE container control, see the Close, Copy CreateEmbed, CreateLink, Delete, DoVerb, FetchVerbs, InsertObjDlg, Paste, PasteSpecialDlg, ReadFromFile, SaveToFile, SaveToOle1File, and Update methods.

Activate

Event

Visual Basic sends an object an `Activate` event when the object receives the focus. This occurs when the user selects the object or when the program calls the object's `Show` or `SetFocus` methods.

Objects That Receive Activate Events

Form

MDIForm

DataReport

Example

A program can respond to an `Activate` event by implementing the target object's `Activate` event procedure. The following code segment shows how a Form object defines an `Activate` event procedure. In this case, the form displays a message box upon activation.

```
Private Sub Form_Activate()
    ' Handle the Activate event here.
    MsgBox ("Form Activated")
End Sub
```

ActiveControl

Property

The `ActiveControl` property represents the currently active control in a form or other type of container object.

Objects with an ActiveControl Property

Form

MDIForm

PropertyPage

Screen

UserControl

Syntax

```
control = container.ActiveControl
```

- *container*—A reference to the container object.
- *control*—The variable that will receive the control with the focus returned by the property.

Example

The following lines determine the currently active control in a form and display the results in a message box. The application's form contains instances of OptionButton, TextBox, and CommandButton controls. The programmer has placed the controls on a Form object named frmForm1.

```
If TypeOf frmForm1.ActiveControl Is OptionButton Then
    MsgBox "OptionButton"
ElseIf TypeOf frmForm1.ActiveControl Is TextBox Then
    MsgBox "TextBox"
ElseIf TypeOf frmForm1.ActiveControl Is CommandButton Then
    MsgBox "CommandButton"
End If
```

ActiveForm

Property

The ActiveForm property represents the currently active form.

Objects with an ActiveForm Property

Form
MDIForm
Screen

Syntax

```
form = object.ActiveForm
```

- *object*—A reference to the object containing the form.
- *form*—The variable that will receive the currently active form returned by the property.

Example

This example application, called ActiveForm Demo, demonstrates one way to use the `ActiveForm` property. The application displays an MDI window that contains two child forms. When you click the MDI window's Mark Active Form button, the caption of the active child form changes to "Active Form" (Figure A-2). When you switch to the other child form, by clicking its window, the program restores the first form's caption. The `btnCommand1_Click` method is where the program uses the `ActiveForm` property.

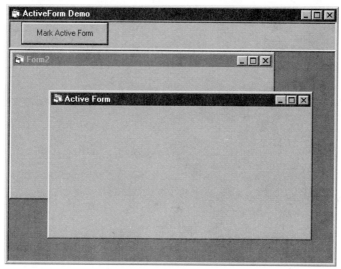

Figure A-2 The ActiveForm Demo application marks its active form.

```
VERSION 5.00
Begin VB.MDIForm MDIForm1
    BackColor       =    &H8000000C&
    Caption         =    "MDIForm1"
    ClientHeight    =    5190
    ClientLeft      =    60
    ClientTop       =    345
    ClientWidth     =    7215
    LinkTopic       =    "MDIForm1"
    StartUpPosition =    3 'Windows Default
    Begin VB.PictureBox Picture1
        Align       =    1 'Align Top
        Height      =    615
        Left        =    0
```

```
                ScaleHeight        =    555
                ScaleWidth         =    7155
                TabIndex           =    0
                Top                =    0
                Width              =    7215
                Begin VB.CommandButton btnCommand1
                    Caption        =    "Mark Active Form"
                    Height         =    495
                    Left           =    240
                    TabIndex       =    1
                    Top            =    0
                    Width          =    1935
                End
            End
        End

        Attribute VB_Name = "MDIForm1"
        Attribute VB_GlobalNameSpace = False
        Attribute VB_Creatable = False
        Attribute VB_PredeclaredId = True
        Attribute VB_Exposed = False

        Private Sub btnCommand1_Click()
            ActiveForm.Caption = "Active Form"
        End Sub

        Private Sub MDIForm_Load()
            ' Show the second child window.
            Dim frmForm2 As New Form2
            frmForm2.Show
        End Sub

        VERSION 5.00
        Begin VB.Form Form1
            Caption        =    "Form1"
            ClientHeight   =    3195
            ClientLeft     =    60
            ClientTop      =    345
            ClientWidth    =    4680
            LinkTopic      =    "Form1"
            MDIChild       =    -1  'True
            ScaleHeight    =    3195
            ScaleWidth     =    4680
        End
```

```
Attribute VB_Name = "Form1"
Attribute VB_GlobalNameSpace = False
Attribute VB_Creatable = False
Attribute VB_PredeclaredId = True
Attribute VB_Exposed = False

Private Sub Form_Deactivate()
    Caption = "Form1"
End Sub

VERSION 5.00
Begin VB.Form Form2
    Caption         =    "Form2"
    ClientHeight    =    3195
    ClientLeft      =    60
    ClientTop       =    345
    ClientWidth     =    4680
    LinkTopic       =    "Form2"
    MDIChild        =    -1  'True
    ScaleHeight     =    3195
    ScaleWidth      =    4680
End

Attribute VB_Name = "Form2"
Attribute VB_GlobalNameSpace = False
Attribute VB_Creatable = False
Attribute VB_PredeclaredId = True
Attribute VB_Exposed = False

Private Sub Form_Deactivate()
    Caption = "Form2"
End Sub
```

ActiveX Controls

Concept

ActiveX controls are like mini-applications that you can embed into other applications. They take the idea of programmable OLE components and separate those components from the server. That is, ActiveX components are complete entities unto themselves, and do not need to be managed by a server application. One of the biggest advantages of ActiveX controls is their capability to provide computing power to Web pages on the Internet. In this way, ActiveX controls can act much like Java applets.

More importantly, though, ActiveX controls enable you to create controls that you can add to your Visual Basic programming environment. In fact, Microsoft includes a large number of ActiveX controls — including common system controls like TreeView, ListView, Slider, RichTextBox, ProgressBar, and more — to the Visual Basic Professional and Enterprise editions. You can add ActiveX controls to your Visual Basic toolbox by selecting the Project menu's Components command.

Add — ButtonMenus Collection

Method

The `Add` method adds a ButtonMenu object to a ButtonMenus collection. Button menus are toolbar buttons that display a drop-down menu when clicked. You create such a menu by adding a Button object to a toolbar. Visual Basic associates the Button object with a ButtonMenus object. You add commands (ButtonMenu objects) to the button menu by calling the ButtonMenus object's `Add` method.

Syntax

`ButtonMenus.Add(position, name, caption)`

- *ButtonMenus* — A reference to a ButtonMenus collection.
- *position* (*) — The position in the collection at which to place the new ButtonMenu object.
- *name* (*) — The name that will be used as an ID for the new ButtonMenu object.
- *caption* — The text that will appear in the menu.

(*) = Optional argument

Example 1

This example application, called ButtonMenus Add Demo, demonstrates how to use the Add method to add ButtonMenu items to a ButtonMenus collection. The application displays a form that contains a toolbar with a single button. When you click the toolbar's button, a drop-down menu appears. You can select an item from the menu (Figure A-3), after which a message box appears, telling you what menu item you chose. Notice that at the end of the

Form_Load method, the program calls the ButtonMenus collection object's Add method to add three menu items to the button menu. Notice also that the Add method returns a reference to the added ButtonMenu.

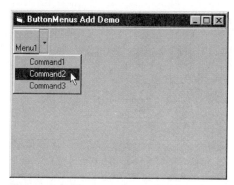

Figure A-3 The sample application demonstrates the ButtonMenus object's Add method.

```
VERSION 5.00
Object = "{6B7E6392-850A-101B-AFC0-4210102A8DA7} _
   #2.0#0"; "MSCOMCTL.OCX"
Begin VB.Form frmForm1
   Caption         =   "ButtonMenus Add Demo"
   ClientHeight    =   3195
   ClientLeft      =   60
   ClientTop       =   345
   ClientWidth     =   4680
   LinkTopic       =   "Form1"
   ScaleHeight     =   3195
   ScaleWidth      =   4680
   StartUpPosition =   3  'Windows Default
   Begin MSComctlLib.Toolbar tlbToolbar1
      Align        =   1  'Align Top
      Height       =   630
      Left         =   0
      TabIndex     =   0
      Top          =   0
      Width        =   4680
      _ExtentX     =   8255
      _ExtentY     =   1111
      ButtonWidth  =   609
      ButtonHeight =   953
```

```
        Appearance       =    1
        _Version         =    393216
     End
  End
End
Attribute VB_Name = "frmForm1"
Attribute VB_GlobalNameSpace = False
Attribute VB_Creatable = False
Attribute VB_PredeclaredId = True
Attribute VB_Exposed = False

Private Sub Form_Load()
    Dim btnButton As Button
    Set btnButton = tlbToolbar1.Buttons.Add _
        (1, "Menu1", "Menu1", tbrDropdown)
    btnButton.ButtonMenus.Add 1, "Command1", "Command1"
    btnButton.ButtonMenus.Add 2, "Command2", "Command2"
    btnButton.ButtonMenus.Add 3, "Command3", "Command3"
End Sub

Private Sub tlbToolbar1_ButtonMenuClick _
    (ByVal ButtonMenu As MSComctlLib.ButtonMenu)
    If ButtonMenu.Index = 1 Then
        MsgBox "Command1"
    ElseIf ButtonMenu.Index = 2 Then
        MsgBox "Command2"
    Else
        MsgBox "Command3"
    End If
End Sub
```

Example 2

In the following lines, the program leaves off the Add method's optional arguments, providing only the menu item's text. Substituting this version of the Form_Load method for the one in the previous example will not change the way the ButtonMenus Add Demo program runs.

```
Private Sub Form_Load()
    Dim btnButton As Button
    Set btnButton = tlbToolbar1.Buttons.Add _
        (1, "Menu1", "Menu1", tbrDropdown)
```

```
        btnButton.ButtonMenus.Add , , "Command1"
        btnButton.ButtonMenus.Add , , "Command2"
        btnButton.ButtonMenus.Add , , "Command3"
    End Sub
```

CROSS-REFERENCE

For more information, see ButtonMenu, ButtonMenus, and Toolbar.

Add — Buttons Collection

Method

The Add method adds a Button object to a Buttons collection. A Buttons collection usually holds the buttons for a toolbar.

Syntax

Buttons.Add(*position, name, caption, style, image*)

- *Buttons* — A reference to a Buttons collection.
- *position* (⋆) — The position in the collection at which to place the new Button object.
- *name* (⋆) — The name that will be used as an ID for the new Button object.
- *caption* (⋆) — The text that will appear on the button.
- *style* (⋆) — The button's style. Can be tbrDefault, tbrCheck, tbrButtonGroup, tbrSeparator, tbrPlaceholder, or tbrDropDown.
- *image* (⋆) — The index or name of an image in an ImageList.

(⋆) = Optional argument

Example

This example application, called Buttons Add Demo, demonstrates how to use the Add method to add Button objects to a toolbar's Buttons collection. As shown in Figure A-4, the application displays a form that contains a toolbar with three buttons. Take special note of the Form_Load method, where the buttons are added to the toolbar.

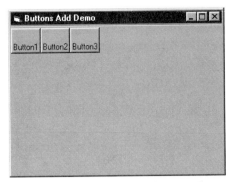

Figure A-4 The sample application demonstrates the Buttons
collection's Add method.

```
VERSION 5.00
Object = "{6B7E6392-850A-101B-AFC0-4210102A8DA7} _
    #2.0#0"; "MSCOMCTL.OCX"
Begin VB.Form Form1
    Caption         =    "Buttons Add Demo"
    ClientHeight    =    3195
    ClientLeft      =    60
    ClientTop       =    345
    ClientWidth     =    4680
    LinkTopic       =    "Form1"
    ScaleHeight     =    3195
    ScaleWidth      =    4680
    StartUpPosition =    3   'Windows Default
    Begin MSComctlLib.Toolbar tlbToolbar1
        Align         =    1   'Align Top
        Height        =    630
        Left          =    0
        TabIndex      =    0
        Top           =    0
        Width         =    4680
        _ExtentX      =    8255
        _ExtentY      =    1111
        ButtonWidth   =    609
        ButtonHeight  =    953
        Appearance    =    1
        _Version      =    393216
    End
End

Attribute VB_Name = "Form1"
```

```
Attribute VB_GlobalNameSpace = False
Attribute VB_Creatable = False
Attribute VB_PredeclaredId = True
Attribute VB_Exposed = False

Private Sub Form_Load()
    tlbToolbar1.Buttons.Add _
        1, "Button1", "Button1", tbrDefault
    tlbToolbar1.Buttons.Add _
        2, "Button2", "Button2", tbrDefault
    tlbToolbar1.Buttons.Add _
        3, "Button3", "Button3", tbrDefault
End Sub
```

CROSS-REFERENCE

For more information, see Button, Buttons, and Toolbar.

Add—ColumnHeaders Collection

Method

The Add method adds a ColumnHeader object to a ColumnHeaders collection. A ColumnHeaders collection represents the column headers in a ListView control.

Syntax

ColumnHeaders.Add(*id, name, caption, width, align, icon*)

- *ColumnHeaders* — A reference to a ColumnHeaders collection.
- *id* (★) — An integer that identifies the new ColumnHeader object.
- *name* (★) — The name that will be used as an ID for the new ColumnHeader object.
- *caption* (★) — The text that will appear in the new ColumnHeader object.
- *width* (★) — The width of the new ColumnHeader object.
- *align* (★) — The alignment of the new ColumnHeader object. Can be lvwColumnCenter, lvwColumnLeft, or lvwColumnRight.
- *icon* (★) — The index or name of an icon in an ImageList representing the small icons.

(★) = Optional argument

Example

In this example, the program adds three ColumnHeader objects to a ListView control's ColumnHeaders collection object. (The programmer has already added the ListView control, called `lvwListView1`, to the form.) Notice that the `Add` method returns a reference to the new ColumnHeader object. Also notice that, in order for the ColumnHeader objects to appear, the ListView control must be in its report view. You set the report view by setting the ListView control's `View` property to `lvwReport`. Finally, remember that the first column requires the `lvwColumnLeft` alignment style. Figure A-5 shows the ColumnHeader objects created by this example.

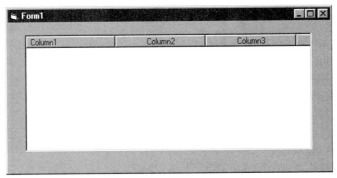

Figure A-5 This ListView control displays three ColumnHeader objects.

```
Dim ColHeader1 As ColumnHeader
Dim ColHeader2 As ColumnHeader
Dim ColHeader3 As ColumnHeader

Set ColHeader1 = lvwListView1.ColumnHeaders. _
    Add(1, "column1", "Column1", 2000, lvwColumnLeft)
Set ColHeader2 = lvwListView1.ColumnHeaders. _
    Add(2, "column2", "Column2", 2000, lvwColumnCenter)
Set ColHeader3 = lvwListView1.ColumnHeaders. _
    Add(3, "column3", "Column3", 2000, lvwColumnCenter)

lvwListView1.View = lvwReport
```

CROSS-REFERENCE
For more information, see ColumnHeader, ColumnHeaders, and ListView.

Add — Controls Collection

Method

The Add method adds a Control object to a Controls collection. You can use the Add method to add controls to a form at runtime.

Syntax

```
Controls.Add(id, name, container)
```

- *Controls* — A reference to a Controls collection.
- *id* — The ID for the control to be added.
- *name* — The name that will be used as an ID for the new Control object.
- *container* (*) — A reference to the container in which the new Control object should be placed.

(*) = Optional argument

Example

In this example, the program adds a CheckBox to the main form, frmForm1. Notice that the Add method returns a reference to the new Control object, which the program uses to access the control's properties.

```
Dim chkCheckBox As CheckBox
Set chkCheckBox = frmForm1.Controls.Add _
    ("VB.CheckBox", "chkbox", frmForm1)
chkCheckBox.Caption = "CheckBox"
chkCheckBox.Top = 500
chkCheckBox.Left = 500
chkCheckBox.Width = 2500
chkCheckBox.Visible = True
chkCheckBox.Visible = True
```

CROSS-REFERENCE
For more information, see Controls and Form.

Add — ListImages Collection

Method

The `Add` method adds a ListImage object to a ListImages collection, which holds the images for an ImageList control. An ImageList control can be used as a general storage place for images, but is most often used to store the images needed for ListView, TreeView, TabStrip, and Toolbar controls.

Syntax

`ListImages.Add(`*id, name, image*`)`

- *ListImages* — A reference to a ListImages collection.
- *id* (*) — The ID for the image to be added.
- *name* (*) — The name for the new image.
- *image* — A reference to the Picture object for the image.

(*) = Optional argument

Example

In this example, the program adds three images to an ImageList control. The programmer previously added the ImageList to the form and named it `ilsImageList1`. Note that the `Add` method returns a reference to the new ListImage object, as you can see in the first call to the `Add` method.

```
Dim image As ListImage
Set image = ilsImageList1.ListImages.Add _
    1, "ImageA", LoadPicture("image1.bmp")
ilsImageList1.ListImages.Add _
    2, "ImageB", LoadPicture("image2.bmp")
ilsImageList1.ListImages.Add _
    3, "ImageC", LoadPicture("image3.bmp")
```

 CROSS-REFERENCE
For more information, see ListImage, ListImages, and ImageList.

Add — ListItems Collection

Method

The `Add` method adds a ListItem object to a ListItems collection, which holds the items for a ListView control.

Syntax

```
ListItems.Add(position, name, caption, icon, smallIcon)
```

- *ListItems* — A reference to a ListItems collection.
- *position* (⋆) — The position at which you want to place the new item.
- *name* (⋆) — The name for the new item.
- *caption* (⋆) — The text that will appear for the item in the ListView control.
- *icon* (⋆) — An index into the ImageList control that contains the regular icons.
- *smallIcon* (⋆) — An index into the ImageList control that contains the small icons.

(⋆) = Optional argument

Example

In this example, the program adds three items to a ListView control. The programmer previously added the ListView to the form and named it lvwListView1. Note that the Add method returns a reference to the new ListItem object, as you can see in the first call to the Add method.

```
Dim item As ListItem
Set item = lvwListView1.ListItems.Add _
    (1, "item1", "Item1", 1, 1)
lvwListView1.ListItems.Add 2, "item2", "Item2", 1, 1
lvwListView1.ListItems.Add 3, "item3", "Item3", 1, 1
```

 CROSS-REFERENCE

For more information, see ListItem, ListItems, and ListView.

Add — ListSubItems Collection

Method

The Add method adds a ListSubItem object to a ListSubItems collection, which holds the subitems for a ListView control. Subitems come into play when a ListView control is in its report view. Then each item in the first column can have subitems in the remaining columns. For example, a ListView control showing files might have file names in the first column and file attributes (such as size, date of creation, etc.) as subitems.

Syntax

```
ListSubItems.Add(position, name, caption, icon, tooltip)
```

- *ListSubItems*—A reference to a ListSubItems collection.
- *position* (*)—The position at which you want to place the new subitem.
- *name* (*)—The name for the new subitem.
- *caption* (*)—The text that will appear for the subitem in the ListView control.
- *icon* (*)—An index into the ImageList control that contains the report icon.
- *tooltip* (*)—The text that will appear when the mouse pointer is over the subitem.

(*) = Optional argument

Example

In this example, the program adds two subitems to each of the three main items in a ListView control. The programmer previously added the ListView to the form and named it lvwListView1. Note that the Add method returns a reference to the new ListSubItem object, as you can see in the first call to the ListSubItems collection's Add method. Figure A-6 shows the ListView control created by this example.

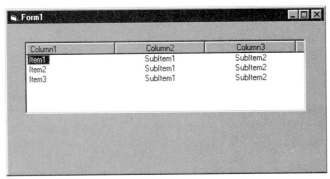

Figure A-6 This ListView control displays items that each have three subitems.

```
Dim item1 As ListItem
Dim item2 As ListItem
Dim item3 As ListItem
Dim SubItem As ListSubItem
```

```
lvwListView1.View = lvwReport

lvwListView1.ColumnHeaders.Add _
    1, "column1", "Column1", 2000, lvwColumnLeft
lvwListView1.ColumnHeaders.Add _
    2, "column2", "Column2", 2000, lvwColumnCenter
lvwListView1.ColumnHeaders.Add _
    3, "column3", "Column3", 2000, lvwColumnCenter

Set item1 = lvwListView1.ListItems.Add _
    (1, "item1", "Item1")
Set item2 = lvwListView1.ListItems.Add _
    (2, "item2", "Item2")
Set item3 = lvwListView1.ListItems.Add _
    (3, "item3", "Item3")

Set SubItem = item1.ListSubItems.Add _
    (1, "subitem1", "SubItem1")
item1.ListSubItems.Add 2, "subitem2", "SubItem2"
item1.ListSubItems.Add 3, "subitem3", "SubItem3"

item2.ListSubItems.Add 1, "subitem1", "SubItem1"
item2.ListSubItems.Add 2, "subitem2", "SubItem2"
item2.ListSubItems.Add 3, "subitem3", "SubItem3"

item3.ListSubItems.Add 1, "subitem1", "SubItem1"
item3.ListSubItems.Add 2, "subitem2", "SubItem2"
item3.ListSubItems.Add 3, "subitem3", "SubItem3"
```

CROSS-REFERENCE
For more information, see ListSubItem, ListSubItems, and ListView.

Add—Nodes Collection

Method

The Add method adds a Node object to a Nodes collection, which holds the nodes for a TreeView control. In spite of its fancy name, a *node* is simply an entry in the TreeView control's displayed tree. The main node is called the *root node*, and the nodes that branch from the root node are called *child nodes*.

Syntax

```
Nodes.Add(node, placement, name, caption, image, selectImage)
```

- *Nodes*—A reference to a Nodes collection.
- *node* (*) — The index or name of an existing node.
- *placement* (*) — The relationship between *node* and the new node. Can be tvwFirst, tvwLast, tvwNext, tvwPrevious, or tvwChild.
- *name* (*) — The name of the new node.
- *caption*—The text that will appear on the node in the TreeView control.
- *image* (*) — An index into the ImageList control that contains the node's image.
- *selectImage* (*) — An index into the ImageList control that contains the node's "selected" image.

(*) = Optional argument

Example

In this example, the program adds to a TreeView control a main node with three child nodes. The programmer previously added the TreeView to the form and named it treTreeView1. Note that the Add method returns a reference to the new Node object, as you can see in the first call to the Add method. Figure A-7 shows the TreeView control created by this example.

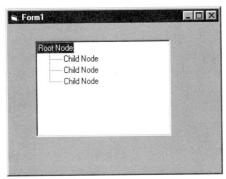

Figure A-7 This TreeView control displays a root node with three children.

```
Dim Nod As Node
Set Nod = treTreeView1.Nodes.Add _
    (, , "Root", "Root Node")
treTreeView1.Nodes.Add "Root", tvwChild, _
```

```
        "Child1", "Child Node"
    treTreeView1.Nodes.Add "Root", tvwChild, _
        "Child2", "Child Node"
    treTreeView1.Nodes.Add "Root", tvwChild, _
        "Child3", "Child Node"
```

 CROSS-REFERENCE
For more information, see Node, Nodes, and TreeView.

Add—OLEObjects Collection

Method

The Add method adds an OLEObject object to an OLEObjects collection, which holds the OLE objects for a RichTextBox control. In this case, an OLE object is any embedded object that you place in a RichTextBox control's RTF file. This can include anything from text to spreadsheet data. An application's user can also place OLEObjects into the RichTextBox control simply by dragging objects from Windows Explorer and dropping the objects on the control. These objects, too, are each represented by a Visual Basic OLEObject object.

Syntax

```
OLEObjects.Add id, name, fileName, oleClass
```

- *OLEObjects*—A reference to an OLEObjects collection.
- *id* (★)—The index of the OLEObject in the collection after which the new object should be placed.
- *name* (★)—The name of the new OLE object.
- *fileName*—The file name of the document to embed. Can also be an empty string.
- *oleClass* (★)—The new object's OLE class name, which is the name in the system registry for the type of object. If *fileName* is not an empty string, *oleClass* has no effect.

(★) = Optional argument

Example 1

In this example, the program embeds a Word document named test.doc into a RichTextBox control. The programmer previously added the RichTextBox control to the form and named it rtfRichTextBox1.

```
rtfRichTextBox1.OLEObjects.Add , , "test.doc"
```

Example 2

Here, the program embeds a new Word document into a RichTextBox control. Of course, to embed a new object like this, you need to know the registered name for the document type. You can find the registered name easily enough by using REGEDIT to look up the file extension associated with the document type in the Registry. Figure A-8 shows REGEDIT displaying the Word document type and its registered name. You can find the REGEDIT application in your main Windows directory.

```
rtfRichTextBox1.OLEObjects.Add , , , "Word.Document.8"
```

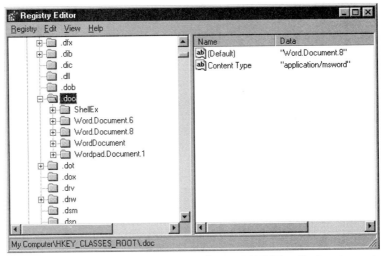

Figure A-8 You can use the Registry editor, REGEDIT, to find registered document names.

Example 3

Finally, in this example, the program embeds into a RichTextBox control a new Microsoft Works spreadsheet and names the new object WorksSheet.

```
rtfRichTextBox1.OLEObjects.Add _
    , "WorksSheet", , "MSWorks.Sheet.4"
```

CROSS-REFERENCE
For more information, see OLEObject, OLEObjects, and RichTextBox.

Add — Panels Collection

Method

The `Add` method adds a Panel object to a Panels collection, which holds the panel objects for a StatusBar control. Status bar panels are the small boxes that appear in a status bar to separate the various types of information displayed in the status bar.

Syntax

```
Panels.Add(position, name, caption, style, image)
```

- *Panels* — A reference to a Panels collection.
- *position* (*) — The position at which the new panel should be placed.
- *name* (*) — The name of the new Panel object.
- *style* (*) — The new panel's style. Can be `sbrText`, `sbrCaps`, `sbrNum`, `sbrIns`, `sbrScrl`, `sbrTime`, `sbrDate`, or `sbrKana`.
- *image* (*) — A reference to a Picture object that will be displayed in the panel.

  (*) = Optional argument

Example

In this example, the program creates four new panels in a StatusBar control. (The programmer previously added the StatusBar control to the form and named it `staStatusBar1`.) The four panels show a text string, the status of the Caps key, the date, and an image, respectively. Figure A-9 shows the status bar created by these lines. Notice that the `Add` method returns a reference to the new Panel, as you can see in the first call to `Add` in the example. Notice also that, although the example lines add only four panels, the status bar has five panels. This is because a status bar always starts with one panel.

```
Dim Pan As Panel
Set Pan = staStatusBar1.Panels.Add _
    (, "text", "Text Panel", sbrText)
staStatusBar1.Panels.Add , "caps", , sbrCaps
staStatusBar1.Panels.Add , "date", , sbrDate
staStatusBar1.Panels.Add , "image", , sbrText, _
    LoadPicture("image1.bmp")
```

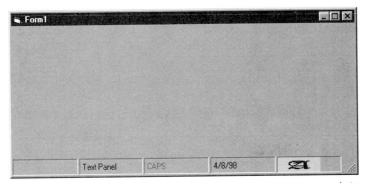

Figure A-9 The Add method enables a program to create panels in a StatusBar control.

 CROSS-REFERENCE
For more information, see Panel, Panels, and StatusBar.

Add—Tabs Collection

Method

The Add method adds a Tab object to a Tabs collection, which holds the tab objects for a TabStrip control. TabStrip controls look like the tabbed areas in a property sheet, being comprised of various pages with an associated tab. Clicking a tab displays the associated page.

Syntax

```
Tabs.Add(position, name, caption, image)
```

- *Tabs*—A reference to a Tabs collection.
- *position* (*)—The position at which the new tab should be placed.
- *name* (*)—The name of the new Panel object.
- *caption* (*)—The text that will appear on the new Tab object.
- *image* (*)—The index of the ImageList image to display on the tab.

(*) = Optional argument

Example

In this example, the program adds two new tabs to the default single tab in a TabStrip control. (The programmer previously added the TabStrip control to the form and named it `tabTabStrip1`.) Notice that the first line below sets the first tab's text. Every TabStrip control starts with one tab. Figure A-10 shows the TabStrip control created by this example.

```
tabTabStrip1.Tabs(1).Caption = "Tab 1"
tabTabStrip1.Tabs.Add 2, "Tab2", "Tab 2"
tabTabStrip1.Tabs.Add 3, "Tab3", "Tab 3"
```

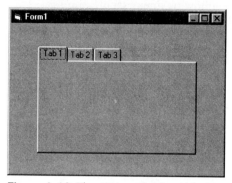

Figure A-10 The Add method enables a program to create tabs in a TabStrip control.

CROSS-REFERENCE
For more information, see Tab, Tabs, and TabStrip.

AddItem

Method

The `AddItem` method adds an entry to a ListBox or ComboBox object's list.

Objects with an AddItem Method

ComboBox
ListBox

Syntax

object.AddItem *string, index*

- *object* — A reference to a ListBox or ComboBox control.

- *string* — The new string entry to add to the list.
- *index* (*) — The position in the list at which to place the new entry.

(*) = Optional argument

Example 1

In this example, the programmer has added a ListBox named lstList1 to the application's form. After the following lines execute, the lstList1 ListBox will contain the list shown in Figure A-11.

```
Private Sub Form_Initialize()
    lstList1.AddItem "Oranges"
    lstList1.AddItem "Apples"
    lstList1.AddItem "Pears"
    lstList1.AddItem "Grapes"
    lstList1.AddItem "Bananas"
End Sub
```

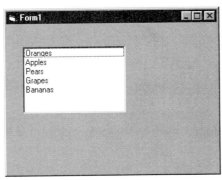

Figure A-11 In this ListBox, the entries appear in the order they were added to the control.

Example 2

Here, after the following lines execute, the lstList1 ListBox will contain the list shown in Figure A-12. Notice the addition of indexes to the AddItem call. The program places the first three entries at indexes 0, 1, and 2, respectively. Then, the fourth and fifth entries use indexes of 0 and 1, forcing those entries to the top of the list.

```
Private Sub Form_Initialize()
    lstList1.AddItem "Oranges", 0
    lstList1.AddItem "Apples", 1
```

```
        lstList1.AddItem "Pears", 2
        lstList1.AddItem "Grapes", 0
        lstList1.AddItem "Bananas", 1
End Sub
```

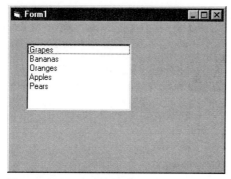

Figure A-12 In this ListBox, the entries appear in a different order, thanks to the use of indexes.

CROSS-REFERENCE

For more information, see ListBox and ComboBox.

AddressCaption

Property

The AddressCaption property represents the caption that appears at the top of the Address Book dialog box. The caption appears, however, only in the default Address Book dialog box. That is, the AddressCaption property is ignored when the program calls the Show method with a value of True.

Objects with an AddressCaption Property

MAPIMessages

Syntax

MAPIMessages.AddressCaption = *caption*

- *MAPIMessages* — A reference to a MAPIMessages object.
- *caption* — A string containing the caption to be displayed.

CROSS-REFERENCE

For more information, see MAPIMessages.

AddressEditFieldCount

Property

The AddressEditFieldCount property determines the edit controls that appear in the Address Book dialog box. This property, however, affects only the default Address Book dialog box. That is, the AddressEditFieldCount property is ignored when the program calls the Show method with a value of True. The AddressEditFieldCount property can be one of the values shown in Table A-5.

Table A-5 Possible Values for the AddressEditFieldCount Property

Value	Description
0	Displays no edit boxes
1	Displays the To edit box (default)
2	Displays the To and CC edit boxes
3	Displays the To, CC, and BCC edit boxes
4	Display only system-supported edit boxes

Objects with an AddressEditFieldCount Property

MAPIMessages

Syntax

MAPIMessages.AddressEditFieldCount = value

- *MAPIMessages* — A reference to a MAPIMessages object.
- *value* — An integer from 0 to 4.

CROSS-REFERENCE

For more information, see MAPIMessages.

a
b
c

AddressLabel

Property

The `AddressLabel` property determines the label that appears on the Address Book dialog box's To edit box. This property, however, affects only the default Address Book dialog box. That is, the `AddressLabel` property is ignored when the program calls the `Show` method with a value of `True`.

Objects with an AddressLabel Property

MAPIMessages

Syntax

`MAPIMessages.AddressLabel = label`

- *MAPIMessages* — A reference to a MAPIMessages object.
- *label* — A string containing the caption to be displayed.

CROSS-REFERENCE
For more information, see MAPIMessages.

AddressModifiable

Property

The `AddressModifiable` property determines whether the user can modify the Address Book.

Objects with an AddressModifiable Property

MAPIMessages

Syntax

`MAPIMessages.AddressModifiable = value`

- *MAPIMessages* — A reference to a MAPIMessages object.
- *value* — A value of `True` or `False`. The default is `False`.

CROSS-REFERENCE
For more information, see MAPIMessages.

AddressOf

Operator

The `AddressOf` operator generates the address of a procedure. This operator has little use in normal Visual Basic programs. However, its usefulness manifests when you need to call Windows API functions from Visual Basic. Many Windows API functions require the types of pointers a program can create with the `AddressOf` operator.

Syntax

`AddressOf procedure`

- *procedure* — The name of the procedure whose address the operator will generate.

AddressResolveUI

Property

The `AddressResolveUI` property determines whether the program will display a dialog box that displays recipient names that closely match the given name.

Objects with an AddressResolveUI Property

MAPIMessages

Syntax

`MAPIMessages.AddressResolveUI = value`

- *MAPIMessages* — A reference to a MAPIMessages object.
- *value* — A value of `True` or `False`. The default is `False`.

 CROSS-REFERENCE
For more information, see MAPIMessages.

AfterLabelEdit

Event

Visual Basic sends a ListView or TreeView control an `AfterLabelEdit` event when the user has finished editing a Node or ListItem object in the control. This enables the program to evaluate the user's changes, usually to determine whether the changes are acceptable.

Objects That Receive AfterLabelEdit Events

ListView

TreeView

Example

A program can respond to an `AfterLabelEdit` event by implementing the target object's `AfterLabelEdit` event procedure. The following code segment shows how a TreeView object can reject a user's changes to a node label. The `AfterLabelEdit` event procedure receives two parameters, which are a flag indicating whether the edit should be accepted and the string that the user entered. In this example, the program checks to see whether the user entered the name "Fred." If he didn't, the program sets `Cancel` to `True`, which causes the node's label to revert to its original state, declining the user's changes.

```
Private Sub TreeView1_AfterLabelEdit _
    (Cancel As Integer, NewString As String)
    If NewString <> "Fred" Then Cancel = True
End Sub
```

 CROSS-REFERENCE
For more information, see ListView and TreeView.

Align

Property

The `Align` property determines whether the position and appearance of an object. The `Align` property can be one of the values shown in Table A-6.

Table A-6 Possible Values for the Align Property

Value	Description
vbAlignBottom	The object is positioned at the top of the container, and its width is automatically the same as the container's.
vbAlignLeft	The object is positioned at the left of the container, and its height is automatically the same as the container's.
vbAlignNone	Alignment is set at design time or by the program (default).
vbAlignRight	The object is positioned at the right of the container, and its height is automatically the same as the container's.
vbAlignTop	The object is positioned at the top of the container, and its width is automatically the same as the container's.

Objects with an Align Property

PictureBox

ProgressBar

StatusBar

Toolbar

Syntax

```
object.Align = value1
```

or

```
value2 = object.Align
```

- *object* — A reference to an object with an `Align` property.
- *value1* — The new alignment.
- *value2* — The variable that will receive the current alignment returned by the property.

Example

A toolbar normally uses the `vbAlignTop` setting for the `Align` property, which places the toolbar across the top of the form. (The programmer previously added the toolbar to the application, naming it `tlbToolbar1`.) However, you can use other alignments, as well. In this example, the program sets the toolbar to appear on the left of the form. Figure A-13 shows the result, with the toolbar looking more like a toolbox.

```
Private Sub Form_Load()
    tlbToolbar1.Align = vbAlignLeft
End Sub
```

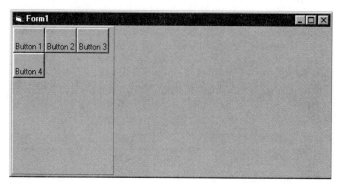

Figure A-13 Here is a toolbar aligned to the left.

CROSS-REFERENCE

For more information, see PictureBox, ProgressBar, StatusBar, and Toolbar.

Alignable

Property

The `Alignable` property determines whether a control is alignable, which means that it supports the `Align` property. The `Alignable` property is accessible only at design time.

Objects with an Alignable Property

UserControl

Syntax

UserControl.Alignable = *value1*

or

value2 = *UserControl*.Alignable

- *UserControl* — A reference to a UserControl object.
- *value1* — A value of `True` or `False`.
- *value2* — The variable that will receive the current alignable setting returned by the property.

CROSS-REFERENCE

For more information, see UserControl and Align.

Alignment—CheckBox and OptionButton

Property

The Alignment property determines whether the text on the control is aligned to the left or right. This property, which can be one of the values in Table A-7, can be set only at design time and is read-only at run time.

Table A-7 Possible Values for the Alignment Property

Value	Description
vbLeftJustify	Aligns text on the left (default).
vbRightJustify	Aligns text on the right.

Syntax

```
value = Control.Alignment
```

- *Control*—A reference to a CheckBox or OptionButton object.
- *value*—The variable that will receive the current alignment setting returned by the property.

Example

In Figure A-14, the CheckBox controls display right alignment (the default), whereas the OptionButton controls display left alignment.

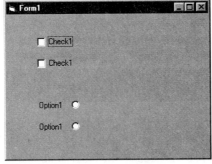

Figure A-14 Text on these controls can be left or right justified.

CROSS-REFERENCE
For more information, see CheckBox and OptionButton.

Alignment—ColumnHeader Object

Property

The `Alignment` property determines whether the text in the control is aligned to the left, right, or center. This property can be one of the values in Table A-8.

Table A-8 Possible Values for the Alignment Property

Value	Description
lvwColumnCenter	Aligns text in the center.
lvwColumnLeft	Aligns text on the left (default).
lvwColumnRight	Aligns text on the right.

Syntax

```
Control.Alignment = value1
```

or

```
value2 = Control.Alignment
```

- *Control*—A reference to a CheckBox or OptionButton object.
- *value1*—The new alignment setting.
- *value2*—The variable that will receive the current alignment setting returned by the property.

Example

In this example, the lines below set three column headers in a ListView control to the three possible alignments. The programmer previously added the ListView control, `lvwListView1`, to the application and created three columns for the control. In Figure A-15, you can see the effect of the alignment settings on the control.

```
lvwListView1.ColumnHeaders(1).Alignment = lvwColumnLeft
lvwListView1.ColumnHeaders(2).Alignment = lvwColumnCenter
lvwListView1.ColumnHeaders(3).Alignment = lvwColumnRight
```

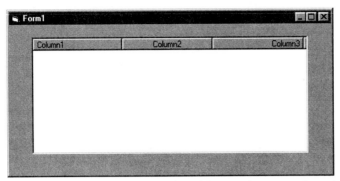

Figure A-15 Here are the three possible text alignments for column headers in a ListView control.

 CROSS-REFERENCE
For more information, see ListView.

Alignment — Panel Objects

Property

The Alignment property determines whether the text in the panel is aligned to the left, right, or center. This property can be one of the values in Table A-9.

Table A-9 Possible Values for the Alignment Property

Value	Description
sbrCenter	Aligns text in the center.
sbrLeft	Aligns text on the left (default).
sbrRight	Aligns text on the right.

Syntax

```
Panel.Alignment = value1
```

or

```
value2 = Panel.Alignment
```

- *Panel* — A reference to a Panel object.
- *value1* — The new alignment setting.

- *value2*—The variable that will receive the current alignment setting returned by the property.

Example

In this example, the lines below set three panels in a StatusBar control to the three possible alignments. The programmer previously added the StatusBar control, staStatusBar1, to the application and created three additional panels for the control. In Figure A-16, you can see the effect of the alignment settings on the panels.

```
staStatusBar1.Panels(2).Alignment = sbrLeft
staStatusBar1.Panels(3).Alignment = sbrCenter
staStatusBar1.Panels(4).Alignment = sbrRight
```

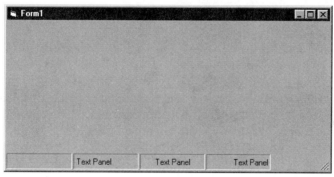

Figure A-16 Here are the three possible text alignments for panels in a StatusBar control.

CROSS-REFERENCE
For more information, see StatusBar.

Alignment—UpDown Control

Property

The Alignment property determines the respective alignment of an UpDown control and its associated buddy control. A *buddy control* is a control, usually an edit box, that displays the UpDown control's current setting. The Alignment property can be one of the values in Table A-10.

Table A-10 Possible Values for the Alignment Property

Value	Description
cc2AlignmentLeft	Aligns the control to the left of its buddy control.
cc2AlignmentRight	Aligns the control to the right of its buddy control (default).

Syntax

```
UpDown.Alignment = value1
```

or

```
value2 = UpDown.Alignment
```

- *UpDown*—A reference to an UpDown control.
- *value1*—The new alignment setting.
- *value2*—The variable that will receive the current alignment setting returned by the property.

Example

In this example, the lines below set the alignment of UpDown controls and their associated buddy controls. The programmer previously added the controls to the application, with the alignments being set in the form's `Load` method. In Figure A-17, you can see the effect of the alignment settings on the controls.

```
updUpDown1.Alignment = cc2AlignmentLeft
updUpDown2.Alignment = cc2AlignmentRight
```

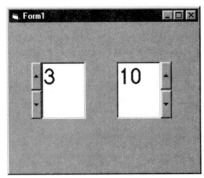

Figure A-17 Here are the two possible alignments for UpDown controls and their buddy controls.

CROSS-REFERENCE
For more information, see UpDown.

AllowColumnReorder

Property

The `AllowColumnReorder` property determines whether the user can reposition the columns in a ListView control. This property can be set to `True` or `False`.

Objects with an AllowColumnReorder Property

ListView

Syntax

`ListView.AllowColumnReorder = value1`

or

`value2 = ListView.AllowColumnReorder`

- *ListView* — A reference to a ListView control.
- *value1* — A value of `True` or `False`. The default is `False`.
- *value2* — A variable that will receive current `AllowColumnReorder` setting returned by the property.

CROSS-REFERENCE
For more information, see ListView.

AllowCustomize

Property

The `AllowCustomize` property determines whether the user can customize the application's toolbar. If this property is set to `True`, the user can double-click the toolbar in order to display the Customize Toolbar dialog box, from which the user can add, delete, or reposition toolbar buttons.

Objects with an AllowCustomize Property

Toolbar

Syntax

```
Toolbar.AllowCustomize = value1
```

or

```
value2 = Toolbar.AllowCustomize
```

- *ListView*—A reference to a ListView control.
- *value1*—A value of `True` or `False`. The default is `True`.
- *value2*—A variable that will receive current `AllowCustomize` setting returned by the property.

 CROSS-REFERENCE
For more information, see Toolbar.

AllowVertical

Property

The `AllowVertical` property determines whether a CoolBar control can display bands when in its vertical orientation. This property can be set to `True` or `False`.

Objects with an AllowVertical Property

Band

Syntax

```
Band.AllowVertical = value1
```

or

```
value2 = Band.AllowVertical
```

- *Band*—A reference to an Band object.
- *value1*—The new property setting of `True` or `False`. The default is `True`.
- *value2*—The variable that will receive the current setting returned by the property.

CROSS-REFERENCE
For more information, see Band and CoolBar.

Ambient

Property

The `Ambient` property enables a program to access a control's AmbientProperties object. You can think of *ambient properties* as properties of a control that are determined by the properties of the control's container. For example, when you place a control in a container, you'll probably want the control to use the same background color as the container. `BackColor` is one of the ambient properties. When your control uses `BackColor` to determine its background color, the control will always have the same background color as the container.

Objects with an Ambient Property

UserControl

Syntax

`UserControl.Ambient`

- *UserControl* — A reference to a UserControl object.

CROSS-REFERENCE
For more information, see AmbientChanged and UserControl.

AmbientChanged

Event

Visual Basic sends a user control an `AmbientChanged` event when the control's container object changes an ambient property. This event enables the user control to determine whether it needs to make a similar change to its own properties.

Objects That Receive AmbientChanged Events

UserControl

Example

A user control can respond to an AmbientChanged event by implementing the target object's AmbientChanged event procedure. The following program shows a Form that changes its BackColor property when the user clicks the form's BackColor button. When you run the program, you see the window shown in Figure A-18. The black rectangle contains a UserControl object.

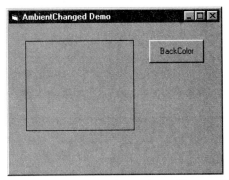

Figure A-18 Here's the AmbientChanged Demo program when you first run it.

When you click the BackColor button, the form's background color changes to purple and a message box appears, letting you know that the UserControl object has received the AmbientChanged event. Figure A-19 shows the program at this point. Notice how the UserControl object still retains its original background color. Finally, when you dismiss the message box, the UserControl object's background color changes to that of its container form.

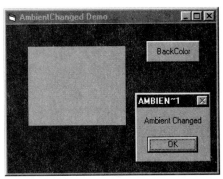

Figure A-19 Here's the program after the form changes its background color.

```
VERSION 5.00
Begin VB.Form frmForm1
   BackColor       =    &H8000000A&
   Caption         =    "AmbientChanged Demo"
   ClientHeight    =    3195
   ClientLeft      =    60
   ClientTop       =    345
   ClientWidth     =    4680
   LinkTopic       =    "Form1"
   ScaleHeight     =    3195
   ScaleWidth      =    4680
   StartUpPosition =    3   'Windows Default
   Begin VB.CommandButton Command1
      Caption      =    "BackColor"
      Height       =    495
      Left         =    3120
      TabIndex     =    1
      Top          =    360
      Width        =    1215
   End
   Begin Project1.UserControl1 UserControl11
      Height       =    1695
      Left         =    480
      TabIndex     =    0
      Top          =    480
      Width        =    2175
      _ExtentX     =    3836
      _ExtentY     =    2990
   End
   Begin VB.Shape Shape1
      Height       =    1935
      Left         =    360
      Top          =    360
      Width        =    2415
   End
End

Attribute VB_Name = "frmForm1"
Attribute VB_GlobalNameSpace = False
Attribute VB_Creatable = False
Attribute VB_PredeclaredId = True
Attribute VB_Exposed = False

Private Sub Command1_Click()
```

```
        BackColor = QBColor(5)
    End Sub
```

The source code lines below show a user control that responds to the color change in its AmbientChanged event procedure. This is, in fact, the source code for the UserControl object that's contained in the program's main form.

```
VERSION 5.00
Begin VB.UserControl UserControl1
    ClientHeight    =    3600
    ClientLeft      =    0
    ClientTop       =    0
    ClientWidth     =    4800
    ScaleHeight     =    3600
    ScaleWidth      =    4800
End

Attribute VB_Name = "UserControl1"
Attribute VB_GlobalNameSpace = False
Attribute VB_Creatable = True
Attribute VB_PredeclaredId = False
Attribute VB_Exposed = False

Private Sub UserControl_AmbientChanged(PropertyName As String)
    MsgBox "Ambient Changed"
    If PropertyName = "BackColor" Then
        BackColor = Ambient.BackColor
    End If
End Sub
```

When you click the BackColor button, the form's Command1_Click procedure changes the form's background color to purple. Because BackColor is an ambient property, this color change sends an AmbientChanged event to the UserControl object, which handles the event in its AmbientChanged event procedure. In the AmbientChanged procedure, the control first displays a message box, giving you time to see the form's background color change before the control's changes. Then, the control checks whether it's the BackColor property that's been changed. If so, the control sets its own BackColor property to the ambient BackColor property, giving the control the same background color as its container form.

CROSS-REFERENCE
For more information, see Ambient and UserControl.

AmbientProperties

Object

The AmbientProperties object represents a UserControl's ambient properties, which are properties of a control that are determined by the properties of the control's container. For example, when you place a control in a container, you'll probably want the control to use the same background color as the container. `BackColor` is one of the ambient properties. When your control uses `BackColor` to determine its background color, the control will always have the same background color as the container. A UserControl control accesses its AmbientProperties object through its `Ambient` property.

Properties

The AmbientProperties object has 16 properties, which are listed in Table A-11. For more information on using a property shown in the following table, look up the property's entry elsewhere in this book.

Table A-11 Properties of the AmbientProperties Object

Property	Description
BackColor	Represents the control's background color.
DisplayAsDefault	Represents whether, in the case of button controls, the control will be the default.
DisplayName	Represents the text string that can be used to identify the control in error messages.
Font	Represents the control's font.
ForeColor	Represents the control's foreground color.
LocaleID	Represents the locale and language of the control's users.
MessageReflect	Represents the control's ability to handle message reflection automatically.
Palette	Represents the color palette for the control, taken from the given image.
RightToLeft	Represents whether text should run from right to left or left to right.
ScaleUnits	Represents the measurement units used with the control.
ShowGrabHandles	Represents whether the control should display grab handles.
ShowHatching	Represents whether the control should display a hatch design when a control has the focus at design time.

Continued

Table A-11 *Continued*

Property	Description
SupportsMnemonics	Represents whether the control can respond to hotkeys.
TextAlign	Represents the type of text alignment the container requests the control to use.
UIDead	Represents whether the user can interact with the control.
UserMode	Represents whether the control is in design mode or user mode.

Methods

The AmbientProperties object has no methods.

Events

The AmbientProperties object responds to no events.

 CROSS-REFERENCE
See also UserControl and Ambient.

Ampersand (&)

Operator

The ampersand (&) operator performs string concatenation on two or more expressions. The operator can concatenate any type of expression, but the result is always a String or Variant object.

Syntax

```
string = exp1 & exp2
```

- *string*—The result of the concatenation.
- *exp1*—Any valid expression.
- *exp2*—Any valid expression.

Example 1

After the following lines execute, vntString1 will contain the string Word1Word2.

```
Dim vntString1
vntString1 = "Word1" & "Word2"
```

Example 2

After the following lines execute, `vntString1` will contain the string Word1999Word2.

```
Dim vntString1
vntString1 = "Word1" & 999 & "Word2"
```

And

Operator

The `And` operator performs Boolean operations on expressions. The result of a Boolean expression is always `True` or `False`. If both expressions being evaluated by `And` are `True`, then the result of the `And` operation is `True`. If either expression is `False`, the `And` operation yields `False`. You can also use `And` to perform a bit-by-bit comparison of two numerical expressions. In this case, the matching bit in the result will be 1 if both bits in the compared expressions are 1, and 0 otherwise.

Syntax

```
boolean = exp1 And exp2
```

or

```
bits = exp3 And exp4
```

- *bits* — The result of the bit-by-bit comparison.
- *boolean* — The result of the `And` operation.
- *exp1* — Any valid expression.
- *exp2* — Any valid expression.
- *exp3* — Any valid numerical expression.
- *exp4* — Any valid numerical expression.

Example 1

In this example, the program sets both `expr1` and `expr2` to `True` and then uses the `And` operator to compare the two expressions. Because both expressions are `True`, the result of the `And` operation is `True` and the program displays the message box.

```
Dim expr1, expr2 As Boolean
expr1 = True
expr2 = True
```

```
If expr1 And expr2 Then
    MsgBox ("The expression is True")
End If
```

Example 2

In this example, the program sets expr1 to True and expr2 to False. Because one of the expressions is False, the result of the And operation is False and the program does not display the message box.

```
Dim expr1, expr2 As Boolean
expr1 = True
expr2 = False
If expr1 And expr2 Then
    MsgBox ("The expression is True")
End If
```

Example 3

In this example, the program uses And to compare two more complex Boolean expressions. Because both of the expressions are True, the result of the And operation is True and the program displays the message box.

```
Dim expr1, expr2 As Integer
expr1 = 10
expr2 = 20
If expr1 = 10 And expr2 = 20 Then
    MsgBox ("The expression is True")
End If
```

Example 4

Here, the program uses And to perform a bit-by-bit comparison of two integers. The binary representation of expr1 is 1101, and the binary representation of expr2 is 1011. The comparison results in the binary number 1001, which is 9 in decimal.

```
Dim expr1, expr2, result As Integer
expr1 = 13   ' 1101 in binary
expr2 = 11   ' 1011 in binary
result = expr1 And expr2
If result = 9 Then MsgBox ("Bitwise operation worked")
```

Animation

Control

An Animation control enables programs to display animation sequences easily. (Animations must be stored in .avi files.) Windows 98, for example, uses the animation control to display the animations that accompany file processing, such as when Windows Explorer copies a file. The Animation control is part of Visual Basic's Microsoft Windows Common Controls-2 6.0 components. You can load these components into your project by selecting the Project menu's Components command and selecting the component package from the Components property sheet, as shown in Figure A-20.

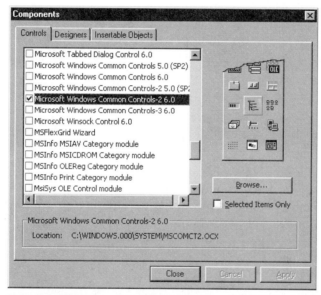

Figure A-20 You can load the animation control from the Components property sheet.

General Properties

The Animation control has 24 general properties, which are listed as follows. Because many Visual Basic controls have similar properties, the general properties' descriptions are listed under their own names elsewhere in this book.

```
BackColor
CausesValidation
Center
Container
```

```
DragIcon
DragMode
Enabled
Height
Help
hWnd
Index
Left
Name
Object
OLEDropMode
Parent
TabIndex
TabStop
Tag
ToolTipText
Top
Visible
WhatsThisHelpID
Width
```

Custom Properties

The Animation control has two custom properties, shown in Table A-12. These custom properties enable you to control how the Animation control, specifically, looks and acts. You can find more complete descriptions of these properties by looking up the property name elsewhere in this book.

Table A-12 The Animation Control's Custom Properties

Property	Description
AutoPlay	Determines whether the control automatically plays the animation sequence upon loading the .avi file.
BackStyle	Determines whether the control displays an animation's background color as transparent or opaque. Can be cc2BackstyleTransparent or cc2BackstyleOpaque. Figure A-21 shows the transparent background style, whereas Figure A-22 shows the opaque background style.

Figure A-21 This animation has a transparent background.

Figure A-22 This animation has an opaque background.

General Methods

The Animation control has six general methods, which are listed below. Because many Visual Basic controls have similar methods, the general methods' descriptions are listed under their own names elsewhere in this book.

```
Drag
Move
OLEDrag
SetFocus
ShowWhatsThis
ZOrder
```

Custom Methods

The Animation control has four custom methods, shown in Table A-13. These custom methods enable you to control how the Animation control, specifically, looks and acts. You can find more complete descriptions of these methods by looking up the method name elsewhere in this book.

Table A-13 The Animation Control's Custom Methods

Method	Description
Close	Closes the currently open .avi file.
Open	Opens the given .avi file.
Play	Plays the currently loaded .avi.
Stop	Stops playing the currently loaded .avi file.

General Events

The Animation control responds to 19 events, which are listed below. Because many Visual Basic controls respond to similar events, the general events' descriptions are listed under their own names elsewhere in this book.

```
Click
DblClick
DragDrop
DragOver
```

```
GotFocus
KeyDown
KeyPress
KeyUp
LostFocus
MouseDown
MouseMove
MouseUp
OLECompleteDrag
OLEDragDrop
OLEDragOver
OLEGiveFeedback
OLESetData
OLEStartDrag
Validate
```

Example

This sample program displays a window into which you can load and play an animation file. Click the Load Animation button to display a dialog box with which you can select the .avi file you want to view. (There's a file called `filecopy.avi`, which is one of Windows' animations, included in the program's directory.) Then click the Play button to start the animation and the Stop button to stop the animation. Figure A-23 shows the running application. The program's source code follows.

Figure A-23 Here's the example program displaying the filecopy.avi animation file.

```
VERSION 5.00
Object = "{FE0065C0-1B7B-11CF-9D53-00AA003C9CB6}#2.0#0"; _
    "MSCOMCT2.OCX"
Object = "{F9043C88-F6F2-101A-A3C9-08002B2F49FB}#1.2#0";  _
    "COMDLG32.OCX"
```

```
Begin VB.Form frmForm1
   Caption         =   "Animation Control Demo"
   ClientHeight    =   3225
   ClientLeft      =   60
   ClientTop       =   345
   ClientWidth     =   4680
   LinkTopic       =   "Form1"
   ScaleHeight     =   3225
   ScaleWidth      =   4680
   StartUpPosition =   3  'Windows Default
   Begin VB.CommandButton btnStop
      Caption      =   "Stop"
      Height       =   375
      Left         =   2520
      TabIndex     =   3
      Top          =   2520
      Width        =   1815
   End
   Begin VB.CommandButton btnPlay
      Caption      =   "Play"
      Height       =   375
      Left         =   480
      TabIndex     =   2
      Top          =   2520
      Width        =   1815
   End
   Begin MSComDlg.CommonDialog dlgCommonDialog1
      Left         =   0
      Top          =   1680
      _ExtentX     =   847
      _ExtentY     =   847
      _Version     =   393216
      DefaultExt   =   "avi (*.avi)"
      DialogTitle  =   "Open AVI File"
      FileName     =   "*.avi"
      Filter       =   "*.avi"
   End
   Begin VB.CommandButton btnLoad
      Caption      =   "Load Animation"
      Height       =   615
      Left         =   600
      TabIndex     =   1
      Top          =   1680
      Width        =   3615
```

```
      End
      Begin MSComCtl2.Animation Animation1
         Height          =    975
         Left            =    360
         TabIndex        =    0
         Top             =    360
         Width           =    3975
         _ExtentX        =    7011
         _ExtentY        =    1720
         _Version        =    393216
         FullWidth       =    265
         FullHeight      =    65
      End
      Begin VB.Shape Shape1
         BorderWidth     =    2
         Height          =    1215
         Left            =    240
         Top             =    240
         Width           =    4215
      End
   End
End

Attribute VB_Name = "frmForm1"
Attribute VB_GlobalNameSpace = False
Attribute VB_Creatable = False
Attribute VB_PredeclaredId = True
Attribute VB_Exposed = False

Private Sub btnLoad_Click()
   dlgCommonDialog1.Action = 1
   On Error GoTo ErrorHandler
   Animation1.Open dlgCommonDialog1.FileName
   Exit Sub
ErrorHandler:
   MsgBox "Couldn't Open the File"
End Sub

Private Sub btnPlay_Click()
   Animation1.Play
End Sub

Private Sub btnStop_Click()
   Animation1.Stop
End Sub
```

App
Object

The App object represents the context of the running application. Through the App object, a program can get information about the running application, including the names of associated files and the application's name and version.

Properties

The App object has 29 properties, which are listed in Table A-14. For more information on using a property shown in the following table, look up the property's entry elsewhere in this book.

Table A-14 Properties of the App Object

Property	Description
Comments	Represents a string that contains the application's comments.
CompanyName	Represents a string that contains the name of the company that developed the application.
EXEName	Represents the name of the running application's executable file, or, if the application is running under the Visual Basic programming environment, the name of the project.
FileDescription	Represents a string that contains the application's file description.
HelpFile	Represents the complete path and file name of the application's help file.
Hinstance	Represents the application's instance handle.
LegalCopyright	Represents a string that contains the application's copyright information.
LegalTrademarks	Represents a string that contains the application's trademark information.
LogMode	Controls the type of message logging associated with the LogEvent message.
LogPath	Represents the complete path and file name of the application's log file.
Major	Represents the application's major version number.
Minor	Represents the application's minor version number.
NonModalAllowed	Controls whether the application's form can be modeless.

Continued

Table A-14 *Continued*

Property	Description
OLERequestPendingMsgText	Represents the text that's displayed when a busy automation object (one that's processing an automation request) receives mouse or keyboard input from the user.
OLERequestPendingMsgTitle	Represents the caption that's displayed when a busy automation object receives mouse or keyboard input from the user.
OLERequestPendingTimeout	Represents, for a busy automation object, the number of milliseconds between mouse and keyboard input and the appearance of the Component Request Pending dialog box.
OLEServerBusyMsgText	Represents the text that's displayed when an automation server object cannot process an automation request.
OLEServerBusyMsgTitle	Represents the caption that's displayed when an automation server object cannot process an automation request.
OLEServerBusyRaiseError	Controls whether a busy automation object receiving mouse or keyboard input displays the default dialog box or generates an error.
OLEServerBusyTimeout	Represents, for a busy automation server, the number of milliseconds between an automation request and the appearance of the Component Busy dialog box.
Path	Represents the application's current path.
PrevInstance	Represents the instance handle of the previously executed application instance.
ProductName	Represents a string that contains the application's product name.
Revision	Represents the application's revision number.
StartMode	Controls whether the application runs as a standalone program or as an ActiveX component.
TaskVisible	Controls whether the application's name appears in the Windows task list.
ThreadID	Represents the ID of the currently executing thread.
Title	Represents the application's title as it appears in Windows task list.
UnattendedApp	Controls whether the application will display a user interface.

a
b
c

Methods

The App object has two methods, which are listed in Table A-15. For more information on using a method shown in the following table, look up the method's entry elsewhere in this book.

Table A-15 Methods of the App Object

Method	Description
LogEvent	Logs messages to the current log file.
StartLogging	Sets the logging file and logging mode.

AppActivate

Statement

The AppActivate statement activates another application's window.

Syntax

```
AppActivate title, focus
```

- *focus* (*) — A Boolean value indicating whether the application immediately activates the other window or waits until the application has the focus. The default is False.

- *title* — The title of the window to activate. This is the title found in the window's title bar.

(*) = Optional

Example

The following line shows how to use the AppActivate statement:

```
AppActivate "My Application", False
```

CROSS-REFERENCE
See also Shell.

Appearance—General Controls

Property

The `Appearance` property determines whether Visual Basic paints a control with 2-D or 3-D graphics. Figure A-24 shows a Form containing a Frame control, both drawn with the default 3-D graphics, whereas Figure A-25 shows the same form and control drawn with 2-D graphics.

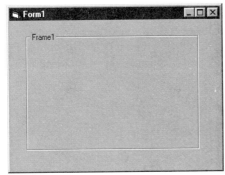

Figure A-24 Here's an example of a 3-D window and control.

Figure A-25 Here's an example of a 2-D window and control.

Objects with an Appearance Property

CheckBox

ComboBox

CommandButton

DirListBox

DriveListBox

FileListBox

Form

Frame

Image

Label

ListBox

ListView

MDIForm

OLEContainer

OptionButton

PictureBox

ProgressBar

PropertyPage

RichTextBox

TextBox

ToolBar

TreeView

UserControl

Syntax

```
control.Appearance = value1
```

or

```
value2 = control.Appearance
```

- *control*—A reference to a control object.
- *value1*—The integer value 0 or 1, where 1 (3-D) is the default.
- *value2*—The integer variable that will receive the property's current value.

ApplsRunning

Property

The `ApplsRunning` property indicates whether the application that created an embedded object is currently running. For example, you might have an OLE Container control that has embedded a Microsoft Word document. If the Word application is running, Visual Basic sets `ApplsRunning` to `True`. Setting

`AppIsRunning` to `True` in a program runs the embedded object's application, whereas setting `AppIsRunning` to `False` closes the application when the embedded object no longer has the focus.

Objects with an AppIsRunning Property
OLEContainer

Syntax
`OLEContainer.AppIsRunning = value1`

or

`value2 = OLEContainer.AppIsRunning`

- *OLEContainer*—A reference to an OLE container control.
- *value1*—A value of `True` or `False`.
- *value2*—The variable that will receive the property's current value.

ApplyChanges

Event

Visual Basic sends a PropertyPage control an `ApplyChanges` event when the user clicks the property page's OK or Apply buttons or when the user switches from one property page to another. To respond to this event, the program should apply the user's new settings to the application as appropriate.

Objects That Receive ApplyChanges Events
PropertyPage

Example
As with any Visual Basic event, you respond to a property page's `ApplyChanges` event by implementing the property page's event procedure of the same name, the skeleton for which looks like this:

```
Private Sub PropertyPage_ApplyChanges()
    ' Respond to the event here.
End Sub
```

CROSS-REFERENCE
For more information, see PropertyPage and TabStrip.

a
b
c

Archive

Property

The `Archive` determines whether a FileListBox control displays files with their archive bits set.

Objects with an Archive Property

FileListBox

Syntax

`FileListBox.Archive = value1`

or

`value2 = FileListBox.Archive`

- *FileListBox* — A reference to a control object.
- *value1* — The value `True` or `False`. The default is `True`.
- *value2* — The variable that will receive the property's current value.

Arrange

Method

The `Arrange` method arranges the windows or icons in an MDIForm window. You can call the `Arrange` method with one of the values shown in Table A-16.

Table A-16 Possible Values for the Arrange Method

Value	Description
vbArrangeIcons	Arranges the icons that represent minimized MDI child windows.
vbCascade	Cascades MDI child windows.
vbTileHorizontal	Horizontally tiles MDI child windows.
vbTileVertical	Vertically tiles MDI child windows.

Objects with an Arrange Method

MDIForm

Syntax

```
MDIForm.Arrange value
```

- *MDIForm* — A reference to an MDIForm object.
- *value* — A value from Table A-16.

Example

The following line arranges an MDI form's document icons into rows at the bottom of the window:

```
MDIForm1.Arrange vbArrangeIcons
```

 CROSS-REFERENCE
For more information, see MDIForm.

Arrange

Property

The Arrange property determines how a ListView control arranges its contents when in icon or small-icon view. This property can be set to one of the values shown in Table A-17.

Table A-17 Possible Values for the Arrange Property

Value	Description
LvwAutoLeft	Automatically aligns list-view items to the left.
LvwAutoTop	Automatically aligns list-view items to the top.
LvwNone	The default setting of no auto arrangement.

Objects with an Arrange Property

ListView

Syntax

```
ListView.Arrange = value1
```

or

```
value2 = ListView.Arrange
```

- *ListView* — A reference to a ListView control.
- *value1* — One of the values from Table A-17.
- *value2* — The variable that will receive the property's current value.

Array

Function

Array is a function that returns an array of given values. To reference a value in the array, add a subscript in parentheses to the array variable name.

Syntax

```
variant = Array(arg1, ...)
```

- *arg1* — The first value to add to the array.
- *variant* — The variable that will receive the array.
- *...* — Any number of additional values to add to the array.

Example

In this example, the program creates two arrays, one containing integers and another containing strings. The program then displays a message box containing a value from each array. Notice how the example references values in the arrays. Unless you use the Option Base statement, the first element of the array is at index 0.

```
Dim array1 As Variant
Dim array2 As Variant
array1 = Array(10, 11, 12, 13, 14, 15)
array2 = Array("One", "Two", "Three", "Four")
MsgBox array1(0) & " " & array2(2)
```

CROSS-REFERENCE
For more information, see Option Base.

As

Keyword

The As keyword specifies data types. You will use As most often when declaring variables and constants or when defining function arguments and return types. However, As is also a part of many other types of Visual Basic statements. Those statements are listed as follows. Please refer to the statement entries elsewhere in this book for more complete descriptions.

```
Const
Declare
Dim
Function
Name
Open
Private
Property Get
Property Let
Property Set
Public
ReDim
Static
Sub
Type
```

Asc

Function

The Asc function returns the ASCII code of the first character in a string.

Syntax

```
code = Asc(string)
```

- *code* — The variable that will receive the ASCII value.
- *string* — The string from which Asc will calculate the ASCII code of the first character.

Example

In this example, the program gets the ASCII code of the first character in a string and displays the code in a message box. In this case, the message box will display the value 88, which is the ASCII code for the letter "X."

```
Dim code As Integer
code = Asc("XYZ")
MsgBox code
```

 CROSS-REFERENCE
See also AscB and AscW.

AscB

Function

The AscB function returns the ASCII value of the first byte in a string.

Syntax

```
code = AscB(string)
```

- *code* — The variable that will receive the ASCII value.
- *string* — The string from which AscB will calculate the ASCII code of the first byte.

 CROSS-REFERENCE
See also Asc and AscW.

AscW

Function

The AscW function returns the Unicode value of the first character in a string. If the platform on which the program is running does not support Unicode, AscW returns the ASCII code of the first character in a string.

Syntax

```
code = AscW(string)
```

- *code* — The variable that will receive the Unicode value.
- *string* — The string from which AscW will calculate the Unicode or ASCII code of the first character.

 CROSS-REFERENCE
See also Asc and AscB.

Assert

Method

The Assert method suspends execution of a program when the given Boolean expression evaluates to False.

Objects with an Assert Method

Debug

Syntax

```
Debug.Assert value
```

- *value* — The expression that Assert will evaluate.

Example

The following lines cause an assertion that suspends program execution on the Assert line. The assertion occurs because the Boolean expression (Value > 20) is False. Figure A-26 shows the suspended program highlighting the line that caused the assertion.

```
Dim value As Integer
value = 10
Debug.Assert (value > 20)
```

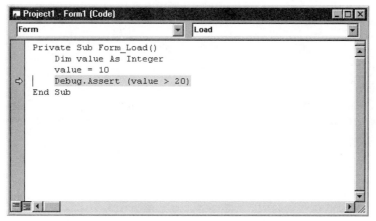

Figure A-26 When an assertion occurs, Visual Basic highlights the code line that caused the assertion.

CROSS-REFERENCE
For more information, see Debug.

Asterisk (*)

Operator

The asterisk (*) operator multiplies two values or expressions.

Syntax

```
result = exp1 * exp2
```

- *result* — The result of the multiplication.
- *exp1* — Any valid numerical expression.
- *exp2* — Any valid numerical expression.

Example 1

In this example, the program lines multiply two values and display the result in a message box. In this case, the result of the multiplication is 250.

```
Dim value1, value2 As Integer
Dim result As Integer
value1 = 10
```

```
value2 = 25
result = value1 * value2
MsgBox result
```

Example 2

Here, the program lines multiply two numerical expressions and display the result in a message box. In this case, the result of the multiplication is 600.

```
Dim value1, value2 As Integer
Dim result As Integer
value1 = 10
value2 = 25
result = (value1 + 10) * (value2 + 5)
MsgBox result
```

AtEndOfLine

Property

The AtEndOfLine property indicates whether a file pointer has reached the end of a line in a text file.

Objects with an AtEndOfLine Property

TextStream

Syntax

TextStream.AtEndOfLine

- *TextStream* — A reference to a TextStream object.

Example

In this example, the program reads three lines of text, one character at a time, from a text file. When reaching the end of a line, the program displays the most recently read line in a message box.

```
Dim fileSystem, stream
Dim str As String

' Create the text stream.
Set fileSystem =
CreateObject("Scripting.FileSystemObject")
```

```
Set stream = fileSystem.OpenTextFile("c:\text.txt", 1)

' Read three lines of text one character at a time.
For Lines = 1 To 3
    str = ""
    Do While stream.AtEndOfLine <> True
        str = str & stream.Read(1)
    Loop
    stream.Skip (2) ' Skip the CR/LF
    MsgBox str
Next Lines

stream.Close
```

CROSS-REFERENCE
For more information, see TextStream.

AtEndOfStream

Property

The AtEndOfStream property indicates whether a file pointer has reached the end of a text file.

Objects with an AtEndOfStream Property

TextStream

Syntax

TextStream.AtEndOfStream

- *TextStream* — A reference to a TextStream object.

Example

In this example, the program reads lines of text from a text file, displaying each line in a message box. The program stops reading from the file when the AtEndOfStream property indicates the file pointer is at the end of the file.

```
Dim fileSystem, stream
Dim str As String

' Create the text stream.
```

```
Set fileSystem = CreateObject("Scripting.FileSystemObject")
Set stream = fileSystem.OpenTextFile("c:\text.txt", 1)

' Read lines from a text file.
Do While stream.AtEndOfStream <> True
    str = stream.ReadLine
    MsgBox str
Loop

stream.Close
```

CROSS-REFERENCE
For more information, see TextStream.

Atn

Function

The Atn function calculates the arctangent of a given value.

Syntax

result = Atn(*value*)

- *result* — The variable that will receive the calculated arctangent.
- *value* — The value whose arctangent Atn will calculate.

CROSS-REFERENCE
See also Tan.

AttachmentCount

Property

The AttachmentCount property indicates the number of attachments in a message.

Objects with an AttachmentCount Property

MAPIMessages

Syntax

```
count = MAPIMessages.AttachmentCount
```

- *count* — The variable that will receive the attachment count.
- *MAPIMessages* — A reference to a MAPIMessages object.

CROSS-REFERENCE
For more information, see MAPIMessages, AttachmentIndex, AttachmentName, AttachmentPathName, AttachmentPosition, and AttachmentType.

AttachmentIndex

Property

The `AttachmentIndex` property determines the current message attachment.

Objects with an AttachmentIndex Property

MAPIMessages

Syntax

```
MAPIMessages.AttachmentIndex = index
```

- *index* — The index number of a message attachment.
- *MAPIMessages* — A reference to a MAPIMessages object.

CROSS-REFERENCE
For more information, see MAPIMessages, AttachmentCount, AttachmentName, AttachmentPathName, AttachmentPosition, and AttachmentType.

AttachmentName

Property

The `AttachmentName` property specifies the file name of the current message attachment. You can set this property only when the MAPIMessages control's `MsgIndex` property is set to –1.

Objects with an AttachmentName Property
MAPIMessages

Syntax

```
MAPIMessages.AttachmentName = name1
```

or

```
name2 = MAPIMessages.AttachmentName
```

- *MAPIMessages*—A reference to a MAPIMessages object.
- *name1*—The file name of a message attachment.
- *name2*—The variable that will receive the attachment file name.

CROSS-REFERENCE
For more information, see MAPIMessages, MsgIndex, AttachmentCount, AttachmentIndex, AttachmentPathName, AttachmentPosition, and AttachmentType.

AttachmentPathName

Property

The `AttachmentPathName` property specifies the complete path name of the current message attachment. You can set this property only when the MAPIMessages control's `MsgIndex` property is set to –1.

Objects with an AttachmentPathName Property
MAPIMessages

Syntax

```
MAPIMessages.AttachmentPathName = name1
```

or

```
name2 = MAPIMessages.AttachmentPathName
```

- *MAPIMessages*—A reference to a MAPIMessages object.
- *name1*—The full path name of a message attachment.
- *name2*—The variable that will receive the attachment path name.

CROSS-REFERENCE
For more information, see MAPIMessages, MsgIndex, AttachmentCount, AttachmentIndex, AttachmentName, AttachmentPosition, and AttachmentType.

a
b
c

AttachmentPosition

Property

The `AttachmentPosition` property specifies the location of an attachment in a message. You can set this property only when the MAPIMessages control's `MsgIndex` property is set to –1. The actual position is the zero-based character position within the message at which the attachment should be placed.

Objects with an AttachmentPosition Property

MAPIMessages

Syntax

`MAPIMessages.AttachmentPosition = position1`

or

`position2 = MAPIMessages.AttachmentPosition`

- *MAPIMessages* — A reference to a MAPIMessages object.
- *position1* — The character position at which to position the attachment.
- *position2* — The variable that will receive the attachment position.

CROSS-REFERENCE
For more information, see MAPIMessages, MsgIndex, AttachmentCount, AttachmentIndex, AttachmentName, AttachmentPathName, and AttachmentType.

AttachmentType

Property

The `AttachmentType` property specifies the current attachment's type. You can set this property only when the MAPIMessages control's `MsgIndex` property is set to –1. The `AttachmentType` property can be one of the values shown in Table A-18.

Table A-18 Possible Values for the AttachmentType Property

Value	Description
mapData	The attachment is a file.
mapEOLE	The attachment is an embedded OLE object.
mapSOLE	The attachment is a static OLE object.

Objects with an AttachmentType Property

MAPIMessages

Syntax

```
MAPIMessages.AttachmentType = type1
```

or

```
type2 = MAPIMessages.AttachmentType
```

- *MAPIMessages*—A reference to a MAPIMessages object.
- *type1* — The message attachment type.
- *type2* — The variable that will receive the attachment type.

 CROSS-REFERENCE
For more information, see MAPIMessages, MsgIndex, AttachmentCount, AttachmentIndex, AttachmentName, AttachmentPosition, and AttachmentPathName.

Attributes

Property

The Attributes property represents the file attributes of a File or Folder object. The Attributes property can be one of the values shown in Table A-19. As you can see by the values in the table, each bit in the Attributes property represents a different attribute, enabling one value to hold all attributes for a File or Folder object. You must use bit manipulations to set or extract bit values.

Table A-19 Possible Values for the Attributes Property

Value	Description
0	Represents a normal file with no special attributes.
1	Represents a read-only file.
2	Represents a hidden file.
4	Represents a system file.
8	Represents a drive volume label.
16	Represents a directory.
32	Represents a file that's been changed since its last backup.
64	Represents a shortcut.
128	Represents a compressed file.

a
b
c

Objects with an Attributes Property

File

Folder

Syntax

object.Attributes = *attributes1*

or

attributes2 = *object*.Attributes

- *object* — A reference to a File or Folder object.
- *attributes1* — The attributes to set.
- *attributes2* — The variable that will receive the file attributes.

Example 1

In this example, the program gets a File object and examines its archive bit to see whether the file has been backed up since its last change. A message box reveals the results.

```
Dim fileSystem, stream

Set fileSystem = CreateObject("Scripting.FileSystemObject")
Set stream = fileSystem.GetFile("c:\text.txt")
If stream.Attributes And 32 Then
```

```
        MsgBox "This file needs to be backed up"
    Else
        MsgBox "This file is backed up"
    End If
```

Example 2

Here, the program gets a File object and reverses the file's read-only bit. A message box tells you whether the program cleared or set the read-only bit.

```
Dim fileSystem, stream

Set fileSystem = CreateObject("Scripting.FileSystemObject")
Set stream = fileSystem.GetFile("c:\text.txt")
If stream.Attributes And 1 Then
    stream.Attributes = stream.Attributes - 1
    MsgBox "Read-only bit has been cleared."
Else
    stream.Attributes = stream.Attributes + 1
    MsgBox "Read-only bit has been set"
End If
```

CROSS-REFERENCE
For more information, see File and Folder.

AutoActivate

Property

The AutoActivate property determines whether the user can activate an embedded object by double-clicking the OLE Container control or by giving the controls the focus. The AutoActivate property can be one of the values shown in Table A-20.

Table A-20 Possible Values for the AutoActivate Property

Value	Description
vbOLEActivateAuto	Activate an embedded object automatically when the OLE container is activated.
vbOLEActivateDoubleClick	Activate an embedded object with a double-click (default).
vbOLEActivateGetFocus	Activate an embedded object when the OLE container receives the focus.
vbOLEActivateManual	No automatic activation.

Objects with an AutoActivate Property
OLE Container

Syntax

OLEContainer.AutoActivate = *value1*

or

value2 = *OLEContainer*.AutoActivate

- *OLEContainer*—A reference to an OLE Container control.
- *value1*—A value from Table A-20.
- *value2*—The variable that will receive the property's current setting.

CROSS-REFERENCE
For more information, see OLE Container.

AutoBuddy

Property

The AutoBuddy property determines whether an UpDown control automatically associates itself with another control, called a *buddy control*. Usually, the buddy control is an edit box that automatically displays the current value of the UpDown control. The UpDown control uses the tab order to determine which control to make the buddy control. If AutoBuddy is set to True, the control makes the previous control in the tab order the buddy control. If there is no previous control, the UpDown control will look for the next highest control in the tab order. If AutoBuddy is False, the UpDown control relies on its BuddyControl property to find its buddy control.

Objects with an AutoBuddy Property
UpDown

Syntax

UpDown.AutoBuddy = *value1*

or

value2 = *UpDown*.AutoBuddy

- *UpDown* — A reference to an UpDown control.
- *value1* — A value of True or False. The default is False.
- *value2* — The variable that will receive the property's current setting.

 CROSS-REFERENCE
For more information, see UpDown.

AutoEnable

Property

The AutoEnable property determines whether a Multimedia MCI control can automatically enable or disable buttons based on its currently set mode and the abilities of the device it's controlling.

Objects with an AutoEnable Property

Multimedia MCI

Syntax

```
MCIControl.AutoEnable = value1
```

or

```
value2 = MCIControl.AutoEnable
```

- *MCIControl* — A reference to a Multimedia MCI control.
- *value1* — A value of True or False. The default is True.
- *value2* — The variable that will receive the property's current setting.

 CROSS-REFERENCE
For more information, see Multimedia MCI Control.

AutoPlay

Property

The `AutoPlay` property determines whether an Animation control automatically plays an animation sequence loaded from an .avi file. If `AutoPlay` is `False`, the control's `Play` method must be called to play the animation sequence.

Objects with an AutoPlay Property

Animation

Syntax

```
Animation.AutoPlay = value1
```

or

```
value2 = Animation.AutoPlay
```

- *Animation* — A reference to an Animation control.
- *value1* — A value of `True` or `False`. The default is `False`.
- *value2* — The variable that will receive the property's current setting.

 CROSS-REFERENCE
For more information, see Animation.

AutoRedraw

Property

The `AutoRedraw` property determines whether an object will automatically redraw itself from an image stored in memory. If `AutoRedraw` is `False`, Visual Basic must call the object's `Paint` method to redraw the object, which is a longer process.

Objects with an AutoRedraw Property

Form

PictureBox

PropertyPage

UserControl

Syntax

```
control.AutoRedraw = value1
```

or

```
value2 = control.AutoRedraw
```

- *control*—A reference to a control that supports the AutoRedraw property.
- *value1*—A value of `True` or `False`. The default is `False`.
- *value2*—The variable that will receive the property's current setting.

 CROSS-REFERENCE
For more information, see PropertyPage, UserControl, Form, and PictureBox.

AutoShowChildren

Property

The `AutoShowChildren` property determines whether an MDI form automatically displays child forms when the child forms are loaded. If `AutoShowChildren` is `False`, a program can display child forms by calling their `Show` methods.

Objects with an AutoShowChildren Property

MDIForm

Syntax

```
MDIForm.AutoShowChildren = value1
```

or

```
value2 = MDIForm.AutoShowChildren
```

- *MDIForm* — A reference to an MDIForm object.
- *value1* — A value of `True` or `False`. The default is `True`.
- *value2* — The variable that will receive the property's current setting.

CROSS-REFERENCE
For more information, see MDIForm.

AutoSize — Label and PictureBox Controls

Property

The `AutoSize` property determines whether a control automatically resizes itself in order to accommodate its contents. If `AutoSize` is `False`, all of a control's contents cannot be seen if the contents are larger than the control. That is, Visual Basic clips contents to the control.

Syntax

```
control.AutoSize = value1
```

or

```
value2 = control.AutoSize
```

- *control* — A reference to a Label or PictureBox control.
- *value1* — A value of `True` or `False`. The default is `False`.
- *value2* — The variable that will receive the property's current setting.

CROSS-REFERENCE
For more information, see Label and PictureBox.

AutoSize — Panel Object

Property

The `AutoSize` property determines how Visual Basic resizes Panel objects when a status bar is resized. The property can be one of the values shown in Table A-21.

Table A-21 Possible Values for the AutoSize Property

Value	Description
sbrContents	The panel is sized such that it fits its contents.
sbrNoAutoSize	The panel always stays set at the width specified by its Width property (default).
sbrSpring	The panel will stretch to accommodate all extra space in the status bar.

Syntax

```
Panel.AutoSize = value1
```

or

```
value2 = control.AutoSize
```

- *Panel* — A reference to a Panel object.
- *value1* — A value from Table A-21.
- *value2* — The variable that will receive the property's current setting.

Example

In this example, the program adds two new panels to a status bar, giving the status bar three panels in all. The second panel (the first one added in the example program lines) sets its AutoSize property to sbrContents, meaning that the panel will always stay large enough to hold its contents. The second new panel sets its AutoSize property to sbrSpring, meaning that this panel will always stretch in order to fill the remaining area of the status bar. Figure A-27 shows the application when it is initially run. Notice how the second panel is just large enough to contain its text. In Figure A-28, the application's window has been enlarged horizontally. Notice how the third panel stretches to fill the extra space.

```
Dim P As Panel
Set P = staStatusBar1.Panels.Add _
    (, "text", "This is a Text Panel", sbrText)
P.AutoSize = sbrContents
P.Alignment = sbrCenter
Set P = staStatusBar1.Panels.Add _
    (, "caps", , sbrDate)
P.AutoSize = sbrSpring
P.Alignment = sbrCenter
```

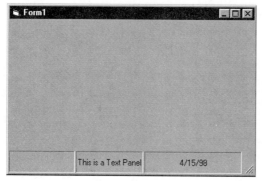

Figure A-27 Here are the panels when the application first runs.

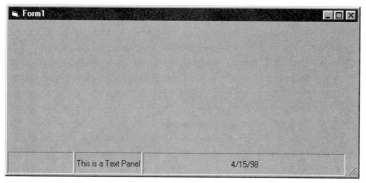

Figure A-28 Here, the third panel stretches to fill the enlarged status bar.

 CROSS-REFERENCE
For more information, see Panel.

AutoVerbMenu

Property

The AutoVerbMenu property determines whether Visual Basic displays a popup menu listing an embedded object's OLE verbs when the user right-clicks an OLE Container control. Figure A-29 shows an application that contains an OLE Container control that the user has right-clicked. Because this OLE Container's AutoVerbMenu property is True (the default setting), Visual Basic displays a popup menu that contains the embedded object's verbs.

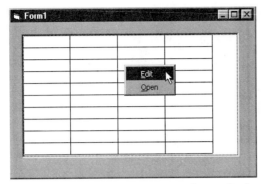

Figure A-29 OLE Container controls can display OLE verbs in a popup menu.

Objects with an AutoVerbMenu Property

OLE Container

Syntax

OLEContainer.AutoVerbMenu = *value1*

or

value2 = *OLEContainer*.AutoVerbMenu

- *OLEContainer*—A reference to an OLE Container control.
- *value1*—A value of True or False. The default is True.
- *value2*—The variable that will receive the property's current setting.

CROSS-REFERENCE
For more information, see OLE Container.

AvailableSpace

Property

The AvailableSpace property represents the amount of available space on a drive represented by a Drive object.

Objects with an AvailableSpace Property

Drive

Syntax

```
space = Drive.AvailableSpace
```

- *Drive* — A reference to a Drive object.
- *space* — The variable that will receive the value representing the drive's available space.

Example

In this example, the program gets a Drive object and determines its available space, displaying the result in a message box.

```
Dim fileSystem, stream
Set fileSystem = _
    CreateObject("Scripting.FileSystemObject")
Set stream = fileSystem.GetDrive("c:")
MsgBox stream.AvailableSpace
```

 CROSS-REFERENCE

For more information, see Drive and FreeSpace.

B

BackClick

Event

Visual Basic sends a Multimedia MCI control a `BackClick` event when the user clicks the control's Back button. By responding to this event, a program can stop the default action of the Back button from occurring.

Objects with a BackClick Event

Multimedia MCI

Example

A program can respond to a `BackClick` event by implementing the Multimedia MCI control's `BackClick` event procedure. By setting the procedure's `Cancel` parameter to `True`, the program can halt the Back button's default action.

```
Private Sub mciMMControl1_BackClick(Cancel As Integer)
    If something Then Cancel = True
End Sub
```

 CROSS-REFERENCE
For more information, see BackCompleted and Multimedia MCI.

BackColor

Property

The `BackColor` property represents an object's background color. This property can be set to any valid color value, including those returned by the `RGB` and `QBColor` functions.

Objects with a BackColor Property

AmbientProperties
Animation
Band
CheckBox
ComboBox
CommandButton
CoolBar
DirListBox
DriveListBox
FileListBox
Form
Frame
Image
ImageList
Label
ListBox
MDIForm
OLE Container
OptionButton
PictureBox
Printer
PropertyPage
RichTextBox
Shape
TextBox
UserControl

Syntax

```
object.BackColor = color1
```

or

```
color2 = object.BackColor
```

- *color1* — The color value to which to set the property.

- *color2* — The variable that will receive the color returned by the property.
- *object* — A reference to an object with a `BackColor` property.

Example 1

In this example, the program calls the `QBColor` function to change the form's background color to green.

```
Private Sub Form_Load()
    BackColor = QBColor(10)
End Sub
```

Example 2

Here, the program calls the `RGB` function to change the form's background color to red.

```
Private Sub Form_Load()
    BackColor = RGB(255,0,0)
End Sub
```

Example 3

Finally, in this example, the program uses a hexadecimal value to set the form's background color to a dark aqua.

```
Private Sub Form_Load()
    BackColor = &H80000001
End Sub
```

CROSS-REFERENCE
See also ForeColor, RGB, and QBColor.

BackCompleted

Event

Visual Basic sends a Multimedia MCI control a `BackCompleted` event after the button's action has been executed. By responding to this event, a program can determine whether any errors occurred.

Objects with a BackCompleted Event

Multimedia MCI

Example

A program can respond to a `BackCompleted` event by implementing the Multimedia MCI control's `BackCompleted` event procedure, which receives an error value as its single parameter.

```
Private Sub mciMMControl1_BackCompleted(Errorcode As Long)
    ' Handle the event here.
End Sub
```

 CROSS-REFERENCE
For more information, see BackClick and Multimedia MCI.

BackEnabled

Property

The `BackEnabled` property represents the enabled status of a Multimedia MCI control's Back button. This property is `True` when the control's Back button is enabled and is `False` when the button is disabled.

Objects with a BackEnabled Property

Multimedia MCI

Syntax

`Multimedia.BackEnabled = value1`

or

`value2 = Multimedia.BackEnabled`

- *Multimedia* — A reference to a Multimedia MCI control.
- *value1* — The value `True` or `False`.
- *value2* — The variable that will receive the value returned by the property.

Example

The following lines show how to get and set the enabled status of a Multimedia control's Back button.

```
Dim enable
enable = mciMMControl1.BackEnabled
mciMMControl1.BackEnabled = True
```

 CROSS-REFERENCE
See also Multimedia MCI.

BackGotFocus

Event

Visual Basic sends a Multimedia MCI control a `BackGotFocus` event when the control's Back button receives the focus.

Objects with a BackGotFocus Event

Multimedia MCI

Example

A program can respond to a `BackGotFocus` event by implementing the Multimedia MCI control's `BackGotFocus` event procedure, which receives no parameters, as shown here.

```
Private Sub mciMMControl1_BackGotFocus()
    ' Handle the event here.
End Sub
```

 CROSS-REFERENCE
For more information, see BackLostFocus and Multimedia MCI.

BackLostFocus

Event

Visual Basic sends a Multimedia MCI control a `BackLostFocus` event when the control's Back button loses the focus.

Objects with a BackLostFocus Event
Multimedia MCI

Example
A program can respond to a `BackLostFocus` event by implementing the Multimedia MCI control's `BackLostFocus` event procedure, which receives no parameters, as shown here.

```
Private Sub mciMMControl1_BackLostFocus()
    ' Handle the event here.
End Sub
```

 CROSS-REFERENCE
For more information, see BackGotFocus and Multimedia MCI.

Backslash (\)

Operator

The backslash (\) operator performs integer division, returning an integer result regardless of the data type of the values used.

Syntax
```
result = exp1 \ exp2
```

- *exp1* — Any valid numerical expression.
- *exp2* — Any valid numerical expression.
- *result* — The integer result of the division.

Example 1
After the following lines execute, `result` will contain the value 3.

```
Dim result
result = 12 \ 4
```

Example 2
Here, after the following lines execute, `result` will also contain the value 3.

```
Dim result
result = 12.5 \ 4.2
```

Example 3

Finally, after the following lines execute, `result` will contain the value 2.

```
Dim result, num1, num2, num3
num1 = 12.5
num2 = 4.2
num3 = 7
result = (num1 + num2) \ (num3 + 1)
```

CROSS-REFERENCE
See also Slash (/).

BackStyle — General Objects

Property

The `BackStyle` property determines whether an object has a transparent or opaque background. This property can be set to 0 (transparent) or 1 (opaque).

Objects with a BackStyle Property

Animation
Label
OLE Container
Shape
UserControl

Syntax

object`.BackStyle = ` *style1*

or

style2 ` = ` *object*`.BackStyle`

- *object* — A reference to an object with a `BackStyle` property.
- *style1* — A value of 0 or 1.
- *style2* — The variable that will receive the style returned by the property.

Example 1

In this example, the program sets a Label control's background style to opaque. Because the form's background color is a different color than the label's, the label's background is clearly visible, as you can see in Figure B-1.

```
Private Sub Form_Load()
    lblLabel1.BackStyle = 1
End Sub
```

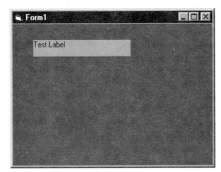

Figure B-1 This label has an opaque background.

Example 2

Here, the program sets a Label control's background style to transparent. The fact that the form's background color is different from the label's doesn't matter, because the label's background doesn't show through, as you can see in Figure B-2.

```
Private Sub Form_Load()
    lblLabel1.BackStyle = 0
End Sub
```

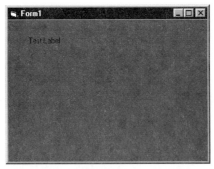

Figure B-2 This label has a transparent background.

a
b
c

BackStyle — UserControl

Property

The BackStyle property determines whether a UserControl object has a transparent, opaque, or invisible background. This property can be set to 0 (transparent), 1 (opaque), or 2 (invisible). The invisible setting only affects a control whose Windowless property is set to True.

Syntax

```
UserControl.BackStyle = style1
```

or

```
style2 = UserControl.BackStyle
```

- *UserControl* — A reference to a UserControl object.
- *style1* — A value of 0, 1, or 2. The default is 1 for opaque.
- *style2* — The variable that will receive the style returned by the property.

BackVisible

Property

The BackVisible property represents the visible status of a Multimedia MCI control's Back button. This property is True when the control's Back button is visible and is False when the button is not visible.

Objects with a BackVisible Property
Multimedia MCI

Syntax

```
Multimedia.BackVisible = value1
```

or

```
value2 = Multimedia.BackVisible
```

- *Multimedia* — A reference to a Multimedia MCI control.
- *value1* — The value True or False. The default is True.

■ *value2* — The variable that will receive the value returned by the property.

Example

The following lines show how to get and set the visible status of a Multimedia control's Back button.

```
Dim visible
visible = mciMMControl1.BackVisible
mciMMControl1.BackVisible = True
```

CROSS-REFERENCE
See also Multimedia MCI.

Band

Object

A Band object represents areas in a CoolBar control that the user can move and resize. A CoolBar control can have multiple bands, each of which can contain a child control.

Properties

The Band object has 24 properties, which are listed in Table B-1. For more information on using a property shown in the following table, look up the individual property's entry, provided alphabetically in this book.

Table B-1 Properties of the Band Object

Property	Description
AllowVertical	Represents whether a CoolBar control can display the band when the control is in the vertical orientation.
BackColor	Represents the band's background color.
Caption	Represents the text that appears on the band.
Child	Represents the band's child control.
EmbossHighlight	Represents the highlight color of the band's picture.
EmbossPicture	Represents whether the band's picture is displayed in full color or with a two-color, embossed effect.
EmbossShadow	Represents the shadow color used to display a band's image.
FixedBackground	Represents whether a CoolBar's image is tiled over its bands or is tiled within each band.

Property	Description
ForeColor	Represents the band's foreground color.
Height	Represents the band's height.
Image	Represents the index of an image in an ImageList control.
Index	The band's index within its parent control.
Key	A text string used to identify the band.
MinHeight	The band's minimum height.
MinWidth	The band's minimum width.
NewRow	Determines whether the band will start a new row of bands in the CoolBar control.
Picture	Represents the picture that will be displayed in the band.
Position	Represents the band's location in the CoolBar control.
Style	Controls whether a busy automation object receiving mouse or keyboard input displays the default dialog box or generates an error.
Tag	Represents user-defined data for the band.
UseCoolBarColors	Determines whether the band will be displayed with the CoolBar control's colors or with its own colors.
UseCoolBarPicture	Determines whether the band will display the CoolBar control's picture or its own picture.
Visible	Determines whether the object is visible.
Width	Represents the band's width.

Methods

The Band object has no methods.

 CROSS-REFERENCE
For more information, see CoolBar.

BandBorders

Property

The BandBorders property determines whether a CoolBar control draws its bands with a 3-D border. This property can be set to True or False.

Objects with a BandBorders Property

CoolBar

Syntax

```
CoolBar.BandBorders = value1
```

or

```
value2 = CoolBar.BandBorders
```

- *CoolBar*—A reference to a CoolBar control.
- *value1*—A value of `True` or `False`. The default is `True`.
- *value2*—The variable that will receive the value returned by the property.

Example 1

In this example, the program turns on a CoolBar control's band borders. (`BandBorders = True` is the default.) Figure B-3 shows the result. Notice how you can clearly see each band's borders.

```
Private Sub Form_Load()
    CoolBar1.BandBorders = True
End Sub
```

Figure B-3 The bands in this CoolBar control have band borders.

Example 2

Here, the program turns off a CoolBar control's band borders. Figure B-4 shows the result. Notice that you can no longer see each band's borders.

```
Private Sub Form_Load()
    CoolBar1.BandBorders = False
End Sub
```

Figure B-4 The bands in this CoolBar control have no band borders.

CROSS-REFERENCE

For more information, see CoolBar.

Bands

Collection

A Bands collection holds the bands displayed in a CoolBar control. You can access a CoolBar's Bands collection through the CoolBar's `Bands` property.

Syntax

```
value1 = CoolBar.Bands
```

- *CoolBar* — A reference to a CoolBar control.
- *value1* — A variable that will receive a reference to the Bands object.

Properties

A Bands collection has one property, `Count`, which represents the number of bands in the collection. For more information on using this property, look up the individual property's entry, provided alphabetically in this book.

Methods

A Bands collection has four methods, which are listed in Table B-2. For more information on a method, look up the individual method's name, provided alphabetically in this book.

Table B-2 Methods of a Bands Collection

Method	Description
Add	Adds a Band object to the collection.
Clear	Removes all Band objects from the collection.
Item	Represents a Band object in the collection. You can access a band by calling Item with an index.
Remove	Removes a Band object from the collection.

Example

In this example, the program uses a Bands collection's `Item` method to access a band and set its caption. Note that you can perform the same operation without the `Item` method, simply by adding an index directly to the Bands collection, like this: `CoolBar1.Bands(1).Caption = "A band caption"`.

```
CoolBar1.Bands.Item(1).Caption = "A band caption"
```

CROSS-REFERENCE
For more information, see Band, Bands (property), and CoolBar.

Bands

Property

The `Bands` property represents a CoolBar control's Bands collection. You can use the `Bands` property to call the collection's methods or to get the collection's band count. By adding an index to the `Bands` property, you can also access individual bands in the collection.

Objects with a Bands Property

CoolBar

Syntax

```
value1 = CoolBar.Bands
```

- *CoolBar*—A reference to a CoolBar control.
- *value1*—A variable that will receive a reference to the Bands object.

Example

In this example, the program uses the `Bands` property to access a band's `Caption` property.

```
CoolBar1.Bands(2).Caption = "This is band 2"
```

CROSS-REFERENCE
For more information, see Band, Bands (collection), and CoolBar.

Base

Keyword

The Base keyword is part of the Option Base statement, which determines whether Visual Basic considers arrays to have a minimum index of 0 or 1. For example, the following line specifies that the first element in arrays will be at index 1.

```
Option Base 1
```

CROSS-REFERENCE
For more information, see Option Base.

BatteryFullTime

Property

The BatteryFullTime property represents the number of seconds the system's battery will last when the battery is fully charged. This property returns &HFFFFFFFF if the time cannot be determined.

Objects with a BatteryFullTime Property

SysInfo

Syntax

```
time = SysInfo.BatteryFullTime
```

- *SysInfo* — A reference to a SysInfo control.
- *time* — The variable that will receive the property's value.

CROSS-REFERENCE
See also BatteryLifePercent, BatteryLifeTime, BatteryStatus, and SysInfo.

BatteryLifePercent

Property

The BatteryLifePercent property represents the percentage of life left in the system's battery. This property returns 255 if the time cannot be determined.

Objects with a BatteryLifePercent Property
SysInfo

Syntax

`time = SysInfo.BatteryLifePercent`

- *SysInfo* — A reference to a SysInfo control.
- *time* — The variable that will receive the property's value.

CROSS-REFERENCE
See also BatteryFullTime, BatteryLifeTime, BatteryStatus, and SysInfo.

BatteryLifeTime

Property

The `BatteryLifeTime` property represents the number of seconds of life left in the system's battery. This property returns &HFFFFFFFF if the time cannot be determined.

Objects with a BatteryLifeTime Property
SysInfo

Syntax

`time = SysInfo.BatteryLifeTime`

- *SysInfo* — A reference to a SysInfo control.
- *time* — The variable that will receive the property's value.

CROSS-REFERENCE
See also BatteryFullTime, BatteryLifePercent, BatteryStatus, and SysInfo.

BatteryStatus

Property

The `BatteryStatus` property represents the general charge status of the system's battery. This property returns one of the values shown in Table B-3.

Table B-3 Possible Values for the BatteryStatus Property

Value	Description
1	High battery charge.
2	Low battery charge.
4	Dangerously low battery charge.
8	Battery currently charging.
128	No battery in the system.
255	The battery status cannot be determined.

Objects with a BatteryStatus Property

SysInfo

Syntax

```
status = SysInfo.BatteryStatus
```

- *status* — The variable that will receive the property's value.
- *SysInfo* — A reference to a SysInfo control.

 CROSS-REFERENCE
See also BatteryFullTime, BatteryLifePercent, BatteryLifeTime, and SysInfo.

Beep

Statement

The Beep statement causes the system speaker to beep. Under Windows, the Beep statement plays, through the system's sound card, the wave file that's currently set for the system's beep sound.

Syntax

```
Beep
```

Example

In this example, the computer beeps whenever the user clicks a button displayed in the application's form. The programmer previously added the btnCommand1 CommandButton to the form.

```
Private Sub btnCommand1_Click()
    Beep
End Sub
```

BeforeClick

Event

Visual Basic sends a BeforeClick event just before generating a Click event for a Tab object in a TabStrip control. You can use the BeforeClick event to validate the entries in the current tab before the control activates the newly selected tab.

Objects That Receive BeforeClick Events

TabStrip

Example

A program can respond to a BeforeClick event by implementing the target TabStrip control's BeforeClick event procedure. The following code segment shows how a TabStrip control defines a BeforeClick event procedure. In this case, the TabStrip displays a message box when receiving the event. The program then sets BeforeClick's Cancel parameter to True, which disallows the activation of the selected Tab. That is, when you want to stop the new tab from being selected, probably because of invalid data in the current tab, you set Cancel to True. If you leave Cancel with its default value (False), the control activates the new tab that the user clicked.

```
Private Sub tabTabStrip1_BeforeClick(Cancel As Integer)
    ' Handle the BeforeClick event here.
    MsgBox ("BeforeClick received")
    Cancel = True
End Sub
```

CROSS-REFERENCE
For more information, see Tab and TabStrip.

BeforeLabelEdit

Event

Visual Basic sends a ListView or TreeView control a `BeforeLabelEdit` event when the user clicks a list item or tree node twice, signaling that the user wants to edit the item or node. (The first click generates a standard `Click` event.) This event enables the program to disallow the editing of specific items or nodes.

Objects That Receive BeforeLabelEdit Events

ListView

TreeView

Example

A program can respond to a `BeforeLabelEdit` event by implementing the target object's `BeforeLabelEdit` event procedure. The following example application displays a ListView control containing five items. If you try to edit the first item, a message box appears, informing you that the item is not editable. You can, however, edit any other item in the first column. As you can see in the source code, the ListView control's `BeforeLabelEdit` event procedure is responsible for rejecting any attempts at editing item 1. Figure B-5 shows the application when the user tries to edit the first item.

Figure B-5 In this application, you can't edit the first ListView item.

```
VERSION 5.00
Object = "{6B7E6392-850A-101B-AFC0-4210102A8DA7} _
    #2.0#0"; "MSCOMCTL.OCX"
Begin VB.Form Form1
   Caption         =    "BeforeLabelEdit Demo"
   ClientHeight    =    3195
   ClientLeft      =    60
   ClientTop       =    345
   ClientWidth     =    4680
   LinkTopic       =    "Form1"
   ScaleHeight     =    3195
   ScaleWidth      =    4680
   StartUpPosition =    3  'Windows Default
   Begin MSComctlLib.ListView lvwListView1
      Height        =    1935
      Left          =    360
      TabIndex      =    0
      Top           =    840
      Width         =    3975
      _ExtentX      =    7011
      _ExtentY      =    3413
      LabelWrap     =    -1  'True
      HideSelection =    -1  'True
      _Version      =    393217
      ForeColor     =    -2147483640
      BackColor     =    -2147483643
      BorderStyle   =    1
      Appearance    =    1
      NumItems      =    0
      _Items        =    "Form1.frx":0000
   End
   Begin VB.Label Label1
      Caption       =        _
         "You can edit every item in column 1 except the
first."
      Height        =    255
      Left          =    480
      TabIndex      =    1
      Top           =    360
      Width         =    3735
   End
End
Attribute VB_Name = "Form1"
Attribute VB_GlobalNameSpace = False
```

```
Attribute VB_Creatable = False
Attribute VB_PredeclaredId = True
Attribute VB_Exposed = False

Private Sub Form_Load()
    Dim Item As ListItem
    Dim ColHead As ColumnHeader

    Set ColHead = lvwListView1.ColumnHeaders. _
        Add(1, "column1", "Column 1", 1140, lvwColumnLeft)
    Set ColHead = lvwListView1.ColumnHeaders. _
        Add(2, "column2", "Column 2", 1140, lvwColumnCenter)
    Set ColHead = lvwListView1.ColumnHeaders. _
        Add(3, "column3", "Column 3", 1140, lvwColumnCenter)

    Set Item = lvwListView1.ListItems.Add(1, "item1", _
        "Item 1")
    Item.SubItems(1) = "SubItem 1"
    Item.SubItems(2) = "SubItem 2"
    Set Item = lvwListView1.ListItems.Add(2, "item2",_
        "Item 2")
    Item.SubItems(1) = "SubItem 1"
    Item.SubItems(2) = "SubItem 2"
    Set Item = lvwListView1.ListItems.Add(3, "item3", _
        "Item 3")
    Item.SubItems(1) = "SubItem 1"
    Item.SubItems(2) = "SubItem 2"
    Set Item = lvwListView1.ListItems.Add(4, "item4", _
        "Item 4")
    Item.SubItems(1) = "SubItem 1"
    Item.SubItems(2) = "SubItem 2"
    Set Item = lvwListView1.ListItems.Add(5, "item5", _
        "Item 5")
    Item.SubItems(1) = "SubItem 1"
    Item.SubItems(2) = "SubItem 2"

    lvwListView1.View = lvwReport
End Sub

Private Sub lvwListView1_BeforeLabelEdit(Cancel As Integer)
    If lvwListView1.SelectedItem.Index = 1 Then
        MsgBox "Cannot edit this item.", , "BeforeLabelEdit"
        Cancel = True
    End If
End Sub
```

CROSS-REFERENCE
For more information, see ListView and TreeView.

Bevel

Property

The `Bevel` property represents the bevel style used with a StatusBar control's panels. This property can be one of the values shown in Table B-4.

Table B-4 Possible Values for the Bevel Property

Value	Description
sbrInset	Panels have indented edges (default).
sbrNoBevel	Panels have no beveled edges.
sbrRaised	Panels have raised edges.

Objects with a Bevel Property

Panel

Syntax

```
Panel.Bevel = value1
```

or

```
value2 = Panel.Bevel
```

- *Panel* — A reference to a Panel object.
- *value1* — A value from Table B-4.
- *value2* — The variable that will receive the value returned by the property.

Example

In this example, the program sets the StatusBar's panels to all three styles of edges. The first panel has no bevels, the second panel has a raised bevel, and the third has an inset bevel. Figure B-6 shows the result.

```
Private Sub Form_Load()
    StatusBar1.Panels(1).Bevel = sbrNone
    StatusBar1.Panels(1).Text = "No Bevel"
    StatusBar1.Panels(2).Bevel = sbrRaised
    StatusBar1.Panels(2).Text = "Raised Bevel"
    StatusBar1.Panels(3).Bevel = sbrInset
    StatusBar1.Panels(3).Text = "Inset Bevel"
End Sub
```

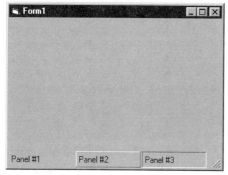

Figure B-6 The panels in this StatusBar show the three bevel styles.

CROSS-REFERENCE
See also Panel and StatusBar.

Binary

Keyword

The Binary keyword is used with the Open statement to specify binary file operations or used with the Option Compare statement to specify how string data should be compared. You will probably use Binary most often when opening files, an example of which is the following statement:

```
Open "datafile.dat" For Binary Access Write As #1
```

CROSS-REFERENCE
See also Open and Option Compare.

Bold—Font Object

Property

The `Bold` property determines whether a font represented by a Font object will be displayed as bold. This property can be set to `True` or `False`.

Syntax

```
Font.Bold = value1
```

or

```
value2 = Font.Bold
```

- *Font*—A reference to a Font object.
- *value1*—A value of `True` or `False`. The default is `False`.
- *value2*—The variable that will receive the value returned by the property.

Example

In this example, the program displays a line of bold text when the user clicks a button, named `btnCommand1`, that the programmer added to the form. This example shows the button's `Click` event procedure.

```
Private Sub btnCommand1_Click()
    Font.Bold = True
    Font.Size = 18
    Print "Button Clicked"
End Sub
```

 **CROSS-REFERENCE**
See also Font.

Bold—ListItem and Node Objects

Property

The `Bold` property determines whether ListView items or TreeView nodes are displayed with bold text. This property can be set to `True` or `False`.

Syntax

```
object.Bold = value1
```

or

```
value2 = object.Bold
```

- *object*—A reference to a ListItem or Node object.
- *value1*—A value of True or False. The default is False.
- *value2*—The variable that will receive the value returned by the property.

Example

In this example, the program adds two items to a ListView control, giving one item a bold font and the other a nonbold font.

```
Private Sub Form_Load()
    Dim Item As ListItem

    Set Item = lvwListView1.ListItems. _
        Add(1, "item1", "Item 1")
    Item.Bold = True
    Set Item = lvwListView1.ListItems. _
        Add(2, "item2", "Item 2")
    Item.Bold = False
End Sub
```

 CROSS-REFERENCE
See also ListItem, Node, ListView, and TreeView.

Boolean

Keyword

The Boolean keyword can be used to declare variables that can hold the Boolean value True or False. The following example declares a Boolean variable named Value and sets it to True.

```
Dim Value As Boolean
Value = True
```

BorderColor

Property

The BorderColor property determines the color of a Line or Shape object's border. This property can be set to any valid color value, including those returned by the RGB and QBColor functions.

Objects with a BorderColor Property

Line

Shape

Syntax

object.BorderColor = *value1*

or

value2 = *object*.BorderColor

- *object* — A reference to a Line or Shape object.
- *value1* — The color value to which to set property.
- *value2* — The variable that will receive the value returned by the property.

Example

The following line shows how to set a Shape object's border color to red.

shpShape1.BorderColor = RGB(255, 0, 0)

 CROSS-REFERENCE
See also Line and Shape.

BorderStyle — Form Object

Property

The BorderStyle property determines how a Form object's border looks and the controls that are included in the border. This property can be one of the values shown in Table B-5.

Table B-5 Possible Values for the BorderStyle Property

Value	Description
vbBSNone	Form has no border or border controls.
vbFixedDouble	Form has a dialog-style border with a control menu, close button, and a title bar.
vbFixedSingle	Form has a fixed border with a minimize button, maximize button, title bar, and control menu.
vbFixedToolWindow	Form has a fixed border with a close button, title bar, and small font.
vbSizable	Form has a resizable border with a minimize button, maximize button, close button, title bar, and control menu. This is the default.
vbSizableToolWindow	Form has a resizable border with a close button, title bar, and small font.

Syntax

```
value = Form.BorderStyle
```

- *Form* — A reference to a Form object.
- *value* — The variable that will receive the value returned by the property.

Example

The following lines show how to get a Form object's border style. Figure B-7 shows a form with the `vbBSNone` border style, whereas Figure B-8 shows a form with the `vbFixedToolWindow` style and Figure B-9 shows a form with the `vbFixedDouble` border style.

```
Dim style
style = frmForm1.BorderStyle
```

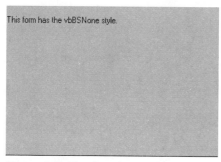

This form has the vbBSNone style.

Figure B-7 This form has no border.

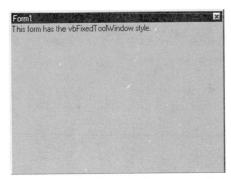

Figure B-8 This form displays as a tool window.

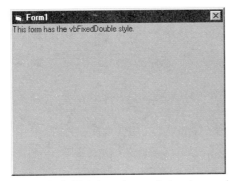

Figure B-9 This form has a dialog-box style.

CROSS-REFERENCE
See also Form.

BorderStyle — General Controls

Property

The BorderStyle property determines how an object's border looks. This property can be one of the values shown in Table B-6.

Table B-6 Possible Values for the BorderStyle Property

Value	Description
0	Control has no border.
1	Control has single fixed border.

Objects with a BorderStyle Property

Frame

Image

Label

OLE Container

PictureBox

Slider

TextBox

UserControl

Syntax

```
object.BorderStyle = value1
```

or

```
value2 = object.BorderStyle
```

- *object* — A reference to an object with the `BorderStyle` property.
- *value1* — The style value to which to set property.
- *value2* — The variable that will receive the value returned by the property.

Example

The following line shows how to set a Label object's border style. Figure B-10 shows a form that contains two label controls, one without a border and one with a border.

```
lblLabel1.BorderStyle = 1
```

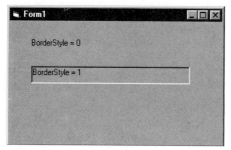

Figure B-10 A border can make a big difference in a control's appearance.

BorderStyle — Line and Shape Objects

Property

The `BorderStyle` property determines the graphics style used to display a Line or Shape object's border. This property can be one of the values shown in Table B-7.

Table B-7 Possible Values for the BorderStyle Property

Value	Description
vbBSDash	Object has a dashed border.
vbBSDashDot	Object has a dash-dot border.
vbBSDashDotDot	Object has a dash-dot-dot border.
vbBSDot	Object has a dotted border.
vbBSSolid	Object has a solid border (default).
vbInsideSolid	Object's outside border edges are also the object's edges.
vbTransparent	Object has a transparent border.

Syntax

```
object.BorderStyle = value1
```

or

```
value2 = object.BorderStyle
```

- *object* — A reference to a Line or Shape object.
- *value1* — The style value to which to set property.
- *value2* — The variable that will receive the value returned by the property.

Example

The following line shows how to set a Shape object's border style.

```
shpShape1.BorderStyle = vbBSSolid
```

CROSS-REFERENCE
See also Line and Shape.

BorderWidth

Property

The `BorderWidth` property represents the width of a Line or Shape object's border. This property can be set to any value from 1 to 8192 pixels.

Objects with a BorderWidth Property

Line

Shape

Syntax

`object.BorderWidth = value1`

or

`value2 = object.BorderWidth`

- *object* — A reference to a Line or Shape object.
- *value1* — The width value to which to set property. The default is 1.
- *value2* — The variable that will receive the value returned by the property.

Example

The following line shows how to set a Shape object's border width.

`shpShape1.BorderWidth = 10`

CROSS-REFERENCE
See also Line and Shape.

BuddyControl

Property

The BuddyControl property represents a UpDown control's buddy control. A *buddy control*, usually an edit box, displays the UpDown control's current setting.

Objects with a BuddyControl Property

UpDown

Syntax

```
UpDown.BuddyControl = value1
```

or

```
value2 = UpDown.BuddyControl
```

- *UpDown* — A reference to an UpDown control.
- *value1* — A reference to the control that will be the buddy control.
- *value2* — The variable that will receive the value returned by the property.

Example

The following line shows how to set an UpDown control's buddy control to a TextBox. The object named updUpDown1 is the UpDown control, and the object named txtText1 is a TextBox control. The programmer added both controls to the form at design time.

```
updUpDown1.BuddyControl = txtText1
```

CROSS-REFERENCE
See also AutoBuddy and UpDown.

BuddyProperty

Property

The `BuddyProperty` determines which of the UpDown control's properties is tracked by the buddy control when its `SyncBuddy` property is set to `True`. Normally, this would be the UpDown control's `Value` property. A *buddy control*, usually an edit box, displays the UpDown control's current setting.

Objects with a BuddyProperty Property

UpDown

Syntax

```
UpDown.BuddyProperty = value1
```

or

```
value2 = UpDown.BuddyProperty
```

- *UpDown* — A reference to an UpDown control.
- *value1* — A reference to the property to be tracked.
- *value2* — The variable that will receive the value returned by the property.

Example

The following line shows how to set an UpDown control to track its `Value` property (which is the normal setting). The object named `updUpDown1` is an UpDown control that the programmer added to the form at design time.

```
updUpDown1.BuddyProperty = updUpDown1.Value
```

 CROSS-REFERENCE
See also AutoBuddy, BuddyControl, and UpDown.

BuildPath

Method

The `BuildPath` method creates a path string from a path name and a file (or folder) name.

Objects with a BuildPath Method

FileSystemObject

Syntax

```
string = FileSystemObject.BuildPath(path, file)
```

- *FileSystemObject* — A reference to a FileSystemObject object.
- *file* — The file (or folder) name to append to the path.
- *path* — The path name to which *file* will be added.
- *string* — The new path.

Example

The following lines create a FileSystemObject and then assemble a complete path from a path name and a file name. In this case, the variable `fullpath` ends up set to "c:\Test\File.dat."

```
Dim fs
Dim fullpath
Set fs = CreateObject("Scripting.FileSystemObject")
fullpath = fs.buildpath("c:\Test", "File.dat")
```

CROSS-REFERENCE
See also FileSystemObject.

BulletIndent

Property

The `BulletIndent` property determines the amount of indent applied to bulleted items in a RichTextBox control.

Objects with a BulletIndent Property
RichTextBox

Syntax

```
RichTextBox.BulletIndent = value1
```

or

```
value2 = RichTextBox.BulletIndent
```

- *RichTextBox* — A reference to a RichTextBox control.
- *value1* — The amount of indentation. The default is 0.
- *value2* — The variable that will receive the value returned by the property.

Example

The following line shows how to set a RichTextBox control's bullet indentation. For the `BulletIndent` property to have an effect, the RichTextBox must set its `SelBullet` property to `True`, which causes text to appear as a bulleted list.

```
rtfRichTextBox1.SelBullet = True
rtfRichTextBox1.BulletIndent = 500
```

 CROSS-REFERENCE
See also RichTextBox and SelBullet.

Button

Object

The Button object represents a button in a Toolbar control's Buttons collection. You can add buttons to a toolbar both at design time, using the Toolbar control's Property Pages property sheet, or at runtime by calling the Buttons collection's `Add` method. Toolbar buttons can contain text, an image, or both text and an image.

Properties

The Button object has 17 properties, which are listed in Table B-8. For more information on using a property shown in the following table, look up the individual property's entry, provided alphabetically in this book.

Table B-8 Properties of the Button Object

Property	Description
ButtonMenus	Represents the object's ButtonMenus collection.
Caption	Represents a string that contains the button's caption.
Description	Represents the button's description that's displayed in the Customize Toolbar dialog box.
Enabled	Determines whether the button is enabled and can respond to user clicks.
Height	Represents the button's height.
Image	Represents the index into an ImageList of the image to display on the button.
Index	Represents the button's position in the Buttons collection.
Key	Represents a string that acts as an ID for the button.
Left	Represents the position of the button's left edge.
MixedState	Determines whether the button is in a mixed (indeterminate) state.
Style	Represents the button's style, which determines how the button looks and acts.
Tag	Represents user-defined data for the button.
ToolTipText	Represents the text that's displayed when the mouse pointer hovers over the button.
Top	Represents the position of the button's top edge.
Value	Represents the pressed or unpressed state of the button.
Visible	Determines whether the button is visible.
Width	Represents the button's width.

Methods

The Button object has no methods.

Example

This sample program displays a window with a Toolbar containing five buttons. The program adds the buttons to the Toolbar in the form's Load method, as well as sets the button's tooltip text. When you run the program, click any button and a message box appears, telling you which button you clicked. If you click the first button in the toolbar, the button remains pressed because of its tbrCheck style. Click the button again to set it back to its unselected state. If you leave the mouse pointer over a button for a second or two, the button's tooltip text appears. Figure B-11 shows the application with the first button clicked and displaying the third button's tooltip text.

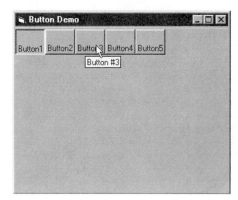

Figure B-11 Here's the example application with its toolbar full of Button objects.

```
VERSION 5.00
Object = "{6B7E6392-850A-101B-AFC0-4210102A8DA7} _
    #2.0#0"; "MSCOMCTL.OCX"
Begin VB.Form Form1
    Caption         =   "Button Demo"
    ClientHeight    =   3540
    ClientLeft      =   60
    ClientTop       =   345
    ClientWidth     =   4680
    LinkTopic       =   "Form1"
    ScaleHeight     =   3540
    ScaleWidth      =   4680
    StartUpPosition =   3  'Windows Default
    Begin MSComctlLib.Toolbar tlbToolbar1
        Align       =   1  'Align Top
        Height      =   630
        Left        =   0
        TabIndex    =   0
        Top         =   0
        Width       =   4680
        _ExtentX    =   8255
        _ExtentY    =   1111
        ButtonWidth =   1164
        ButtonHeight =  953
        Appearance  =   1
        _Version    =   393216
    End
End
Attribute VB_Name = "Form1"
Attribute VB_GlobalNameSpace = False
```

```
Attribute VB_Creatable = False
Attribute VB_PredeclaredId = True
Attribute VB_Exposed = False

Private Sub Form_Load()
    Dim btn As Button

    Set btn = tlbToolbar1.Buttons.Add _
        (1, , "Button1", tbrCheck)
    btn.ToolTipText = "Button #1"
    Set btn = tlbToolbar1.Buttons.Add(2, , "Button2")
    btn.ToolTipText = "Button #2"
    Set btn = tlbToolbar1.Buttons.Add(3, , "Button3")
    btn.ToolTipText = "Button #3"
    Set btn = tlbToolbar1.Buttons.Add(4, , "Button4")
    btn.ToolTipText = "Button #4"
    Set btn = tlbToolbar1.Buttons.Add(5, , "Button5")
    btn.ToolTipText = "Button #5"
End Sub

Private Sub tlbToolbar1_ButtonClick _
    (ByVal Button As MSComctlLib.Button)
    MsgBox Button.ToolTipText
End Sub
```

CROSS-REFERENCE
See also Buttons and Toolbar.

ButtonClick — Toolbar Control

Event

Visual Basic sends a Toolbar control a `ButtonClick` event when the user clicks one of the Toolbar's buttons. By responding to this event, a program can execute whatever command the button represents.

Example 1

A program can respond to a `ButtonClick` event by implementing the Toolbar's `ButtonClick` event procedure, which receives a reference to the clicked button as its single parameter. You can access the clicked button's properties through this reference. For example, the following sample displays a message box that contains the Button object's tooltip text.

```
Private Sub tlbToolbar1_ButtonClick _
    (ByVal Button As MSComctlLib.Button)
    MsgBox Button.ToolTipText
End Sub
```

Example 2

Here, the program uses a `Select Case` statement to determine which button to respond to. In this case, the application's toolbar has three buttons with the captions "Button1," "Button2," and "Button3." As you can see, the program can determine which button was clicked by examining the buttons' captions.

```
Private Sub tlbToolbar1_ButtonClick(ByVal Button As
MSComctlLib.Button)
    Select Case Button.Caption
    Case "Button1"
        ' Respond to button 1 here.
        MsgBox "Button1 clicked.", , "Button Clicked"
    Case "Button2"
        ' Respond to button 2 here.
        MsgBox "Button2 clicked.", , "Button Clicked"
    Case "Button3"
        ' Respond to button 3 here.
        MsgBox "Button3 clicked.", , "Button Clicked"
    End Select
End Sub
```

CROSS-REFERENCE

For more information, see Button and Toolbar.

ButtonDropDown

Event

Visual Basic sends a Toolbar control a `ButtonDropDown` event when the user clicks a Button object's drop-down arrow, which appears on Button objects with the `tbrDropDown` style.

Objects with a ButtonDropDown Event

Toolbar

Example

A program can respond to a ButtonDropDown event by implementing the Toolbar control's ButtonDropDown event procedure. The following sample program demonstrates this technique. When you run the program, you see a window that has a toolbar with two menu buttons. Click either button's drop-down arrow, and the application displays a message box (Figure B-12), indicating which button arrow you clicked. When you dismiss the message box, the button's menu appears.

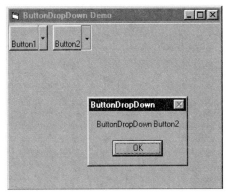

Figure B-12 A Button object's drop-down arrow generates ButtonDropDown events.

```
VERSION 5.00
Object = "{6B7E6392-850A-101B-AFC0-4210102A8DA7} _
    #2.0#0"; "MSCOMCTL.OCX"
Begin VB.Form Form1
    Caption         =   "ButtonDropDown Demo"
    ClientHeight    =   3540
    ClientLeft      =   60
    ClientTop       =   345
    ClientWidth     =   4680
    LinkTopic       =   "Form1"
    ScaleHeight     =   3540
    ScaleWidth      =   4680
    StartUpPosition =   3  'Windows Default
    Begin MSComctlLib.Toolbar tlbToolbar1
        Align       =       1  'Align Top
        Height      =       630
        Left        =       0
        TabIndex    =       0
```

```
            Top             =    0
            Width           =    4680
            _ExtentX        =    8255
            _ExtentY        =    1111
            ButtonWidth     =    1164
            ButtonHeight    =    953
            Appearance      =    1
            _Version        =    393216
        End
End
Attribute VB_Name = "Form1"
Attribute VB_GlobalNameSpace = False
Attribute VB_Creatable = False
Attribute VB_PredeclaredId = True
Attribute VB_Exposed = False

Private Sub Form_Load()
    Dim btn As Button

    Set btn = tlbToolbar1.Buttons.Add _
        (1, , "Button1", tbrDropdown)
    btn.ButtonMenus.Add 1, , "Item 1"
    btn.ButtonMenus.Add 2, , "Item 2"
    btn.ButtonMenus.Add 3, , "Item 3"

    tlbToolbar1.Buttons.Add 2, , , tbrSeparator

    Set btn = tlbToolbar1.Buttons.Add _
        (3, , "Button2", tbrDropdown)
    btn.ButtonMenus.Add 1, , "Item 1"
    btn.ButtonMenus.Add 2, , "Item 2"
    btn.ButtonMenus.Add 3, , "Item 3"
End Sub

Private Sub tlbToolbar1_ButtonDropDown _
    (ByVal Button As MSComctlLib.Button)
    If Button.Caption = "Button1" Then
        MsgBox "ButtonDropDown Button1"
    Else
        MsgBox "ButtonDropDown Button2"
    End If
End Sub
```

```
Private Sub tlbToolbar1_ButtonMenuClick _
    (ByVal ButtonMenu As MSComctlLib.ButtonMenu)
    MsgBox "ButtonMenuClick"
End Sub
```

 CROSS-REFERENCE
For more information, see Button, ButtonMenus, and Toolbar.

ButtonHeight

Property

The `ButtonHeight` determines the height of a Toolbar control's buttons. The property affects all buttons on the toolbar.

Objects with a ButtonHeight Property

Toolbar

Syntax

```
Toolbar.ButtonHeight = value1
```

or

```
value2 = Toolbar.ButtonHeight
```

- *Toolbar*—A reference to a Toolbar control.
- *value1*—The new button height.
- *value2*—The variable that will receive the current button height returned by the property.

Example

The following line shows how to set and get a Toolbar control's button height at runtime. The object named `tlbToolbar1` is a Toolbar control that the programmer added to the form at design time.

```
Dim height
height = tlbToolbar1.ButtonHeight
tlbToolbar1.ButtonHeight = 500
```

CROSS-REFERENCE
See also Button, ButtonWidth, and Toolbar.

ButtonMenu

Object

The ButtonMenu object represents a Toolbar button's drop-down menu. A toolbar button can display a drop-down menu when the button's style is set to tbrDropDown. Each of a toolbar button's menu items is a member of the button's ButtonMenus collection.

Properties

The ButtonMenu object has seven properties, which are listed in Table B-9. For more information on using a property shown in the following table, look up the individual property's entry, provided alphabetically in this book.

Table B-9 Properties of the ButtonMenu Object

Property	Description
Enabled	Determines whether the menu item is enabled.
Index	Represents the menu item's position in its ButtonMenus collection.
Key	Represents a string that acts as an ID for the menu item.
Parent	Represents the Button object that contains the ButtonMenu object.
Tag	Represents user-defined data for the object.
Text	Represents the text displayed in the menu item.
Visible	Determines whether the item is visible.

Methods

The ButtonMenu object has no methods.

Example

The following example adds a button with a drop-down menu to a Toolbar control. The button's menu contains three menu items, represented by the three ButtonMenu objects that the program adds to the button's ButtonMenus collection. The control named tlbToolbar1 is a Toolbar control that the programmer added to the form as design time.

```
Dim btn As Button
Set btn = tlbToolbar1.Buttons.Add _
    (1, , "Button1", tbrDropdown)
btn.ButtonMenus.Add 1, , "Item 1"
btn.ButtonMenus.Add 2, , "Item 2"
btn.ButtonMenus.Add 3, , "Item 3"
```

CROSS-REFERENCE
See also Button, ButtonDropDown, ButtonMenus, and Toolbar.

ButtonMenuClick

Event

Visual Basic sends a Toolbar control a `ButtonMenuClick` event when the user clicks an item (called a ButtonMenu object) in a Button object's drop-down menu. This menu appears when a button has the `tbrDropDown` style.

Objects that Receive ButtonMenuClick Events

Toolbar

Example

A program can respond to a `ButtonMenuClick` event by implementing the Toolbar control's `ButtonMenuClick` event procedure. The following example shows how to respond to the user's menu-item selections. The `ButtonMenuClick` event procedure receives a reference to the clicked ButtonMenu object as its single parameter. By accessing the ButtonMenu object's properties, a program can easily determine exactly which item was clicked and respond to it as appropriate. In this example's case, the program uses the ButtonMenu object's `Text` property to determine which menu item was selected.

```
Private Sub tlbToolbar1_ButtonMenuClick _
    (ByVal ButtonMenu As MSComctlLib.ButtonMenu)
    Select Case ButtonMenu.Text
    Case "Command #1"
        ' Respond to first menu item here.
        MsgBox "Command #1 clicked."
    Case "Command #2"
```

```
        ' Respond to second menu item here.
        MsgBox "Command #2 clicked."
      Case "Command #3"
        ' Respond to third menu item here.
        MsgBox "Command #3 clicked."
      End Select
    End Sub
```

CROSS-REFERENCE
For more information, see Button, ButtonMenus, and Toolbar.

ButtonMenus

Collection

A ButtonMenus collection represents the ButtonMenu objects of a button on a Toolbar control. A Toolbar button can display a drop-down menu when the button's style is set to `tbrDropDown`. Each of a Toolbar button's menu items is a member of the button's ButtonMenus collection.

Syntax

value1 = *Button*.ButtonMenus

- *Button* — A reference to a Button object.
- *value1* — A variable that will receive a reference to the ButtonMenus object.

Properties

The ButtonMenus collection has one property, called `Count`, that represents the number of objects currently in the collection. For more information on `Count`, look up the individual property's name, provided alphabetically in this book.

Methods

A ButtonMenus collection has four methods, which are listed in Table B-10. For more information on a method, look up the individual method's name, provided alphabetically in this book.

Table B-10 Methods of a ButtonMenus Collection

Method	Description
Add	Adds a ButtonMenu object to the collection.
Clear	Removes all ButtonMenu objects from the collection.
Item	Represents a ButtonMenu object in the collection. You can access a ButtonMenu object by calling Item with an index.
Remove	Removes a ButtonMenu object from the collection.

Example

The following example adds a button with a drop-down menu to a Toolbar control. The button's menu contains three menu items, represented by the three ButtonMenu objects that the program adds to the button's ButtonMenus collection. The control named tlbToolbar1 is a Toolbar control that the programmer added to the form at design time.

```
Dim btn As Button
Set btn = tlbToolbar1.Buttons.Add _
    (1, , "Button1", tbrDropdown)
btn.ButtonMenus.Add 1, , "Item 1"
btn.ButtonMenus.Add 2, , "Item 2"
btn.ButtonMenus.Add 3, , "Item 3"
```

CROSS-REFERENCE
See also Button, ButtonDropDown, ButtonMenu, ButtonMenus (property), and Toolbar.

ButtonMenus

Property

The ButtonMenus property represents a Toolbar button's ButtonMenus collection. A toolbar button can display a drop-down menu when the button's style is set to tbrDropDown. Each of a toolbar button's menu items is a member of the button's ButtonMenus collection.

Objects with a ButtonMenus Property

Button

Syntax

```
value1 = Button.ButtonMenus
```

- *Button* — A reference to a Button object.
- *value1* — A variable that will receive a reference to the ButtonMenus object.

Example

The following lines show how the `ButtonMenus` property can return a valid reference to a Toolbar button's ButtonMenus object. The object named `tlbToolbar1` is a Toolbar control that the programmer added to the form at design time. The second line below sets `menu` equal to the ButtonMenus object associated with the first button on the Toolbar. The third line uses that reference to change the second menu item's text.

```
Dim menu
Set menu = tlbToolbar1.Buttons(1).ButtonMenus
menu(2).Text = "Test"
```

 CROSS-REFERENCE

See also Button, ButtonDropDown, ButtonMenu, ButtonMenus (object), and Toolbar.

Buttons

Collection

A `Buttons` collection contains all of a Toolbar control's buttons.

Syntax

```
value1 = Toolbar.Buttons
```

- *Toolbar* — A reference to a Toolbar control.
- *value1* — A variable that will receive a reference to the Buttons object.

Properties

The Buttons collection has a single property, called `Count`, that represents the number of objects currently in the collection. For more information on `Count`, look up the individual property's name, provided alphabetically in this book.

Methods

A Buttons collection has four methods, which are listed in Table B-11. For more information on a method, look up the individual method's name, provided alphabetically in this book.

Table B-11 Methods of a Buttons Collection

Method	Description
Add	Adds a Button object to the collection.
Clear	Removes all Button objects from the collection.
Item	Represents a Button object in the collection. You can access a button by calling Item with an index.
Remove	Removes a Button object from the collection.

Example

The following example adds five buttons, the first of which can display a drop-down menu, to a Toolbar control. The first button's menu contains three menu items, represented by the three ButtonMenu objects that the program adds to the button's ButtonMenus collection. The control named tlbToolbar1 is a Toolbar control that the programmer added to the form at design time. Figure B-13 shows the resultant toolbar, with the first button's drop-down menu displayed.

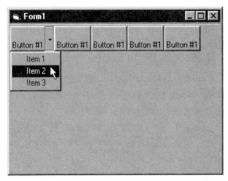

Figure B-13 A Buttons collection can hold normal command buttons or buttons with menus.

```
Dim button
Set button = tlbToolbar1.Buttons.Add _
    (1, , "Button #1", tbrDropdown)
button.ButtonMenus.Add 1, , "Item 1"
button.ButtonMenus.Add 2, , "Item 2"
button.ButtonMenus.Add 3, , "Item 3"

tlbToolbar1.Buttons.Add 2, , "Button #2"
tlbToolbar1.Buttons.Add 3, , "Button #3"
tlbToolbar1.Buttons.Add 4, , "Button #4"
tlbToolbar1.Buttons.Add 5, , "Button #5"
```

 CROSS-REFERENCE
See also Button, Buttons (property), and Toolbar.

Buttons

Property

The Buttons property represents a Toolbar's Buttons collection. The Buttons collection holds all the Button objects in the Toolbar.

Objects with a Buttons Property

Toolbar

Syntax

value1 = *Toolbar*.Buttons

- *Toolbar*—A reference to a Toolbar control.
- *value1*—A variable that will receive a reference to the Buttons object.

Example

The following lines show how the Buttons property can return a valid reference to a Toolbar's Buttons object. The object named tlbToolbar1 is a Toolbar control that the programmer added to the form at design time. The second line below sets buttons equal to the toolbar's Buttons object. The remaining lines use that reference to create a button with a drop-down menu. In this example, you can also see how to call a Buttons collection's Add method.

```
Dim buttons
Set buttons = tlbToolbar1.Buttons
buttons.Add 1, , "Button #1"
buttons(1).Style = tbrDropdown
buttons(1).ButtonMenus.Add 1, , "Item 1"
buttons(1).ButtonMenus.Add 2, , "Item 2"
buttons(1).ButtonMenus.Add 3, , "Item 3"
```

 CROSS-REFERENCE
See also Button, Buttons (collection), and Toolbar.

ButtonWidth

Property

The ButtonWidth determines the width of a Toolbar control's buttons. The property affects all buttons on the toolbar.

Objects with a ButtonWidth Property

Toolbar

Syntax

```
Toolbar.ButtonWidth = value1
```

or

```
value2 = Toolbar.ButtonWidth
```

- *Toolbar*—A reference to a Toolbar control.
- *value1*—The new button width.
- *value2*—The variable that will receive the current button width returned by the property.

Example

The following line shows how to get and set a Toolbar control's button width at runtime. The object named tlbToolbar1 is a Toolbar control that the programmer added to the form at design time.

```
Dim width
width = tlbToolbar1.ButtonWidth
tlbToolbar1.ButtonWidth = 500
```

CROSS-REFERENCE
See also Button, ButtonHeight, and Toolbar.

ByRef

Keyword

The `ByRef` keyword specifies that the associated argument should be passed *by reference*, which means an actual reference to the argument is passed to the receiver. Passing an object by reference is similar to passing an object's address, which means when you change the value of the passed object, you change the value of the original object, as well. The following two procedures demonstrate how `ByRef` works. The procedure `MySub2` receives `var1` as a `ByRef` argument, naming it `value1`. In the procedure, the program changes `value1` to 30. Because `value1` and `var1` are references to the same object, `var1` also becomes 30. So, the message box displayed in `MySub2` displays the value 30, and the message box in `MySub1` also displays 30.

```
Private Sub MySub1()
    Dim var1
    var1 = 10
    MySub2 var1
    MsgBox var1
End Sub

Private Sub MySub2(ByRef value1)
    value1 = 30
    MsgBox value1
End Sub
```

CROSS-REFERENCE
See also ByVal.

Byte

Keyword

The `Byte` keyword can be used to declare variables that can hold the byte (8-bit) values. The following example declares a Byte variable named `Value` and sets it to 128.

```
Dim Value As Byte
Value = 128
```

ByVal

Keyword

The ByVal keyword specifies that the associated argument should be passed *by value*, which means only the current value of the object is passed to the receiver, rather than an actual reference to the object. Passing an object by reference causes Visual Basic to create a copy of the object, which means when you change the value of the passed object, the original object is unaffected. The following two procedures demonstrate how ByVal works. The procedure MySub2 receives var1 as a ByVal argument, naming it value1. In the procedure, the program changes value1 to 30. Because value1 and var1 are not references to the same object, var1 is unchanged. So, the message box displayed in MySub2 displays the value 30, and the message box in MySub1 displays 10.

```
Private Sub MySub1()
    Dim var1
    var1 = 10
    MySub2 var1
    MsgBox var1
End Sub

Private Sub MySub2(ByVal value1)
    value1 = 30
    MsgBox value1
End Sub
```

CROSS-REFERENCE
See also ByRef.

Call

Statement

The `Call` statement is used to transfer program execution to a procedure or function. The `Call` keyword is actually an optional part of the `Call` statement. That is, you can call procedures and functions without using the `Call` keyword. When you do use `Call`, however, you must enclose any procedure- or function-call arguments within parentheses.

Syntax

```
Call Proc
```

or

```
Proc
```

or

```
Call Proc(arg1, arg2, ...)
```

or

```
Proc arg1, arg2, ...
```

- ... — Any number of arguments.
- *arg1* — Procedure or function call's first argument.
- *arg2* — Procedure or function call's second argument.
- *Proc* — Procedure or function name.

Example

In this example, the `Proc3` procedure shows the various ways you can construct a `Call` statement by calling the `Proc1` and `Proc2` procedures. Notice the addition of parentheses when specifying the `Call` keyword and procedure arguments.

```
Private Sub Proc1()
    ' Procedure code goes here.
End Sub

Private Sub Proc2(value1 As Integer, value2 As Integer)
    ' Procedure code goes here.
End Sub

Private Sub Proc3()
    Call Proc1
    Proc1
    Call Proc2(10, 20)
    Proc2 10, 20
End Sub
```

CallByName

Function

CallByName is a function that calls an object's methods or accesses an object's properties.

Syntax

```
CallByName object, name, type, arg
```

or

```
value = CallByName(object, name, type, arg)
```

- *arg* — Method call or property arguments.
- *name* — The method or property name.
- *object* — The object's name.
- *type* — The type of method call, which can be vbLet, vbSet, vbGet, or vbMethod.
- *value* — The variable that will receive the call's return value.

Example

In this example, the program uses the CallByName function to call a button object's Move method, as well as to set and get the button's Enabled property. The programmer added the CommandButton object, btnCommand1, to the form at design time.

```
Dim result
CallByName btnCommand1, "Move", vbMethod, 200, 200
CallByName btnCommand1, "Enabled", vbLet, False
Result = CallByName(btnCommand1, "Enabled", vbGet)
```

Note that you can perform the above operations on the button object using simpler and more direct syntax. The following lines perform exactly the same functions as the previous ones:

```
Dim result
btnCommand1.Move 200, 200
btnCommand1.Enabled = False
result = btnCommand1.Enabled
```

Cancel

Property

The `Cancel` property determines whether a CommandButton control acts as the cancel button on a form. A form's cancel button usually closes a form, ignoring any changes made to the form. For example, the cancel button on a dialog box enables the user to change his or her mind about entries in the dialog box, without having to reset the entries manually to their original states. The `Cancel` property can be set to `True` or `False`.

Objects with a Cancel Property

CommandButton

Syntax

CommandButton.Cancel = *value1*

or

value2 = *CommandButton*.Cancel

- *CommandButton* — A reference to a CommandButton object.
- *value1* — The value `True` or `False`.
- *value2* — The variable that will receive the value returned by the property.

Example

In this example, the program makes a button object the form's cancel button. The programmer added the CommandButton control, `btnCommand1`, to the form at design time.

```
btnCommand1.Enabled = True
```

 CROSS-REFERENCE
See also CommandButton.

CancelError

Property

The `CancelError` property determines whether Visual Basic generates the `cdlCancel` error (error number 32755) when the user clicks a dialog box's Cancel button. A form's cancel button usually closes a form, ignoring any changes made to the form. For example, the cancel button on a dialog box enables the user to change his or her mind about entries in the dialog box, without having to reset the entries manually to their original states. The `CancelError` property can be set to `True` or `False`.

Objects with a CancelError Property

CommonDialog

Syntax

```
CommonDialog.CancelError = value1
```

or

```
value2 = CommonDialog.CancelError
```

- *CommonDialog* — A reference to a CommonDialog control.
- *value1* — The value `True` or `False`.
- *value2* — The variable that will receive the value returned by the property.

Example

In this example, the program sets up a common dialog box so that it generates `cdlCancel` errors when the user clicks the Cancel button. The programmer added the CommonDialog control, dlgCommonDialog1, to the form at design time.

```
dlgCommonDialog1.CancelError = True
```

 CROSS-REFERENCE
See also CommonDialog.

CanEject

Property

The CanEject property represents whether a multimedia device can eject its media. For example, a CD player that can eject its CD under software control will have a CanEject property of True. However, a wave-file device probably can't eject its media, because wave files are usually stored on the user's hard disk. This type of device will have a CanEject property of False.

Objects with a CanEject Property

Multimedia MCI

Syntax

```
value = Multimedia.CanEject
```

- *Multimedia* — A reference to a Multimedia MCI control.
- *value* — The variable that will receive the True or False value returned by the property.

Example

In this example, the program gets the CanEject status of the device associated with a Multimedia control. The programmer added the Multimedia control, mciMMControl1, to the form at design time.

```
Dim result As Boolean
result = mciMMControl1.CanEject
```

 CROSS-REFERENCE
For more information, see Multimedia MCI.

CanGetFocus

Property

The `CanGetFocus` property represents whether a control can get the focus. Because this property is available only when a programmer is creating the control, it cannot be accessed at runtime.

Objects with a CanGetFocus Property

UserControl

 CROSS-REFERENCE
For more information, see UserControl.

CanPlay

Property

The `CanPlay` property represents whether a multimedia device can play, pause, and stop its media. For example, a CD player can play, pause, and stop its media and so will have a `CanPlay` property of `True`.

Objects with a CanPlay Property

Multimedia MCI

Syntax

```
value = Multimedia.CanPlay
```

- *Multimedia* — A reference to a Multimedia MCI control.
- *value* — The variable that will receive the `True` or `False` value returned by the property.

Example

In this example, the program gets the `CanPlay` status of the device associated with a Multimedia control. The programmer added the Multimedia control, `mciMMControl1`, to the form at design time.

```
Dim result As Boolean
result = mciMMControl1.CanPlay
```

CROSS-REFERENCE
For more information, see Multimedia MCI.

CanRecord

Property

The `CanRecord` property represents whether a multimedia device can record, pause, and stop its media. For example, a VCR can record, pause, and stop its media and so will have a `CanRecord` property of `True`. However, a CD player probably can't record and so will have a `CanRecord` property of `False`.

Objects with a CanRecord Property

Multimedia MCI

Syntax

```
value = Multimedia.CanRecord
```

- *Multimedia* — A reference to a Multimedia MCI control.
- *value* — The variable that will receive the `True` or `False` value returned by the property.

Example

In this example, the program gets the `CanRecord` status of the device associated with a Multimedia control. The programmer added the Multimedia control, `mciMMControl`, to the form at design time.

```
Dim result As Boolean
result = mciMMControl1.CanRecord
```

CROSS-REFERENCE
For more information, see Multimedia MCI.

CanStep

Property

The `CanStep` property represents whether a multimedia device can step through its media one frame at a time. For example, a VCR can display images frame by frame and so will have a `CanStep` property of `True`. However, a CD player probably can't step frame by frame and so will have a `CanStep` property of `False`.

Objects with a CanStep Property
Multimedia MCI

Syntax

```
value = Multimedia.CanStep
```

- *Multimedia* — A reference to a Multimedia MCI control.
- *value* — The variable that will receive the `True` or `False` value returned by the property.

Example

In this example, the program gets the `CanStep` status of the device associated with a Multimedia control. The programmer added the Multimedia control, `mciMMControl1`, to the form at design time.

```
Dim result As Boolean
result = mciMMControl1.CanStep
```

CROSS-REFERENCE
For more information, see Multimedia MCI.

Caption

Property

The `Caption` property determines the text that appears in a control or object. For example, a CommandButton control's `Caption` property holds the text that appears on the button, whereas a CheckBox control's `Caption` property determines the text that appears next to the check box. In the case of a form, the `Caption` property determines the text that appears in the form's title bar.

Objects with a Caption Property
Band
CheckBox
CommandButton

Form
Frame
Label
MDIForm
Menu
OptionButton
PropertyPage
Tab

Syntax

```
object.Caption = value1
```

or

```
value2 = object.Caption
```

- *object* — A reference to an object with a `Caption` property.
- *value1* — The string to which to set the `Caption` property.
- *value2* — The variable that will receive the string value returned by the property.

Example

In this example, the program sets a CommandButton control's `Caption` property. Figure C-1 shows the resultant button. The programmer added the CommandButton control, `btnCommand1`, to the form at design time.

```
btnCommand1.Caption = "Click Me"
```

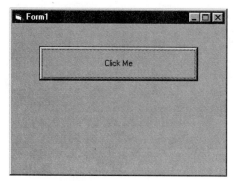

Figure C-1 This button's Caption property holds the text "Click Me."

Caret (^)

Operator

The caret (^) operator indicates an exponent. That is, you use this operator (called an exponentiation operator) to raise a value to a power.

Syntax

```
result = exp1 ^ exp2
```

- *exp1* — Any valid numerical expression.
- *exp2* — Any valid numerical expression used as an exponent.
- *result* — The result of the operation.

Example 1

After the following lines execute, `result` will contain the value 1000.

```
Dim result
result = 10 ^ 3
```

Example 2

Here, after the following lines execute, `result` will also contain the value 1000.

```
Dim result
result = 10 ^ (1 + 2)
```

Example 3

Finally, after the following lines execute, `result` will contain the value 278.89.

```
Dim result, num1, num2, num3
num1 = 12.5
num2 = 4.2
num3 = 1
result = (num1 + num2) ^ (num3 + 1)
```

Case

Keyword

The Case keyword is used as part of the Select Case statement, which enables a program to control program execution based on the result of a comparison of values. The Select Case statement is often used to replace complex If/Then/Else statements. In the following example, the program displays a message box containing the message "num1 = 3." Because the program sets num1 to 3, the Case 3 clause of the Select Case statement executes.

```
Dim num1
num1 = 3

Select Case num1
Case 1
    MsgBox "num1 = 1"
Case 2
    MsgBox "num1 = 2"
Case 3
    MsgBox "num1 = 3"
Case 4
    MsgBox "num1 = 4"
Case Else
    MsgBox "Error"
End Select
```

CROSS-REFERENCE
For more information, see Select Case.

CausesValidation

Property

The CausesValidation property determines whether a control that's gaining the focus triggers a Validate event for the control losing the focus. Specifically, when the user attempts to switch focus from control A to control B, if control B's CausesValidation property is set to True, control A will fire its Validate event. If control B's CausesValidation property is set to False, control A will not fire its Validate event. The Validate event enables a program to determine whether the data entered into a control is valid, and, if not, to force the control to retain the focus.

Objects with a CausesValidation Property

Animation

CheckBox

ComboBox

CommandButton

DirListBox

DriveListBox

FileListBox

Frame

HScrollBar

ListBox

ListView

Multimedia MCI

OLE Container

OptionButton

PictureBox

RichTextBox

Slider

TabStrip

TextBox

TreeView

UpDown

VScrollBar

Syntax

```
object.CausesValidation = value1
```

or

```
value2 = object.CausesValidation
```

- *object*—A reference to an object with a `CausesValidation` property.
- *value1*—A value of `True` or `False`.
- *value2*—The variable that will receive the value returned by the property.

Example

When you run the following program, you see the window shown in Figure C-2. Press your keyboard's Tab key several times to see that you can change the focus between all the controls. Then, click the Toggle button to toggle the value of the Test Validation button's CausesValidation property. Now, press the Tab key twice. When you try to tab out of the check box, a message box appears asking you to check the box. This is because the Test Validation button to which you just tried to change the focus now has a CausesValidation property of True. The button's CausesValidation property causes the previous control (the check box) to fire its Validate event.

In the check box's Validate event procedure, the program checks to see whether the check box is checked. If it isn't, the procedure displays the message box and sets Cancel to True, which forces the focus to stay on the check box. If you dismiss the message box and click the check box to check it, you can again tab between the control, because the Validate event procedure no longer sets Cancel to True. Clicking the Toggle button again resets the Test Validation button's CausesValidation property to False, which enables you to tab between the controls, regardless of the check box's state.

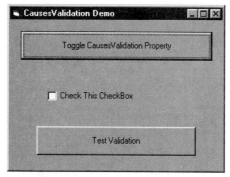

Figure C-2 Tabbing between the controls in this demo will help you understand the CausesValidation property.

```
VERSION 5.00
Begin VB.Form frmForm1
    Caption        =    "CausesValidation Demo"
    ClientHeight   =    3195
    ClientLeft     =    60
```

```
                    ClientTop       =    345
                    ClientWidth     =    4680
                    LinkTopic       =    "Form1"
                    ScaleHeight     =    3195
                    ScaleWidth      =    4680
                    StartUpPosition =    3   'Windows Default
                    Begin VB.CommandButton btnTest
                       Caption        =     "Test Validation"
                       Height         =     615
                       Left           =     600
                       TabIndex       =     2
                       Top            =     2280
                       Width          =     3495
                    End
                    Begin VB.CheckBox chkCheck1
                       Caption        =     "Check This CheckBox"
                       Height         =     375
                       Left           =     840
                       TabIndex       =     1
                       Top            =     1440
                       Width          =     2655
                    End
                    Begin VB.CommandButton btnToggle
                       Caption        =     "Toggle CausesValidation Property"
                       Height         =     615
                       Left           =     240
                       TabIndex       =     0
                       Top            =     240
                       Width          =     4215
                    End
                 End
                 Attribute VB_Name = "frmForm1"
                 Attribute VB_GlobalNameSpace = False
                 Attribute VB_Creatable = False
                 Attribute VB_PredeclaredId = True
                 Attribute VB_Exposed = False

                 Private Sub btnToggle_Click()
                    If btnTest.CausesValidation = True Then
                        btnTest.CausesValidation = False
                    Else: btnTest.CausesValidation = True
```

```
            End If
    End Sub

    Private Sub chkCheck1_Validate(Cancel As Boolean)
        If chkCheck1.Value = False Then
            MsgBox "Please check the box"
            Cancel = True
        End If
    End Sub

    Private Sub Form_Load()
        btnTest.CausesValidation = False
        btnToggle.CausesValidation = False
    End Sub
```

CROSS-REFERENCE
For more information, see Validate.

Center

Property

The Center property determines whether an Animation control centers its animation display. This property can be set to True (centered) or False (not centered). Figure C-3 shows an Animation control with a Center property of False, whereas Figure C-4 shows the same control when Center is True.

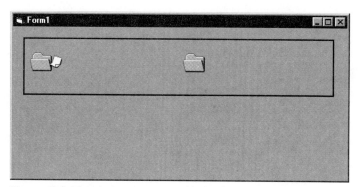

Figure C-3 This Animation control's display is not centered.

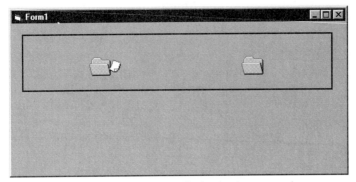

Figure C-4 This Animation control's display is centered.

Objects with a Center Property

Animation

Syntax

```
Animation.Center = value1
```

or

```
value2 = Animation.Center
```

- *Animation* — A reference to an Animation control.
- *value1* — A value of True or False.
- *value2* — The variable that will receive the value returned by the property.

Example

In this example, the program sets an Animation control's Center property to True, which centers the control's display.

```
Animation1.Center = True
```

CROSS-REFERENCE
For more information, see Animation.

Change

Event

Visual Basic sends an object a Change event when the user or the program changes the object's editable contents. For example, when the user types into a TextBox control, the control receives a Change event for each key press, because each key press changes the contents of the control. Similarly, a ComboBox control receives a Change event when the user types text into the control's edit box, a Slider control receives a Change event when the user changes the position of the slider (which changes the slider's value), and a Toolbar control receives a Change event when the user changes the toolbar's contents with the Customize Toolbar dialog box.

Objects with a Change Event

ComboBox

DirListBox

DriveListBox

HScrollBar

Label

PictureBox

RichTextBox

Slider

TextBox

Toolbar

UpDown

VScrollBar

Example

A program can respond to a Change event by implementing a control's Change event procedure. This sample program enables you to see several types of controls—a TextBox, a ComboBox, a DirListBox, and an HScrollBar—respond to their Change events. When you run the application, you see a window in which each of the main controls is associated with a text box that mirrors the changes made in the main control. For example, if you type into the TextBox control, its mirror control mirrors the control's contents. Similarly, if you change the contents of the other controls, their mirror controls will display the changes (see Figure C-5).

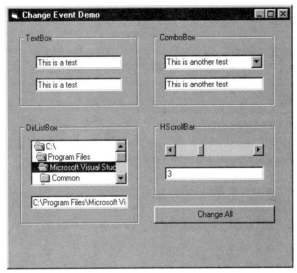

Figure C-5 The Change event makes it possible to synchronize the contents of various controls.

If you examine the source code, you can see that the program keeps the mirror controls up to date by responding to the main controls' Change events. Note that the ComboBox control doesn't fire a Change event when you select an item from its list, but only when you type into the control's edit box.

To prove that programmatically changing a control's contents also fires Change events, try clicking the Change All button. When you do, the program changes the contents of all the main controls, and the mirror controls automatically mirror the changes thanks to the resultant Change events fired by all the main controls. Figure C-6 shows the results of clicking the Change All button.

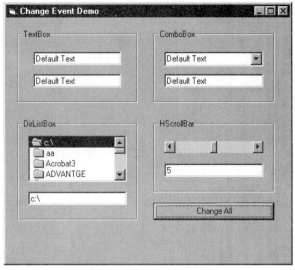

Figure C-6 Changing a control's contents programmatically also fires Change events for the controls.

```
VERSION 5.00
Begin VB.Form Form1
   Caption         =   "Change Event Demo"
   ClientHeight    =   5235
   ClientLeft      =   60
   ClientTop       =   345
   ClientWidth     =   6240
   LinkTopic       =   "Form1"
   ScaleHeight     =   5235
   ScaleWidth      =   6240
   StartUpPosition =   3  'Windows Default
   Begin VB.CommandButton cmdChangeAll
      Caption      =   "Change All"
      Height       =   375
      Left         =   3240
      TabIndex     =   12
      Top          =   3960
      Width        =   2655
   End
   Begin VB.Frame Frame4
      Caption      =   "HScrollBar"
      Height       =   1575
      Left         =   3240
      TabIndex     =   9
```

```
               Top              =    2160
               Width            =    2655
               Begin VB.TextBox txtHSBMirror
                  Height        =    285
                  Left          =    240
                  TabIndex      =    11
                  Top           =    960
                  Width         =    2175
               End
               Begin VB.HScrollBar hsbHScroll
                  Height        =    255
                  Left          =    240
                  TabIndex      =    10
                  Top           =    480
                  Width         =    2175
               End
            End
            Begin VB.Frame Frame3
               Caption          =    "DirListBox"
               Height           =    2175
               Left             =    240
               TabIndex         =    6
               Top              =    2160
               Width            =    2655
               Begin VB.TextBox txtDLBMirror
                  Height        =    285
                  Left          =    240
                  TabIndex      =    8
                  Top           =    1560
                  Width         =    2175
               End
               Begin VB.DirListBox dirDirectories
                  Height        =    990
                  Left          =    240
                  TabIndex      =    7
                  Top           =    360
                  Width         =    2175
               End
            End
            Begin VB.Frame Frame2
               Caption          =    "ComboBox"
               Height           =    1575
               Left             =    3240
               TabIndex         =    3
```

```
    Top              =    240
    Width            =    2655
    Begin VB.TextBox txtCBMirror
        Height       =    285
        Left         =    240
        TabIndex     =    5
        Top          =    960
        Width        =    2175
    End
    Begin VB.ComboBox cboCombo
        Height       =    315
        ItemData     =    "Form1.frx":0000
        Left         =    240
        List         =    "Form1.frx":0002
        TabIndex     =    4
        Top          =    480
        Width        =    2175
    End
End
Begin VB.Frame Frame1
    Caption          =    "TextBox"
    Height           =    1575
    Left             =    240
    TabIndex         =    0
    Top              =    240
    Width            =    2655
    Begin VB.TextBox txtTBMirror
        Height       =    285
        Left         =    360
        TabIndex     =    2
        Top          =    960
        Width        =    1935
    End
    Begin VB.TextBox txtText
        Height       =    285
        Left         =    360
        TabIndex     =    1
        Top          =    480
        Width        =    1935
    End
    End
End
End
Attribute VB_Name = "Form1"
Attribute VB_GlobalNameSpace = False
```

```
            Attribute VB_Creatable = False
            Attribute VB_PredeclaredId = True
            Attribute VB_Exposed = False
            Private Sub cboCombo_Change()
                txtCBMirror.Text = cboCombo.Text
            End Sub

            Private Sub cmdChangeAll_Click()
                txtText.Text = "Default Text"
                cboCombo.Text = "Default Text"
                dirDirectories.Path = "c:\"
                hsbHScroll.Value = 5
            End Sub

            Private Sub dirDirectories_Change()
                txtDLBMirror.Text = dirDirectories.Path
            End Sub

            Private Sub Form_Load()
                cboCombo.AddItem "Fred"
                cboCombo.AddItem "Sam"
                cboCombo.AddItem "Mary"
                cboCombo.AddItem "Lucy"
                cboCombo.AddItem "Alex"

                hsbHScroll.Max = 10
            End Sub

            Private Sub hsbHScroll_Change()
                txtHSBMirror = hsbHScroll.Value
            End Sub

            Private Sub txtText_Change()
                txtTBMirror.Text = txtText.Text
            End Sub
```

Changed

Property

The Changed property represents whether the user has changed properties in a PropertyPage object. This property can be set to True (changed) or False (not changed). When the Changed property becomes True, the property sheet's Apply button becomes available, enabling the user to apply the changes she's made to the control.

Objects with a Changed Property

PropertyPage

Syntax

PropertyPage.Changed = *value1*

or

value2 = *PropertyPage*.Changed

- *PropertyPage* — A reference to a PropertyPage object.
- *value1* — A value of True or False.
- *value2* — The variable that will receive the value returned by the property.

Example

In this example, the program sets a PropertyPage object's Changed property to True, which causes the Property Pages property sheet to enable the Apply button. A program should set the property whenever the user changes the contents of a control on the property page, probably in response to the control's Change event. Figure C-7 shows a Property Pages property sheet with its Apply button enabled.

PropertyPage1.Changed = True

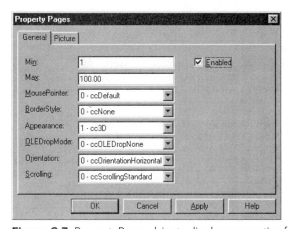

Figure C-7 PropertyPage objects display properties for ActiveX controls.

CROSS-REFERENCE
For more information, see PropertyPage and ActiveX Controls.

Charset

Property

The `Charset` property represents the character set associated with a Font object. Table C-1 shows typical values to which this property can be set.

Table C-1 Typical Settings for the Charset Property

Value	Description
0	Windows' standard character set.
2	The symbol character set.
255	Extended DOS character set.

Objects with a Charset Property

Font

Syntax

```
Font.Charset = value1
```

or

```
value2 = Font.Charset
```

- *Font* — A reference to a Font object.
- *value1* — An integer that represents the desired character set.
- *value2* — The variable that will receive the value returned by the property.

Example

In this example, the program sets a Font object's `Charset` property to display standard Windows characters. The `btnCommand1` control is a CommandButton control that the programmer added to the form at design time.

```
btnCommand1.Font.Charset = 0
```

ChDir

Statement

The ChDir statement changes the current default directory.

Syntax

```
ChDir dir
```

- *dir*— A string containing the new directory path.

Example 1

In this example, the program sets the current default directory to C:\MyStuff before displaying an Open dialog box. Assuming that the current drive is C:, when the dialog box appears, it will open to the C:\MyStuff directory. The programmer added the dlgCommonDialog1 control to the form at design time.

```
Private Sub btnLoad_Click()
    ChDir "C:\MyStuff"
    dlgCommonDialog1.Action = 1
    On Error GoTo ErrorHandler
    ' Open a file here.
    Exit Sub
ErrorHandler:
    MsgBox "Couldn't Open the File"
End Sub
```

Example 2

In this example, the program sets the current default directory on drive C: to C:\MyStuff and changes the current default directory on drive D: to D:\MoreStuff. If the current drive is C:, the Open dialog box will open to C:\MyStuff directory, regardless of the ChDir call that changes the current directory to D:\MoreStuff. This illustrates that changing a default directory is not the same thing as changing the default drive. That is, to access the default directory on the D: drive, this example would also have to call ChDrive to change the current default drive to D:.

```
Private Sub btnLoad_Click()
    ChDir "C:\MyStuff"
    ChDir "D:\MoreStuff"
    dlgCommonDialog1.Action = 1
    On Error GoTo ErrorHandler
    ' Open a file here.
```

```
        Exit Sub
ErrorHandler:
        MsgBox "Couldn't Open the File"
End Sub
```

CROSS-REFERENCE
See also ChDrive.

ChDrive

Statement

The ChDrive statement changes the current default drive.

Syntax

```
ChDir drive
```

- *drive* — A string containing the new drive letter.

Example

In this example, the program sets the current default drive to C: before displaying an Open dialog box. The dialog box will open to the C: drive's current default directory. The programmer added the dlgCommonDialog1 control to the form at design time.

```
Private Sub btnLoad_Click()
    ChDrive "C"
    dlgCommonDialog1.Action = 1
    On Error GoTo ErrorHandler
    ' Open a file here.
    Exit Sub
ErrorHandler:
    MsgBox "Couldn't Open the File"
End Sub
```

CROSS-REFERENCE
See also ChDir.

CheckBox

Control

A CheckBox is a control that a program's user can click to toggle an option or some other sort of command. The control gets its name from the fact that the button displays a check mark when in its selected state. The control also sports a caption that a program can set to a descriptive line of text. Figure C-8 shows CheckBox controls in a form. Notice that the first control is selected (check marked), whereas the other two are not. The CommandButton control is available on Visual Basic's toolbox.

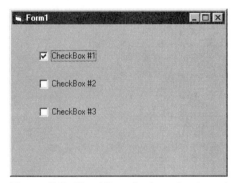

Figure C-8 CheckBox displays check marks when clicked.

Properties

The CheckBox control has 43 properties, which are listed as follows. Because many Visual Basic controls have similar properties, the properties' descriptions are listed under their own names elsewhere in this book.

```
Alignment
Appearance
BackColor
Caption
CausesValidation
Container
DisabledPicture
DownPicture
DragIcon
DragMode
Enabled
Font
FontBold
```

```
FontItalic
FontName
FontSize
FontStrikethru
FontUnderline
ForeColor
Height
HelpContextID
hWnd
Index
Left
MaskColor
MouseIcon
MousePointer
Name
OLEDropMode
Parent
Picture
RightToLeft
Style
TabIndex
TabStop
Tag
ToolTipText
Top
UseMaskColor
Value
Visible
WhatsThisHelpID
Width
```

Methods

The CheckBox control has seven methods, which are listed below. Because many Visual Basic controls have similar methods, the methods' descriptions are listed under their own names elsewhere in this book.

```
Drag
Move
OLEDrag
Refresh
SetFocus
ShowWhatsThis
ZOrder
```

Events

The CheckBox control responds to 17 events, which are listed below. Because many Visual Basic controls respond to similar events, the events' descriptions are listed under their own names elsewhere in this book.

```
Click
DragDrop
DragOver
GotFocus
KeyDown
KeyPress
KeyUp
LostFocus
MouseDown
MouseMove
MouseUp
OLECompleteDrag
OLEDragDrop
OLEDragOver
OLEGiveFeedback
OLESetData
OLEStartDrag
```

The CheckBox control's most commonly used event is Click, which the button generates when the user clicks the button with the mouse. A program responds to the button's Click event in the Click event procedure. A button called chkCheck1 will have a Click event procedure called chkCheck1_Click, which is where the program should handle the event. In the following example, when the user clicks the chkCheck1 button, the program plays the computer's beep sound:

```
Private Sub chkCheck1_Click()
    ' Handle the Click event here.
    Beep
End Sub
```

CheckBoxes

Property

The CheckBoxes property represents whether the items in a ListView or TreeView control are displayed with check boxes. The check boxes enable the user visually to select multiple items in either control. The CheckBoxes property can be set to True (show check boxes) or False (show no check boxes).

Objects with a CheckBoxes Property

ListView

TreeView

Syntax

```
object.CheckBoxes = value1
```

or

```
value2 = object.CheckBoxes
```

- *object* — A reference to a ListView or TreeView control.
- *value1* — The value True or False.
- *value2* — The variable that will receive the value returned by the property.

Example

In this example, the program sets a TreeView control's CheckBoxes property to display check boxes. (The treTreeView1 control is a TreeView control that the programmer added to the form at design time.) Figure C-9 shows the TreeView control created by the example. Notice the check boxes on each item in the control, as well as the selected Child Node #2 item.

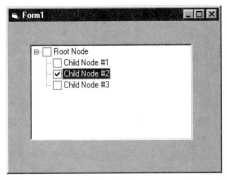

Figure C-9 The CheckBoxes property controls the display of check boxes in the ListView and TreeView controls.

```
Private Sub Form_Load()
    treTreeView1.Checkboxes = True
    treTreeView1.LineStyle = tvwRootLines
    treTreeView1.Indentation = 200
```

```
    With treTreeView1.Nodes
        .Add , , "Root", "Root Node"
        .Add "Root", tvwChild, "Child1", "Child Node #1"
        .Add "Root", tvwChild, "Child2", "Child Node #2"
        .Add "Root", tvwChild, "Child3", "Child Node #3"
    End With
End Sub
```

CROSS-REFERENCE
See also Checked, TreeView, and ListView.

Checked

Property

The Checked property represents whether an item in a ListView, TreeView, or Menu control is check marked, as shown in Figure C-10. The Checked property can be set to True (check marked) or False (not check marked).

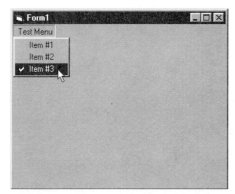

Figure C-10 The third menu item in the Test Menu menu has a Checked property of True.

Objects with a Checked Property
ListView

Menu

TreeView

Syntax

```
object.Checked = value1
```

or

```
value2 = object.Checked
```

- *object* — A reference to a ListView, TreeView, or Menu control.
- *value1* — The value `True` or `False`.
- *value2* — The variable that will receive the value returned by the property.

Example

In this example, the program turns a menu item's check mark on or off when the user clicks the menu item. The `mnuItem3` object is a menu item that the programmer added to a menu on the application's menu bar at design time.

```
Private Sub mnuItem3_Click()
    If mnuItem3.Checked Then
        mnuItem3.Checked = False
    Else
        mnuItem3.Checked = True
    End If
End Sub
```

CROSS-REFERENCE
See also CheckBoxes, TreeView, ListView, and Menu.

Child — Band

Property

The `Child` property represents a Band object's child control.

Syntax

```
Set Band.Child = value1
```

or

```
Set value2 = Band.Child
```

- *Band*—A reference to a Band object.
- *value1*—A reference to the control that will become the band's child control.
- *value2*—The variable that will receive the control returned by the property.

Example

In this example, the program retrieves a reference to a child control on a CoolBar's second Band object. The `CoolBar1` object is a CoolBar control that the programmer added to the program at design time.

```
Set cntrl = CoolBar1.Bands(2).Child
```

CROSS-REFERENCE
See also CoolBar and Band.

Child — Node

Property

The `Child` property represents a Node object's first child object.

Syntax

```
Set value1 = Node.Child
```

- *Node*—A reference to a Node object.
- *value1*—The variable that will receive the node returned by the property.

Example

In this example, the program populates a TreeView control with nodes, and then changes the text of the root node's first child to "New Text," as shown in Figure C-11. The program gets a reference to the child node through the root node's (the first node's) `Child` property. The `treTreeView1` object is a TreeView control that the programmer added to the program at design time.

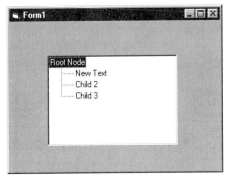

Figure C-11 The program uses the Child property to change the text of the root node's first child node.

```
Dim Nod As Node

With treTreeView1.Nodes
    Set Nod = .Add(, , "Root", "Root Node")
    Set Nod = .Add("Root", tvwChild, "Child1", _
        "Child 1")
    Set Nod = .Add("Root", tvwChild, "Child2", _
        "Child 2")
    Set Nod = .Add("Root", tvwChild, "Child3", _
        "Child 3")
End With

Set Node = treTreeView1.Nodes(1).Child
Node.Text = "New Text"
```

CROSS-REFERENCE
See also TreeView, Node, FirstSibling, LastSibling, Previous, Parent, Next, and Root.

Children

Property

The Children property represents the number of child nodes associated with a Node object.

Objects with a Children Property

Node

Syntax

```
value1 = Node.Children
```

- *Node*—A reference to a Node object.
- *value1*—The variable that will receive the number of child nodes.

Example

In this example, the program displays a message box whenever the user clicks a node in a TreeView control. The message box displays the number of child nodes associated with the clicked Node object. The treTreeView1 object is a TreeView control that the programmer added to the program at design time.

```
Private Sub treTreeView1_NodeClick(ByVal Node As
MSComctlLib.Node)
    Dim nodeCount As Integer
    nodeCount = Node.Children
    MsgBox nodeCount
End Sub
```

 CROSS-REFERENCE
See also TreeView and Node.

Choose

Function

Choose is a function that returns a value from a list based on a given index.

Syntax

```
value1 = Choose (index, item1, item2, ...)
```

- *index*—The value that determines which list member the function returns.
- *item1*—The first item in the list.
- *item2* (*)—The second item in the list.
- ... (*)—Any number of additional list items.
- *value1*—The variable that will receive the selected item from the list.

(*) = Optional argument

Example

In this example, the program enables the user to enter an index value into a text box. When the user clicks the application's Select button, the program uses the given index value in a call to the Choose function. If the user enters a valid index (from 1 to 3), the second text box displays the string returned from the Choose function. If the user enters an invalid index, the second text box displays the error message "Invalid Index." Figure C-12 shows the program after the user has entered the index 3. Note that if you call Choose with an invalid index, the function returns Null.

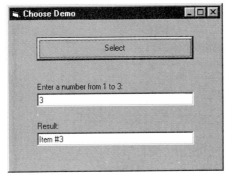

Figure C-12 This program displays text strings based on an index entered by the user.

```
VERSION 5.00
Begin VB.Form Form1
    Caption         =   "Choose Demo"
    ClientHeight    =   3195
    ClientLeft      =   60
    ClientTop       =   345
    ClientWidth     =   4680
    LinkTopic       =   "Form1"
    ScaleHeight     =   3195
    ScaleWidth      =   4680
    StartUpPosition =   3  'Windows Default
    Begin VB.TextBox txtText2
        Height          =   285
        Left            =   600
        TabIndex        =   3
        Top             =   2400
        Width           =   3495
    End
```

```
        Begin VB.TextBox txtText1
            Height          =   285
            Left            =   600
            TabIndex        =   1
            Top             =   1560
            Width           =   3495
        End
        Begin VB.CommandButton btnCommand1
            Caption         =   "Select"
            Height          =   495
            Left            =   600
            TabIndex        =   0
            Top             =   360
            Width           =   3495
        End
        Begin VB.Label Label2
            Caption         =   "Result:"
            Height          =   255
            Left            =   600
            TabIndex        =   4
            Top             =   2160
            Width           =   1935
        End
        Begin VB.Label Label1
            Caption         =   "Enter a number from 1 to 3:"
            Height          =   255
            Left            =   600
            TabIndex        =   2
            Top             =   1320
            Width           =   2295
        End
    End
Attribute VB_Name = "Form1"
Attribute VB_GlobalNameSpace = False
Attribute VB_Creatable = False
Attribute VB_PredeclaredId = True
Attribute VB_Exposed = False

Private Sub btnCommand1_Click()
    Dim intIndex As Integer
    Dim strSelection As String

    intIndex = Val(txtText1.Text)
```

```
    If intIndex > 0 And intIndex < 4 Then
        strSelection = Choose(intIndex, _
            "Item #1", "Item #2", "Item #3")
        txtText2.Text = strSelection
    Else
        txtText2.Text = "Invalid Index"
    End If
End Sub
```

Chr

Function

Chr is a function that returns the character associated with the given character code.

Syntax

```
value1 = Chr (code)
```

- *code* — The character code.
- *value1* — The variable that will receive the character.

Example

In this example, the program gets a value from a text box and uses that value as a character code in a call to the Chr function. A second text box displays the character associated with the character code (assuming the character code represents a printable character). The txtText1 and txtText2 objects are TextBox controls that the programmer added to the application's form at design time.

```
Dim lngCode As Long
Dim strChar As String

lngCode = Val(txtText1.Text)
If lngCode > 0 And lngCode < 256 Then
    strChar = Chr(lngCode)
    txtText2.Text = strChar
Else
    txtText2.Text = "Invalid Character Code"
End If
```

CROSS-REFERENCE
See also ChrB and ChrW.

ChrB

Function

ChrB is a function that returns the byte character associated with the given character code.

Syntax

```
value1 = ChrB (code)
```

- *code* — The character code.
- *value1* — The variable that will receive the byte character.

Example

In this example, the program gets a value from a text box and uses that value as a character code in a call to the ChrB function. A second text box displays the byte character associated with the character code (assuming the character code represents a printable character). The txtText1 and txtText2 objects are TextBox controls that the programmer added to the application's form at design time.

```
Dim lngCode As Long
Dim strChar As String

lngCode = Val(txtText1.Text)
If lngCode > 0 And lngCode < 256 Then
    strChar = ChrB(lngCode)
    txtText2.Text = strChar
Else
    txtText2.Text = "Invalid Character Code"
End If
```

CROSS-REFERENCE
See also Chr and ChrW.

ChrW

Function

ChrW is a function that returns the Unicode character associated with the given character code. If the system doesn't support Unicode characters, ChrW works just like Chr.

Syntax

```
value1 = ChrW(code)
```

- *code* — The character code.
- *value1* — The variable that will receive the Unicode character.

Example

In this example, the program gets a value from a text box and uses that value as a character code in a call to the ChrW function. A second text box displays the Unicode character associated with the character code (assuming the character code represents a printable character). The txtText1 and txtText2 objects are TextBox controls that the programmer added to the application's form at design time.

```
Dim lngCode As Long
Dim strChar As String

lngCode = Val(txtText1.Text)
If lngCode > 0 And lngCode < 256 Then
    strChar = ChrW(lngCode)
    txtText2.Text = strChar
Else
    txtText2.Text = "Invalid Character Code"
End If
```

 CROSS-REFERENCE
See also Chr and ChrB.

Circle

Method

The Circle method draws an ellipse, arc, or circle.

Objects with a Circle Method

Form

PictureBox

Printer

PropertyPage

UserControl

Syntax

```
object.Circle Step (xPos, yPos), radius, _
    color, radStart, radEnd, ratio
```

- *color* (*) — The color in which to draw the shape.
- *object* (*) — A reference to an object with a `Circle` method.
- *radEnd* (*) — The position in radians at which to stop drawing the shape.
- *radius* — The radius of the shape.
- *radStart* (*) — The position in radians at which to start drawing the shape.
- *ratio* (*) — The aspect ratio to use when drawing the shape.
- *xPos* — The horizontal position of the center of the shape.
- *xPos* — The vertical position of the center of the shape.

(*) = Optional

NOTE

The `Step` keyword is optional and determines whether the `xPos` and `yPos` values are relative to the `CurrentX` and `CurrentY` object properties. If you leave `Step` off from the call to `Circle`, the shape's position is relative to the object's upper-left corner.

Example

With this example program, you can manipulate most of the `Circle` method's arguments and instantly see the results of your choices, which will go a long way towards helping you understand the method. When the application's window appears, you'll see several text boxes into which you can type different values for the method's arguments. To see the results of your selections, click the Draw button, which causes the application to draw the selected ellipse, arc, or circle in the application's PictureBox control. Figure C-13, for example, shows the circle you get if you use the default arguments.

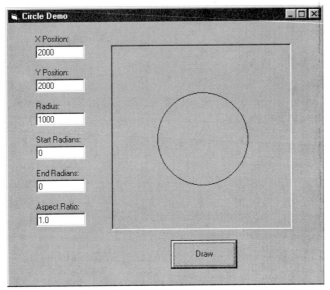

Figure C-13 The Circle Demo application enables you to experiment with the Circle method.

```
VERSION 5.00
Begin VB.Form Form1
    Caption         =   "Circle Demo"
    ClientHeight    =   5595
    ClientLeft      =   60
    ClientTop       =   345
    ClientWidth     =   6915
    LinkTopic       =   "Form1"
    ScaleHeight     =   5595
    ScaleWidth      =   6915
    StartUpPosition =   3  'Windows Default
    Begin VB.CommandButton btnDraw
        Caption     =   "Draw"
        Height      =   615
        Left        =   3600
        TabIndex    =   13
        Top         =   4680
        Width       =   1455
    End
    Begin VB.PictureBox picPicture1
        Height      =   3975
        Left        =   2280
        ScaleHeight =   3915
```

```
      ScaleWidth      =    3915
      TabIndex        =    12
      Top             =    480
      Width           =    3975
   End
   Begin VB.TextBox txtAspectRatio
      Height          =    285
      Left            =    600
      TabIndex        =    10
      Text            =    "1.0"
      Top             =    4080
      Width           =    1095
   End
   Begin VB.TextBox txtEndRadians
      Height          =    285
      Left            =    600
      TabIndex        =    8
      Text            =    "0"
      Top             =    3360
      Width           =    1095
   End
   Begin VB.TextBox txtStartRadians
      Height          =    285
      Left            =    600
      TabIndex        =    6
      Text            =    "0"
      Top             =    2640
      Width           =    1095
   End
   Begin VB.TextBox txtRadius
      Height          =    285
      Left            =    600
      TabIndex        =    4
      Text            =    "1000"
      Top             =    1920
      Width           =    1095
   End
   Begin VB.TextBox txtYPosition
      Height          =    285
      Left            =    600
      TabIndex        =    1
      Text            =    "2000"
      Top             =    1200
      Width           =    1095
   End
```

```
Begin VB.TextBox txtXPosition
   Height        =    285
   Left          =    600
   TabIndex      =    0
   Text          =    "2000"
   Top           =    480
   Width         =    1095
End
Begin VB.Label Label6
   Caption       =    "Aspect Ratio:"
   Height        =    255
   Left          =    600
   TabIndex      =    11
   Top           =    3840
   Width         =    1215
End
Begin VB.Label Label5
   Caption       =    "End Radians:"
   Height        =    255
   Left          =    600
   TabIndex      =    9
   Top           =    3120
   Width         =    1215
End
Begin VB.Label Label4
   Caption       =    "Start Radians:"
   Height        =    255
   Left          =    600
   TabIndex      =    7
   Top           =    2400
   Width         =    1215
End
Begin VB.Label Label3
   Caption       =    "Radius:"
   Height        =    255
   Left          =    600
   TabIndex      =    5
   Top           =    1680
   Width         =    855
End
```

```
          Begin VB.Label Label2
             Caption         =    "Y Position:"
             Height          =    255
             Left            =    600
             TabIndex        =    3
             Top             =    960
             Width           =    855
          End
          Begin VB.Label Label1
             Caption         =    "X Position:"
             Height          =    255
             Left            =    600
             TabIndex        =    2
             Top             =    240
             Width           =    855
          End
       End
       Attribute VB_Name = "Form1"
       Attribute VB_GlobalNameSpace = False
       Attribute VB_Creatable = False
       Attribute VB_PredeclaredId = True
       Attribute VB_Exposed = False
       Private Sub btnDraw_Click()
          Dim xPos, yPos, radius
          Dim startRads, endRads, ratio

          xPos = Val(txtXPosition.Text)
          yPos = Val(txtYPosition.Text)
          radius = Val(txtRadius.Text)
          startRads = Val(txtStartRadians.Text)
          endRads = Val(txtEndRadians.Text)
          ratio = Val(txtAspectRatio.Text)

          picPicture1.Cls
          picPicture1.Circle (xPos, yPos), radius, , _
             startRads, endRads, ratio
       End Sub
```

CROSS-REFERENCE

For more information, see ColumnHeader, ColumnHeaders, and ListView.

Class

Property

The Class property represents the name of an ActiveX object. ActiveX class names usually comprise the application's name, the object's type name, and a version number. For example, a Microsoft Word document has the class name Word.Document.8, whereas a Microsoft Works spreadsheet object has the name MSWorks.Sheet.4.

Objects with a Class Property

OLE Container

OLEObject

Syntax

```
object.Class = value1
```

or

```
value2 = object.Class
```

- *object* — A reference to an OLE Container control or OLEObject object.
- *value1* — A string containing the class name.
- *value2* — The variable that will receive the class name.

Note that, in the case of the OLEObject object, the Class property is read-only.

Example

In this example, the program retrieves the class name of an embedded object and displays the name in a message box. The oleOLEContainer object is an OLE container control that the programmer added to the application's form at design time.

```
Dim className
className = oleOLEContainer.Class
MsgBox className
```

CROSS-REFERENCE
See also OLE Container and OLEObject.

Clear

Method

The Clear method removes all objects from a collection, or, in the case of the Clipboard, ComboBox, and ListBox object, the Clear method removes the object's contents.

Objects with a Clear Method

Bands

ButtonMenus

Buttons

Clipboard

ColumnHeaders

ComboBox

ComboItems

ListBox

ListImages

ListItems

Nodes

OLEObjects

Panels

Tabs

Syntax

```
object.Clear
```

- *object* — A reference to a collection or object with a Clear method.

Example

With this example program, you can click buttons to clear and add items to a ListView control. When you run the application, you see the window shown in Figure C-14. Click the Clear button to remove all items from the ListView control, and then click the Add button to add the items back to the control. As you can see in the listing, the btnClear_Click event procedure is where the program calls the ListItems collection's Clear method, which handles the task of removing all list items from the ListView control.

Figure C-14 The Clear Demo application demonstrates the Clear method.

```
VERSION 5.00
Object = "{6B7E6392-850A-101B-AFC0-4210102A8DA7} _
    #2.0#0"; "MSCOMCTL.OCX"
Begin VB.Form Form1
    Caption         =   "Clear Demo"
    ClientHeight    =   3195
    ClientLeft      =   60
    ClientTop       =   345
    ClientWidth     =   4740
    LinkTopic       =   "Form1"
    ScaleHeight     =   3195
    ScaleWidth      =   4740
    StartUpPosition =   3   'Windows Default
    Begin VB.CommandButton btnAdd
        Caption     =   "Add"
        Enabled     =   0   'False
        Height      =   735
        Left        =   2520
        TabIndex    =   2
        Top         =   2280
        Width       =   1575
    End
    Begin VB.CommandButton btnClear
        Caption     =   "Clear"
        Height      =   735
        Left        =   600
        TabIndex    =   1
        Top         =   2280
        Width       =   1575
    End
```

```
      Begin MSComctlLib.ListView ListView1
         Height          =    1695
         Left            =    360
         TabIndex        =    0
         Top             =    240
         Width           =    3975
         _ExtentX        =    7011
         _ExtentY        =    2990
         LabelWrap       =    -1   'True
         HideSelection   =    -1   'True
         _Version        =    393217
         ForeColor       =    -2147483640
         BackColor       =    -2147483643
         BorderStyle     =    1
         Appearance      =    1
         NumItems        =    0
         _Items          =    "Form1.frx":0000
      End
   End
End
Attribute VB_Name = "Form1"
Attribute VB_GlobalNameSpace = False
Attribute VB_Creatable = False
Attribute VB_PredeclaredId = True
Attribute VB_Exposed = False

Private Sub btnAdd_Click()
    ListView1.ListItems.Add 1, "item1", "Item 1"
    ListView1.ListItems.Add 2, "item2", "Item 2"
    ListView1.ListItems.Add 3, "item3", "Item 3"
    btnClear.Enabled = True
    btnAdd.Enabled = False
End Sub

Private Sub btnClear_Click()
    ListView1.ListItems.Clear
    btnClear.Enabled = False
    btnAdd.Enabled = True
End Sub

Private Sub Form_Load()
    btnAdd_Click
End Sub
```

CROSS-REFERENCE
See also Remove.

ClearSel

Method

The `ClearSel` method removes a selected range from a Slider control. To do this, the method sets the control's `SelStart` property to the current value of the `Value` property and sets the `SelLength` property to 0.

Objects with a ClearSel Method

Slider

Syntax

```
Slider.ClearSel
```

- *Slider*—A reference to a Slider control.

Example

The following line removes the current range selection from a slider control. The `sldSlider1` object is a Slider control that the programmer added to the form at design time.

```
sldSlider1.ClearSel
```

CROSS-REFERENCE
See also Slider, SelStart, and SelLength.

Click

Event

Visual Basic sends an object a `Click` event when the user clicks an object with the mouse. A program can also fire a `Click` event when the user clicks an object like a CommandButton by pressing the keyboard's spacebar, or pressing Enter or Esc to click a default button or cancel button, respectively. Button hotkeys can also trigger `Click` events.

Objects with a Click Event

Animation

CheckBox

ComboBox

CommandButton

CoolBar

DirListBox

FileListBox

Form

Frame

Image

Label

ListBox

ListView

MDIForm

Menu

OLE Container

OptionButton

PictureBox

ProgressBar

PropertyPage

RichTextBox

Slider

StatusBar

TabStrip

TextBox

Toolbar

UserControl

Example

A program can respond to a `Click` event by implementing a control's `Click` event procedure. For example, the following lines show how clicking a button can display a message box. The `btnCommand1` object is a CommandButton control that the programmer added to the form at design time.

```
Private Sub btnCommand1_Click()
    MsgBox "Button clicked."
End Sub
```

 CROSS-REFERENCE
See also DblClick, MouseDown, and MouseUp.

ClientHeight

Property

The `ClientHeight` property represents the height of a TabStrip control's client area. The units used with `ClientHeight` are those of the containing form's `ScaleMode` property, which can be twip, pixel, point, character, inch, millimeter, centimeter, or user-defined. The `ClientHeight` property is available only at runtime, when it is read-only.

Objects with a ClientHeight Property

TabStrip

Syntax

value1 = *TabStrip*.ClientHeight

- *TabStrip* — A reference to a TabStrip control.
- *value1* — The variable that will receive the client height.

Example

In this example, the program retrieves the height of a TabStrip control's client area. The `tabTabStrip1` object is a TabStrip control that the programmer added to the application's form at design time.

```
Dim CHeight As Integer
CHeight = tabTabStrip1.ClientHeight
```

 CROSS-REFERENCE
See also TabStrip, ClientLeft, ClientTop, and ClientWidth.

ClientLeft

Property

The ClientLeft property represents the left coordinate of a TabStrip control's client area. The units used with ClientHeight are those of the containing form's ScaleMode property, which can be twip, pixel, point, character, inch, millimeter, centimeter, or user-defined. The ClientLeft property is available only at runtime, when it is read-only.

Objects with a ClientLeft Property

TabStrip

Syntax

```
value1 = TabStrip.ClientLeft
```

- *TabStrip* — A reference to a TabStrip control.
- *value1* — The variable that will receive the client's left coordinate.

Example

In this example, the program retrieves the left coordinate of a TabStrip control's client area. The tabTabStrip1 object is a TabStrip control that the programmer added to the application's form at design time.

```
Dim CLeft As Integer
CLeft = tabTabStrip1.ClientLeft
```

 CROSS-REFERENCE
See also TabStrip, ClientHeight, ClientTop, and ClientWidth.

ClientTop

Property

The ClientTop property represents the top coordinate of a TabStrip control's client area. The units used with ClientTop are those of the containing form's ScaleMode property, which can be twip, pixel, point, character, inch, millimeter, centimeter, or user-defined. The ClientTop property is available only at runtime, when it is read-only.

Objects with a ClientTop Property

TabStrip

Syntax

```
value1 = TabStrip.ClientTop
```

- *TabStrip* — A reference to a TabStrip control.
- *value1* — The variable that will receive the client's top coordinate.

Example

In this example, the program retrieves the top coordinate of a TabStrip control's client area. The `tabTabStrip1` object is a TabStrip control that the programmer added to the application's form at design time.

```
Dim CTop As Integer
CTop = tabTabStrip1.ClientTop
```

 CROSS-REFERENCE
See also TabStrip, ClientHeight, ClientLeft, and ClientWidth.

ClientWidth

Property

The `ClientWidth` property represents the width of a TabStrip control's client area. The units used with `ClientWidth` are those of the containing form's `ScaleMode` property, which can be twip, pixel, point, character, inch, millimeter, centimeter, or user-defined. The `ClientWidth` property is available only at runtime, when it is read-only.

Objects with a ClientWidth Property

TabStrip

Syntax

```
value1 = TabStrip.ClientWidth
```

- *TabStrip* — A reference to a TabStrip control.
- *value1* — The variable that will receive the client area's width.

Example

In this example, the program retrieves the width of a TabStrip control's client area. The `tabTabStrip1` object is a TabStrip control that the programmer added to the application's form at design time.

```
Dim CWidth As Integer
CWidth = tabTabStrip1.ClientWidth
```

 CROSS-REFERENCE
See also TabStrip, ClientHeight, ClientTop, and ClientLeft.

ClipBehavior

Property

The `ClipBehavior` property determines where drawing can be performed inside a UserControl control. This property can be set to 0 (graphics can be drawn anywhere inside the control) or 1 (graphics can appear only in the area of the control defined by the control's MaskRegion).

Objects with a ClipBehavior Property

UserControl

Syntax

```
UserControl.ClipBehavior = value1
```

or

```
value2 = UserControl.ClipBehavior
```

- *UserControl* — A reference to a UserControl object.
- *value1* — The value 0 or 1.
- *value2* — The variable that will receive the property's current setting.

Example

In this example, the program enables graphics methods to draw anywhere within the control object.

```
Private Sub UserControl_Initialize()
    UserControl.ClipBehavior = 0
End Sub
```

CROSS-REFERENCE
See also UserControl.

Clipboard

Object

The Clipboard object represents the system's Clipboard, which applications can use to cut and paste data. You don't need to create an instance of the Clipboard object in order to access the Clipboard in your applications. Just use the global Clipboard object directly.

Properties

The Clipboard object has no properties.

Methods

The Clipboard object has six methods, which are listed in Table C-2. For more information on using a method shown in the following table, look up the method's entry elsewhere in this book.

Table C-2 Methods of the Clipboard Object

Method	Description
Clear	Clears the Clipboard's contents.
GetData	Gets graphical data from the Clipboard. This data can be a bitmap, a DIB, a palette, or a metafile.
GetFormat	Determines whether the Clipboard contains the given data format.
GetText	Gets text data from the Clipboard.
SetData	Places graphical data in the Clipboard. This data can be a bitmap, a DIB, a palette, or a metafile.
SetText	Places text data in the Clipboard.

Events

The CheckBox control does not respond to events.

Example

In this example, when the user clicks a button, the program checks whether the Clipboard contains text data. If it does, a message box displays the text in the

Clipboard. If the Clipboard doesn't contain text, the program places text in the Clipboard, after which, if the user clicks the button again, the message box will display the text. The `btnCommand1` object is a CommandButton control that the programmer added to the application's form at design time.

```
Private Sub btnCommand1_Click()
    Dim formatOK
    Dim msg

    formatOK = Clipboard.GetFormat(vbCFText)
    If formatOK Then
        msg = Clipboard.GetText
        MsgBox msg
    Else
        Clipboard.SetText "Clipboard Text"
    End If
End Sub
```

ClipControls

Property

The `ClipControls` property controls where, within an object, a graphics method can draw. When `ClipControls` is set to `True`, graphics methods won't draw over most objects contained inside the parent object. When `ClipControls` is `False`, however, graphics methods can draw anywhere within the parent object. Figure C-15 shows the result of a call to the `Circle` method when a form's `ClipControls` property is set to `True`, whereas Figure C-16 shows the results when `ClipControls` is set to `False`. Notice in the latter case how the program draws the circle right over the controls.

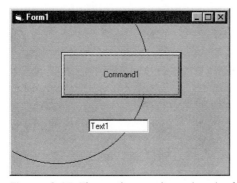

Figure C-15 This circle was clipped to the form's controls.

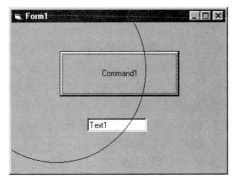

Figure C-16 This circle was drawn with no clipping.

Objects with a ClipControls Property

Form

Frame

PictureBox

PropertyPage

UserControl

Syntax

```
object.ClipControls = value1
```

or

```
value2 = object.ClipControls
```

- *object* — A reference to an object with a `ClipControls` property.
- *value1* — The value `True` or `False`.
- *value2* — The variable that will receive the property's current setting.

Example

In this example, the program turns on control clipping.

```
frmForm1.ClipControls = True
```

Close

Statement

The Close statement closes a file that was opened with the Open statement.

Syntax

```
Close #num
```

- *#num* (*) — The file number to close.

(*) = Optional

 NOTE
If the optional file number is not included in the statement, Visual Basic closes all open files.

Example

In this example, a program opens a file for text output, writes a line of text to the file, and then closes the file.

```
Open "DataFile.dat" For Output As #1
Print #1, "Text data for the file"
Close
```

 CROSS-REFERENCE
For more information, see Open.

Close — Animation

Method

The Close method closes the currently loaded animation file in an Animation control.

Syntax

```
Animation.Close
```

- *Animation* — A reference to an Animation control.

Example

The following line closes an Animation control's AVI file. The `aniAnimation1` object is an Animation control the programmer added to the application's form at design time.

```
aniAnimation1.Close
```

CROSS-REFERENCE
For more information, see Animation.

Close—OLE Container

Method

The `Close` method closes the embedded object in an OLE Container control. Closing the object terminates the connection between the object and its server application.

Syntax

```
OLEContainer.Close
```

- *OLEContainer*—A reference to an OLE Container control.

Example

The following line closes an object in an OLE Container control. The `oleContainer1` object is an OLE Container control the programmer added to the application's form at design time.

```
oleContainer1.Close
```

CROSS-REFERENCE
For more information, see OLE Container.

Close—TextStream

Method

The `Close` method closes the file associated with a TextStream object.

Syntax

TextStream.Close

- *TextStream* — A reference to a TextStream object.

Example

In this example, the program reads lines of text from a text file, displaying each line in a message box. The program stops reading from the file when the AtEndOfStream property indicates the file pointer is at the end of the file. When the file has been processed, the Close method closes the file.

```
Dim fileSystem, stream
Dim str As String

' Create the text stream.
Set fileSystem = CreateObject("Scripting.FileSystemObject")
Set stream = fileSystem.OpenTextFile("c:\text.txt", 1)

' Read lines from a text file.
Do While stream.AtEndOfStream <> True
    str = stream.ReadLine
    MsgBox str
Loop

stream.Close
```

CROSS-REFERENCE
For more information, see TextStream.

Cls

Method

The Cls method erases an object's display area.

Objects with a Cls Method

Form
PictureBox
PropertyPage
UserControl

Syntax

```
object.Cls
```

- *object* — A reference to an object with a Cls method.

Example

The following line clears graphics and text from a form's window. Controls contained in the window are unaffected.

```
frmForm1.Cls
```

CROSS-REFERENCE
For more information, see Animation.

Collapse

Event

Visual Basic sends a TreeView control a Collapse event when the user collapses a node in the tree.

Objects with a Collapse Event

TreeView

Example

A program can respond to a Collapse event by implementing a TreeView control's Collapse event procedure. For example, the following lines display a message box whenever the user collapses a TreeView control's node. The treTreeView1 object is a TreeView control that the programmer added to the form at design time.

```
Private Sub treTreeView1_Collapse _
  (ByVal Node As MSComctlLib.Node)
     MsgBox "A node just collpased"
End Sub
```

CROSS-REFERENCE
See also TreeView.

Collection

Object

A Collection object holds a series of items that can be accessed through the collection using an index or the collection's `Item` method. For example, collections are used to store the Column objects for a ListView control or to store the Pane objects for a StatusBar control.

Properties

A Collection object has one property, called `Count`, which represents the number of items in the collection.

Methods

The Collection object has four methods, which are listed in Table C-3. For more information on using a method shown in the following table, look up the method's entry elsewhere in this book.

Table C-3 Methods of the Collection Object

Method	Description
Add	Adds an item to the collection.
Clear	Removes all items from the collection.
Item	Returns an item from the collection.
Remove	Removes an item from the collection.

Example

In this example, a program adds nodes to a TreeView control by calling the Nodes collection's `Add` method. The `treTreeView1` object is a TreeView control that the programmer added to the application's form at design time.

```
treTreeView1.Nodes.Add _
    , , "Root", "Root Node"
treTreeView1.Nodes.Add "Root", tvwChild, _
    "Child1", "Child Node"
treTreeView1.Nodes.Add "Root", tvwChild, _
    "Child2", "Child Node"
treTreeView1.Nodes.Add "Root", tvwChild, _
    "Child3", "Child Node"
```

Color

Property

The `Color` property represents the currently selected color in a CommonDialog control. This property's value can be set by the `RGB` or `QBColor` functions or using one of Visual Basic's predefined color constants.

Objects with a Color Property

CommonDialog

Syntax

```
CommonDialog.Color = value1
```

or

```
value2 = CommonDialog.Color
```

- *CommonDialog* — A reference to a CommonDialog control.
- *value1* — The new color value.
- *value2* — The variable that will receive the color from the property.

Example

In this example, the program displays a Color dialog box and stores the color the user selected. The `dlgCommonDialog1` object is a CommonDialog control that the programmer added to the application's form at design time.

```
Private Sub Command1_Click()
    dlgCommonDialog1.ShowColor
    selectedColor = dlgCommonDialog1.Color
End Sub
```

CROSS-REFERENCE
See also CommonDialog.

ColorMode

Property

The `ColorMode` property represents whether a Printer object outputs in color or monochrome. This property can be one of two values: `vbPRCMMonochrome` or `vbPRCMColor`. Note that not all printers support color printing. Monochrome printers are unaffected by the `ColorMode` property.

Objects with a ColorMode Property

Printer

Syntax

```
Printer.Class = value1
```

or

```
value2 = Printer.Class
```

- *Printer* — A reference to a Printer object.
- *value1* — The value `vbPRCMMonochrome` or `vbPRCMColor`.
- *value2* — The variable that will receive the current `ColorMode` setting.

Example

In this example, the program sets a printer to color output. Note that you don't need to create an instance of the Printer object, which is a global object that can be referenced directly in your programs.

```
Printer.ColorMode = vbPRCMColor
```

CROSS-REFERENCE
See also Printer.

Column

Property

The Column property represents the current character position in a file associated with a TextStream object. The first character in the file is in column 1, as is every character after a newline character.

Objects with a Column Property

TextStream

Syntax

value1 = *TextStream*.Column

- *TextStream*—A reference to a TextStream object.
- *value1*—The variable that will receive the current column value.

Example

In this example, the program creates a TextStream object and reads a line of text, one character at a time. A message box appears for each character, displaying the character's column position. A message box also displays the complete line after the line has been read in from the file.

```
Dim fileSystem, stream
Dim str As String

Set fileSystem = CreateObject("Scripting.FileSystemObject")
Set stream = fileSystem.OpenTextFile("c:\text.txt", 1)
str = ""
Do While stream.AtEndOfLine <> True
    MsgBox stream.Column
    str = str & stream.Read(1)
Loop
MsgBox str
```

CROSS-REFERENCE
See also TextStream.

ColumnClick

Event

Visual Basic sends a ListView control a `ColumnClick` event when the user clicks one of the control's column headers, which the control displays only in report view.

Objects That Receive ColumnClick Events

ListView

Example

A program can respond to a `ColumnClick` event by implementing the target object's `ColumnClick` event procedure. The following code segment shows how a ListView object defines a `ColumnClick` event procedure. In this case, the form displays a message box each time the user clicks a column in the ListView control. The `lvwListView1` object is a ListView control that the programmer added to the form at design time.

```
Private Sub lvwListView1_ColumnClick _
  (ByVal ColumnHeader As MSComctlLib.ColumnHeader)
    ' Handle the Activate event here.
    MsgBox "User clicked a column"
End Sub
```

CROSS-REFERENCE
See also ListView.

ColumnHeader

Object

The ColumnHeader object represents the column headers in a ListView control that's set to report view. A ColumnHeaders collection holds all of a ListView control's ColumnHeader objects.

Properties

The ColumnHeader object has nine properties, which are listed in Table C-4. For more information on using a property shown in the following table, look up the property's entry elsewhere in this book.

Table C-4 Properties of the ColumnHeader Object

Property	Description
Alignment	Determines the alignment of text in the column header. Can be lvwColumnLeft, lvwColumnRight, or lvwColumnCenter.
Icon	Determines the icon that will be displayed in the column header.
Index	Represents the column header's position in its ColumnHeaders collection.
Left	Represents the position of the column header's left edge in the row of column headers.
Position	Determines the column header's position in the row of column headers.
SubItemIndex	Represents the index of the subitems associated with the column.
Tag	Represents user-defined text data for the object.
Text	Represents the text that will appear in the column header object.
Width	Represents the column header's width.

Methods

The ColumnHeader object has no methods.

Events

The ColumnHeader object does not respond to events.

Example

In this example, a program sets a ListView control to report view, and then adds three ColumnHeader objects to the control. Figure C-17 shows how the column headers appear. The lvwListView1 object is a ListView control that the programmer added to the application's form at design time.

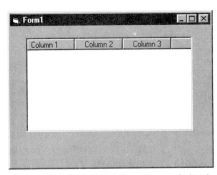

Figure C-17 This ListView control displays three ColumnHeader objects.

```
lvwListView1.View = lvwReport
lvwListView1.ColumnHeaders. _
    Add 1, "column1", "Column 1", 1140, lvwColumnLeft
lvwListView1.ColumnHeaders. _
    Add 2, "column2", "Column 2", 1140, lvwColumnCenter
lvwListView1.ColumnHeaders. _
    Add 3, "column3", "Column 3", 1140, lvwColumnCenter
```

 **CROSS-REFERENCE**
See also ListView.

ColumnHeaderIcons

Property

The `ColumnHeaderIcons` property represents the ImageList that holds the images for the ColumnHeader objects in a ListView control's ColumnHeaders collection.

Objects with a ColumnHeaderIcons Property

ListView

Syntax

```
ListView.ColumnHeaderIcons = value1
```

or

```
value2 = ListView.ColumnHeaderIcons
```

- *ListView* — A reference to a ListView control.
- *value1* — A reference to an ImageList control.
- *value2* — The variable that will receive the current ImageList control.

Example

In this example, the program sets the column headers images to the images stored in an ImageList control. The `lvwListView1` and `ilsImageList1` objects are the ListView and ImageList controls, respectively, that the programmer added to the application's form at design time.

```
lvwListView1.ColumnHeaderIcons = ilsImageList1
```

CROSS-REFERENCE
See also ListView, ColumnHeader, ColumnHeaders, ImageList, ListImage, and ListImages.

ColumnHeaders

Collection

A `ColumnHeaders` collection holds the ColumnHeader objects that are associated with the columns of a ListView control in report view.

Properties

A ColumnHeaders collection has one property, called `Count`, which represents the number of items in the collection.

Methods

A ColumnHeaders collection has four methods, which are listed in Table C-5. For more information on using a method shown in the following table, look up the method's entry elsewhere in this book.

Table C-5 Methods of the ColumnHeaders Object

Method	Description
Add	Adds a ColumnHeader to the collection.
Clear	Removes all ColumnHeaders from the collection.
Item	Returns a ColumnHeader from the collection.
Remove	Removes a ColumnHeader from the collection.

CROSS-REFERENCE
See also ColumnHeaders (property).

ColumnHeaders

Property

The `ColumnHeaders` property represents the ColumnHeaders collection that's associated with an ImageList control.

Objects with a ColumnHeaders Property

ListView

Syntax

```
value1 = ListView.ColumnHeaders
```

- *ListView* — A reference to a ColumnHeaders collection.
- *value1* — The variable that will receive a reference to the current ColumnHeaders collection.

Example

In this example, the program retrieves a reference to a ListView control's ColumnHeaders collection and then uses that reference to change the text in the second ColumnHeader object held in the collection. The `lvwListView1` object is a ListView control that the programmer added to the application's form at design time.

```
Dim colHeaders As ColumnHeaders
Set colHeaders = lvwListView1.ColumnHeaders
colHeaders.Item(2).Text = "New Text"
```

 CROSS-REFERENCE
See also ListView and ColumnHeader.

Columns

Property

The `Columns` property determines whether items in a ListBox control are organized into a single column or multiple columns. A value of 0 (which is the default) causes the ListBox to organize its items into a single, vertically scrolling column. A value greater than 0 causes the ListBox to organize its contents into multiple columns with horizontal scrolling. The `Columns` value determines how many of the columns are visible in the control. That is, a value of 1 arranges the items into multiple columns with one column at a time displayed in the control (see Figure C-18). On the other hand, a value of 3 arranges the items into multiple columns with three columns at a time displayed in the control, as shown in Figure C-19. Note that, at runtime, a program cannot change a single-column ListBox to a multiple-column ListBox or vice-versa.

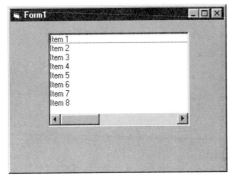

Figure C-18 Here is a multiple-column ListBox displaying a single column.

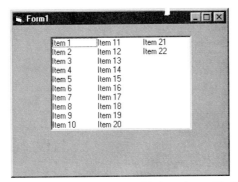

Figure C-19 Here is a multiple-column ListBox displaying three columns.

Objects with a Columns Property

ListBox

Syntax

```
ListBox.Columns = value1
```

or

```
value2 = ListBox.Columns
```

- *ListBox* — A reference to a ListBox control.
- *value1* — 0 or the number of columns.
- *value2* — The variable that will receive the current property setting.

Example

The following line sets a ListBox to display three columns of items with a horizontal scrollbar (if needed). The lstList1 object is a ListBox control that the programmer added to the application's form at design time.

```
lstList1.Columns = 3
```

CROSS-REFERENCE
See also ListBox.

ComboBox

Control

A ComboBox is a control that enables a program's user to select items from a list, much like a ListBox control. The main difference between a ListBox and a ComboBox is that a ComboBox combines a TextBox with the list so that the user can also type a selection into the control. Figure C-20 shows a ComboBox control as it first appears. The user can type a selection into the control's text box or click the control's arrow to display a list of selections (see Figure C-21). The ComboBox control is available on Visual Basic's standard toolbox.

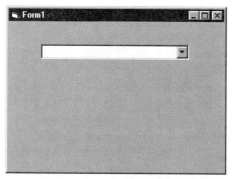

Figure C-20 Here's a ComboBox as it first appears to the user.

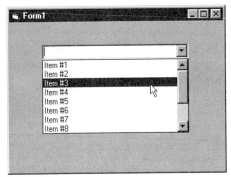

Figure C-21 Here's the ComboBox after the user clicks the control's arrow.

There are actually three types of ComboBox controls you can create. The control's `Style` property determines the type of control you get. A *drop-down combo box* includes the text box and the drop-down list. A *simple combo box* has both the text box and the list, but the list doesn't drop down and is always visible. In this case, the ComboBox control's `Height` property determines the size of the list. Finally, you can create a *drop-down list combo box*, in which the user can select items only from the drop-down list and not by typing into the text box.

Properties

The ComboBox control has 50 properties, which are listed below. Because many Visual Basic controls have similar properties, the properties' descriptions are listed under their own names elsewhere in this book.

```
Appearance
BackColor
CausesValidation
Container
DragIcon
DragMode
Enabled
Font
FontBold
FontItalic
FontName
FontSize
FontStrikethru
FontUnderline
```

```
ForeColor
Height
HelpContextID
hWnd
Index
IntegralHeight
ItemData
Left
List
ListCount
ListIndex
Locked
MouseIcon
MousePointer
Name
NewIndex
OLEDrag
OLEDragMode
OLEDropMode
Parent
RightToLeft
SelLength
SelStart
SelText
Sorted
Style
TabIndex
TabStop
Tag
Text
ToolTipText
Top
TopIndex
Visible
WhatsThisHelpID
Width
```

Methods

The ComboBox control has ten methods, which are listed below. Because many Visual Basic controls have similar methods, the methods' descriptions are listed under their own names elsewhere in this book.

```
AddItem
Clear
Drag
Move
OLEDrag
Refresh
RemoveItem
SetFocus
ShowWhatsThis
ZOrder
```

Events

The ComboBox control responds to 18 events, which are listed below. Because many Visual Basic controls respond to similar events, the events' descriptions are listed under their own names elsewhere in this book.

```
Change
Click
DblClick
DragDrop
DragOver
DropDown
GotFocus
KeyDown
KeyPress
KeyUp
LostFocus
OLECompleteDrag
OLEDragDrop
OLEDragOver
OLEGiveFeedback
OLESetData
OLEStartDrag
Scroll
Validate
```

The ComboBox control's most commonly used events are Change and Click. The Change event occurs when the user types into the control's text box, and the Click event occurs when the user selects an item from the control's list. A program responds to the control's Change and Click events in the Change and Click event procedures. For example, a combo box called cboCombo1 will have a Click event procedure called cboCombo1_Click, which is where the program should handle the Click event. In the following example, when the user selects an item from the cboCombo1 combo box, the program displays the selected item in a message box:

```
Private Sub cboCombo1_Click()
    MsgBox cboCombo1.Text
End Sub
```

Command

Function

Command is a function that returns the command line that was used to run the program. The user might, for example, run the program by following the .exe file's name with a document file name. By examining the string returned by Command, the program can automatically load the given file for the user.

Syntax

```
Command
```

Example

In this example, the program displays the program's command line in a message box.

```
MsgBox Command
```

Command

Property

The Command property represents an MCI command that the Multimedia MCI control should execute. The valid commands are Back, Close, Eject, Next, Open, Pause, Play, Prev, Record, Save, Seek, Sound, Step, and Stop. Note that the successful execution of an MCI command also depends upon the settings of other Multimedia MCI control properties, as described in Table C-6. Some of these properties have default values.

Table C-6 MCI Commands and their Associated Multimedia
Control Properties

Command	Associated Properties
Back	Notify, Wait, and Frames
Close	Notify and Wait
Eject	Notify and Wait
Next	Notify and Wait
Open	DeviceType, FileName, Notify, Shareable, and Wait
Pause	Notify and Wait
Play	From, To, Notify, and Wait
Prev	Notify and Wait
Record	From, To, RecordMode, Notify, and Wait
Save	FileName, Notify, and Wait
Seek	To, Notify, and Wait
Sound	FileName, Notify, and Wait
Step	Frames, Notify, and Wait
Stop	Notify and Wait

Objects with a Command Property

Multimedia MCI

Syntax

```
MultimediaMCI.Command = value1
```

- *MultimediaMCI* — A reference to a Multimedia MCI control.
- *value1* — A string containing the command.

Example

The following line closes the currently open device that's associated with a Multimedia MCI control. The `mciMMControl1` object is a Multimedia MCI control that the programmer added to the application's form at design time.

```
mciMMControl1.Notify = False
mciMMControl1.Wait = True
mciMMControl1.Command = "Close"
```

CROSS-REFERENCE
See also Multimedia MCI.

CommandButton

Control

A CommandButton (often called a pushbutton) is a control that a program's user can click to initiate some sort of action. The control gets its name from the fact that the button sends a command—in the form of a `Click` event—to the program. Figure C-22 shows several CommandButton controls in a form. Notice that the controls are graphical pushbuttons that contain a label describing the command triggered by the control. The CommandButton control is available on Visual Basic's standard toolbox.

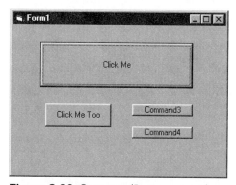

Figure C-22 CommandButton controls are pushbuttons that trigger commands in a program.

Properties

The CommandButton control has 43 properties, which are listed below. Because many Visual Basic controls have similar properties, the properties' descriptions are listed under their own names elsewhere in this book.

```
Appearance
BackColor
Cancel
Caption
CausesValidation
```

```
Container
Default
DisabledPicture
DownPicture
DragIcon
DragMode
Enabled
Font
FontBold
FontItalic
FontName
FontSize
FontStrikethru
FontUnderline
Height
HelpContextID
hWnd
Index
Left
MaskColor
MouseIcon
MousePointer
Name
OLEDropMode
Parent
Picture
RightToLeft
Style
TabIndex
TabStop
Tag
ToolTipText
Top
UseMaskColor
Value
Visible
WhatsThisHelpID
Width
```

Methods

The CommandButton control has seven methods, which are listed below. Because many Visual Basic controls have similar methods, the methods' descriptions are listed under their own names elsewhere in this book.

```
Drag
Move
OLEDrag
Refresh
SetFocus
ShowWhatsThis
ZOrder
```

Events

The CommandButton control responds to 17 events, which are listed below. Because many Visual Basic controls respond to similar events, the events' descriptions are listed under their own names elsewhere in this book.

```
Click
DragDrop
DragOver
GotFocus
KeyDown
KeyPress
KeyUp
LostFocus
MouseDown
MouseMove
MouseUp
OLECompleteDrag
OLEDragDrop
OLEDragOver
OLEGiveFeedback
OLESetData
OLEStartDrag
```

The CommandButton's most commonly used event is `Click`, which the button generates when the user clicks the button with the mouse. A program responds to the button's `Click` event in the `Click` event procedure. A button called `btnCommand1` will have a `Click` event procedure called `btnCommand1_Click`, which is where the program should handle the event. In the following example, when the user clicks the `btnCommand1` button, the program plays the computer's beep sound:

```
Private Sub btnCommand1_Click()
    ' Handle the Click event here.
    Beep
End Sub
```

Comments

Property

The `Comments` property represents a text string that holds comments about the application. You can set the value of this property name by selecting the Properties command from the Project menu, which displays the Project Properties property sheet. The `Comments` property is on the Make page of the property sheet, as shown in Figure C-23. The `Comments` property is read-only at runtime.

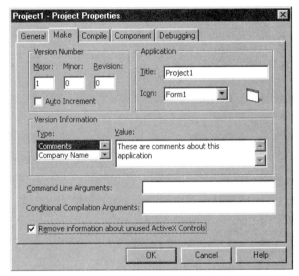

Figure C-23 You can set an App object's Comments property using the Project Properties property sheet.

Objects with a Comments Property

App

Syntax

```
value1 = App.Comments
```

- *value1* — The variable that will receive the text from the `Comments` property.

Example

The following line displays the application's comments in a message box. Because the `App` object is a global Visual Basic object, you don't need to create an instance of the object in your program and can just reference the object directly.

```
MsgBox App.Comments
```

 **CROSS-REFERENCE**
See also App.

CommonDialog

Control

The CommonDialog control represents Windows' common dialog boxes, which include Open, Save, Font, Color, Print, and Help. Figure C-24, for example, shows a Color dialog box.

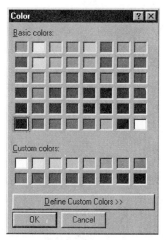

Figure C-24 The Color dialog box is one of Windows' common dialog boxes.

Properties

The CommonDialog control has 35 properties, which are listed as follows. Because many Visual Basic controls have similar properties, the properties' descriptions are listed under their own names elsewhere in this book.

```
Action
CancelError
Color
Copies
DefaultExt
DialogTitle
FileName
FileTitle
Filter
Flags
FontBold
FontItalic
FontName
FontSize
FontStrikethru
FontUnderline
FromPage
hDC
HelpCommand
HelpContext
HelpFile
HelpKey
HelpContextID
Index
InitDir
Max
MaxFileSize
Min
Name
Object
Orientation
Parent
PrinterDefault
Tag
TopPage
```

Methods

The CommonDialog control has six methods, which are listed below. Because many Visual Basic controls have similar methods, the methods' descriptions are listed under their own names elsewhere in this book.

```
ShowColor
ShowFont
ShowHelp
ShowOpen
ShowPrinter
ShowSave
```

Events

The CommonDialog control does not respond to events.

 CROSS-REFERENCE
See also ShowColor, ShowFont, ShowHelp, ShowOpen, ShowPrinter, and ShowSave.

CompanyName

Property

The CompanyName property represents the name of the company that developed and/or distributes the application. You can get or set the CompanyName property through a running application's App object.

Objects with a CompanyName Property

App

Syntax

```
string = App.CompanyName
```

- *string* — The string that will hold the company name.

Example 1

Because the CompanyName property is read-only at runtime, you must set the property in the Project Properties dialog box before compiling the project. To display the Project Properties dialog box, select the *ProjectName* Properties command from Visual Basic's Project menu. (*ProjectName* is the name of the current project.) Figure C-25 shows the CompanyName property being set to "Acme Software" in the Project Properties dialog box.

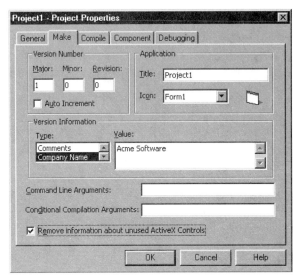

Figure C-25 You can set the App object's properties in the Project Properties
dialog box.

Example 2

The following example obtains the value of the `CompanyName` property when
the user clicks the application's form. The program then displays the property's
value in a message box.

```
Private Sub Form_Click()
    Dim vntName
    vntName = App.CompanyName
    MsgBox vntName
End Sub
```

Compare

Keyword

The `Compare` keyword is part of the `Option Compare` statement, which determines how Visual Basic compares string data. For example, the following line
specifies that string information should be compared as text. Other settings
are `Binary` and `Database`.

```
Option Compare Text
```

CROSS-REFERENCE
For more information, see Option Compare.

Compose

Method

The `Compose` method sets up the MAPIMessages control to compose a new message.

Objects with a Compose Method

MAPIMessages

Syntax

`MAPIMessages.Compose`

- *MAPIMessages* — A reference to a MAPIMessages control.

CROSS-REFERENCE
For more information, see MAPIMessages.

ConfigChangeCancelled

Event

Visual Basic sends a SysInfo control a `ConfigChangeCancelled` event when a change to the system's hardware configuration is canceled.

Objects That Receive ConfigChangeCancelled Events

SysInfo

Example

A program can respond to a `ConfigChangeCancelled` event by implementing the SysInfo control's `ConfigChangeCancelled` event procedure. The following code segment shows how a SysInfo object defines a `ConfigChangeCancelled` event procedure. In this case, the form displays a message box when the event arrives. The SysInfo1 object in this example is a SysInfo control that the programmer added to the form at design time.

```
Private Sub SysInfo1_ConfigChangeCancelled()
    ' Respond to the event here
    MsgBox "Hardware configuration cancelled"
End Sub
```

CROSS-REFERENCE
See also SysInfo and ConfigChanged.

ConfigChanged

Event

Visual Basic sends a SysInfo control a ConfigChanged event when a change to the system's hardware configuration is completed.

Objects That Receive ConfigChanged Events

SysInfo

Example

A program can respond to a ConfigChanged event by implementing the SysInfo control's ConfigChanged event procedure. The following code segment shows how a SysInfo object defines a ConfigChanged event procedure. In this case, the form displays a message box when the event arrives. (The SysInfo1 object in this example is a SysInfo control that the programmer added to the form at design time.) ConfigChanged's two parameters are the Windows registry key for the old hardware configuration and the Windows registry key for the new hardware configuration.

```
Private Sub SysInfo1_ConfigChanged _
    (ByVal OldConfigNum As Long, ByVal NewConfigNum As Long)
        ' Respond to the event here
    MsgBox "Hardware configuration completed"
End Sub
```

CROSS-REFERENCE
See also SysInfo and ConfigChangeCancelled.

Const

Statement

The `Const` statement enables the programmer to declare constants that can take the place of literal values in a program. By using carefully named constants in place of literal values, program listings are easier to read and understand. You can declare a constant as `Public` or `Private`, as well as specify a data type.

Syntax

`access Const name type`

- *access* (*) — The keyword `Public` or `Private`.
- *name* — The constant's name.
- *type* (*) — The keyword `As` followed by the value's data type.

(*) = Optional

Example 1

The following line defines an integer constant called `MemberCount` that represents the value 25 in the current module. The constant `MemberCount` can then be used in the program in the place of the literal value 25.

```
Private Const MemberCount As Integer = 25
```

Example 2

You could also define the `MemberCount` constant as shown in this example, because `Private` access is the default and Visual Basic knows that 25 is an integer. However, this form is not as descriptive and could lead to some confusion, as well as cause side effects if you're not certain how Visual Basic will interpret the data type of the expression.

```
Const MemberCount = 25
```

 CROSS-REFERENCE
See also As, Public, Private, and Data Types.

ContainedControls

Property

The ContainedControls property represents, as a collection, the controls that were added to the UserControl object at runtime. This property is available only at runtime, when it is read-only.

Objects with a ContainedControls Property

UserControl

Syntax

`value1 = UserControl.ContainedControls`

- *UserControl*—A reference to a UserControl object.
- *value1*—The variable that will receive the control collection.

CROSS-REFERENCE
See also UserControl and ControlContainer.

Container

Property

The Container property represents a control's container object, which can be a Form, Frame, or PictureBox control. This property cannot be accessed at design time.

Objects with a Container Property

Animation
CheckBox
ComboBox
CommandButton
CoolBar
DirListBox
DriveListBox
FileListBox
Frame

b
c
d

HScrollBar

Image

Label

Line

ListBox

ListView

Multimedia MCI

OLE Container

OptionButton

PictureBox

ProgressBar

RichTextBox

Shape

Slider

StatusBar

TabStrip

TextBox

Toolbar

TreeView

UpDown

VScrollBar

Syntax

```
Set value1 = object.Container
```

- *object* — A reference to an object with a `Container` property.
- *value1* — The variable that will receive a reference to the container object.

Example

The following lines get a reference to a button's container object and then use the reference to change the container's caption. The `btnCommand1` object is a CommandButton control that the programmer added to the application's form at design time.

```
Set btnParent = btnCommand1.Container
btnParent.Caption = "Container Caption"
```

ContainerHWnd

Property

The `ContainerHWnd` property represents the Windows handle of a UserControl object's container.

Objects with a ContainerHWnd Property

UserControl

Syntax

`value1 = UserControl.ContainerHWnd`

- *UserControl*—A reference to a UserControl object.
- *value1*—The variable that will receive the handle.

Control

Object

The Control object represents all Visual Basic controls. That is, a variable of the Control type can hold a reference to any Visual Basic control.

Properties

The Control object has no properties.

Methods

The Control object has no methods.

Events

The Control object does not respond to events.

Example

The following lines dimension a variable named `butn` as a Control reference and then set the variable to represent a button control. The program changes the button's caption through the `butn` control reference. The `btnCommand1` object is a

CommandButton control that the programmer added to the application's form at design time.

```
Dim butn As Control
Set butn = btnCommand1
butn.Caption = "Button Caption"
```

Control Array

Concept

When a set of controls are related to each other, it often makes sense to organize the controls into a *control array*. When controls are added to a control array, all the controls get the same name. You then access a specific control through the use of an index, just as with any other type of array. You might, for example, have a set of CommandButton controls that would be convenient to handle in a single event procedure. To accomplish this, organize the buttons into a control array.

To create a control array, begin by adding the first control to the control's container. Then, with the control selected, press Ctrl-C to copy the control. To add a second button to the array, press Ctrl-V to paste the copied control to the container. When you do, Visual Basic asks whether you want to create a control array. Answer yes. You can then continue adding controls to the array by pressing Ctrl-V.

The control array's event procedures will receive as a parameter an index into the control array. This index indicates which control generated the event. For example, the following program shows how to define a control array in source code, as well as shows the event procedure for a CommandButton control array. Notice, in the first part of the listing, how the three button controls are all assigned the same name, `btnCommand1`. Also notice, in the `btnCommand1_Click` event procedure how the program uses `Index` to access the clicked control, changing its caption.

```
VERSION 5.00
Begin VB.Form frmForm1
   Caption        =   "Control Array Demo"
   ClientHeight   =   3195
   ClientLeft     =   60
   ClientTop      =   345
   ClientWidth    =   4680
   LinkTopic      =   "Form1"
```

```
ScaleHeight     =     3195
ScaleWidth      =     4680
StartUpPosition =     3  'Windows Default
Begin VB.CommandButton btnCommand1
   Caption          =     "Command1"
   Height           =     495
   Index            =     2
   Left             =     840
   TabIndex         =     2
   Top              =     1920
   Width            =     3015
End
Begin VB.CommandButton btnCommand1
   Caption          =     "Command1"
   Height           =     495
   Index            =     1
   Left             =     840
   TabIndex         =     1
   Top              =     1200
   Width            =     3015
End
Begin VB.CommandButton btnCommand1
   Caption          =     "Command1"
   Height           =     495
   Index            =     0
   Left             =     840
   TabIndex         =     0
   Top              =     480
   Width            =     3015
   End
End
Attribute VB_Name = "frmForm1"
Attribute VB_GlobalNameSpace = False
Attribute VB_Creatable = False
Attribute VB_PredeclaredId = True
Attribute VB_Exposed = False

Private Sub btnCommand1_Click(Index As Integer)
    btnCommand1(Index).Caption = "Click!"
End Sub
```

ControlBox

Property

The `ControlBox` property represents whether a Form has a control box. Note that only Fixed-Single, Sizable, or Fixed-Dialog border styles can support the control box. (A control box represents the system menu in the upper-left corner of a window.)

Objects with a ControlBox Property

Form

Syntax

`value1 = Form.ControlBox`

- *Form* — A reference to a Form object.
- *value1* — The variable that will receive the current property setting.

Example

In this example, the program displays a message box that indicates whether the form has a control box. The `frmForm1` object is the application's form.

```
If frmForm1.ControlBox Then
    MsgBox "The form has a control box."
Else
    MsgBox "The form has no control box."
End If
```

 CROSS-REFERENCE
See also Form.

ControlContainer

Property

The `ControlContainer` property determines whether a UserControl object can act as a container for other controls. The property can be set to `True` (can contain controls) or `False` (cannot contain controls).

Objects with a ControlContainer Property

UserControl

Syntax

```
UserControl.ControlContainer = value1
```

or

```
value2 = UserControl.ControlContainer
```

- *UserControl* — A reference to a UserControl control.
- *value1* — The value True or False.
- *value2* — The variable that will receive the property's current setting.

 CROSS-REFERENCE
See also UserControl and ContainedControls.

Controls

Collection

A Controls collection holds the controls that are associated with an object such as a form or toolbar.

Properties

A Controls collection has one property, called Count, which represents the number of items in the collection.

Methods

A Controls collection has one method, Item, which returns a reference to a control in the collection.

Example 1

In this example, the program changes the captions of three buttons in the form. Figure C-26 shows the result. The frmForm1 object is the application's form.

```
frmForm1.Controls(0).Caption = "Control One"
frmForm1.Controls(1).Caption = "Control Two"
frmForm1.Controls(2).Caption = "Control Three"
```

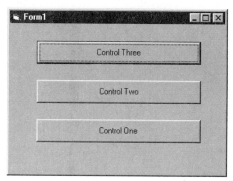

Figure C-26 These buttons' captions were changed by accessing the controls through a Controls collection.

Example 2

The previous example could be rewritten using the `Item` method as follows:

```
frmForm1.Controls.Item(0).Caption = "Control One"
frmForm1.Controls.Item(1).Caption = "Control Two"
frmForm1.Controls.Item(2).Caption = "Control Three"
```

Example 3

Finally, a third way to get similar results would be to use the controls' captions as the index into the control collection, as follows:

```
frmForm1.Controls("Command1").Caption = "Control One"
frmForm1.Controls("Command2").Caption = "Control Two"
frmForm1.Controls("Command3").Caption = "Control Three"
```

Controls

Property

The `Controls` property represents a container's Controls collection.

Objects with a Controls Property
PropertyPage

UserControl

Form

MDIForm

Toolbar

Syntax

`value1 = object.Controls`

- *object* — A reference to an object with a `Controls` property.
- *value1* — The variable that will receive the Controls collection reference.

 CROSS-REFERENCE
See also Controls (collection).

Copies

Property

The `Copies` property represents the number of copies of a document that will be printed by a Printer object. The number of copies can also be obtained from the Print common dialog box, which also has a `Copies` property representing the value the user entered into the dialog's Copies text box.

Objects with a Copies Property
CommonDialog

Printer

Syntax

`object.Copies = value1`

or

`value2 = object.Copies`

- *object* — A reference to a CommonDialog or Printer object.

- *value1* — The number of copies to print.
- *value2* — The variable that will receive the property's current setting.

Example

In this example, the program sets the number of copies to print to 10. Note that Printer is a global Visual Basic object, so you don't need to create an instance of Printer. Just access the Printer object directly.

```
Printer.Copies = 10
```

 CROSS-REFERENCE
See also CommonDialog and Printer.

CopyFile

Method

The `CopyFile` method copies a file — or multiple files specified with wildcard characters — from a given source path to a given destination path.

Objects with a CopyFile Method

FileSystemObject

Syntax

`FileSystemObject.CopyFile src dest overwrite`

- *dest* — The path to which the file or files should be copied.
- *FileSystemObject* — A reference to a FileSystemObject object.
- *src* — The name of file or files to be copied.
- *overwrite* (*) — A value of `True` or `False`, indicating whether an existing file of the same name should be overwritten with the copy. The default is `True`.

(*) = Optional argument

Example 1

The following lines copy a file called `MyText.txt` to a directory called c:\TextFiles, providing overwrite protection. Notice that, when copying a single file, the destination must specify a file name, as well as the destination path. An exception is when the destination path ends with a backslash (\), as shown in Example 2.

```
Dim fileSystem
Set fileSystem = CreateObject("Scripting.FileSystemObject")
fileSystem.CopyFile "c:\MyText.txt", _
    "c:\TextFiles\MyText.txt", False
```

Example 2

If you want to copy a single file to a directory without specifying a destination file name, add a backslash (\) to the destination's path name. Then Visual Basic knows that you want to copy the file to the given directory using the same file name, as shown here:

```
Dim fileSystem
Set fileSystem = CreateObject("Scripting.FileSystemObject")
fileSystem.CopyFile "c:\MyText.txt", "c:\TextFiles\", False
```

Example 3

Finally, to copy multiple files, use valid DOS-style wildcard characters in the source file name. For example, the following lines copy all files in the root directory of drive C: to a directory called c:\TextFiles, allowing files with the same name to be overwritten.

```
Dim fileSystem
Set fileSystem = CreateObject("Scripting.FileSystemObject")
fileSystem.CopyFile "c:\*.txt", "c:\TextFiles\", True
```

CROSS-REFERENCE
For more information, see File, Folder, FileSystemObject, CopyFolder, and Copy.

Copy — File and Folder

Method

The `Copy` method copies a file or folder.

Syntax

```
object.Copy newName overwrite
```

- *newName* — The new file's path and name.
- *object* — A reference to a File or Folder object.
- *overwrite* (*) — A value of True or False, indicating whether an existing file of the same name should be overwritten with the copy. The default is True.

(*) = Optional argument

Example

The following lines open and copy a file. The text2.txt file will be an exact duplicate of the text.txt file.

```
Dim fileSystem, file
Set fileSystem = CreateObject("Scripting.FileSystemObject")
Set file = fileSystem.GetFile("c:\text.txt")
file.Copy "c:\text2.txt"
```

CROSS-REFERENCE
For more information, see File, Folder, FileSystemObject, CopyFile, and CopyFolder.

Copy — MAPIMessages

Method

The Copy method duplicates the current message, placing the copy in the compose buffer and setting the MsgIndex property to –1.

Syntax

```
MAPIMessages.Copy
```

- *MAPIMessages* — A reference to a MAPIMessages control.

CROSS-REFERENCE
See also MAPIMessages.

Copy — OLE Container

Method

The Copy method copies an embedded object to the Clipboard from which the object can be pasted into another document. For example, if an OLE Container holds a Microsoft Word document, the Copy method can copy the document to the Clipboard, after which the document could be pasted into any other application that supports ActiveX objects.

Syntax

```
OLEContainer.Copy
```

- *OLEContainer* — A reference to an OLE Container control.

 CROSS-REFERENCE
See also OLE Container.

CopyFolder

Method

The CopyFolder method copies a folder — or multiple folders specified with wildcard characters — from a given source path to a given destination path.

Objects with a CopyFolder Method

FileSystemObject

Syntax

```
FileSystemObject.CopyFolder src dest overwrite
```

- *dst* — The path to which the folder or folders should be copied.
- *FileSystemObject* — A reference to a FileSystemObject object.
- *src* — The name of the folder or folders to be copied.
- *overwrite* (*) — A value of True or False, indicating whether an existing file of the same name should be overwritten with the copy. The default is True.

(*) = Optional argument

Example 1

The following lines copy a folder called TextFiles to a folder called MyText, creating the MyText folder and providing overwrite protection. Visual Basic knows to create the folder because the destination name doesn't end with a backslash (\).

```
Dim fileSystem
Set fileSystem = CreateObject("Scripting.FileSystemObject")
fileSystem.CopyFolder "c:\TextFiles", "c:\MyText", False
```

Example 2

If you want to copy a folder to an existing folder, you must end the destination name with a backslash (\), as shown here:

```
Dim fileSystem
Set fileSystem = CreateObject("Scripting.FileSystemObject")
fileSystem.CopyFolder "c:\TextFiles", "c:\MyText\", False
```

Example 3

Finally, to copy multiple folders, use valid DOS-style wildcard characters in the source folder name. For example, the following lines copy all folders inside the MyText folder to the existing Backup folder:

```
Dim fileSystem
Set fileSystem = CreateObject("Scripting.FileSystemObject")
fileSystem.CopyFolder "c:\MyText\*", "c:\Backup\"
```

 CROSS-REFERENCE
For more information, see File, Folder, FileSystemObject, CopyFile, and Copy.

Cos

Function

Cos is a function that calculates the cosine of an angle.

Syntax

```
value = Cos(angle)
```

- *angle*—A Double value containing the angle in radians.
- *value*—The Double variable that will receive the angle's cosine.

Example

The following line calculates the cosine of a 45-degree angle. Note that a 45-degree angle is 0.79 in radians, which is the result of the calculation 45 * PI / 180.

```
cosine = Cos(0.79)
```

Count

Property

The Count property represents the number of items contained in a collection.

Objects with a Count Property

Bands

ButtonMenus

Buttons

Collection

ColumnHeaders

ComboItems

Controls

Drives

Files

Folders

ListImages

ListItems

Nodes

Panels

Tabs

Syntax

```
value1 = object.Count
```

- *object* — A reference to a collection object.
- *value1* — The variable that will receive the collection item count.

Example

The following example program gives you a chance to see collections and the `Count` property in action. When you run the program, you see the window shown in Figure C-27. Click the Set Widths button, and the program sets the three top buttons to a smaller width, as shown in Figure C-28. Click the Set Widths button again to restore the button widths to their original size. As you can see in the listing, the `btnSetWidths_Click` event procedure is where all the action happens. The program uses the form's Controls collection to access the buttons, taking advantage of the collection's `Count` property to initialize a loop variable. To see how valuable the `Count` property can be, experiment with the program by adding more buttons to the form. No matter how many you add, or where you add them, the program still works.

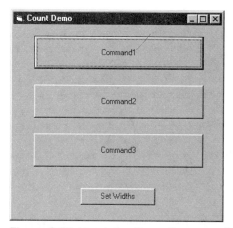

Figure C-27 Here's the Count Demo application when it first appears.

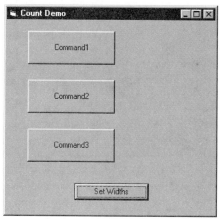

Figure C-28 Here's the program after the user has clicked the Set Widths button.

```
VERSION 5.00
Begin VB.Form frmForm1
   Caption         =   "Count Demo"
   ClientHeight    =   4275
   ClientLeft      =   60
   ClientTop       =   345
   ClientWidth     =   4740
   LinkTopic       =   "Form1"
   ScaleHeight     =   4275
   ScaleWidth      =   4740
   StartUpPosition =   3   'Windows Default
   Begin VB.CommandButton btnSetWidths
      Caption      =   "Set Widths"
      Height       =   375
      Left         =   1560
      TabIndex     =   3
      Top          =   3600
      Width        =   1695
   End
   Begin VB.CommandButton btnCommand3
      Caption      =   "Command3"
      Height       =   735
      Left         =   480
      TabIndex     =   2
      Top          =   2400
      Width        =   3855
   End
   Begin VB.CommandButton btnCommand2
      Caption      =   "Command2"
      Height       =   735
      Left         =   480
      TabIndex     =   1
      Top          =   1320
      Width        =   3855
   End
   Begin VB.CommandButton btnCommand1
      Caption      =   "Command1"
      Height       =   735
      Left         =   480
      TabIndex     =   0
      Top          =   240
      Width        =   3855
   End
End
```

```
Attribute VB_Name = "frmForm1"
Attribute VB_GlobalNameSpace = False
Attribute VB_Creatable = False
Attribute VB_PredeclaredId = True
Attribute VB_Exposed = False

Private Sub btnSetWidths_Click()
    Dim newWidth
    Dim ctrlCount

    If btnCommand1.Width = 3855 Then
        newWidth = 2000
    Else
        newWidth = 3855
    End If

    ctrlCount = frmForm1.Controls.Count
    For x = 0 To ctrlCount - 1
        If frmForm1.Controls(x).Caption <> "Set Widths" Then
            frmForm1.Controls(x).Width = newWidth
        End If
    Next x
End Sub
```

CROSS-REFERENCE
See also Collection.

CreateDragImage

Method

The CreateDragImage method creates an image for use with drag-and-drop operations in a ListView or TreeView control. The method creates the drag image from the item's associated image.

Objects with a CreateDragImage Method

ListItem

Node

Syntax

```
object.CreateDragImage
```

- *object* — A reference to a ListItem or Node object.

Example

The following program creates and displays a drag image when the user moves the mouse pointer over the form while holding down the left mouse button. The image represents the item image assigned to the items in the ListView control. Figure C-29 shows the program when the user is dragging the image. The larger image in the window is the one being dragged.

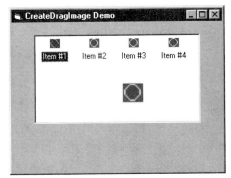

Figure C-29 The CreateDragImage Demo program demonstrates creating and displaying a drag image.

```
VERSION 5.00
Object = "{6B7E6392-850A-101B-AFC0-4210102A8DA7} _
    #2.0#0"; "MSCOMCTL.OCX"
Begin VB.Form Form1
    Caption         =   "CreateDragImage Demo"
    ClientHeight    =   3195
    ClientLeft      =   60
    ClientTop       =   345
    ClientWidth     =   4680
    LinkTopic       =   "Form1"
    ScaleHeight     =   3195
    ScaleWidth      =   4680
    StartUpPosition =   3   'Windows Default
    Begin MSComctlLib.ListView ListView1
        Height      =       1935
        Left        =       480
```

```
            TabIndex        =    0
            Top             =    240
            Width           =    3735
            _ExtentX        =    6588
            _ExtentY        =    3413
            LabelWrap       =    -1   'True
            HideSelection   =    -1   'True
            _Version        =    393217
            ForeColor       =    -2147483640
            BackColor       =    -2147483643
            BorderStyle     =    1
            Appearance      =    1
            NumItems        =    0
            _Items          =    "form1.frx":0000
         End
         Begin MSComctlLib.ImageList ImageList1
            Left            =    1200
            Top             =    2400
            _ExtentX        =    1005
            _ExtentY        =    1005
            BackColor       =    -2147483643
            MaskColor       =    12632256
            _Version        =    393216
         End
      End
End
Attribute VB_Name = "Form1"
Attribute VB_GlobalNameSpace = False
Attribute VB_Creatable = False
Attribute VB_PredeclaredId = True
Attribute VB_Exposed = False
Private Sub Form_Load()
    ImageList1.ListImages.Add , , LoadPicture("c:\reddot.ico")
    ListView1.Icons = ImageList1
    ListView1.SmallIcons = ImageList1
    ListView1.ListItems.Add , , "Item #1", 1, 1
    ListView1.ListItems.Add , , "Item #2", 1, 1
    ListView1.ListItems.Add , , "Item #3", 1, 1
    ListView1.ListItems.Add , , "Item #4", 1, 1
End Sub

Private Sub ListView1_MouseMove(Button As Integer, _
    Shift As Integer, x As Single, y As Single)
    If Button = vbLeftButton Then
```

```
        ListView1.DragIcon =
ListView1.SelectedItem.CreateDragImage
        ListView1.Drag vbBeginDrag
    End If
End Sub
```

 CROSS-REFERENCE
For more information, see ListView, TreeView, Node, and ListItem.

CreateEmbed

Method

The `CreateEmbed` method creates an ActiveX object and embeds it into an OLE Container control. You can embed an existing document by giving a file name or create a new document by giving the class name for the new object. ActiveX class names usually comprise the application's name, the object's type name, and a version number. For example, a Microsoft Word document has the class name Word.Document.8, whereas a Microsoft Works spreadsheet object has the name MSWorks.Sheet.4.

Objects with a CreateEmbed Method

OLE Container

Syntax

`OLEContainer.CreateEmbed fileName, className`

- *fileName* — The file name of the document to embed or an empty string to create a new document of the *className* type.
- *className* (*) — The ActiveX class name of the object to embed.
- *OLEContainer* — A reference to an OLE Container control.

(*) = Optional argument

Example 1

The following line creates an embedded object from an existing Works spreadsheet. The `oleContainer` object is an OLE Container control the programmer added to the application's form at design time.

```
oleContainer.CreateEmbed "c:\MySheet.wks"
```

Example 2

The following line creates a new Word embedded object. Again, the `oleContainer` object is an OLE Container control the programmer added to the application's form at design time. For this example to work, you must have Word installed and registered on your system.

```
oleContainer.CreateEmbed "", "Word.Document.8"
```

CROSS-REFERENCE

For more information, see OLE Container.

CreateFolder

Method

The `CreateFolder` method creates a new folder. If the given folder already exists, the method generates an error.

Objects with a CreateFolder Method

FileSystemObject

Syntax

```
FileSystemObject.CreateFolder
```

- *FileSystemObject* — A reference to a FileSystemObject.

Example

The following lines create a new folder called MyNewFolder on drive C:.

```
Dim fileSystem, stream
Dim str As String

Set fileSystem = CreateObject("Scripting.FileSystemObject")
fileSystem.CreateFolder "c:\MyNewFolder"
```

CROSS-REFERENCE

For more information, see FileSystemObject.

CreateLink

Method

The CreateLink method creates an ActiveX object from a file and links it into an OLE Container control.

Objects with a CreateLink Method

OLE Container

Syntax

OLEContainer.CreateLink fileName, data

- *fileName* — The file name of the document to link.
- *data* (*) — The data from the file to be linked.
- *OLEContainer* — A reference to an OLE Container control.

(*) = Optional argument

Example

The following line creates a linked object from a Works spreadsheet. The oleContainer object is an OLE Container control the programmer added to the application's form at design time.

```
oleContainer.CreateLink "c:\MySheet.wks"
```

 CROSS-REFERENCE
For more information, see OLE Container.

CreateObject

Function

The CreateObject function creates an ActiveX object given a class name. ActiveX class names usually comprise the application's name, the object's type name, and a version number. For example, a Microsoft Word document has the class name Word.Document.8, whereas a Microsoft Works spreadsheet object has the name MSWorks.Sheet.4.

Syntax

```
value = CreateObject(class, server)
```

- *class* — The ActiveX class name of the object to create.
- *server* — The network server on which to create the object.
- *value* — The variable that will receive the reference to the object.

Example

In this example, the program creates a Word document as an ActiveX object. To show that the object was successfully created, the third line causes the server application to run. For this example to work, you must have Word installed and registered on your system.

```
Dim doc As Object
Set doc = CreateObject("Word.Document.8")
doc.Application.Visible = True
```

CreateTextFile

Method

The CreateTextFile method creates a TextStream object that's associated with a new text file.

Objects with a CreateTextFile Method

FileSystemObject

Syntax

```
value = FileSystemObject.CreateTextFile(fileName, _
    overwrite, type)
```

- *fileName* — The name of the file to create.
- *FileSystemObject* — A reference to a FileSystemObject object.
- *overwrite* (*) — The value True or False, indicating whether an existing file should be overwritten with the new file. The default is False.
- *type* (*) — A value of True (create a Unicode file) or False (create an ASCII file). The default is an ASCII file.

- *value*—The variable that will receive the reference to the object.

(*) = Optional argument

Example 1

The following lines create an ASCII text file called `MyTextFile.txt` on drive C:. In this case, if the file already exists, Visual Basic generates an error. That is, overwriting of an existing file is disallowed.

```
Dim fileSystem, stream
Dim str As String

Set fileSystem = CreateObject("Scripting.FileSystemObject")
Set stream = fileSystem.CreateTextFile("c:\MyTextFile.txt")
stream.write ("This text goes to the file.")
stream.Close
```

Example 2

The following lines create a Unicode text file called `MyTextFile.txt` on drive C:. In this case, Visual Basic will overwrite an existing file.

```
Dim fileSystem, stream
Dim str As String

Set fileSystem = CreateObject("Scripting.FileSystemObject")
Set stream = fileSystem.CreateTextFile("c:\MyTextFile.txt",
True, True)
stream.write ("This text goes to the file.")
stream.Close
```

CROSS-REFERENCE
For more information, see FileSystemObject, TextStream, and OpenTextFile.

CurDir

Function

The `CurDir` function returns the current default path.

Syntax

```
value = CurDir(drive)
```

- *drive* — The drive for which to get the default directory.
- *value* — The variable that will receive the path.

Example 1

The following lines get the current directory on the current drive and display the result in a message box. The path returned is for the current drive because the CurDir call doesn't specify a drive.

```
Dim strDir As String
strDir = CurDir
MsgBox strDir
```

Example 2

The following lines get the current directory on drive D:.

```
Dim strDir As String
strDir = CurDir("D")
MsgBox strDir
```

CurrentX

Property

The CurrentX property represents the horizontal position at which the next drawing operation will occur. When a program draws with graphics methods, Visual Basic sets the value of CurrentX based on the coordinates given to the graphics method. The CurrentX property is accessible only at runtime.

Objects with a CurrentX Property

Form

PictureBox

Printer

Property Page

UserControl

Syntax

```
object.CurrentX = value1
```

or

```
value2 = object.CurrentX
```

- *object*—A reference to an object with a `CurrentX` property.
- *value1* — The new horizontal position.
- *value2* — The variable that will receive the current horizontal position.

Example

In this example, the program draws three lines using the settings of the `CurrentX` and `CurrentY` properties. In the first two code lines, the program sets the `CurrentX` and `CurrentY` properties' starting values. In the third line, the program draws a line from the coordinate 500,700 (the current setting of `CurrentX` and `CurrentY`) to 1000,3000. This action sets `CurrentX` and `CurrentY` to 1000 and 3000, respectively. So, the fourth code line draws a line from 1000,3000 to 3000,3000, which resets `CurrentX` and `CurrentY` to 3000 and 3000. Finally, the last code line draws a line from 3000,3000 to 3000,1000. Figure C-30 shows the results.

```
frmForm1.CurrentX = 500
frmForm1.CurrentY = 750
Line -(1000, 3000)
Line -(3000, 3000)
Line -(3000, 1000)
```

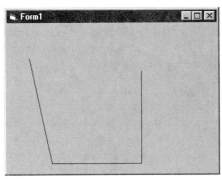

Figure C-30 Here are the results of the drawing operations shown in the sample code.

CROSS-REFERENCE
See also CurrentY.

CurrentY

Property

The CurrentY property represents the vertical position at which the next drawing operation will occur. When a program draws with graphics methods, Visual Basic sets the value of CurrentY based on the coordinates given to the graphics method. The CurrentY property is accessible only at runtime.

Objects with a CurrentY Property

Form

PictureBox

Printer

Property Page

UserControl

Syntax

```
object.CurrentY = value1
```

or

```
value2 = object.CurrentY
```

- *object* — A reference to an object with a CurrentY property.
- *value1* — The new horizontal position.
- *value2* — The variable that will receive the number of child nodes.

Example

In this example, the program draws three lines using the settings of the CurrentX and CurrentY properties. In the first code line, the program clears the window, which automatically sets CurrentX and CurrentY to 0. In the second code line, the program draws a line from the coordinate 0,0 (the current setting of CurrentX and CurrentY) to 1000,3000. This action sets CurrentX and CurrentY to 1000 and 3000, respectively. So, the fourth code line draws a line from 1000,3000 to 3000,3000, which resets CurrentX and CurrentY to 3000 and 3000. Finally, the last code line draws a line from 3000,3000 to 3000,1000. Figure C-31 shows the results of the drawing.

```
Cls
Line -(1000, 3000)
Line -(3000, 3000)
Line -(3000, 1000)
```

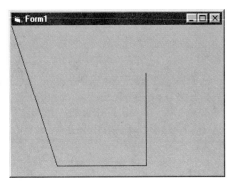

Figure C-31 Here are the results of the drawing operations shown in the sample code.

CROSS-REFERENCE
See also CurrentX.

Customize

Method

The Customize method displays the Customize Toolbar dialog box (see Figure C-32) on behalf of a Toolbar control. The user can then add or delete buttons to and from the toolbar.

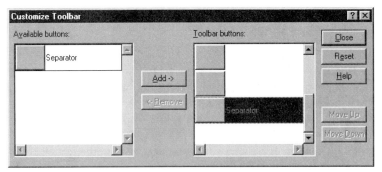

Figure C-32 The Customize Toolbar dialog box enables a user to change which buttons the toolbar displays.

Objects with a Customize Method

Toolbar

Syntax

```
Toolbar.Customize
```

- *Toolbar*—A reference to a Toolbar control.

Example

The following line displays a toolbar's Customize Toolbar dialog box. The `tlbToolbar1` object is a Toolbar control the programmer added to the application's form at design time.

```
tlbToolbar1.Customize
```

 CROSS-REFERENCE
For more information, see Toolbar, SaveToolbar, and RestoreToolbar.

CVErr

Function

The `CVErr` function enables user-written functions to return user-defined errors.

Syntax

```
CVErr(error)
```

- *error*—The error number to return.

Example

In this example, the program defines a function called `MyFunc` that doubles a value between 0 and 5 and returns an error for any value less than zero or greater than 5. The program calls the function from the `btnCommand1_Click` event procedure, where the `IsError` function evaluates `MyFunc`'s return value. If the call to `MyFunc` generates an error (because `CVErr` gets called), a message box appears informing the user of the problem. Otherwise, a message box appears, informing the user that the return value was OK.

```
Private Function MyFunc(value As Integer)
    If value < 0 Or value > 5 Then
        MyFunc = CVErr(10)
    Else
        MyFunc = value * 2
```

```
        End If
End Function

Private Sub btnCommand1_Click()
    Dim result
    result = MyFunc(5)
    If IsError(result) Then
        MsgBox ("Got an error.")
    Else
        MsgBox ("Return value OK")
    End If
End Sub
```

CROSS-REFERENCE
See also IsError.

Data

Property

The Data property represents an object handle for data that will be sent to an ActiveX server.

Objects with a Data Property

OLE Container

Syntax

```
OLEContainer.Data = value1
```

or

```
value2 = OLEContainer.Data
```

Description

- *OLEContainer* — A reference to an OLE Container control.
- *value1* — A handle to a data object.
- *value2* — The variable that will receive the currently set handle.

 CROSS-REFERENCE
See also OLE Container.

DataObject

Object

The DataObject object represents data that will be transferred from one component to another, usually in the context of Clipboard or drag-and-drop operations. For example, the data object might represent the list of files a user dragged from or to Windows Explorer.

Properties

The DataObject object has one property, called `Files`, which is a reference to a DataObjectFiles collection. The DataObjectFiles collection contains the file names associated with the DataObject object when the DataObject data is of the `vbCFFiles` type. For more information on using the `Files` property, look up the property's entry elsewhere in this book.

Methods

The DataObject object has four methods, which are listed in Table D-1. For more information on using a method shown in the following table, look up the method's entry elsewhere in this book.

Table D-1 Methods of the DataObject Object

Method	Description
Clear	Clears the object's DataObjectFiles collection.
GetData	Gets the data associated with the object.
GetFormat	Gets the format of the data associated with the object.
SetData	Sets the data associated with the object.

DataObjectFiles

Collection

A `DataObjectFiles` collection holds a list of file names associated with a DataObject object when the object's data is of the `vbCFFiles` type. For example, the file names might represent the list of files a user dragged from or to Windows Explorer.

Properties

A DataObjectFiles object has one property, called `Count`, which represents the number of file names in the collection.

Methods

A DataObjectFiles object has four methods, which are listed in Table D-2. For more information on using a method shown in the following table, look up the method's entry elsewhere in this book.

Table D-2 Methods of the DataObjectFiles Object

Method	Description
Add	Adds a file name to the collection.
Clear	Removes all file names from the collection.
Item	Returns a file name from the collection.
Remove	Removes a file name from the collection.

CROSS-REFERENCE
See also DataObject.

DataText

Property

The `DataText` property represents a string of text that's associated with an embedded object in an OLE Container control.

Objects with a DataText Property

OLE Container

Syntax

```
OLEContainer.DataText = value1
```

or

```
value2 = OLEContainer.DataText
```

- *OLEContainer* — A reference to an OLE Container control.
- *value1* — The string to send to the object.
- *value2* — The variable that will receive the current string from the object.

Example

When you run this sample program, type a text message into the text box and then click the Transfer Text button to load the Microsoft Word server, embed a Word document into the OLE Container control, and transfer the text message to the Word document. Figure D-1 shows the application after the user has transferred the text "This is a test." Notice in the `btnTransferText_Click` event procedure that the program sets the OLE Container control's `Format` property to `CF_TEXT` before attempting to transfer the string.

NOTE
This program will run only if you have Microsoft Word installed on your system.

Figure D-1 The DataText Demo program shows how the DataText property transfers text to an embedded object.

```
VERSION 5.00
Begin VB.Form Form1
   Caption         =   "Form1"
   ClientHeight    =   4785
   ClientLeft      =   60
   ClientTop       =   345
   ClientWidth     =   4680
   LinkTopic       =   "Form1"
   ScaleHeight     =   4785
   ScaleWidth      =   4680
   StartUpPosition =   3  'Windows Default
   Begin VB.TextBox txtText
      Height       =   375
      Left         =   720
      TabIndex     =   2
      Top          =   3720
      Width        =   3255
   End
```

```
      Begin VB.CommandButton btnTransferText
         Caption         =       "Transfer Text"
         Height          =       495
         Left            =       1200
         TabIndex        =       0
         Top             =       2520
         Width           =       2415
      End
      Begin VB.Label Label1
         Caption         =       "Type text below:"
         Height          =       255
         Left            =       720
         TabIndex        =       3
         Top             =       3480
         Width           =       1455
      End
      Begin VB.OLE oleContainer
         Class           =       "WordPad.Document.1"
         Height          =       1815
         Left            =       480
         OleObjectBlob   =       "Form1.frx":0000
         TabIndex        =       1
         Top             =       360
         Width           =       3615
      End
   End
End
Attribute VB_Name = "Form1"
Attribute VB_GlobalNameSpace = False
Attribute VB_Creatable = False
Attribute VB_PredeclaredId = True
Attribute VB_Exposed = False

Private Sub btnTransferText_Click()
    oleContainer.Format = "CF_TEXT"
    oleContainer.CreateEmbed "", "Word.Document"
    If oleContainer.AppIsRunning Then
        oleContainer.DataText = txtText.Text
        oleContainer.Update
    Else
        MsgBox "Word not available."
    End If
End Sub
```

CROSS-REFERENCE
See also OLE Container.

Data Types

Concept

Visual Basic's data types determine the kinds of information variables can hold. When you declare a variable, you can also declare a data type for the variable. If you choose not to declare a data type, Visual Basic gives the variable the default Variant data type. Variant variables can hold just about any type of data, and Visual Basic can automatically interpret such a variable's value as needed. However, because Visual Basic must work harder to manage Variant data, your programs will run more efficiently if you declare data types for your variables. Table D-3 lists Visual Basic's data types.

Table D-3 Visual Basic Data Types

Data Type	Description
Integer	Whole number values.
Long	Larger whole number values.
Single	Single-precision floating point values.
Double	Double-precision floating point values.
Currency	Monetary values.
Byte	Binary values.
String	Text values.
Boolean	True or False values.
Date	Date and time values.
Object	References to objects.
Variant	All types of data.

Date

Function

The Date function returns the system date as a string in the form mm/dd/yy.

Syntax

```
value = Date
```

- *value*— The variable that will receive the date string.

Example

In this example, the program displays the system date in a message box, as shown in Figure D-2.

```
Dim strDate As String
strDate = Date
MsgBox strDate
```

Figure D-2 This message box shows the date string returned by the Date function.

CROSS-REFERENCE

See also Date (keyword), Date (statement), DateAdd, DateDiff, DatePart, DateSerial, DateValue, Day, Month, and Year.

Date

Keyword

The Date keyword can be used to define a variable of the Date type or to construct a call to the Date function or to the Date statement. The Date data type is a floating-point value that can hold a date or time. Valid dates range from January 1, 100 to December 31, 9999, and valid times range from 00:00:00 to 23:59:59. The following lines declare two variables of the Date data type and assign a date to one variable and a time to the other. Notice how date and time literals are enclosed in pound signs (#).

```
Dim dtmDate As Date
Dim dtmTime As Date
dtmDate = #1/21/1951#
dtmDate = #12:23:34 AM#
```

CROSS-REFERENCE
For more information, see Date (function), Date (statement), DateAdd, DateDiff, DatePart, DateSerial, DateValue, Day, Month, and Year.

Date

Statement

The Date statement sets the system date. Valid dates for Windows 95 range from January 1, 1980 through December 31, 2099.

Syntax

```
Date = value
```

- *value*—A Date value that contains the date to set.

Example

The following lines change the system date to January 21, 1998. Notice how Date literals are enclosed in pound signs (#).

```
Dim dtmDate As Date
dtmDate = #1/21/98#
Date = dtmDate
```

CROSS-REFERENCE
See also Date (function), Date (keyword), DateAdd, DateDiff, DatePart, DateSerial, DateValue, Day, Month, and Year.

DateAdd

Function

The DateAdd function adds or subtracts a given amount of time to or from a date. The amount of time to add or subtract is determined by a string value from Table D-4.

Table D-4 Time Values for the DateAdd Function

Value	Description
"d"	Day
"h"	Hour
"m"	Month
"n"	Minute
"q"	Quarter
"s"	Second
"w"	Weekday
"ww"	Week
"y"	Day of year
"yyyy"	Year

Syntax

```
value = DateAdd(time, amount, date)
```

- *amount* — The number of *time* units to add to *date*.
- *date* — The date to which to add the time.
- *time* — The amount of time to add to *date*.
- *value* — The variable that will receive the new date string.

Example 1

The following lines declare a Date variable called dtmDate and set it to January 21, 1951. The call to DateAdd then adds a year to the date, resulting in January 21, 1952, the date that the program displays in a message box.

```
Dim dtmDate As Date
dtmDate = #1/21/1951#
dtmDate = DateAdd("yyyy", 1, dtmDate)
MsgBox dtmDate
```

Example 2

Here, the following lines declare a Date variable called dtmDate and set it to October 31, 1999. The call to DateAdd then adds a month to the date, resulting in November 30, 1999. Notice that the function is intelligent enough to know that there is no day 31 in November.

```
Dim dtmDate As Date
dtmDate = #10/31/1999#
dtmDate = DateAdd("m", 1, dtmDate)
MsgBox dtmDate
```

Example 3

In this example, the following lines subtract a month from dtmDate. The dtmDate variable starts with the date October 31, 1999, and ends up with September 30, 1999. Notice that, just as with November, the function is intelligent enough to know that there is no day 31 in September.

```
Dim dtmDate As Date
dtmDate = #10/31/1999#
dtmDate = DateAdd("m", -1, dtmDate)
MsgBox dtmDate
```

Example 4

Finally, the following lines add three days to the date May 14, 1999, and end up displaying the result of May 17, 1999, in the message box.

```
Dim dtmDate As Date
dtmDate = #5/14/1999#
dtmDate = DateAdd("d", 3, dtmDate)
MsgBox dtmDate
```

 CROSS-REFERENCE
See also Date (statement), Date (function), Date (keyword), DateDiff, DatePart, DateSerial, DateValue, Day, Month, and Year.

DateCreated

Property

The DateCreated property represents the date and time that a file was created.

Objects with a DateCreated Property

File

Folder

Syntax

```
value = object.DateCreated
```

- *object*— A reference to a File or Folder object.
- *value*— The variable that will receive the date string.

Example

In this example, the program associates a File object with a text file named `text.txt` and displays, in a message box, the date the file was created. Figure D-3 shows the format of the returned date as it's displayed in the message box.

```
Dim strDate As String
Dim fileSystem
Dim file
Set fileSystem = CreateObject("Scripting.FileSystemObject")
Set file = fileSystem.GetFile("c:\text.txt")
MsgBox file.DateCreated
```

Figure D-3 This message box shows the date string returned by the DateCreated property.

CROSS-REFERENCE
See also File, Folder, FileSystemObject, DateLastAccessed, and DateLastModified.

DateDiff

Function

The `DateDiff` function calculates the difference between two dates. The time unit to use in the calculation is determined by a string value from Table D-5. The function's optional arguments can be taken from Tables D-6 and D-7, as described in the "Syntax" and "Description" sections that follow.

Table D-5 Time Unit Values for the DateDiff Function

Value	Description
"d"	Day
"h"	Hour
"m"	Month
"n"	Minute
"q"	Quarter
"s"	Second
"w"	Weekday
"ww"	Week
"y"	Day of year
"yyyy"	Year

Table D-6 Values for the DateDiff Function's First Optional Argument

Value	Description
vbFriday	First day of the week is Friday.
vbMonday	First day of the week is Monday.
vbSaturday	First day of the week is Saturday.
vbSunday	First day of the week is Sunday. This is the default.
vbThursday	First day of the week is Thursday.
vbTuesday	First day of the week is Tuesday.
vbUseSystem	First day of the week is determined by the NLS API setting.
vbWednesday	First day of the week is Wednesday.

Table D-7 Values for the DateDiff Function's Second Optional Argument

Value	Description
vbFirstFourDays	The first week is considered to be the first week that contains four days in the new year.
vbFirstFullWeek	The first week is considered to be the first full week in the new year.
vbFirstJan1	The first week is considered to be the week that contains January 1 of the new year. This is the default.
vbUseSystem	The first week in the new year is determined by the NLS API setting.

Syntax

```
value = DateDiff(time, date1, date2, firstDay, firstWeek)
```

- *date1* — The first date used in the calculation.
- *date2* — The second date used in the calculation.
- *firstDay* (⋆) — A value from Table D-6 indicating how to determine the first day of the week.
- *firstWeek* (⋆) — A value from Table D-7 indicating how to determine the first week of the year.
- *time* — The type of time unit to use in the calculation (from Table D-5).
- *value* — The variable that will receive the calculated difference.

(⋆) = Optional

Example

When you run the following program, you see the window shown in Figure D-4. Type a valid date into the text box and click the Calculate Hours button. The program calculates and displays the number of hours between January 1, 1998, and the date you entered.

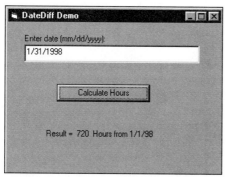

Figure D-4 This is the DateDiff Demo application when you first run it.

```
VERSION 5.00
Begin VB.Form Form1
   Caption        =    "DateDiff Demo"
   ClientHeight   =    3195
```

```
            ClientLeft      =   60
            ClientTop       =   345
            ClientWidth     =   4680
            LinkTopic       =   "Form1"
            ScaleHeight     =   3195
            ScaleWidth      =   4680
            StartUpPosition =   3   'Windows Default
            Begin VB.CommandButton btnCalcHours
               Caption      =   "Calculate Hours"
               Height       =   375
               Left         =   1080
               TabIndex     =   1
               Top          =   1320
               Width        =   2055
            End
            Begin VB.TextBox txtDate
               Height       =   375
               Left         =   360
               TabIndex     =   0
               Top          =   480
               Width        =   3855
            End
            Begin VB.Label lblResult
               Caption      =   "Result = "
               Height       =   255
               Left         =   840
               TabIndex     =   3
               Top          =   2280
               Width        =   3375
            End
            Begin VB.Label Label1
               Caption      =   "Enter date (mm/dd/yyyy):"
               Height       =   255
               Left         =   360
               TabIndex     =   2
               Top          =   240
               Width        =   2895
            End
         End
         Attribute VB_Name = "Form1"
         Attribute VB_GlobalNameSpace = False
         Attribute VB_Creatable = False
```

```
Attribute VB_PredeclaredId = True
Attribute VB_Exposed = False

Private Sub btnCalcHours_Click()
    Dim dtmDate1, dtmDate2 As Date
    Dim strMsg As String
    Dim hours As Integer
    dtmDate1 = #1/1/1998#
    dtmDate2 = txtDate.Text
    hours = DateDiff("h", dtmDate1, dtmDate2)
    strMsg = "Result =  " & hours & "  Hours from 1/1/98"
    lblResult.Caption = strMsg
End Sub

Private Sub Form_Load()
    txtDate.Text = "1/31/1998"
    btnCalcHours_Click
End Sub
```

CROSS-REFERENCE
See also Date (statement), Date (function), Date (keyword), DateAdd, DatePart, DateSerial, DateValue, Day, Month, and Year.

DateLastAccessed

Property

The DateLastAccessed property represents the date and time that a file was last accessed.

Objects with a DateLastAccessed Property

File

Folder

Syntax

value = object.DateLastAccessed

- *object* — A reference to a File or Folder object.
- *value* — The variable that will receive the date string.

Example

In this example, the program associates a File object with a text file named `text.txt` and displays, in a message box, the date the file was last accessed. Figure D-5 shows the format of the returned date as it's displayed in the message box.

```
Dim strDate As String
Dim fileSystem
Dim file
Set fileSystem = CreateObject("Scripting.FileSystemObject")
Set file = fileSystem.GetFile("c:\text.txt")
MsgBox file.DateLastAccessed
```

Figure D-5 This message box shows the date string returned by the DateLateAccessed property.

 CROSS-REFERENCE
See also File, Folder, FileSystemObject, DateCreated, and DateLastModified.

DateLastModified

Property

The `DateLastModified` property represents the date and time that a file was last changed.

Objects with a DateLastModified Property

File

Folder

Syntax

```
value = object.DateLastModified
```

- *object* — A reference to a File or Folder object.
- *value* — The variable that will receive the date string.

Example

In this example, the program associates a File object with a text file named `text.txt` and displays, in a message box, the date the file was last edited. Figure D-6 shows the format of the returned date as it's displayed in the message box.

```
Dim strDate As String
Dim fileSystem
Dim file
Set fileSystem = CreateObject("Scripting.FileSystemObject")
Set file = fileSystem.GetFile("c:\text.txt")
MsgBox file.DateLastModified
```

Figure D-6 This message box shows the date string returned by the DateLastModified property.

CROSS-REFERENCE
See also File, Folder, FileSystemObject, DateCreated, and DateLastAccessed.

DatePart

Function

The `DatePart` function calculates the requested part of a date. For example, the function can determine in which quarter of the year a date falls, determine in which week of the month a date falls, and so on. The time part to use in the calculation is determined by a string value from Table D-8. The function's optional arguments can be taken from Tables D-9 and D-10, as described in the "Syntax" and "Description" sections that follow.

Table D-8 Time Part Values for the DatePart Function

Value	Description
"d"	Day
"h"	Hour
"m"	Month
"n"	Minute
"q"	Quarter
"s"	Second
"w"	Weekday
"ww"	Week
"y"	Day of year
"yyyy"	Year

Table D-9 Values for the DatePart Function's First Optional Argument

Value	Description
vbFriday	First day of the week is Friday.
vbMonday	First day of the week is Monday.
vbSaturday	First day of the week is Saturday.
vbSunday	First day of the week is Sunday. This is the default.
vbThursday	First day of the week is Thursday.
vbTuesday	First day of the week is Tuesday.
vbUseSystem	First day of the week is determined by the NLS API setting.
vbWednesday	First day of the week is Wednesday.

Table D-10 Values for the DatePart Function's Second Optional Argument

Value	Description
vbFirstFourDays	The first week is considered to be the first week that contains four days in the new year.
vbFirstFullWeek	The first week is considered to be the first full week in the new year.
vbFirstJan1	The first week is considered to be the week that contains January 1 of the new year. This is the default.
vbUseSystem	The first week in the new year is determined by the NLS API setting.

Syntax

```
value = DatePart(part, date, firstDay, firstWeek)
```

- *date* — The date to be used in the calculation.
- *firstDay* (★) — A value from Table D-9 indicating how to determine the first day of the week.
- *firstWeek* (★) — A value from Table D-10 indicating how to determine the first week of the year.
- *part* — The type of time part to use in the calculation (from Table D-8).
- *value* — The variable that will receive the calculated date-part value.

(★) = Optional

Example

The following lines determine and display the week in which the date 3/17/99 falls. In this case, the message box displays the message "Week #3," because the 17th falls in the third week of March.

```
Dim dtmDate As Date
Dim strMsg As String
Dim week As Integer
dtmDate = #3/17/1999#
week = DatePart("w", dtmDate)
msgbox "Week #" & week
```

CROSS-REFERENCE

See also Date (statement), Date (function), Date (keyword), DateAdd, DateDiff, DateSerial, DateValue, Day, Month, and Year.

DateSerial

Function

The `DateSerial` function constructs a complete date from a given year, month, and day.

Syntax

```
value = DateSerial(year, month, day)
```

- *day* — The day part of the date.

- *month* — The month part of the date.
- *value* — The variable that will receive the date.
- *year* — The year part of the date.

Example 1

The following lines display the date 3/17/99 in a message box. The date is constructed by a call to the DateSerial function.

```
Dim dtmDate As Date
dtmDate = DateSerial(1999, 3, 17)
MsgBox dtmDate
```

Example 2

In this example, the program calculates the date from the given numerical expressions, demonstrating that you don't have to use literals as arguments to the DateSerial function. Like the previous example, the following lines also display the date 3/17/99 in a message box.

```
Dim dtmDate As Date
Dim year, month, day As Integer
year = 1996
month = 5
day = 10
dtmDate = DateSerial(year + 3, month - 2, day + 7)
MsgBox dtmDate
```

CROSS-REFERENCE
See also Date (statement), Date (function), Date (keyword), DateAdd, DateDiff, DatePart, DateValue, Day, Month, and Year.

DateValue

Function

The DateValue function converts a string or expression to a date.

Syntax

```
value = DateValue(expr)
```

- *expr*—The expression (usually a string) that represents the date to convert.
- *value*—The variable that will receive the date.

Example

The following lines display the date 3/17/99 in a message box. The date is constructed by a call to the DateValue function.

```
Dim dtmDate As Date
dtmDate = DateValue("March 17, 1999")
MsgBox dtmDate
```

CROSS-REFERENCE
See also Date (statement), Date (function), Date (keyword), DateAdd, DateDiff, DatePart, DateSerial, Day, Month, and Year.

Day

Function

The Day function returns the day part of a date. The valid return values are 1 through 31, inclusive.

Syntax

```
value = Day(date)
```

- *date*—The date from which to get the day.
- *value*—The variable that will receive the day.

Example

The following lines display the message "Day #17" in a message box.

```
Dim dtmDate As Date
Dim dayPart As Integer
dtmDate = DateValue("March 17, 1999")
dayPart = Day(dtmDate)
MsgBox "Day #" & dayPart
```

CROSS-REFERENCE
See also Date (statement), Date (function), Date (keyword), DateAdd, DateDiff, DatePart, DateSerial, DateValue, Month, and Year.

DblClick

Event

Visual Basic sends a control a `DblClick` event when the user double-clicks (presses and releases the mouse button twice in rapid succession) the control.

Objects That Receive DblClick Events

Animation
ComboBox
CoolBar
FileListBox
Form
Frame
Image
Label
ListBox
ListBox
ListView
MDIForm
OLE Container
OptionButton
PropertyPage
RichTextBox
StatusBar
TextBox
Toolbar
TreeView
UserControl

Example 1

A program can respond to a `DblClick` event by implementing the target object's `DblClick` event procedure. The following code segment shows how a Form object defines a `DblClick` event procedure. In this case, the form displays a message box each time the user double-clicks the form.

```
Private Sub Form_DblClick()
    ' Handle event here.
    MsgBox "Got double-click"
End Sub
```

Example 2

Controls that are part of a control array define a slightly different form of the DblClick event procedure. This form of the event procedure receives an index into the control array as a parameter, the index indicating which of the controls in the array received the double-click. In this example, the programmer has added three TextBox controls to the application's form, making the controls members of a control array called txtText1. When the user double-clicks one of these TextBox controls, the DblClick event procedure sets the control's text to "Got the double-click."

```
Private Sub txtText1_DblClick(Index As Integer)
    txtText1(Index).Text = "Got the double-click"
End Sub
```

CROSS-REFERENCE
See also Click, MouseDown, and MouseUp.

DDB

Function

The DDB function calculates asset depreciation over a given period of time.

Syntax

```
value = DDB(startValue, endingValue, lifetime, time, rate)
```

- *endingValue* — The asset's value at the end of its lifetime.
- *startValue* — The asset's value at the start of its lifetime.
- *lifetime* — The lifetime of the asset.
- *rate* (*) — The rate of depreciation. The default is 2.
- *time* — The period of time over which the depreciation should be calculated.
- *value* — The variable that will receive the depreciated value.

(*) = Optional argument

Example

The following lines calculate depreciation for an item that was worth $1,000 when new and will be worth $200 at the end of its lifetime, which is ten years. The lines perform ten depreciation calculations, one for each year in the product's lifetime, displaying a message box with the depreciation for each year. The depreciation values produced by this example are, starting at the first year, 200, 160, 128, 102.40, 81.92, 65.54, 52.43, 9.72, 0, and 0, which total 800.01. The total of the depreciation values for each year is the difference between the item's starting and ending values (taking into consideration a small rounding error).

```
depValue = DDB(1000, 200, 10, 1)
MsgBox "Year #1: " & depValue
depValue = DDB(1000, 200, 10, 2)
MsgBox "Year #2: " & depValue
depValue = DDB(1000, 200, 10, 3)
MsgBox "Year #3: " & depValue
depValue = DDB(1000, 200, 10, 4)
MsgBox "Year #4: " & depValue
depValue = DDB(1000, 200, 10, 5)
MsgBox "Year #5: " & depValue
depValue = DDB(1000, 200, 10, 6)
MsgBox "Year #6: " & depValue
depValue = DDB(1000, 200, 10, 7)
MsgBox "Year #7: " & depValue
depValue = DDB(1000, 200, 10, 8)
MsgBox "Year #8: " & depValue
depValue = DDB(1000, 200, 10, 9)
MsgBox "Year #9: " & depValue
depValue = DDB(1000, 200, 10, 10)
MsgBox "Year #10: " & depValue
```

Deactivate

Event

Visual Basic sends an object a `Deactivate` event when the object loses the focus.

Objects That Receive Deactivate Events

Form

MDIForm

Example

A program can respond to a `Deactivate` event by implementing the target object's `Deactivate` event procedure. The following code segment shows how a Form object defines a `Deactivate` event procedure. In this case, the form displays a message box upon deactivation.

```
Private Sub Form_Deactivate()
    ' Handle the Deactivate event here.
    MsgBox ("Form Deactivated")
End Sub
```

Debug

Object

The Debug object enables a program to display trace information in Visual Basic's Immediate window, as well as to suspend program execution under specified conditions.

Properties

The Debug object has no properties.

Methods

The Debug object has two methods. The `Assert` method enables the object to suspend program execution when a given condition is false. The `Print` method enables the object to display messages in the Immediate window.

Events

The Debug object does not respond to events.

Example

In this example, Visual Basic displays the value of `var1` in the Immediate window and then suspends program execution on the `Assert` line because the conditional expression in the `Assert` evaluates to `False`.

```
Dim var1
var1 = 5
Debug.Print var1
Debug.Assert var1 = 10
```

Declare

Statement

The Declare statement enables a programmer to declare external procedures or functions that are located in a DLL. One common example would be declaring Windows SDK functions that you want to call from your Visual Basic program.

Syntax for a Procedure

```
access Declare Sub procName Lib "dllName" alias args
```

- *access* (*) — The keyword Public or Private.
- *alias* (*) — The keyword Alias followed by the name of the procedure in the DLL, if the name is different from the declared name.
- *args* (*) — A list of arguments that are passed to the procedure.
- *dllName* — The name of the DLL that contains the procedure.
- *procName* — The name of the external procedure.

(*) = Optional

Syntax for a Function

```
access Declare Function funcName Lib "dllName" alias args type
```

- *access* (*) — The keyword Public or Private.
- *alias* (*) — The keyword Alias followed by the name of the procedure in the DLL, if the name is different from the declared name.
- *args* (*) — A list of arguments that are passed to the procedure. The argument list follows the same rules as the argument list for any Visual Basic function or procedure.
- *dllName* — The name of the DLL that contains the procedure.
- *funcName* — The name of the external function.
- *type* (*) — The keyword As followed by the function's return type.

(*) = Optional

Example

The following lines declare a function from the Windows multimedia library DLL.

```
Private Declare Function mciSendCommandA Lib "WinMM" (ByVal _
    DeviceID As Integer, ByVal Message As Integer, _
    ByVal Param1 As Long, Param2 As Any) As Long
```

Default

Property

The Default property determines which button on a form can be automatically selected with the keyboard's Enter key. The property can be set to True or False. However, only one button on a form can have its default property set to True. Setting a button's Default property to True automatically changes any other buttons' Default properties to False.

Objects with a Default Property

CommandButton

OLE Container

Syntax

object.Default = *value1*

or

value2 = *object*.Default

- *object* — A reference to a CommandButton or an OLE Container control.
- *value1* — The value True or False.
- *value2* — The variable that will receive the current property setting.

Example

The following line makes the button named btnCommand1 the default button for the form.

```
btnCommand1.Default = True
```

CROSS-REFERENCE

See also CommandButton and OLE Container.

DefaultCancel

Property

The DefaultCancel property determines whether a UserControl object can respond as the default Cancel button. The property can be set to True or False, but only at design time. A UserControl that has a DefaultCancel property of True gains the Default and Cancel extended properties.

Objects with a DefaultCancel Property

UserControl

Example

Set the DefaultCancel property in the control's property window, as shown in Figure D-7.

Figure D-7 You can set a control's DefaultCancel property in its property window.

CROSS-REFERENCE
See also UserControl.

DefaultExt

Property

The DefaultExt property represents the file extension that the CommonDialog control automatically adds to a file name when the user fails to provide the file extension himself. For example, if you have an application whose document file names end with the extension .xyz, you can set the CommonDialog control's DefaultExt property to "xyz" to ensure that file names without extensions get saved with the correct extension.

Objects with a DefaultExt Property

CommonDialog

Syntax

```
CommonDialog.DefaultExt = value1
```

or

```
value2 = CommonDialog.DefaultExt
```

- *CommonDialog* — A reference to a CommonDialog control.
- *value1* — A string containing the default file-name extension.
- *value2* — The variable that will receive the current default file-name extension.

Example

The following lines set a dialog box's DefaultExt property to "xyz" and then display the Save As dialog box to the user. If the user should enter a file name like MyFile, without an extension, the dialog box adds the extension automatically. The final line in the example displays the complete file name. Note that if the user enters a file name with a different extension than the default, the dialog box will not change the extension. That is, if the user enters a file name like MyFile.txt, the final file name will remain MyFile.txt.

```
dlgCommonDialog1.DefaultExt = "xyz"
dlgCommonDialog1.ShowSave
MsgBox dlgCommonDialog1.FileName
```

CROSS-REFERENCE
See also CommonDialog and Filter.

DefBool

Statement

The `DefBool` statement is used to associate a `Boolean` default data type with variable names that start with specified characters.

Syntax

```
DefBool chrs ...
```

- ... — Other character ranges.
- *chrs* — A range of characters that specify the variable-name start characters associated with the data type.

Example

The following line tells Visual Basic to default all variables starting with the letters A, B, C, and D to the `Boolean` data type.

```
DefBool A-D
```

DefByte

Statement

The `DefByte` statement is used to associate a `Byte` default data type with variable names that start with specified characters.

Syntax

```
DefByte chrs ...
```

- ... — Other character ranges.
- *chrs* — A range of characters that specify the variable-name start characters associated with the data type.

Example

The following line tells Visual Basic to default all variables starting with the letters A, B, C, and D to the `Byte` data type.

```
DefByte A-D
```

DefCur

Statement

The DefCur statement is used to associate a Currency default data type with variable names that start with specified characters.

Syntax

DefCur *chrs* ...

- ... — Other character ranges.
- *chrs* — A range of characters that specify the variable-name start characters associated with the data type.

Example

The following line tells Visual Basic to default all variables starting with the letters A, B, C, and D to the Currency data type.

DefCur A-D

DefDate

Statement

The DefDate statement is used to associate a Date default data type with variable names that start with specified characters.

Syntax

DefDate *chrs* ...

- ... — Other character ranges.
- *chrs* — A range of characters that specify the variable-name start characters associated with the data type.

Example

The following line tells Visual Basic to default all variables starting with the letters A, B, C, and D to the Date data type.

DefDate A-D

DefDbl

Statement

The `DefDbl` statement is used to associate a `Double` default data type with variable names that start with specified characters.

Syntax

```
DefDbl chrs ...
```

- ... — Other character ranges.
- *chrs* — A range of characters that specify the variable-name start characters associated with the data type.

Example

The following line tells Visual Basic to default all variables starting with the letters A, B, C, and D to the `Double` data type.

```
DefDbl A-D
```

DefDec

Statement

The `DefDec` statement is used to associate a `Decimal` default data type with variable names that start with specified characters.

Syntax

```
DefDec chrs ...
```

- ... — Other character ranges.
- *chrs* — A range of characters that specify the variable-name start characters associated with the data type.

Example

The following line tells Visual Basic to default all variables starting with the letters A, B, C, and D to the `Decimal` data type.

```
DefDec A-D
```

DefInt

Statement

The `DefInt` statement is used to associate an `Integer` default data type with variable names that start with specified characters.

Syntax

```
DefInt chrs ...
```

- ... — Other character ranges.
- *chrs* — A range of characters that specify the variable-name start characters associated with the data type.

Example

The following line tells Visual Basic to default all variables starting with the letters A, B, C, and D to the `Integer` data type.

```
DefInt A-D
```

DefLng

Statement

The `DefLng` statement is used to associate a `Long` default data type with variable names that start with specified characters.

Syntax

```
DefLng chrs ...
```

- ... — Other character ranges.
- *chrs* — A range of characters that specify the variable-name start characters associated with the data type.

Example

The following line tells Visual Basic to default all variables starting with the letters A, B, C, and D to the `Long` data type.

```
DefLng A-D
```

DefObj

Statement

The `DefObj` statement is used to associate an `Object` default data type with variable names that start with specified characters.

Syntax

```
DefObj chrs ...
```

- ... — Other character ranges.
- *chrs* — A range of characters that specify the variable-name start characters associated with the data type.

Example

The following line tells Visual Basic to default all variables starting with the letters A, B, C, and D to the `Object` data type.

```
DefObj A-D
```

DefSng

Statement

The `DefSng` statement is used to associate a `Single` default data type with variable names that start with specified characters.

Syntax

```
DefSng chrs ...
```

- ... — Other character ranges.
- *chrs* — A range of characters that specify the variable-name start characters associated with the data type.

Example

The following line tells Visual Basic to default all variables starting with the letters A, B, C, and D to the `Single` data type.

```
DefSng A-D
```

DefStr

Statement

The `DefStr` statement is used to associate a `String` default data type with variable names that start with specified characters.

Syntax

```
DefStr chrs ...
```

- ... — Other character ranges.
- *chrs* — A range of characters that specify the variable-name start characters associated with the data type.

Example

The following line tells Visual Basic to default all variables starting with the letters A, B, C, and D to the `String` data type.

```
DefStr A-D
```

DefVar

Statement

The `DefVar` statement is used to associate a `Variant` default data type with variable names that start with specified characters.

Syntax

```
DefVar chrs ...
```

- ... — Other character ranges.
- *chrs* — A range of characters that specify the variable-name start characters associated with the data type.

Example

The following line tells Visual Basic to default all variables starting with the letters A, B, C, and D to the `Variant` data type.

```
DefVar A-D
```

DeleteFile

Method

The `DeleteFile` method deletes a file.

Objects with a DeleteFile Method

FileSystemObject

Syntax

```
FileSystemObject.DeleteFile fileName, readOnly
```

- *fileName* — The name of the file to delete. Wildcard characters can be used to delete multiple files.
- *FileSystemObject* — A reference to a FileSystemObject object.
- *readOnly* (*) — A flag indicating whether read-only files should be deleted. A value of `True` causes read-only files to be deleted, whereas a value of `False` does not.

(*) = Optional argument

Example 1

The following lines demonstrate how to delete a single file with the `DeleteFile` method.

```
Dim fileSystem
Dim file

Set fileSystem = _
    CreateObject("Scripting.FileSystemObject")
fileSystem.DeleteFile "c:\MyText.txt", True
```

Example 2

In this example, the sample code lines delete all files, in the given path, that end with the .bak extension.

```
Dim fileSystem
Dim file

Set fileSystem = _
    CreateObject("Scripting.FileSystemObject")
fileSystem.DeleteFile "c:\*.bak", True
```

CROSS-REFERENCE
For more information, see FileSystemObject, File, Folder, Delete, and
DeleteFolder.

Delete — File or Folder

Method

The `Delete` method deletes a file or folder. In the case of a folder, the folder is
deleted whether or not it contains files or subdirectories.

Syntax

`object.Delete readOnly`

- *object* — A reference to a File or Folder object.
- *readOnly* (*) — A flag indicating whether read-only files should be
  deleted. A value of `True` causes read-only files to be deleted,
  whereas a value of `False` does not.

(*) = Optional argument

Example

The following sample program demonstrates deleting a file with the `Delete`
method. When you run the program, you see the window shown in Figure D-8.
Click the Delete a File button, and a dialog box appears from which you can
select the file to delete (Figure D-9). When you select a file a message box asks
whether you want to delete the file. This is your last chance to change your
mind. Click Yes to delete the selected file, or click No to cancel the operation.
You can also cancel the delete operation by clicking the dialog box's Cancel
button.

Figure D-8 This simple utility deletes a file that you choose.

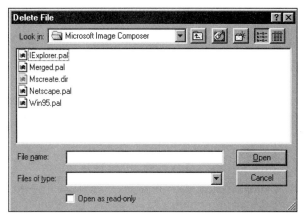

Figure D-9 You select the file to delete from an instance of the CommonDialog control.

```
VERSION 5.00
Object = "{F9043C88-F6F2-101A-A3C9-08002B2F49FB} _
    #1.2#0"; "COMDLG32.OCX"
Begin VB.Form frmForm1
    Caption         =   "Delete Demo"
    ClientHeight    =   3195
    ClientLeft      =   1695
    ClientTop       =   1620
    ClientWidth     =   4680
    LinkTopic       =   "Form1"
    ScaleHeight     =   3195
    ScaleWidth      =   4680
    Begin MSComDlg.CommonDialog dlgCommonDialog1
        Left            =    3840
```

```
        Top             =    2640
        _ExtentX        =    847
        _ExtentY        =    847
        _Version        =    393216
     End
     Begin VB.CommandButton btnDeleteFile
        Caption         =    "Delete a File"
        Height          =    1575
        Left            =    480
        TabIndex        =    0
        Top             =    600
        Width           =    3735
     End
End
Attribute VB_Name = "frmForm1"
Attribute VB_GlobalNameSpace = False
Attribute VB_Creatable = False
Attribute VB_PredeclaredId = True
Attribute VB_Exposed = False

Private Sub btnDeleteFile_Click()
    Dim fileSystem
    Dim file
    Dim fileName
    Dim result

    dlgCommonDialog1.CancelError = True
    On Error GoTo CancelErr
    dlgCommonDialog1.DialogTitle = "Delete File"
    dlgCommonDialog1.ShowOpen
    fileName = dlgCommonDialog1.fileName

    result = MsgBox("Delete " & fileName & "?", _
        vbQuestion Or vbYesNo, "Delete File")
    If result = vbYes Then
        Set fileSystem = _
            CreateObject("Scripting.FileSystemObject")
        Set file = fileSystem.GetFile(fileName)
        file.Delete True
    End If

CancelErr:
End Sub
```

CROSS-REFERENCE
For more information, see FileSystemObject, File, Folder, DeleteFile, and DeleteFolder.

Delete — MAPIMessages

Method

The `Delete` method deletes a message from an email session. It can also be used to delete message attachments or recipients.

Syntax

```
MAPIMessages.Delete item
```

- *MAPIMessages* — A reference to a MAPIMessages object.
- *item* — A value that specifies what type of item to delete. This can be `mapMessageDelete` to delete a message, `mapRecipientDelete` to delete a recipient, and `mapAttachmentDelete` to delete an attachment.

Example

The following line deletes the currently indexed message.

```
MAPIMessages.Delete mapMessageDelete
```

CROSS-REFERENCE
For more information, see MAPIMessages.

Delete — OLE Container

Method

The `Delete` method deletes an object from an OLE Container control.

Syntax

```
OLEContainer.Delete
```

- *OLEContainer* — A reference to an OLE Container object.

Example

The following line deletes the currently embedded object from a OLE Container control. The `oleContainer` object is an OLE Container control that the programmer added to the form at design time.

```
oleContainer.Delete
```

 CROSS-REFERENCE
For more information, see OLE Container.

DeleteFolder

Method

The `DeleteFolder` method deletes a directory, as well as all the directory's contents.

Objects with a DeleteFolder Method

FileSystemObject

Syntax

```
FileSystemObject.DeleteFolder folderName, readOnly
```

- *FileSystemObject* — A reference to a FileSystemObject object.
- *folderName* — The name of the folder to delete. Wildcard characters can be used to delete multiple folders.
- *readOnly* (*) — A flag indicating whether read-only folders should be deleted. A value of `True` causes read-only folders to be deleted, whereas a value of `False` does not.

(*) = Optional argument

Example 1

The following lines demonstrate how to delete a folder with the `DeleteFolder` method.

```
Dim fileSystem
Dim file

Set fileSystem = _
    CreateObject("Scripting.FileSystemObject")
fileSystem.DeleteFolder "c:\MyFolder"
```

Example 2

In this example, the sample code lines delete all folders within the given folder, MyFolder, thanks to the wildcard character specified in the last part of the path name.

```
Dim fileSystem
Dim file

Set fileSystem = _
    CreateObject("Scripting.FileSystemObject")
fileSystem.DeleteFolder "c:\MyFolder\*", True
```

CROSS-REFERENCE
For more information, see FileSystemObject, File, Folder, Delete, and DeleteFile.

DeleteSetting

Statement

The DeleteSetting statement removes a section or a key from an entry in the Windows Registry.

Syntax

```
DeleteSetting app, section, key
```

- *app* — The application's name in the registry.
- *section* — The name of the registry section to be deleted or the name of the section that contains the key to be deleted.
- *key* (*) — The name of the registry key to be deleted. If this argument is not present, the entire registry section is deleted.

(*) = Optional

Example 1

The following line removes the StatusBar key from the registry entry for the AnyApp application. Figure D-10 shows the registry entry for AnyApp as it appears in the registry editor before the following line deletes the key.

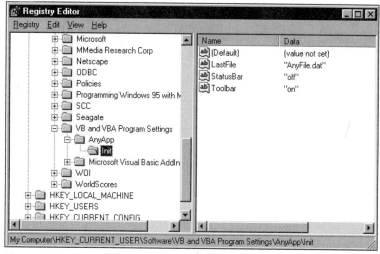

Figure D-10 Here is AnyApp's Init registry section with its three keys: LastFile, StatusBar, and Toolbar.

```
DeleteSetting "AnyApp", "Init", "StatusBar"
```

Example 2

The following line removes the entire Init section from the registry entry for the AnyApp application.

```
DeleteSetting "AnyApp", "Init"
```

 CROSS-REFERENCE
See also SaveSetting.

Description — Button

Property

The Description property represents a button object's description, which is the text that's displayed in a toolbar's Customize Toolbar dialog box.

Syntax

```
Button.Description = value1
```

or

```
value2 = Button.Description
```

- *Button* — A reference to a Button object.
- *value1* — A string containing the button's description.
- *value2* — The variable that will receive the button's current description.

Example

The following lines add three buttons to a toolbar and set the button objects' descriptions. Figure D-11 shows how the buttons' descriptions appear in the Customize Toolbar dialog box, should the user display the dialog box from the application. The `tlbToolbar1` object is a Toolbar control that the programmer added to the form at design time.

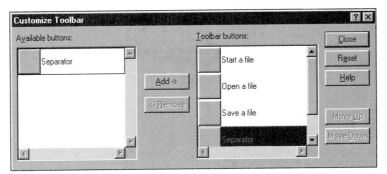

Figure D-11 A button's description text appears next to the button in the Customize Toolbar dialog box.

```
Dim btn As Button
Set btn = tlbToolbar1.Buttons.Add(1, , "New")
btn.Description = "Start a file"
Set btn = tlbToolbar1.Buttons.Add(2, , "Open")
btn.Description = "Open a file"
Set btn = tlbToolbar1.Buttons.Add(3, , "Save")
btn.Description = "Save a file"
```

CROSS-REFERENCE

See also Button, Customize, and Toolbar.

Description — Err

Property

The `Description` property represents a line of text that describes the error associated with an Err object.

Syntax

```
Err.Description = value1
```

or

```
value2 = Err.Description
```

- *Err* — A reference to an Err object.
- *value1* — A string containing the error's description.
- *value2* — The variable that will receive the error's description.

Example

The following line assigns description text to an Err object.

```
Err.Description = "Cannot create a new object"
```

 CROSS-REFERENCE
See also Err.

DeselectAll

Method

The `DeselectAll` method deselects all selected tabs in a TabStrip control that has its `MultiSelect` property set to `True`.

Objects with a DeselectAll Method
TabStrip

Syntax

```
TabStrip.DeselectAll
```

- *TabStrip* — A reference to a TabStrip control.

Example

The following line deselects all tabs in a TabStrip control called `tabTabStrip1`. The programmer added `tabTabStrip1` to the form at design time.

```
tabTabStrip1.DeselectAll
```

 CROSS-REFERENCE
For more information, see Tab and TabStrip.

DeviceArrival

Event

Visual Basic sends a SysInfo control a `DeviceArrival` event when the user installs a new device into her system.

Objects That Receive DeviceArrival Events

SysInfo

Example

A program can respond to a `DeviceArrival` event by implementing the SysInfo control's `DeviceArrival` event procedure. The following code segment shows how Visual Basic defines the `DeviceArrival` event procedure. The event procedure has five parameters, which are described as follows:

- The SysInfo control's index if it's in a control array. This parameter doesn't appear otherwise.
- The new device's type, which can be `DeviceTypeNet`, `DeviceTypeDevNode`, `DeviceTypeOEM`, `DeviceTypePort`, or `DeviceTypeVolume`.
- The new device's ID, which can be `dbcn_resource` (for `DeviceTypeNet`), `dbcd_devnode` (for `DeviceTypeDevNode`), `dbco_identifier` (for `DeviceTypeOEM`), `Null` (for `DeviceTypePort`), or `dbcv_unitmask` (for `DeviceTypeVolume`).
- The new device's name, which is `dbcp_name` when the device type is `DeviceTypePort` and `Null` otherwise.
- The device's data setting, which can be `dbcn_flags` for `DeviceTypeNet`, `Null` for `DeviceTypeDevNode`, `dbco_suppfunc` for `DeviceTypeOEM`, `Null` for `DeviceTypePort`, or `dbcv_flags` for `DeviceTypeVolume`.

```
Private Sub SysInfo1_DeviceArrival(index As Integer, _
   ByVal DeviceType As Long, ByVal DeviceID As Long, _
   ByVal DeviceName As String, ByVal DeviceData As Long)
      ' Respond to the event here.
End Sub
```

CROSS-REFERENCE

See also SysInfo, DevModeChange, DeviceOtherEvent, DeviceQueryRemove, DeviceQueryRemoveFailed, DeviceRemoveComplete, and DeviceRemovePending.

DeviceID

Property

The `DeviceID` property represents the ID of the device currently associated with the Multimedia control. This property is available only at runtime, when it is read-only.

Objects with a DeviceID Property

Multimedia MCI

Syntax

```
value = MultimediaMCI.DeviceID
```

- *MultimediaMCI* — A reference to a Multimedia MCI control.
- *value* — The variable that will receive the ID.

Example

The following line gets the ID of a multimedia device from a multimedia control. The `mciMultimedia` object is a Multimedia MCI control that the programmer added to the form at design time.

```
devID = mciMultimedia.DeviceID
```

CROSS-REFERENCE

See also Multimedia MCI.

DeviceName

Property

The `DeviceName` property represents the name of a printer device. An example of a printer device name is "Epson ActionLaser 1500."

Objects with a DeviceName Property

Printer

Syntax

```
value = Printer.DeviceName
```

- *Printer*—A reference to the Printer object.
- *value*—The variable that will receive the device name.

Example

The following line gets the name of the system's default printer device. The Printer object is a global Visual Basic object that you can reference directly, without having to create an instance of the object.

```
devName = Printer.DeviceName
```

CROSS-REFERENCE
See also Printer.

DeviceOtherEvent

Event

Visual Basic sends a SysInfo control a `DeviceOtherEvent` event for unknown device events.

Objects That Receive DeviceOtherEvent Events

SysInfo

Example

A program can respond to a `DeviceOtherEvent` event by implementing the SysInfo control's `DeviceOtherEvent` event procedure. The following code segment shows how Visual Basic defines the `DeviceOtherEvent` event procedure. The event procedure has four parameters, which are described as follows:

- The SysInfo control's index if it's in a control array. This parameter doesn't appear otherwise.
- The device's type, which can be `DeviceTypeNet`, `DeviceTypeDevNode`, `DeviceTypeOEM`, `DeviceTypePort`, or `DeviceTypeVolume`.
- The event name.
- A pointer to data associated with the device.

```
Private Sub SysInfo1_DeviceOtherEvent _
  (ByVal DeviceType As Long, _
  ByVal EventName As String, ByVal DataPointer As Long)
    ' Respond to the event here.
End Sub
```

CROSS-REFERENCE
See also SysInfo, DeviceArrival, DevModeChange, DeviceQueryRemove, DeviceQueryRemoveFailed, DeviceRemoveComplete, and DeviceRemovePending.

DeviceQueryRemove

Event

Visual Basic sends a SysInfo control a `DeviceQueryRemove` event immediately before a device is removed. Responding to this event enables a program to approve or cancel the device removal.

Objects That Receive DeviceQueryRemove Events

SysInfo

Example

A program can respond to a `DeviceQueryRemove` event by implementing the SysInfo control's `DeviceQueryRemove` event procedure. The following code segment shows how Visual Basic defines the `DeviceQueryRemove` event procedure. The event procedure has six parameters, which are described as follows:

- The SysInfo control's index if it's in a control array. This parameter doesn't appear otherwise.
- The device's type, which can be `DeviceTypeNet`, `DeviceTypeDevNode`, `DeviceTypeOEM`, `DeviceTypePort`, or `DeviceTypeVolume`.
- The device's ID, which can be `dbcn_resource` (for `DeviceTypeNet`), `dbcd_devnode` (for `DeviceTypeDevNode`), `dbco_identifier` (for `DeviceTypeOEM`), `Null` (for `DeviceTypePort`), or `dbcv_unitmask` (for `DeviceTypeVolume`).
- The device's name, which is `dbcp_name` when the device type is `DeviceTypePort` and `Null` otherwise.
- The device's data setting, which can be `dbcn_flags` for `DeviceTypeNet`, `Null` for `DeviceTypeDevNode`, `dbco_suppfunc` for `DeviceTypeOEM`, `Null` for `DeviceTypePort`, or `dbcv_flags` for `DeviceTypeVolume`.
- A `Boolean` variable that, when set to `True`, cancels the device removal.

```
Private Sub SysInfo1_DeviceQueryRemove(index As Integer, _
    ByVal DeviceType As Long, ByVal DeviceID As Long, _
    ByVal DeviceName As String, ByVal DeviceData As Long, _
    Cancel As Boolean)
        ' Respond to the event here.
End Sub
```

CROSS-REFERENCE
See also SysInfo, DeviceArrival, DevModeChange, DeviceOtherEvent, DeviceQueryRemoveFailed, DeviceRemoveComplete, and DeviceRemovePending.

DeviceQueryRemoveFailed

Event

Visual Basic sends a SysInfo control a `DeviceQueryRemoveFailed` event if a program sets the `Cancel` parameter of the `DeviceQueryRemove` event procedure to `True`, canceling the device removal.

Objects That Receive DeviceQueryRemoveFailed Events

SysInfo

Example

A program can respond to a `DeviceQueryRemoveFailed` event by implementing the SysInfo control's `DeviceQueryRemoveFailed` event procedure. The following code segment shows how Visual Basic defines the `DeviceQueryRemoveFailed` event procedure. The event procedure has five parameters, which are described as follows:

- The SysInfo control's index if it's in a control array. This parameter doesn't appear otherwise.
- The device's type, which can be `DeviceTypeNet`, `DeviceTypeDevNode`, `DeviceTypeOEM`, `DeviceTypePort`, or `DeviceTypeVolume`.
- The device's ID, which can be `dbcn_resource` (for `DeviceTypeNet`), `dbcd_devnode` (for `DeviceTypeDevNode`), `dbco_identifier` (for `DeviceTypeOEM`), `Null` (for `DeviceTypePort`), or `dbcv_unitmask` (for `DeviceTypeVolume`).
- The device's name, which is `dbcp_name` when the device type is `DeviceTypePort` and `Null` otherwise.
- The device's data setting, which can be `dbcn_flags` for `DeviceTypeNet`, `Null` for `DeviceTypeDevNode`, `dbco_suppfunc` for `DeviceTypeOEM`, `Null` for `DeviceTypePort`, or `dbcv_flags` for `DeviceTypeVolume`.

```
Private Sub SysInfo1_DeviceQueryRemoveFailed(index As Integer, _
    ByVal DeviceType As Long, ByVal DeviceID As Long, _
    ByVal DeviceName As String, ByVal DeviceData As Long)
        ' Respond to the event here.
End Sub
```

 CROSS-REFERENCE
See also SysInfo, DeviceArrival, DevModeChange, DeviceOtherEvent, DeviceQueryRemove, DeviceRemoveComplete, and DeviceRemovePending.

DeviceRemoveComplete

Event

Visual Basic sends a SysInfo control a `DeviceRemoveComplete` event when the device removal is complete.

Objects That Receive DeviceRemoveComplete Events

SysInfo

Example

A program can respond to a `DeviceRemoveComplete` event by implementing the SysInfo control's `DeviceRemoveComplete` event procedure. The following code segment shows how Visual Basic defines the `DeviceRemoveComplete` event procedure. The event procedure has five parameters, which are described as follows:

- The SysInfo control's index if it's in a control array. This parameter doesn't appear otherwise.

- The device's type, which can be `DeviceTypeNet`, `DeviceTypeDevNode`, `DeviceTypeOEM`, `DeviceTypePort`, or `DeviceTypeVolume`.

- The device's ID, which can be `dbcn_resource` (for `DeviceTypeNet`), `dbcd_devnode` (for `DeviceTypeDevNode`), `dbco_identifier` (for `DeviceTypeOEM`), `Null` (for `DeviceTypePort`), or `dbcv_unitmask` (for `DeviceTypeVolume`).

- The device's name, which is `dbcp_name` when the device type is `DeviceTypePort` and `Null` otherwise.

- The device's data setting, which can be `dbcn_flags` for `DeviceTypeNet`, `Null` for `DeviceTypeDevNode`, `dbco_suppfunc` for `DeviceTypeOEM`, `Null` for `DeviceTypePort`, or `dbcv_flags` for `DeviceTypeVolume`.

```
Private Sub SysInfo1_DeviceRemoveComplete(index As Integer, _
    ByVal DeviceType As Long, ByVal DeviceID As Long, _
    ByVal DeviceName As String, ByVal DeviceData As Long)
        ' Respond to the event here.
End Sub
```

CROSS-REFERENCE

See also SysInfo, DeviceArrival, DevModeChange, DeviceOtherEvent, DeviceQueryRemove, DeviceQueryRemoveFailed, and DeviceRemovePending.

DeviceRemovePending

Event

Visual Basic sends a SysInfo control a `DeviceRemovePending` when all applications have approved the device removal.

Objects That Receive DeviceRemovePending Events

SysInfo

Example

A program can respond to a `DeviceRemovePending` event by implementing the SysInfo control's `DeviceRemovePending` event procedure. The following code segment shows how Visual Basic defines the `DeviceRemovePending` event procedure. The event procedure has five parameters, which are described as follows:

- The SysInfo control's index if it's in a control array. This parameter doesn't appear otherwise.
- The device's type, which can be `DeviceTypeNet`, `DeviceTypeDevNode`, `DeviceTypeOEM`, `DeviceTypePort`, or `DeviceTypeVolume`.
- The device's ID, which can be `dbcn_resource` (for `DeviceTypeNet`), `dbcd_devnode` (for `DeviceTypeDevNode`), `dbco_identifier` (for `DeviceTypeOEM`), `Null` (for `DeviceTypePort`), or `dbcv_unitmask` (for `DeviceTypeVolume`).
- The device's name, which is `dbcp_name` when the device type is `DeviceTypePort` and `Null` otherwise.
- The device's data setting, which can be `dbcn_flags` for `DeviceTypeNet`, `Null` for `DeviceTypeDevNode`, `dbco_suppfunc` for `DeviceTypeOEM`, `Null` for `DeviceTypePort`, or `dbcv_flags` for `DeviceTypeVolume`.

```
Private Sub SysInfo1_DeviceRemovePending(index As Integer, _
    ByVal DeviceType As Long, ByVal DeviceID As Long, _
    ByVal DeviceName As String, ByVal DeviceData As Long)
        ' Respond to the event here.
End Sub
```

CROSS-REFERENCE
See also SysInfo, DeviceArrival, DevModeChange, DeviceOtherEvent, DeviceQueryRemove, DeviceQueryRemoveFailed, and DeviceRemoveComplete.

DeviceType

Property

The `DeviceType` property represents the type of device that should be opened and associated with a multimedia control. The device types are AVIAudio, CDAudio, DAT, DigitalVideo, MMMovie, Overlay, Scanner, Sequencer, VCR, Videodisc, WaveAudio, and Other.

Objects with a DeviceType Property
Multimedia MCI

Syntax

```
MultimediaMCI.DeviceType = value1
```

or

```
value2 = MultimediaMCI.DeviceType
```

- *MultimediaMCI*—A reference to a Multimedia MCI control.
- *value1*—A string containing the device type.
- *value2*—The variable that will receive the device type.

Example

This sample program not only shows how to use the DeviceName property, but also how to load and play a wave file with the Multimedia MCI control. When you run the program, click the Load Wave File button. When you do, the Choose Wave File dialog box appears from which you can select a wave file to play. (The MySound.wav file is included with the program on this book's CD-ROM.) Make sure that you select a valid wave file, because the program does no error checking. Once the file is loaded, click the Multimedia MCI control's Play button to hear the file. (To play the file again, you must first click the rewind button.) Figure D-12 shows the application after it has loaded a wave file.

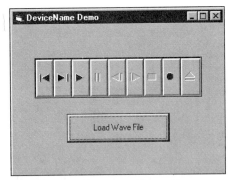

Figure D-12 The DeviceName Demo program plays any wave file you select.

```
VERSION 5.00
Object = "{C1A8AF28-1257-101B-8FB0-0020AF039CA3} _
    #1.1#0"; "MCI32.OCX"
Object = "{F9043C88-F6F2-101A-A3C9-08002B2F49FB} _
    #1.2#0"; "COMDLG32.OCX"
Begin VB.Form Form1
    Caption         =   "DeviceName Demo"
    ClientHeight    =   3195
    ClientLeft      =   60
    ClientTop       =   345
    ClientWidth     =   4680
    LinkTopic       =   "Form1"
    ScaleHeight     =   3195
    ScaleWidth      =   4680
    StartUpPosition =   3  'Windows Default
    Begin MSComDlg.CommonDialog dlgCommonDialog1
        Left        =   3840
        Top         =   2640
        _ExtentX    =   847
        _ExtentY    =   847
        _Version    =   393216
    End
    Begin MCI.MMControl mciMMControl1
        Height      =   855
        Left        =   480
        TabIndex    =   1
        Top         =   720
        Width       =   3735
        _ExtentX    =   6588
        _ExtentY    =   1508
        _Version    =   393216
        DeviceType  =   ""
        FileName    =   ""
    End
    Begin VB.CommandButton btnLoadWave
        Caption     =   "Load Wave File"
        Height      =   615
        Left        =   1200
        TabIndex    =   0
        Top         =   1920
        Width       =   2295
    End
End
```

```
         Attribute VB_Name = "Form1"
         Attribute VB_GlobalNameSpace = False
         Attribute VB_Creatable = False
         Attribute VB_PredeclaredId = True
         Attribute VB_Exposed = False

         Private Sub btnLoadWave_Click()
             Dim fileName

             dlgCommonDialog1.CancelError = True
             On Error GoTo CancelErr
             dlgCommonDialog1.DialogTitle = "Choose Wave File"
             dlgCommonDialog1.fileName = "*.wav"
             dlgCommonDialog1.ShowOpen
             fileName = dlgCommonDialog1.fileName

             mciMMControl1.DeviceType = "WaveAudio"
             mciMMControl1.Shareable = False
             mciMMControl1.Wait = True
             mciMMControl1.Notify = False
             mciMMControl1.fileName = fileName
             mciMMControl1.Command = "Open"
         CancelErr:
         End Sub
```

CROSS-REFERENCE
See also Multimedia MCI.

DevModeChanged

Event

Visual Basic sends a SysInfo control a DevModeChanged event when the mode settings of a device are changed.

Objects That Receive DevModeChanged Events

SysInfo

Example

A program can respond to a `DevModeChanged` event by implementing the SysInfo control's `DevModeChanged` event procedure. The following code segment shows how Visual Basic defines the `DevModeChange` event procedure.

```
Private Sub SysInfo1_DevModeChanged()
    ' Respond to the event here.
End Sub
```

 CROSS-REFERENCE

See also SysInfo, DeviceArrival, DeviceRemoveComplete, DeviceOtherEvent, DeviceQueryRemove, DeviceQueryRemoveFailed, and DeviceRemovePending.

DialogTitle

Property

The `DialogTitle` property represents the title that's displayed in a dialog box generated by the CommonDialog control. You can set the dialog title only on the Open and Save As dialog boxes.

Objects with a DialogTitle Property

CommonDialog

Syntax

`CommonDialog.DialogTitle = value1`

or

`value2 = CommonDialog.DialogTitle`

- *CommonDialog* — A reference to a CommonDialog control.
- *value1* — A string containing the dialog title.
- *value2* — The variable that will receive the dialog title.

Example

The following lines set a common dialog's title and file-name type, and then display the dialog box. Figure D-13 shows the results. The `dlgCommonDialog1` object is a CommonDialog control that the programmer added to the application's form at design time.

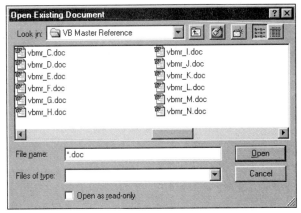

Figure D-13 This dialog's title comes from the CommonDialog control's DialogTitle property.

```
dlgCommonDialog1.DialogTitle = "Open Existing Document"
dlgCommonDialog1.fileName = "*.doc"
dlgCommonDialog1.ShowOpen
```

CROSS-REFERENCE
See also CommonDialog.

Dim

Statement

The Dim statement enables you to declare variables. The Dim statement also allocates space for the declared variable. Declaring variables in Visual Basic with the Dim statement is optional unless you've specified the Option Explicit option. Specifying this option is usually the best programming practice because it prevents you from accidentally defining new variables by misspelling another variable's name.

Syntax

Dim *events name type*

- *events* (*) — The keyword WithEvents, which specifies that the variable is used with an ActiveX object's events.
- *name* — The variable's name, which can include subscripts for declaring an array.

- *type* (*) — The keyword As followed by the variable type. The New keyword can also be used (such as As New *object*) to create a new object with which to associate the variable. If you leave off the type, the variable's data type defaults to Variant.

(*) = Optional

NOTE
You can define several variables with one Dim statement by separating the declarations with commas.

Example 1

The following lines declare the variables var1 and var2 as Variant.

```
Dim var1
Dim var2 As Variant
```

Example 2

Here, the following line uses a single Dim statement to declare two variables of differing types.

```
Dim var1 As Integer, var2 As Variant
```

Example 3

Finally, the following lines declare two arrays.

```
Dim var1(10) As Integer
Dim var2(5, 10) As Integer
```

CROSS-REFERENCE
See also Private, Public, Static, and ReDim.

Dir

Function

The Dir function enables you to locate files and directories based on given criteria. For example, you can find all the files in a directory with the .bak extension or look for files with their read-only attribute set. The Dir function returns the name of a file or folder that meets the given criteria.

Syntax

```
Dir path, attribute
```

- *attribute* (*) — The file attributes to match.
- *path* (*) — The file name with path to match.

(*) = Optional

Example 1

In this example, the program checks whether the `MyText.txt` file in the root directory exists. If it does, the `Dir` function will assign `strResult` the file name "MyText.txt." Otherwise, `strResult` ends up with an empty string.

```
Dim strResult As String
strResult = Dir("c:\MyText.txt")
```

Example 2

Here, the program gets the names of all .txt files in the root directory and displays them one by one in a message box. Note that calling `Dir` without arguments causes the function to locate the next file that matches the arguments given in the first call to `Dir`.

```
Dim strResult As String
strResult = Dir("c:\*.txt")
Do While strResult <> ""
    MsgBox strResult
    strResult = Dir
Loop
```

DirListBox

Control

A DirListBox is a control that displays the directories on a drive, enabling the user to select a directory. Figure D-14 shows a DirListBox control in a form. At design time, the DirListBox control is available on Visual Basic's toolbox.

Figure D-14 DirListBox controls provide an easy way for users to select directories.

Properties

The DirListBox control has 39 properties, which are listed as follows. Because many Visual Basic controls have similar properties, the following list does not include the properties' descriptions. For information on using a property, look up the individual property's entry, provided alphabetically in this book.

```
Appearance
BackColor
CausesValidation
Container
DragIcon
DragMode
Enabled
Font
FontBold
FontItalic
FontName
FontSize
FontStrikethru
FontUnderline
ForeColor
Height
HelpContextID
hWnd
Index
Left
List
ListCount
ListIndex
```

```
MouseIcon
MousePointer
Name
OLEDragMode
OLEDropMode
Parent
Path
TabIndex
TabStop
Tag
ToolTipText
Top
TopIndex
Visible
WhatsThisHelpID
Width
```

Methods

The DirListBox control has seven methods, which are listed below. Because many Visual Basic controls have similar methods, the following list does not include the methods' descriptions. For information on using a method, look up the individual method's entry, provided alphabetically in this book.

```
Drag
Move
OLEDrag
Refresh
SetFocus
ShowWhatsThis
ZOrder
```

Events

The DirListBox control responds to 20 events, which are listed below. Because many Visual Basic controls respond to similar events, the following list does not include the events' descriptions. For information on using an event, look up the individual event's entry, provided alphabetically in this book.

```
Change
Click
DragDrop
DragOver
GotFocus
```

```
KeyDown
KeyPress
KeyUp
LostFocus
MouseDown
MouseMove
MouseUp
OLECompleteDrag
OLEDragDrop
OLEDragOver
OLEGiveFeedback
OLESetData
OLEStartDrag
Scroll
Validate
```

The DirListBox's most commonly used event is Change, which the control generates when the user selects a directory. A program responds to the button's Change event in the Change event procedure. For example, the following program uses a DirListBox's Change event procedure to display the currently selected directory in a text box. When you run the program, each time you double-click a directory, the selected directory gets updated, as shown in Figure D-15.

Figure D-15 This simple application displays a selected directory.

```
VERSION 5.00
Begin VB.Form Form1
   Caption        =    "DirListBox Demo"
   ClientHeight   =    3195
   ClientLeft     =    60
   ClientTop      =    345
   ClientWidth    =    4680
```

```
        LinkTopic        =    "Form1"
        ScaleHeight      =    3195
        ScaleWidth       =    4680
        StartUpPosition =    3  'Windows Default
        Begin VB.TextBox txtText1
           Height           =     375
           Left             =     480
           TabIndex         =     1
           Top              =     240
           Width            =     3735
        End
        Begin VB.DirListBox dirDirectoryList
           Height           =     1890
           Left             =     480
           TabIndex         =     0
           Top              =     840
           Width            =     3735
        End
     End
  End
  Attribute VB_Name = "Form1"
  Attribute VB_GlobalNameSpace = False
  Attribute VB_Creatable = False
  Attribute VB_PredeclaredId = True
  Attribute VB_Exposed = False

  Private Sub dirDirectoryList_Change()
      txtText1.Text = dirDirectoryList.Path
  End Sub

  Private Sub Form_Load()
      dirDirectoryList.Path = "c:\"
  End Sub
```

DisabledImageList

Property

The DisabledImageList property represents the images for disabled buttons in a Toolbar control. That is, when a button on a toolbar has been disabled, the button displays the disabled image from the associated ImageList control.

Objects with a DisabledImageList Property

Toolbar

Syntax

```
Toolbar.DisabledImageList = value1
```

or

```
value2 = Toolbar.DisabledImageList
```

- *Toolbar* — A reference to a Toolbar control.
- *value1* — A reference to the image list that contains the images for disabled buttons.
- *value2* — The variable that will receive a reference to the image list.

Example

When you run this sample program, you see the window shown in Figure D-16. Click the Disable Buttons button, and the program disables all of the toolbar buttons, displaying the images stored in the toolbar's DisabledImageList image list (called ilsImageList2 in the program). Figure D-17 shows the application with its disabled buttons. Clicking the button (which now has the caption "Enable Buttons") a second time causes the program to restore all the buttons to their enabled state. Notice how the image lists and the toolbar are constructed in the Form_Load method, and also notice how the program enables and disables the buttons in the btnEnable_Click event procedure.

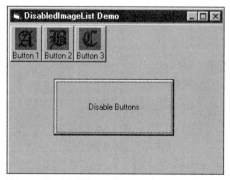

Figure D-16 When the application first appears, the toolbar's buttons are all enabled.

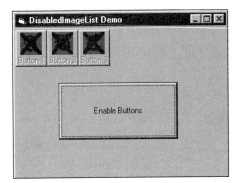

Figure D-17 Here's the application with its toolbar buttons disabled.

```
VERSION 5.00
Object = "{6B7E6392-850A-101B-AFC0-4210102A8DA7} _
    #2.0#0"; "MSCOMCTL.OCX"
Begin VB.Form Form1
    Caption         =   "DisabledImageList Demo"
    ClientHeight    =   3195
    ClientLeft      =   60
    ClientTop       =   345
    ClientWidth     =   4680
    LinkTopic       =   "Form1"
    ScaleHeight     =   3195
    ScaleWidth      =   4680
    StartUpPosition =   3  'Windows Default
    Begin MSComctlLib.Toolbar tlbToolbar1
        Align       =   1  'Align Top
        Height      =   630
        Left        =   0
        TabIndex    =   0
        Top         =   0
        Width       =   4680
        _ExtentX    =   8255
        _ExtentY    =   1111
        ButtonWidth =   609
        ButtonHeight =  953
        Appearance  =   1
        _Version    =   393216
    End
    Begin VB.CommandButton btnEnable
        Caption     =   "Disable Buttons"
```

```
            Height          =    1215
            Left            =    960
            TabIndex        =    1
            Top             =    1200
            Width           =    2655
         End
         Begin MSComctlLib.ImageList ilsImageList2
            Left            =    3120
            Top             =    2520
            _ExtentX        =    1005
            _ExtentY        =    1005
            BackColor       =    -2147483643
            MaskColor       =    12632256
            _Version        =    393216
         End
         Begin MSComctlLib.ImageList ilsImageList1
            Left            =    3840
            Top             =    2520
            _ExtentX        =    1005
            _ExtentY        =    1005
            BackColor       =    -2147483643
            MaskColor       =    12632256
            _Version        =    393216
         End
      End
   End
Attribute VB_Name = "Form1"
Attribute VB_GlobalNameSpace = False
Attribute VB_Creatable = False
Attribute VB_PredeclaredId = True
Attribute VB_Exposed = False

Private Sub btnEnable_Click()
    With tlbToolbar1
        If .Buttons(1).Enabled = True Then
            .Buttons(1).Enabled = False
            .Buttons(2).Enabled = False
            .Buttons(3).Enabled = False
            btnEnable.Caption = "Enable Buttons"
        Else
            .Buttons(1).Enabled = True
            .Buttons(2).Enabled = True
            .Buttons(3).Enabled = True
```

```
                        btnEnable.Caption = "Disable Buttons"
                End If
            End With
    End Sub

    Private Sub Form_Load()
        ilsImageList1.ListImages.Add , , _
            LoadPicture("but1.bmp")
        ilsImageList1.ListImages.Add , , _
            LoadPicture("but2.bmp")
        ilsImageList1.ListImages.Add , , _
            LoadPicture("but3.bmp")

        ilsImageList2.ListImages.Add , , _
            LoadPicture("but1d.bmp")
        ilsImageList2.ListImages.Add , , _
            LoadPicture("but2d.bmp")
        ilsImageList2.ListImages.Add , , _
            LoadPicture("but3d.bmp")

        tlbToolbar1.ImageList = ilsImageList1
        tlbToolbar1.DisabledImageList = ilsImageList2
        tlbToolbar1.Buttons.Add , , "Button 1", , 1
        tlbToolbar1.Buttons.Add , , "Button 2", , 2
        tlbToolbar1.Buttons.Add , , "Button 3", , 3
    End Sub
```

 CROSS-REFERENCE
See also Button and Toolbar.

DisabledPicture

Property

The DisabledPicture property represents the image that appears on a control when the control is disabled. To have any type of graphic appear on a control, the control's Style property must be set to graphical.

Objects with a DisabledPicture Property

CheckBox

CommandButton

OptionButton

Syntax

```
object.DisabledPicture = value1
```

or

```
value2 = object.DisabledPicture
```

- *object* — A reference to a control with a `DisabledPicture` property.
- *value1* — A reference to the picture object that will be the control's disabled picture.
- *value2* — The variable that will receive a reference to the control's disabled picture.

Example

In this example, the program loads and sets images for a graphical pushbutton. The `btnCommand1` object is a CommandButton control that the programmer added to the application's form at design time.

```
btnCommand1.Picture = LoadPicture("but1.bmp")
btnCommand1.DownPicture = LoadPicture("but1dn.bmp")
btnCommand1.DisabledPicture = LoadPicture("but1d.bmp")
```

 CROSS-REFERENCE
See also CommandButton, OptionButton, CheckBox, Picture, and DownPicture.

DisableNoScroll

Property

The `DisableNoScroll` property represents whether a RichTextBox control's scroll bars are displayed all the time but disabled when not needed. If this property is set to `True`, the RichTextBox's scroll bars are grayed out when they aren't needed. If set to `False`, the scroll bars work normally, not even appearing in the RichTextBox control until they're actually needed. This property is read-only at runtime, so it must be set in the control's Properties window at design time.

Objects with a DisableNoScroll Property

RichTextBox

Syntax

```
value = RichTextBox.DisableNoScroll
```

- *RichTextBox* — A reference to a RichTextBox control.
- *value* — The variable that will receive the property's current setting.

Example

Figure D-18 shows a RichTextBox control with its DisableNoScroll property set to False. Because the control contains only a single line of text, it doesn't need to scroll. Therefore, no scroll bars appear. Figure D-19, on the other hand, shows the same control with the DisableNoScroll property set to True. Now the scroll bars appear whether they are needed or not, although, in this case, they are disabled. Note, however, that if the ScrollBars property is set to rftNone, scroll bars never appear in the control, no matter how the DisableNoScroll property is set.

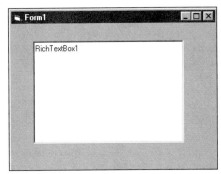

Figure D-18 Here, the RichTextBox control displays no scroll bars.

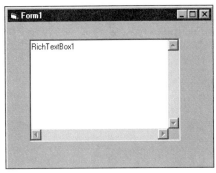

Figure D-19 Thanks to the DisableNoScroll property, this RichTextBox control displays grayed-out scroll bars when scroll bars aren't needed to view the text.

CROSS-REFERENCE
See also RichTextBox.

DisplayAsDefault

Property

The `DisplayAsDefault` property specifies whether a control is the default control in the container.

Objects with a DisplayAsDefault Property

AmbientProperties

Syntax

`value = AmbientProperties.DisplayAsDefault`

- *AmbientProperties* — A reference to an AmbientProperties object.
- *value* — The variable that will receive the property's current setting.

Example

In this example, the program retrieves the status of a UserControl's `DisplayAsDefault` status.

```
Dim defaultCntr As Boolean
defaultCntr = UserControl.Ambient.DisplayAsDefault
```

CROSS-REFERENCE
See also UserControl, Ambient, and AmbientProperties.

DisplayChanged

Event

Visual Basic sends a SysInfo control a `DisplayChanged` event when the screen resolution is changed. This gives an application the opportunity to make whatever changes are necessary to accommodate the new screen resolution.

Objects That Receive DisplayChanged Events

SysInfo

Example

A program can respond to a `DisplayChanged` event by implementing the SysInfo control's `DisplayChanged` event procedure. The following code segment shows how a SysInfo control defines a `DisplayChanged` event procedure. The `SysInfo1` object is a SysInfo control that the programmer added to the form at design time.

```
Private Sub SysInfo1_DisplayChanged()
    ' Handle the event here.
End Sub
```

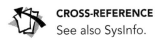

CROSS-REFERENCE
See also SysInfo.

DisplayName

Property

The `DisplayName` property represents the text string that can be used to identify a UserControl in error messages. This text string comes from the control's container.

Objects with a DisplayName Property

AmbientProperties

Syntax

```
value = AmbientProperties.DisplayName
```

- *AmbientProperties* — A reference to an AmbientProperties object.
- *value* — The variable that will receive the name string.

Example

In this example, the program retrieves a UserControl's display name.

```
Dim dispName as String
dispName = UserControl.Ambient.DisplayName
```

CROSS-REFERENCE
See also UserControl, Ambient, and AmbientProperties.

DisplayType

Property

The `DisplayType` property represents whether an object displays its contents or just an icon.

Objects with a DisplayType Property

OLE Container

OLEObject

Syntax

```
object.DisplayType = value1
```

or

```
value2 = object.DisplayType
```

- *object* — A reference to an OLE Container control or OLEObject object.
- *value1* — The value `vbOLEDisplayContent` or `vbOLEDisplayIcon`.
- *value2* — The variable that will receive the property's current setting.

Example

The following line shows how to set an OLE container to display an icon. Normally, you would specify an icon in the Insert Object dialog box when you place the OLE Container control at design time. Figure D-20 shows an OLE Container control in its icon display mode.

```
oleOLEContainer.DisplayType = vbOLEDisplayIcon
```

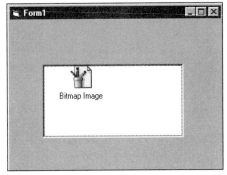

Figure D-20 This OLE Container's bitmap contents are being displayed as an icon.

CROSS-REFERENCE
See also OLE Container and OLEObject.

Do

Statement

The Do statement enables you to set up various types of loops, including Do-While and Do-Until loops.

Syntax

```
Do condition
    ' Loop body statements here.
Loop
```

or

```
Do
    ' Loop body statements here.
Loop condition
```

- *condition* (*) — The keyword While or Until followed by an expression that evaluates to True or False.

(*) = Optional

NOTE
You can use the Exit Do statement anywhere within the loop to force the end of the loop.

Example 1

In this example, a `Do-While` loop continues to display values of x in a message box until x becomes 0. With this type of loop, the body of the loop may or may not execute. For example, if x were to start with a value of 0, rather than 5, the message box would never appear.

```
Dim x As Integer
x = 5
Do While x > 0
    MsgBox x
    x = x - 1
Loop
```

Example 2

Here, this `Do-Until` loop performs exactly as Example 1's `Do-While` loop, displaying values of x in a message box until x becomes 0.

```
Dim x As Integer
x = 5
Do Until x = 0
    MsgBox x
    x = x - 1
Loop
```

Example 3

Here, this `Do-Until` loop evaluates its condition after executing the loop body statements. You can do the same thing with a `Do-While` loop. With this type of loop, the body of the loop always gets executed at least once.

```
Dim x As Integer
x = 5
Do
    MsgBox x
    x = x - 1
Loop Until x = 0
```

Example 4

Finally, in this example, a message box appears for values of x from 5 to 2, but when x becomes 1, the `Exit Do` statement stops the loop. Notice that this version of the loop has no conditional expression. Without the `Exit Do` statement, this loop will run forever.

```
x = 5
Do
    MsgBox x
    x = x - 1
    If x = 1 Then Exit Do
Loop
```

DoEvents

Function

The DoEvents function suspends the application's execution so that the system can process events. Control returns to the application when the system finishes its processing, with the DoEvents function returning the number of open forms. You might want to use this function when your application must perform a lengthy task so that other processes don't get bogged down as well.

Syntax

```
value = DoEvents
```

■ *value* — The variable that will receive the function's return value.

Example

This example shows how to call the DoEvents function. The function will return execution to the application when the system has completed its processing.

```
Dim formCount As Integer
formCount = DoEvents
```

Done

Event

Visual Basic sends a Multimedia MCI control a Done event when an MCI command has finished executing. In order to receive such events, the control's Notify property must be set to True for the command.

Objects That Receive Done Events
Multimedia MCI

Example

A program can respond to a Done event by implementing the multimedia control's Done event procedure. The following code segment shows two event procedures. The Command1_Click event procedure opens a wave file using the MCI Open command. Because the procedure sets the multimedia control's Notify property to True, the multimedia control's Done event procedure will get called after the wave is loaded. Here, the btnCommand1 and mciMMControl1 objects are CommandButton and Multimedia MCI controls that the programmer added to the form at design time.

```
Private Sub btnCommand1_Click()
    mciMMControl1.DeviceType = "WaveAudio"
    mciMMControl1.Shareable = False
    mciMMControl1.Wait = True
    mciMMControl1.Notify = True
    mciMMControl1.FileName = "c:\MySound.wav"
    mciMMControl1.Command = "Open"
End Sub

Private Sub mciMMControl1_Done(NotifyCode As Integer)
    MsgBox "Command Executed"
End Sub
```

CROSS-REFERENCE
See also Multimedia MCI.

DoVerb

Method

The DoVerb method executes an OLE command on behalf of an embedded object. For example, by executing an OLE verb, an application can open an embedded Word document for editing. Table D-11 lists the verb types.

Table D-11 Values for the DoVerb Method

Value	Description
vbOLEDiscardUndoState	Upon activation, clears all modifications that can be undone.
vbOLEHide	Hides the application that created the object.
vbOLEInPlaceActivate	Activates the object for editing when the object gets the focus.
vbOLEOpen	Opens the object in its own window.
vbOLEPrimary	Executes the object's default verb.
vbOLEShow	Opens the document for editing.
vbOLEUIActivate	Activates the object in-place, displaying the associated user interface.

Objects with a DoVerb Method

OLE Container

OLEObject

Syntax

`object.DoVerb verb`

- *object* — A reference to an OLE Container control or an OLEObject object.
- *verb* — One of the values from Table D-11.

Example

The following line opens an embedded document for editing. The `oleContainer` object is an OLE Container control that the programmer added to the application's form at design time.

`oleContainer.DoVerb vbOLEShow`

CROSS-REFERENCE

For more information, see OLE Container and OLEObject.

DownClick

Event

Visual Basic sends an UpDown control a `DownClick` event when the user clicks the control's left or down arrow buttons.

Objects That Receive DownClick Events

UpDown

Example

A program can respond to a `DownClick` event by implementing the UpDown control's `DownClick` event procedure. The following code segment shows how an UpDown control defines a `DownClick` event procedure. The `updUpDown1` object is an UpDown control that the programmer added to the form at design time.

```
Private Sub updUpDown1_DownClick()
    ' Respond to event here.
End Sub
```

 **CROSS-REFERENCE**
See also UpDown.

DownloadMail

Property

The `DownloadMail` property determines when the MAPISession control downloads new mail from the user's mail server. If this property is set to `True`, the control downloads new mail upon connection to the server. If this property is `False`, new messages get downloaded at a time specified by the user.

Objects with a DownloadMail Property

MAPISession

Syntax

```
MAPISession.DownloadMail = value1
```

or

```
value2 = MAPISession.DownloadMail
```

- *MAPISession* — A reference to a MAPISession control.
- *value1* — The value `True` or `False`.
- *value2* — The variable that will receive the property's current setting.

Example

The following line sets a MAPISession control to download mail immediately after signing on to the server. The `MAPISession1` object is a MAPISession control that the programmer added to the application's form at design time.

```
MAPISession1.DownloadMail = True
```

CROSS-REFERENCE
See also MAPISession and MAPIMessages.

DownPicture

Property

The `DownPicture` property represents the image that appears on a control when it's being clicked. For example, in the case of a CommandButton control, the down-picture image appears when the button is in its depressed state.

NOTE
To have any type of graphic appear on a control, the control's `Style` property must be set to graphical.

Objects with a DownPicture Property

CheckBox

CommandButton

OptionButton

Syntax

```
object.DownPicture = value1
```

or

```
value2 = object.DownPicture
```

- *object* — A reference to a control with a `DownPicture` property.
- *value1* — A reference to the picture object that will be the control's down picture.
- *value2* — The variable that will receive a reference to the control's down picture.

Example

In this example, the program loads and sets images for a graphical pushbutton. The `btnCommand1` object is a CommandButton control that the programmer added to the application's form at design time.

```
btnCommand1.Picture = LoadPicture("but1.bmp")
btnCommand1.DownPicture = LoadPicture("but1dn.bmp")
btnCommand1.DisabledPicture = LoadPicture("but1d.bmp")
```

 CROSS-REFERENCE
See also CommandButton, OptionButton, CheckBox, Picture, and DisabledPicture.

Drag

Method

The `Drag` method begins, ends, or cancels a drag operation on behalf of a control.

Objects with a Drag Method

Animation

CheckBox

ComboBox

CommandButton

CoolBar

DirListBox

DriveListBox

FileListBox

Frame

HScrollBar

Image

Label

ListBox

ListView

OLE Container

OptionButton

PictureBox

ProgressBar

RichTextBox

Slider

StatusBar

TabStrip

TextBox

Toolbar

TreeView

UpDown

VScrollBar

Syntax

`object.Drag command`

- *object* — A reference to an object with a `Drag` method.
- *command* (★) — The value `vbBeginDrag`, `vbCancel`, or `vbEndDrag`. If this argument is missing, `vbBeginDrag` is the default.

(★) = Optional argument

Example

The following program gives you a chance to experiment with drag-and-drop operations, as well as to see how the basic drag-and-drop operations work. When you run the program, you see the window shown in Figure D-21. Click the Command1 button, and a message box appears, proving that the button responds to its clicks. Next, click the Enable Dragging button. When you do, you'll be able to reposition the Command1 button by dragging it to a new location. If you drag the Command1 button on top of the Enable Dragging button (which now has the caption "Disable Dragging"), the mouse cursor changes to indicate that you cannot drop the Command1 button there (Figure D-22). After dragging the Command1 button to its new location (Figure D-23), click the Disable Dragging button to restore the Command1 button to working order. Then, when you click the Command1 button, it again shows its message box.

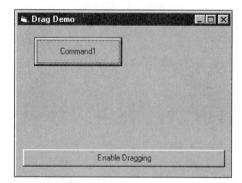

Figure D-21 This is the Drag Demo application when you first run it.

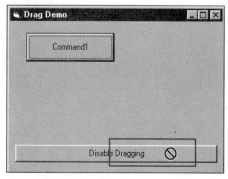

Figure D-22 The mouse cursor changes when over a control that cannot act as a drag-and-drop target.

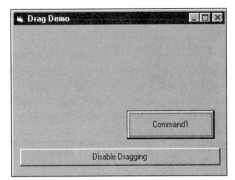

Figure D-23 Here's the Drag Demo application after the user has repositioned the Command1 button.

```
VERSION 5.00
Begin VB.Form Form1
   Caption         =    "Drag Demo"
   ClientHeight    =    3195
   ClientLeft      =    60
   ClientTop       =    345
   ClientWidth     =    4680
   LinkTopic       =    "Form1"
   ScaleHeight     =    3195
   ScaleWidth      =    4680
   StartUpPosition =    3  'Windows Default
   Begin VB.CommandButton btnEnableDrag
      Caption      =    "Enable Dragging"
      Height       =    375
      Left         =    120
      TabIndex     =    1
      Top          =    2640
      Width        =    4455
   End
   Begin VB.CommandButton Command1
      Caption      =    "Command1"
      Height       =    615
      Left         =    360
      TabIndex     =    0
      Top          =    240
      Width        =    1935
   End
End
Attribute VB_Name = "Form1"
Attribute VB_GlobalNameSpace = False
```

```
Attribute VB_Creatable = False
Attribute VB_PredeclaredId = True
Attribute VB_Exposed = False
Dim blnDrag As Boolean
Dim xClickPos, yClickPos

Private Sub btnEnableDrag_Click()
    If blnDrag = False Then
        blnDrag = True
        btnEnableDrag.Caption = "Disable Dragging"
    Else
        blnDrag = False
        btnEnableDrag.Caption = "Enable Dragging"
    End If
End Sub

Private Sub btnEnableDrag_DragOver(Source As Control, _
        X As Single, Y As Single, State As Integer)
    If State = 0 Then
        Source.MousePointer = 12
    ElseIf State = 1 Then
        Source.MousePointer = 0
    End If
End Sub

Private Sub Command1_Click()
    If blnDrag = False Then MsgBox "Button Clicked"
End Sub

Private Sub Command1_MouseDown (Button As Integer, _
        Shift As Integer, X As Single, Y As Single)
    If blnDrag Then
        xClickPos = X
        yClickPos = Y
        Command1.Drag vbBeginDrag
    End If
End Sub

Private Sub Form_DragDrop _
        (Source As Control, X As Single, Y As Single)
    Source.Left = X - xClickPos
    Source.Top = Y - yClickPos
End Sub
```

```
Private Sub Form_Load()
    blnDrag = False
End Sub
```

CROSS-REFERENCE
For more information, see DragDrop, DragOver, DragIcon, DragMode, and MousePointer.

DragDrop

Event

Visual Basic sends a control a `DragDrop` event when the user ends a drag-and-drop operation over the control. This event enables an application to perform whatever tasks are needed to complete the drag-and-drop operation. For example, if the user is dragging a control to a new location, the program would update the control's position in the `DragDrop` event procedure.

Objects That Receive DragDrop Events

Animation

CheckBox

ComboBox

CommandButton

CoolBar

DirListBox

DriveListBox

FileListBox

Form

Frame

HScrollBar

Image

Label

ListBox

ListView

MDIForm

OLE Container

OptionButton

PictureBox

ProgressBar

PropertyPage

RichTextBox

Slider

StatusBar

TabStrip

TextBox

TreeView

UpDown

UserControl

VScrollBar

Example 1

A program can respond to a `DragDrop` event by implementing the target object's `DragDrop` event procedure. The following code segment shows how a Form object defines a `DragDrop` event procedure. The event procedure's three arguments are the control that was dropped and the X and Y position of the mouse pointer at the time of the drop.

```
Private Sub frmForm_DragDrop _
   (Source As Control, X As Single, Y As Single)
      ' Respond to DragDrop event here.
End Sub
```

Example 2

The drag-and-drop target can be a member of a control array. In this case, the `DragDrop` event procedure receives an extra argument, which is the index of the control in the array, as follows:

```
Private Sub btnCommand1_DragDrop (Index as Integer, _
   Source As Control, X As Single, Y As Single)
      ' Respond to DragDrop event here.
End Sub
```

CROSS-REFERENCE

For more information, see Drag, DragOver, DragIcon, DragMode, and MousePointer.

DragIcon

Property

The DragIcon property represents the mouse-pointer image that appears during a drag-and-drop operation. This image must be an icon and not a bitmap or some other type of image.

Objects with a DragIcon Property

CheckBox

ComboBox

CommandButton

CoolBar

DirListBox

DriveListBox

FileListBox

Frame

HScrollBar

Image

Label

ListBox

ListView

OLE Container

OptionButton

PictureBox

ProgressBar

RichTextBox

Slider

StatusBar

TabStrip

TextBox

Toolbar

TreeView

UpDown

VScrollBar

Syntax

```
object.DragIcon = value1
```

or

```
value2 = object.DragIcon
```

- *object* — A reference to an object with a `DragIcon` property.
- *value1* — A reference to the new icon.
- *value2* — The variable that will receive a reference to the icon.

Example

Typically, a program sets a control's drag icon in the `MouseDown` event procedure, like this:

```
Private Sub Command1_MouseDown _
   (Button As Integer, Shift As Integer, _
      X As Single, Y As Single)
    Command1.DragIcon = LoadPicture("MyIcon.ico")
    Command1.Drag
End Sub
```

 CROSS-REFERENCE
For more information, see Drag, DragOver, DragDrop, DragMode, and MousePointer.

DragMode

Property

The `DragMode` property represents whether the control is set for manual or automatic drag-and-drop. A control with manual drag-and-drop must start a drag-and-drop operation by calling its `Drag` method. Automatic drag-and-drop, on the other hand, begins as soon as the user clicks the control. The `DragMode` property can be set to `vbManual` or `vbAutomatic`. Keep in mind, however, that a control set to automatic drag-and-drop cannot respond to mouse clicks normally. For example, a CommandButton control won't generate `Click` events when set to automatic drag-and-drop.

Objects with a DragMode Property

CheckBox

ComboBox

CommandButton

CoolBar

DirListBox

DriveListBox

FileListBox

Frame

HScrollBar

Image

Label

ListBox

ListView

OLE Container

OptionButton

PictureBox

ProgressBar

RichTextBox

Slider

StatusBar

TabStrip

TextBox

Toolbar

TreeView

UpDown

VScrollBar

Syntax

`object.DragMode = value1`

or

`value2 = object.DragMode`

- *object* — A reference to an object with a `DragMode` property.
- *value1* — The value `vbManual` or `vbAutomatic`.
- *value2* — The variable that will receive the property's current setting.

Example

The following line sets a control's `DragMode` property when the program is first run. The `btnCommand1` object is a CommandButton control that the programmer added to the form at design time.

```
Private Sub Form_Load()
    btnCommand1.DragMode = vbAutomatic
End Sub
```

 CROSS-REFERENCE
For more information, see Drag, DragOver, DragDrop, and DragIcon.

DragOver

Event

Visual Basic sends a control a `DragOver` event when the user drags a drag-and-drop source over the control. This event enables an application to perform whatever tasks are needed to respond to this portion of a drag-and-drop operation. For example, the program may want to change the mouse pointer depending upon whether the target control (the control over which the user is dragging the drag-and-drop source) can be the drop target.

Objects That Receive DragOver Events

Animation

CheckBox

ComboBox

CommandButton

CoolBar

DirListBox

DriveListBox

FileListBox

Form

Frame

HScrollBar

Image

Label

ListBox

ListView

MDIForm

OLE Container

OptionButton

PictureBox

ProgressBar

PropertyPage

RichTextBox

Slider

StatusBar

TabStrip

TextBox

TreeView

UpDown

UserControl

VScrollBar

Example 1

A program can respond to a DragOver event by implementing the target object's DragOver event procedure. The following code segment shows how a Form object defines a DragOver event procedure. The event procedure's four arguments are the control that's being dragged, the X and Y positions of the mouse pointer at the time of the event, and the state of the event. State is 0 when the drag operation enters the object, 1 when the drag operation leaves the object, and 2 when the drag operation moves within the object.

```
Private Sub frmForm_DragOver(Source As Control, _
    X As Single, Y As Single, State As Integer)
    ' Respond to DragOver event here.
End Sub
```

Example 2

The drag-over target can be a member of a control array. In this case, the DragOver event procedure receives an extra argument, which is the index of the control in the array, as follows:

```
Private Sub btnCommand1_DragOver(Index as Integer, _
    Source As Control, X As Single, Y As Single, _
    State As Integer)
    ' Respond to DragOver event here.
End Sub
```

CROSS-REFERENCE
For more information, see Drag, DragDrop, DragIcon, DragMode, and MousePointer.

Draw

Method

The Draw method draws images stored in an ImageList control. The images can be drawn in various styles.

Objects with a Draw Method

ListImage

Syntax

```
ListImage.Draw hdc, x, y, operation
```

- *ListImage* — A reference to a ListImage object.
- *hdc* — A reference to the source object's device context.
- *x* (*) — The horizontal coordinate at which to draw the image.
- *y* (*) — The vertical coordinate at which to draw the image.
- *operation* (*) — The drawing style to use, which can be imlNormal, imlTransparent, imlSelected, or imlFocus.

(*) = Optional argument

Example

The following lines load an ImageList control with images and then display those images in the form's window. The ilsImageList1 object is an ImageList control the programmer added to the application's form at design time.

```
ilsImageList1.ListImages.Add , , _
    LoadPicture("butn1.bmp")
ilsImageList1.ListImages.Add , , _
    LoadPicture("butn2.bmp")
ilsImageList1.ListImages.Add , , _
    LoadPicture("butn3.bmp")

ilsImageList1.ListImages(1).Draw Form1.hDC, _
    100, 100, imlNormal
```

```
ilsImageList1.ListImages(2).Draw Form1.hDC, _
    1100, 100, imlNormal
ilsImageList1.ListImages(3).Draw Form1.hDC, _
    2100, 100, imlNormal
```

CROSS-REFERENCE
For more information, see ImageList, ListImage, and ListImages.

DrawMode

Property

The DrawMode property represents the way the source and destination pixels of a drawing operation are combined. The DrawMode property can be one of the values shown in Table D-12.

Table D-12 Values for the DrawMode Property

Value	Description
vbBlackness	Output is drawn all black.
vbCopyPen	Output is the ForeColor color.
vbInvert	Output is the inversion of the destination pixels.
vbMaskNotPen	Output is the colors shared by the inverted pen and the destination pixels.
vbMaskPen	Output is the colors shared by the pen and the destination pixels.
vbMaskPenNot	Output is the colors shared by the pen and the inverted destination pixels.
vbMergeNotPen	Output combines the inverted pen with the destination pixels.
vbMergePen	Output combines the pen and destination pixels.
vbMergePenNot	Output combines the pen with the inverted destination pixels.
vbNop	Output is unchanged.
vbNotCopyPen	Output is the inverted ForeColor color.
vbNotMaskPen	Output is the inverted colors shared by the pen and the destination pixels.
vbNotMergePen	Output combines the pen and destination pixels and inverts the result.
vbNotXorPen	Output is the colors that appear in either the pen or the destination pixel, but not both, and then inverted.
vbWhiteness	Output is all white.
vbXorPen	Output is the colors that appear in either the pen or the destination pixel, but not both.

Objects with a DrawMode Property
Form
Line
PictureBox
Printer
PropertyPage
Shape
UserControl

Syntax

```
object.DrawMode = value1
```

or

```
value2 = object.DrawMode
```

- *object*—A reference to a control with a `DrawMode` property.
- *value1*—The new draw-mode setting.
- *value2*—The variable that will receive the property's current setting.

Example

In this example, the program sets the drawing mode of a form so that Visual Basic draws graphics output with the color specified by the form's `ForeColor` property.

```
Private Sub Form_Load()
    DrawMode = vbCopyPen
End Sub
```

DrawStyle

Property

The `DrawStyle` property represents the style Visual Basic uses to draw lines. The property can be set to `vbDash`, `vbDashDot`, `vbDashDotDot`, `vbDot`, `vbInsideSolid`, `vbInvisible`, or `vbSolid`.

 NOTE
Dashed and dotted lines can be drawn only when the object's `DrawWidth` property is set to 1.

Objects with a DrawStyle Property

Form
PictureBox
Printer
PropertyPage
UserControl

Syntax

object`.DrawStyle = `*value1*

or

value2` = object.DrawStyle`

- *object* — A reference to a control with a `DrawStyle` property.
- *value1* — The new draw-style setting.
- *value2* — The variable that will receive the property's current setting.

Example

In this example, the program sets the drawing mode of a form so that Visual Basic draws lines with single dashes and dots.

```
Private Sub Form_Load()
    DrawStyle = vbDashDot
End Sub
```

CROSS-REFERENCE
See also DrawWidth.

DrawWidth

Property

The `DrawWidth` property represents the width Visual Basic uses to draw lines. This property can be set to any value from 1 to 32,767.

Objects with a DrawWidth Property

Form
PictureBox

Printer

PropertyPage

UserControl

Syntax

```
object.DrawWidth = value1
```

or

```
value2 = object.DrawWidth
```

- *object* — A reference to a control with a `DrawWidth` property.
- *value1* — The new line-width setting.
- *value2* — The variable that will receive the property's current setting.

Example

In this example, the program sets the line-drawing width of a form so that Visual Basic draws lines that are four pixels wide.

```
Private Sub Form_Load()
    DrawWidth = 4
End Sub
```

 CROSS-REFERENCE
See also DrawStyle.

Drive

Object

The Drive object represents the attributes of a disk drive.

Properties

The Drive object has 12 properties, which are listed in Table D-13. For more information on using a property shown in the following table, look up the individual property's entry, provided alphabetically in this book.

Table D-13 Properties of the Drive Object

Property	Description
AvailableSpace	Represents the amount of available space on the drive.
DriveLetter	Represents the drive letter associated with the drive.
DriveType	Represents the type of the drive.
FileSystem	Represents the type of file system associated with the drive.
FreeSpace	Represents the amount of free space on the drive.
IsReady	Represents whether the drive is ready to access its media.
Path	Represents the drive's path.
RootFolder	Represents a Folder object that's associated with the drive's root folder.
SerialNumber	Represents the drive's volume serial number.
ShareName	Represents the drive's network share name.
TotalSize	Represents the total amount of space on the drive.
VolumeName	Represents the drive's volume name.

Methods

The Drive object has no methods.

Events

The Drive object does not respond to events.

Example

In this example, the program creates a FileSystemObject and uses it to get a Drive object for drive C:. A message box then displays the total amount of space on the drive.

```
Dim fileSystem
Dim drv

Set fileSystem = CreateObject("Scripting.FileSystemObject")
Set drv = fileSystem.GetDrive("c")
MsgBox drv.TotalSize
```

CROSS-REFERENCE
See also FileSystemObject.

Drive — DriveListBox

Property

The Drive property represents the selected drive in a DriveListBox.

Syntax

```
DriveListBox.Drive = value1
```

or

```
value2 = DriveListBox.Drive
```

- *DriveListBox* — A reference to a DriveListBox control.
- *value1* — A string containing the drive identifier.
- *value2* — The variable that will receive the current drive identifier.

Example

In this example, the program starts by setting the current drive in a DriveListBox control to c:, after which the program displays the currently selected drive whenever the user changes it. For example, if the user changes the selected drive to d:, the message box displays the string "d:." The drvDrive1 object is a DriveListBox control that the programmer added to the application's form at design time.

```
Private Sub Form_Load()
    drvDrive1.Drive = "c"
End Sub

Private Sub drvDrive1_Change()
    MsgBox drvDrive1.Drive
End Sub
```

CROSS-REFERENCE
See also DirListBox and FileListBox.

Drive — File and Folder

Property

The Drive property represents the drive that's associated with a File or Folder object.

Syntax

```
value = object.Drive
```

- *object* — A reference to a File or Folder object.
- *value* — The variable that will receive the string containing the drive letter.

Example

In this example, the program opens a text file and then displays the associated drive in a message box. In this case, the message box displays the string "c:."

```
Dim fileSystem, file
Set fileSystem = _
    CreateObject("Scripting.FileSystemObject")
Set file = _
    fileSystem.GetFile("c:\testfile.txt")
MsgBox file.Drive
```

CROSS-REFERENCE
See also File and Folder.

DriveExists

Method

The `DriveExists` method represents whether a given drive exists.

Objects with a DriveExists Method

FileSystemObject

Syntax

```
value = FileSystemObject.DriveExists(drv)
```

- *drv* — The drive's letter or path.
- *FileSystemObject* — A reference to a FileSystemObject object.
- *value* — The variable that will receive the return value of `True` or `False`.

Example

The following lines create a FileSystemObject and use that object to determine whether the system has a drive D:. If drive D: exists, the message box displays the string "True"; otherwise, it displays the string "False."

```
Dim fileSystem
Dim exists As Boolean

Set fileSystem = CreateObject("Scripting.FileSystemObject")
exists = fileSystem.DriveExists("d")
MsgBox exists
```

CROSS-REFERENCE
For more information, see FileSystemObject.

DriveLetter

Property

The `DriveLetter` property represents the drive letter associated with a Drive object.

Objects with a DriveLetter Property

Drive

Syntax

`value = Drive.DriveLetter`

- *Drive* — A reference to a Drive object.
- *value* — The variable that will receive the driver letter.

Example

In this example, the program creates a FileSystemObject and uses the object to obtain a Drive object associated with the C: drive. A message box then displays the drive letter associated with the Drive object. In this case, it's obvious that the drive letter is C.

```
Dim fileSystem
Dim drv
```

```
Set fileSystem = CreateObject("Scripting.FileSystemObject")
Set drv = fileSystem.GetDrive("c")
MsgBox drv.DriveLetter
```

CROSS-REFERENCE
See also Drive and FileSystemObject.

DriveListBox

Control

A DriveListBox is a control that a program's user can use to select a drive. Figure D-24 shows a DriveListBox control in a form. The figure shows the list box's drop-down portion (which the user displays by clicking the control's arrow button) from which the user can select a drive. The DriveListBox control is available on Visual Basic's standard toolbox.

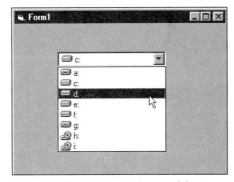

Figure D-24 A DriveListBox enables a user to select a drive.

Properties

The DriveListBox control has 38 properties, which are listed as follows. Because many Visual Basic controls have similar properties, the following list does not include the properties' descriptions. For information on using a property, look up the individual property's entry, provided alphabetically in this book.

```
Appearance
BackColor
CausesValidation
```

```
Container
DragIcon
DragMode
Drive
Enabled
Font
FontBold
FontItalic
FontName
FontSize
FontStrikethru
FontUnderline
ForeColor
Height
HelpContextID
hWnd
Index
Left
List
ListCount
ListIndex
MouseIcon
MousePointer
Name
OLEDropMode
Parent
TabIndex
TabStop
Tag
ToolTipText
Top
TopIndex
Visible
WhatsThisHelpID
Width
```

Methods

The DriveListBox control has seven methods, which are listed below. Because many Visual Basic controls have similar methods, the following list does not include the methods' descriptions. For information on using a method, look up the individual method's entry, provided alphabetically in this book.

```
Drag
Move
OLEDrag
Refresh
SetFocus
ShowWhatsThis
ZOrder
```

Events

The DriveListBox control responds to 16 events, which are listed below. Because many Visual Basic controls respond to similar events, the following list does not include the events' descriptions. For information on using an event, look up the individual event's entry, provided alphabetically in this book.

```
Change
DragDrop
DragOver
GotFocus
KeyDown
KeyPress
KeyUp
LostFocus
OLECompleteDrag
OLEDragDrop
OLEDragOver
OLEGiveFeedback
OLESetData
OLEStartDrag
Scroll
Validate
```

The DriveListBox control's most commonly used event is Change, which the control generates when the user or the program changes the currently selected drive. A program responds to the control's Change event in the Change event procedure. A DriveListBox called drvDrive1 will have a Change event procedure called drvDrive11_Change, which is where the program should handle the event. In the following example, when the user selects a drive, a message box displays the selected drive:

```
Private Sub drvDrive1_Change()
    MsgBox drvDrive1.Drive
End Sub
```

DriverName

Property

The `DriverName` property represents the name of the printer driver associated with the Printer object. An example of a driver name is "HPPCL5MS."

Objects with a DriverName Property

Printer

Syntax

```
value = Printer.DriverName
```

- *Printer*—A reference to the Printer object.
- *value*—The variable that will receive the printer driver name.

Example

In this example, a message box displays the current printer driver name. Note that the Printer object is a global Visual Basic object that you don't need to create in your program.

```
MsgBox Printer.DriverName
```

 CROSS-REFERENCE
See also Printer and DeviceName.

Drives

Collection

A Drives collection holds a list of Drive objects that represent all the available drives on the system.

Properties

A Drives collection has one property, called `Count`, which represents the number of items in the collection.

Methods

A Drives collection has one method, `Item`, which returns a Drive object from the Drives collection.

CROSS-REFERENCE

See also Drives (property).

Drives

Property

The `Drives` property represents a Drives collection that contains Drive objects for each of the drives on the system. You can use the Drives collection to access any available drive.

Objects with a Drives Property

FileSystemObject

Syntax

```
value = FileSystemObject.Drives
```

- *FileSystemObject* — A reference to a FileSystemObject object.
- *value* — The variable that will receive the Drives collection.

Example

In this example, the program creates a FileSystemObject and uses the object to access all the drives on the system. A message box displays each drive letter, one by one.

```
Dim fileSystem
Dim drv

Set fileSystem = CreateObject("Scripting.FileSystemObject")
For Each drv In fileSystem.Drives
    MsgBox drv.driveletter
Next
```

CROSS-REFERENCE

See also FileSystemObject and Drives (collection).

DriveType

Property

The DriveType property represents the type of drive that's associated with a Drive object. The property can be one of the values shown in Table D-14.

Table D-14 Values of the DriveType Property

Value	Description
0	Unknown drive
1	Removable drive
2	Fixed drive
3	Network drive
4	CD-ROM drive
5	RAM disk

Objects with a DriveType Property

Drive

Syntax

```
value = Drive.DriveType
```

- *Drive* — A reference to a Drive object.
- *value* — The variable that will receive the driver type.

Example

In this example, the program creates a FileSystemObject and uses the object to obtain a Drive object associated with the C: drive. A message box then displays the drive type associated with the Drive object.

```
Dim fileSystem
Dim drv

Set fileSystem = CreateObject("Scripting.FileSystemObject")
Set drv = fileSystem.GetDrive("c")
MsgBox drv.DriveType
```

CROSS-REFERENCE
See also Drive and FileSystemObject.

DropDown

Event

Visual Basic sends a ComboBox control a DropDown event right before the ComboBox's list is about to be displayed.

Objects That Receive DropDown Events

ComboBox

Example

A program can respond to a DropDown event by implementing a ComboBox's DropDown event procedure. The following code segment shows how a ComboBox object defines a DropDown event procedure. The cboCombo1 object is a ComboBox control that the programmer added to the form at design time.

```
Private Sub cboCombo1_DropDown()
    ' Handle the DropDown event here.
End Sub
```

CROSS-REFERENCE
See also ComboBox.

DropHighlight

Property

The DropHighlight property represents the Node or ListItem object that is highlighted in response to the mouse cursor's passing over the object during a drag-and-drop operation.

Objects with a DropHighlight Property

ListView
TreeView

Syntax

object.DropHighlight = *value1*

or

value2 = *object*.DropHightlight

- *object* — A reference to a ListView or TreeView control.
- *value1* — A reference to the Node or ListItem object to be highlighted.
- *value2* — The variable that will receive Node or ListItem reference.

Example

The following line highlights the item returned by a ListView control's HitTest method. The lstListView1 object is a ListView control that the programmer added to the form at design time.

lstListView1.DropHighlight = lstListView1.HitTest(x, y)

CROSS-REFERENCE

See also ListView, ListItem, TreeView, and Node.

Duplex

Property

The Duplex property represents whether a Printer object prints on both sides of the paper. Table D-15 shows the possible values for this property. A printer will respond to this property only if the printer supports double-sided printing.

Table D-15 Values of the Duplex Property

Value	Description
vbPRDPHorizontal	Front and back of page printed with the same orientation.
vbPRDPSimplex	Normal, one-sided printing.
vbPRDPVertical	Front of page has the reverse orientation of the back.

Objects with a Duplex Property

Printer

Syntax

```
Printer.Duplex = value1
```

or

```
value2 = Printer.Duplex
```

- *Printer*—A reference to the Printer object.
- *value1*—A value from Table D-15.
- *value2*—The variable that will receive the property's current setting.

Example

In this example, the program sets the printer object to normal, one-side printing. Note `Printer` is a global Visual Basic object that you don't need to create in your programs.

```
Printer.Duplex = vbPRDPSimplex
```

CROSS-REFERENCE
See also Printer.

E

EditAtDesignTime

Property

The EditAtDesignTime property represents whether a UserControl can be activated by a developer at design time. If this property is set to True, an Edit command appears on the control's context menu, which appears when the control is right-clicked. Selecting the Edit command causes the control to behave just as it would at runtime.

Objects with an EditAtDesignTime Property

UserControl

Example

You can set the EditAtDesignTime property from the UserControl's Properties window, as shown in Figure E-1.

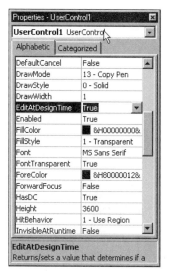

Figure E-1 The EditAtDesignTime property appears in a control's Properties window.

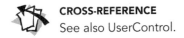

CROSS-REFERENCE
See also UserControl.

EditProperty

Event

Visual Basic sends a PropertyPage object an `EditProperty` event when the user opens a control's property page by clicking the ellipsis button on the Properties window.

Objects That Receive EditProperty Events

PropertyPage

Example

A program can respond to an `EditProperty` event by implementing the PropertyPage's `EditProperty` event procedure. The following code segment shows how a PropertyPage object defines an `EditProperty` event procedure. The procedure's single parameter, `PropertyName`, is the name of the property that's being edited.

```
Private Sub PropertyPage_EditProperty(PropertyName As String)
    ' Handle the EditProperty event here.
End Sub
```

CROSS-REFERENCE
See also PropertyPage.

EjectClick

Event

Visual Basic sends a Multimedia MCI control an `EjectClick` event when the user clicks the control's Eject button. By responding to this event, a program can stop the default action of the Eject button from occurring.

Objects with an EjectClick Event

Multimedia MCI

Example

A program can respond to a `EjectClick` event by implementing the Multimedia MCI control's `EjectClick` event procedure. By setting the procedure's `Cancel` parameter to `True`, the program can halt the Eject button's default action.

```
Private Sub mciMMControl1_EjectClick(Cancel As Integer)
    If something Then Cancel = True
End Sub
```

CROSS-REFERENCE

For more information, see EjectCompleted and Multimedia MCI.

EjectCompleted

Event

Visual Basic sends a Multimedia MCI control an `EjectCompleted` event after the Eject button's action has been executed. By responding to this event, a program can determine whether any errors occurred.

Objects with an EjectCompleted Event

Multimedia MCI

Example

A program can respond to a `EjectCompleted` event by implementing the Multimedia MCI control's `EjectCompleted` event procedure, which receives an error value as its single parameter.

```
Private Sub mciMMControl1_EjectCompleted(Errorcode As Long)
    ' Handle the event here.
End Sub
```

CROSS-REFERENCE

For more information, see EjectClick and Multimedia MCI.

EjectEnabled

Property

The EjectEnabled property represents the enabled status of a Multimedia MCI control's Eject button. This property is True when the control's Eject button is enabled and is False when the button is disabled.

Objects with an EjectEnabled Property

Multimedia MCI

Syntax

```
Multimedia.EjectEnabled = value1
```

or

```
value2 = Multimedia.EjectEnabled
```

- *Multimedia*—A reference to a Multimedia MCI control.
- *value1*—The value True or False.
- *value2*—The variable that will receive the value returned by the property.

Example

The following lines show how to get and set the enabled status of a Multimedia control's Eject button.

```
Dim enable
enable = mciMMControl1.EjectEnabled
mciMMControl1.EjectEnabled = True
```

 CROSS-REFERENCE
See also Multimedia MCI.

EjectGotFocus

Event

Visual Basic sends a Multimedia MCI control an EjectGotFocus event when the control's Eject button receives the focus.

Objects with an EjectGotFocus Event

Multimedia MCI

Example

A program can respond to an `EjectGotFocus` event by implementing the Multimedia MCI control's `EjectGotFocus` event procedure, which receives no parameters, as shown here.

```
Private Sub mciMMControl1_EjectGotFocus()
    ' Handle the EjectGotFocus event here.
End Sub
```

 CROSS-REFERENCE

For more information, see EjectLostFocus and Multimedia MCI.

EjectLostFocus

Event

Visual Basic sends a Multimedia MCI control an `EjectLostFocus` event when the control's Eject button loses the focus.

Objects with an EjectLostFocus Event

Multimedia MCI

Example

A program can respond to an `EjectLostFocus` event by implementing the Multimedia MCI control's `EjectLostFocus` event procedure, which receives no parameters, as shown here.

```
Private Sub mciMMControl1_EjectLostFocus()
    ' Handle the event here.
End Sub
```

 CROSS-REFERENCE

For more information, see EjectGotFocus and Multimedia MCI.

EjectVisible

Property

The `EjectVisible` property represents the visible status of a Multimedia MCI control's Eject button. This property is `True` when the control's Eject button is visible and is `False` when the button is not visible.

Objects with an EjectVisible Property
Multimedia MCI

Syntax

`Multimedia.EjectVisible = value1`

or

`value2 = Multimedia.EjectVisible`

- *Multimedia* — A reference to a Multimedia MCI control.
- *value1* — The value `True` or `False`.
- *value2* — The variable that will receive the value returned by the property.

Example
The following lines show how to get and set the visible status of a Multimedia control's Eject button.

```
Dim visible
visible = mciMMControl1.EjectVisible
mciMMControl1.EjectVisible = True
```

 CROSS-REFERENCE
See also Multimedia MCI.

Else

Keyword

The `Else` keyword is used as part of the `If/Then` statement, which enables a program to control program execution based on the result of a comparison of values. The `Else` portion of an `If/Then` statement executes when other conditionals in the `If/Then` statement evaluate to `False`. For example, in the following case, a message box with the message "Else portion executed" will appear.

```
Dim x As Integer
x = 10
If x = 5 Then
    MsgBox "First condition met."
Else
    MsgBox "Else portion executed."
End If
```

 CROSS-REFERENCE
For more information, see If.

EmbossHighlight

Property

The `EmbossHighlight` property represents the image-highlight color of a CoolBar control. For this property to have an effect, the control's `EmbossPicture` property must be set to `True`. The `EmbossHighlight` property can be set to a color determined by the `RGB` or `QBColor` functions or by a Visual Basic color constant.

Objects with an EmbossHighlight Property

CoolBar

Syntax

`CoolBar.EmbossHighlight = value1`

or

`value2 = CoolBar.EmbossHighlight`

- *CoolBar*—A reference to a CoolBar control.
- *value1*—The image-highlight color.
- *value2*—The variable that will receive the current image-highlight color.

Example

In this example, the program sets a CoolBar control's image-highlight color to blue. The `CoolBar1` object is a CoolBar control that the programmer added to the application's form at design time.

```
CoolBar1.EmbossHighlight = RGB(0, 0, 255)
```

 CROSS-REFERENCE
See also CoolBar, EmbossPicture, and EmbossShadow.

EmbossPicture

Property

The `EmbossPicture` property represents whether Visual Basic displays an image on a CoolBar control in full color or embossed using the two colors defined by the `EmbossHighlight` and `EmbossShadow` properties. This property can be set to `True` or `False`.

Objects with an EmbossPicture Property

CoolBar

Syntax

```
CoolBar.EmbossPicture = value1
```

or

```
value2 = CoolBar.EmbossPicture
```

- *CoolBar* — A reference to a CoolBar control.
- *value1* — The value `True` or `False`.
- *value2* — The variable that will receive the current property setting.

Example

In this example, the program sets a CoolBar control's image to be displayed as embossed. The `CoolBar1` object is a CoolBar control that the programmer added to the application's form at design time.

```
CoolBar1.EmbossPicture = True
```

CROSS-REFERENCE
See also CoolBar, EmbossHighlight, and EmbossShadow.

EmbossShadow

Property

The `EmbossShadow` property represents the image-shadow color of a CoolBar control. For this property to have an effect, the control's `EmbossPicture` property must be set to `True`. The `EmbossShadow` property can be set to a color determined by the `RGB` or `QBColor` functions or by a Visual Basic color constant.

Objects with an EmbossShadow Property

CoolBar

Syntax

```
CoolBar.EmbossShadow = value1
```

or

```
value2 = CoolBar.EmbossShadow
```

- *CoolBar* — A reference to a CoolBar control.
- *value1* — The image-shadow color.
- *value2* — The variable that will receive the current image-shadow color.

Example

In this example, the program sets a CoolBar control's image-shadow color to dark blue. The `CoolBar1` object is a CoolBar control that the programmer added to the application's form at design time.

```
CoolBar1.EmbossShadow = RGB(0, 0, 64)
```

CROSS-REFERENCE
See also CoolBar, EmbossPicture, and EmbossHighlight.

Empty

Keyword

The Empty keyword is used to determine whether or not a variable has been initialized. That is, a variable that has not yet been set to a specific value will have Empty as its default value. For example, the following lines display a message box that indicates that the var1 variable has not yet been initialized.

```
Dim var1
If var1 = Empty Then MsgBox "var1 uninitialized"
```

Enabled

Property

The Enabled property represents whether a control can be manipulated by the user. For example, an enabled button will generate Click events when clicked by the user, but a disabled button will not respond to the user's clicks. Visual Basic grays out disabled controls.

Objects with an Enabled Property

Animation
Button
CheckBox
ComboBox
CommandButton
CoolBar
DirListBox
DriveListBox
FileListBox
Form
Frame
HScrollBar
Image
Label
ListBox
ListView

MDIForm

Menu

Multimedia MCI

OLE Container

OptionButton

Panel

PictureBox

RichTextBox

Slider

StatusBar

TabStrip

TextBox

Timer

Toolbar

TreeView

UpDown

UserControl

VScrollBar

Syntax

```
object.Enabled = value1
```

or

```
value2 = object.Enabled
```

- *object* — A reference to an object with an `Enabled` property.
- *value1* — The value `True` or `False`.
- *value2* — The variable that will receive the property's current setting.

Example

The following sample program enables and disables controls when you click a button. When you run the program, you see the window shown in Figure E-2. At this point, all the controls in the window are enabled. Click the Disable Controls button, and the program disables the upper four controls, as shown in Figure E-3, as well as changes the Disable Controls button's caption to "Enable Controls." If you click the button again, the program re-enables all the controls.

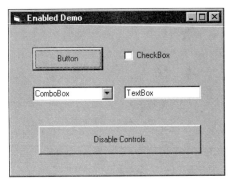

Figure E-2 At startup, all the application's controls are enabled.

Figure E-3 Here's the application with the controls disabled.

```
VERSION 5.00
Begin VB.Form Form1
    Caption         =   " Enabled Demo"
    ClientHeight    =   3195
    ClientLeft      =   60
    ClientTop       =   345
    ClientWidth     =   4680
    LinkTopic       =   "Form1"
    ScaleHeight     =   3195
    ScaleWidth      =   4680
    StartUpPosition =   3  'Windows Default
    Begin VB.CommandButton btnEnable
        Caption     =   "Disable Controls"
        Height      =   615
        Left        =   600
        TabIndex    =   4
        Top         =   2160
```

```
      Width            =    3615
   End
   Begin VB.TextBox txtText1
      Height           =    285
      Left             =    2520
      TabIndex         =    3
      Text             =    "TextBox"
      Top              =    1320
      Width            =    1695
   End
   Begin VB.ComboBox cboCombo1
      Height           =    315
      Left             =    480
      TabIndex         =    2
      Text             =    "ComboBox"
      Top              =    1320
      Width            =    1815
   End
   Begin VB.CheckBox chkCheck1
      Caption          =    "CheckBox"
      Height           =    375
      Left             =    2520
      TabIndex         =    1
      Top              =    480
      Width            =    1575
   End
   Begin VB.CommandButton btnCommand1
      Caption          =    "Button"
      Height           =    495
      Left             =    480
      TabIndex         =    0
      Top              =    480
      Width            =    1575
   End
End
Attribute VB_Name = "Form1"
Attribute VB_GlobalNameSpace = False
Attribute VB_Creatable = False
Attribute VB_PredeclaredId = True
Attribute VB_Exposed = False

Private Sub btnEnable_Click()
    If btnCommand1.Enabled = True Then
        btnCommand1.Enabled = False
```

d
e
f

```
                chkCheck1.Enabled = False
                cboCombo1.Enabled = False
                txtText1.Enabled = False
                btnEnable.Caption = "Enable Controls"
            Else
                btnCommand1.Enabled = True
                chkCheck1.Enabled = True
                cboCombo1.Enabled = True
                txtText1.Enabled = True
                btnEnable.Caption = "Disable Controls"
            End If
        End Sub
```

End

Statement

The End statement immediately closes open files and ends program execution.

Syntax

```
End
```

Example

In this example, the Proc1 procedure ends program execution if var1 is equal to 25.

```
Private Sub Proc1()
    If var1 = 25 Then End
End Sub
```

EndDoc

Method

The EndDoc method ends the document currently being printed by the Printer object.

Objects with an EndDoc Method

Printer

Syntax

```
Printer.EndDoc
```

- *Printer*— A reference to the Printer object.

Example

The following lines print a document with a single line of text.

```
Printer.CurrentX = 100
Printer.CurrentY = 100
Printer.Print " This is a test message."
Printer.NewPage
Printer.EndDoc
```

 CROSS-REFERENCE
For more information, see Printer.

End Enum

Statement

The `End Enum` statement immediately ends an enumeration definition.

Syntax

```
End Enum
```

Example

In this example, the symbols `one`, `two`, `three`, and `five` are assigned the values 1, 2, 3, and 5, respectively. Notice how the `End Enum` statement ends the enumeration.

```
Private Enum digits
    one = 1
    two = 2
    three = 3
    five = 5
End Enum
```

 CROSS-REFERENCE
See also Enum.

End Function

Concept

A function is a special type of procedure that returns a value to the caller. By writing functions, you can process various types of data and return the results. For example, the following function sums two values and returns the result. The first line is the line that calls the function, which means the variable result will receive the value 10.

```
result = SumValues(6, 4)

Function SumValues(val1 As Integer, val2 As Integer)
    SumValues = val1 + val2
End Function
```

CROSS-REFERENCE
See also Event Procedure and Procedure.

End Function

Statement

The End Function statement marks the end of a Visual Basic function.

Syntax

```
End Function
```

Example

The following lines define a function that returns the larger of two integers. Note how the End Function statement ends the function.

```
Private Function Max(var1 As Integer, var2 As Integer) _
    As Integer
    If var1 > var2 Then
        Max = var1
    Else
        Max = var2
    End If
End Function
```

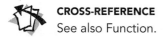

CROSS-REFERENCE
See also Function.

End If
Statement

The `End If` statement marks the end of a multiple line `If/Then` block. If an `If/Then` statement comprises only a single line, you don't need to include the `End If` statement.

Syntax

```
End If
```

Example

The following lines show how to write a multiple-line `If/Then` block, which must end with the `End If` statement.

```
If var1 > var2 Then
    Max = var1
Else
    Max = var2
End If
```

CROSS-REFERENCE
See also If.

End Property
Statement

The `End Property` statement marks the end of `Property Let`, `Property Set`, or `Property Get` procedure. You use these procedures when defining properties for a UserControl control.

Syntax

```
End Property
```

Example

The following lines show a `Property Get` procedure for a UserControl control. Note how the procedure ends with the `End Property` statement.

```
Public Property Get TextColor() As Integer
    TextColor = UserControl.TextColor
End Property
```

 CROSS-REFERENCE
See also UserControl, Property Let, Property Set, and Property Get.

End Select

Statement

The `End Select` statement marks the end of `Select Case` block.

Syntax

```
End Select
```

Example

The following lines show how to write a `Select Case` block, which must end with an `End Select` statement.

```
Select Case var1
    Case 0
        MsgBox "var1 = 0"
    Case 1
        MsgBox "var1 = 1"
    Case 2
        MsgBox "var1 = 2"
End Select
```

 CROSS-REFERENCE
See also Select Case.

End Sub

Statement

The End Sub statement marks the end of a Visual Basic procedure (also called a subroutine).

Syntax

```
End Sub
```

Example

The following lines define a procedure that displays the values of two integers in a message box. Note how the End Sub statement ends the procedure.

```
Private Sub ShowVals(var1 As Integer, var2 As Integer)
    MsgBox var1 & " - " & var2
End Sub
```

CROSS-REFERENCE
See also Procedure.

End Type

Statement

The End Type statement marks the end of a user-defined data type.

Syntax

```
End Type
```

Example

The following lines declare a user-defined data type that holds the coordinates of a point. Note how the End Type statement ends the definition.

```
Private Type Point
    X As Integer
    Y As Integer
End Type
```

CROSS-REFERENCE
See also Type.

End With

Statement

The End With statement marks the end of a With block.

Syntax

```
End With
```

Example

The following lines show how to use a With statement to access more easily the properties of a CommandButton control. Note how the End With statement ends the With block. The btnCommand1 object is a CommandButton control that the programmer added to the form at design time.

```
With btnCommand1
    .Caption = "Click Me"
    .Cancel = False
    .Left = 1000
    .Top = 1000
End With
```

CROSS-REFERENCE
See also With.

EnsureVisible

Method

The EnsureVisible method guarantees that a given Node or ListItem object is visible in its respective TreeView or ListView control.

Objects with an EnsureVisible Method

ListItem

Node

Syntax

`object.EnsureVisible`

- *object* — A reference to a ListItem or Node object.

Example

The following program demonstrates how the `EnsureVisible` method works. When you first run the program, you see the window shown in Figure E-4. As you can see, the TreeView control is in its fully collapsed state. The TreeView contains a node named Root and a set of child nodes named Child1, Child2, and so on up to Child9. To display any node, type its name into the text box, and click the Show Item button. If the node you requested exists, the TreeView control expands as needed to display the chosen node (Figure E-5). If the node doesn't exist, a message box warns you of the error.

 NOTE

The node names are case sensitive.

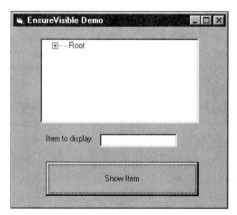

Figure E-4 Here's the application before the program expands the TreeView control.

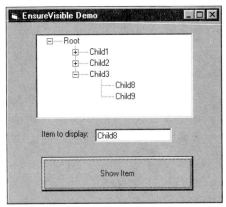

Figure E-5 Here's the application after the user requests to see the Child8 node.

```
VERSION 5.00
Object = "{6B7E6392-850A-101B-AFC0-4210102A8DA7} _
    #2.0#0"; "MSCOMCTL.OCX"
Begin VB.Form Form1
   Caption         =   "EnsureVisible Demo"
   ClientHeight    =   3825
   ClientLeft      =   60
   ClientTop       =   345
   ClientWidth     =   4680
   LinkTopic       =   "Form1"
   ScaleHeight     =   3825
   ScaleWidth      =   4680
   StartUpPosition =   3   'Windows Default
   Begin VB.TextBox txtItemKey
      Height       =   285
      Left         =   1920
      TabIndex     =   3
      Top          =   2280
      Width        =   1695
   End
   Begin VB.CommandButton btnShowItem
      Caption      =   "Show Item"
      Height       =   735
      Left         =   720
      TabIndex     =   1
      Top          =   2880
      Width        =   3375
   End
```

```
      Begin MSComctlLib.TreeView treTreeView1
         Height          =    1815
         Left            =    600
         TabIndex        =    2
         Top             =    240
         Width           =    3495
         _ExtentX        =    6165
         _ExtentY        =    3201
         _Version        =    393217
         Style           =    7
         Appearance      =    1
         _Nodes          =    "Form1.frx":0000
      End
      Begin VB.Label Label1
         Caption         =    "Item to display:"
         Height          =    255
         Left            =    720
         TabIndex        =    0
         Top             =    2280
         Width           =    1095
      End
   End
End
Attribute VB_Name = "Form1"
Attribute VB_GlobalNameSpace = False
Attribute VB_Creatable = False
Attribute VB_PredeclaredId = True
Attribute VB_Exposed = False

Private Sub btnShowItem_Click()
    Dim keyText As String
    Dim selNode As Node
    Dim found As Boolean

    found = False
    keyText = txtItemKey.Text
    For Each Nod In treTreeView1.Nodes
        If Nod.Key = keyText Then
            Set selNode = Nod
            found = True
        End If
    Next Nod

    If found Then
        selNode.EnsureVisible
```

```
        Else
            MsgBox "No such node"
        End If
End Sub

Private Sub Form_Load()
    treTreeView1.Style = tvwTreelinesPlusMinusPictureText
    treTreeView1.LineStyle = tvwRootLines

    With treTreeView1.Nodes
        .Add , , "Root", "Root"
        .Add "Root", tvwChild, "Child1", "Child1"
        .Add "Root", tvwChild, "Child2", "Child2"
        .Add "Root", tvwChild, "Child3", "Child3"
        .Add "Child1", tvwChild, "Child4", "Child4"
        .Add "Child1", tvwChild, "Child5", "Child5"
        .Add "Child2", tvwChild, "Child6", "Child6"
        .Add "Child2", tvwChild, "Child7", "Child7"
        .Add "Child3", tvwChild, "Child8", "Child8"
        .Add "Child3", tvwChild, "Child9", "Child9"
    End With
End Sub
```

CROSS-REFERENCE
For more information, see Node, ListItem, ListView, and TreeView.

EnterFocus

Event

Visual Basic sends a UserControl control an EnterFocus event when the UserControl, or a control contained in the UserControl (called a *constituent control*), is getting the focus. This event occurs before the GotFocus event, which is generated for the control that actually obtains the focus.

Objects That Receive EnterFocus Events

UserControl

Example

A program can respond to an `EnterFocus` event by implementing the UserControl's `EnterFocus` event procedure. The following code segment shows how a UserControl object defines an `EnterFocus` event procedure.

```
Private Sub UserControl_EnterFocus()
    ' Handle the EnterFocus event here.
End Sub
```

CROSS-REFERENCE

See also UserControl, ExitFocus, Got Focus, and LostFocus.

Enum

Statement

The `Enum` statement is used to define an *enumeration*, which is a set of related symbols with numerical values. These symbols can be used as constants in a program.

Syntax

```
access Enum typeName
    member expr
    . . .
End Enum
```

- ... — Additional enumeration members.
- *access* (*) — The keyword `Public` or `Private`.
- *expr* (*) — The member's value.
- *member* — The member's name.
- *typeName* — The enumeration's name.

(*) = Optional

Example 1

The following lines declare an enumeration that sets the symbols `one`, `two`, `three`, and `five` to the values 1, 2, 3, and 5, respectively. The symbols `one`, `two`, `three`, and `five` can then be used as constants in the program.

```
Private Enum digits
    one = 1
    two = 2
    three = 3
    five = 5
End Enum
```

Example 2

You don't have to provide values for the members. If you leave the values off, Visual Basic assigns the first member 0, and then increments the value of each member in the enumeration. In the following example, the symbols zero, one, two, and three are assigned the values 0, 1, 2, and 3, respectively.

```
Private Enum digits
    zero
    one
    two
    three
End Enum
```

Example 3

Finally, you can assign a value for one member and let Visual Basic take care of the rest. You can also force Visual Basic to skip over values. In this example, the symbols five, six, seven, ten, and eleven get the values 5, 6, 7, 10, and 11, respectively.

```
Private Enum digits
    five = 5
    six
    seven
    ten = 10
    eleven
End Enum
```

Environ

Function

The Environ function returns a string containing the setting of an environment variable. For example, most systems define an environment variable called TEMP, which holds the path of the temporary directory.

Syntax

```
value = Environ(envVar)
```

- *envVar*—The name of the environment variable or the variable's position in the environment-variable table.
- *value*—The variable that will receive the string returned from the function.

Example 1

In this example, the program uses the Environ function to get the settings for a Sound Blaster sound card that are stored in the environment variable named BLASTER. The program displays the returned string in a message box, as shown in Figure E-6.

Figure E-6 This message box displays the system's BLASTER environment-variable setting.

```
Dim strEnvVar As String
strEnvVar = Environ("BLASTER")
MsgBox strEnvVar
```

Example 2

Here, the program iterates through the entire environment-variable table, displaying each variable and its setting in a message box. Notice that, in this case, the Environ function's argument is an integer specifying a position in the environment-variable table. Figure E-7 shows one of the returned strings, which shows both the variable's name and its setting. When the table position given to the Environ function is invalid, the function returns an empty string.

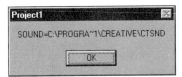

Figure E-7 When you specify a table position as the function's argument, you get both the name of the variable and its setting.

```
Dim strEnvVar As String
Dim index As Integer

index = 1
Do
    strEnvVar = Environ(index)
    If strEnvVar <> "" Then MsgBox strEnvVar
    index = index + 1
Loop Until strEnvVar = ""
```

EOF

Function

The EOF function returns True when the end of a file has been reached.

Syntax

```
value = EOF(fileNum)
```

- *fileNum* — The file's file number as given in the Open statement.
- *value* — The variable that will receive the value returned from the function.

Example

In this example, the program opens a file and reads through the file line by line, displaying each line in a message box. When the EOF function returns False, the Do-While loop ends.

```
Dim strLine As String

Open "c:\TEXTFILE.TXT" For Input As #1
Do While Not EOF(1)
    Line Input #1, strLine
```

```
      MsgBox strLine
   Loop
   Close #1
```

CROSS-REFERENCE
See also LOF and Loc.

Equals (=)

Operator

The equals (=) operator is Visual Basic's assignment operator, enabling programs to assign values to variables. The equals operator can also be used to construct Boolean logic, which compares the values of two objects ands returns a True or False result. You often see this type of comparison in If/Then statements and other program-control blocks. Whether Visual Basic interprets the equals operator as an assignment operator or as a Boolean operator depends on the context in which the operator is used.

Syntax

```
value1 = value2
```

- *value1* — The name of the variable to be assigned the value value2 or to be compared with the value of value2.
- *value2* — The value that will be assigned to value1 or that will be compared to value1.

Example

In this example, the first use of the equals operator, shown in the third and fourth lines, assigns values to the variables var1 and var2. In the fifth line, the equals operator compares the value of var1 and var2 in an If/Then statement. If the two variables have the same value (which, in this case, they don't), the message "The variables are the same value." appears in a message box. Otherwise, the message "The variables are different values." appears in the message box.

```
   Dim var1 As Integer
   Dim var2 As Integer

   var1 = 10
   var2 = 15
```

```
If var1 = var2 Then
    MsgBox "The variables are the same value."
Else
    MsgBox "The variables are different values."
End If
```

Eqv

Operator

The Eqv operator is Visual Basic's logical equivalence operator, which is often used to compare Boolean expressions, but can be used to compare other types of expressions, as well.

Syntax

```
value1 = value2 Eqv value3
```

- *value1* — The True or False result returned from the expression.
- *value2* — The first expression to evaluate.
- *value3* — The second expression to evaluate.

Example 1

In this example, the Eqv operator compares two Boolean expressions. Because both Boolean expressions are True, a message box appears with the message "The expressions are equivalent."

```
Dim var1, var2, var3, var4 As Integer

var1 = 10
var2 = 15
var3 = 25
var4 = 10

If var1 = var4 Eqv var3 > var2 Then
    MsgBox "The expressions are equivalent."
Else
    MsgBox "The expressions are not equivalent."
End If
```

Example 2

Here, the Eqv operator compares two slightly different Boolean expressions. Because both Boolean expressions are False, a message box appears with the message "The expressions are equivalent."

```
Dim var1, var2, var3, var4 As Integer

var1 = 10
var2 = 15
var3 = 25
var4 = 10

If var1 < var4 Eqv var3 = var2 Then
    MsgBox "The expressions are equivalent."
Else
    MsgBox "The expressions are not equivalent."
End If
```

Example 3

In this case, both Boolean expressions evaluate to different results. The first is True and the second is False, so a message box appears with the message "The expressions are not equivalent."

```
Dim var1, var2, var3, var4 As Integer

var1 = 10
var2 = 15
var3 = 25
var4 = 10

If var1 = var4 Eqv var3 = var2 Then
    MsgBox "The expressions are equivalent."
Else
    MsgBox "The expressions are not equivalent."
End If
```

Example 4

Finally, in this case, both numerical expressions compared by the Eqv operator evaluate to 17, so a message box appears with the message "The expressions are equivalent."

```
If 3 * 4 + 5 Eqv 5 * 2 + 7 Then
    MsgBox "The expressions are equivalent."
Else
    MsgBox "The expressions are not equivalent."
End If
```

Erase

Statement

The Erase statement erases the contents of an array and initializes the array to its default values. For example, an erased integer array contains all zeroes, whereas an erased string array contains all empty strings. The Erase statement can also release memory allocated to a dynamic array.

Syntax

```
Erase arrays
```

■ *arrays*—One or more array names separated by commas.

Example 1

In this example, the Erase statement initializes all elements of the intArray array to zeroes.

```
Dim intArray(5) As Integer
Erase intArray
```

Example 2

Here, the program declares a string array and sets one of its elements to the text "Test string". A message box then displays the string, proving that it's in the array. After the Erase statement, the string array contains all empty strings, which the second message box shows by displaying the same string that was indexed by the first call to MsgBox.

```
Dim strArray(5) As String
strArray(1) = "Test string"
MsgBox strArray(1)
Erase strArray
MsgBox strArray(1)
```

Example 3

Finally, here the program declares a dynamic array, sets its size to five elements, and then initializes its last element to 100. A message box displays the initialized element, proving that the array is valid. Then the `Erase` statement releases the memory associated with the array, causing the second call to `MsgBox` to generate a "subscript out of range" error .

```
Dim myArray() As Integer
ReDim myArray(5)
myArray(5) = 100
MsgBox myArray(5)
Erase myArray

' The following line generates an error.
MsgBox myArray(5)
```

Err

Object

The Err object is a global Visual Basic object that contains information about the last generated runtime error. Such errors can be generated by Visual Basic itself or generated programmatically from within an application. Because Err is a global Visual Basic object, you do not need to create it in your programs.

Properties

The Err object has six properties, which are listed in Table E-1. For more information on using a property shown in the following table, look up the individual property's entry, provided alphabetically in this book.

Table E-1 Properties of the Err Object

Property	Description
Description	Represents a string that contains the error's description.
HelpContext	Represents a string that contains a context ID in a help file.
HelpFile	Represents a string that contains the path name of the associated help file.
LastDLLError	Represents the code returned from a call to a DLL.
Number	Represents the error number.
Source	Represents a string that contains the name of the object that generated the error.

Methods

The Err object has two methods, which are listed in Table E-2. For more information on using a method shown in the following table, look up the individual method's entry, provided alphabetically in this book.

Table E-2 Methods of the Err Object

Method	Description
Clear	Clears all properties of an Err object.
Raise	Generates an error at runtime.

Events

The Err object does not respond to events.

Example

This example attempts to open a file. If the file doesn't exist, Visual Basic generates a runtime error, which is displayed in a message box. The program generates the message box's title and message text from the Err object's properties. Figure E-8 shows the message box that appears if the file does not exist.

Figure E-8 The text in this message box was generated in part from the Err object's contents.

```
Dim strMsgBoxTitle As String
Dim strMsgBoxText As String

On Error Resume Next
Open "c:\ZZZZZ.ZZZ" For Input As #1

If Err.Number <> 0 Then
    strMsgBoxTitle = Err.Source
    strMsgBoxText = "Error " & Err.Number & _
```

```
      ": " & Err.Description
   MsgBox strMsgBoxText, vbExclamation, strMsgBoxTitle
   End If
```

Error

Function

The `Error` function returns the message text that's associated with an error number.

Syntax

```
value = Error(number)
```

- *(number)* (*) — The error number enclosed in parentheses.
- *value* — The variable that will receive the returned string.

(*) = Optional

Example 1

In this example, the program attempts to open a file, which generates an error if the file doesn't exist. The call to `Error` includes no argument, which causes the function to return the text description associated with the last error generated. This text description (which, if the file doesn't exist, is "File not found") is then displayed in a message box.

```
Dim strMsg As String
On Error Resume Next
Open "c:\ZZZZZ.ZZZ" For Input As #1
strMsg = Error
MsgBox strMsg
```

Example 2

In this example, the program displays a message box containing the text "Expression too complex," which is the description associated with error number 16.

```
Dim strMsg As String
strMsg = Error(16)
MsgBox strMsg
```

Error

Keyword

The Error keyword is used as part of the On Error statement, which enables a program to respond to runtime errors. For example, the following lines attempt to open and read a file. If the file fails to open successfully, the On Error GoTo statement causes program execution to jump to the lines following the ErrorHandler label.

```
Private Sub btnCommand1_Click()
    On Error GoTo ErrorHandler
    Open "c:\ZZZZZ.ZZZ" For Input As #1
    Do While Not EOF(1)
        Line Input #1, strLine
        MsgBox strLine
    Loop
    Close #1
    Exit Sub
ErrorHandler:
    MsgBox Err.Description
End Sub
```

 CROSS-REFERENCE
For more information, see Err, Error (function), and On Error.

Error

Property

The Error property represents the code number of the error last generated by an MCI command issued by the Multimedia MCI control.

Objects with an Error Property
Multimedia MCI

Syntax
```
value = Multimedia.Error
```

- *Multimedia* — A reference to the Multimedia MCI control.
- *value* — The variable that will receive the error code.

Example

In this example, the program retrieves an error code from a Multimedia MCI control and displays the code in a message box. The `MMControl1` object is a Multimedia MCI control that the programmer added to the application's form at design time.

```
Dim errorNum As Integer
errorNum = MMControl1.Error
MsgBox errorNum
```

CROSS-REFERENCE
See also Multimedia MCI.

Error

Statement

The `Error` statement enables a program to generate a runtime error by number. However, the `Error` statement is obsolete and is supported only to provide compatibility with older Visual Basic programs. New programs should use the Err object's `Raise` method to generate errors.

Syntax

```
Error number
```

- *number* — The number of the error to generate.

Example

This example simulates the occurrence of a "Return without GoSub" error.

```
Error 3
```

ErrorMessage

Property

The `ErrorMessage` property represents the text description of the error associated with a Multimedia MCI control's `Error` property.

Objects with an ErrorMessage Property

Multimedia MCI

Syntax

`value = Multimedia.ErrorMessage`

- *Multimedia* — A reference to the Multimedia MCI control.
- *value* — The variable that will receive the error text.

Example

In this example, the program retrieves error text from a Multimedia MCI control and displays the text in a message box. The `MMControl` object is a Multimedia MCI control that the programmer added to the application's form at design time.

```
Dim errorText As String
errorText = MMControl1.ErrorMessage
MsgBox errorText
```

CROSS-REFERENCE
See also Multimedia MCI.

Event

Statement

The `Event` statement enables a program to declare a user-defined event.

Syntax

`access Event name args`

- *access* (*) — The keyword `Public`.

- *name* — The event procedure's name.
- *args* (*) — The argument list normally used to define Visual Basic procedures.

(*) = Optional

Example

The following program demonstrates how to create a simple class that defines a user-defined event, as well as how to create an object of that class and respond to the class's events. The first listing below defines a class module called Class1, which is the class that defines and generates a user event named MyEvent. Much of this listing was generated automatically by Visual Basic, with the programmer's code lines starting with the Option Explicit statement.

```
VERSION 1.0 CLASS
BEGIN
   MultiUse = -1    'True
   Persistable = 0    'NotPersistable
   DataBindingBehavior = 0    'vbNone
   DataSourceBehavior  = 0    'vbNone
   MTSTransactionMode  = 0    'NotAnMTSObject
END
Attribute VB_Name = "Class1"
Attribute VB_GlobalNameSpace = False
Attribute VB_Creatable = True
Attribute VB_PredeclaredId = False
Attribute VB_Exposed = False

Option Explicit
Public Event MyEvent()

Public Sub SendEvent()
    RaiseEvent MyEvent
End Sub
```

The second listing defines the main program, which creates an object of the Class1 class. When the user clicks the Trigger User-Defined Event button, the program calls the Class1 class's SendEvent procedure through the myObject object. In the SendEvent procedure, the Class1 class calls RaiseEvent to generate the user-defined MyEvent event. The main program responds to this event in the myObject_MyEvent event procedure, which displays a message box proving that the event arrived. Figure E-9 shows the application after the user clicks the form's button.

Figure E-9 The message box proves that the user-defined event arrived.

```
VERSION 5.00
Begin VB.Form Form1
    Caption         =   "Form1"
    ClientHeight    =   3195
    ClientLeft      =   60
    ClientTop       =   345
    ClientWidth     =   4680
    LinkTopic       =   "Form1"
    ScaleHeight     =   3195
    ScaleWidth      =   4680
    StartUpPosition =   3 'Windows Default
    Begin VB.CommandButton btnTriggerEvent
        Caption     =   "Trigger User-Defined Event"
        Height      =   855
        Left        =   720
        TabIndex    =   0
        Top         =   600
        Width       =   3255
    End
End
Attribute VB_Name = "Form1"
Attribute VB_GlobalNameSpace = False
Attribute VB_Creatable = False
Attribute VB_PredeclaredId = True
Attribute VB_Exposed = False

Option Explicit
Private WithEvents myObject As Class1
Attribute myObject.VB_VarHelpID = -1

Private Sub btnTriggerEvent_Click()
```

```
        myObject.SendEvent
End Sub

Private Sub Form_Load()
    Set myObject = New Class1
End Sub

Private Sub myObject_MyEvent()
    MsgBox "Event received"
End Sub
```

d
e
f

Event Procedure

Concept

An event procedure is a special type of procedure that responds to events generated by controls or other objects in an application. By writing event procedures,
you can specify the way your program interacts with its user. For example, the
following event procedure responds to a click on a CommandButton control.
Because of this procedure, whenever the user clicks the `btnCommand1` button, a
message box appears.

```
Private Sub btnCommand1_Click()
    MsgBox "You clicked the button"
End Sub
```

CROSS-REFERENCE
See also Function and Procedure.

EventsFrozen

Property

The `EventsFrozen` property represents whether a control's container is
responding to events generated by the control. This property, which can be
`True` or `False`, is available only at runtime, when it is read-only.

Objects with an EventsFrozen Property

UserControl

Syntax

```
value = UserControl.EventsFrozen
```

- *UserControl*—A reference to a UserControl control.
- *value*—The variable that will receive the property's current setting.

Example

In this example, the program retrieves the setting of a UserControl object's EventsFrozen property.

```
Dim frozen As Boolean
frozen = UserControl.EventsFrozen
```

CROSS-REFERENCE
See also UserControl.

EXEName

Property

The EXEName property represents the name of the running application's executable file.

Objects with an EXEName Property

App

Syntax

```
string = App.EXEName
```

- *string*—The string that will receive the executable's name.

Example

The following example obtains the value of the EXEName property when the user clicks the application's form. The program then displays the property's value in a message box.

```
Private Sub Form_Click()
    Dim strName as String
    strName = App.EXEName
    MsgBox strName
End Sub
```

Exit

Statement

The Exit statement enables a program to exit a Do, For, Sub, Property, or Function program block immediately.

Syntax

Exit *blockName*

- *blockName* — The keyword Do, For, Function, Property, or Sub.

Example

In this example, the program uses the Exit Sub statement to exit the procedure right before the code for the error handler. The procedure will get to the Exit Sub line if the MyText.txt file opens and reads successfully.

```
Private Sub btnCommand1_Click()
    On Error GoTo ErrorHandler
    Open "c:\MyText.txt" For Input As #1
    Do While Not EOF(1)
        Line Input #1, strLine
        MsgBox strLine
    Loop
    Close #1
    Exit Sub
ErrorHandler:
    MsgBox Err.Description
End Sub
```

ExitFocus

Event

Visual Basic sends a UserControl control an ExitFocus event when the UserControl, or a control contained in the UserControl (called a *constituent control*), is losing the focus. This event occurs after the LostFocus event, which Visual Basic triggers for the control actually losing the focus.

Objects That Receive ExitFocus Events

UserControl

Example

A program can respond to an ExitFocus event by implementing the UserControl's ExitFocus event procedure. The following code segment shows how a UserControl object defines an ExitFocus event procedure.

```
Private Sub UserControl_ExitFocus()
    ' Handle the EnterFocus event here.
End Sub
```

CROSS-REFERENCE
See also UserControl, EnterFocus, Got Focus, and LostFocus.

Expand

Event

Visual Basic sends a TreeView control an Expand event when the user expands a node (reveals child nodes) in the tree.

Objects That Receive Expand Events

TreeView

Example

A program can respond to an Expand event by implementing the TreeView control's Expand event procedure. The following code segment shows how a TreeView object defines an Expand event procedure. The treTreeView1 object is a TreeView control that the programmer added to the form at design time.

```
Private Sub treTreeView1_Expand(ByVal Node As ComctlLib.Node)
    ' Handle the expand event here.
End Sub
```

CROSS-REFERENCE
See also TreeView.

Expanded

Property

The `Expanded` property represents whether a node in a TreeView control is in its expanded (has revealed any child nodes) state. The property can also be used to expand a node.

Objects with an Expanded Property

Node

Syntax

`Node.Expanded = value1`

or

`value2 = Node.Expanded`

- *Node* — A reference to a Node object.
- *value1* — The value `True` or `False`.
- *value2* — The variable that will receive the property's current setting.

Example

In this example, the program expands the second node in a TreeView control. The `TreeView1` object is a TreeView control that the programmer added to the application's form at design time.

`TreeView1.Nodes(2).Expanded = True`

CROSS-REFERENCE
See also Node and TreeView.

ExpandedImage

Property

The `ExpandedImage` property represents the index in an ImageList control of the image to display on a node when the node is in its expanded state.

Objects with a ExpandedImage Property

Node

Syntax

Node.ExpandedImage = *value1*

or

value2 = *Node*.ExpandedImage

- *Node* — A reference to a Node object.
- *value1* — The index of the expanded image in an ImageList control.
- *value2* — The variable that will receive the currently set expanded image index.

Example

In the following program, you can see the ExpandedImage property in action. When you run the program, you see the window shown in Figure E-10. Expand the root node, and the node's icon changes from blue to red. You can now expand the Child1 node, which also changes its image from blue to red, as shown in Figure E-11. (Unfortunately, the figure is in black and white, but the program is on this book's CD-ROM, so you can see the color changes for yourself.)

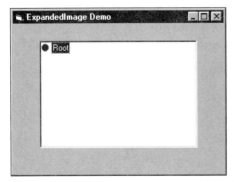

Figure E-10 When first run, the application's tree is fully collapsed.

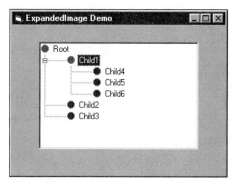

Figure E-11 Here's the application with the tree's nodes fully expanded.

```
VERSION 5.00
Object = "{6B7E6392-850A-101B-AFC0-4210102A8DA7} _
    #2.0#0"; "MSCOMCTL.OCX"
Begin VB.Form Form1
   Caption         =   "ExpandedImage Demo"
   ClientHeight    =   3195
   ClientLeft      =   60
   ClientTop       =   345
   ClientWidth     =   4680
   LinkTopic       =   "Form1"
   ScaleHeight     =   3195
   ScaleWidth      =   4680
   StartUpPosition =   3  'Windows Default
   Begin ComctlLib.ImageList ilsImageList1
      Left         =   4080
      Top          =   2640
      _ExtentX     =   1005
      _ExtentY     =   1005
      BackColor    =   -2147483643
      MaskColor    =   12632256
      _Version     =   393216
   End
   Begin ComctlLib.TreeView treTreeView1
      Height       =   2295
      Left         =   600
      TabIndex     =   0
      Top          =   360
      Width        =   3495
      _ExtentX     =   6165
      _ExtentY     =   4048
      _Version     =   393217
```

```
        Style           =   7
        Appearance      =   1
      End
End
Attribute VB_Name = "Form1"
Attribute VB_GlobalNameSpace = False
Attribute VB_Creatable = False
Attribute VB_PredeclaredId = True
Attribute VB_Exposed = False
Private Sub Form_Load()
    ilsImageList1.ListImages.Add , , _
        LoadPicture("circle1.bmp")
    ilsImageList1.ListImages.Add , , _
        LoadPicture("circle2.bmp")

    treTreeView1.ImageList = ilsImageList1

    With treTreeView1.Nodes
        .Add , , "Root", "Root", 1
        .Add "Root", tvwChild, "Child1", "Child1", 1
        .Add "Root", tvwChild, "Child2", "Child2", 1
        .Add "Root", tvwChild, "Child3", "Child3", 1
        .Add "Child1", tvwChild, "Child4", "Child4", 1
        .Add "Child1", tvwChild, "Child5", "Child5", 1
        .Add "Child1", tvwChild, "Child6", "Child6", 1
    End With

    treTreeView1.Nodes(1).ExpandedImage = 2
    treTreeView1.Nodes(2).ExpandedImage = 2
End Sub
```

CROSS-REFERENCE

See also Node and TreeView.

Explicit

Keyword

The Explicit keyword is part of the `Option Explicit` statement, which determines whether Visual Basic requires all variables to be declared before they are used. For example, the following line specifies that all variables must be previously declared.

```
Option Explicit
```

CROSS-REFERENCE

For more information, see Option Explicit.

Extender

Object

The Extender object represents the properties of a control that are supplied by the control's container. Not all Extender properties, methods, and events are supported by all containers. Only five of the properties—Cancel, Default, Name, Parent, and Visible—are standard to all containers.

Properties

The Extender object has 23 properties, which are listed as follows. Because many Visual Basic objects and controls have similar properties, the following list does not include the properties' descriptions. For information on using a property, look up the individual property's entry, provided alphabetically in this book.

```
Align
Cancel
CausesValidation
Container
Default
DragIcon
DragMode
Enabled
Height
HelpContextID
Index
Left
Name
Object
Parent
TabIndex
TabStop
Tag
ToolTipText
Top
Visible
WhatsThisHelpID
Width
```

Methods

The Extender object has five methods, which are listed as follows. Because many Visual Basic objects and controls have similar methods, the following list does not include the methods' descriptions. For information on using a method, look up the individual method's entry, provided alphabetically in this book.

```
Drag
Move
SetFocus
ShowWhatsThis
ZOrder
```

Events

The Extender object responds to six events, which are listed below. Because many Visual Basic objects and controls respond to similar events, the following list does not include the events' descriptions. For information on using an event, look up the individual event's entry, provided alphabetically in this book.

```
DragDrop
DragOver
GotFocus
LostFocus
ObjectEvent
Validate
```

CROSS-REFERENCE
See also Extender (property).

Extender

Property

The Extender property represents a UserControl's Extender object, which provides access to the container's extender properties.

Objects with an Extender Property

UserContainer

Syntax

```
value = UserControl.Extender
```

- *UserControl* — A reference to a UserControl control.
- *value* — The variable that will receive the reference to the Extender object.

Example

In this example, the program gets the value of the Extender object's `Name` property and displays the result in a message box.

```
Dim strName As String
strName = UserControl.Extender.Name
MsgBox strName
```

CROSS-REFERENCE
See also UserControl and Extender (object).

ExtractIcon

Method

The `ExtractIcon` method creates an icon from a bitmap stored in an ImageList control.

Objects with an ExtractIcon Method

ListImage

Syntax

```
value = ListImage.ExtractIcon
```

- *ListImage* — A reference to a ListImage object.
- *value* — The variable that will hold the reference to the icon returned from the method.

Example

The following line creates an icon from the second image in an ImageList control. The `ilsImageList1` object is an ImageList control the programmer added to the application's form at design time.

```
myIcon = ilsImageList1.ListImages(2).ExtractIcon
```

 CROSS-REFERENCE
For more information, see ImageList and ListImage.

False

Keyword

The False keyword represents the false Boolean condition, which results from a Boolean expression that evaluates to False. For example, if x = 10, then the expression x = 15 yields a Boolean value of False. Also, variables can be declared to be of the Boolean data type and so used as flags for tracking conditions in a program. Such variables can hold the value True or False, like this:

```
Dim gotResult As Boolean
gotResult = False
```

CROSS-REFERENCE
See also True.

Fetch

Method

The Fetch method extracts messages from the user's InBox based on the settings of the FetchMsgType, FetchSorted, and FetchUnreadOnly properties of the MAPIMessages control.

Objects with a Fetch Method

MAPIMessages

Syntax

MAPIMessages.Fetch

- *MAPIMessages* — A reference to a MAPIMessages control.

Example

The following extracts a set of messages from the user's InBox. The `mpmMAPIMessages1` object is a MAPIMessages control that the programmer added to the form at design time.

```
mpmMAPIMessages1.Fetch
```

CROSS-REFERENCE
For more information, see FetchMsgType, FetchSorted, FetchUnreadOnly, MAPIMessages, and MAPISession.

FetchMsgType

Property

The `FetchMsgType` property determines the type of messages extracted by the MAPIMessages control's `Fetch` method. The default message type is IPM (interpersonal message), which is automatically selected when this property is set to `Null` or an empty string. Other types of messages depend upon the user's message system.

Objects with a FetchMsgType Property

MAPIMessages

Syntax

```
MAPIMessages.FetchMsgType = value1
```

or

```
value2 = MAPIMessages.FetchMsgType
```

- *MAPIMessages* — A reference to a MAPIMessages control.
- *value1* — A string containing the message type.
- *value2* — The variable that will receive the current message type.

Example

In this example, the program sets the message type to the default IPM. The `mpmMAPIMessages1` object is a MAPIMessages control that the programmer added to the application's form at design time.

```
mpmMAPIMessages1.FetchMsgType = ""
```

CROSS-REFERENCE

For more information, see Fetch, FetchSorted, FetchUnreadOnly, MAPIMessages, and MAPISession.

FetchSorted

Property

The `FetchSorted` property determines the order in which messages are extracted by the MAPIMessages control's `Fetch` method. A value of `True` causes the messages to be extracted in the order in which they were received, whereas a value of `False` causes the messages to be extracted in the order determined by the settings of the user's InBox.

Objects with a FetchSorted Property

MAPIMessages

Syntax

```
MAPIMessages.FetchSorted = value1
```

or

```
value2 = MAPIMessages.FetchSorted
```

- *MAPIMessages* — A reference to a MAPIMessages control.
- *value1* — The value `True` or `False`.
- *value2* — The variable that will receive the property's current setting.

Example

In this example, the program sets the `Fetch` method to the retrieve messages in the order in which they were received. The `mpmMAPIMessages1` object is a MAPIMessages control that the programmer added to the application's form at design time.

```
mpmMAPIMessages1.FetchSorted = True
```

CROSS-REFERENCE

For more information, see Fetch, FetchMsgType, FetchUnreadOnly, MAPIMessages, and MAPISession.

FetchUnreadOnly

Property

The `FetchUnreadOnly` property determines whether the MAPIMessages control's `Fetch` method will retrieve only unread messages from the user's InBox.

Objects with a FetchUnreadOnly Property

MAPIMessages

Syntax

`MAPIMessages.FetchUnreadOnly = value1`

or

`value2 = MAPIMessages.FetchUnreadOnly`

- *MAPIMessages* — A reference to a MAPIMessages control.
- *value1* — The value `True` or `False`.
- *value2* — The variable that will receive the property's current setting.

Example

In this example, the program sets the `Fetch` method to the retrieve only unread messages. The `mpmMAPIMessages1` object is a MAPIMessages control that the programmer added to the application's form at design time.

`mpmMAPIMessages1.FetchUnreadOnly = True`

CROSS-REFERENCE
For more information, see Fetch, FetchMsgType, FetchSorted, MAPIMessages, and MAPISession.

FetchVerbs

Method

The `FetchVerbs` method fetches the list of actions (called verbs) that can be performed on an ActiveX object.

Objects with a FetchVerbs Method
OLEObject

OLE Container

Syntax

`object.FetchVerbs`

- *object*—A reference to an OLEObject object or OLE Container control.

Example

The following line updates an OLE Container control's verb list. The `oleContainer1` object is an OLE Container control that the programmer added to the form at design time.

`oleContainer1.FetchVerbs`

File

Object

The File object enables a program to retrieve the properties and attributes of a file, including the file's size, date created, date last accessed, and so on.

Properties

The File object has 12 properties, which are listed in Table F-1. For more information on using a property shown in the following table, look up the property's entry provided alphabetically in this book.

Table F-1 Properties of the File Object

Property	Description
Attributes	Represents the file's attributes, such as whether the file is read-only or hidden.
DateCreated	Represents the date and time the file was created.
DateLastAccessed	Represents the date and time the file was last accessed.
DateLastModified	Represents the date and time the file was last modified.
Drive	Represents the drive letter for the drive on which the file is located.

Continued

Table F-1 *Continued*

Property	Description
Name	Represents the name of the file.
ParentFolder	Represents the name of the folder in which the file is located.
Path	Represents the file's complete path name.
ShortName	Represents the file's 8.3 DOS file name.
ShortPath	Represents the file's 8.3 path name.
Size	Represents the file's size in bytes.
Type	Represents the file's type.

Methods

The File object has four methods, which are listed in Table F-2. For more information on using a method shown in the following table, look up the method's entry provided alphabetically in this book.

Table F-2 Methods of the File Object

Method	Description
Copy	Copies a file or folder.
Delete	Deletes a file or folder.
Move	Moves a file or folder.
OpenAsTextStream	Opens a file as a TextStream object.

Events

The File object does not respond to events.

Example

The following lines open a file and display the file's size in a message box.

```
Dim fileSystem
Dim file
Set fileSystem = CreateObject("Scripting.FileSystemObject")
Set file = fileSystem.GetFile("c:\TextFile.txt")
MsgBox file.Size
```

FileAttr

Function

The FileAttr function returns the mode for which a file was opened with the
Open statement. The returned modes are input (1), output (2), random-access
(4), append (8), and binary (32).

Syntax

```
value = FileAttr(num, type)
```

- *num* — The file number given in the Open statement.
- *type* — The type of information to return: 1 for the mode and 2 to
  get a file handle (only on 16-bit systems).
- *value* — The variable that will receive the return value.

Example

In this example, the program opens a file and then displays the file's mode in
a message box. Because the file was opened for input, the call to FileAttr
returns 1, which causes the message box to display the message "Input."

```
Dim fileMode
Open "c:\TextFile.txt" For Input As #1
fileMode = FileAttr(1, 1)

Select Case fileMode
Case 1
    MsgBox "Input"
Case 2
    MsgBox "Output"
Case 4
    MsgBox "Random-access"
Case 8
    MsgBox "Append"
Case 32
    MsgBox "Binary"
End Select

Close #1
```

FileCopy

Statement

The `FileCopy` statement copies a file. You cannot copy a file that is currently open.

Syntax

```
FileCopy src, dest
```

- *dest* — The path and name of the new copy.
- *src* — The path and name of the file to copy.

Example

The following line copies a file named `TextFile.txt` to a file named `Text2.txt`.

```
FileCopy "C:\TextFile.txt", "C:\Text2.txt"
```

FileDateTime

Function

The `FileDateTime` function returns the time and date a file was created or last modified.

Syntax

```
value = FileDateTime(name)
```

- *name* — The file's name.
- *value* — The variable that will receive the return value.

Example

In this example, the program retrieves the date and time for a file and displays it in a message box. Figure F-1 shows the format in which the function returns the time and date.

Figure F-1 This message box shows the time and date returned by the FileDateTime function.

```
Dim fileInfo As String
fileInfo = FileDateTime("c:\TextFile.txt")
MsgBox fileInfo
```

FileDescription

Property

The FileDescription property represents the text description of the running application's file.

Objects with a FileDescription Property

App

Syntax

```
value = App.FileDescription
```

- *App* — A reference to the App object.
- *value* — The variable that will receive the file description.

Example

The following lines get the application's file description and display it in a message box. To set the FileDescription property, you must use the Make page of the Project Properties property sheet, as shown in Figure F-2. You display this property sheet by selecting the Project menu's *project* Properties command, where *project* is the name of the currently loaded project.

```
Dim strFileDesc As String
strFileDesc = App.FileDescription
MsgBox strFileDesc
```

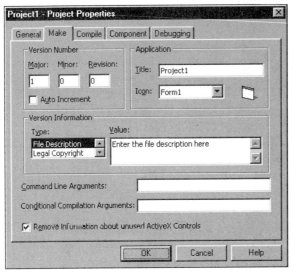

Figure F-2 You can set the FileDescription property in this property sheet.

CROSS-REFERENCE
See also App.

FileExists

Method

The FileExists method returns True if the specified file exists.

Objects with a FileExists Method

FileSystemObject

Syntax

```
value = FileSystemObject.FileExists(name)
```

- *FileSystemObject* — A reference to a FileSystemObject object.
- *name* — The path and name of the file for which to check.
- *value* — The variable that will receive the return value of True or False.

Example

The following lines create a FileSystemObject and use it to determine whether a file named `TextFile.txt` exists on the root directory of drive C. A message box displays the results.

```
Dim fileSystem As Object
Dim exists As Boolean

Set fileSystem = CreateObject("Scripting.FileSystemObject")
exists = fileSystem.FileExists("c:\TextFile.txt")
If exists Then
    MsgBox "File exists"
Else
    MsgBox "File does not exist"
End If
```

CROSS-REFERENCE

For more information, see FileSystemObject.

FileLen

Function

The `FileLen` function returns the size of a file in bytes.

Syntax

`value = FileLen(name)`

- *name* — The file's name.
- *value* — The variable that will receive the return value.

Example

In this example, the program retrieves the size of a file and displays it in a message box.

```
Dim fileSize As Long
fileSize = FileLen("c:\TextFile.txt")
MsgBox fileSize
```

FileListBox

Control

A FileListBox is a control that displays the files contained in a specified folder. The user can select a file from the list by clicking a file name with the mouse. Figure F-3 shows a FileListBox (which is available in Visual Basic's standard toolbox) placed in a form. Note that the FileListBox control is often used in conjunction with the DriveListBox and DirListBox to create a complete interface for browsing a drive and selecting files.

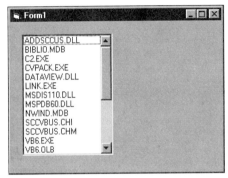

Figure F-3 A FileListBox enables the user to select files from a list.

Properties

The FileListBox control has 48 properties, which are listed as follows. Because many Visual Basic controls have similar properties, the properties' descriptions are listed under their own names provided alphabetically in this book.

```
Appearance
Archive
BackColor
CausesValidation
Container
DragIcon
DragMode
Enabled
FileName
Font
FontBold
```

```
FontItalic
FontName
FontSize
FontStrikethru
FontUnderline
ForeColor
Height
HelpContextID
Hidden
hWnd
Index
Left
List
ListCount
ListIndex
MouseIcon
MousePointer
MultiSelect
Name
Normal
OLEDragMode
OLEDropMode
Parent
Path
Pattern
ReadOnly
Selected
System
TabIndex
TabStop
Tag
ToolTipText
Top
TopIndex
Visible
WhatsThisHelpID
Width
```

Methods

The FileListBox control has seven methods, which are listed below. Because many Visual Basic controls have similar methods, the methods' descriptions are listed under their own names provided alphabetically in this book.

```
Drag
Move
OLEDrag
Refresh
SetFocus
ShowWhatsThis
ZOrder
```

Events

The FileListBox control responds to 22 events, which are listed below. Because many Visual Basic controls respond to similar events, the events' descriptions are listed under their own names provided alphabetically in this book.

```
Click
DblClick
DragDrop
DragOver
GotFocus
KeyDown
KeyPress
KeyUp
LostFocus
MouseDown
MouseMove
MouseUp
OLECompleteDrag
OLEDragDrop
OLEDragOver
OLEGiveFeedback
OLESetData
OLEStartDrag
PathChange
PatternChange
Scroll
Validate
```

The FileListBox's most commonly used event is DblClick, which the control generates when the user double-clicks a file in the list. A program responds to the control's DblClick event in the DblClick event procedure. A FileListBox called filFile1 will have a DblClick event procedure called `filFile1_DblClick`, which is where the program should handle the event. In the following example, when the user clicks the `filFile1` control, the program displays the selected file in a message box. The `filFile1` object is a FileListBox control that the programmer placed on the form at design time.

```
Private Sub filFile1_DblClick()
    MsgBox filFile1.FileName
End Sub
```

 CROSS-REFERENCE
See also DirListBox, DriveListBox, and FileName.

FileName — CommonDialog and FileListBox

Property

The `FileName` property represents the currently selected file in a FileListBox or CommonDialog control.

Syntax

`object.FileName = value1`

or

`value2 = object.FileName`

- *object* — A reference to a CommonDialog or FileListBox control.
- *value1* — A string containing the path and file name.
- *value2* — The variable that will receive the selected file name.

Example

The following program shows how you can link together the DriveListBox, DirListBox, and FileListBox controls in order to enable the user to select any file on any drive. When you run the program, you see the window shown in Figure F-4. Use the DriveListBox to select a drive, the DirListBox to select a directory, and, finally, double-click a file in the FileListBox to select the file. Whenever you change the contents of one control, the other controls update themselves as appropriate.

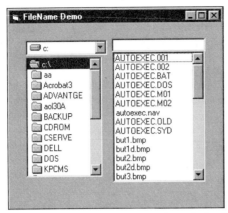

Figure F-4 Here, the DriveListBox, DirListBox, and FileListBox controls work together to enable the user to select a file anywhere on the system.

```
VERSION 5.00
Begin VB.Form Form1
    Caption         =   "FileName Demo"
    ClientHeight    =   3930
    ClientLeft      =   60
    ClientTop       =   345
    ClientWidth     =   4680
    LinkTopic       =   "Form1"
    ScaleHeight     =   3930
    ScaleWidth      =   4680
    StartUpPosition =   3   'Windows Default
    Begin VB.DirListBox dirDir1
        Height      =   2565
        Left        =   360
        TabIndex    =   3
        Top         =   720
        Width       =   1695
    End
    Begin VB.DriveListBox drvDrive1
        Height      =   315
        Left        =   360
        TabIndex    =   2
        Top         =   360
        Width       =   1815
    End
    Begin VB.TextBox txtFileName
        Height      =   285
```

```
        Left            =    2280
        TabIndex        =    1
        Text            =    "Text1"
        Top             =    330
        Width           =    2055
     End
     Begin VB.FileListBox filFile1
        Height          =    2820
        Left            =    2280
        TabIndex        =    0
        Top             =    600
        Width           =    2055
     End
End
Attribute VB_Name = "Form1"
Attribute VB_GlobalNameSpace = False
Attribute VB_Creatable = False
Attribute VB_PredeclaredId = True
Attribute VB_Exposed = False

Private Sub dirDir1_Change()
    filFile1.Path = dirDir1.Path
    txtFileName.Text = ""
End Sub

Private Sub drvDrive1_Change()
    dirDir1.Path = drvDrive1.Drive
    txtFileName.Text = ""
End Sub

Private Sub filFile1_DblClick()
    txtFileName.Text = filFile1.FileName
End Sub

Private Sub Form_Load()
    drvDrive1.Drive = "C"
    dirDir1.Path = "c:\"
    filFile1.Path = "c:\"
    txtFileName = ""
End Sub
```

CROSS-REFERENCE
See also FileListBox, DirListBox, DriveListBox, and CommonDialog.

FileName—Multimedia MCI

Property

The FileName property represents the name of the file that will be acted upon by the Open or Save commands of a Multimedia MCI control.

Syntax

```
MultimediaMCI.FileName = value1
```

or

```
value2 = MultimediaMCI.FileName
```

- *MultimediaMCI*—A reference to a Multimedia MCI control.
- *value1*—A string containing the file name.
- *value2*—The variable that will receive the file name.

Example

The following lines show how the FileName property is used in the context of an Open command, opening a wave file for the WaveAudio device. The mciMMControl1 object is a Multimedia MCI control that the programmer added to the form at design time.

```
mciMMControl1.DeviceType = "WaveAudio"
mciMMControl1.Shareable = False
mciMMControl1.Wait = True
mciMMControl1.Notify = False
mciMMControl1.fileName = "c:\MySound.wav"
mciMMControl1.Command = "Open"
```

CROSS-REFERENCE
See also Multimedia MCI.

FileName—RichTextBox

Property

The FileName property represents the name of the file that is currently displayed in a RichTextBox control. This file must be either plain text or an .rtf file. Setting the FileName property causes the control to display the file.

Syntax

```
RichTextBox.FileName = value1
```

or

```
value2 = RichTextBox.FileName
```

- *RichTextBox* — A reference to a RichTextBox control.
- *value1* — A string containing the file name.
- *value2* — The variable that will receive the file name.

Example

The following line shows how to set a RichTextBox control's `FileName` property. The `rtfRichTextBox1` object is a RichTextBox control that the programmer added to the form at design time.

```
rtfRichTextBox1.FileName = "C:\TextFile.txt"
```

 CROSS-REFERENCE
See also RichTextBox.

FileNumber

Property

The `FileNumber` property represents the file number associated with an object or the last file number issued. However, this property of the OLE Container control is obsolete and should not be used in new programs. Refer to the `SaveToFile` and `ReadFromFile` methods.

Objects with a FileNumber Property

OLE Container

Syntax

```
value = OLEContainer.FileNumber
```

- *OLEContainer* — A reference to an OLE Container control.
- *value* — The variable that will receive the file number.

Example

The following line shows how to retrieve the value of an OLE Container control's `FileNumber` property. The `oleContainer1` object is an OLE Container control that the programmer added to the form at design time.

```
Dim fileNum As Integer
fileNum = oleContainer1.FileNumber
```

CROSS-REFERENCE
See also OLE Container, ReadFromFile, SaveToFile, and SaveToOle1File.

Files

Collection

The Files collection object represents all of the files contained in a folder.

Properties

A Files collection has one property, called `Count`, which represents the number of items in the collection.

Methods

A Files collection has one method, `Item`, which returns a reference to a control in the collection.

Example

The following lines display, in a message box, the number of files in the C: root directory.

```
Dim fileSystem, folder As Object
Dim numFiles As Integer

Set fileSystem = CreateObject("Scripting.FileSystemObject")
Set folder = fileSystem.GetFolder("c:\")
numFiles = folder.Files.Count
MsgBox numFiles
```

CROSS-REFERENCE
See also Files (property) and FileSystemObject.

Files

Property

The Files property represents the Files collection for a Folder object.

Objects with a Files Property

Folder

Syntax

```
value = Folder.Files
```

- *Folder*—A reference to a Folder object.
- *value*—The variable that will receive the reference to the Files collection.

Example

The following lines display, one by one, the names of all the files in the C: root directory.

```
Dim fileSystem, folder As Object
Dim filex As Object

Set fileSystem = CreateObject("Scripting.FileSystemObject")
Set folder = fileSystem.GetFolder("c:\")
For Each filex In folder.Files
    MsgBox filex.Name
Next
```

CROSS-REFERENCE

See also Files (collection) and FileSystemObject.

FileSystem

Property

The FileSystem property represents the type of file system in use on a drive. The possible types include FAT, NTFS, and CDFS.

Objects with a FileSystem Property

Drive

Syntax

```
value = Drive.FileSystem
```

- *Drive* — A reference to a Drive object.
- *value* — The variable that will receive the file system string.

Example

The following lines display the file system used on drive C.

```
Dim fileSystem, drv As Object

Set fileSystem = CreateObject("Scripting.FileSystemObject")
Set drv = fileSystem.GetDrive("C")
MsgBox drv.fileSystem
```

CROSS-REFERENCE

See also Drive and FileSystemObject.

FileSystemObject

Object

The FileSystemObject object represents a computer's file system. Through a FileSystemObject, a program can create File, Folder, and Drive objects that enable the program to manipulate the file system. A FileSystemObject can also open and create files.

Properties

The FileSystemObject object has one property, `Drives`, which represents the drives on the system.

Methods

The FileSystemObject object has 24 methods, which are listed in Table F-3. For more information on using a method shown in the following table, look up the method's entry provided alphabetically in this book.

Table F-3 Methods of the FileSystemObject Object

Method	Description
BuildPath	Adds a name to a path.
CopyFile	Copies a file.
CopyFolder	Copies a folder.
CreateFolder	Creates a folder.
CreateTextFile	Creates a file associated with a TextStream object.
DeleteFile	Deletes a file.
DeleteFolder	Deletes a folder.
DriveExists	Returns True if the given drive exists.
FileExists	Returns True if the given file exists.
FolderExists	Returns True if the given folder exists.
GetAbsolutePathName	Creates a full path from a given specification.
GetBaseName	Extracts a base name without a file extension from a given path.
GetDrive	Returns a Drive object for the given drive specification.
GetDriveName	Returns a drive's name.
GetExtensionName	Extracts an extension from a given path.
GetFile	Returns a File object for the given path.
GetFileName	Extracts a file's name, including the extension, from a given path.
GetFolder	Returns a Folder object for the given path.
GetParentFolderName	Extracts the name of the parent folder from a given path.
GetSpecialFolder	Returns the Windows, System, or Temp folder.
GetTempName	Generates a random name for a temporary folder.
MoveFile	Moves a file.
MoveFolder	Moves a folder.
OpenTextFile	Opens a file and associates a TextStream object with the file.

Events

The FileSystemObject object does not respond to events.

Example

The following lines check whether the file TextFile.txt exists on the root directory of drive C.

```
Dim fileSystem
Dim exists As Boolean
```

```
Set fileSystem = CreateObject("Scripting.FileSystemObject")
exists = fileSystem.FileExists("c:\TextFile.txt")
If exists Then MsgBox "File exists"
```

FileTitle

Property

The FileTitle property represents the name of the selected file, without the path, in a CommonDialog control.

Objects with a FileTitle Property

CommonDialog

Syntax

```
value = CommonDialog.FileTitle
```

- *CommonDialog* — A reference to a CommonDialog control.
- *value* — The variable that will receive the file name.

Example

The following program enables you to select a file with a CommonDialog box. When you do, the application's text boxes show the difference between the file's name and the file's title, as shown in Figure F-5. To display the CommonDialog box, click the Choose File button. When you've selected a file, its name and title appear in the text boxes.

Figure F-5 The text boxes display the file name and file title for the selected file.

```
VERSION 5.00
Object = "{F9043C88-F6F2-101A-A3C9-08002B2F49FB} _
   #1.2#0"; "COMDLG32.OCX"
Begin VB.Form Form1
   Caption         =       "FileTitle Demo"
   ClientHeight    =       3195
   ClientLeft      =       60
   ClientTop       =       345
   ClientWidth     =       4680
   LinkTopic       =       "Form1"
   ScaleHeight     =       3195
   ScaleWidth      =       4680
   StartUpPosition =       3   'Windows Default
   Begin VB.TextBox txtFileTitle
      Height       =       375
      Left         =       720
      TabIndex     =       3
      Text         =       "Text1"
      Top          =       1200
      Width        =       3135
   End
   Begin VB.CommandButton btnChooseFile
      Caption      =       "Command1"
      Height       =       735
      Left         =       1080
      TabIndex     =       1
      Top          =       2160
      Width        =       2535
   End
   Begin VB.TextBox txtFileName
      Height       =       375
      Left         =       720
      TabIndex     =       0
      Text         =       "Text1"
      Top          =       360
      Width        =       3135
   End
   Begin MSComDlg.CommonDialog dlgCommonDialog1
      Left         =       4080
      Top          =       2520
      _ExtentX     =       847
      _ExtentY     =       847
      _Version     =       393216
   End
```

```
Begin VB.Label Label2
   Caption         =    "File Title:"
   Height          =    255
   Left            =    720
   TabIndex        =    4
   Top             =    960
   Width           =    2175
End
Begin VB.Label Label1
   Caption         =    "File Name:"
   Height          =    255
   Left            =    720
   TabIndex        =    2
   Top             =    120
   Width           =    2175
End
End
Attribute VB_Name = "Form1"
Attribute VB_GlobalNameSpace = False
Attribute VB_Creatable = False
Attribute VB_PredeclaredId = True
Attribute VB_Exposed = False

Private Sub btnChooseFile_Click()
   dlgCommonDialog1.ShowOpen
   txtFileName.Text = dlgCommonDialog1.FileName
   txtFileTitle.Text = dlgCommonDialog1.FileTitle
End Sub
```

CROSS-REFERENCE
See also FileName and CommonDialog.

FillColor

Property

The FillColor property represents the color Visual Basic uses to fill graphical objects, including those drawn with graphics methods such as Circle and Line. You can use the RGB or QBColor functions to set this property, or you can use Visual Basic's color constants.

Objects with a FillColor Property

> Form
> PictureBox
> Printer
> PropertyPage
> Shape
> UserControl

Syntax

> `object.FillColor = value1`
>
> or
>
> `value2 = object.FillColor`

- *object* — A reference to an object with a `FillColor` property.
- *value1* — The fill color.
- *value2* — The variable that will receive the property's current value.

Example

> The following line sets the fill color of a form to bright red.
>
> `frmForm1.FillColor = RGB(255, 0, 0)`

 CROSS-REFERENCE
See also FillStyle.

FillStyle

Property

> The `FillStyle` property represents the pattern Visual Basic uses to fill graphical objects, including those drawn with graphics methods such as `Circle` and `Line`. This property can be set to one of eight pattern types: `vbFSSolid`, `vbFSTransparent`, `vbHorizontalLine`, `vbVerticalLine`, `vbUpwardDiagonal`, `vbDownwardDiagonal`, `vbCross`, or `vbDiagonalCross`.

Objects with a FillStyle Property

Form
PictureBox
Printer
PropertyPage
Shape
UserControl

Syntax

object.FillStyle = *value1*

or

value2 = *object*.FillStyle

- *object* — A reference to an object with a FillStyle property.
- *value1* — The style value.
- *value2* — The variable that will receive the property's current value.

Example

The following line sets the fill style of a Shape control to the cross pattern. Figure F-6 shows the shape as it appears when the program that contains it runs. The shpShape1 object is a Shape control the programmer added to the form at design time.

```
shpShape1.FillStyle = vbCross
```

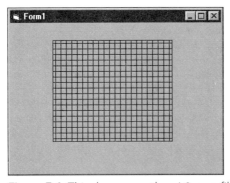

Figure F-6 This shape uses the vbCross fill style.

CROSS-REFERENCE
See also FillColor.

Filter

Function

The Filter function extracts strings from a string array based on given criteria.

Syntax

value = Filter(*srcArray, str, substrings, type*)

- *srcArray* — The source string array.
- *str* — The string or substring for which to search.
- *substrings* (*) — A Boolean value that indicates whether the function should consider str to be a substring for which to search. A value of True specifies that the function should return all strings that contain str, whereas a value of False specifies that the function should return all strings that do not contain str.
- *type* (*) — The type of comparison to make, which can be a value from Table F-4.

(*) = Optional

Table F-4 Settings for the *type* Argument

Value	Description
vbBinaryCompare	Performs a binary comparison.
vbDatabaseCompare	Performs a comparison using Access database information.
vbTextCompare	Compares values as text.
vbUseCompareOption	Compares values based on the program's Option Compare setting.

Example 1

In this example, after the following lines execute, the array dstArray will contain the single string "Betty".

```
Dim srcArray(5) As String
Dim dstArray() As String

srcArray(0) = "Fred"
srcArray(1) = "Betty"
srcArray(2) = "Frederick"
srcArray(3) = "Mary"
srcArray(4) = "Margo"
srcArray(5) = "Thomas"

dstArray = Filter(srcArray, "Betty")
```

Example 2

In this example, the array dstArray will contain the strings "Fred" and "Frederick". Notice that the Filter function's third argument is True, which means that the function should return all strings that contain the substring "Fred".

```
Dim srcArray(5) As String
Dim dstArray() As String

srcArray(0) = "Fred"
srcArray(1) = "Betty"
srcArray(2) = "Frederick"
srcArray(3) = "Mary"
srcArray(4) = "Margo"
srcArray(5) = "Thomas"

dstArray = Filter(srcArray, "Fred", True, vbTextCompare)
```

Example 3

Finally, in this example, the array dstArray will contain the strings "Betty", "Mary", "Margo", and "Thomas". Notice that the Filter function's third argument is False, which means that the function should return all strings that do not contain the substring "Fred".

```
Dim srcArray(5) As String
Dim dstArray() As String

srcArray(0) = "Fred"
srcArray(1) = "Betty"
srcArray(2) = "Frederick"
srcArray(3) = "Mary"
```

```
srcArray(4) = "Margo"
srcArray(5) = "Thomas"

dstArray = Filter(srcArray, "Fred", False, vbTextCompare)
```

CROSS-REFERENCE
See also Replace.

Filter

Property

The `Filter` property determines the type of files that appear in a CommonDialog dialog box when it first appears. For example, a filter of *.bmp will cause only files with the *.bmp file extension to appear in the dialog box. You can also specify multiple filters that enable the user to select different filters from the dialog box's Files of Type box. File filters are strings that are constructed like this:

description | filter

Here, *description* is the text description that the user will see in the Files of Type box and *filter* is the actual file filter. For example, a filter for text files might look like this:

Text Files (*.txt) | *.txt

You can create multiple filters by stringing the filters together separating them with the | symbol, like this:

Text Files (*.txt) | *.txt | Bitmap Files (*.bmp) | *.bmp

Objects with a Filter Property

CommonDialog

Syntax

```
CommonDialog.Filter = value1
```

or

```
value2 = CommonDialog.Filter
```

- *CommonDialog* — A reference to a CommonDialog control.
- *value1* — A string containing the file filter.
- *value2* — The variable that will receive the current file filter.

Example

In this example, the program shows an Open dialog box that displays either text or Word documents, depending on the filter the user selects. Figure F-7 shows the dialog box set to the text filter and the filters available to the user in the Files of Type box. The `dlgCommonDialog1` object is a CommonDialog control that the programmer added to the form at design time.

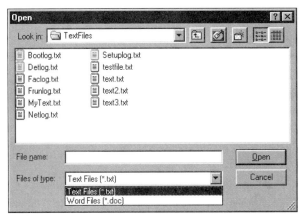

Figure F-7 This dialog box is set to the text filter and shows all the filters available in the Files of Type box.

```
dlgCommonDialog1.Filter = _
    "Text Files (*.txt)|*.txt|Word Files (*.doc)|*.doc"
dlgCommonDialog1.FilterIndex = 1
dlgCommonDialog1.ShowOpen
```

CROSS-REFERENCE
See also CommonDialog and FilterIndex.

FilterIndex

Property

The `FilterIndex` property works in conjunction with the CommonDialog control's `Filter` property to determine which of the dialog box's file filters is active when the dialog box appears. The `FilterIndex` property also contains the selected filter index when the user closes the dialog box. The first filter has an index of 1, the second has an index of 2, and so on.

Objects with a FilterIndex Property
CommonDialog

Syntax

`CommonDialog.FilterIndex = value1`

or

`value2 = CommonDialog.FilterIndex`

- *CommonDialog* — A reference to a CommonDialog control.
- *value1* — The file filter index.
- *value2* — The variable that will receive the current filter index.

Example

In this example, the program shows an Open dialog box that displays either text or Word documents, depending on the filter the user selects. Because the `FilterIndex` property is set to 2, the *.doc filter will be active when the dialog box appears. The `dlgCommonDialog1` object is a CommonDialog control that the programmer added to the form at design time.

```
dlgCommonDialog1.Filter = _
    "Text Files (*.txt)|*.txt|Word Files (*.doc)|*.doc"
dlgCommonDialog1.FilterIndex = 2
dlgCommonDialog1.ShowOpen
```

CROSS-REFERENCE
See also CommonDialog and Filter.

Find

Method

The `Find` method searches for string matches in the contents of a RichTextBox control.

Objects with a Find Method
RichTextBox

Syntax

```
value = RichTextBox.Find(str, start, end, type)
```

- *end (*)* — The last character index to include in the search.
- *RichTextBox* — A reference to a RichTextBox control.
- *start (*)* — The first character index to include in the search.
- *str* — The text for which to search.
- *type (*)* — The type of search to perform. Can be one or more of rtfWholeWord (search for whole words only), rtfMatchCase (search is case sensitive), and rtfNoHighlight (do not highlight found text). Use the Or operator to combine the options.
- *value* — The character index of the found text or –1 if no match is found.

(*) = Optional argument

Example

The following program gives you a chance to experiment with a RichTextBox and its Find method. To search for text, type the text into the String to Find box and click the Search button. The program highlights any text it finds, as well as displays a message box telling you the position of the text, as shown in Figure F-8. If the Find method discovers no match, the message box notifies you as well. You can set one of three options before performing a search. Select the options you want in the Options group.

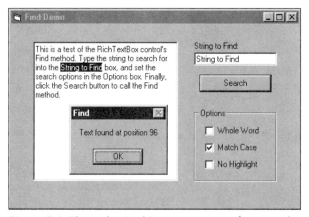

Figure F-8 This is the Find Demo program after completing a search.

```
VERSION 5.00
Object = "{3B7C8863-D78F-101B-B9B5-04021C009402} _
    #1.2#0"; "RICHTX32.OCX"
Begin VB.Form Form1
   Caption         =    "Find Demo"
   ClientHeight    =    3915
   ClientLeft      =    60
   ClientTop       =    345
   ClientWidth     =    6375
   LinkTopic       =    "Form1"
   ScaleHeight     =    3915
   ScaleWidth      =    6375
   StartUpPosition =    3   'Windows Default
   Begin VB.CheckBox chkMatchCase
      Caption      =    "Match Case"
      Height       =    255
      Left         =    4320
      TabIndex     =    6
      Top          =    2520
      Width        =    1335
   End
   Begin VB.Frame Frame1
      Caption      =    "Options"
      Height       =    1575
      Left         =    4080
      TabIndex     =    4
      Top          =    1800
      Width        =    1815
      Begin VB.CheckBox chkNoHighlight
         Caption   =    "No Highlight"
         Height    =    255
         Left      =    240
         TabIndex  =    7
         Top       =    1080
         Width     =    1335
      End
      Begin VB.CheckBox chkWholeWord
         Caption   =    "Whole Word"
         Height    =    255
         Left      =    240
         TabIndex  =    5
         Top       =    360
```

```
                       Width            =    1335
               End
        End
        Begin VB.CommandButton btnSearch
           Caption           =    "Search"
           Height            =    375
           Left              =    4200
           TabIndex          =    3
           Top               =    1080
           Width             =    1575
        End
        Begin VB.TextBox txtString
           Height            =    285
           Left              =    4080
           TabIndex          =    1
           Top               =    600
           Width             =    1815
        End
        Begin RichTextLib.RichTextBox rtfRichTextBox1
           Height            =    3015
           Left              =    480
           TabIndex          =    0
           Top               =    360
           Width             =    3255
           _ExtentX          =    5741
           _ExtentY          =    5318
           _Version          =    393217
           Enabled           =    -1   'True
           TextRTF           =    $"Form1.frx":0000
        End
        Begin VB.Label Label1
           Caption           =    "String to Find:"
           Height            =    255
           Left              =    4080
           TabIndex          =    2
           Top               =    360
           Width             =    1695
        End
     End
     Attribute VB_Name = "Form1"
     Attribute VB_GlobalNameSpace = False
     Attribute VB_Creatable = False
     Attribute VB_PredeclaredId = True
```

```
Attribute VB_Exposed = False

Private Sub Form_Load()
    Dim contents As String

    contents = "This is a test of the RichTextBox "
    contents = contents & _
        "control's Find method. Type the string "
    contents = contents & _
        "to search for into the String to Find box, "
    contents = contents & _
        "and set the search options in the Options "
    contents = contents & _
        "box. Finally, click the Search button to "
    contents = contents & "call the Find method."
    rtfRichTextBox1.Text = contents
    rtfRichTextBox1.HideSelection = False
End Sub

Private Sub btnSearch_Click()
    Dim strSearchString As String
    Dim rtnValue, options As Integer

    rtfRichTextBox1.SelStart = 0
    rtfRichTextBox1.SelLength = 0
    options = 0

    If chkWholeWord.Value = 1 Then _
        options = options Or rtfWholeWord
    If chkMatchCase.Value = 1 Then _
        options = options Or rtfMatchCase
    If chkNoHighlight.Value = 1 Then _
        options = options Or rtfNoHighlight
    strSearchString = txtString.Text
    rtnValue = rtfRichTextBox1.Find _
        (strSearchString, , , options)

    If rtnValue = -1 Then
        MsgBox "Text not found"
    Else
        MsgBox "Text found at position " & rtnValue
    End If
End Sub
```

CROSS-REFERENCE
For more information, see RichTextBox.

FindItem

Method

The FindItem method searches for a ListItem in a ListView control.

Objects with a FindItem Method

ListView

Syntax

```
value = ListView.FindItem(str, type, begin, option)
```

- *begin* (⋆) — The ListItem index or key at which to begin the search.
- *ListView* — A reference to a ListView control.
- *option* (⋆) — Determines whether the ListItem text must match a whole word at the start of the text or just begin with the specified text. This can be set to lvwWholeWord or lvwPartial.
- *str* — The string for which to search.
- *type* (⋆) — Determines whether the search will be performed on the ListItem's text, subitems, or tag. Can be the values lvwText, lvwSubitem, or lvwTag.
- *value* — The variable that will receive the returned reference to the ListItem object.

(⋆) = Optional argument

Example

The following program gives you a chance to experiment with a ListView control and its FindItem method. To search for an item, type the item text into the Item Label box, and then click the Search button. If the FindItem method finds a match, it changes the matching ListItem's label to "Found Me," as shown in Figure F-9.

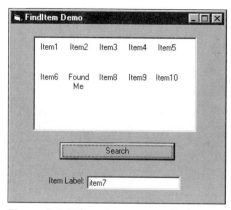

Figure F-9 When the program finds a match, it changes the matching ListItem's Text property.

```
VERSION 5.00
Object = "{6B7E6392-850A-101B-AFC0-4210102A8DA7} _
    #2.0#0"; "MSCOMCTL.OCX"
Begin VB.Form Form1
    Caption         =   "FindItem Demo"
    ClientHeight    =   3780
    ClientLeft      =   60
    ClientTop       =   345
    ClientWidth     =   4680
    LinkTopic       =   "Form1"
    ScaleHeight     =   3780
    ScaleWidth      =   4680
    StartUpPosition =   3   'Windows Default
    Begin VB.TextBox txtItemLabel
        Height          =   285
        Left            =   1680
        TabIndex        =   3
        Top             =   3240
        Width           =   2055
    End
    Begin VB.CommandButton btnSearch
        Caption         =   "Search"
        Height          =   375
        Left            =   1080
        TabIndex        =   1
        Top             =   2520
        Width           =   2535
    End
```

```
        Begin MSComctlLib.ListView lvwListView1
           Height          =   2055
           Left            =   480
           TabIndex        =   0
           Top             =   240
           Width           =   3615
           _ExtentX        =   6376
           _ExtentY        =   3625
           LabelWrap       =   -1   'True
           HideSelection   =   -1   'True
           _Version        =   393217
           ForeColor       =   -2147483640
           BackColor       =   -2147483643
           BorderStyle     =   1
           Appearance      =   1
           NumItems        =   0
        End
        Begin VB.Label Label1
           Caption         =   "Item Label:"
           Height          =   255
           Left            =   840
           TabIndex        =   2
           Top             =   3240
           Width           =   855
        End
     End
     Attribute VB_Name = "Form1"
     Attribute VB_GlobalNameSpace = False
     Attribute VB_Creatable = False
     Attribute VB_PredeclaredId = True
     Attribute VB_Exposed = False

     Private Sub btnSearch_Click()
        Dim foundItem As ListItem
        Dim itemLabel As String

        itemLabel = txtItemLabel.Text
        Set foundItem = lvwListView1.FindItem(itemLabel)
        foundItem.Text = "Found Me"
     End Sub
```

```
Private Sub Form_Load()
    lvwListView1.ListItems.Add , , "Item1"
    lvwListView1.ListItems.Add , , "Item2"
    lvwListView1.ListItems.Add , , "Item3"
    lvwListView1.ListItems.Add , , "Item4"
    lvwListView1.ListItems.Add , , "Item5"
    lvwListView1.ListItems.Add , , "Item6"
    lvwListView1.ListItems.Add , , "Item7"
    lvwListView1.ListItems.Add , , "Item8"
    lvwListView1.ListItems.Add , , "Item9"
    lvwListView1.ListItems.Add , , "Item10"
End Sub
```

CROSS-REFERENCE
For more information, see ListView.

FirstSibling

Property

The FirstSibling property represents the first sibling — a sibling is a node at the same level as another node — of a node in a TreeView control.

Objects with a FirstSibling Property

Node

Syntax

value = Node.FirstSibling

- *Node* — A reference to a Node object.
- *value* — The variable that will receive the reference to the node.

Example

The following lines populate a TreeView control with nodes, get a reference to the first sibling below the root node, and change that node's text. Figure F-10 shows the resultant TreeView control. The treTreeView1 object is a TreeView control that the programmer added to the application's form at design time.

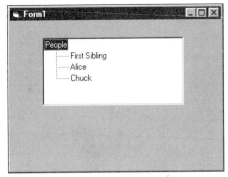

Figure F-10 In this TreeView control, the first sibling below the root has had its text changed.

```
Dim sibNode As Node
treTreeView1.Nodes.Add , , "Root", "People"
treTreeView1.Nodes.Add "Root", tvwChild, "Child1", "Fred"
treTreeView1.Nodes.Add "Root", tvwChild, "Child2", "Alice"
treTreeView1.Nodes.Add "Root", tvwChild, "Child3", "Chuck"

Set sibNode = treTreeView1.Nodes(2).FirstSibling
sibNode.Text = "First Sibling"
```

CROSS-REFERENCE
See also Node, Nodes, and TreeView.

Fix

Function

The Fix function truncates the decimal portion from a number, returning the resultant integer value. If the given number is negative, the function returns the next negative value greater than or equal to the given number. That is, Fix truncates the value –4.3 to –4.

Syntax

```
value = Fix(num)
```

- *num* — The number to truncate.
- *value* — The variable that will receive the returned integer value.

Example

After the following lines execute, the variable result will contain the value 3.

```
Dim value, result As Integer
value = 3.6
result = Fix(value)
```

 CROSS-REFERENCE
See also Int.

FixedBackground

Property

The FixedBackground property represents whether the picture assigned to the band of a CoolBar control moves when the band moves or stays fixed in place.

Objects with a FixedBackground Property
Band

Syntax

```
Band.FixedBackground = value1
```

or

```
value2 = Band.FixedBackground
```

- *Band*—A reference to a Band object.
- *value1*—The value True or False.
- *value2*—The variable that will receive the property's current setting.

Example

The following line sets three bands in a CoolBar control to a fixed background. The CoolBar1 object is a CoolBar control that the programmer added to the form at design time.

```
CoolBar1.Bands(1).FixedBackground = True
CoolBar1.Bands(2).FixedBackground = True
CoolBar1.Bands(3).FixedBackground = True
```

CROSS-REFERENCE
See also Band, Bands, and CoolBar.

FixedOrder

Property

The `FixedOrder` property represents whether the user can reposition the order of bands in a CoolBar control by dragging and dropping a band with the band's handle.

Objects with a FixedOrder Property

CoolBar

Syntax

`CoolBar.FixedOrder = value1`

or

`value2 = CoolBar.FixedOrder`

- *CoolBar*—A reference to a CoolBar control.
- *value1* — The value `True` or `False`.
- *value2*—The variable that will receive the property's current setting.

Example

The following line sets a CoolBar control so that the user can reposition the bands. The `CoolBar1` object is a CoolBar control that the programmer added to the form at design time.

`CoolBar1.FixedOrder = False`

CROSS-REFERENCE
See also CoolBar.

Flags — Color CommonDialog

Property

The Flags property determines the way a Color dialog box looks and acts. The property can be set to one of the values in Table F-5. Or, you can set multiple flags by combining the constants with the Or operator.

Table F-5 Settings for the Color Dialog's Flags Property

Value	Description
cdlCCFullOpen	Displays the full Color dialog box, which includes the custom color selections.
cdlCCHelpButton	Displays a Help button in the dialog box.
cdlCCPreventFullOpen	Prevents the user from displaying the dialog box's custom color selections.
cdlCCRGBInit	Sets the Color dialog's initial color.

Syntax

```
CommonDialog.Flags = value1
```

or

```
value2 = CommonDialog.Flags
```

- *CommonDialog* — A reference to a CommonDialog control.
- *value1* — The flags setting.
- *value2* — The variable that will receive the current flags.

Example

The following lines display a fully open Color dialog box that includes a Help button, as shown in Figure F-11. The dlgCommonDialog1 object is a CommonDialog control that the programmer added to the application's form at design time.

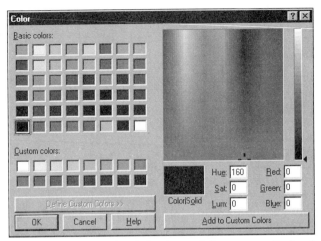

Figure F-11 This Color dialog box is fully open to display the custom color area.

```
dlgCommonDialog1.Flags = cdlCCFullOpen Or cdlCCHelpButton
dlgCommonDialog1.ShowColor
```

CROSS-REFERENCE
See also CommonDialog.

Flags—Font CommonDialog

Property

The Flags property determines the way a Font dialog box looks and acts. The property can be set to one of the values in Table F-6, or you can set multiple flags by combining the constants with the Or operator.

Table F-6 Settings for the Font Dialog's Flags Property

Value	Description
cdlCFANSIOnly	Allows the user to select only fonts that contain a standard character set.
cdlCFApply	Enables the Font dialog's Apply button.
cdlCFBoth	Specifies that the Font dialog should display both screen and printer fonts.

Value	Description
cdlCFEffects	Enables the underline, strikethrough, and color attributes in the Font dialog.
cdlCFFixedPitchOnly	Specifies that the Font dialog should display only fixed-pitch fonts.
cdlCFForceFontExist	Causes an error to appear if the user attempts to select a nonexistent font.
cdlCFHelpButton	Displays a Help button in the Font dialog.
cdlCFLimitSize	Limits the font sizes to those specified in the dialog box's Min and Max properties.
cdlCFNoFaceSel	Selects no initial font in the dialog.
cdlCFNoSimulations	Disallows GDI font simulations.
cdlCFNoSizeSel	Selects no initial font size.
cdlCFNoStyleSel	Selects no initial font style.
cdlCFNoVectorFonts	Disables the selection of vector fonts.
cdlCFPrinterFonts	Displays only printer fonts.
cdlCFScalableOnly	Allows the selection of only scalable fonts.
cdlCFScreenFonts	Displays only screen fonts.
cdlCFTTOnly	Displays only TrueType fonts.
cdlCFWYSIWYG	Displays only fonts that can be used on both the screen and the printer.

Syntax

```
CommonDialog.Flags = value1
```

or

```
value2 = CommonDialog.Flags
```

- *CommonDialog* — A reference to a CommonDialog control.
- *value1* — A flags setting from Table F-6.
- *value2* — The variable that will receive the current flags.

Example

The following lines display a Font dialog box that displays fonts supported by both the screen and the printer, as shown in Figure F-12. The dlgCommonDialog1 object is a CommonDialog control that the programmer added to the application's form at design time.

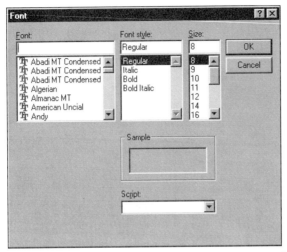

Figure F-12 This Font dialog box displays screen and printer fonts.

```
dlgCommonDialog1.Flags = cdlCFWYSIWYG Or cdlCFBoth _
    Or cdlCFScalableOnly
dlgCommonDialog1.ShowFont
```

CROSS-REFERENCE
See also CommonDialog.

Flags—Open and Save As CommonDialog

Property

The Flags property determines the way an Open or Save As dialog box looks and acts. The property can be set to one of the values in Table F-7, or you can set multiple flags by combining the constants with the Or operator. As you can see in the table, some of the Open or Save As dialog flags return values that you can check after the user closes the dialog box. To check the value of a flag, use the And operator to compare the Flags property with the appropriate constant from Table F-7, like this:

```
If CommonDialog1.Flags And cdlOFNExtensionDifferent then _
    MsgBox "The extension is different from DefaultExt."
```

Table F-7 Settings for the Open or Save As Dialog's Flags Property

Value	Description
cdlOFNAllowMultiselect	Allows the user to select multiple files.
cdlOFNCreatePrompt	Asks the user whether he wants to create a file when the selected file doesn't exist.
cdlOFNExplorer	Displays an Explorer-type Open dialog box under Windows 98 or Windows NT 4.0.
cdlOFNExtensionDifferent	Set if the selected file has a different file extension than that specified in the `DefaultExt` property.
cdlOFNFileMustExist	Enables the user to type only the names of existing files into the dialog's File Name box.
cdlOFNHelpButton	Displays a Help button in the dialog.
cdlOFNHideReadOnly	Removes the Read-Only option from the dialog.
cdlOFNLongNames	Enables the use of long file names in the dialog.
cdlOFNNoChangeDir	Prevents the dialog box from changing the current directory.
cdlOFNNoDereferenceLinks	Disallows dereferencing of shortcuts.
cdlOFNNoLongNames	Disallows long file names.
cdlOFNNoReadOnlyReturn	Disallows the selected file to be read-only or located in a write-protected folder.
cdlOFNNoValidate	Validation not performed on characters in the selected file name.
cdlOFNOverwritePrompt	Displays a warning if the selected file will be overwritten.
cdlOFNPathMustExist	Allows the user to select only existing paths.
cdlOFNReadOnly	Selects the dialog's Read-Only check box.
cdlOFNShareAware	Causes the dialog to ignore sharing violations.

Syntax

```
CommonDialog.Flags = value1
```

or

```
value2 = CommonDialog.Flags
```

- `CommonDialog` — A reference to a CommonDialog control.
- *value1* — A flags setting from Table F-7.
- *value2* — The variable that will receive the current flags.

Example

The following lines display an Explorer-style Open dialog box in which the user can select multiple files, as shown in Figure F-13. The `dlgCommonDialog1` object is a CommonDialog control that the programmer added to the application's form at design time.

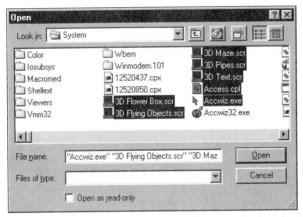

Figure F-13 This Open dialog box allows multiple selections.

```
dlgCommonDialog1.Flags = cdlOFNExplorer Or
cdlOFNAllowMultiselect
dlgCommonDialog1.ShowOpen
```

CROSS-REFERENCE
See also CommonDialog.

Flags—Print CommonDialog

Property

The `Flags` property determines the way a Print dialog box looks and acts. The property can be set to one of the values in Table F-8, or you can set multiple flags by combining the constants with the `Or` operator. As you can see in the table, some of the Printer dialog flags return values that you can check after the user closes the dialog box. To check the value of a flag, use the `And` operator to compare the `Flags` property with the appropriate constant from Table F-8, like this:

```
If CommonDialog1.Flags And cdlPDAllPages then _
    MsgBox "The All Pages option is selected."
```

Table F-8 Settings for the Print Dialog's Flags Property

Value	Description
cdlPDAllPages	Holds the setting of the Print dialog's All Pages option.
cdlPDCollate	Holds the setting of the Print dialog's Collate option.
cdlPDDisablePrintToFile	Disables the Print dialog's Print To File option.
cdlPDHelpButton	Displays a Help button in the dialog.
cdlPDHidePrintToFile	Removes the Print to File option from the dialog box.
cdlPDNoPageNums	Disables the Print dialog's Pages option.
cdlPDNoSelection	Disables the Print dialog's Selection option.
cdlPDNoWarning	Stops a no-default-printer warning from appearing.
cdlPDPageNums	Holds the setting of the Pages option.
cdlPDPrintSetup	Displays the Print Setup dialog box.
cdlPDPrintToFile	Holds the setting of the Print to File option.
cdlPDReturnDC	Holds the printer's device context.
cdlPDReturnDefault	Holds the default printer's name.
cdlPDReturnIC	Holds the selected printer's information context.
cdlPDSelection	Holds the setting of the Selection option.
cdlPDUseDevModeCopies	Controls the availability of the Number of Copies option, based on whether the selected printer supports the option.

Syntax

```
CommonDialog.Flags = value1
```

or

```
value2 = CommonDialog.Flags
```

- *CommonDialog* — A reference to a CommonDialog control.
- *value1* — A flags setting from Table F-8.
- *value2* — The variable that will receive the current flags.

Example

The following lines display a Print dialog box in which the Print to File and Pages options have been disabled, as shown in Figure F-14. The `dlgCommonDialog1` object is a CommonDialog control that the programmer added to the application's form at design time.

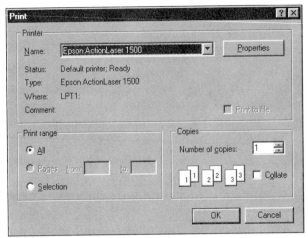

Figure F-14 This Print dialog box has disabled Print to File and Pages options.

```
dlgCommonDialog1.Flags = cdlPDDisablePrintToFile Or
cdlPDNoPageNums
dlgCommonDialog1.ShowPrinter
```

CROSS-REFERENCE
See also CommonDialog.

Folder

Object

The Folder object represents a directory on a drive.

Properties

The Folder object has 15 properties, which are listed in Table F-9. For more information on using a property shown in the following table, look up the property's entry provided alphabetically in this book.

Table F-9 Properties of the Folder Object

Property	Description
Attributes	Represents the folder's attributes.
DateCreated	Represents the date and time the folder was created.
DateLastAccessed	Represents the date and time the folder was last accessed.

Property	Description
DateLastModified	Represents the date and time the folder was last modified.
Drive	Represents the drive letter for the drive on which the folder is located.
Files	Represents all the files in the folder as File objects.
IsRootFolder	Represents whether the folder is the root folder.
Name	Represents the name of the folder.
ParentFolder	Represents the name of the folder in which the folder is located.
Path	Represents the folder's complete path name.
ShortName	Represents the folder's 8.3 DOS file name.
ShortPath	Represents the folder's 8.3 path name.
Size	Represents the folder's size in bytes, which includes all the folder's contents.
SubFolders	Represents, as a Folders collection, the folders contained in the folder.
Type	Represents the folder's type.

Methods

The Folder object has two methods, which are listed in Table F-10. For more information on using a method shown in the following table, look up the method's entry provided alphabetically in this book.

Table F-10 Methods of the File Object

Method	Description
Copy	Copies a folder.
CreateTextFile	Creates a text file and associates the file with a TextStream object.
Delete	Deletes a folder.
Move	Moves a folder.

Events

The Folder object does not respond to events.

Example

The following lines create a Folder object and display the folder's size in a message box.

```
Dim fileSystem
Dim folder
Set fileSystem = CreateObject("Scripting.FileSystemObject")
Set folder = fileSystem.GetFolder("c:\Program Files")
MsgBox folder.Size
```

FolderExists

Method

The FolderExists method returns True if the specified folder exists.

Objects with a FolderExists Method

FileSystemObject

Syntax

value = FileSystemObject.FolderExists(name)

- *FileSystemObject* — A reference to a FileSystemObject object.
- *name* — The path and name of the Folder for which to check.
- *value* — The variable that will receive the return value of True or False.

Example

The following lines create a FileSystemObject and use it to determine whether a folder named "Program Files" exists on the root directory of drive C. A message box displays the results.

```
Dim fileSystem As Object
Dim exists As Boolean

Set fileSystem = CreateObject("Scripting.FileSystemObject")
exists = fileSystem.FolderExists("c:\Program Files")
If exists Then
    MsgBox "Folder exists"
Else
    MsgBox "Folder does not exist"
End If
```

CROSS-REFERENCE

For more information, see FileSystemObject.

Folders

Collection

A `Folders` collection represents as Folder objects the subfolders contained in a folder.

Properties

A Folders collection has one property, called `Count`, which represents the number of items in the collection.

Methods

A Folders collection has one method, `Add`, which adds a folder to the collection.

Example

The following lines display the number of subfolders contained in the Program Files folder on drive C.

```
Dim fileSystem As Object
Dim folder, folders As Object
Set fileSystem = CreateObject("Scripting.FileSystemObject")
Set folder = fileSystem.GetFolder("c:\Program Files")
Set folders = folder.subfolders
MsgBox folders.Count
```

CROSS-REFERENCE

For more information, see Folder and FileSystemObject.

Font

Object

The Font object represents the typeface used to display text. By changing a Font object's properties, you can change the way text appears.

Properties

The Font object has eight properties, which are listed in Table F-11. For more information on using a property shown in the following table, look up the property's entry provided alphabetically in this book.

Table F-11 Properties of the Font Object

Property	Description
Bold	Determines whether the font will be bold.
Charset	Determines the character set. This property can be set to 0 (standard Windows character set), 2 (symbol character set), 128 (double-byte character set), or 255 (extended character set).
Italic	Determines whether the font will be italic.
Name	Represents the font's name.
Size	Determines the font's point size.
StrikeThrough	Determines whether the font will be strikethrough.
Underline	Determines whether the font will be underlined.
Weight	Determines the thickness of characters in the font, similar to bold.

Methods

The Font object has no methods.

Events

The Font object does not respond to events.

Example

The following line displays the name of the form's current font in a message box.

```
Dim fontName As String
fontName = Form1.Font.Name
MsgBox fontName
```

Font

Property

The Font property represents the font object being used to display text in a control. You can use the Font object returned by the Font property to change the way text appears in the control. For example, you might want to change the size of the font or use an underlined font.

Objects with a Font Property

CheckBox

ComboBox

CommandButton

DirListBox

DriveListBox

FileListBox

Form

Frame

Label

ListBox

ListView

OptionButton

PictureBox

Printer

PropertyPage

RichTextBox

StatusBar

TabStrip

TreeView

TextBox

UserControl

Syntax

```
Set value = object.Font
```

- *object* — A reference to an object with a `Font` property.
- *value* — The variable that will receive the current Font object.

Example

In this example, the program sets a button's caption to a 24-point italic font. The `btnCommand1` object is a CommandButton control that the programmer added to the application's form at design time.

```
Dim fnt As Font
Set fnt = btnCommand1.Font
fnt.Italic = True
fnt.Size = 24
```

 CROSS-REFERENCE
See also FontBold, FontItalic, FontStrikethru, FontUnderline, FontSize, and
FontName.

FontBold

Property

The FontBold property represents whether an object's text will be displayed in
a bold font.

Objects with a FontBold Property

AmbientProperties

CheckBox

ComboBox

CommandButton

CommonDialog

DirListBox

DriveListBox

FileListBox

Form

Frame

Label

ListBox

OptionButton

PictureBox

Printer

PropertyPage

TextBox

UserControl

Syntax

`object.FontBold = value1`

or

`value2 = object.FontBold`

- *object* — A reference to an object with a `FontBold` property.
- *value1* — The value `True` or `False`.
- *value2* — The variable that will receive the property's current setting.

Example

In this example, the program sets a button's caption to a bold font. The `btnCommand1` object is a CommandButton control that the programmer added to the application's form at design time.

`btnCommand1.FontBold = True`

 CROSS-REFERENCE
See also FontItalic, FontStrikethru, FontUnderline, and FontName.

FontCount

Property

The `FontCount` property represents the number of fonts that are available for use with the screen or printer display.

Objects with a FontCount Property

Printer
Screen

Syntax

`value = object.FontCount`

- *object* — A reference to the Screen or Printer object.
- *value* — The variable that will receive the property's current setting.

Example

In this example, the program gets the number of fonts that can be used with the screen display. The Screen object is a Visual Basic global object that you don't need to create in your program.

```
Dim numFonts As Integer
numFonts = Screen.FontCount
```

CROSS-REFERENCE
See also Fonts, Printer, and Screen.

FontItalic

Property

The FontItalic property represents whether an object's text will be displayed in an italic font.

Objects with a FontItalic Property

AmbientProperties

CheckBox

ComboBox

CommandButton

CommonDialog

DirListBox

DriveListBox

FileListBox

Form

Frame

Label

ListBox

OptionButton

PictureBox

Printer

PropertyPage

TextBox

UserControl

Syntax

object.FontItalic = *value1*

or

value2 = *object*.FontItalic

- *object* — A reference to an object with a FontItalic property.
- *value1* — The value True or False.
- *value2* — The variable that will receive the property's current setting.

Example

In this example, the program sets a button's caption to an italic font. The btnCommand1 object is a CommandButton control that the programmer added to the application's form at design time.

```
btnCommand1.FontItalic = True
```

CROSS-REFERENCE
See also FontBold, FontStrikethru, FontUnderline, FontSize, and FontName.

FontName

Property

The FontName property represents the name of the typeface used to display text in a control.

Objects with a FontName Property

CheckBox

ComboBox

CommandButton

CommonDialog

DirListBox

DriveListBox

FileListBox

Form

Frame

Label

ListBox
OptionButton
PictureBox
Printer
PropertyPage
TextBox
UserControl

Syntax

```
object.FontName = value1
```

or

```
value2 = object.FontName
```

- *object* — A reference to an object with a `FontName` property.
- *value1* — A string containing the font's name.
- *value2* — The variable that will receive the current font's name.

Example

In this example, the program sets a button's font to Times New Roman. The `btnCommand1` object is a CommandButton control that the programmer added to the application's form at design time.

```
btnCommand1.FontName = "Times New Roman"
```

CROSS-REFERENCE
See also FontBold, FontItalic, FontStrikethru, FontUnderline, and FontSize.

Fonts

Property

The `Fonts` property represents the names of all fonts that are available for use with the screen or printer display.

Objects with a Fonts Property

Printer
Screen

Syntax

```
value = object.Font(num)
```

- *object* — A reference to the Screen or Printer object.
- *num* — The number of the font for which to get the name.
- *value* — The variable that will receive the font name.

Example

In this example, the program displays, in message boxes, the names of all the fonts that the Printer object can use. The Printer object is a Visual Basic global object that you don't need to create in your program.

```
Dim fntName As String
Dim fntcount As Integer
Dim x As Integer

fntcount = Printer.FontCount
For x = 1 To fntcount - 1
    fntName = Printer.Fonts(x)
    MsgBox fntName
Next
```

CROSS-REFERENCE
See also FontCount, Printer, and Screen.

FontSize

Property

The FontSize property represents the size of the typeface used to display text in a control.

Objects with a FontSize Property

CheckBox

ComboBox

CommandButton

CommonDialog

DirListBox

DriveListBox

FileListBox

Form

Frame

Label

ListBox

OptionButton

PictureBox

Printer

PropertyPage

TextBox

UserControl

Syntax

```
object.FontSize = value1
```

or

```
value2 = object.FontSize
```

- *object* — A reference to an object with a `FontSize` property.
- *value1* — The point size of the font.
- *value2* — The variable that will receive the current font size.

Example

In this example, the program sets a button's font to 24-point text. The `btnCommand1` object is a CommandButton control that the programmer added to the application's form at design time.

```
btnCommand1.FontSize = 24
```

 CROSS-REFERENCE
See also FontBold, FontItalic, FontStrikethru, FontUnderline, and FontName.

FontStrikethru

Property

The `FontStrikethru` property represents whether an object's text will be displayed in a strikethrough font.

Objects with a FontStrikethru Property

AmbientProperties

CheckBox

ComboBox

CommandButton

CommonDialog

DirListBox

DriveListBox

FileListBox

Form

Frame

Label

ListBox

OptionButton

PictureBox

Printer

PropertyPage

TextBox

UserControl

Syntax

```
object.FontStrikethru = value1
```

or

```
value2 = object.FontStrikethru
```

- *object* — A reference to an object with a `FontStrikethru` property.
- *value1* — The value `True` or `False`.
- *value2* — The variable that will receive the property's current setting.

Example

In this example, the program sets a button's caption to a strikethrough font. The `btnCommand1` object is a CommandButton control that the programmer added to the application's form at design time.

```
btnCommand1.FontStrikethru = True
```

CROSS-REFERENCE
See also FontBold, FontItalic, FontUnderline, FontSize, and FontName.

FontTransparent

Property

The `FontTransparent` property represents whether an object's background will show between the letters in text (a setting of `True`) or whether the text will completely overwrite the background (a setting of `False`).

Objects with a FontTransparent Property

Form
PictureBox
Printer
PropertyPage
UserControl

Syntax

```
object.FontTransparent = value1
```

or

```
value2 = object.FontTransparent
```

- *object* — A reference to an object with a `FontTransparent` property.
- *value1* — The value `True` or `False`.
- *value2* — The variable that will receive the property's current setting.

Example

In this example, the program sets a form's text to transparent.

```
Form1.FontTransparent = True
```

FontUnderline

Property

The `FontUnderline` property represents whether an object's text will be displayed in an underline font.

Objects with a FontUnderline Property

AmbientProperties

CheckBox

ComboBox

CommandButton

CommonDialog

DirListBox

DriveListBox

FileListBox

Form

Frame

Label

ListBox

OptionButton

PictureBox

Printer

PropertyPage

TextBox

UserControl

Syntax

`object.FontUnderline = value1`

or

`value2 = object.FontUnderline`

- *object* — A reference to an object with a `FontUnderline` property.
- *value1* — The value `True` or `False`.
- *value2* — The variable that will receive the property's current setting.

Example

In this example, the program sets a button's caption to an underline font. The `btnCommand1` object is a CommandButton control that the programmer added to the application's form at design time.

```
btnCommand1.FontUnderline = True
```

CROSS-REFERENCE
See also FontBold, FontItalic, FontStrikethru, FontSize, and FontName.

For

Keyword

The `For` keyword is used as part of the `For Each`, `For/Next`, and `Open` statements.

CROSS-REFERENCE
For more information, see For Each, For/Next (statement), and Open.

For Each

Statement

The `For Each` statement enables a program to iterate through the elements of an array or through the members of a collection.

Syntax

```
For Each member In src
    ' Body statements go here.
Next
```

or

```
For Each member In src
```

```
        ' Body statements go here.
        Exit For
        ' Body statements here.
    Next
```

- *member* — The loop variable that represents an element of the array or collection.
- *src* — The array or collection through which to iterate.

Example

The following lines initialize a string array, and then use the For Each statement to iterate through the array, displaying each string element in a message box.

```
Dim strArray(3) As String
Dim vntElement As Variant

strArray(0) = "Zero"
strArray(1) = "One"
strArray(2) = "Two"
strArray(3) = "Three"
For Each vntElement In strArray
    MsgBox vntElement
Next
```

ForeColor

Property

The ForeColor property represents an object's foreground color, which determines the color used to display text and graphics. This property can be set to any valid color value, including those returned by the RGB and QBColor functions.

Objects with a ForeColor Property

AmbientProperties

Animation

Band

CheckBox

ComboBox

CommandButton

CoolBar

DirListBox

DriveListBox

FileListBox

Form

Frame

Image

ImageList

Label

ListBox

MDIForm

OLE Container

OptionButton

PictureBox

Printer

PropertyPage

RichTextBox

Shape

TextBox

UserControl

Syntax

```
object.ForeColor = color1
```

or

```
color2 = object.ForeColor
```

- *color1* — The color value to which to set the property.
- *color2* — The variable that will receive the color returned by the property.
- *object* — A reference to an object with a ForeColor property.

Example 1

In this example, the program calls the QBColor function to change the form's foreground color to green.

```
Private Sub Form_Load()
    ForeColor = QBColor(10)
End Sub
```

Example 2

Here, the program calls the RGB function to change the form's foreground color to red.

```
Private Sub Form_Load()
    ForeColor = RGB(255,0,0)
End Sub
```

Example 3

Finally, in this example, the program uses a hexadecimal value to set the form's foreground color to a dark aqua.

```
Private Sub Form_Load()
    ForeColor = &H80000001
End Sub
```

CROSS-REFERENCE
See also BackColor, RGB, and QBColor.

Form

Object

The Form object represents a window in a Visual Basic application. Virtually all Visual Basic programs begin with a form onto which the programmer places the various controls that make up the application's user interface.

Properties

The Form object has 65 properties, which are listed as follows. Because many Visual Basic controls have similar properties, the properties' descriptions are listed under their own names provided alphabetically in this book.

```
ActiveControl
Appearance
AutoRedraw
BackColor
BorderStyle
Caption
ClipControls
ControlBox
```

```
Controls
Count
CurrentX
CurrentY
DrawMode
DrawStyle
DrawWidth
DragIcon
Enabled
FillColor
FillStyle
Font
FontBold
FontItalic
FontName
FontSize
FontStrikethru
FontTransparent
FontUnderline
ForeColor
HasDC
hDC
Height
HelpContextID
hWnd
Icon
Image
KeyPreview
Left
LinkMode
LinkTopic
MaxButton
MDIChild
MinButton
MouseIcon
MousePointer
Movable
Name
OLEDropMode
Palette
PaletteMode
Picture
RightToLeft
ScaleHeight
```

```
ScaleLeft
ScaleMode
ScaleTop
Scalewidth
Style
ShowInTaskbar
StartUpPosition
Tag
Visible
WhatsThisButton
WhatsThisHelp
Width
WindowState
```

e
f
g

Methods

The Form object has 22 methods, which are listed as follows. Because many Visual Basic controls have similar methods, the methods' descriptions are listed under their own names provided alphabetically in this book.

```
Circle
Cls
Hide
Line
Move
OLEDrag
PaintPicture
Point
PopupMenu
PrintForm
PSet
Refresh
Scale
ScaleX
ScaleY
SetFocus
Show
TextHeight
TextWidth
ValidateControls
WhatsThisMode
ZOrder
```

Events

The Form object responds to 31 events, which are listed below. Because many Visual Basic controls respond to similar events, the events' descriptions are listed under their own names provided alphabetically in this book.

```
Activate
Click
DblClick
Deactivate
DragDrop
DragOver
GotFocus
Initialize
KeyDown
KeyPress
KeyUp
LinkClose
LinkError
LinkExecute
LinkOpen
Load
LostFocus
MouseDown
MouseMove
MouseUp
OLECompleteDrag
OLEDragDrop
OLEDragOver
OLEGiveFeedback
OLESetData
OLEStartDrag
Paint
QueryUnload
Resize
Terminate
Unload
```

Format

Function

The Format function formats expressions in various ways. For example, you could choose to format a date in the form 01/21/99 or in the form January 21, 1999.

Syntax

```
value = Format(exp, formatName, firstDay, firstWeek)
```

- *exp*—The expression to be formatted.
- *firstDay* (*) — A value that specifies the first day of the week. Can be vbUseSystem, vbSunday, vbMonday, vbTuesday, vbWednesday, vbThursday, vbFriday, or vbSaturday.
- *firstWeek* (*) — A value that specifies the first week of the year. Can be vbFirstJan1, vbFirstFourDays, vbFirstFullWeek, or vbUseSystem.
- *formatName* (*) — The system-defined format name or a user-defined format.
- *value* — The variable that will receive the formatted string.

(*) = Optional

Example

The following lines show several examples of using the Format function. In the four lines, Visual Basic sets strResult to the values "01:32:15 PM," "Thursday," "1-21-99," and "12,354.20," respectively. Note that the actual formatting depends on your system's regional settings.

```
strResult = Format("13:32:15", "hh:mm:ss AMPM")
strResult = Format("January 21, 1999", "dddd")
strResult = Format("January 21, 1999", "m-d-yy")
strResult = Format(12354.2, "#,##0.00")
```

CROSS-REFERENCE
See also FormatCurrency, FormatDateTime, FormatNumber, and FormatPercent.

FormatCurrency

Function

The FormatCurrency function formats expressions as currency.

Syntax

```
value = FormatCurrency(exp, decimalDigits, _
    leadingDigit, negParens, group)
```

- *exp* — The expression to be formatted.
- *decimalDigits* (★) — The number of places to the right of the decimal point. The value –1, which selects the current regional settings, is the default.
- *group* (★) — A value that specifies whether the regional settings' group delimiter is used to group numbers. Can be set to vbTrue, vbFalse, or vbUseDefault.
- *leadingDigit* (★) — A value that specifies whether leading zeroes should be displayed. Can be set to vbTrue, vbFalse, or vbUseDefault.
- *negParens* (★) — A value that specifies whether negative values should appear inside parentheses. Can be set to vbTrue, vbFalse, or vbUseDefault.
- *value* — The variable that will receive the formatted string.

(★) = Optional

Example

The following lines display the value $1,436.40 in a message box. Note that the actual formatting depends on your system's regional settings.

```
Dim strCurrency As String
strCurrency = FormatCurrency(1436.4, -1, _
    vbFalse, vbTrue, vbUseDefault)
MsgBox strCurrency
```

 CROSS-REFERENCE
See also Format, FormatDateTime, FormatNumber, and FormatPercent.

FormatDateTime

Function

The `FormatDateTime` function formats expressions as dates and times.

Syntax

```
value = FormatDateTime(exp, format)
```

- *exp* — The expression to be formatted.
- *format* (*) — A value that specifies the date and time format. Can be set to `vbGeneralDate` (the default), `vbLongDate`, `vbLongTime`, `vbShortDate`, or `vbLongDate`.
- *value* — The variable that will receive the formatted string.

(*) = Optional

Example

The following lines display the string "Wednesday, January 21, 1999" in a message box. Note that the actual formatting depends on your system's regional settings.

```
Dim strDateTime As String
strDateTime = FormatDateTime("1/21/99", vbLongDate)
MsgBox strDateTime
```

 CROSS-REFERENCE
See also Format, FormatCurrency, FormatNumber, and FormatPercent.

FormatNumber

Function

The `FormatNumber` function formats expressions as numbers.

Syntax

```
value = FormatNumber(exp, decimalDigits, _
    leadingDigit, negParens, group)
```

- *exp* — The expression to be formatted.

- *decimalDigits* (*) — The number of places to the right of the decimal point. The value –1, which selects the current regional settings, is the default.
- *group* (*) — A value that specifies whether the regional settings' group delimiter is used to group numbers. Can be set to `vbTrue`, `vbFalse`, or `vbUseDefault`.
- *leadingDigit* (*) — A value that specifies whether leading zeroes should be displayed. Can be set to `vbTrue`, `vbFalse`, or `vbUseDefault`.
- *negParens* (*) — A value that specifies whether negative values should appear inside parentheses. Can be set to `vbTrue`, `vbFalse`, or `vbUseDefault`.
- *value* — The variable that will receive the formatted string.

(*) = Optional

Example

The following lines display the value 1,436.40 in a message box. Note that the actual formatting depends on your system's regional settings.

```
Dim strNumber As String
strNumber = FormatNumber(1436.4, -1, _
    vbFalse, vbTrue, vbUseDefault)
MsgBox strNumber
```

CROSS-REFERENCE
See also Format, FormatCurrency, FormatDateTime, and FormatPercent.

Format—OLE Container

Property

The `Format` property represents the format in which an embedded object transfers data. You can retrieve supported formats by calling the `ObjectGetFormats` method.

Syntax

```
OLEContainer.Format = value1
```

or

```
value2 = OLEContainer.Format
```

- *OLEContainer*—A reference to an OLE Container control.
- *value1*—A string containing the format name.
- *value2*—The variable that will receive the format name.

Example

The following line sets an OLE Container's data format to `CF_TEXT`. The `oleContainer` object is an OLE container control that the programmer added to the application's form at design time.

```
oleContainer.Format = "CF_TEXT"
```

CROSS-REFERENCE
See also OLE Container, ObjectAcceptFormats, ObjectAcceptFormatCounts, ObjectGetFormats, and ObjectGetFormatsCount.

FormatPercent

Function

The `FormatPercent` function formats expressions as percentages.

Syntax

```
value = FormatPercent(exp, decimalDigits, _
    leadingDigit, negParens, group)
```

- *exp*—The expression to be formatted.
- *decimalDigits* (⋆)—The number of places to the right of the decimal point. The value –1, which selects the current regional settings, is the default.
- *group* (⋆)—A value that specifies whether the regional settings' group delimiter is used to group numbers. Can be set to vbTrue, vbFalse, or vbUseDefault.
- *leadingDigit* (⋆)—A value that specifies whether leading zeroes should be displayed. Can be set to vbTrue, vbFalse, or vbUseDefault.
- *negParens* (⋆)—A value that specifies whether negative values should appear inside parentheses. Can be set to vbTrue, vbFalse, or vbUseDefault.
- *value*—The variable that will receive the formatted string.

(⋆) = Optional

Example

The following lines display the value "15.00%" in a message box. Note that the actual formatting depends on your system's regional settings.

```
Dim strPercent As String
strPercent = FormatPercent(0.15, -1, _
    vbFalse, vbTrue, vbUseDefault)
MsgBox strPercent
```

 CROSS-REFERENCE
See also Format, FormatCurrency, FormatDateTime, and FormatNumber.

Forms

Collection

A Forms collection holds references to Form objects that represent all the application's currently loaded forms.

Properties

A Forms collection has one property, called Count, which represents the number of items in the collection.

Methods

A Forms collection has one method, Item, which returns a reference to a form in the collection.

Example

In this example, the program displays the name of each loaded form in a message box.

```
Dim x As Integer
Dim formCount As Integer

formCount = Forms.Count
For x = 0 To formCount - 1
    MsgBox Forms.Item(I).Caption
Next
```

Note that the line that displays the message box could be rewritten without the `Item` method as follows:

```
MsgBox Forms(I).Caption
```

CROSS-REFERENCE

See also Form and Forms (property).

Forms

Property

The `Forms` property represents an application's Forms collection.

Objects with a Forms Property

Global object

Syntax

```
value = Forms(index)
```

- *Forms*—A reference to the global Forms object.
- *value*—The variable that will receive the indexed Form object.

Example

In this example, the program displays the name of each loaded form in a message box.

```
Dim x As Integer
Dim formCount As Integer

formCount = Forms.Count
For x = 0 To formCount - 1
    MsgBox Forms(I).Caption
Next
```

CROSS-REFERENCE

See also Form and Forms (collection).

For/Next

Statement

The `For/Next` statement is used to execute a set of statements a given number of times.

Syntax

```
For var1 = startValue To endValue step
    ' Body statements go here.
Next var2
```

or

```
For var1 = startValue To endValue step
    ' Body statements go here.
    Exit For
    ' Body statements here.
Next var2
```

- *endValue* — The last value for which the loop will iterate.
- *startValue* — The first value for which the loop will iterate.
- *step* (*) — The keyword `Step` followed by the amount that the loop counter should be incremented each time through the loop.
- *var1* — The variable that will hold the current value of the loop counter.
- *var2* (*) — The same variable used as `var1`.

(*) = Optional

Example 1

The following lines loop through the values 1 through 5, displaying the current value of the loop counter in a message box each time through the loop.

```
Dim x As Integer
For x = 1 To 5
    MsgBox x
Next x
```

Example 2

The following lines loop through the values 10 through 50, displaying the current value of the loop counter in a message box each time through the loop. In this case, the `Step` portion of the statement causes the loop counter to increment by 10 each time through the loop. That is, the message box will display the values 10, 20, 30, 40, and 50.

```
Dim x As Integer
For x = 10 To 50 Step 10
    MsgBox x
Next x
```

Forward

Method

The `Forward` method forwards the current message in a MAPIMessages control.

Objects with a Forward Method

MAPIMessages

Syntax

`MAPIMessages.Forward`

- *MAPIMessages* — A reference to a MAPIMessages control.

Example

The following line forwards a message from a MAPIMessages control. The `MAPIMessages1` object is a MAPIMessages control the programmer added to the application's form at design time.

`MAPIMessages1.Forward`

CROSS-REFERENCE
For more information, see MAPIMessages.

ForwardFocus

Property

The `ForwardFocus` property represents whether, when a UserControl's access key is pressed, Visual Basic will forward the focus to the next control in the tab order or the UserControl itself will receive the focus. This property is available only at the control's authoring time.

Objects with a ForwardFocus Property

UserControl

CROSS-REFERENCE
See also UserControl.

Frame

Control

A Frame is a control that enables a program to organize other controls into a named group. Figure F-15 shows several OptionButton controls grouped into a frame named Options. The Frame control is available on Visual Basic's standard toolbox.

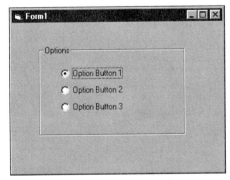

Figure F-15 The Frame control organizes sets of related controls.

Properties

The Frame control has 34 properties, which are listed as follows. Because many Visual Basic controls have similar properties, the properties' descriptions are listed under their own names provided alphabetically in this book.

```
Appearance
BackColor
BorderStyle
```

Caption
ClipControls
Container
DragIcon
DragMode
Enabled
Font
FontBold
FontItalic
FontName
FontSize
FontStrikethru
FontUnderline
Height
HelpContextID
hWnd
Index
Left
MouseIcon
MousePointer
Name
OLEDropMode
Parent
RightToLeft
TabIndex
Tag
ToolTipText
Top
Visible
WhatsThisHelpID
Width

Methods

The Frame control has six methods, which are listed below. Because many Visual Basic controls have similar methods, the methods' descriptions are listed under their own names provided alphabetically in this book.

Drag
Move
OLEDrag

```
Refresh
ShowWhatsThis
ZOrder
```

Events

The Frame control responds to 13 events, which are listed below. Because many Visual Basic controls respond to similar events, the events' descriptions are listed under their own names provided alphabetically in this book.

```
Click
DblClick
DragDrop
DragOver
MouseDown
MouseMove
MouseUp
OLECompleteDrag
OLEDragDrop
OLEDragOver
OLEGiveFeedback
OLESetData
OLEStartDrag
```

Frames

Property

The Frames property represents the frame step rate for the Multimedia MCI control's Step and Back commands. That is, the property determines how many frames forward or backward to step.

Objects with a Frame Property

Multimedia MCI

Syntax

```
MultimediMCI.Frames = value1
```

or

```
value2 = MultimediMCI.Frames
```

- *MultimediaMCI*—A reference to a Multimedia MCI control.

- *value1* — The frame rate setting.
- *value2* — The variable that will receive the current frame rate setting.

Example

In this example, the program sets a Multimedia MCI control's step rate to 10. The `mciMMControl1` object is a Multimedia MCI control that the programmer added to the application's form at design time.

```
mciMMControl1.Frames = 10
```

 CROSS-REFERENCE
See also Multimedia MCI.

FreeFile

Function

The `FreeFile` function returns the next available file number.

Syntax

```
value = FreeFile(range)
```

- *range* (*) — A value that specifies the range from which to return the file number. Set this argument to 0 (the default) to return a file number from the range 1 to 255, and set to 1 to return a file number from the range 256 to 511.
- *value* — The variable that will receive the file number.

(*) = Optional

Example

In this example, the program uses the `FreeFile` function to get a file number for a new text file. The program then creates the text file, writes a line of text to the file, and closes the file.

```
Dim fileNum As Integer
fileNum = FreeFile
Open "c:\Text.txt" For Output As #fileNum
Write #fileNum, "Text for a text file"
Close #fileNum
```

FreeSpace

Property

The FreeSpace property represents the amount of free space on a drive.

Objects with a FreeSpace Property

Drive

Syntax

```
value = Drive.FreeSpace
```

- *Drive* — A reference to a Drive object.

Example

The following lines display the amount of free space on drive C.

```
Dim fileSystem
Dim drive
Set fileSystem = CreateObject("Scripting.FileSystemObject")
Set drive = fileSystem.GetDrive("c")
MsgBox drive.FreeSpace
```

 CROSS-REFERENCE
See also Drive and FileSystemObject.

Friend

Keyword

The Friend keyword specifies that a procedure in a form or class module can be called from other modules in the project, but cannot be called by class-instance controllers, as would be the case if the procedure were declared Public. The following is an example of a procedure declared as Friend:

```
Friend Sub MyProcedure()
    ' Body of procedure here.
End Sub
```

CROSS-REFERENCE
See also Public and Private.

From

Property

The `From` property represents the position at which a Play or Record command should begin. The value to set this property depends upon the setting of the `TimeFormat` property.

Objects with a From Property
Multimedia MCI

Syntax

```
MultimediaMCI.From = value1
```

or

```
value2 = MultimediaMCI.From
```

- *MultimediaMCI* — A reference to a Multimedia MCI control.
- *value1* — The position at which to start.
- *value2* — The variable that will receive the property's current setting.

Example

The following lines set a Multimedia MCI control's time format to milliseconds and sets the starting point to 10 seconds from the start of the file.

```
MMControl1.TimeFormat = 0
MMControl1.From = 10000
```

CROSS-REFERENCE
See also Multimedia MCI, TimeFormat, and To.

FromPage

Property

The FromPage property represents the value that will appear in a Print dialog box's From text box.

Objects with a FromPage Property
CommonDialog

Syntax

```
CommonDialog.FromPage = value1
```

or

```
value2 = CommonDialog.FromPage
```

- *CommonDialog*—A reference to a CommonDialog control.
- *value1*—The starting page number.
- *value2*—The variable that will receive the starting page number.

Example

In this example, the program sets a Print dialog box's From box to 1. The dlgCommonDialog1 object is a CommonDialog control that the programmer added to the application's form at design time.

```
CommonDialog1.FromPage = 1
```

 CROSS-REFERENCE
See also Flags and ToPage.

FullPath

Property

The FullPath property represents the full path of a node in a TreeView control. This path includes the name of the target node appended to the names of all the nodes that must be expanded to get to the target node.

Objects with a FullPath Property

Node

Syntax

```
value = Node.FullPath
```

- *Node* — A reference to a Node object.
- *value* — The variable that will receive the node path.

Example

In this example, the program populates a TreeView control with nodes, and then displays the path of the fourth node. In this case, the message box displays the path "People/Alice/Grant." Figure F-16 shows the TreeView control created by this example, with the path to the Grant node fully expanded. The treTreeView1 object is a TreeView control that the programmer added to the application's form at design time.

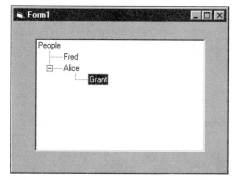

Figure F-16 This TreeView controls shows the path to the Grant node.

```
Dim nodePath As String
treTreeView1.Nodes.Add , , "Root", "People"
treTreeView1.Nodes.Add "Root", tvwChild, "Child1", "Fred"
treTreeView1.Nodes.Add "Root", tvwChild, "Child2", "Alice"
treTreeView1.Nodes.Add "Child2", tvwChild, "Child3", "Grant"
nodePath = treTreeView1.Nodes(4).FullPath
MsgBox nodePath
```

CROSS-REFERENCE
See also Node and TreeView.

FullRowSelect

Property

The FullRowSelect property represents whether an entire row is selected in a ListView (set to report view) or TreeView control. When set to True in a TreeView control, a selected node highlights from the node's text all the way to the right edge of the control. When set to True in a ListView control that's displayed in report view, the selected item highlights the entire width of the control.

Objects with a FullRowSelect Property

ListView

TreeView

Syntax

object.FullRowSelect = *value1*

or

value2 = *object*.FullRowSelect

- *object* — A reference to a ListView or TreeView control.
- *value1* — The value True or False.
- *value2* — The variable that will receive the property's current setting.

Example

The following line sets a ListView control to highlight a selected row completely. The lvwListView1 object is a ListView control that the programmer added to the application's form at design time.

lvwListView1.FullRowSelect = True

CROSS-REFERENCE
See also ListView and TreeView.

Function

Keyword

The Function keyword is used to declare Visual Basic functions. The keyword specifies the function's starting line and ending line. It can also be used in the Exit Function statement to exit the function from anywhere within the function's body statements. The following lines illustrate the definition of a Visual Basic function.

```
Private Function Min(val1 As Integer, val2 As Integer) As
Integer
    If val < val2 Then
        Min = val1
    Else
        Min = val2
    End If
End Function
```

CROSS-REFERENCE

For more information, see End Function (concept).

FV

Function

The FV function calculates the future value of an annuity.

Syntax

```
value = PV(intRate, numPayments, payment, presValue, payDue)
```

- *intRate* — The interest rate per period.
- *numPayments* — The number of payments.
- *payDue* (*) — The value 0 if payments are made at the end of the period and 1 if payments are made at the start of the period. The default is 0.
- *payment* — The amount of a payment.
- *presValue* (*) — The annuity's present value.
- *value* — The variable that will receive the future value.

(*) = Optional

Example

The following program is a future-value calculator that demonstrates the FV function. When you run the program, enter the following values into the text boxes:

- Enter the amount of each payment into the Amount of Payment box.
- Enter the yearly interest rate into the Annual Interest Rate box.
- Enter the number of payments into the Number of Payments box.
- Enter the annuity's present value (the amount already in the account) into the Present Value box.

After entering the data, click the Calculate button. The annuity's future value then appears at the bottom of the window. For example, the future value of an annuity that will require 24 annual payments of $100 each, with an annual interest rate of 10% and a present value of $1,000, is $3,865.08.

```
VERSION 5.00
Begin VB.Form Form1
    Caption         =   "FV Demo"
    ClientHeight    =   4305
    ClientLeft      =   165
    ClientTop       =   450
    ClientWidth     =   5235
    LinkTopic       =   "Form1"
    ScaleHeight     =   4305
    ScaleWidth      =   5235
    StartUpPosition =   3   'Windows Default
    Begin VB.TextBox txtPresValue
        Height          =   375
        Left            =   240
        TabIndex        =   8
        Top             =   2040
        Width           =   1695
    End
    Begin VB.CommandButton btnCalculate
        Caption         =   "Calculate"
        Height          =   1095
        Left            =   2520
        TabIndex        =   6
        Top             =   1200
        Width           =   1815
    End
End
```

```
Begin VB.TextBox txtNumPayments
   Height        =  375
   Left          =  240
   TabIndex      =  5
   Top           =  1200
   Width         =  1695
End
Begin VB.TextBox txtIntRate
   Height        =  375
   Left          =  2520
   TabIndex      =  3
   Top           =  360
   Width         =  1815
End
Begin VB.TextBox txtPayment
   Height        =  375
   Left          =  240
   TabIndex      =  1
   Top           =  360
   Width         =  1695
End
Begin VB.Label Label4
   Caption       =  "Present Value:"
   Height        =  255
   Left          =  240
   TabIndex      =  9
   Top           =  1800
   Width         =  1575
End
Begin VB.Label lblFutValue
   BorderStyle   =  1  'Fixed Single
   Caption       =  "Future Value:"
   BeginProperty Font
      Name          =  "MS Sans Serif"
      Size          =  13.5
      Charset       =  0
      Weight        =  400
      Underline     =  0   'False
      Italic        =  0   'False
      Strikethrough =  0   'False
   EndProperty
   Height        =  615
   Left          =  240
   TabIndex      =  7
```

```
            Top             =    3120
            Width           =    4815
         End
         Begin VB.Label Label3
            Caption         =    "Number of Payments:"
            Height          =    255
            Left            =    240
            TabIndex        =    4
            Top             =    960
            Width           =    1575
         End
         Begin VB.Label Label2
            Caption         =    "Annual Interest Rate:"
            Height          =    255
            Left            =    2520
            TabIndex        =    2
            Top             =    120
            Width           =    1575
         End
         Begin VB.Label Label1
            Caption         =    "Amount of payment:"
            Height          =    255
            Left            =    240
            TabIndex        =    0
            Top             =    120
            Width           =    1695
         End
      End
Attribute VB_Name = "Form1"
Attribute VB_GlobalNameSpace = False
Attribute VB_Creatable = False
Attribute VB_PredeclaredId = True
Attribute VB_Exposed = False
Private Sub btnCalculate_Click()
    Dim intRate As Double
    Dim numPayments As Integer
    Dim paymentAmt As Double
    Dim futValue As Double
    Dim presValue As Double
    Dim strResult As String

    On Error GoTo ErrorHandler
```

```
    intRate = txtIntRate.Text
    intRate = intRate / 100 / 12
    paymentAmt = txtPayment.Text
    numPayments = txtNumPayments.Text
    presValue = txtPresValue

    futValue = FV(intRate, numPayments, -paymentAmt, _
        -presValue, 0)
    futValue = futValue + 0.005
    strResult = "$" & Format(futValue, "###,###,##0.00")
    lblFutValue.Caption = "Future Value: " & strResult
    Exit Sub

ErrorHandler:
    MsgBox "An error occurred.", vbExclamation
End Sub
```

G

Get

Statement

The Get statement retrieves data from a disk file.

Syntax

```
Get #num, offset, buf
```

- *buf* — The variable into which the data will be stored.
- *num* — The file number.
- *offset* (*) — The offset at which to start reading data.

(*) = Optional

Example

The following lines open a file and read an integer value using the Get statement.

```
Dim intData As Integer
Open "c:\MyFile.dat" For Binary As #1
Get #1, , intData
Close #1
```

 CROSS-REFERENCE
See also Put, Open, and Close.

GetAbsolutePathName

Method

The GetAbsolutePathName method constructs a complete path name based on the current directory and the given path specification.

Objects with a GetAbsolutePathName Method

FileSystemObject

Syntax

```
value = FileSystemObject.GetAbsolutePathName
```

- *FileSystemObject* — A reference to a FileSystemObject.
- *value* — The variable that will receive the returned path.

Example

If the current directory were c:\MyStuff\Pics, the message box produced by the following lines would display "c:\MyStuff\Pics."

```
Dim strPath As String
Dim fileSystem
Set fileSystem = CreateObject("Scripting.FileSystemObject")
strPath = fileSystem.GetAbsolutePathName("c:")
MsgBox strPath
```

 CROSS-REFERENCE
See also FileSystemObject, GetBaseName, GetFileName, GetDriveName, GetExtensionName, GetParentFolderName, and GetTempName.

GetAllSettings

Function

The GetAllSettings function retrieves an application's settings from the Registry.

Syntax

```
value = GetAllSettings(app, regSection)
```

- *app* — The application's name.
- *regSection* — The name of the Registry section containing the required keys.

- *value* — The Variant variable that will receive the return values as a two-dimensional array.

Example

The following lines extract the Registry keys from the Init section of the PicMachine application. (PicMachine is a fictional application whose name is used only for the example.)

```
Dim regKeys as Variant
regKeys = GetAllSettings("PicMachine", "Init")
```

CROSS-REFERENCE
See also GetSetting, SaveSetting, and DeleteSetting.

GetAttr

Function

The GetAttr function returns an integer value that contains flags that indicate file or folder attributes. The flags can be a combination of vbArchive, vbDirectory, vbHidden, vbNormal, vbReadOnly, and vbSystem.

Syntax

```
value = GetAttr(path)
```

- *path* — The path to the file or folder.
- *value* — The variable that will receive the attribute flags.

Example

The following lines determine whether the file MyFile.dat on drive C has its read-only attribute set.

```
Dim attrFlags As Integer
attrFlags = GetAttr("c:\MyFile.dat")
If attrFlags And vbReadOnly Then
    MsgBox "File is read-only"
Else
    MsgBox "File is read/write"
End If
```

GetBaseName

Method

The `GetBaseName` method returns the last portion, not including a file extension, of a given path.

Objects with a GetBaseName Method

FileSystemObject

Syntax

```
value = FileSystemObject.GetBaseName(path)
```

- *FileSystemObject*—A reference to a FileSystemObject.
- *path*—The path from which to extract the base name.
- *value*—The variable that will receive the base name.

Example

The following lines create a FileSystemObject and call its `GetBaseName` function on the path c:\MyFiles\MyText.txt. A message box then displays the results "MyText."

```
Dim strBaseName As String
Dim fileSystem
Set fileSystem = CreateObject("Scripting.FileSystemObject")
strBaseName = fileSystem.GetBaseName("c:\MyFiles\MyText.txt")
MsgBox strBaseName
```

CROSS-REFERENCE
See also FileSystemObject, GetAbsolutePathName, GetFileName, GetDriveName, GetExtensionName, GetParentFolderName, and GetTempName.

GetData

Method

The `GetData` method retrieves graphical data from the Clipboard.

Objects with a GetData Method

Clipboard

Syntax

value = ClipBoard.GetData(*dataType*)

- *Clipboard* — A reference to the Clipboard object.
- *dataType* (*) — The type of graphical data to retrieve, which can be vbCFBitmap, vbCFDIB, vbCFMetafile, or vbCFPalette.
- *value* — The variable that will receive the image.

(*) = Optional

Example

The following line gets graphical data from the Clipboard and displays it in the form. The Clipboard object is a Visual Basic global object that you don't need to create in your programs.

```
frmForm1.Picture = Clipboard.GetData
```

 CROSS-REFERENCE
For more information, see Clipboard, GetFormat, GetText, SetData, and SetText.

GetDrive

Method

The GetDrive method returns a Drive object for the given path.

Objects with a GetDrive Method

FileSystemObject

Syntax

value = FileSystemObject.GetDrive(*path*)

- *FileSystemObject* — A reference to a FileSystemObject.
- *path* — The path from which to create the Drive object.
- *value* — The variable that will receive the Drive object.

Example

The following lines create a FileSystemObject and call its GetDrive function to get a Drive object for drive C. The message box then displays the amount of free space on the drive.

```
Dim drive, fileSystem As Object
Set fileSystem = CreateObject("Scripting.FileSystemObject")
Set drive = fileSystem.GetDrive("c:")
MsgBox drive.freespace
```

 CROSS-REFERENCE
See also FileSystemObject, Drive, GetFile, GetFolder, and GetSpecialFolder.

GetDriveName

Method

The GetDriveName method returns the name of a drive from a given path.

Objects with a GetDriveName Method

FileSystemObject

Syntax

```
value = FileSystemObject.GetDriveName(path)
```

- *FileSystemObject* — A reference to a FileSystemObject.
- *path* — The path from which to get the drive name.
- *value* — The variable that will receive the drive name.

Example

The following lines create a FileSystemObject and call its GetDriveName function on the path c:\MyFiles\MyText.txt. The message box then displays the result "c:".

```
Dim fileSystem As Object
Dim drvName As String
Set fileSystem = CreateObject("Scripting.FileSystemObject")
drvName = fileSystem.GetDriveName("c:\MyFiles\MyText.txt")
MsgBox drvName
```

CROSS-REFERENCE

See also FileSystemObject, GetAbsolutePathName, GetBaseName, GetFileName, GetExtensionName, GetParentFolderName, and GetTempName.

GetExtensionName

Method

The GetExtensionName method returns the file extension from a given path.

Objects with a GetExtensionName Method

FileSystemObject

Syntax

```
value = FileSystemObject.GetExtensionName(path)
```

- *FileSystemObject* — A reference to a FileSystemObject.
- *path* — The path from which to get the extension name.
- *value* — The variable that will receive the extension name.

Example

The following lines create a FileSystemObject and call its GetExtensionName function on the path c:\MyFiles\MyText.txt. The message box then displays the result "txt."

```
Dim fileSystem As Object
Dim extName As String
Set fileSystem = CreateObject("Scripting.FileSystemObject")
extName = fileSystem.GetExtensionName("c:\MyFiles\MyText.txt")
MsgBox extName
```

CROSS-REFERENCE

See also FileSystemObject, GetAbsolutePathName, GetBaseName, GetDriveName, GetFileName, GetParentFolderName, and GetTempName.

GetFile

Method

The GetFile method returns a File object for the given path.

Objects with a GetFile Method
FileSystemObject

Syntax

```
value = FileSystemObject.GetFile(path)
```

- *FileSystemObject*—A reference to a FileSystemObject.
- *path*—The path from which to create the File object.
- *value*—The variable that will receive the File object.

Example

The following lines create a FileSystemObject and call its GetFile function to get a File object from the path c:\TextFile.txt. The message box then displays the size of the file.

```
Dim file, fileSystem As Object
Set fileSystem = CreateObject("Scripting.FileSystemObject")
Set file = fileSystem.GetFile("c:\TextFile.txt")
MsgBox file.Size
```

 CROSS-REFERENCE
See also FileSystemObject, File, GetDrive, GetFolder, and GetSpecialFolder.

GetFileName

Method

The GetFileName method returns the file name from a given path.

Objects with a GetFileName Method
FileSystemObject

Syntax

```
value = FileSystemObject.GetFileName(path)
```

- *FileSystemObject* — A reference to a FileSystemObject.
- *path* — The path from which to get the file name.
- *value* — The variable that will receive the file name.

Example

The following lines create a FileSystemObject and call its `GetFileName` function on the path c:\MyFiles\MyText.txt. The message box then displays the result "MyFile.txt."

```
Dim fileSystem As Object
Dim fileName As String
Set fileSystem = CreateObject("Scripting.FileSystemObject")
fileName = fileSystem.GetFileName("c:\MyFiles\MyText.txt")
MsgBox fileName
```

CROSS-REFERENCE

See also FileSystemObject, GetAbsolutePathName, GetBaseName, GetDriveName, GetExtensionName, GetParentFolderName, and GetTempName.

GetFirstVisible

Method

The `GetFirstVisible` method gets the first visible ListItem object displayed in a ListView control.

Objects with a GetFirstVisible Method

ListView

Syntax

```
value = ListView.GetFirstVisible
```

- *ListView* — A reference to a ListView control.
- *value* — The variable that will receive the returned ListItem object.

Example

The following program demonstrates how the `GetFirstVisible` method works. When you run the program, scroll the ListView control to any position you like and then click the Mark First button. The program calls the `GetFirstVisible` method to determine the first visible ListItem object in the ListView control and changes that ListItem object's text to "First Item," as shown in Figure G-1.

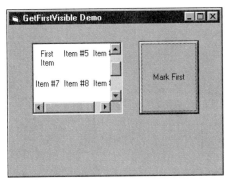

Figure G-1 The first visible item in this ListView control has had its text changed to "First Item."

```
VERSION 5.00
Object = "{6B7E6392-850A-101B-AFC0-4210102A8DA7} _
   #2.0#0"; "MSCOMCTL.OCX"
Begin VB.Form Form1
   Caption         =   "GetFirstVisible Demo"
   ClientHeight    =   3195
   ClientLeft      =   60
   ClientTop       =   345
   ClientWidth     =   4680
   LinkTopic       =   "Form1"
   ScaleHeight     =   3195
   ScaleWidth      =   4680
   StartUpPosition =   3   'Windows Default
   Begin VB.CommandButton btnMarkFirstVisible
      Caption      =   "Mark First"
      Height       =   1575
      Left         =   2880
      TabIndex     =   1
      Top          =   360
      Width        =   1335
   End
```

```
    Begin MSComctlLib.ListView lvwListView1
        Height          =   1575
        Left            =   480
        TabIndex        =   0
        Top             =   360
        Width           =   2055
        _ExtentX        =   3625
        _ExtentY        =   2778
        LabelWrap       =   -1  'True
        HideSelection   =   -1  'True
        _Version        =   393217
        ForeColor       =   -2147483640
        BackColor       =   -2147483643
        BorderStyle     =   1
        Appearance      =   1
        NumItems        =   0
    End
End
Attribute VB_Name = "Form1"
Attribute VB_GlobalNameSpace = False
Attribute VB_Creatable = False
Attribute VB_PredeclaredId = True
Attribute VB_Exposed = False

Private Sub btnMarkFirstVisible_Click()
    Dim visItem As ListItem
    Set visItem = lvwListView1.GetFirstVisible
    visItem.Text = "First Item"
End Sub

Private Sub Form_Load()
    lvwListView1.ListItems.Add , , "Item #1"
    lvwListView1.ListItems.Add , , "Item #2"
    lvwListView1.ListItems.Add , , "Item #3"
    lvwListView1.ListItems.Add , , "Item #4"
    lvwListView1.ListItems.Add , , "Item #5"
    lvwListView1.ListItems.Add , , "Item #6"
    lvwListView1.ListItems.Add , , "Item #7"
    lvwListView1.ListItems.Add , , "Item #8"
    lvwListView1.ListItems.Add , , "Item #9"
    lvwListView1.ListItems.Add , , "Item #10"
    lvwListView1.ListItems.Add , , "Item #11"
    lvwListView1.ListItems.Add , , "Item #12"
End Sub
```

CROSS-REFERENCE
For more information, see ListView, ListItem, and ListItems.

GetFolder

Method

The `GetFolder` method returns a Folder object for the given path.

Objects with a GetFolder Method

FileSystemObject

Syntax

```
value = FileSystemObject.GetFolder(path)
```

- *FileSystemObject*—A reference to a FileSystemObject.
- *path*—The path from which to create the Folder object.
- *value*—The variable that will receive the Folder object.

Example

The following lines create a FileSystemObject and call its `GetFolder` function to get a Folder object from the path c:\My Documents. The message box then displays the folder's size.

```
Dim folder, fileSystem As Object
Set fileSystem = CreateObject("Scripting.FileSystemObject")
Set folder = fileSystem.GetFolder("c:\My Documents")
MsgBox folder.Size
```

CROSS-REFERENCE
See also FileSystemObject, Folder, GetDrive, GetFile, and GetSpecialFolder.

GetFormat

Method

The `GetFormat` method determines whether the Clipboard contains the type of data given as the method's single argument, which can be one of the values `vbCFBitmap`, `vbCFDIB`, `vbCFLink`, `vbCFMetafile`, `vbCFPalette`, or `vbCFText`.

Objects with a GetFormat Method

Clipboard

Syntax

```
value = Clipboard.GetFormat(dataType)
```

- *Clipboard*—A reference to the Clipboard object.
- *dataType*—A value specifying the type of data for which to check.
- *value*—The variable that will receive the return value of `True` or `False`.

Example

The following lines determine whether the Clipboard currently contains text data. A message box displays the result. Note that the Clipboard object is a Visual Basic global object that you don't need to create in your programs.

```
Dim gotFormat As Boolean
gotFormat = Clipboard.GetFormat(vbCFText)
If gotFormat Then
    MsgBox "Clipboard contains text"
Else
    MsgBox "Clipboard does not contain text"
End If
```

CROSS-REFERENCE

For more information, see Clipboard, GetData, GetText, SetData, and SetText.

GetLineFromChar

Method

The `GetLineFromChar` method determines the text line on which a specified character index is located.

Objects with a GetLineFromChar Method

RichTextBox

Syntax

```
value = RichTextBox.GetLineFromChar(index)
```

- *index* — The position of the character whose line number the method should determine.
- *RichTextBox* — A reference to a RichTextBox control.
- *value* — The variable that will receive the line number.

Example

The following lines determine the line number on which the 50th character is located. The rtfRichTextBox1 object is a RichTextBox control the programmer added to the application's form at design time.

```
Dim charLine As Integer
charLine = rtfRichTextBox1.GetLineFromChar(50)
```

 CROSS-REFERENCE
For more information, see RichTextBox.

GetNumTicks

Method

The GetNumTicks method determines the number of ticks between a Slider control's Min and Max property settings.

Objects with a GetNumTicks Method

Slider

Syntax

```
value = Slider.GetNumTicks
```

- *Slider* — A reference to a Slider control.
- *value* — The variable that will receive the number of ticks.

Example

The following lines get the number of ticks on a Slider control and display the result in a message box. The sldSlider1 object is a Slider control the programmer added to the application's form at design time.

```
Dim numClicks As Integer
numClicks = sldSlider1.GetNumTicks
MsgBox numClicks
```

CROSS-REFERENCE
For more information, see Slider, Min, and Max.

GetObject

Function

The `GetObject` function associates an Object object with an object supplied by an ActiveX component.

Syntax

```
value = GetObject(path, class)
```

- *class* (✲) — The object's class name. Either this argument or the *path* argument (or both) must be specified. If only *class* is specified, `CreateObject` creates a new object.
- *path* (✲) — The file from which to create the object. Either this argument or the *class* argument (or both) must be specified. If *path* is specified, `CreateObject` creates the object from the specified file.
- *value* — The variable that will receive the returned object.

(✲) = Optional

Example

The following lines create an object from a Word document.

```
Dim obj As Object
Set obj = GetObject("c:\MyDoc.doc", "Word.Document.8")
```

GetParentFolderName

Method

The `GetParentFolderName` method returns the name of the parent folder of a folder in the given path.

Objects with a GetParentFolderName Method

FileSystemObject

Syntax

```
value = FileSystemObject.GetParentFolderName(path)
```

- *FileSystemObject* — A reference to a FileSystemObject.
- *path* — The path from which to get the folder name.
- *value* — The variable that will receive the folder name.

Example

The following lines create a FileSystemObject and call its `GetParentFolderName` function to get a folder name from the path c:\MyFiles\TextFiles. The message box then displays the result "c:\MyFiles."

```
Dim fileSystem As Object
Dim folderName As String
Set fileSystem = CreateObject("Scripting.FileSystemObject")
folderName =
fileSystem.GetParentFolderName("c:\MyFiles\TextFiles")
MsgBox folderName
```

CROSS-REFERENCE
See also FileSystemObject, GetAbsolutePathName, GetBaseName, GetDriveName, GetExtensionName, GetFileName, and GetTempName.

GetSetting

Function

The `GetSetting` function retrieves a key setting from the Registry.

Syntax

```
value = GetSetting(app, regSection, regKey, defaultVal)
```

- *app* — The application's name.
- *regSection* — The name of the Registry section.
- *regKey* — The name of the Registry key.
- *defaultVal* (*) — The default value to return if the key value doesn't exist.
- *value* — The variable that will receive the key setting.

(*) = Optional

Example

The following lines extract the value of the Width key from the Init section of the PicMachine application's Registry entry. (PicMachine is a fictional application whose name is used for this example.)

```
Dim regKeys as Integer
regKeys = GetSetting("PicMachine", "Init", "Width", 50)
```

CROSS-REFERENCE
See also GetAllSettings, SaveSetting, and DeleteSetting.

GetSpecialFolder

Method

The GetSpecialFolder method returns a Folder object for the system's Windows folder, system folder, or temporary folder.

Objects with a GetSpecialFolder Method

FileSystemObject

Syntax

```
value = FileSystemObject.GetSpecialFolder(type)
```

- *FileSystemObject* — A reference to a FileSystemObject.
- *type* — A value specifying the type of folder to get. Can be WindowsFolder, SystemFolder, or TemporaryFolder.
- *value* — The variable that will receive the Folder object.

Example

The following lines create a FileSystemObject and call its GetSpecialFolder function to get a Folder object for the user's Windows folder. The message box then displays the folder's name.

```
Dim folder, fileSystem As Object
Set fileSystem = CreateObject("Scripting.FileSystemObject")
Set folder = fileSystem.GetSpecialFolder(WindowsFolder)
MsgBox folder.Name
```

CROSS-REFERENCE
See also FileSystemObject, Folder, GetDrive, GetFile, and GetFolder.

GetTempName

Method

The `GetTempName` method generates a random folder name that can be used as the name for a temporary folder.

Objects with a GetTempName Method

FileSystemObject

Syntax

```
value = FileSystemObject.GetTempName
```

- *FileSystemObject* — A reference to a FileSystemObject.
- *value* — The variable that will receive the folder name.

Example

The following lines create and display a random name for a temporary folder. An example of the type of name created by this method is "rad73ABF.tmp."

```
Dim fileSystem As Object
Dim folderName As String
Set fileSystem = CreateObject("Scripting.FileSystemObject")
folderName = fileSystem.GetTempName
MsgBox folderName
```

CROSS-REFERENCE
See also FileSystemObject, GetAbsolutePathName, GetBaseName, GetDriveName, GetExtensionName, GetFileName, and GetParentFolderName.

GetText

Method

The `GetText` method retrieves text data from the Clipboard.

Objects with a GetText Method

Clipboard

Syntax

```
value = ClipBoard.GetText(dataType)
```

- *Clipboard*—A reference to the Clipboard object.
- *dataType* (*) — The type of text data to retrieve, which can be `vbCFLink`, `vbCFText`, or `vbCFRTF`.
- *value*—The variable that will receive the text.

(*) = Optional

Example

The following line gets text data from the Clipboard and displays it in a message box. If the Clipboard contains no text, the method returns an empty string. The Clipboard object is a Visual Basic global object that you don't need to create in your programs.

```
Dim strText As String
strText = Clipboard.GetText(vbCFText)
MsgBox strText
```

CROSS-REFERENCE

For more information, see Clipboard, GetFormat, GetData, SetData, and SetText.

GetVisibleCount

Method

The `GetVisibleCount` method determines how many nodes can be displayed in a TreeView control.

Objects with a GetVisibleCount Method

TreeView

Syntax

```
value = TreeView.GetVisibleCount
```

- *TreeView* — A reference to a TreeView control.
- *value* — The variable that will receive the returned value.

Example

The following line gets the number of nodes that will fit in a TreeView control's display. The `treTreeView1` object is a TreeView control the programmer added to the form at design time.

```
Dim numNodes As Integer
numNodes = treTreeView1.GetVisibleCount
```

CROSS-REFERENCE
For more information, see TreeView.

Ghosted

Property

The `Ghosted` property represents whether a ListItem in a ListView control is displayed dimmed out and is not selectable by the user.

Objects with a Ghosted Property

ListItem

Syntax

```
ListItem.Ghosted = value1
```

or

```
value2 = ListItem.Ghosted
```

- *ListItem* — A reference to a ListItem object.
- *value1* — The value `True` or `False`.
- *value2* — The variable that will receive the property's current setting.

Example

The following line sets a ListItem in a ListView control to ghosted. The lvwListView1 object is a ListView control the programmer added to the form at design time.

```
lvwListView1.ListItems(2).Ghosted = True
```

 CROSS-REFERENCE
See also ListItem and ListView.

Global

Object

The Global object represents a group of application-level objects that enable a program to get information about, as well as to manipulate, system features such as the Clipboard, the screen, and the current printer. You never need to refer to the Global object explicitly. Instead, use the object's properties directly to access the desired system feature.

Properties

The Global object has seven properties, which are listed in Table G-1. For more information on using an object associated with a property shown in the following table, look up the object's entry provided alphabetically in this book.

Table G-1 Properties of the Global Object

Property	Description
App	Represents the App object.
Clipboard	Represents the Clipboard object.
Forms	Represents the Forms collection.
Licenses	Represents the Licenses object.
Printer	Represents the Printer object.
Printers	Represents the Printers collection.
Screen	Represents the Screen object.

f
g
h

Methods

The Global object has seven methods, which are listed in Table G-2. For more information on using a method shown in the following table, look up the method's entry provided alphabetically in this book.

Table G-2 Methods of the Global object

Method	Description
Load	Loads a form or control.
LoadPicture	Loads a picture file.
LoadResData	Loads data from a resource file.
LoadResPicture	Loads an image from a resource file.
LoadResString	Loads a string from a resource file.
SavePicture	Saves a picture to a file.
Unload	Unloads a form or control.

Events

The Global object does not respond to events.

Example 1

The following lines determine whether the Clipboard contains text data.

```
Dim gotFormat As Boolean
gotFormat = Clipboard.GetFormat(vbCFText)
If gotFormat Then
    MsgBox "Clipboard contains text"
Else
    MsgBox "Clipboard does not contain text"
End If
```

Example 2

The following line loads a bitmap into the Picture property of the current form.

```
Picture = LoadPicture("c:\but1.bmp")
```

GoSub

Statement

The GoSub statement causes program execution to jump to a subroutine within the current procedure. The Return statement causes program execution to jump to the line immediately following the GoSub statement.

Syntax

```
GoSub LineID
```

- *LineID* — The line number or line label to where program execution should jump.

Example

In this example, if x equals five, the procedure calls a subroutine named FiveSub. The Return statement in the FiveSub subroutine causes program execution to jump back to the Exit Sub statement immediately following the GoSub statement.

```
Private Sub Command1_Click()
    If x = 5 Then
        GoSub FiveSub
        Exit Sub
    Else
        ' Additional statements here.
        Exit Sub
    End If

FiveSub:
    ' Subroutine statements here.
    Return
End Sub
```

GotFocus

Event

Visual Basic sends a control a GotFocus event when the control receives the input focus. This can occur programmatically by calling the SetFocus method, or it can occur by the user's selection of the control.

Objects That Receive GotFocus Events

Animation

CheckBox

ComboBox

CommandButton

DirListBox

DriveListBox

FileListBox

Form

HScrollBar

ListBox

ListView

OLE Container

OptionButton

PictureBox

PropertyPage

RichTextBox

Slider

TabStrip

TextBox

TreeView

UpDown

UserControl

VScrollBar

Example

A program can respond to a `GotFocus` event by implementing the target object's `GotFocus` event procedure. The following code segment shows how a CommandButton object defines a `GotFocus` event procedure. The `btnCommand1` object is a CommandButton control that the programmer added to the form at design time.

```
Private Sub btnCommand1_GotFocus()
    ' respond to the GotFocus event here.
End Sub
```

CROSS-REFERENCE
See also LostFocus and SetFocus.

GoTo

Statement

The GoTo statement causes program execution to jump to the specified line.

Syntax

```
GoTo LineID
```

- *LineID* — The line number or line label to where program execution should jump.

Example

In this example, a procedure uses the GoTo statement to direct errors to the error handler segment of the code, which begins with the label ErrorHandler.

```
Private Sub btnLoad_Click()
    dlgCommonDialog1.ShowOpen
    On Error GoTo ErrorHandler
    Animation1.Open dlgCommonDialog1.FileName
    Exit Sub
ErrorHandler:
    MsgBox "Couldn't Open the File"
End Sub
```

GridLines

Property

The GridLines property represents whether a ListView control in report view displays grid lines.

Objects with a GridLines Property

ListView

Syntax

```
ListView.GridLines = value1
```

or

```
value2 = ListView.GridLines
```

- *ListView*—A reference to a ListView control.
- *value1*—The value `True` or `False`.
- *value2*—The variable that will receive the property's current setting.

Example

The following lines set a ListView control to report view and to display grid lines. The `lvwListView1` object is a ListView control that the programmer added to the application's form at design time.

```
lvwListView1.View = lvwReport
lvwListView1.GridLines = True
```

CROSS-REFERENCE

For more information, see ListView and View.

Handle

Property

The `Handle` property represents the handle of a Picture object's image. Normally, you use the `Handle` property only when you need a reference to a Picture image in order to call a function in a DLL.

Objects with a Handle Property

Picture

Syntax

`value = Picture.Handle`

- *Picture* — A reference to a Picture object.
- *value* — The variable that will receive the handle.

Example

In this example, the program loads an image into a form and then obtains the handle of the image from the resultant Picture object. In the following lines, note that the symbol `Picture`, which is a reference to a Picture object, is a property of the Form object.

```
Dim picHnd As Integer
frmForm1.Picture = LoadPicture("c:\MyImage.bmp")
picHnd = frmForm1.Picture.handle
```

 CROSS-REFERENCE
See also Picture.

HasDC

Property

The HasDC property represents whether a control has a device-context handle.

Objects with a HasDC Property

Form
PictureBox
PropertyPage
UserControl

Syntax

```
object.HasDC = value1
```

or

```
value2 = object.HasDC
```

- *object* — A reference to a control with a HasDC property.
- *value1* — The value True or False.
- *value2* — The variable that will receive the property's current setting.

Example

The following lines determine whether or not a Form object has a handle to a device context.

```
Dim result As Boolean
result = frmForm1.HasDC
```

 **CROSS-REFERENCE**
See also hDC.

hDC

Property

The hDC property represents the handle of a control's device context.

Objects with an hDC Property

CommonDialog

Form

PictureBox

Printer

PropertyPage

UserControl

Syntax

```
value = object.hDC
```

- *object* — A reference to a control with an hDC property.
- *value* — The variable that will receive the device-context handle.

Example

The following lines get the handle to a form's device context.

```
Dim frmDCHnd As Integer
If frmForm1.HasDC Then
    frmDCHnd = frmForm1.hDC
Else
    frmDCHnd = -1
End If
```

CROSS-REFERENCE
See also HasDC.

Height

Property

The Height property represents the height of a control or object. Except for the Form, Printer, Screen, and Picture objects, the value of the Height property depends on the setting of the control container's ScaleMode property. That is, a CommandButton object's height is measures in pixels, for example, if the container's ScaleMode property is set to pixels. The Form, Printer, and Screen objects always return Height values in twips, whereas the Picture object returns HiMetric measurements. The Printer object returns the height of a page, and the Screen object returns the height of the screen.

Objects with a Height Property

CheckBox

ComboBox

CommandButton

DirListBox

DriveListBox

FileListBox

Form

Frame

HScrollBar

Image

Label

ListBox

MDIForm

OLE Container

OptionButton

Picture

PictureBox

Printer

PropertyPage

Screen

Shape

TextBox

UserControl

VScrollBar

Syntax

```
object.Height = value1
```

or

```
value2 = object.Height
```

- *object*—A reference to an object with a `Height` property.
- *value1*—The object's new height setting. (Not all objects can be resized.)
- *value2*—The variable that will receive the object's current height.

Example

In this example, the program sets the height of a CommandButton control. The `btnCommand1` object is a CommandButton control that the programmer added to the application's form at design time.

```
btnCommand1.Height = 500
```

 CROSS-REFERENCE
See also Left, Top, and Width.

HeightChanged

Event

Visual Basic sends a CoolBar control a `HeightChanged` event when the CoolBar's height changes.

Objects That Receive HeightChanged Events

CoolBar

Example

A program can respond to a `HeightChanged` event by implementing the target object's `HeightChanged` event procedure. The following code segment shows how a CoolBar control defines a `HeightChanged` event procedure. The single parameter, `NewHeight`, is the CoolBar control's new height. In the example, the `CoolBar1` object is a CoolBar control that the programmer added to the form at design time.

```
Private Sub CoolBar1_HeightChanged(ByVal NewHeight As Single)
    ' Respond to the HeightChanged event here.
End Sub
```

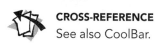 **CROSS-REFERENCE**
See also CoolBar.

HelpCommand

Property

The `HelpCommand` property represents the type of help a CommonDialog control should display. This property can be set to one of the values in Table H-1.

Table H-1 Settings for the HelpCommand Property

Setting	Description
cdlHelpCommand	Performs a help macro.
cdlHelpContents	Shows the help contents.
cdlHelpContext	Shows help based on the HelpContext property.
cdlHelpContextPopup	Shows a popup help window based on a context number.
cdlHelpForceFile	Ensures that the correct help file is currently displayed.
cdlHelpHelpOnHelp	Shows help on using the Help feature.
cdlHelpIndex	Shows the help file's index.
cdlHelpKey	Shows help based on the setting of the HelpKey property.
cdlHelpPartialKey	Searches for a given topic.
cdlHelpQuit	Specifies that the help file is no longer being used.
cdlHelpSetContents	Specifies the help topic to display when the F1 key is pressed.
cdlHelpSetIndex	Sets the help index based on the setting of the HelpContext property.

Objects with a HelpCommand Property

CommonDialog

Syntax

```
CommonDialog.HelpCommand = value1
```

or

```
value2 = CommonDialog.HelpCommand
```

- *CommonDialog* — A reference to a CommonDialog control.
- *value1* — A command value from Table H-1.
- *value2* — The variable that will receive the property's current setting.

Example

In this example, the program sets a CommonDialog box's help command to display the help contents. The `dlgCommonDialog1` object is a CommonDialog control that the programmer added to the application's form at design time.

```
dlgCommonDialog1.HelpCommand = cdlHelpContents
```

CROSS-REFERENCE
See also HelpFile, HelpKey, and HelpContext.

HelpContext — CommonDialog

Property

The `HelpContext` property of the CommonDialog control represents the context ID for the Help system to display.

Syntax

```
CommonDialog.HelpContext = value1
```

or

```
value2 = CommonDialog.HelpContext
```

- *CommonDialog* — A reference to a CommonDialog control.
- *value1* — The context ID for the help file topic.
- *value2* — The variable that will receive the current context ID.

Example

In this example, the program sets a CommonDialog box's help context ID. The `dlgCommonDialog1` object is a CommonDialog control that the programmer added to the application's form at design time.

```
dlgCommonDialog1.HelpContext = 500
```

CROSS-REFERENCE
See also HelpFile, HelpKey, and HelpCommand.

HelpContext — Err

Property

The HelpContext property of the Err object represents the context ID for the Help system to display. Usually, Visual Basic sets the properties of the Err object when a runtime error occurs. However, you can use the Err object's Raise method to generate your own errors.

Syntax

```
Err.HelpContext = value1
```

or

```
value2 = Err.HelpContext
```

- *Err* — A reference to an Err object.
- *value1* — The context ID for the help file topic.
- *value2* — The variable that will receive the current context ID.

Example

In this example, the program retrieves the Err object's help context ID. Note that the Err object is a Visual Basic global object that you don't need to create in your programs.

```
Dim hlpContext As Long
hlpContext = Err.HelpContext
```

 **CROSS-REFERENCE**
See also Err.

HelpContextID

Property

The HelpContextID property represents the context ID for an object's context-sensitive help topic. If you supply help topics for objects in your application, the user can get help on an object by pressing F1 while the object has the focus.

Objects with a HelpContextID Property

Animation

CheckBox

ComboBox

CommandButton

DirListBox

DriveListBox

FileListBox

Form

Frame

HScrollBar

ListBox

ListView

MDIForm

Menu

OLE Container

OptionButton

PictureBox

PropertyPage

RichTextBox

Slider

TabStrip

TextBox

TreeView

UpDown

VScrollBar

Syntax

object.HelpContextID = *value1*

or

value2 = *object*.HelpContextID

- *object* — A reference to an object with a `HelpContextID` property.
- *value1* — The object's context-sensitive help context ID.
- *value2* — The variable that will receive the context ID.

Example

In this example, the program sets a CommandButton control's help context ID. The `btnCommand1` object is a CommandButton control that the programmer added to the application's form at design time.

```
btnCommand1.HelpContextID = 500
```

CROSS-REFERENCE
See also HelpFile.

HelpContextID — Toolbar

Property

The `HelpContextID` property represents the context ID for a topic in a Toolbar control's Help file. Visual Basic displays the Help file when the user presses the Help button in the Customize Toolbar dialog box.

Syntax

```
Toolbar.HelpContextID = value1
```

or

```
value2 = Toolbar.HelpContextID
```

- *Toolbar* — A reference to a Toolbar control.
- *value1* — The context ID.
- *value2* — The variable that will receive the context ID.

Example

In this example, the program sets a Toolbar control's `HelpContextID` property. The `tlbToolbar1` object is a Toolbar control that the programmer added to the form at design time.

```
tlbToolbar1.HelpContextID = 500
```

 CROSS-REFERENCE
See also Toolbar.

HelpFile — App and CommonDialog

Property

The `HelpFile` property represents an object's Help file name and location. Visual Basic displays the Help file when the user presses the F1 key.

Syntax

```
object.HelpFile = value1
```

or

```
value2 = object.HelpFile
```

- *object* — A reference to an object with a `HelpFile` property.
- *value1* — The complete path to the help file.
- *value2* — The variable that will receive the path to the help file.

Example

In this example, the program sets the App object's Help file. You can also set the App object's Help file from the Project Properties property sheet, as shown in Figure H-1. Note that the App object is a Visual Basic global object that you don't need to create in your programs.

```
App.HelpFile = "c:\MyHelp.hlp"
```

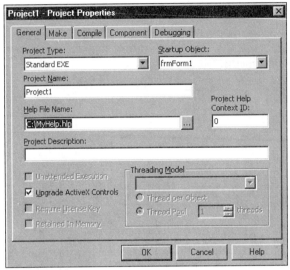

Figure H-1 The Project Properties property sheet gives you access to many of the App object's properties.

CROSS-REFERENCE
See also App and CommonDialog.

HelpFile — Err

Property

The `HelpFile` property represents an Err object's Help file name and location. Visual Basic displays the Help file when the user presses the F1 key while the Error dialog box is displayed. If no Help file is specified, Visual Basic automatically displays its own Help file.

Syntax

```
Err.HelpFile = value1
```

or

```
value2 = Err.HelpFile
```

- *Err* — A reference to the Err object.
- *value1* — The complete path to the help file.
- *value2* — The variable that will receive the path to the help file.

Example

In this example, the program sets the Err object's Help file. Note that the Err object is a Visual Basic global object that you don't need to create in your programs.

```
Err.HelpFile = "c:\MyHelp.hlp"
```

CROSS-REFERENCE
See also Err.

HelpFile — Toolbar

Property

The `HelpFile` property represents a Toolbar control's Help file name and location. Visual Basic displays the Help file when the user presses the Help button in the Customize Toolbar dialog box, shown in Figure H-2.

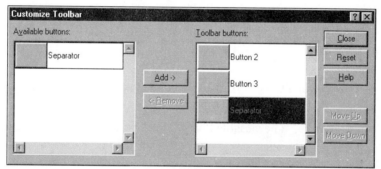

Figure H-2 A Toolbar can display help from its Customize Toolbar dialog box.

Syntax

```
Toolbar.HelpFile = value1
```

or

```
value2 = Toolbar.HelpFile
```

- *Toolbar* — A reference to a Toolbar control.
- *value1* — The complete path to the help file.
- *value2* — The variable that will receive the path to the help file.

Example

In this example, the program sets a Toolbar control's Help file. The `tlbToolbar1` object is a Toolbar control that the programmer added to the form at design time.

```
tlbToolbar1.HelpFile = "c:\MyHelp.hlp"
```

 CROSS-REFERENCE
See also Toolbar.

HelpKey

Property

The `HelpKey` property of the CommonDialog control represents a keyword in a Help file.

Syntax

```
CommonDialog.HelpKey = value1
```

or

```
value2 = CommonDialog.HelpKey
```

- *CommonDialog*—A reference to a CommonDialog control.
- *value1*—The help keyword.
- *value2*—The variable that will receive the current help keyword.

Example

In this example, the program sets a CommonDialog box's `HelpKey` property. The `dlgCommonDialog1` object is a CommonDialog control that the programmer added to the application's form at design time.

```
dlgCommonDialog1.HelpKey = "Lines"
```

 CROSS-REFERENCE
See also HelpFile, HelpKey, and HelpCommand.

Hex

Function

The Hex function converts a number to a string containing the equivalent hexadecimal number.

Syntax

```
value1 = Hex(value2)
```

- *value1* — The variable that will receive the call's return value.
- *value2* — The number to convert to hexadecimal notation.

Example

The following lines convert the number 256 to its hexadecimal value and display the result, 100, in a message box.

```
Dim hexResult As String
hexResult = hex(256)
MsgBox hexResult
```

Hide

Event

Visual Basic sends a UserControl control a Hide event when the control's Visible property is set to False.

Objects That Receive Hide Events

UserControl

Example

A program can respond to a Hide event by implementing the target object's Hide event procedure. The following code segment shows how a UserControl object defines a Hide event procedure.

```
Private Sub UserControl_Hide()
    ' Respond to Hide event here.
End Sub
```

CROSS-REFERENCE
See also UserControl and Visible.

Hide

Method

The Hide method hides a form without removing the form from memory. That is, the form can be redisplayed with the Show method.

Objects with a Hide Method

Form

MDIForm

Syntax

object.Hide

- *object* — A reference to a Form or MDI Form object.

Example

The following line hides a form in response to a button click. The btnCommand1 object is a CommandButton control the programmer added to the application's form at design time.

```
Private Sub btnCommand1_Click()
    frmForm1.Hide
End Sub
```

CROSS-REFERENCE
For more information, see Form, MDIForm, Show, Load, and Unload.

HideColumnHeaders

Property

The HideColumnHeaders property represents whether a ListView control hides its ColumnHeader objects when the control is in report view.

Objects with a HideColumnHeaders Property

ListView

Syntax

ListView.HideColumnHeaders = *value1*

or

value2 = *ListView*.HideColumnHeaders

- *ListView* — A reference to a ListView control.
- *value1* — The value True or False.
- *value2* — The variable that will receive the property's current setting.

Example

The following program gives you a chance to see the HideColumnHeaders property working in a ListView control. When you run the program, you see the window shown in Figure H-3. Click the Toggle Column Headers button, and the program hides the ListView control's column headers, as shown in Figure H-4.

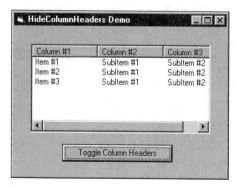

Figure H-3 Here's the application with the column headers displayed.

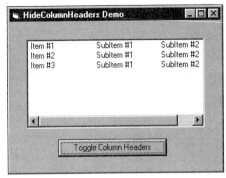

Figure H-4 Here's the application with the column headers hidden.

```
VERSION 5.00
Object = "{6B7E6392-850A-101B-AFCO-4210102A8DA7}#2.0#0";
"MSCOMCTL.OCX"
Begin VB.Form frmForm1
   Caption         =    "HideColumnHeaders Demo"
   ClientHeight    =    3195
   ClientLeft      =    60
   ClientTop       =    345
   ClientWidth     =    4680
   LinkTopic       =    "Form1"
   ScaleHeight     =    3195
   ScaleWidth      =    4680
   StartUpPosition =    3  'Windows Default
   Begin MSComctlLib.ListView lvwListView1
      Height        =    1935
      Left          =    360
      TabIndex      =    1
      Top           =    360
      Width         =    3975
      _ExtentX      =    7011
      _ExtentY      =    3413
      LabelWrap     =    -1  'True
      HideSelection =    -1  'True
      _Version      =    393217
      ForeColor     =    -2147483640
      BackColor     =    -2147483643
      BorderStyle   =    1
      Appearance    =    1
```

```
        NumItems          =      0
    End
    Begin VB.CommandButton btnToggleColumnHeaders
        Caption         =      "Toggle Column Headers"
        Height          =      375
        Left            =      1080
        TabIndex        =      0
        Top             =      2520
        Width           =      2415
    End
End
Attribute VB_Name = "frmForm1"
Attribute VB_GlobalNameSpace = False
Attribute VB_Creatable = False
Attribute VB_PredeclaredId = True
Attribute VB_Exposed = False

Private Sub btnToggleColumnHeaders_Click()
    If lvwListView1.HideColumnHeaders Then
        lvwListView1.HideColumnHeaders = False
    Else
        lvwListView1.HideColumnHeaders = True
    End If
End Sub

Private Sub Form_Load()
    Dim item As ListItem
    lvwListView1.View = lvwReport
    lvwListView1.ColumnHeaders.Add , , "Column #1"
    lvwListView1.ColumnHeaders.Add , , "Column #2"
    lvwListView1.ColumnHeaders.Add , , "Column #3"
    Set item = lvwListView1.ListItems.Add(, , "Item #1")
    item.SubItems(1) = "SubItem #1"
    item.SubItems(2) = "SubItem #2"
    Set item = lvwListView1.ListItems.Add(, , "Item #2")
    item.SubItems(1) = "SubItem #1"
    item.SubItems(2) = "SubItem #2"
    Set item = lvwListView1.ListItems.Add(, , "Item #3")
    item.SubItems(1) = "SubItem #1"
    item.SubItems(2) = "SubItem #2"
End Sub
```

CROSS-REFERENCE

See also ListView, ColumnHeader, and ColumnHeader.

HideSelection

Property

The `HideSelection` property represents whether a control hides highlighted text when the control loses the focus.

Objects with a HideSelection Property

ListView

RichTextBox

TreeView

Syntax

`object.HideSelection = value1`

or

`value2 = object.HideSelection`

- *object* — A reference to a control with a `HideSelection` property.
- *value1* — The value `True` or `False`.
- *value2* — The variable that will receive the property's current setting.

Example

The following program gives you a chance to see the `HideSelection` property working in a RichTextBox control. When you run the program, you see the window shown in Figure H-5. Select some text, and then press your keyboard's Tab key to move the focus to the button. When you do, the RichTextBox hides its selected text. Click the Toggle Selection Mode button, and the program changes the `HideSelection` property to `False`, causing the selected text to remain visible regardless of which control has the focus.

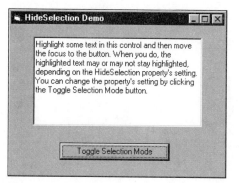

Figure H-5 The HideSelection Demo application demonstrates the HideSelection property of a RichTextBox control.

```
VERSION 5.00
Object = "{3B7C8863-D78F-101B-B9B5-04021C009402} _
    #1.2#0"; "RICHTX32.OCX"
Begin VB.Form frmForm1
    Caption         =   "HideSelection Demo"
    ClientHeight    =   3195
    ClientLeft      =   60
    ClientTop       =   345
    ClientWidth     =   4680
    LinkTopic       =   "Form1"
    ScaleHeight     =   3195
    ScaleWidth      =   4680
    StartUpPosition =   3   'Windows Default
    Begin RichTextLib.RichTextBox rtfRichTextBox1
        Height      =   1935
        Left        =   480
        TabIndex    =   1
        Top         =   240
        Width       =   3735
        _ExtentX    =   6588
        _ExtentY    =   3413
        _Version    =   393217
        Enabled     =   -1   'True
        TextRTF     =   $"Form1.frx":0000
    End
```

```
        Begin VB.CommandButton btnToggleSelectionMode
            Caption         =   "Toggle Selection Mode"
            Height          =   375
            Left            =   1080
            TabIndex        =   0
            Top             =   2520
            Width           =   2415
        End
    End
End
Attribute VB_Name = "frmForm1"
Attribute VB_GlobalNameSpace = False
Attribute VB_Creatable = False
Attribute VB_PredeclaredId = True
Attribute VB_Exposed = False

Private Sub btnToggleSelectionMode_Click()
    If rtfRichTextBox1.HideSelection Then
        rtfRichTextBox1.HideSelection = False
    Else
        rtfRichTextBox1.HideSelection = True
    End If
End Sub

Private Sub Form_Load()
    Dim txt As String
    txt = "Highlight some text in this control "
    txt = txt & "and then move the focus to the button. "
    txt = txt & "When you do, the highlighted text "
    txt = txt & "may or may not stay highlighted, "
    txt = txt & "depending on the HideSelection "
    txt = txt & "property's setting. You can change "
    txt = txt & "the property's setting by clicking the "
    txt = txt & "Toggle Selection Mode button."
    rtfRichTextBox1.Text = txt
End Sub
```

CROSS-REFERENCE
See also ListView, RichTextBox, and TreeView.

HighLighted

Property

The `HighLighted` property represents whether a Tab object in a TabStrip control is highlighted.

Objects with a HighLighted Property

Tab

Syntax

`Tab.HighLighted = value1`

or

`value2 = Tab.HighLighted`

- *Tab* — A reference to a Tab object.
- *value1* — The value `True` or `False`.
- *value2* — The variable that will receive the property's current setting.

Example

In this example, a Tab object in a TabStrip control is set for highlighting. The `tabTabStrip1` object is a TabStrip control that the programmer added to the application's form at design time.

`tabTabStrip1.Tabs(2).HighLighted = True`

CROSS-REFERENCE
See also Tab, Tabs, and TabStrip.

hImageList

Property

The `hImageList` property represents an ImageList control's handle, which a program may need when making Windows API calls from Visual Basic.

Objects with an hImageList Property

ImageList

Syntax

```
value = ImageList.hImageList
```

- *ImageList* — A reference to an ImageList control.
- *value* — The variable that will receive the ImageList's handle.

Example

In this example, the program retrieves an ImageList control's handle. The ilsImageList1 object is an ImageList control that the programmer added to the application's form at design time.

```
Dim ILHandle As Long
ILHandle = ilsImageList1.hImageList
```

 CROSS-REFERENCE
See also ImageList.

hInstance

Property

The hInstance property represents an application's instance handle, which a program may need when making Windows API calls from Visual Basic.

Objects with an hInstance Property

App

Syntax

```
value = App.hInstance
```

- *App* — A reference to the App object.
- *value* — The variable that will receive the instance handle.

Example

In this example, the program retrieves an application's instance handle. The App object is a global Visual Basic object that you don't need to create on your program.

```
Dim ILHandle As Long
ILHandle = App.hInstance
```

 CROSS-REFERENCE
See also App.

HitBehavior

Property

The HitBehavior property represents how a UserControl object performs hit testing. This property can be set to one of the values in Table H-2.

Table H-2 Settings for the HitBehavior Property

Setting	Description
0	Hit result is always 0.
1	Hit result is 3 when the cursor is over the control's MaskRegion. This is the default.
2	Hit result is 3 when the cursor is over the control's painted area.

Objects with a HitBehavior Property

UserControl

Syntax

UserControl.HitBehavior = *value1*

or

value2 = *UserControl*.HitBehavior

- *UserControl*—A reference to a UserControl object.
- *value1*—A value from Table H-2.
- *value2*—The variable that will receive the property's current setting.

Example

The following line sets a UserControl object's hit behavior.

```
UserControl.HitBehavior = 2
```

 CROSS-REFERENCE
See also UserControl, HitTest, MaskPicture, MaskColor, and Windowless.

HitTest

Event

Visual Basic sends a UserControl control a HitTest event when the mouse pointer moves over the control. To get this event, the control must have its Windowless property set to True and its BackStyle property set to transparent.

Objects That Receive HitTest Events

UserControl

Example

A program can respond to a HitTest event by implementing the target object's HitTest event procedure. The following code segment shows how a UserControl object defines a HitTest event procedure. The X and Y parameters are the coordinates of the mouse, and the HitResult parameter is the type of hit, the values for which are shown in Table H-3.

```
Private Sub UserControl_HitTest(X As Single, Y As Single, _
    HitResult As Integer)
        ' Handle the HitTest event here.
End Sub
```

Table H-3 Settings for the HitResult Parameter

Setting	Description
vbHitResultClose	The hit occurred close to the control's visible area.
vbHitResultHit	The hit occurred over the control's visible area.
vbHitResultOutside	The hit occurred outside of the control's visible area.
vbHitResultTransparent	The hit occurred over the control's transparent area.

CROSS-REFERENCE
See also UserControl, HitBehavior, MaskPicture, MaskColor, and Windowless.

HitTest

Method

The `HitTest` method determines whether the given X and Y coordinates are over a Node or ListItem object. If so, the method returns a reference to the Node or ListItem object. Otherwise, the method returns the value `Nothing`.

Objects with a HitTest Method

ListView

TreeView

Syntax

`value = object.HitTest(xCoord, yCoord)`

- *object* — A reference to a ListView or TreeView control.
- *value* — The variable that will receive the returned object.
- *xCoord* — The X coordinate to test.
- *yCoord* — The Y coordinate to test.

Example

The following lines determine whether a ListItem object is located at the coordinates 12,112 in a ListView control. The `lvwListView1` object is a ListView control the programmer added to the application's form at design time.

```
Dim item As ListItem
item = lvwListView1.HitTest(12, 112)
```

CROSS-REFERENCE
See also ListView, ListItem, TreeView, and Node.

HostName

Property

The `HostName` property represents an application's host name.

Objects with a HostName Property

OLE Container

Syntax

```
OLEContainer.HostName = value1
```

or

```
value2 = OLEContainer.HostName
```

- *OLEContainer* — A reference to an OLE Container control.
- *value1* — A string containing the host name.
- *value2* — The variable that will receive the host name.

Example

In this example, the program retrieves the host name of an OLE Container control and displays the name in a message box. The `oleOLEContainer` object is an OLE container control that the programmer added to the application's form at design time.

```
Dim hstName As String
hstName = oleOLEContainer.HostName
MsgBox hstName
```

CROSS-REFERENCE
See also OLE Container.

HotImageList

Property

The `HotImageList` property represents the ImageList that contains the images that Visual Basic displays on a Toolbar button when the mouse is over the button.

Objects with a HotImageList Property

Toolbar

Syntax

`Toolbar.HotImageList = value1`

or

`value2 = Toolbar.HotImageList`

- *Toolbar* — A reference to a Toolbar control.
- *value1* — A reference to the ImageList control that contains the images.
- *value2* — The variable that will receive the reference to the ImageList.

Example

In this example, the program sets a toolbar's hot image list to the ImageList control named `ilsImageList1`. The `tlbToolbar1` and `ilsImageList1` objects are Toolbar and ImageList controls that the programmer added to the application's form at design time.

`tlbToolbar1.HotImageList = ilsImageList1`

 CROSS-REFERENCE
See also ImageList and Toolbar.

HotTracking

Property

The `HotTracking` property represents whether an object becomes highlighted when the mouse is over it.

Objects with a HotTracking Property

ListView
TabStrip
TreeView

Syntax

```
object.HotTracking = value1
```

or

```
value2 = object.HotTracking
```

- *object* — A reference to a control with a HotTracking property.
- *value1* — The value True or False.
- *value2* — The variable that will receive the property's current setting.

Example

In this example, the program turns on a TreeView control's hot tracking. The treeTreeView1 object is a TreeView control that the programmer added to the application's form at design time.

```
treeTreeView1.HotTracking = True
```

CROSS-REFERENCE
See also ListView, TabStrip, and TreeView.

Hour

Function

The Hour function returns the hour portion of a given time. The result is in 24-hour time — that is, a value between 0 and 23.

Syntax

```
value = Hour(time)
```

- *time* — A time expression.
- *value* — The variable that will receive the return value.

Example

In this example, the variable result will be assigned the value 19.

```
Dim result As Integer
result = Hour("7:15:00 PM")
```

HoverSelection

Property

The `HoverSelection` property represents whether Visual Basic selects an item in a ListView control when the mouse pointer hovers over the item.

Objects with a HoverSelection Property

ListView

Syntax

```
ListView.HoverSelection = value1
```

or

```
value2 = ListView.HoverSelection
```

- *ListView* — A reference to a ListView control.
- *value1* — The value `True` or `False`.
- *value2* — The variable that will receive the property's current setting.

Example

The following program gives you a chance to see the `HoverSelection` property working in a ListView control. When you run the program, place the mouse over an item in the ListView control. Nothing happens. Now, click the Toggle Hover Selection button, and place the mouse over an item again. This time, Visual Basic selects the item automatically, as shown in Figure H-6.

Figure H-6 When the HoverSelection property is on, the mouse can select items just by hovering over them.

```
VERSION 5.00
Object = "{6B7E6392-850A-101B-AFC0-4210102A8DA7}#2.0#0";
"MSCOMCTL.OCX"
Begin VB.Form frmForm1
   Caption         =    "HoverSelection Demo"
   ClientHeight    =    3195
   ClientLeft      =    60
   ClientTop       =    345
   ClientWidth     =    4680
   LinkTopic       =    "Form1"
   ScaleHeight     =    3195
   ScaleWidth      =    4680
   StartUpPosition =    3  'Windows Default
   Begin MSComctlLib.ListView lvwListView1
      Height       =    1455
      Left         =    480
      TabIndex     =    1
      Top          =    360
      Width        =    3735
      _ExtentX     =    6588
      _ExtentY     =    2566
      LabelWrap    =    -1  'True
      HideSelection =    -1  'True
      _Version     =    393217
      ForeColor    =    -2147483640
      BackColor    =    -2147483643
      BorderStyle  =    1
      Appearance   =    1
      NumItems     =    0
   End
   Begin VB.CommandButton btnToggle
      Caption      =    "Toggle Hover Selection"
      Height       =    495
      Left         =    1200
      TabIndex     =    0
      Top          =    2160
      Width        =    2295
   End
End
Attribute VB_Name = "frmForm1"
Attribute VB_GlobalNameSpace = False
Attribute VB_Creatable = False
Attribute VB_PredeclaredId = True
Attribute VB_Exposed = False
```

```
Private Sub btnToggle_Click()
    If lvwListView1.HoverSelection Then
        lvwListView1.HoverSelection = False
    Else
        lvwListView1.HoverSelection = True
    End If
End Sub

Private Sub Form_Load()
    lvwListView1.ListItems.Add , , "Orange"
    lvwListView1.ListItems.Add , , "Apple"
    lvwListView1.ListItems.Add , , "Melon"
    lvwListView1.ListItems.Add , , "Peach"
End Sub
```

CROSS-REFERENCE
See also ListView.

hPal

Property

The `hPal` property represents a Picture object's palette handle, which a program may need when making Windows API calls from Visual Basic.

Objects with an hPal Property

Picture

Syntax

```
value = Picture.hPal
```

- *Picture* — A reference to a Picture object.
- *value* — The variable that will receive the palette handle.

Example

In this example, the program retrieves a Picture object's palette handle. The `picPicture1` object is a PictureBox control the programmer added to the form at design time.

```
Dim palHandle As Long
palHandle = picPicture1.Picture.hPal
```

CROSS-REFERENCE
See also Picture.

HScrollBar

Control

An HScrollBar control is comprised of a sliding button within a horizontal track that the user can use to scroll or to select values from a range. Figure H-7 shows several HScrollBar controls in a form. The HScrollBar control is available on Visual Basic's standard toolbox.

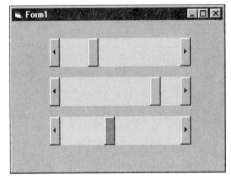

Figure H-7 These three HScrollBar controls could be used for something like selecting RGB values for a color.

Properties

The HScrollBar control has 28 properties, which are listed as follows. Because many Visual Basic controls have similar properties, the properties' descriptions are listed under their own names provided alphabetically elsewhere in this book.

```
CausesValidation
Container
Default
DragIcon
DragMode
Enabled
Height
HelpContextID
hWnd
Index
```

```
LargeChange
Left
Max
Min
MouseIcon
MousePointer
Name
Parent
RightToLeft
SmallChange
TabIndex
TabStop
Tag
Top
Value
Visible
WhatsThisHelpID
Width
```

Methods

The HScrollBar control has six methods, which are listed below. Because many Visual Basic controls have similar methods, the methods' descriptions are listed under their own names provided alphabetically elsewhere in this book.

```
Drag
Move
Refresh
SetFocus
ShowWhatsThis
ZOrder
```

Events

The HScrollBar control responds to ten events, which are listed below. Because many Visual Basic controls respond to similar events, the events' descriptions are listed under their own names provided alphabetically elsewhere in this book.

```
Change
DragDrop
DragOver
GotFocus
KeyDown
```

```
KeyPress
KeyUp
LostFocus
Scroll
Validate
```

The HScrollBar control's most commonly used event is `Change`, which the control generates when the user sets it to a new value. A program responds to the control's `Change` event in the `Change` event procedure. A scroll bar called `hsbHScroll1` will have a `Change` event procedure called `hsbHScroll1_Change`, which is where the program should handle the event. In the following example, a message box displays the scroll bar's new value whenever the user changes the value.

```
Private Sub hsbHScroll1_Change()
    MsgBox hsbHScroll1.Value
End Sub
```

hWnd

Property

The `hWnd` property represents a form or control's handle, which a program may need when making Windows API calls from Visual Basic.

Objects with an hWnd Property

Animation

CheckBox

ComboBox

CommandButton

DirListBox

DriveListBox

FileListBox

Form

Frame

HScrollBar

ListBox

MDIForm

OptionButton

PictureBox

ProgressBar

PropertyPage

RichTextBox

Slider

StatusBar

TabStrip

TextBox

Toolbar

UpDown

UserControl

VScrollBar

Syntax

```
value = object.hWnd
```

- *object*—A reference to an object with an hWnd property.
- *value*—The variable that will receive the handle.

Example

In this example, the program retrieves a PictureBox control's handle. The picPicture1 object is a PictureBox control the programmer added to the form at design time.

```
Dim picHandle As Long
picHandle = picPicture1.hWnd
```

hWndDisplay

Property

The hWndDisplay property represents the handle of an MCI device's output window, which a program may need when making Windows API calls from Visual Basic.

Objects with an hWndDisplay Property

Multimedia MCI

Syntax

```
value = Multimedia.hWndDisplay
```

- *Multimedia* — A reference to a Multimedia MCI control.
- *value* — The variable that will receive the handle.

Example

In this example, the program retrieves a Multimedia MCI control's display-window handle. The MMControl1 object is a Multimedia MCI control the programmer added to the form at design time.

```
Dim dispHandle As Long
dispHandle = MMControl1.hWndDisplay
```

CROSS-REFERENCE
See also Multimedia MCI and UsesWindows.

Icon — ColumnHeader

Property

The `Icon` property holds a reference to the icon that Visual Basic will display in a ListView control's ColumnHeader object.

Syntax

```
ColumnHeader.Icon = value1
```

or

```
value2 = ColumnHeader.Icon
```

- *ColumnHeader* — A reference to a ColumnHeader object.
- *value1* — A key or index to an image in an ImageList control.
- *value2* — The variable that will receive the icon's key or index.

Example

The following lines initialize a ListView control and set the control's icons for the ColumnHeader objects. Figure I-1 shows the resultant ListView control in its form. Note the icons in the column headers. In this example, the `ilsImageList1` and `lvwListView1` objects are ImageList and ListView controls that the programmer added to the form at design time.

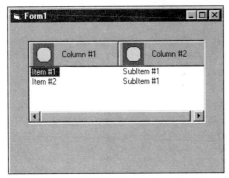

Figure I-1 You can display icons in a ListView control's column headers.

```
Dim item As ListItem
ilsImageList1.ListImages.Add , , LoadPicture("icon1.ico")
lvwListView1.View = lvwReport
lvwListView1.ColumnHeaders.Add , , "Column #1"
lvwListView1.ColumnHeaders.Add , , "Column #2"
Set item = lvwListView1.ListItems.Add(, , "Item #1")
item.SubItems(1) = "SubItem #1"
Set item = lvwListView1.ListItems.Add(, , "Item #2")
item.SubItems(1) = "SubItem #1"
lvwListView1.ColumnHeaders(1).Width = 2000
lvwListView1.ColumnHeaders(2).Width = 2000
lvwListView1.ColumnHeaderIcons = ilsImageList1
lvwListView1.ColumnHeaders(1).Icon = 1
lvwListView1.ColumnHeaders(2).Icon = 1
```

CROSS-REFERENCE
See also ListView, ColumnHeader, ColumnHeaders, and ColumnHeaderIcons.

Icon—Form and MDIForm

Property

The Icon property holds a reference to the icon that represents the form when it is in its minimized state. Under Windows 95 and later, the icon also appears in the form's upper-left corner.

Syntax

object.Icon = *value1*

or

```
value2 = object.Icon
```

- *object* — A reference to a Form or MDIForm object.
- *value1* — A reference to the form's icon, which must be a standard icon file with the .ico extension.
- *value2* — The variable that will receive a reference to the form's icon.

Example

The following line sets the form's icon to the image found in the `MyIcon.ico` file.

```
frmForm1.Icon = LoadPicture("MyIcon.ico")
```

CROSS-REFERENCE
See also Form and MDIForm.

Icon — ListItem

Property

The `Icon` property holds a reference to the icon that Visual Basic will display next to a ListView control's ListItem object.

Syntax

```
ListItem.Icon = value1
```

or

```
value2 = ListItem.Icon
```

- *ListItem* — A reference to a ListItem object.
- *value1* — A key or index to an image in an ImageList control.
- *value2* — The variable that will receive the icon's key or index.

Example

The following program demonstrates the `Icon` and `SmallIcon` properties in a ListView control. When you run the program, you see the window shown in Figure I-2. At this point, the control is in its icon view. Click the Toggle View button to switch the control to its small icon view, as shown in Figure I-3.

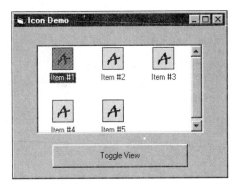

Figure I-2 This ListView control is set to icon view.

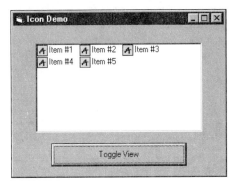

Figure I-3 This ListView control is set to small icon view.

```
VERSION 5.00
Object = "{6B7E6392-850A-101B-AFC0-4210102A8DA7} _
    #2.0#0"; "MSCOMCTL.OCX"
Begin VB.Form frmForm1
   Caption         =    "Icon Demo"
   ClientHeight    =    3195
   ClientLeft      =    60
   ClientTop       =    345
   ClientWidth     =    4680
   LinkTopic       =    "Form1"
   ScaleHeight     =    3195
   ScaleWidth      =    4680
   StartUpPosition =    3   'Windows Default
   Begin MSComctlLib.ImageList ilsImageList2
      Left         =     4080
      Top          =     2520
```

```
            _ExtentX        =    1005
            _ExtentY        =    1005
            BackColor       =    -2147483643
            MaskColor       =    12632256
            _Version        =    393216
         End
         Begin MSComctlLib.ImageList ilsImageList1
            Left            =    120
            Top             =    2520
            _ExtentX        =    1005
            _ExtentY        =    1005
            BackColor       =    -2147483643
            MaskColor       =    12632256
            _Version        =    393216
         End
         Begin VB.CommandButton btnToggleView
            Caption         =    "Toggle View"
            Height          =    495
            Left            =    840
            TabIndex        =    1
            Top             =    2520
            Width           =    3015
         End
         Begin MSComctlLib.ListView lvwListView1
            Height          =    1935
            Left            =    480
            TabIndex        =    0
            Top             =    360
            Width           =    3735
            _ExtentX        =    6588
            _ExtentY        =    3413
            LabelWrap       =    -1   'True
            HideSelection   =    -1   'True
            _Version        =    393217
            ForeColor       =    -2147483640
            BackColor       =    -2147483643
            BorderStyle     =    1
            Appearance      =    1
            NumItems        =    0
         End
      End
   End
   Attribute VB_Name = "frmForm1"
   Attribute VB_GlobalNameSpace = False
```

```
Attribute VB_Creatable = False
Attribute VB_PredeclaredId = True
Attribute VB_Exposed = False

Private Sub btnToggleView_Click()
    If lvwListView1.View = lvwIcon Then
        lvwListView1.View = lvwSmallIcon
    Else
        lvwListView1.View = lvwIcon
    End If
End Sub

Private Sub Form_Load()
    Dim x As Integer

    ilsImageList1.ListImages.Add , , LoadPicture("icon1.ico")
    lvwListView1.Icons = ilsImageList1
    ilsImageList2.ListImages.Add , , LoadPicture("icon2.ico")
    lvwListView1.SmallIcons = ilsImageList2
    lvwListView1.View = lvwIcon

    Set Item = lvwListView1.ListItems.Add(, , "Item #1")
    Set Item = lvwListView1.ListItems.Add(, , "Item #2")
    Set Item = lvwListView1.ListItems.Add(, , "Item #3")
    Set Item = lvwListView1.ListItems.Add(, , "Item #4")
    Set Item = lvwListView1.ListItems.Add(, , "Item #5")

    For x = 1 To 5
        lvwListView1.ListItems(x).Icon = 1
        lvwListView1.ListItems(x).SmallIcon = 1
    Next x
End Sub
```

 CROSS-REFERENCE
See also ListView, ListItem, Icons, and SmallIcon.

Icons

Property

The Icons property represents the ImageList control that contains the large images to be displayed with items in a ListView control.

Objects with an Icons Property

ListView

Syntax

```
ListView.Icons = value1
```

or

```
value2 = ListView.Icons
```

- *ListView* — A reference to a ListView control.
- *value1* — A reference to an ImageList control.
- *value2* — The variable that will receive a reference to the ImageList control.

Example

The following lines initialize an ImageList control with a single image and then set a ListView control's Icons property to the ImageList. The ilsImageList1 and lvwListView1 objects are ImageList and ListView controls that the programmer added to the application's form at design time.

```
ilsImageList1.ListImages.Add , , LoadPicture("reddot.ico")
lvwListView1.Icons = ilsImageList1
```

CROSS-REFERENCE
See also ListView, ListItem, Icon, SmallIcon, and SmallIcons.

If

Statement

The If statement routes program execution based on the evaluation of Boolean expressions.

Syntax

```
If BoolExp Then bodyStatements1 elseSection
```

or

```
If BoolExp Then
    bodyStatements2
```

```
elseifSection
    bodyStatements2
elseSection
    bodyStatements2
End If
```

- *bodyStatements1* — The statement to be executed if *BoolExp* is `True`. Can also be multiple statements separated by colons.
- *bodyStatements2* (*) — The statements to be executed if *BoolExp* is `True`.
- *BoolExp* — The Boolean expression to be evaluated.
- *elseifSection* (*) — The keyword `ElseIf` followed by an alternate *BoolExp* and the keyword `Then`. An `If` statement can have multiple `ElseIf` sections.
- *elseSection* (*) — The keyword `Else` followed by the statements to be executed if *BoolExp* is `False`.

(*) = Optional

Example 1

In this example, the variable y will be assigned the value 1.

```
Dim x, y As Integer
x = 10
If x = 10 Then y = 1 Else y = 2
```

Example 2

Here, the variables y and z will be assigned the values 2 and 20, respectively.

```
Dim x, y, z As Integer
x = 15
If x = 10 Then
    y = 1
    z = 10
Else
    y = 2
    z = 20
End If
```

Example 3

The following is a single-line version of the `If` statement in Example 2.

```
If x = 10 Then y = 1: z = 10 Else y = 2: z = 20
```

Example 4

Finally, the following lines also set the variables y and z to the values 2 and 20, respectively. If you were to initialize x to a value other than 10 or 15, y and z would be assigned 3 and 30.

```
Dim x, y, z As Integer
x = 15
If x = 10 Then
    y = 1
    z = 10
ElseIf x = 15 Then
    y = 2
    z = 20
Else
    y = 3
    z = 30
End If
```

IIf

Function

The IIf function acts as a kind of abbreviated If statement, returning a value based on the evaluation of a Boolean expression.

Syntax

```
value = IIf(BoolExp, trueReturn, falseReturn)
```

- *BoolExp* — The Boolean expression to be evaluated.
- *falseReturn* — The value to return if *BoolExp* is False.
- *trueReturn* — The value to return if *BoolExp* is True.
- *value* — The variable that will receive the return value.

Example

In this example, the program sets the variable result to the string value "Twenty." If x in this example were assigned a value other than 20, result would be set to "Not Twenty."

```
Dim x As Integer
Dim result As String
x = 20
result = IIf(x = 20, "Twenty", "Not Twenty")
```

Image

Control

An Image control (which is similar to a PictureBox control, but is faster due to its fewer properties and methods) displays an image in a form. An Image control can display images contained in bitmap, GIF, JPEG, metafile, or icon files. Figure I-4 shows an Image control in a form. The Image control is available on Visual Basic's standard toolbox.

Figure I-4 The Image control provides a quick and easy way to display many types of images in a form.

Properties

The Image control has 24 properties (not including database-related properties), which are listed as follows. Because many Visual Basic controls have similar properties, the properties' descriptions are listed under their own names provided alphabetically in this book.

```
Appearance
BorderStyle
Container
Caption
DragIcon
DragMode
Enabled
Height
Index
Left
MouseIcon
MousePointer
```

```
Name
OLEDragMode
OLEDropMode
Parent
Picture
Stretch
Tag
ToolTipText
Top
Visible
WhatsThisHelpID
Width
```

Methods

The Image control has six methods, which are listed below. Because many Visual Basic controls have similar methods, the methods' descriptions are listed under their own names provided alphabetically in this book.

```
Drag
Move
OLEDrag
Refresh
ShowWhatsThis
ZOrder
```

Events

The Image control responds to 13 events, which are listed below. Because many Visual Basic controls respond to similar events, the events' descriptions are listed under their own names provided alphabetically in this book.

```
Click
DblClick
DragDrop
DragOver
MouseDown
MouseMove
MouseUp
OLECompleteDrag
OLEDragDrop
OLEDragOver
OLEGiveFeedback
OLESetData
OLEStartDrag
```

The Image control's most commonly used event is `Click`, which the control generates when the user clicks the image with the mouse. A program responds to the control's `Click` event in the `Click` event procedure. An Image control called `imgImage1` will have a `Click` event procedure called `imgImage1_Click`, which is where the program should handle the event. In the following example, when the user clicks the `imgImage1` control, the program plays the computer's beep sound:

```
Private Sub imgImage1_Click()
    ' Handle the Click event here.
    Beep
End Sub
```

Image — ActiveX Controls

Property

The `Image` property represents the image that will be used with the control. The value contained in the property is the index or key of an image stored in an ImageList control.

Objects with an Image Property

Button
CoolBar
Node
Tab

Syntax

```
object.Image = value1
```

or

```
value2 = object.Image
```

- *object* — A reference to an object with an `Image` property.
- *value1* — The index of key of an image in an ImageList control.
- *value2* — The variable that will receive the index or key.

Example

The following lines initialize an ImageList and TreeView control, using the images in the ImageList control as node images. Figure I-5 shows the resultant

TreeView control. The `ilsImageList1` and `treTreeView1` objects are ImageList and TreeView controls that the programmer added to the application's form at design time.

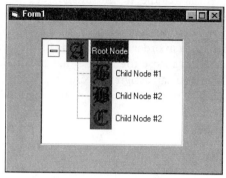

Figure I-5 Various controls, like this TreeView, can display images.

```
ilsImageList1.ListImages.Add , , LoadPicture("c:\but1.bmp")
ilsImageList1.ListImages.Add , , LoadPicture("c:\but2.bmp")
ilsImageList1.ListImages.Add , , LoadPicture("c:\but3.bmp")

treTreeView1.ImageList = ilsImageList1
treTreeView1.Style = tvwTreelinesPlusMinusPictureText
treTreeView1.LineStyle = tvwRootLines
treTreeView1.Indentation = 200

treTreeView1.Nodes.Add , , "Root", "Root Node"
treTreeView1.Nodes.Add "Root", tvwChild, _
    "Child1", "Child Node #1"
treTreeView1.Nodes.Add "Root", tvwChild, _
    "Child2", "Child Node #2"
treTreeView1.Nodes.Add "Root", tvwChild, _
    "Child3", "Child Node #2"

treTreeView1.Nodes(1).Image = 1
treTreeView1.Nodes(2).Image = 2
treTreeView1.Nodes(3).Image = 2
treTreeView1.Nodes(4).Image = 3
```

CROSS-REFERENCE
See also CoolBar, TreeView, TabStrip, Toolbar, and ImageList.

Image—General Controls

Property

The `Image` property represents a handle to the image (called a persistent image) that Visual Basic uses to redraw a window. When a control's `AutoRedraw` property is set to `True`, the persistent image contains a bitmap that Visual Basic can copy to the window's client area in order to update the display without having to redraw it from scratch. You can use the handle that the `Image` property returns in Windows API calls, or you can assign the contents of the `Image` property to another control's `Picture` property and so display the image in that control, as well.

Objects with an Image Property

Form

PictureBox

PropertyPage

UserControl

Syntax

```
value = object.Image
```

- *object*—A reference to an object with an `Image` property.
- *value*—The variable that will receive the image handle.

Example 1

The following lines get a handle for a PictureBox's persistent graphic. The `picPicture1` object is a PictureBox control that the programmer added to the application's form at design time.

```
Dim imageHnd As Long
imageHnd = picPicture1.Image
```

Example 2

The following line assigns one PictureBox's `Image` property to another PictureBox's `Picture` property. The `picPicture1` and `picPicture2` objects are PictureBox controls that the programmer added to the application's form at design time.

```
picPicture2.Picture = picPicture1.Image
```

CROSS-REFERENCE
See also AutoRedraw and Picture.

ImageHeight

Property

The `ImageHeight` property represents the height in pixels of the images in an ImageList control. You can set this property only before images have been added to the ImageList control.

Objects with an ImageHeight Property

ImageList

Syntax

```
ImageList.ImageHeight = value1
```

or

```
value2 = ImageList.ImageHeight
```

- *ImageList* — A reference to an ImageList control.
- *value1* — The image height.
- *value2* — The variable that will receive the image height.

Example

The following line sets the height of an ImageList control's images to 64 pixels. The `ilsImageList1` object is an ImageList control that the programmer added to the application's form at design time.

```
ilsImageList1.ImageHeight = 64
```

CROSS-REFERENCE
See also ImageList, ListImage, and ImageWidth.

ImageList

Control

An ImageList is a control that holds images to be displayed on other controls and is used most often with the TreeView, ListView, TabStrip, and Toolbar controls. Although the images stored in the control can be displayed on the screen, the control itself remains hidden in memory. The ImageList control is one of the Microsoft Windows Common Controls 6.0 components, which you can load into your project from the Components dialog box, as shown in Figure I-6.

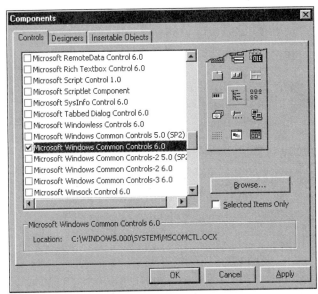

Figure I-6 You can load the ImageList control into the Visual Basic toolbox from the Components dialog box.

Properties

The ImageList control has 12 properties, which are listed as follows. Because many Visual Basic controls have similar properties, the properties' descriptions are listed under their own names provided alphabetically in this book.

```
BackColor
hImageList
ImageHeight
ImageWidth
Index
```

```
ListImages
MaskColor
Name
Object
Parent
Tag
UseMaskColor
```

Methods

The ImageList control has one method, named `Overlay`, which combines two images stored in an ImageList control. For more information on this method, look up its name elsewhere in this book.

Events

The ImageList control does not respond to events.

 CROSS-REFERENCE
See also ImageList (property).

ImageList

Property

The `ImageList` property represents the ImageList control that contains the images to be displayed in a control.

Objects with an ImageList Property

CoolBar
TabStrip
Toolbar
TreeView

Syntax

object.ImageList = *value1*

or

value2 = *object*.ImageList

- *object*—A reference to a control with an `ImageList` property.

- *value1* — A reference to an ImageList control.
- *value2* — The variable that will receive a reference to the ImageList control.

Example

The following lines initialize an ImageList control with a single image and then set a TreeView control's `ImageList` property to the ImageList. The `ilsImageList1` and `treTreeView1` objects are ImageList and TreeView controls that the programmer added to the application's form at design time.

```
ilsImageList1.ListImages.Add , , LoadPicture("icon1.ico")
treTreeView1.ImageList = ilsImageList1
```

 CROSS-REFERENCE
See also ImageList (control).

ImageWidth

Property

The `ImageWidth` property represents the width in pixels of the images in an ImageList control. You can set this property only before images have been added to the ImageList control.

Objects with an ImageWidth Property

ImageList

Syntax

```
ImageList.ImageWidth = value1
```

or

```
value2 = ImageList.ImageWidth
```

- *ImageList* — A reference to an ImageList control.
- *value1* — The image width.
- *value2* — The variable that will receive the image width.

Example

The following line sets the width of an ImageList control's images to 64 pixels. The `ilsImageList1` object is an ImageList control that the programmer added to the application's form at design time.

```
ilsImageList1.ImageWidth = 64
```

 CROSS-REFERENCE
See also ImageList, ListImage, and ImageHeight.

Imp

Operator

The `Imp` operator compares expressions using a logical-implication operation.

Syntax

```
value = exp1 Imp exp2
```

- *exp1* — Any valid expression.
- *exp2* — Any valid expression.
- *value* — The variable that will receive the result of the operation.

Example 1

After the following lines execute, `result` will be `True`.

```
Dim x, y As Integer
Dim result As Boolean
x = 20
y = 30
result = x > 20 Imp y > x
```

Example 2

Here, after the following lines execute, `result` will be `True`.

```
Dim x, y As Integer
Dim result As Boolean
x = 20
y = 30
result = x < 10 Imp y > x
```

Example 3

Finally, after the following lines execute, `result` will be `False`.

```
Dim x, y, z As Integer
Dim result As Boolean
x = 20
y = 30
z = 40
result = x = 20 Imp y > z
```

Increment

Property

The `Increment` property represents how much an UpDown control's value changes when the user clicks the control's arrows.

Objects with an Increment Property

UpDown

Syntax

```
UpDown.Increment = value1
```

or

```
value2 = UpDown.Increment
```

- *UpDown* — A reference to an UpDown control.
- *value1* — The amount to increment.
- *value2* — The variable that will receive the property's current setting.

Example

The following line sets an UpDown control to increment (or decrement) by 2 each time the user clicks the control's arrow buttons. The `updUpDown1` object is an UpDown control that the programmer added to the application's form at design time.

```
updUpDown1.Increment = 2
```

CROSS-REFERENCE
See also UpDown, Max, Min, and Value.

Indentation

Property

The `Indentation` property represents how nodes in a TreeView control should be indented.

Objects with an Indentation Property

TreeView

Syntax

```
TreeView.Indentation = value1
```

or

```
value2 = TreeView.Indentation
```

- *TreeView* — A reference to a TreeView control.
- *value1* — The amount of node indentation.
- *value2* — The variable that will receive the property's current setting.

Example

The following line sets the indentation for nodes in a TreeView control to 200. The `treTreeView1` object is a TreeView control that the programmer added to the application's form at design time.

```
treTreeView1.Indentation = 200
```

CROSS-REFERENCE
See also TreeView, Node, and Nodes.

Index—ActiveX Controls

Property

The Index property represents the index of an object in a collection. By default, the first object added to a collection has an index of 1, with succeeding objects incrementing the index by 1. A collection's Add method, however, enables you to specify indexes for objects. Note that the Index property does not necessarily represent the order in which the objects are stored in the collection, because objects in a collection can be reordered.

Objects with an Index Property

Band

Button

ColumnHeader

Extender

ImageList

ListImage

ListItem

ListView

MAPIMessages

MAPISession

Multimedia MCI

Node

Panel

ProgressBar

RichTextBox

Slider

StatusBar

SysInfo

Tab

TabStrip

Toolbar

TreeView

UpDown

Syntax

```
value = object.Index
```

- *object*—A reference to an object with an `Index` property.
- *value*—The variable that will receive the index.

Example

The following lines populate a ListView control with items and then get the index of the first item in the collection. In this case, the program sets the variable `indx` to 1. The `lvwListView1` object is a ListView control that the programmer added to the application's form at design time.

```
Dim indx As Integer
lvwListView1.ListItems.Add , , "One"
lvwListView1.ListItems.Add , , "Two"
lvwListView1.ListItems.Add , , "Three"
indx = lvwListView1.ListItems(1).Index
```

Index—Control Array

Property

The `Index` property represents the index of a control in a control array. By default, the first object added to a control array has an index of 0, with succeeding controls incrementing the index by 1. However, at design time, a programmer can specify any index for a control, even skipping over index values.

Objects with an Index Property

CheckBox

ComboBox

CommandButton

CommonDialog

DirListBox

DriveListBox

FileListBox

Frame

HScrollBar

Image

Label

Line

ListBox

Menu

OLE Container

OptionButton

PictureBox

Shape

SysInfo

TextBox

Timer

VScrollBar

Syntax

```
value = object.Index
```

- *object*—A reference to an object with an `Index` property.
- *value*—The variable that will receive the index.

InitDir

Property

The `InitDir` property represents the starting directory for a dialog box.

Objects with an InitDir Property

CommonDialog

Syntax

```
CommonDialog.InitDir = value1
```

or

```
value2 = CommonDialog.InitDir
```

- *CommonDialog*—A reference to a CommonDialog control.
- *value1*—A string containing the starting directory.
- *value2*—The variable that will receive the starting directory.

Example

In this example, the program sets a CommonDialog control's starting directory to c:\Program Files and then displays the Open dialog box, which will now automatically open to the c:\Program Files directory. The dlgCommonDialog1 object is a CommonDialog control that the programmer added to the application's form at design time.

```
dlgCommonDialog1.InitDir = "c:\Program Files"
dlgCommonDialog1.ShowOpen
```

CROSS-REFERENCE

See also CommonDialog.

Initialize

Event

Visual Basic sends an object an Initialize event when the object is created.

Objects That Receive Initialize Events

Class

Form

MDIForm

PropertyPage

UserControl

Example

A program can respond to an Initialize event by implementing the target object's Initialize event procedure. The following code segment shows how a Form object defines an Initialize event procedure.

```
Private Sub Form_Initialize()
    ' Handle the Initialize event here.
End Sub
```

CROSS-REFERENCE

See also Load and Terminate.

InitProperties

Event

Visual Basic sends an object an `InitProperties` event when the object is created.

Objects That Receive InitProperties Events

Class

UserControl

Example

A program can respond to an `InitProperties` event by implementing the target object's `InitProperties` event procedure. The following code segment shows how a UserControl object defines an `InitProperties` event procedure.

```
Private Sub UserControl_InitProperties()
    ' Handle the InitProperties event here.
End Sub
```

 CROSS-REFERENCE
See also Initialize, ReadProperties, and WriteProperties.

Input

Function

The `Input` function returns characters from a file, including line feeds, spaces, commas, and other special characters processed differently by the `Input #` statement. The `Input` function works only on files opened in `Input` or `Binary` mode.

Syntax

```
value = Input(numChars, #fileNum)
```

- *fileNum* — The file number given in the `Open` statement. Note that the # symbol is not necessary if the file number is given in a variable.

- *numChars* — The number of characters to read.
- *value* — The variable that will receive the characters read by the function.

Example 1

The following lines open a text file, read the first 10 characters from the file, display the text in a message box, and then close the file.

```
Dim strText As String
Open "c:\TextFile.txt" For Input As #1
strText = Input(10, #1)
MsgBox strText
Close #1
```

Example 2

The following lines work exactly like the code segment in Example 1, except the program now specifies the file number in a variable named fileNum. Note that, because the program gives the file number with a variable, the # symbol in the Open, Input, and Close lines is no longer needed.

```
Dim strText As String
Dim fileNum As Integer
fileNum = 1
Open "c:\TextFile.txt" For Input As fileNum
strText = Input(10, fileNum)
MsgBox strText
Close fileNum
```

CROSS-REFERENCE
See also Input (statement) and InputB.

Input

Keyword

The Input keyword is used as part of the Input function, Input statement, Line Input statement, and the Open statement. The following line, for example, opens a text file in input mode.

```
Open "c:\TextFile.txt" For Input As #1
```

CROSS-REFERENCE
For more information, see Input (function), Input (statement), Line Input, and Open.

Input

Statement

The Input statement returns data from a file and stores the data in the specified variables. Input treats commas in the file as data delimiters and ignores quotation marks. For the Input statement to work properly, data should be written to the file using the Write statement. In addition, Input works only on files opened in Input or Binary mode.

Syntax

```
Input #fileNum, vars
```

- *fileNum* — The file number given in the Open statement. Note that, unlike the Input function, the # symbol is required whether or not the file number is given in a variable.
- *vars* — The list of variables into which the data should be read. Variable names must be separated by commas.

Example 1

The following lines open a file, read a line of text from the file, display the text in a message box, and then close the file.

```
Dim strText As String
Open "c:\TextFile.txt" For Input As #1
Input #1, strText
MsgBox strText
Close #1
```

Example 2

In this case, the following lines open a file, read a line of text and an integer from the file, display the read data in a message box, and then close the file. Note that, even though the program specifies the file number in a variable, the # symbol in the Input statement is still required.

```
Dim strText As String
Dim intValue As Integer
```

```
Dim fileNum As Integer
fileNum = 1
Open "c:\TextFile.txt" For Input As fileNum
Input #fileNum, strText, intValue
MsgBox strText & " — " & intValue
Close fileNum
```

CROSS-REFERENCE
See also Input (function) and InputB.

InputB

Function

The InputB function returns bytes, rather than characters, from a text file. The InputB function works only on files opened in Input or Binary mode.

Syntax

```
value = InputB(numBytes, #fileNum)
```

- *fileNum* — The file number given in the Open statement. Note that the # symbol is not necessary if the file number is given in a variable.
- *numBytes* — The number of bytes to read.
- *value* — The variable that will receive the bytes read by the function.

Example 1

The following lines open a text file, read the first byte from the file, and then close the file.

```
Dim retValue
Open "c:\TextFile.txt" For Input As #1
retValue = InputB(1, #1)
Close #1
```

Example 2

The following lines work exactly like the code segment in Example 1, except the program now specifies the file number in a variable named fileNum. Note that, because the program gives the file number with a variable, the # symbol in the Open, Input, and Close lines is no longer needed.

```
Dim retValue
Dim fileNum As Integer
fileNum = 1
Open "c:\TextFile.txt" For Input As fileNum
retValue = InputB(1, fileNum)
Close fileNum
```

CROSS-REFERENCE
See also Input (function) and Input (statement).

InputBox

Function

The InputBox function displays a dialog box into which the user can type a response.

Syntax

```
value = InputBox(message, title, defaultVal, _
    xPos, yPos, helpFile, helpContext)
```

- *defaultVal* (*) — The data to display in the dialog's text box as the default selection.
- *helpContext* (*) — The context value for the appropriate help topic.
- *helpFile* (*) — The name of the dialog's context help file. The user can press F1 to view the help topic specified by *helpContext*.
- *message* — The message to display in the dialog.
- *title* (*) — The title to display in the dialog.
- *xPos* (*) — The horizontal position in twips at which to position the dialog on the screen.
- *yPos* (*) — The vertical position in twips at which to position the dialog on the screen.
- *value* — The variable that will receive the text the user typed into the dialog's text box.

(*) = Optional

Example 1

The following lines display an input box into which the user can type text, as shown in Figure I-7. A message box then displays the user's response.

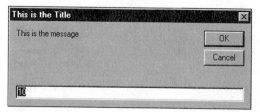

Figure I-7 You can use the InputBox to get a quick response from the user.

```
Dim strResult As String
strResult = InputBox("This is the message", "This is the
Title", 10)
MsgBox strResult
```

Example 2

In this case, the following lines display an input box at the location 1000,1000 (measured in twips) on the screen.

```
Dim strResult As String
strResult = InputBox("This is the message", _
    "This is the Title", 10, 1000, 1000)
MsgBox strResult
```

InsertObjDlg

Method

The InsertObjDlg method displays the Insert Object dialog box on behalf of an OLE Container control. The Insert Object dialog box enables the user to select an object to link or embed in the control.

Objects with an InsertObjDlg Method

OLE Container

Syntax

OLEContainer.InsertObjDlg

- *OLEContainer*—A reference to an OLE Container control.

Example

The following line displays the Insert Object dialog box, as shown in Figure I-8. The `oleContainer1` object is an OLE Container control the programmer added to the application's form at design time.

```
oleContainer1.InsertObjDlg
```

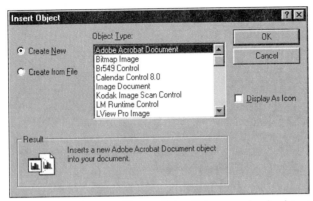

Figure I-8 The Insert Object dialog links or embeds objects into an OLE Container control.

CROSS-REFERENCE
For more information, OLE Container and OLETypeAllowed.

InStr

Function

The `InStr` function returns the position of a specified substring within another string.

Syntax

```
value = InStr(start, srcStr, searchStr, compType)
```

- *compType* (*) — The type of search to perform. Can be a value from Table I-1.
- *searchStr* — The string for which to search.
- *srcStr* — The string to search.

- *start* (*) — The character at which to start the search.
- *value* — The variable that will receive the position of the first occurrence of the given substring, or 0 if the substring is not found.

(*) = Optional

Table I-1 Settings for Instr Search Type

Value	Description
vbBinaryCompare	Searches using a binary comparison.
vbDatabaseCompare	Searches based on data in a Microsoft Access database.
vbTextCompare	Searches using a text comparison.
vbUseCompareOption	Searches based on the program's Option Compare statement.

Example 1

After the following lines execute, pos will contain the value 4, which is the location of the substring "two" within the str1 string.

```
Dim pos As Long
Dim str1, str2 As String
str1 = "onetwothree"
str2 = "two"
pos = InStr(str1, str2)
```

Example 2

After the following lines execute, pos will contain the value 7, which is the location of the second "two" within the str1 string. In this case, the InStr function found the second occurrence of "two" because it started searching at the fifth character in str1.

```
Dim pos As Long
Dim str1, str2 As String
str1 = "onetwotwothree"
str2 = "two"
pos = InStr(5, str1, str2)
```

CROSS-REFERENCE
See also InStrB, InStrRev, and StrComp.

InStrB

Function

The InStrB function returns the byte position of a specified substring within another string.

Syntax

```
value = InStrB(start, srcStr, searchStr, compType)
```

- *compType* (*) — The type of search to perform. Can be a value from Table I-2.
- *searchStr* — The string for which to search.
- *srcStr* — The string to search.
- *start* (*) — The character at which to start the search.
- *value* — The variable that will receive the position of the first occurrence of the given substring, or 0 if the substring is not found.

(*) = Optional

Table I-2 Settings for InStrB Search Type

Value	Description
vbBinaryCompare	Searches using a binary comparison.
vbDatabaseCompare	Searches based on data in a Microsoft Access database.
vbTextCompare	Searches using a text comparison.
vbUseCompareOption	Searches based on the program's Option Compare statement.

Example

After the following lines execute, pos will contain the value 7, which is the byte location of the substring "two" within the str1 string.

```
Dim pos As Long
Dim str1, str2 As String
str1 = "onetwothree"
str2 = "two"
pos = InStrB(str1, str2)
```

CROSS-REFERENCE
See also InStr, InStrRev, and StrComp.

InStrRev

Function

The `InStrRev` function returns the position of a specified substring within another string, with the search starting at the end of the string instead of at the start.

Syntax

```
value = InStrRev(srcStr, searchStr, start, compType)
```

- *compType* (*) — The type of search to perform. Can be a value from Table I-3.
- *searchStr* — The string for which to search.
- *srcStr* — The string to search.
- *start* (*) — The character at which to start the search.
- *value* — The variable that will receive the position of the first occurrence of the given substring, or 0 if the substring is not found.

(*) = Optional

Table I-3 Settings for `InStrRev` Search Type

Value	Description
vbBinaryCompare	Searches using a binary comparison.
vbDatabaseCompare	Searches based on data in a Microsoft Access database.
vbTextCompare	Searches using a text comparison.
vbUseCompareOption	Searches based on the program's `Option Compare` statement.

Example

After the following lines execute, `pos` will contain the value 7, which is the location of the last substring "two" within the `str1` string.

```
Dim pos As Long
Dim str1, str2 As String
str1 = "onetwotwothree"
str2 = "two"
pos = InStrRev(str1, str2)
```

CROSS-REFERENCE
See also InStr and StrComp.

Int

Function

The Int function truncates the decimal portion from a number, returning the resultant integer value. If the given number is negative, the function returns the next negative value less than or equal to the given number. That is, Int truncates the value –4.3 to –5.

Syntax

```
value = Int(num)
```

- *num* — The number to truncate.
- *value* — The variable that will receive the returned integer value.

Example

After the following lines execute, the variable result will contain the value 3.

```
Dim value, result As Integer
value = 3.6
result = Int(value)
```

CROSS-REFERENCE
See also Fix.

IntegralHeight

Property

The IntegralHeight property represents whether a control can display items partially or display only complete items. For example, a ListBox that's large enough to display seven and a half items (Figure I-9) would display only seven items (Figure I-10) if its IntegralHeight property were set to True. The IntegralHeight property can be set only at design time.

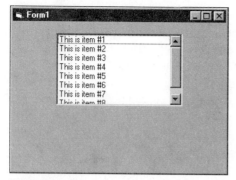

Figure I-9 This ListBox can display partial items.

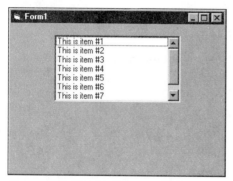

Figure I-10 This ListBox can display only complete items.

Objects with an IntegralHeight Property

ComboBox

ListBox

Syntax

object.IntegralHeight = *value1*

or

value2 = *object*.IntegralHeight

- *object* — A reference to a ComboBox or ListBox control.
- *value1* — The value True or False.
- *value2* — The variable that will receive the property's current setting.

Example

The following lines retrieve the setting of a ListBox control's `IntegralHeight` property. The `lstList1` object is a ListBox control that the programmer added to the application's form at design time.

```
Dim result As Boolean
result = lstList1.IntegralHeight
```

CROSS-REFERENCE
See also ComboBox and ListBox.

Interval

Property

The `Interval` property represents the amount of time in milliseconds between timer events.

Objects with an Interval Property

Timer

Syntax

```
Timer.Interval = value1
```

or

```
value2 = Timer.Interval
```

- *Timer*—A reference to a Timer control.
- *value1*—The interval time in milliseconds.
- *value2*—The variable that will receive the interval time.

Example

In this example, the program sets a Timer control to send timer events once a second. The `tmrTimer1` object is a Timer control that the programmer added to the application's form at design time.

```
tmrTimer1.Interval = 1000
```

CROSS-REFERENCE
See also Timer and Enabled.

InvisibleAtRuntime

Property

The `InvisibleAtRuntime` property represents whether a UserControl object will be invisible. That is, if `InvisibleAtRuntime` is set to `True`, the control will have no visible window. Set this property in the control's Properties window when authoring the control.

Objects with an InvisibleAtRuntime Property

UserControl

 CROSS-REFERENCE
See also OLE Container and OLEObject.

IPmt

Function

The `IPmt` function calculates the interest on an annuity.

Syntax

```
value = IPmt(intRate, payPeriod, numPeriods, _
    presValue, futVal, typeDue)
```

- *intRate* — The interest rate.
- *futVal* (*) — The future value after the final payment.
- *numPeriods* — The total number of payment periods.
- *payPeriod* — The payment period on which to calculate interest.
- *presValue* — The annuity's present value.
- *typeDue* (*) — The value 0 if payments are due at the end of the period and 1 if payments are due at the start of the period.
- *value* — The variable that will receive the calculation's result.

(*) = Optional

Example

The following lines calculate the interest for the first month of a $1,000 loan with a 10% annual interest rate and 12 monthly payments.

```
Dim result As Double
result = IPmt(0.1 / 12, 1, 12, -1000, 0, 0)
```

IRR

Function

The IRR function calculates the internal rate of return on a series of payments and receipts.

Syntax

```
value = IRR(input(), return)
```

- *input* — An array of positive and negative values, with positive values representing receipts and negative values representing payments.
- *return* (*) — The estimated return. The default is 10%.
- *value* — The variable that will receive the calculation's result.

(*) = Optional

Example

The following lines calculate the rate of return on a series of transactions containing one payment of $1,000 and two receipts of $750.

```
Dim result As Double
Dim inVals(3) As Double
inVals(0) = -1000
inVals(1) = 750
inVals(2) = 750
result = IRR(inVals())
```

Is

Operator

The Is operator compares two variables, returning True if the variables refer to the same object and False if they don't.

Syntax

```
value = var1 Is var2
```

- *value* — The variable that will receive the result of the comparison.
- *var1* — A variable name.
- *var2* — A variable name.

Example

The following lines compare `obj1` to `obj2`. If the variables refer to the same object, `result` will equal `True`.

```
Dim result As Boolean
result = obj1 Is obj2
```

 CROSS-REFERENCE
See also IsObject.

IsArray

Function

The `IsArray` function determines whether a variable is an array.

Syntax

```
value = IsArray(variable)
```

- *value* — The variable that will receive the return value of `True` or `False`.
- *variable* — The name of the variable to check.

Example

In this example, the program sets the variable `result` to `True`.

```
Dim intArray(10) As Integer
Dim result As Boolean
result = IsArray(intArray)
```

IsDate

Function

The `IsDate` function determines whether the given expression is a valid date.

Syntax

```
value = IsDate(expr)
```

- *expr*—The expression to check for date format.
- *value*—The variable that will receive the return value of True or False.

Example

In this example, the program sets the variable result to True. If var1 is set to something like "1998" or "This is a test" in the sample lines, result would be False.

```
Dim var1 As String
Dim result As Boolean
var1 = "1/21/98"
result = IsDate(var1)
```

IsEmpty

Function

The IsEmpty function determines whether the given variable has been initialized.

Syntax

```
value = IsEmpty(variable)
```

- *value*—The variable that will receive the return value of True or False.
- *variable*—The name of the variable to check.

Example 1

In this example, the program sets the variable result to False.

```
Dim var1
Dim result As Boolean
var1 = 10
result = IsEmpty(var1)
```

Example 2

Here, the program sets the variable `result` to `True`. The program has not explicitly initialized the variable, and because `var1` has not been declared with a data type, Visual Basic cannot automatically initialize the variable to a starting default value.

```
Dim var1
Dim result As Boolean
result = IsEmpty(var1)
```

Example 3

Here, the program sets the variable `result` to `False`. Although the program has not explicitly initialized the variable, Visual Basic itself automatically initializes integers to 0.

```
Dim var1 As Integer
Dim result As Boolean
result = IsEmpty(var1)
```

IsError

Function

The `IsError` function determines whether the given expression represents an error value.

Syntax

```
value = IsError(expr)
```
- *expr*—The expression to check.
- *value*—The variable that will receive the return value of `True` or `False`.

Example

In this example, the program determines whether an error was returned from the `AnyFunction` function.

```
Dim var1
Dim result As Boolean
var1 = AnyFunction()
result = IsError(var1)
```

IsMissing

Function

The IsMissing function determines if an optional argument was not passed to a procedure.

Syntax

```
value = IsMissing(variable)
```

- *value*—The variable that will receive the return value of True or False.
- *variable*—The name of the variable to check.

Example

The following lines show how to use the IsMissing function to determine whether an optional argument was passed to a procedure or is missing.

```
Private Sub MyProc(Optional var1)
    If IsMissing(var1) Then
        MsgBox "var1 is missing"
    Else
        MsgBox "var1 was passed to the procedure"
    End If
End Sub
```

IsNull

Function

The IsNull function determines whether the given variable is Null.

Syntax

```
value = IsNull(variable)
```

- *value*—The variable that will receive the return value of True or False.
- *variable*—The name of the variable to check.

Example

In this example, the program sets the variable result to True.

```
Dim var1
Dim result As Boolean
var1 = Null
result = IsNull(var1)
```

IsNumeric

Function

The IsNumeric function determines whether a given expression can be resolved to a numeric value.

Syntax

```
value = IsNumeric(expr)
```

- *expr* — The expression to check.
- *value* — The variable that will receive the return value of True or False.

Example 1

In this example, the program sets the variable result to False.

```
Dim var1
Dim result As Boolean
var1 = "OneTwoThree"
result = IsNumeric(var1)
```

Example 2

In this example, the program sets the variable result to True.

```
Dim var1 As String
Dim result As Boolean
var1 = "35"
result = IsNumeric(var1)
```

IsObject

Function

The IsObject function determines whether a given variable is a reference to an Object.

Syntax

```
value = IsObject(variable)
```

- *value* — The variable that will receive the return value of True or False.
- *variable* — The name of the variable to check.

Example 1

In this example, the program sets the variable result to True.

```
Dim var1 As Object
Dim result As Boolean
result = IsObject(var1)
```

Example 2

Here, the program sets the variable result to False.

```
Dim var1 As Integer
Dim result As Boolean
result = IsObject(var1)
```

IsReady

Property

The IsReady property represents whether the given drive is ready to read and write data.

Objects with an IsReady Property

Drive

Syntax

```
value = Drive.IsReady
```

- *Drive* — A reference to a Drive object.
- *value* — The variable that will receive the return value of `True` or `False`.

Example

The following lines determine whether drive C is ready to be accessed.

```
Dim fileSystem, drv As Object
Dim result As Boolean
Set fileSystem = CreateObject("Scripting.FileSystemObject")
Set drv = fileSystem.GetDrive("c")
result = drv.IsReady
```

 CROSS-REFERENCE
See also Drive, DriveExists, DriveLetter, and DriveType.

IsRootFolder

Property

The `IsRootFolder` property represents whether the given path is the drive's root folder.

Objects with an IsRootFolder Property

Folder

Syntax

```
value = Folder.IsRootFolder
```

- *Folder* — A reference to a Folder object.
- *value* — The variable that will receive the return value of `True` or `False`.

Example

After the following lines execute, the variable `result` will contain `True`.

```
Dim fileSystem, folder As Object
Dim result As Boolean
Set fileSystem = CreateObject("Scripting.FileSystemObject")
Set folder = fileSystem.GetFolder("c:\")
result = folder.IsRootFolder
```

 CROSS-REFERENCE
See also Folder.

Italic

Property

The Italic property represents whether a font is italic.

Objects with an Italic Property

Font

Syntax

Font.Italic = *value1*

or

value2 = *Font*.Italic

- *Font* — A reference to a Font object.
- *value1* — The value True or False.
- *value2* — The variable that will receive the property's current setting.

Example

The following line sets a form's font to italic.

```
frmForm1.Font.Italic = True
```

 CROSS-REFERENCE
See also Font, Strikethrough, and Underline.

Item

Method

The Item method returns an item from a collection.

Objects with an Item Method

Collection

Syntax

```
value = Collection.Item(index)
```

- *Collection* — A reference to a Collection object.
- *index* — The index or key of the item to retrieve.
- *value* — The variable that will receive the reference to the item.

Example

The following lines get a reference to a node (which is stored in a Nodes collection) in a TreeView control. The treTreeView1 object is a TreeView control that the programmer added to the application's form at design time.

```
Dim n As Node
Set n = treTreeView1.Nodes.Item(2)
```

CROSS-REFERENCE
See also Collection.

Item

Property

The Item property represents a member of a collection.

Objects with an Item Property

ButtonMenus
ColumnHeaders
ListImages
ListItems

Nodes

Panels

Tabs

Syntax

```
value = object.Item(index)
```

- *index* — The index or key of the item to retrieve.
- *object* — A reference to an object with an Item property.
- *value* — The variable that will receive the reference to the item.

Example

The following lines get a reference to a node in a TreeView control. The treTreeView1 object is a TreeView control that the programmer added to the application's form at design time.

```
Dim n As Node
Set n = treTreeView1.Nodes.Item(2)
```

 CROSS-REFERENCE
See also Collection.

ItemCheck — ListBox

Event

Visual Basic sends a ListBox control an ItemCheck event when the user checks an item in a ListBox with the Style property set to checkboxes.

Example

A program can respond to an ItemCheck event by implementing the target object's ItemCheck event procedure. The following code segment shows how a ListBox object defines an ItemCheck event procedure, whose single parameter is the index of the checked item. The lstList1 object is a ListBox control that the programmer added to the form at design time.

```
Private Sub lstList1_ItemCheck(Item As Integer)
    ' Handle the ItemCheck event here.
End Sub
```

CROSS-REFERENCE
See also ListBox.

ItemCheck — ListView

Event

Visual Basic sends a ListBox control an ItemCheck event when the user checks an item in a ListBox with the Checkboxes property set to True.

Example

A program can respond to an ItemCheck event by implementing the target object's ItemCheck event procedure. The following code segment shows how a ListView object defines an ItemCheck event procedure, whose single parameter is a reference to the checked item. The lvwListView1 object is a ListView control that the programmer added to the form at design time.

```
Private Sub lvwListView1_ItemCheck(ByVal Item As
ComctlLib.ListItem)
    ' Respond to the ItemCheck event here.
End Sub
```

CROSS-REFERENCE
See also ListView.

ItemClick

Event

Visual Basic sends a ListView control an ItemClick event when the user clicks one of the control's items.

Objects That Receive ItemClick Events

ListView

Example

A program can respond to an ItemClick event by implementing the target object's ItemClick event procedure. The following code segment shows how a ListView object defines an ItemClick event procedure, whose single parameter is a reference to the clicked item. The `lvwListView1` object is a ListView control that the programmer added to the form at design time.

```
Private Sub lvwListView1_ItemClick _
    (ByVal Item As MSComctlLib.ListItem)
    ' Respond to the ItemClick event here.
End Sub
```

 **CROSS-REFERENCE**
See also ListView.

ItemData

Property

The `ItemData` property represents an array of values that identify items in a control.

Objects with an ItemData Property

ComboBox
ListBox

Syntax

```
object.ItemData(index) = value1
```

or

```
value2 = object.ItemData(index)
```

- *index* — The index into the array.
- *object* — A reference to a ComboBox or ListBox control.
- *value1* — The number to associate with the item.
- *value2* — The variable that will receive the item's number.

Example

The following lines add items to a ListBox control, and then set the items' values in the `ItemData` array. The `lstList1` object is a ListBox control that the programmer added to the application's form at design time.

```
lstList1.AddItem "Item #1"
lstList1.AddItem "Item #2"
```

```
lstList1.AddItem "Item #3"
lstList1.AddItem "Item #4"
lstList1.AddItem "Item #5"
lstList1.ItemData(0) = 4376
lstList1.ItemData(1) = 1125
lstList1.ItemData(2) = 4387
lstList1.ItemData(3) = 1243
lstList1.ItemData(4) = 9845
```

CROSS-REFERENCE

See also ComboBox and ListBox.

h o

i

j

Key

Property

The Key property represents a string that a programmer can set in order to identify a collection member.

Objects with a Key Property

Buttons

ColumnHeaders

ListImages

ListItems

Nodes

Panels

Tabs

Syntax

```
object.Key = value1
```

or

```
value2 = object.Key
```

- *object* — A reference to an object with a Key property.
- *value1* — A string containing the key.
- *value2* — The variable that will receive the key.

Example

The following line sets the key for the first ListItem object in a ListView control. The lvwListView1 object is a ListView control that the programmer added to the application's form at design time.

```
lvwListView1.ListItems(1).Key = "Item1"
```

CROSS-REFERENCE
See also Collection and Index.

KeyDown

Event

Visual Basic sends a control a KeyDown event when the user presses a key on the keyboard when the control has the input focus. After the KeyDown event, Visual Basic sends the KeyPress and KeyUp events. Use the KeyDown event to respond to a key press the instant the key is pressed.

Objects That Receive KeyDown Events

CheckBox

ComboBox

CommandButton

DirListBox

DriveListBox

FileListBox

Form

HScrollBar

ListBox

ListView

OLE Container

OptionButton

PictureBox

PropertyPage

RichTextBox

Slider

TabStrip

TextBox

TreeView

UserControl

VScrollBar

Example 1

A program can respond to a KeyDown event by implementing the target object's KeyDown event procedure. For example, the following code segment shows how a CommandButton object defines a KeyDown event procedure. Note that the procedure's two parameters are the key code of the pressed key and a flag indicating whether the Shift (bit 0 of Shift is set), Ctrl (bit 1 of Shift is set), or Alt (bit 2 of Shift is set) key was also pressed. Any combination of these special keys can be pressed simultaneously. In the example, the btnCommand1 object is a CommandButton control that the programmer added to the form at design time.

```
Private Sub btnCommand1_KeyDown _
  (KeyCode As Integer, Shift As Integer)
    ' Handle the KeyDown event here.
End Sub
```

Example 2

The following program demonstrates the KeyDown, KeyPress, and KeyUp events. Run the program and press a key. When you do, the events appear in the window, as shown in Figure K-1. Try pressing different combinations of the Shift, Ctrl, and Alt keys to see how the Shift parameter of the KeyDown and KeyUp events changes.

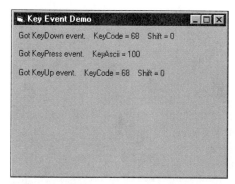

Figure K-1 When you press a key, you see the key events in the program's window.

```
VERSION 5.00
Begin VB.Form frmForm1
   Caption        =    "Key Event Demo"
   ClientHeight   =    3195
   ClientLeft     =    60
   ClientTop      =    345
```

```
        ClientWidth     =    4680
        FontTransparent =    0    'False
        LinkTopic       =    "Form1"
        ScaleHeight     =    3195
        ScaleWidth      =    4680
        StartUpPosition =    3    'Windows Default
End
Attribute VB_Name = "frmForm1"
Attribute VB_GlobalNameSpace = False
Attribute VB_Creatable = False
Attribute VB_PredeclaredId = True
Attribute VB_Exposed = False

Private Sub Form_KeyDown(KeyCode As Integer, Shift As Integer)
    Dim msg As String
    frmForm1.Cls
    frmForm1.CurrentX = 100
    frmForm1.CurrentY = 100
    msg = "Got KeyDown event.   KeyCode = " & KeyCode
    msg = msg & "    Shift = " & Shift
    frmForm1.Print msg
End Sub

Private Sub Form_KeyPress(KeyAscii As Integer)
    Dim msg As String
    frmForm1.CurrentX = 100
    frmForm1.CurrentY = 500
    msg = "Got KeyPress event.   KeyAscii = " & KeyAscii
    frmForm1.Print msg
End Sub

Private Sub Form_KeyUp(KeyCode As Integer, Shift As Integer)
    Dim msg As String
    frmForm1.CurrentX = 100
    frmForm1.CurrentY = 900
    msg = "Got KeyUp event.   KeyCode = " & KeyCode
    msg = msg & "    Shift = " & Shift
    frmForm1.Print msg
End Sub

Private Sub Form_Load()
    frmForm1.FontTransparent = False
End Sub
```

CROSS-REFERENCE
See also KeyPress, KeyUp, and KeyPreview.

KeyPress

Event

Visual Basic sends a control a `KeyPress` event when the user presses and releases a key on the keyboard when the control has the input focus. Before the `KeyPress` event, Visual Basic sends the `KeyDown` event, and after the `KeyPress` event, Visual Basic sends the `KeyUp` event. Use the `KeyPress` event to retrieve the ASCII value of a pressed key.

Objects That Receive KeyPress Events

CheckBox

ComboBox

CommandButton

DirListBox

DriveListBox

FileListBox

Form

HScrollBar

ListBox

ListView

OLE Container

OptionButton

PictureBox

PropertyPage

RichTextBox

Slider

TabStrip

TextBox

TreeView

UserControl

VScrollBar

Example

A program can respond to a KeyPress event by implementing the target object's KeyPress event procedure. For example, the following code segment shows how a CommandButton object defines a KeyPress event procedure. Note that the procedure's single parameter is the ASCII code of the pressed key. In the example, the btnCommand1 object is a CommandButton control that the programmer added to the form at design time.

```
Private Sub btnCommand1_KeyPress(KeyAscii As Integer)
    ' Handle the KeyPress event here.
End Sub
```

 CROSS-REFERENCE
See also KeyDown, KeyUp, and KeyPreview.

KeyPreview

Property

The KeyPreview property represents whether a form will receive key events before the controls in the form receive them.

Objects with a KeyPreview Property

PropertyPage

Form

UserControl

Syntax

object.KeyPreview = *value1*

or

value2 = *object*.KeyPreview

- *object* — A reference to an object with a KeyPreview property.
- *value1* — The value True or False.
- *value2* — The variable that will receive the property's current setting.

Example

The following program demonstrates how the KeyPreview property works. When you first run the program, the application's single button has the input focus. Press a key on your keyboard, and a message box tells you that the button received the key event (Figure K-2). Now, click the button to toggle the KeyPreview property to True. Press a key again, and the message box tells you that the form got the key event first, after which the button gets the event.

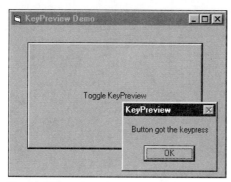

Figure K-2 When the program first runs, the button gets first crack at key events.

```
VERSION 5.00
Begin VB.Form frmForm1
   Caption         =   "KeyPreview Demo"
   ClientHeight    =   3195
   ClientLeft      =   60
   ClientTop       =   345
   ClientWidth     =   4680
   LinkTopic       =   "Form1"
   ScaleHeight     =   3195
   ScaleWidth      =   4680
   StartUpPosition =   3   'Windows Default
   Begin VB.CommandButton btnToggle
      Caption      =   "Toggle KeyPreview"
      Height       =   2295
      Left         =   360
      TabIndex     =   0
      Top          =   360
      Width        =   3855
   End
End
```

```
Attribute VB_Name = "frmForm1"
Attribute VB_GlobalNameSpace = False
Attribute VB_Creatable = False
Attribute VB_PredeclaredId = True
Attribute VB_Exposed = False

Private Sub btnToggle_Click()
    If frmForm1.KeyPreview Then
        frmForm1.KeyPreview = False
    Else
        frmForm1.KeyPreview = True
    End If
End Sub

Private Sub btnToggle_KeyPress(KeyAscii As Integer)
    MsgBox "Button got the keypress"
End Sub

Private Sub Form_KeyPress(KeyAscii As Integer)
    MsgBox "Form got the keypress"
End Sub

Private Sub Form_Load()
    KeyPreview = False
End Sub
```

CROSS-REFERENCE
See also Collection and Index.

KeyUp

Event

Visual Basic sends a control a KeyUp event when the user releases a key on the keyboard when the control has the input focus. Before the KeyUp event, Visual Basic sends the KeyDown and KeyPress events. Use the KeyUp event to respond to a key release.

Objects That Receive KeyUp Events
CheckBox
ComboBox
CommandButton

DirListBox

DriveListBox

FileListBox

Form

HScrollBar

ListBox

ListView

OLE Container

OptionButton

PictureBox

PropertyPage

RichTextBox

Slider

TabStrip

TextBox

TreeView

UserControl

VScrollBar

Example

A program can respond to a KeyUp event by implementing the target object's KeyUp event procedure. For example, the following code segment shows how a CommandButton object defines a KeyUp event procedure. Note that the procedure's two parameters are the key code of the pressed key and a flag indicating whether the Shift (bit 0 of Shift is set), Ctrl (bit 1 of Shift is set), or Alt (bit 2 of Shift is set) key was also pressed. Any combination of these special keys can be pressed simultaneously. In the example, the btnCommand1 object is a CommandButton control that the programmer added to the form at design time.

```
Private Sub btnCommand1_KeyUp _
  (KeyCode As Integer, Shift As Integer)
    ' Handle the KeyUp event here.
End Sub
```

 CROSS-REFERENCE

See also KeyDown, KeyPress, and KeyPreview.

Kill

Statement

The `Kill` statement deletes a disk file. The file's name can include wildcard characters to enable the statement to delete multiple files.

Syntax

```
Kill name
```

■ *name* — The path of the file or files to delete.

Example 1

The following line deletes a file named `MyText.txt` from the C: root directory.

```
Kill "C:\MyText.txt"
```

Example 2

The following line deletes all files with the .txt extension from the C: root directory.

WARNING
Don't try this code example unless you really want to delete all text files on drive C.

```
Kill "C:\*.txt"
```

CROSS-REFERENCE
See also RmDir.

KillDoc

Method

The `KillDoc` method ends a print job.

Objects with a KillDoc Method

Printer

Syntax

`Printer.KillDoc`

- *Printer*—A reference to the Printer object.

Example

The following line ends the current print job. Note that Printer is a Visual Basic global object that you don't need to create in your programs.

`Printer.KillDoc`

CROSS-REFERENCE
See also Printer.

Label

Control

A Label is a control that displays text labels in a program. Figure L-1 shows Label controls in a form. Note that, unlike text in a TextBox control, the user cannot edit the contents of a Label control. For this reason, this type of text is often referred to as *static text*. The Label control is available on Visual Basic's standard toolbox.

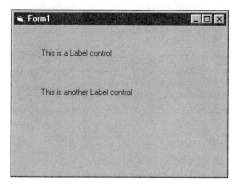

Figure L-1 Label controls represent static text in a program.

Properties

The Label control has 40 properties, which are listed as follows. Because many Visual Basic controls have similar properties, the properties' descriptions are listed under their own names, provided alphabetically elsewhere in this book.

```
Alignment
Appearance
AutoSize
BackColor
BackStyle
BorderStyle
```

```
Caption
Container
DragIcon
DragMode
Enabled
Font
FontBold
FontItalic
FontName
FontSize
FontStrikethru
FontUnderline
ForeColor
Index
Left
LinkItem
LinkMode
LinkTimeout
LinkTopic
MouseIcon
MousePointer
Name
OLEDropMode
Parent
RightToLeft
TabIndex
Tag
ToolTipText
Top
UseMnemonic
Visible
WhatsThisHelpID
Width
WordWrap
```

Methods

The Label control has ten methods, which are listed below. Because many Visual Basic controls have similar methods, the methods' descriptions are listed under their own names, provided alphabetically elsewhere in this book.

```
Drag
LinkExecute
LinkPoke
```

```
LinkRequest
LinkSend
Move
OLEDrag
Refresh
ShowWhatsThis
ZOrder
```

Events

The Label control responds to 18 events, which are listed below. Because many Visual Basic controls respond to similar events, the events' descriptions are listed under their own names elsewhere in this book.

```
Change
Click
DblClick
DragDrop
DragOver
LinkClose
LinkError
LinkNotify
LinkOpen
MouseDown
MouseMove
MouseUp
OLECompleteDrag
OLEDragDrop
OLEDragOver
OLEGiveFeedback
OLESetData
OLEStartDrag
```

The Label control's most commonly used event is `Click`, which the control generates when the user clicks the control with the mouse. A program responds to the control's `Click` event in the `Click` event procedure. A label called `lblLabel1` will have a `Click` event procedure called `lblLabel1_Click`, which is where the program should handle the event. In the following example, when the user clicks the `lblLabel1` Label control, the program plays the computer's beep sound:

```
Private Sub lblLabel1_Click()
    ' Handle the Click event here.
    Beep
End Sub
```

LabelEdit — ListView

Property

The `LabelEdit` property represents whether the user can automatically edit the text associated with a ListItem object. When this property is set to `lvwAutomatic`, which is the default, Visual Basic sends the control a `BeforeLabelEdit` event as soon as the user clicks a selected ListItem's text. When set to `lvwManual`, the program must call the `StartLabelEdit` method in order to trigger the `BeforeLabelEdit` event and allow the user to edit the label.

Syntax

```
ListView.LabelEdit = value1
```

or

```
value2 = ListView.LabelEdit
```

- *ListView* — A reference to a ListView control.
- *value1* — The value `lvwAutomatic` or `lvwManual`.
- *value2* — The variable that will receive the property's current setting.

Example

The following line sets a ListView control to allow automatic editing. The `lvwListView1` object is a ListView control the programmer added to the form at design time.

```
lvwListView1.LabelEdit = lvwAutomatic
```

CROSS-REFERENCE
See also ListView, ListItem, and StartLabelEdit.

LabelEdit — TreeView

Property

The `LabelEdit` property represents whether the user can edit the text associated with a Node object. When this property is set to `tvwAutomatic`, which is the default, Visual Basic sends the control a `BeforeLabelEdit` event as soon as the user clicks a selected Node's text. When set to `tvwManual`, the program must call the `StartLabelEdit` method in order to trigger the `BeforeLabelEdit` event.

Syntax

`TreeView.LabelEdit = value1`

or

`value2 = TreeView.LabelEdit`

- *TreeView* — A reference to a TreeView control.
- *value1* — The value `tvwAutomatic` or `tvwManual`.
- *value2* — The variable that will receive the property's current setting.

Example

The following program demonstrates how the `LabelEdit` property affects a TreeView control's interactivity with the user. When you first run the program, you can edit any node's label simply by selecting the node and then clicking the label (see Figure L-2). However, if you click the Turn Off Auto Editing button, the program takes over control of label editing. Now you can't edit a label by clicking it. Instead, you must select a node and then click the Edit Item button, which causes the program to call the `StartLabelEdit` method.

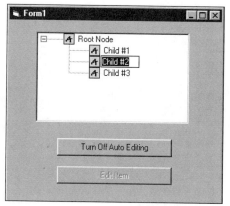

Figure L-2 The selected label in this TreeView control is about to be edited.

```
VERSION 5.00
Object = "{6B7E6392-850A-101B-AFC0-4210102A8DA7} _
    #2.0#0"; "MSCOMCTL.OCX"
Begin VB.Form frmForm1
    Caption         =    "Form1"
    ClientHeight    =    3840
    ClientLeft      =    60
    ClientTop       =    345
    ClientWidth     =    4680
    LinkTopic       =    "Form1"
    ScaleHeight     =    3840
    ScaleWidth      =    4680
    StartUpPosition =    3   'Windows Default
    Begin MSComctlLib.TreeView treTreeView1
        Height      =    1935
        Left        =    600
        TabIndex    =    2
        Top         =    240
        Width       =    3375
        _ExtentX    =    5953
        _ExtentY    =    3413
        _Version    =    393217
        Style       =    7
        Appearance  =    1
    End
    Begin VB.CommandButton btnEditItem
        Caption     =    "Edit Item"
        Height      =    375
        Left        =    1080
        TabIndex    =    1
        Top         =    3120
        Width       =    2535
    End
    Begin MSComctlLib.ImageList ilsImageList1
        Left        =    240
        Top         =    2640
        _ExtentX    =    1005
        _ExtentY    =    1005
        BackColor   =    -2147483643
        MaskColor   =    12632256
        _Version    =    393216
    End
    Begin VB.CommandButton btnToggle
        Caption         =    "Turn Off Auto Editing"
```

```
          Height        =    375
          Left          =    1080
          TabIndex      =    0
          Top           =    2520
          Width         =    2535
       End
   End
   Attribute VB_Name = "frmForm1"
   Attribute VB_GlobalNameSpace = False
   Attribute VB_Creatable = False
   Attribute VB_PredeclaredId = True
   Attribute VB_Exposed = False


   Private Sub btnEditItem_Click()
       treTreeView1.StartLabelEdit
   End Sub


   Private Sub btnToggle_Click()
       If treTreeView1.LabelEdit = lvwAutomatic Then
           treTreeView1.LabelEdit = lvwManual
           btnToggle.Caption = "Turn On Auto Editing"
           btnEditItem.Enabled = True
       Else
           treTreeView1.LabelEdit = lvwAutomatic
           btnToggle.Caption = "Turn Off Auto Editing"
           btnEditItem.Enabled = False
       End If
   End Sub


   Private Sub Form_Load()
       ilsImageList1.ListImages.Add , , LoadPicture("icon2.ico")
       treTreeView1.ImageList = ilsImageList1
       treTreeView1.LabelEdit = lvwAutomatic
       treTreeView1.LineStyle = tvwRootLines

       treTreeView1.Nodes.Add , , , "Root Node", 1
       treTreeView1.Nodes.Add 1, tvwChild, , "Child #1", 1
       treTreeView1.Nodes.Add 1, tvwChild, , "Child #2", 1
       treTreeView1.Nodes.Add 1, tvwChild, , "Child #3", 1

       treTreeView1.Nodes(3).EnsureVisible
       btnEditItem.Enabled = False
   End Sub
```

CROSS-REFERENCE
See also TreeView and Node.

LabelWrap

Property

The `LabelWrap` property represents whether ListItem labels wrap to another line when the ListView control is in icon view, as shown in Figure L-3. Figure L-4 shows the same ListView control with the `LabelWrap` property set to `False`.

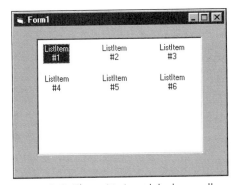

Figure L-3 These ListItem labels are allowed to wrap.

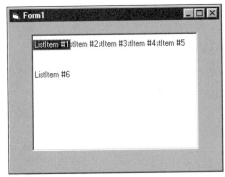

Figure L-4 Visual Basic must display these ListItem labels on a single line.

Objects with a LabelWrap Property

ListView

Syntax

`ListView.LabelWrap = value1`

or

`value2 = ListView.LabelWrap`

- *ListView*—A reference to a ListView control.
- *value1*—The value `True` or `False`.
- *value2*—The variable that will receive the property's current setting.

Example

In this example, the program enables a ListView control to wrap its ListItem labels if necessary. The `lvwListView1` object is a ListView control that the programmer added to the application's form at design time.

`lvwListView1.LabelWrap = True`

CROSS-REFERENCE
See also ListView, Node, and View.

LargeChange—HScrollBar and VScrollBar

Property

The `LargeChange` property represents how far a scroll bar scrolls when the user clicks in the control's channel. If the program doesn't set this property, the property defaults to 1.

Syntax

`Scroll.LargeChange = value1`

or

`value2 = Scroll.LargeChange`

- *Scroll*—A reference to an HScrollBar or VScrollBar control.

- *value1* — The amount the scroll bar should change.
- *value2* — The variable that will receive the property's current setting.

Example

In this example, the program sets an HScrollBar control to scroll 25 units each time the user clicks the scroll bar's channel. The `hsbHScroll1` object is an HScrollBar control that the programmer added to the application's form at design time.

```
hsbHScroll1.LargeChange = 25
```

 CROSS-REFERENCE
See also HScrollBar, VScrollBar, Change, SmallChange, Min, Max, and Value.

LargeChange — Slider

Property

The `LargeChange` property represents how many ticks the slider moves when the user clicks in a Slider control's channel or presses PageUp or PageDown on the keyboard. If the program doesn't set this property, the property defaults to 5.

Syntax

```
Slider.LargeChange = value1
```

or

```
value2 = Slider.LargeChange
```

- *Slider* — A reference to a Slider control.
- *value1* — The amount the slider should change.
- *value2* — The variable that will receive the property's current setting.

Example

In this example, the program sets a Slider control to change 10 ticks each time the user clicks the slider's channel. The `sldSlider1` object is a Slider control that the programmer added to the application's form at design time.

```
sldSlider1.LargeChange = 10
```

CROSS-REFERENCE
See also Slider, Change, SmallChange, Min, Max, and Value.

LastDLLError

Property

The `LastDLLError` property represents the error code returned by the last call to a DLL function.

Objects with a LastDLLError Property
Err

Syntax

```
value = Err.LastDLLError
```

- *Err*—A reference to the Err object.
- *value*—The variable that will receive the error code.

Example

The following lines extract the most recent error code received by a DLL function call. The Err object is a global Visual Basic object that you don't need to create in your programs.

```
Dim errCode As Integer
errCode = Err.LastDllError
```

CROSS-REFERENCE
See also Err.

LastSibling

Property

The `LastSibling` property represents the last sibling of a node in a TreeView control.

NOTE
A *sibling* is a node at the same level as another node.

Objects with a LastSibling Property

Node

Syntax

```
value = Node.LastSibling
```

- *Node* — A reference to a Node object.
- *value* — The variable that will receive the reference to the node.

Example

The following lines populate a TreeView control with nodes, get a reference to the last sibling below the root node, and change that node's text. Figure L-5 shows the resultant TreeView control. The treTreeView1 object is a TreeView control that the programmer added to the application's form at design time.

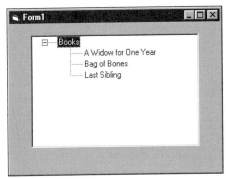

Figure L-5 In this TreeView control, the last sibling below the root has had its text changed.

```
Dim sibNode As Node
treTreeView1.LineStyle = tvwRootLines
treTreeView1.Nodes.Add , , "Root", "Books"
treTreeView1.Nodes.Add "Root", tvwChild, _
    "Child1", "A Widow for One Year"
treTreeView1.Nodes.Add "Root", tvwChild, _
    "Child2", "Bag of Bones"
treTreeView1.Nodes.Add "Root", tvwChild, _
    "Child3", "The Lord of the Rings"

Set sibNode = treTreeView1.Nodes(2).LastSibling
sibNode.Text = "Last Sibling"
```

CROSS-REFERENCE
See also FirstSibling, Node, Nodes, and TreeView.

LBound

Function

The LBound function gets the lowest valid index for a specified dimension of an array. For example, a single-dimension array with three elements with indexes 0, 1, and 2 has a lower bound of 0, which is the value LBound will return for the array. The Option Base statement determines the lower bound for Visual Basic arrays. The default value is 0.

Syntax

```
value = LBound(array, dim)
```

- *array*—The array for which to return the lower bound.
- *dim* (*) — The array dimension for which to return the lower bound.
- *value*—The variable that will receive the lower bound.

(*) = Optional

Example 1

The following lines get the lower bound of a single-dimension array named intArray().

```
Dim intArray(10) As Integer
Dim lowIndex As Integer
lowIndex = LBound(intArray)
```

Example 2

In this case, the following lines get the lower bound of the second dimension of a two-dimensional array named intArray().

```
Dim intArray(10, 25) As Integer
Dim lowIndex As Integer
lowIndex = LBound(intArray, 2)
```

CROSS-REFERENCE
See also UBound and Option Base.

LBound

Property

The LBound property represents the lowest index for a control in a control array. For example, an array of three CommandButton controls with indexes of 0, 1, and 2 have an LBound property setting of 0.

Syntax

```
value = ControlArray.LBound
```

- *ControlArray* — A reference to a control array.
- *value* — The variable that will receive the property's current setting.

Example

The following lines get the lowest index for an array of TextBox controls. The txtText1() object is a TextBox array that the programmer added to the application's form at design time.

```
Dim lowIndex As Integer
lowIndex = txtText1().LBound
```

 CROSS-REFERENCE
See also UBound and Index.

LCase

Function

The LCase function changes the characters in a string to lowercase.

Syntax

```
value = LCase(str)
```

- *str* — The string to change to lowercase.
- *value* — The variable that will receive the converted string.

Example

After the following lines execute, the strLCase variable will contain the text "this is a test."

```
Dim strMsg, strLCase As String
strMsg = "This Is A Test"
strLCase = LCase(strMsg)
```

CROSS-REFERENCE
See also UCase.

Left

Function

The `Left` function returns characters from the left portion of a string.

Syntax

```
value = Left(str, numChars)
```

- *str*—The string from which to get the characters.
- *numChars*—The number of characters to extract from the left portion of the string.
- *value*—The variable that will receive the returned characters.

Example

After the following lines execute, the `strChars` variable will contain the text "This Is."

```
Dim strMsg, strChars As String
strMsg = "This Is A Test"
strChars = Left(strMsg, 7)
```

CROSS-REFERENCE
See also LeftB, Right, RightB, and Mid.

Left

Property

The `Left` property represents the horizontal position of an object inside its container, with the units of measurement depending on the container's `ScaleMode`. The object's horizontal position is measured from the container's left edge.

Objects with a Left Property

Animation

Button

CheckBox

ColumnHeader

ComboBox

CommandButton

CommonDialog

CoolBar

DirListBox

DriveListBox

FileListBox

Form

Frame

HScrollBar

Image

Label

ListBox

ListItem

ListView

MDIForm

Multimedia MCI

OLE Container

OptionButton

Panel

PictureBox

ProgressBar

RichTextBox

Shape

Slider

StatusBar

SysInfo

Tab

TabStrip

TextBox

Timer

Toolbar

TreeView

UpDown

VScrollBar

Syntax

```
object.Left = value1
```

or

```
value2 = object.Left
```

- *object*—A reference to an object with a Left property.
- *value1*—The horizontal position of the object from the left of its container.
- *value2*—The variable that will receive the property's current setting.

Example

The following line positions a CommandButton control 500 twips from the left edge of its form. The btnCommand1 object is a CommandButton control that the programmer added to the application's form at design time.

```
btnCommand1.Left = 500
```

 CROSS-REFERENCE
See also Twips, Top, Height, and Width.

LeftB

Function

The LeftB function returns bytes from the left portion of a string.

Syntax

```
value = LeftB(str, numBytes)
```

- *str*—The string from which to get the bytes.

- *numBytes* — The number of bytes to extract from the left portion of the string.
- *value* — The variable that will receive the returned bytes.

Example

After the following lines execute, the `strBytes` variable will contain the text "This" because four characters normally are represented with eight bytes of data.

```
Dim strMsg, strBytes As String
strMsg = "This Is A Test"
strBytes = LeftB(strMsg, 8)
```

 CROSS-REFERENCE
See also Left, Right, RightB, and Mid.

LegalCopyright

Property

The `LegalCopyright` property represents the application's copyright information. You can get or set the `LegalCopyright` property through a running application's App object.

Objects with a LegalCopyright Property

App

Syntax

```
value = App.LegalCopyright
```

- *string* — The variable that will receive the copyright string.

Example 1

Because the `LegalCopyright` property is read-only at runtime, you must set the property in the Project Properties dialog box before compiling the project. To display the Project Properties dialog box, select the *ProjectName* Properties command from Visual Basic's Project menu. (*ProjectName* is the name of the current project.) Figure L-6 shows the `LegalCopyright` property being set to "Copyright 1998 by Acme Software" in the Project Properties dialog box.

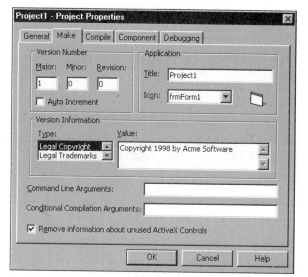

Figure L-6 You can set the application's copyright information in the Project Properties dialog box.

Example 2

The following example obtains the value of the `LegalCopyright` property, and then displays the property's value in a message box. Note that the App object is a Visual Basic global object that you don't need to create in your programs.

```
Dim strCopyright As String
strCopyright = App.LegalCopyright
MsgBox strCopyright
```

 CROSS-REFERENCE
See also App.

LegalTrademarks

Property

The `LegalTrademarks` property represents the application's trademark information. You can get or set the `LegalTrademarks` property through a running application's App object.

Objects with a LegalTrademarks Property

App

Syntax

```
value = App.LegalTrademarks
```

- *string*—The variable that will receive the trademark string.

Example 1

Because the LegalTrademarks property is read-only at runtime, you must set the property in the Project Properties dialog box before compiling the project. To display the Project Properties dialog box, select the *ProjectName* Properties command from Visual Basic's Project menu. (*ProjectName* is the name of the current project.) Figure L-7 shows the LegalTrademarks property being set to "WizTask is a registered trademark of Acme Software" in the Project Properties dialog box.

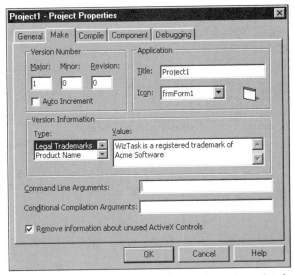

Figure L-7 You can set the application's trademark information in the Project Properties dialog box.

Example 2

The following example obtains the value of the LegalTrademarks property, and then displays the property's value in a message box. Note that the App object is a Visual Basic global object that you don't need to create in your programs.

```
Dim strTrademarks As String
strTrademarks = App.LegalTrademarks
MsgBox strTrademarks
```

 **CROSS-REFERENCE**
See also App.

Len

Function

The Len function calculates the size in characters of a string or the number of bytes used by a variable.

Syntax

```
value = Len(var1)
```

- *value*—The variable that will receive the return value.
- *var1*—The string or variable for which to calculate the length.

Example 1

After the following lines execute, the variable strLen will contain the value 14.

```
Dim strText As String
Dim strLen As Long
strText = "This is a test"
strLen = Len(strText)
```

Example 2

In this case, after the following lines execute, the variable intLen will contain the value 2.

```
Dim intValue As Integer
Dim intLen As Long
intValue = 50
intLen = Len(intValue)
```

Len

Keyword

The Len keyword is used as an optional part of the Open statement for specifying the number of bytes to buffer or the size of a record used in random-access files. For example, the following line opens a random-access file containing records that are 52 bytes in length.

```
Open "DataFile.dat" For Random As #1 Len = 52
```

CROSS-REFERENCE
See also Open and Len (function).

Length

Property

The Length property represents the length of the media currently loaded into a multimedia device. The unit of measurement used to represent the media length depends on the Multimedia MCI control's TimeFormat property setting, which may be milliseconds, frames, SMPTE, and so on. This property is available only at runtime, when it is read-only.

Objects with a Length Property

Multimedia MCI

Syntax

```
value = MultimediaMCI.Length
```

- *MultimediaMCI*—A reference to a Multimedia MCI control.
- *value*—The variable that will receive the media length.

Example

The following lines get the length of the currently active media in a Multimedia MCI control. The mciMMControl1 object is a Multimedia MCI control that the programmer added to the application's form at design time.

```
Dim mediaLen As Long
mediaLen = mciMMControl1.Length
```

CROSS-REFERENCE
See also Multimedia MCI, TimeFormat, From, and To.

Let

Keyword

The Let keyword is used as part of the Let statement or part of a Property Let procedure. For example, the following lines define a Property Let procedure for a property called MsgStr.

```
Property Let MsgStr(Msg As String)
    msgProp = UCase(Msg)
End Property
```

CROSS-REFERENCE
For more information, see Let (statement) and Property Let.

Let

Statement

The Let statement is used to assign a value to a variable. Because the use of the Let keyword in an assignment statement is optional, however, assignment statements often leave off the Let.

Syntax

```
Let var1 = value
```

- *value* — The value to assign to the variable.
- *var1* — The name of the variable to which to assign a value.

Example 1

The following lines set the variable named intVar to 10.

```
Dim intVar As Integer
Let intVar = 10
```

Example 2

The following lines also set the variable named intVar to 10; in this case, the Let keyword has been left off the assignment statement.

```
Dim intVar As Integer
intVar = 10
```

Like

Operator

The Like operator performs string comparisons by determining whether a string matches a given pattern. Patterns can be explicit, or can be constructed from character lists and characters with wildcard symbols. Wildcard symbols that can be used with the Like operator are # (matches any single digit), ? (matches any single character), and * (matches any group of characters). Character lists can be constructed by placing the range of characters within square brackets and using an exclamation point to indicate character exclusions. For example, the list [G-L] includes all uppercase letters from G to L, whereas the list [!G-L] includes all characters except uppercase letters from G to L.

Syntax

```
value = str1 Like str2
```

- *str1* — The string to compare.
- *str2* — The string pattern to which *str1* should be compared.
- *value* — The variable that will receive the returned True or False value.

Example 1

After the following lines execute, result will be True.

```
Dim result As Boolean
result = "aaa" Like "a??"
```

Example 2

After the following lines execute, result will again be True.

```
Dim result As Boolean
result = "AFW" Like "[A-Z]?W"
```

Example 3

In this case, after the following lines execute, result will be False.

```
Dim result As Boolean
result = "AFW" Like "[!A-Z]?W"
```

Example 4

Finally, after the following lines execute, result will be True.

```
Dim result As Boolean
result = "abcdefghi" Like "ab*"
```

Line

Control

A Line control enables a program to display various types of lines, as shown in Figure L-8. The Line control is available on Visual Basic's standard toolbox.

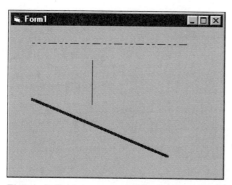

Figure L-8 Line controls display horizontal, vertical, or diagonal lines in various styles.

Properties

The Line control has 14 properties, which are listed as follows. Because many Visual Basic controls have similar properties, the properties' descriptions are listed under their own names, provided alphabetically elsewhere in this book.

```
BorderColor
BorderStyle
BorderWidth
```

```
Container
DrawMode
Index
Name
Parent
Tag
Visible
X1
X2
Y1
Y2
```

Methods

The Line control has two methods, which are listed below. Because many Visual Basic controls have similar methods, the methods' descriptions are listed under their own names, provided alphabetically elsewhere in this book.

```
Refresh
ZOrder
```

Events

The Line control does not respond to events.

Line

Method

The `Line` method draws a line or rectangle.

Objects with a Line Method

Form
PropertyPage
UserControl

Syntax

`object.Line start - end, color, style`

- *color* (*) — The line color, which can be set with the `RGB` or `QBColor` functions. The default is the color specified in the object's `ForeColor` property.

- *end* — The end coordinates for the line, enclosed in parentheses and separated by a comma, such as (100,300). The coordinates can be preceded by the optional Step keyword, which indicates that the end coordinates are relative to the starting coordinates.
- *object* — A reference to an object with a Line method.
- *start* (*) — The starting coordinates for the line, enclosed in parentheses and separated by a comma, such as (2400,4322). The coordinates can be preceded by the optional Step keyword, which indicates that the starting coordinates are relative to the coordinates in the CurrentX and CurrentY properties.
- *style* (*) — The letter B indicates that the method should draw a rectangle. Adding the letter F to the B indicates that the rectangle should be filled with the line color. The FillStyle and FillColor properties determine the appearance of the rectangle when F is not specified.

(*) = Optional

Example 1

The following example draws a line from the coordinates in the CurrentX and CurrentY properties to the coordinate 500,500.

```
Line -(500, 500)
```

Example 2

Here, the following example draws a line from the starting coordinates 500, 250 to ending coordinates 2000,1000.

```
Line (500, 250)-(2000, 1000)
```

Example 3

The following example draws a line from the starting coordinates 500, 250 to ending coordinates 1500,1250.

```
Line (500, 250)-Step(1000, 1000)
```

Example 4

In this case, the following example draws a filled rectangle with the upper-left corner's coordinates at 500,250 and the lower-right corner's coordinates at 1000,1000.

```
Line (500, 250)-(1000, 1000),,BF
```

Example 5

Finally, the following example draws the same filled rectangle as Example 4, except using the color red.

```
Line (500, 250)-(1000, 1000), RGB(255, 0, 0), BF
```

 CROSS-REFERENCE
For more information, see CurrentX, CurrentY, ScaleMode, ForeColor, FillColor, and FillStyle.

Line

Property

The Line property represents the line number of the line about to be read or written from or to a text file. This read-only property starts with the value 1.

Objects with a Line Property

TextStream

Syntax

```
value = TextStream.Line
```

- *TextStream* — A reference to a TextStream object.
- *value* — The variable that will receive the line number.

Example

The following lines create a TextStream object called `file` and write ten lines of text to the file. Before the program writes a line of text, it displays a message box with the file's current line number.

```
Dim fileSystem, file As Object
Dim x As Integer
Dim msg As String
Set fileSystem = CreateObject("Scripting.FileSystemObject")
Set file = fileSystem.CreateTextFile("c:\MyText.txt", True)
For x = 1 To 10
    MsgBox file.Line
```

```
        msg = "This is line #" & x
        file.WriteLine (msg)
    Next x
    file.Close
```

 CROSS-REFERENCE
See also FileSystemObject and TextStream.

Line Input

Statement

The `Line Input` statement gets a line of text from a file, skipping over any carriage-return and linefeed characters.

Syntax

```
Line Input #fileNum, str
```

- *fileNum* — The file number assigned to the file in the `Open` statement.
- *str* — The string variable that will receive the line.

Example 1

The following lines open a file, read a line of text from the file, display the line in a message box, and then close the file.

```
Dim txt As String
Open "c:\MyText.txt" For Input As #1
Line Input #1, txt
MsgBox txt
Close #1
```

Example 2

Here, the following lines perform exactly as the lines in Example 1, except now the file number is stored in a variable named `fileNum`.

```
Dim txt As String
Dim fileNum As Integer
fileNum = 1
```

```
Open "c:\MyText.txt" For Input As fileNum
Line Input #fileNum, txt
MsgBox txt
Close fileNum
```

CROSS-REFERENCE
See also Open and Close.

LineStyle

Property

The LineStyle property represents the type of lines used to connect nodes in a TreeView control. This property can be set to tvwTreeLines (the default, as shown in Figure L-9) or tvwRootLines (Figure L-10). Notice the addition of the line connected to the root node in Figure L-10.

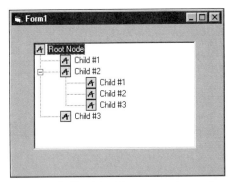

Figure L-9 This TreeView control uses the tvwTreeLines line style.

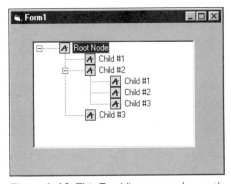

Figure L-10 This TreeView control uses the tvwRootLines line style.

Objects with a LineStyle Property

TreeView

Syntax

TreeView.LineStyle = *value1*

or

value2 = *TreeView*.LineStyle

- *TreeView* — A reference to a TreeView control.
- *value1* — The value `tvwTreeLines` or `tvwRootLines`.
- *value2* — The variable that will receive the property's current setting.

Example

The following lines create the TreeView control shown in Figure L-10. The `treTreeView1` and `ilsImageList1` objects are TreeView and ImageList controls that the programmer added to the application's form at design time.

```
ilsImageList1.ListImages.Add , , LoadPicture("icon2.ico")
treTreeView1.ImageList = ilsImageList1
treTreeView1.LineStyle = tvwRootLines
treTreeView1.Nodes.Add , , , "Root Node", 1
treTreeView1.Nodes.Add 1, tvwChild, , "Child #1", 1
treTreeView1.Nodes.Add 1, tvwChild, , "Child #2", 1
treTreeView1.Nodes.Add 1, tvwChild, , "Child #3", 1
treTreeView1.Nodes.Add 3, tvwChild, , "Child #1", 1
treTreeView1.Nodes.Add 3, tvwChild, , "Child #2", 1
treTreeView1.Nodes.Add 3, tvwChild, , "Child #3", 1
treTreeView1.Nodes(5).EnsureVisible
```

 **CROSS-REFERENCE**
See also TreeView.

LinkClose

Event

Visual Basic sends a control a `LinkClose` event when a DDE communication between applications ends.

Objects That Receive LinkClose Events

Form

Label

MDIForm

PictureBox

TextBox

Example

A program can respond to a LinkClose event by implementing the target object's LinkClose event procedure. The following code segment shows how a TextBox control defines a LinkClose event procedure. The txtText1 object is a TextBox control that the programmer added to the form at design time.

```
Private Sub txtText1_LinkClose()
    ' Handle the LinkClose event here.
End Sub
```

 CROSS-REFERENCE

See also LinkError, LinkExecute, LinkNotify, and LinkOpen.

LinkError

Event

Visual Basic sends a control a LinkError event when a DDE communication between applications results in an error.

Objects That Receive LinkError Events

Form

Label

MDIForm

PictureBox

TextBox

Example

A program can respond to a LinkError event by implementing the target object's LinkError event procedure. The following code segment shows how a TextBox control defines a LinkError event procedure. Note that the event procedure's single argument is the type of DDE error. This value can be 1 (request for data in an invalid format), 6 (DDE communication halted because the source object's LinkMode property is set to 0), 7 (all 128 DDE links are in use), 8 (data update failed), or 11 (not enough memory to perform DDE communication). In this example, the txtText1 object is a TextBox control that the programmer added to the form at design time.

```
Private Sub txtText1_LinkError(LinkErr As Integer)
    ' Handle the LinkError event here.
End Sub
```

CROSS-REFERENCE
See also LinkClose, LinkExecute, LinkNotify, and LinkOpen.

LinkExecute

Event

Visual Basic sends an object a LinkExecute event when the object receives a command from a DDE destination application.

Objects That Receive LinkExecute Events

Form

MDIForm

Example

A program can respond to a LinkExecute event by implementing the target object's LinkExecute event procedure. The following code segment shows how a Form object defines a LinkExecute event procedure. Note that the event procedure's two arguments are the command string and a value that indicates whether the application executed the command. Specifically, setting Cancel to False indicates that the command was executed, whereas setting Cancel to True indicates that the command was not executed.

```
Private Sub Form_LinkExecute(CmdStr As String, Cancel As
Integer)
    ' Handle the LinkExecute event here.
End Sub
```

CROSS-REFERENCE
See also LinkClose, LinkError, LinkNotify, and LinkOpen.

LinkExecute

Method

The `LinkExecute` method sends a command to a DDE source application.

Objects with a LinkExecute Method

Label

PictureText

TextBox

Syntax

`object.LinkExecute command`

- *command* — The command string to send.
- *object* — A reference to an object with a `LinkExecute` method.

 CROSS-REFERENCE

For more information, see LinkPoke, LinkExecute (event), LinkRequest, LinkSend, LinkTopic, LinkItem, and LinkMode.

LinkItem

Property

The `LinkItem` property represents the data to be passed in a DDE communication. This property is used in conjunction with the `LinkTopic` property to define a full DDE link.

Objects with a LinkItem Property

Label

PictureBox

TextBox

Syntax

`object.LinkItem = value1`

or

```
value2 = object.LinkItem
```

- *object* — A reference to an object with a `LinkItem` property.
- *value1* — A string containing the DDE item information.
- *value2* — The variable that will receive the property's current setting.

Example

The following line sets a TextBox control's DDE `LinkItem` property to the first cell in a spreadsheet. The `txtText1` object is a TextBox control that the programmer added to the application's form at design time.

```
txtText1.LinkItem = "A1"
```

 CROSS-REFERENCE
See also LinkTopic, LinkMode, and LinkTimeout.

LinkMode

Property

The `LinkMode` property represents the type of link to set up for a DDE communication. This property can be set to one of the values in Table L-1. Note the different settings for DDE source and destination applications. Also note that the link depends on the `LinkTopic` and `LinkItem` properties.

Table L-1 Settings for the LinkMode Property

Value	Application	Description
vbLinkAutomatic	Destination	Automatic data update
vbLinkManual	Destination	LinkRequest method updates data
vbLinkNone	Destination and source	DDE communications disallowed
vbLinkNotify	Destination	LinkNotify event enabled
vbLinkSource	Source	DDE links for Label, TextBox, and PictureBox controls enabled

Objects with a LinkMode Property

Form
Label
MDIForm
PictureBox
TextBox

Syntax

```
object.LinkMode = value1
```

or

```
value2 = object.LinkMode
```

- *object* — A reference to an object with a LinkMode property.
- *value1* — The link type from Table L-1.
- *value2* — The variable that will receive the property's current setting.

Example

The following line sets a TextBox to act as a DDE source. The txtText1 object is a TextBox control that the programmer added to the application's form at design time.

```
txtText1.LinkMode = vbLinkSource
```

 CROSS-REFERENCE
See also LinkTopic, LinkItem, and LinkTimeout.

LinkNotify

Event

Visual Basic sends an object a LinkNotify event when the object changes the data associated with its DDE link.

Objects That Receive LinkNotify Events

Label
PictureBox
TextBox

Example

A program can respond to a `LinkNotify` event by implementing the target object's `LinkNotify` event procedure. The following code segment shows how a TextBox control defines a `LinkNotify` event procedure. In this example, the `txtText1` object is a TextBox control that the programmer added to the form at design time.

```
Private Sub txtText1_LinkNotify()
    ' Handle the LinkNotify event here.
End Sub
```

 CROSS-REFERENCE
See also LinkClose, LinkError, LinkExecute, LinkOpen, and LinkMode.

LinkOpen

Event

Visual Basic sends a control a `LinkOpen` event when a DDE communication between applications begins.

Objects That Receive LinkOpen Events

Form
Label
MDIForm
PictureBox
TextBox

Example

A program can respond to a `LinkOpen` event by implementing the target object's `LinkOpen` event procedure. The following code segment shows how a TextBox control defines a `LinkOpen` event procedure. Note that the procedure's single argument enables the program to accept or cancel the DDE communication. Specifically, setting `Cancel` to `False` establishes the link, whereas setting `Cancel` to `True` refuses the link. The `txtText1` object is a TextBox control that the programmer added to the form at design time.

```
Private Sub txtText1_LinkOpen(Cancel As Integer)
    ' Handle the LinkOpen event here.
End Sub
```

CROSS-REFERENCE
See also LinkClose, LinkError, LinkExecute, and LinkNotify.

LinkPoke

Method

The LinkPoke method sends a control's contents to a DDE source application.

Objects with a LinkPoke Method

Label

PictureBox

TextBox

Syntax

object.LinkPoke

■ *object*—A reference to an object with a LinkPoke method.

Example

The following line transfers the contents of a TextBox control to the DDE source application. The txtText1 object is a TextBox control the programmer added to the application's form at design time.

txtText1.LinkPoke

 CROSS-REFERENCE
See also LinkRequest, LinkSend, LinkExecute, LinkTopic, LinkItem, and LinkMode.

LinkRequest

Method

The LinkRequest method sends a request to a DDE source application to update the contents of the control associated with the DDE communication. If the destination control's LinkMode property is set to vbLinkAutomatic, the program doesn't need to call LinkRequest to update the control.

Objects with a LinkRequest Method

Label

PictureBox

TextBox

Syntax

```
object.LinkRequest
```

- *object* — A reference to an object with a `LinkRequest` method.

Example

The following lines make a DDE update request on behalf of a TextBox control. The `txtText1` object is a TextBox control the programmer added to the application's form at design time.

```
txtText1.LinkTopic = "Excel|MySheet"
txtText1.LinkItem = "A1F1"
txtText1.LinkMode = vbLinkManual
txtText1.LinkRequest
```

 CROSS-REFERENCE

See also LinkPoke, LinkSend, LinkExecute, LinkTopic, LinkItem, and LinkMode.

LinkSend

Method

The `LinkSend` method sends a PictureBox control's contents to a DDE destination application.

Objects with a LinkSend Method

PictureBox

Syntax

```
PictureBox.LinkSend
```

- *PictureBox* — A reference to a PictureBox control.

Example

The following line sends the contents of a PictureBox control to the destination application associated with the control's DDE link. The `picPicture1` object is a PictureBox control the programmer added to the application's form at design time.

```
picPicture1.LinkSend
```

 CROSS-REFERENCE
See also LinkPoke, LinkRequest, LinkExecute, LinkTopic, LinkItem, and LinkMode.

LinkTimeout

Property

The `LinkTimeout` property represents how long (in tenths of a second) an object will wait for a response to a DDE communication. The default is 50 tenths of a second.

Objects with a LinkTimeout Property

Label
PictureBox
TextBox

Syntax

```
object.LinkTimeout = value1
```

or

```
value2 = object.LinkTimeout
```

- *object* — A reference to a control with a `LinkTimeout` property.
- *value1* — The timeout value in tenths of a second.
- *value2* — The variable that will receive the timeout value.

Example

The following line sets a TextBox control's DDE timeout to 15 seconds. The `txtText1` object is a TextBox control that the programmer added to the application's form at design time.

```
txtText1.LinkTimeout = 150
```

CROSS-REFERENCE
See also LinkItem, LinkMode, and LinkTopic.

LinkTopic

Property

The `LinkTopic` property represents a DDE link's source application and topic. This property is used in conjunction with the `LinkItem` property to define a full DDE link.

Objects with a LinkTopic Property

Form
Label
MDIForm
PictureBox
TextBox

Syntax

```
object.LinkTopic = value1
```

or

```
value2 = object.LinkTopic
```

- *object* — A reference to an object with a `LinkTopic` property.
- *value1* — A string containing the DDE link topic information.
- *value2* — The variable that will receive the property's current setting.

Example

The following line sets a TextBox control's DDE timeout to 15 seconds. The `txtText1` object is a TextBox control that the programmer added to the application's form at design time.

```
txtText1.LinkTopic = "Excel|MySheet"
```

CROSS-REFERENCE
See also LinkItem, LinkMode, and LinkTimeout.

List

Property

The List property represents a control's list of items as an array of strings.

Objects with a List Property

ComboBox

DirListBox

DriveListBox

FileListBox

ListBox

Syntax

```
object.List(index) = value1
```

or

```
value2 = object.List(index)
```

- *index* — The zero-based index into the list array.
- *object* — A reference to a control with a List property.
- *value1* — A string containing the item text.
- *value2* — The variable that will receive the item text.

Example

The following lines extract the fourth item from a ListBox control's list and display the item in a message box. The lstList1 object is a ListBox control that the programmer added to the application's form at design time.

```
Dim itemText As String
itemText = lstList1.List(3)
MsgBox itemText
```

CROSS-REFERENCE
See also AddItem and RemoveItem.

ListBox

Control

A ListBox control enables a program's user to select one or more items from a list. Figure L-11 shows a ListBox control—which is available on Visual Basic's standard toolbox—in a form.

Figure L-11 ListBox controls display lists of items from which the user can select.

Properties

The ListBox control has 49 properties, which are listed as follows. Because many Visual Basic controls have similar properties, the properties' descriptions are listed under their own names, provided alphabetically elsewhere in this book.

```
Appearance
BackColor
CausesValidation
Columns
Container
DragIcon
DragMode
Enabled
Font
FontBold
FontItalic
```

```
FontName
FontSize
FontStrikethru
FontUnderline
ForeColor
Height
HelpContextID
hWnd
Index
IntegralHeight
ItemData
Left
List
ListCount
ListIndex
MouseIcon
MousePointer
MultiSelect
Name
NewIndex
OLEDragMode
OLEDropMode
Parent
RightToLeft
SelCount
Selected
Sorted
Style
TabIndex
TabStop
Tag
Text
ToolTipText
Top
TopIndex
Visible
WhatsThisHelpID
Width
```

Methods

The ListBox control has ten methods, which are listed below. Because many Visual Basic controls have similar methods, the methods' descriptions are listed under their own names, provided alphabetically elsewhere in this book.

```
AddItem
Clear
Drag
Move
OLEDrag
Refresh
RemoveItem
SetFocus
ShowWhatsThis
ZOrder
```

Events

The ListBox control responds to 21 events, which are listed below. Because many Visual Basic controls respond to similar events, the events' descriptions are listed under their own names, provided alphabetically elsewhere in this book.

```
Click
DblClick
DragDrop
DragOver
GotFocus
ItemCheck
KeyDown
KeyPress
KeyUp
LostFocus
MouseDown
MouseMove
MouseUp
OLECompleteDrag
OLEDragDrop
OLEDragOver
OLEGiveFeedback
OLESetData
OLEStartDrag
Scroll
Validate
```

The ListBox's most commonly used event is Click, which the control generates when the user clicks a list item with the mouse. A program responds to the control's Click event in the Click event procedure. A ListBox called lstList1 will have a Click event procedure called lstList1_Click, which is where the program should handle the event. In the following example, when the user clicks an item in the ListBox control, a message box displays the selected item.

```
Private Sub lstList1_Click()
    Dim selItem As Integer
    selItem = lstList1.ListIndex
    MsgBox lstList1.List(selItem)
End Sub
```

ListCount

Property

The ListCount property represents the number of items in a control's list.

Objects with a ListCount Property

ComboBox

DirListBox

DriveListBox

FileListBox

ListBox

Syntax

value = object.ListCount

- *object* — A reference to a control with a ListCount property.
- *value* — The variable that will receive the number of items in the list.

Example

The following lines retrieve the number of items in a ListBox control. The lstList1 object is a ListBox control that the programmer added to the application's form at design time.

```
Dim numItems As Integer
numItems = lstList1.ListCount
```

CROSS-REFERENCE

See also AddItem and RemoveItem.

ListImage

Object

The ListImage object represents an image stored in an ImageList control.

Properties

The ListImage object has four properties. For more information on using a property shown in the following list, look up the property's entry, provided alphabetically elsewhere in this book.

```
Index
Key
Picture
Tag
```

Methods

The ListImage object has two methods. For more information on using a method shown in the following list, look up the method's entry, provided alphabetically elsewhere in this book.

```
Draw
ExtractIcon
```

Events

The ListItem object does not respond to events.

Example

The following lines add an image to an ImageList control and display the image in the form's window. The `ilsImageList1` object is an ImageList control that the programmer added to the application's form at design time.

```
ilsImageList1.ListImages.Add , , LoadPicture("but1.bmp")
ilsImageList1.ListImages(1).Draw frmForm1.hDC, 100, 100,
imlNormal
```

CROSS-REFERENCE
See also ImageList and ListImages.

ListImages

Collection

A ListImages collection holds the images that are associated with an ImageList control.

Properties

A ListImages collection has one property, called `Count`, which represents the number of images in the collection.

Methods

A ListImages collection has four methods. For more information on a method, look up the method's name, provided alphabetically elsewhere in this book.

```
Add
Clear
Item
Remove
```

Events

The ListImages object does not respond to events.

Example

The following lines load three picture files into an ImageList control, which adds the images to the control's ListImages collection. The `ilsImageList1` object is an ImageList control the programmer added to the form at design time.

```
ilsImageList1.ListImages.Add , , LoadPicture("but1.bmp")
ilsImageList1.ListImages.Add , , LoadPicture("but2.bmp")
ilsImageList1.ListImages.Add , , LoadPicture("but3.bmp")
```

ListImages

Property

The `ListImages` property represents an ImageList control's ListImages collection.

Objects with a ListImages Property

ImageList

Syntax

Set *value* = *ImageList*.ListImages

- *ImageList* — A reference to an ImageList control.
- *value* — The variable that will receive a reference to the ListImages collection.

Example

The following lines get a reference to an ImageList control's ListImages collection and use that reference to add an image to the collection. The ilsImageList1 object is an ImageList control that the programmer added to the application's form at design time.

```
Dim lstImages As ListImages
Set lstImages = ilsImageList1.ListImages
lstImages.Add , , LoadPicture("c:\but2.bmp")
```

CROSS-REFERENCE
See also ImageList and ListImage.

ListIndex

Property

The ListIndex property represents the zero-based index of the currently selected item in a control's list. In the case of a control that allows multiple selection, ListIndex is the index of the item displaying the focus rectangle. For the DirListBox and DriveListBox, a value of –1 in this property means that the user has selected no new directory or drive. For the ComboBox control, a ListIndex of –1 means that the user has typed an unlisted item into the control's text box.

Objects with a ListIndex Property

ComboBox

DirListBox

DriveListBox

FileListBox

ListBox

Syntax

`object.ListIndex = value1`

or

`value2 = object.ListIndex`

- *object* — A reference to a control with a `ListIndex` property.
- *value1* — The index of the item to be selected.
- *value2* — The variable that will receive the index of the currently selected item.

Example

The following program displays a combo box in which you can select an item by clicking the item with the mouse (Figure L-12). The program uses the `ListIndex` property to retrieve the text of the selected item and display it in a message box.

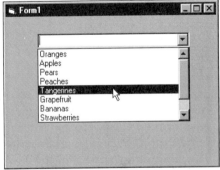

Figure L-12 The ListIndex Demo program demonstrates the use of the ListIndex property.

```
VERSION 5.00
Begin VB.Form frmForm1
    Caption        =    "ListIndex Demo"
    ClientHeight   =    3195
    ClientLeft     =    60
```

```
    ClientTop       =    345
    ClientWidth     =    4680
    ScaleHeight     =    3195
    ScaleWidth      =    4680
    StartUpPosition =    3    'Windows Default
    Begin VB.ComboBox cboCombo1
        Height      =    315
        Left        =    720
        TabIndex    =    0
        Top         =    360
        Width       =    3375
    End
End
Attribute VB_Name = "frmForm1"
Attribute VB_GlobalNameSpace = False
Attribute VB_Creatable = False
Attribute VB_PredeclaredId = True
Attribute VB_Exposed = False

Private Sub cboCombo1_Click()
    Dim selIndex As Integer
    Dim selText As String
    selIndex = cboCombo1.ListIndex
    selText = cboCombo1.List(selIndex)
    MsgBox selText
End Sub

Private Sub Form_Load()
    cboCombo1.AddItem "Oranges"
    cboCombo1.AddItem "Apples"
    cboCombo1.AddItem "Pears"
    cboCombo1.AddItem "Peaches"
    cboCombo1.AddItem "Tangerines"
    cboCombo1.AddItem "Grapefruit"
    cboCombo1.AddItem "Bananas"
    cboCombo1.AddItem "Strawberries"
    cboCombo1.AddItem "Watermelons"
    cboCombo1.AddItem "Plums"
End Sub
```

CROSS-REFERENCE
See also List and ListCount.

ListItem

Object

The ListItem object represents the items displayed in a ListView control.

Properties

The ListItem object has 18 properties. For more information on using a property shown in the following list, look up the property's entry, provided alphabetically elsewhere in this book.

```
Bold
Checked
ForeColor
Ghosted
Height
Icon
Index
Key
Left
ListSubItems
Selected
SmallIcon
SubItems
Tag
Text
ToolTipText
Top
Width
```

Methods

The ListItem object has two methods. For more information on using a method shown in the following table, look up the method's entry, provided alphabetically elsewhere in this book.

```
CreateDragImage
EnsureVisible
```

Events

The ListItem object does not respond to events.

Example

The following lines add three items to a ListView control and set the items to display bold, blue text. The `lvwListView1` object is a ListView control that the programmer added to the application's form at design time.

```
lvwListView1.ListItems.Add , , "Item #1"
lvwListView1.ListItems.Add , , "Item #2"
lvwListView1.ListItems.Add , , "Item #3"
lvwListView1.ListItems(1).Bold = True
lvwListView1.ListItems(2).Bold = True
lvwListView1.ListItems(3).Bold = True
lvwListView1.ListItems(1).ForeColor = RGB(0, 0, 255)
lvwListView1.ListItems(2).ForeColor = RGB(0, 0, 255)
lvwListView1.ListItems(3).ForeColor = RGB(0, 0, 255)
```

CROSS-REFERENCE
See also ListView and ListItems.

ListItems

Collection

A ListItems collection holds the ListItem objects associated with a ListView control.

Properties

A ListItems collection has one property, called `Count`, which represents the number of items in the collection.

Methods

A ListItems collection has four methods. For more information on a method, look up the method's name, provided alphabetically elsewhere in this book.

```
Add
Clear
Item
Remove
```

Events

The ListItems object does not respond to events.

Example

The following lines add five ListItem objects to a ListView control and display the items in the list-type view, as shown in Figure L-13. The `lvwListView1` object is a ListView control that the programmer added to the form at design time.

```
lvwListView1.ListItems.Add 1, "#1", "Item #1"
lvwListView1.ListItems.Add 2, "#2", "Item #2"
lvwListView1.ListItems.Add 3, "#3", "Item #3"
lvwListView1.ListItems.Add 4, "#4", "Item #4"
lvwListView1.ListItems.Add 5, "#5", "Item #5"
lvwListView1.View = lvwList
```

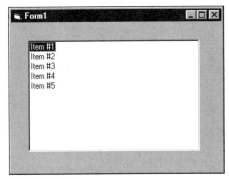

Figure L-13 This ListView control displays the items created by the ListItems example.

CROSS-REFERENCE
See also ListView, ListItem, ListItems (property), ListSubItem, and ListSubItems.

ListItems

Property

The `ListItems` property represents a ListView control's ListItem collection.

Objects with a ListItems Property

ListView

Syntax

```
Set value = ListView.ListItems
```

- *ListView* — A reference to a ListView control.
- *value* — The variable that will receive a reference to the ListItems collection.

Example

The following lines get a reference to a ListView control's ListItems collection and use that reference to add an item to the collection. The `lvwListView1` object is a ListView control that the programmer added to the application's form at design time.

```
Dim lstItems As ListItems
Set lstItems = lvwListView1.ListItems
lstItems.Add 1, "#1", "Item #1"
```

 CROSS-REFERENCE
See also ListView, ListItem, ListItems (collection), ListSubItem, and ListSubItems.

ListSubItem

Object

The ListSubItem object represents the subitems displayed in a ListView control when the control is in report view.

Properties

The ListSubItem object has eight properties. For more information on using a property shown in the following list, look up the property's entry, provided alphabetically elsewhere in this book.

```
Bold
ForeColor
Index
Key
ReportIcon
Tag
Text
ToolTipText
```

Methods

The ListSubItem object has no methods.

Events

The ListSubItem object does not respond to events.

Example

The following lines set a ListView control to report view, add three column headers to the control, and add three items, each with two subitems. Figure L-14 shows the result. In this example, the lvwListView1 object is a ListView control that the programmer added to the application's form at design time.

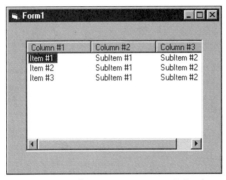

Figure L-14 This ListView control displays two subitems for each item.

```
Dim lstItem As ListItem

lvwListView1.View = lvwReport
lvwListView1.ColumnHeaders.Add , , "Column #1"
lvwListView1.ColumnHeaders.Add , , "Column #2"
lvwListView1.ColumnHeaders.Add , , "Column #3"

Set lstItem = lvwListView1.ListItems.Add(, , "Item #1")
lstItem.ListSubItems.Add , , "SubItem #1"
lstItem.ListSubItems.Add , , "SubItem #2"

Set lstItem = lvwListView1.ListItems.Add(, , "Item #2")
lstItem.ListSubItems.Add , , "SubItem #1"
lstItem.ListSubItems.Add , , "SubItem #2"
```

```
Set lstItem = lvwListView1.ListItems.Add(, , "Item #3")
lstItem.ListSubItems.Add , , "SubItem #1"
lstItem.ListSubItems.Add , , "SubItem #2"
```

 CROSS-REFERENCE
See also ListView, ListItem, ListItems, and ListSubItems.

ListSubItems

Collection

A ListSubItems collection holds the ListSubItem objects associated with a ListView control.

Properties

A ListSubItems collection has one property, called Count, which represents the number of items in the collection.

Methods

A ListSubItems collection has four methods. For more information on a method, look up the method's name, provided alphabetically elsewhere in this book.

```
Add
Clear
Item
Remove
```

Events

The ListSubItems object does not respond to events.

Example

The following lines add a ListItem object with two subitems to a ListView control. The lvwListView1 object is a ListView control the programmer added to the form at design time.

```
lvwListView1.ListItems.Add , , "Item #1"
lvwListView1.ListItems(1).ListSubItems.Add , , "SubItem #1"
lvwListView1.ListItems(1).ListSubItems.Add , , "SubItem #1"
```

CROSS-REFERENCE
See also ListView, ListItem, ListItems, ListSubItem, and ListSubItems (property).

ListSubItems

Property

The `ListSubItems` property represents a ListItem object's ListSubItems collection.

Objects with a ListSubItems Property

ListItem

Syntax

```
Set value = ListItem.ListSubItems
```

- *ListItem* — A reference to a ListItem object.
- *value* — The variable that will receive a reference to the ListSubItems collection.

Example

The following lines get a reference to a ListItem object's ListSubItems collection and use that reference to add two subitems to the collection. The `lvwListView1` object is a ListView control that the programmer added to the application's form at design time.

```
Dim lstSubItems As ListSubItems
lvwListView1.ListItems.Add , , "Item #1"
Set lstSubItems = lvwListView1.ListItems(1).ListSubItems
lstSubItems.Add , , "SubItem #1"
lstSubItems.Add , , "SubItem #2"
```

CROSS-REFERENCE
See also ListView, ListItem, ListItems, ListSubItem, and ListSubItems (collection).

ListView

Control

A ListView control displays a set of items in various views, including icon, small-icon, and report view. Figure L-15, for example, shows a ListView control in icon view, whereas Figure L-16 shows the same control in report view. The ListView control is included in the Microsoft Windows Common Controls 6.0 control set, which you can add to your project using the Components dialog box, as shown in Figure L-17.

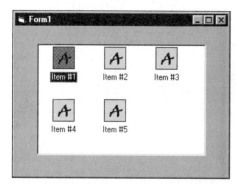

Figure L-15 This ListView control is in icon view.

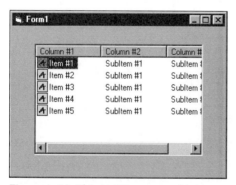

Figure L-16 This ListView control is in report view.

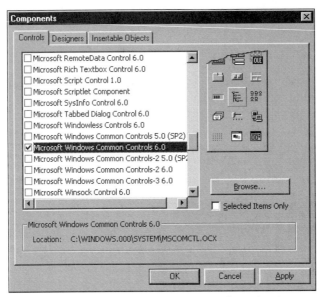

Figure L-17 You load the ListView control from the Components dialog box.

Properties

The ListView control has 57 properties, which are listed as follows. Because many Visual Basic controls have similar properties, the properties' descriptions are listed under their own names, provided alphabetically elsewhere in this book.

```
AllowColumnReorder
Appearance
Arrange
BackColor
BorderStyle
CausesValidation
CheckBoxes
ColumnHeaderIcons
ColumnHeaders
Container
DragIcon
DragMode
DropHighlight
Enabled
FlatScrollBar
```

Font
ForeColor
FullRowSelect
GridLines
Height
HelpContextID
HideColumnHeaders
HideSelection
HotTracking
HoverSelection
hWnd
Icons
Index
LabelEdit
LabelWrap
Left
ListItems
MouseIcon
MousePointer
MultiSelect
Name
Object
OLEDragMode
OLEDropMode
Parent
Picture
PictureAlignment
SelectedItem
SmallIcons
Sorted
SortKey
SortOrder
TabIndex
TabStop
Tag
TextBackground
ToolTipText
Top
View
Visible
WhatsThisHelpID
Width

k
l
m

Methods

The ListView control has 11 methods, which are listed below. Because many Visual Basic controls have similar methods, the methods' descriptions are listed under their own names, provided alphabetically elsewhere in this book.

```
Drag
FindItem
GetFirstVisible
HitTest
Move
OLEDrag
Refresh
SetFocus
ShowWhatsThis
StartLabelEdit
ZOrder
```

Events

The ListView control responds to 24 events, which are listed below. Because many Visual Basic controls respond to similar events, the events' descriptions are listed under their own names, provided alphabetically elsewhere in this book.

```
AfterLabelEdit
BeforeLabelEdit
Click
ColumnClick
DblClick
DragDrop
DragOver
GotFocus
ItemCheck
ItemClick
KeyDown
KeyPress
KeyUp
LostFocus
MouseDown
MouseMove
MouseUp
OLECompleteDrag
OLEDragDrop
```

```
OLEDragOver
OLEGiveFeedback
OLESetData
OLEStartDrag
Validate
```

One of the ListView control's most commonly used events is Click, which the control generates when the user clicks an item in the control. A program responds to the Click event in the Click event procedure. A ListView control called lvwListView1 will have a Click event procedure called lvwListView1_Click, which is where the program should handle the event. In the following example, when the user clicks an item in the ListView control, a message box displays the selected item's text label.

```
Private Sub lvwListView1_Click()
    Dim selItem As ListItem
    Dim itemText As String
    Set selItem = lvwListView1.SelectedItem
    itemText = selItem.Text
    MsgBox itemText
End Sub
```

Load

Event

Visual Basic sends an object a Load event when the object is loaded. This event occurs right after the Initialize event and is often used to perform initialization for the object.

Objects That Receive Load Events

Form

MDIForm

PropertyPage

Example

A program can respond to a Load event by implementing the target object's Load event procedure. The following code segment shows how a Form object defines a Load event procedure.

```
Private Sub Form_Load()
    ' Handle the Load event here.
End Sub
```

 CROSS-REFERENCE
See also Initialize and Unload.

Load

Statement

The Load statement loads a form or control.

Syntax

```
Load object
```

- *object* — The form or control to load.

Example

The following line loads a form named frmForm1.

```
Load frmForm1
```

LoadFile

Method

The LoadFile method loads a file into a RichTextBox control. The file can be in the .rtf or plain text format.

Objects with a LoadFile Method

RichTextBox

Syntax

```
RichTextBox.OpenFile fileName
```

- *fileName* — The path of the file to open.
- *RichTextBox* — A reference to a RichTextBox control.

Example

The following program demonstrates how to load files into a RichTextBox control. When you run the program, click the Load File button, which displays the Open dialog box. Choose a plain text or RTF file, and the file appears in the window, as shown in Figure L-18.

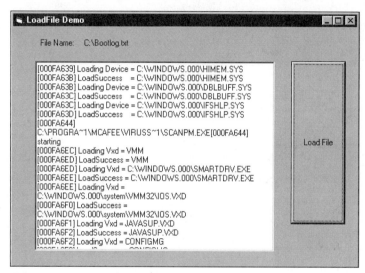

Figure L-18 Here's the LoadFile Demo program after the user has loaded a file.

```
VERSION 5.00
Object = "{F9043C88-F6F2-101A-A3C9-08002B2F49FB} _
    #1.2#0"; "COMDLG32.OCX"
Object = "{3B7C8863-D78F-101B-B9B5-04021C009402} _
    #1.2#0"; "RICHTX32.OCX"
Begin VB.Form frmForm1
   Caption         =   "LoadFile Demo"
   ClientHeight    =   5100
   ClientLeft      =   60
   ClientTop       =   345
   ClientWidth     =   7590
   ScaleHeight     =   5100
   ScaleWidth      =   7590
   StartUpPosition =   3  'Windows Default
   Begin MSComDlg.CommonDialog dlgCommonDialog1
      Left         =     6960
```

```
            Top             =       4440
            _ExtentX        =       847
            _ExtentY        =       847
            _Version        =       393216
         End
         Begin VB.CommandButton btnLoadFile
            Caption         =       "Load File"
            Height          =       3495
            Left            =       6120
            TabIndex        =       1
            Top             =       720
            Width           =       1215
         End
         Begin RichTextLib.RichTextBox rtfRichTextBox1
            Height          =       4095
            Left            =       480
            TabIndex        =       0
            Top             =       720
            Width           =       5295
            _ExtentX        =       9340
            _ExtentY        =       7223
            _Version        =       393217
            TextRTF         =       $"form1.frx":0000
         End
         Begin VB.Label lblLabel2
            Height          =       255
            Left            =       1560
            TabIndex        =       3
            Top             =       240
            Width           =       4095
         End
         Begin VB.Label Label1
            Caption         =       "File Name:"
            Height          =       255
            Left            =       600
            TabIndex        =       2
            Top             =       240
            Width           =       855
         End
      End
   End
Attribute VB_Name = "frmForm1"
Attribute VB_GlobalNameSpace = False
```

```
Attribute VB_Creatable = False
Attribute VB_PredeclaredId = True
Attribute VB_Exposed = False

Private Sub btnLoadFile_Click()
    Dim strFileName As String
    dlgCommonDialog1.Filter = _
        "RTF (*.rtf)|*.rtf|Text (*.txt)|*.txt"
    dlgCommonDialog1.FileName = "*.txt"
    dlgCommonDialog1.ShowOpen
    On Error GoTo ErrorHandler
    strFileName = dlgCommonDialog1.FileName
    rtfRichTextBox1.LoadFile strFileName
    lblLabel2 = strFileName
    Exit Sub
ErrorHandler:
    MsgBox "Couldn't Open the File"
End Sub
```

CROSS-REFERENCE
See also RichTextBox, FileName, and SaveFile.

LoadPicture

Function

The LoadPicture function loads a picture, icon, or cursor from disk. The LoadPicture function can also be used to clear a picture from a control by calling the function with no arguments. This function can load images in various formats, including .bmp, .cur, .ico, .gif, .wmf, .emf, .rle, and .jpg.

Syntax

```
value = LoadPicture(fileName, size, colors, width, height)
```

- *colors* (*) — The color depth of a cursor or icon, which can be a value from Table L-2.
- *height* (*) — The height of the image, which is used only when *colors* is set to vbLPCustom. The *width* argument must be included if the *height* argument is included and vice versa.
- *fileName* (*) — The file name of the image to load.

- *size* (*) — The size of a cursor or icon, which can be a value from Table L-3.
- *width* (*) — The width of the image, which is used only when *colors* is set to vbLPCustom. The *width* argument must be included if the *height* argument is included and vice versa.
- *value* — The variable that will receive the reference to the Picture object.

(*) = Optional

Table L-2 Settings for the *colors* Argument

Value	Description
vbLPColor	256 colors
vbLPDefault	Best match
vbLPMonochrome	2 colors
vbLPVGAColor	16 colors

Table L-3 Settings for the *size* Argument

Value	Description
vbLPCustom	Size specified by the width and height arguments
vbLPLarge	Large icon size
vbLPLargeShell	Shell large icon size
vbLPSmall	Small icon size
vbLPSmallShell	Shell small icon size

Example

The following program demonstrates how to load pictures into a PictureBox control. When you run the program, click the Load File button, which displays the Open dialog box. Choose a graphic file, and the image appears in the window, as shown in Figure L-19. Note that, in order to load different types of files, you must change the setting of the Open dialog's Files of Type box.

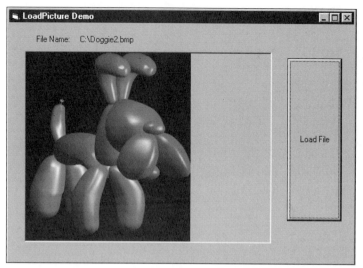

Figure L-19 Here's the LoadPicture Demo program after the user has loaded an image.

```
VERSION 5.00
Object = "{F9043C88-F6F2-101A-A3C9-08002B2F49FB}#1.2#0";
"COMDLG32.OCX"
Begin VB.Form frmForm1
   Caption        =   "LoadPicture Demo"
   ClientHeight   =   5100
   ClientLeft     =   60
   ClientTop      =   345
   ClientWidth    =   7590
   ScaleHeight    =   5100
   ScaleWidth     =   7590
   StartUpPosition =  3   'Windows Default
   Begin VB.PictureBox picPicture1
      Height      =   4095
      Left        =   360
      ScaleHeight =   4035
      ScaleWidth  =   5355
      TabIndex    =   3
      Top         =   600
      Width       =   5415
   End
```

```
            Begin MSComDlg.CommonDialog dlgCommonDialog1
                Left            =    6960
                Top             =    4440
                _ExtentX        =    847
                _ExtentY        =    847
                _Version        =    393216
            End
            Begin VB.CommandButton btnLoadFile
                Caption         =    "Load File"
                Height          =    3495
                Left            =    6120
                TabIndex        =    0
                Top             =    720
                Width           =    1215
            End
            Begin VB.Label lblLabel2
                Height          =    255
                Left            =    1560
                TabIndex        =    2
                Top             =    240
                Width           =    4095
            End
            Begin VB.Label Label1
                Caption         =    "File Name:"
                Height          =    255
                Left            =    600
                TabIndex        =    1
                Top             =    240
                Width           =    855
            End
        End
    End
    Attribute VB_Name = "frmForm1"
    Attribute VB_GlobalNameSpace = False
    Attribute VB_Creatable = False
    Attribute VB_PredeclaredId = True
    Attribute VB_Exposed = False

    Private Sub btnLoadFile_Click()
        Dim strFileName As String
        Dim strFilter As String
        Dim pic As Picture
```

```
strFilter = "Bitmap (*.bmp)|*.bmp|GIF (*.gif)|*.gif"
strFilter = strFilter & _
    "|JPEG (*.jpg)|*.jpg|Icon (*.ico)|*.ico"
strFilter = strFilter & _
    "|Cursor (*.cur)|*.cur|Metafile (*.wmf)|*.wmf"
strFilter = strFilter & _
    "|Extended Metafile (*.emf)|*.emf"
strFilter = strFilter & _
    "|Run Length Encoded (*.rle)|*.rle"

dlgCommonDialog1.Filter = strFilter
dlgCommonDialog1.FileName = "*.bmp"
dlgCommonDialog1.ShowOpen
On Error GoTo ErrorHandler
strFileName = dlgCommonDialog1.FileName
Set pic = LoadPicture(strFileName)
picPicture1.Picture = pic
lblLabel2 = strFileName
Exit Sub
ErrorHandler:
    MsgBox "Couldn't Open the File"
End Sub
```

CROSS-REFERENCE

See also LoadResPicture, Picture, and SavePicture.

LoadResData

Function

The LoadResData function loads various types of data from a resource file.

Syntax

`value` = LoadResData(`resID, type`)

- *resID* — The resource ID of the data to load.
- *type* — The type of resource to load, which can be a value from Table L-4.
- *value* — The variable that will receive the returned Byte array.

Table L-4 Settings for the *type* Argument

Value	Description
1	Cursor
2	Bitmap
3	Icon
4	Menu
5	Dialog box
6	String
7	Font directory
8	Font
9	Accelerator table
10	User-defined resource
12	Group cursor
14	Group icon

Example

The following lines load a bitmap as a `Byte` array from a resource file.

```
Dim byteArray() As Byte
byteArray = LoadResData(101, 2)
```

 CROSS-REFERENCE
See also LoadResPicture and LoadResString.

LoadResPicture

Function

The `LoadResPicture` function loads a bitmap, cursor, or icon from a resource file.

Syntax

```
value = LoadResPicture(resID, type)
```

- *resID*—The resource ID of the data to load.
- *type*—The type of resource to load, which can be a value from Table L-5.
- *value*—The variable that will receive the returned Picture object.

Table L-5 Settings for the *type* Argument

Value	Description
vbResBitmap	Bitmap
vbResCursor	Cursor
vbResIcon	Icon

Example

The following lines load an icon from a resource file and assign the icon's image to a PictureBox control. The picPicture1 object is a PictureBox control that the programmer added to the form at design time.

```
Dim pic As Picture
Set pic = LoadResPicture(101, vbResIcon)
picPicture1.Picture = pic
```

CROSS-REFERENCE
See also LoadResData and LoadResString.

LoadResString

Function

The LoadResString function loads a string from a string table in a resource file.

Syntax

```
value = LoadResString(resID)
```

- *resID* — The resource ID of the data to load.
- *value* — The variable that will receive the returned string.

Example

The following lines load a string from a string table in a resource file and display the string in a message box.

```
Dim str As String
str = LoadResString(101)
MsgBox str
```

CROSS-REFERENCE
See also LoadResData and LoadResPicture.

Loc

Function

The Loc function returns the position of the file pointer in a currently open file. For a binary file, the file pointer is the position of the last byte that was read or written, whereas the file pointer in a random-access file is the last record number.

Syntax

```
value = Loc(fileNum)
```

- *fileNum* — The file number used in the Open statement.
- *value* — The variable that will receive the file pointer's position.

Example

The following lines open a binary file and read fifty characters — five characters at a time — from the file. After reading each block of five characters, the program displays the data that was read, as well as the current value of the file pointer, in a message box.

```
Dim x As Integer
Dim data As String
Dim filePointer As Long
Open "c:\textfile.txt" For Binary As #1
For x = 1 To 10
    data = Input(5, #1)
    filePointer = Loc(1)
    MsgBox data & "-" & filePointer
Next x
Close #1
```

CROSS-REFERENCE
See also Seek.

LocaleID

Property

The LocaleID property represents the application's locale ID, which identifies the language and country of the user.

Objects with a LocaleID Property

AmbientProperties

Syntax

```
value = Ambient.LocaleID
```

- *Ambient* — A reference to an AmbientProperties object.
- *value* — The variable that will receive the ID.

Example

The following lines get the value of the LocaleID property for a UserControl object.

```
Dim locID As Long
locID = Ambient.LocaleID
```

Lock

Keyword

The Lock keyword is used as part of the Lock and Open statements, which, respectively, lock file access and open a file. In the following example, the program opens a binary file that cannot be accessed by other programs.

```
Open "MyFile.dat" For Binary Access Read Lock Read As #1
```

 CROSS-REFERENCE
For more information, see Lock and Open.

Lock

Statement

The Lock statement locks part or all of a file from being accessed by other programs.

Syntax

```
Lock #fileNum, lockRange
```

- *fileNum* — The file number given in the file's Open statement.
- *lockRange* (*) — The range of records to lock in a random-access file. The range can be a single record number or a range of records formed by the starting record number followed the keyword To and the ending record number, such as Lock #1, 10 To 25. If you leave off the starting record number, Lock assumes the first record, as in the statement Lock #1, To 25. If you leave off the optional record range, Lock locks the entire file.

(*) = Optional

Example 1

The following lines open a random-access file and read ten records from the file, displaying each record in a message box. The program locks each record before reading the data and then unlocks the record when finished with it. Note that a Lock statement must always be matched with the equivalent Unlock statement.

```
Dim recNum As Integer
Dim data As String
Open "TextFile.txt" For Random Shared As #1 Len = 20
For recNum = 1 To 10
    Lock #1, recNum
    Get #1, recNum, data
    MsgBox data
    Unlock #1, recNum
Next recNum
Close #1
```

Example 2

The following line locks a range of records, from record 2 to record 10.

```
Lock #1, 2 To 10
```

Example 3

Here, the following line locks a range of records, from the first record to record 10.

```
Lock #1, To 10
```

Example 4

Finally, the following line locks the entire file.

```
Lock #1
```

Locked

Property

The `Locked` property represents whether the contents of a control can be edited.

Objects with a Locked Property

RichTextBox

TextBox

Syntax

```
object.Locked = value1
```

or

```
value2 = object.Locked
```

- *object*—A reference to a RichTextBox or TextBox control.
- *value1*—The value `True` or `False`.
- *value2*—The variable that will receive the property's current setting.

Example

The following program demonstrates how the `Locked` property works with a RichTextBox control. When you first run the program, type some text into the control (Figure L-20). Then, click the Lock File button to lock the text from further editing. You'll be able to move the cursor around the text and even highlight text, but you won't be able to change any of the text. Click the button a second time to unlock the text.

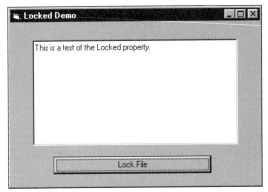

Figure L-20 Click the Lock File button to lock the text in the RichTextBox.

```
VERSION 5.00
Object = "{3B7C8863-D78F-101B-B9B5-04021C009402} _
    #1.2#0": "RICHTX32.OCX"
Begin VB.Form frmForm1
    Caption         =   "Locked Demo"
    ClientHeight    =   3495
    ClientLeft      =   60
    ClientTop       =   345
    ClientWidth     =   5535
    ScaleHeight     =   3495
    ScaleWidth      =   5535
    StartUpPosition =   3  'Windows Default
    Begin VB.CommandButton btnLock
        Caption     =   "Lock File"
        Height      =   375
        Left        =   960
        TabIndex    =   1
        Top         =   2880
        Width       =   3495
    End
    Begin RichTextLib.RichTextBox rtfRichTextBox1
        Height      =   2295
        Left        =   480
        TabIndex    =   0
        Top         =   360
        Width       =   4575
        _ExtentX    =   8070
        _ExtentY    =   4048
        _Version    =   393217
```

```
        Enabled         =    -1   'True
        TextRTF         =    $"form1.frx":0000
     End
  End
End
Attribute VB_Name = "frmForm1"
Attribute VB_GlobalNameSpace = False
Attribute VB_Creatable = False
Attribute VB_PredeclaredId = True
Attribute VB_Exposed = False

Private Sub btnLock_Click()
   If rtfRichTextBox1.Locked Then
      rtfRichTextBox1.Locked = False
      btnLock.Caption = "Lock File"
      rtfRichTextBox1.SetFocus
   Else
      rtfRichTextBox1.Locked = True
      btnLock.Caption = "Unlock File"
      rtfRichTextBox1.SetFocus
   End If
End Sub
```

CROSS-REFERENCE
See also RichTextBox and TextBox.

LOF

Function

The LOF function returns the length of an open file.

Syntax

```
value = LOF(fileNum)
```

- *fileNum* — The file number given to the file in the Open statement.
- *value* — The variable that will receive the file's length.

Example

The following lines open a file, get the file's length, and then close the file.

```
Dim fileLen As Long
Open "TextFile.txt" For Input As #1
fileLen = LOF(1)
Close #1
```

CROSS-REFERENCE
See also FileLen and EOF.

Log

Function

The Log function calculates the natural logarithm of a given number.

Syntax

```
value = Log(number)
```

- *number*—The number for which to calculate the logarithm.
- *value*—The variable that will receive the logarithm.

Example

The following lines calculate the natural logarithm of 10.

```
Dim dblLog As Double
dblLog = Log(10)
```

LogEvent

Method

The LogEvent method writes messages to the application's event log. On Windows 95, the App object's LogPath property determines the location of the log file. The default is vbevents.log.

Objects with a LogEvent Method

App

Syntax

```
App.LogEvent(msg, type)
```

- *App*—A reference to the App object.
- *msg*—The string to send to the log file.
- *type* (*)—The type of log event, which can be `vbLogEventTypeError`, `vbLogEventTypeInformation`, or `vbLogEventTypeWarning`.

(*) = Optional

Example

The following line sends a message to a log file. Note that the App object is a Visual Basic global object that you don't need to create in your programs.

```
App.LogEvent("Log message goes here.")
```

CROSS-REFERENCE
For more information, see App, LogMode, and LogPath.

LogMode

Property

The `LogMode` property represents the type of logging that the application will use with the `LogEvent` method. This property can be one of the values shown in Table L-6.

Table L-6 Settings for the LogMode Property

Value	Description
vbLogAuto	Sends log messages to the log file set in the LogPath property or to Windows NT's event log.
vbLogOff	Turns logging off.
vbLogOverwrite	Starts a new log file each time the application runs.
vbLogThreadID	Adds the current thread ID to the log message.
vbLogToFile	Sends log messages to the file set by the LogPath property.
vbLogToNT	Sends log messages to Windows NT's event log.

Objects with a LogMode Property

App

Syntax

```
value = App.LogMode
```

- *App* — A reference to the App object.
- *value* — The variable that will receive the property's current setting.

Example

The following lines get the current logging mode. Note that the App object is a Visual Basic global object that you don't need to create in your programs.

```
Dim logMde As Long
logMde = App.LogMode
```

CROSS-REFERENCE
For more information, see App, LogEvent, and LogPath.

LogonUI

Property

The LogonUI property determines whether sign-on for a mail session is done with a dialog box in which the user must enter his user name and password.

Objects with a LogonUI Property

MAPISession

Syntax

```
MAPISession.LogonUI = value1
```

or

```
value2 = MAPISession.LogonUI
```

- *MAPISession* — A reference to a MAPISession control.

- *value1* — The value `True` or `False`.
- *value2* — The variable that will receive the property's current setting.

Example

The following line sets the MAPISession object so that the user signs on with a dialog box. The `MAPISession1` object is a MAPISession control that the programmer added to the application's form at design time.

```
MAPISession1.LogonUI = True
```

CROSS-REFERENCE
See also MAPISession.

LogPath

Property

The `LogPath` property represents the path to the application's logging file.

Objects with a LogPath Property

App

Syntax

```
value = App.LogPath
```

- *App* — A reference to the App object.
- *value* — The variable that will receive the logging path.

Example

The following lines get the current logging path. Note that the App object is a Visual Basic global object that you don't need to create in your programs.

```
Dim logPth As String
logPth = App.LogPath
```

CROSS-REFERENCE
For more information, see App, LogEvent, and LogMode.

LostFocus

Event

Visual Basic sends a control a LostFocus event when the control loses the input focus. This can occur in two ways: programmatically by calling the SetFocus method on behalf of a control, or by the user's selection of another control.

Objects That Receive LostFocus Events

Animation	OptionButton
CheckBox	PictureBox
ComboBox	PropertyPage
CommandButton	RichTextBox
DirListBox	Slider
DriveListBox	TabStrip
FileListBox	TextBox
Form	TreeView
HScrollBar	UpDown
ListBox	UserControl
ListView	VScrollBar
OLE Container	

Example

A program can respond to a LostFocus event by implementing the target object's LostFocus event procedure. The following code segment shows how a CommandButton object defines a LostFocus event procedure. The btnCommand1 object is a CommandButton control that the programmer added to the form at design time.

```
Private Sub btnCommand1_LostFocus()
    ' Respond to the LostFocus event here.
End Sub
```

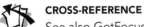

CROSS-REFERENCE
See also GotFocus and SetFocus.

lpOleObject

Property

The lpOleObject property represents a pointer to the object embedded or linked into an OLE Container control. This pointer makes it possible to call ActiveX functions that require the address of an object.

Objects with an lpOleObject Property

OLE Container

Syntax

```
value = OLEContainer.lpOleObject
```

- *OLEContainer* — A reference to an OLE Container control.
- *value2* — The variable that will receive the object address.

Example

The following lines get a pointer to an embedded ActiveX object. The oleContainer1 object is an OLE container control that the programmer added to the application's form at design time.

```
Dim objectPtr As Long
objectPtr = oleContainer1.lpOleObject
```

 CROSS-REFERENCE
See also OLE Container.

LSet

Statement

The LSet statement copies a string into the left portion of a string variable, filling any remaining characters with spaces.

Syntax

```
LSet var1 = str
```

- *var1* — The string variable to which to copy *str*.
- *str* — The string to copy.

Example 1

After the following lines execute, msg contains the string "XXXX   " (four *x*'s followed by ten spaces).

```
Dim msg As String
msg = "This is a test"
LSet msg = "XXXX"
```

Example 2

Here, after the following lines execute, msg will contain the string "12345678901234." Note that the source string gets truncated if the destination string isn't big enough to hold all the characters.

```
Dim msg As String
msg = "This is a test"
LSet msg = "12345678901234567890"
```

 CROSS-REFERENCE
See also RSet.

LTrim

Function

The LTrim function removes leading spaces from a string.

Syntax

```
value = Trim(str)
```

- *str* — The string from which to remove leading spaces.
- *value* — The variable that will receive the new string.

Example

After the following lines execute, `newMsg` will contain the string "This is a test."

```
Dim msg As String
Dim newMsg As String
msg = "        This is a test"
newMsg = LTrim(msg)
```

 CROSS-REFERENCE
See also RTrim and Trim.

Major

Property

The Major property represents the application's major version number. You can set this property in the Project Properties property sheet, as shown in Figure M-1.

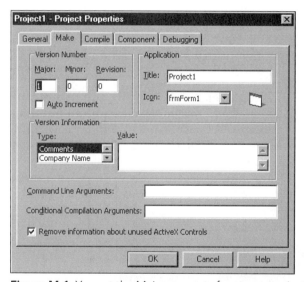

Figure M-1 You set the Major property from your project's Project Properties property sheet.

Objects with a Major Property

App

Syntax

```
value = App.Major
```

- *App*—A reference to the App object.
- *value*—The variable that will receive the major version number.

Example

In this example, the program retrieves an application's major version number. Note that the App object is a global Visual Basic object that you don't need to add to your programs.

```
Dim majVersion As Integer
majVersion = App.Major
```

CROSS-REFERENCE
See also App, Minor, Revision.

MAPIMessages

Control

A MAPIMessages control handles the sending and receiving of email messages, as well as other email related functions such managing recipients, attachments, and the Address Book. Figure M-2 shows a MAPIMessages control in a form at design time. (The control is not visible at runtime.) You can add the MAPIMessages control to your Visual Basic toolbox from the Components property sheet, as shown in Figure M-3. Note, however, that the control will function properly only if the user has MAPI services installed on his machine.

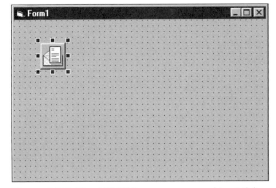

Figure M-2 The MAPIMessages control is visible only at design time.

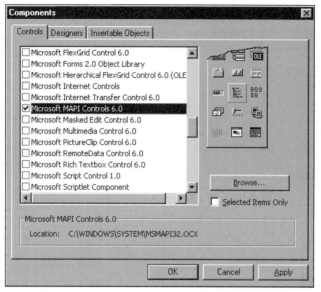

Figure M-3 Use the Components property sheet to add the MAPIMessages control to your Visual Basic project.

Properties

The MAPIMessages control has 39 properties, which are listed as follows. Because many Visual Basic controls have similar properties, the properties' descriptions are listed under their own names, provided alphabetically elsewhere in this book.

```
Action
AddressCaption
AddressEditFieldCount
AddressLabel
AddressModifiable
AddressResolveUI
AttachmentCount
AttachmentIndex
AttachmentName
AttachmentPathName
AttachmentPosition
AttachmentType
FetchMsgType
FetchSorted
```

```
FetchUnreadOnly
Index
MsgConversationID
MsgCount
MsgDateReceived
MsgID
MsgIndex
MsgNoteText
MsgOrigAddress
MsgOrigDisplayName
MsgRead
MsgReceiptRequested
MsgSent
MsgSubject
MsgType
Name
Object
Parent
RecipAddress
RecipCount
RecipDisplayName
RecipIndex
RecipType
SessionID
Tag
```

Methods

The **MAPIMessages** control has 11 methods, which are listed below. Because many Visual Basic controls have similar methods, the methods' descriptions are listed under their own names, provided alphabetically elsewhere in this book.

```
Compose
Copy
Delete
Fetch
Forward
Reply
ReplyAll
ResolveName
Save
Send
Show
```

Events

The MAPIMessages control does not respond to events.

MAPISession

Control

A MAPISession control handles the start and end of an email session. Figure M-4 shows a MAPISession control in a form at design time. (The control is not visible at runtime.) You can add the MAPISession control to your Visual Basic toolbox from the Components property sheet. Note, however, that the control will function properly only if the user has MAPI services installed on his machine.

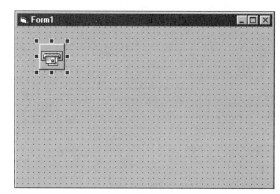

Figure M-4 The MAPISession control is visible only at design time.

Properties

The MAPISession control has 12 properties, which are listed as follows. Because many Visual Basic controls have similar properties, the properties' descriptions are listed under their own names, provided alphabetically elsewhere in this book.

```
Action
DownloadMail
Index
LogonUI
Name
NewSession
Object
Parent
Password
```

```
SessionID
Tag
UserName
```

Methods

The MAPISession control has two methods, which are listed below. Because many Visual Basic controls have similar methods, the methods' descriptions are listed under their own names elsewhere in this book.

```
SignOff
SignOn
```

Events

The MAPISession control does not respond to events.

MaskColor—Button Controls

Property

The MaskColor property represents a control's transparent color. The transparent color affects the control only when the control has an image assigned to its Picture property, when its UseMaskColor property is set to True, and its Style property is set to graphical. The MaskColor property can be set with the Visual Basic color constants or with the RGB and QBColor functions.

Objects with a MaskColor Property

CheckBox
CommandButton
OptionButton

Syntax

```
object.MaskColor = value1
```

or

```
value2 = object.MaskColor
```

- *object*—A reference to a control with a MaskColor property.

- *value1* — The control's mask color. The default is &H00C0C0C0, which is light gray.
- *value2* — The variable that will receive the current mask color.

Example

The following lines add an image to a CommandButton control and set its MaskColor property. Note that the Style property is read-only at runtime and so must be set at design time in the control's Properties window. In this example, the btnCommand1 object is a CommandButton control that the programmer added to the application's form at design time.

```
btnCommand1.Picture = LoadPicture("c:\but1.bmp")
btnCommand1.UseMaskColor = True
btnCommand1.MaskColor = RGB(255, 0, 0)
```

CROSS-REFERENCE
See also UseMaskColor, Picture, and Style.

MaskColor — ImageList

Property

The MaskColor property represents the transparent mask color used with Overlay and Draw functions in an ImageList control. The MaskColor property can be set with the Visual Basic color constants or with the RGB and QBColor functions.

Syntax

```
ImageList.MaskColor = value1
```

or

```
value2 = ImageList.MaskColor
```

- *ImageList* — A reference to an ImageList control.
- *value1* — The control's mask color. The default is &H00C0C0C0, which is light gray.
- *value2* — The variable that will receive the current mask color.

Example

The following line sets an ImageList control's `MaskColor` property. The `ilsImageList1` object is an ImageList control that the programmer added to the application's form at design time.

```
ilsImageList1.MaskColor = RGB(255, 0, 0)
```

CROSS-REFERENCE
See also ImageList.

MaskColor—UserControl

Property

The `MaskColor` property represents the part of a control that becomes transparent when parts of an image that are the same color as `MaskColor` cover the control. For this property to have an effect on the control, the control must have a bitmap assigned to its `MaskPicture` property and its `BackStyle` property set to transparent. The `MaskColor` property can be set with the Visual Basic color constants or with the `RGB` and `QBColor` functions.

Syntax

```
UserControl.MaskColor = value1
```

or

```
value2 = UserControl.MaskColor
```

- *UserControl*—A reference to a UserControl control.
- *value1*—The control's mask color. The default is &H8000000F, which is the light gray, system button-face color.
- *value2*—The variable that will receive the current mask color.

Example

The following line sets a UserControl control's `MaskColor` property to red.

```
UserControl.MaskColor = RGB(255, 0, 0)
```

CROSS-REFERENCE
See also UserControl, BackStyle, and MaskPicture.

MaskRegion

Concept

The MaskRegion of a control determines where graphical operations can draw. A control's MaskRegion is the area containing subcontrols, as well as any area specified in the `MaskColor` and `MaskPicture` properties. If graphical operations attempt to draw outside of the control's MaskRegion, the graphical output will not appear.

MaxButton

Property

The `MaxButton` property represents whether a form has a maximize button with which the user can enlarge the window to its maximum size. A maximize button can be added only to a form whose `BorderStyle` property is set to fixed-single, sizable, or fixed-double. Moreover, the `MaxButton` property can be set only at design time. That is, the property is read-only at runtime.

Objects with a MaxButton Property

Form

Syntax

```
value = Form.MaxButton
```

- *Form* — A reference to a Form object.
- *value* — The variable that will receive the property's current setting of `True` or `False`.

Example

The following lines retrieve the current value of a form's `MaxButton` property.

```
Dim maxBut As Boolean
maxBut = frmForm1.MaxButton
```

CROSS-REFERENCE
See also Form, MinButton, BorderStyle, and WindowState.

Max — CommonDialog Font

Property

The Max property in a Font dialog box represents the maximum font size (in points) included on the dialog's Size box. This property affects the dialog box only when the dialog's cdlCLLimitSize flag is set.

Syntax

CommonDialog.Max = *value1*

or

value2 = *CommonDialog*.Max

- *CommonDialog* — A reference to a CommonDialog control.
- *value1* — The maximum font size. The default is 0.
- *value2* — The variable that will receive the current maximum font size.

Example

The following lines display a font dialog box with a maximum font size of 72 points. Figure M-5 shows the resultant dialog box with its maximum font size highlighted in the Size box. In this example, the btnCommand1 and dlgCommonDialog1 objects are a CommandButton control and a CommonDialog control that the programmer added to the application's form at design time.

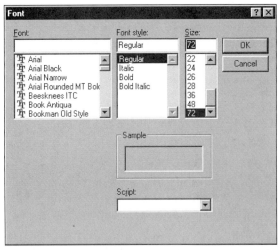

Figure M-5 This Font dialog box lists 72 points as the largest font size selectable in the Size box.

```
Private Sub btnCommand1_Click()
    dlgCommonDialog1.Flags = cdlCFBoth Or cdlCFLimitSize
    dlgCommonDialog1.Max = 72
    dlgCommonDialog1.ShowFont
End Sub
```

CROSS-REFERENCE
See also CommonDialog, Min, and Flags.

Max — CommonDialog Print

Property

The Max property in a Print dialog box represents the value used for the maximum page number in the dialog's Print Range section. Specifically, the Max property determines the highest acceptable value for the To box, as well as the value displayed in the All option.

Syntax

```
CommonDialog.Max = value1
```

or

```
value2 = CommonDialog.Max
```

- *CommonDialog* — A reference to a CommonDialog control.
- *value1* — The maximum page number. The default is 0.
- *value2* — The variable that will receive the current maximum page number.

Example

The following lines display a Print dialog box with a maximum page number of 10 pages. Figure M-6 shows the resultant dialog box with its maximum page number shown in the To box. Notice also the dialog's All 10 Pages option, the value for which was determined by the Max and Min properties. In this example, the btnCommand1 and dlgCommonDialog1 objects are a CommandButton control and a CommonDialog control that the programmer added to the application's form at design time.

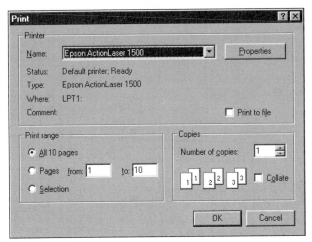

Figure M-6 This Print dialog box lists 10 as the highest page number to print.

```
Private Sub btnCommand1_Click()
    dlgCommonDialog1.Min = 1
    dlgCommonDialog1.Max = 10
    dlgCommonDialog1.FromPage = 1
    dlgCommonDialog1.ToPage = 10
    dlgCommonDialog1.ShowPrinter
End Sub
```

CROSS-REFERENCE
See also CommonDialog and Min.

Max — HScrollBar

Property

The Max property represents the highest value returned by a scroll bar. That is, Max is the horizontal scroll bar's value when the scroll bar's thumb is in its far right position.

Syntax

HScrollBar.Max = *value1*

or

value2 = *HScrollBar*.Max

- *HScrollBar* — A reference to an HScrollBar control.
- *value1* — The maximum scroll value. The default value is 32,767.
- *value2* — The variable that will receive the current maximum scroll value.

Example

The following line sets a horizontal scroll bar's `Max` property. In this example, the `hsbHScroll1` object is an HScrollBar control that the programmer added to the application's form at design time.

```
hsbHScroll1.Max = 1000
```

 CROSS-REFERENCE
See also HScrollBar and Min.

Max — ProgressBar

Property

The `Max` property represents the progress bar's highest value. That is, when the progress bar's value is equal to `Max`, the progress bar's display is fully filled, as shown in Figure M-7.

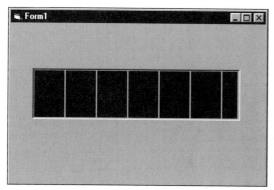

Figure M-7 This progress bar control is set to its maximum value.

Syntax

```
ProgressBar.Max = value1
```

or

```
value2 = ProgressBar.Max
```

- *ProgressBar*—A reference to a ProgressBar control.
- *value1*—The maximum value. The default is 100.
- *value2*—The variable that will receive the current maximum value.

Example

The following line sets a progress bar's `Max` property. In this example, the `prgProgressBar1` object is a ProgressBar control that the programmer added to the application's form at design time.

```
prgProgressBar1.Max = 1000
```

 CROSS-REFERENCE
See also ProgressBar and Min.

Max—Slider

Property

The `Max` property represents the Slider control's highest value. That is, when the user has moved the slider fully to the right, the slider's value is equal to `Max`.

Syntax

```
Slider.Max = value1
```

or

```
value2 = Slider.Max
```

- *Slider*—A reference to a Slider control.
- *value1*—The maximum value. The default is 10.
- *value2*—The variable that will receive the current maximum value.

Example

The following line sets a Slider control's `Max` property. In this example, the `sldSlider1` object is a Slider control that the programmer added to the application's form at design time.

```
sldSlider1.Max = 1000
```

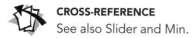

CROSS-REFERENCE
See also Slider and Min.

Max — UpDown

Property

The `Max` property represents the UpDown control's highest value. That is, when the user has clicked the control's up arrow button until the control can go no higher, the control's value is `Max`.

Syntax

```
UpDown.Max = value1
```

or

```
value2 = UpDown.Max
```

- *UpDown* — A reference to an UpDown control.
- *value1* — The maximum value. The default is 10.
- *value2* — The variable that will receive the current maximum value.

Example

The following line sets an UpDown control's `Max` property. In this example, the `updUpDown1` object is an UpDown control that the programmer added to the application's form at design time.

```
updUpDown1.Max = 1000
```

CROSS-REFERENCE
See also UpDown and Min.

Max — VScrollBar

Property

The `Max` property represents the highest value returned by a scroll bar. That is, `Max` is the vertical scroll bar's value when the scroll bar's thumb is in its bottom-most position.

Syntax

```
VScrollBar.Max = value1
```

or

```
value2 = VScrollBar.Max
```

- *VScrollBar*—A reference to a VScrollBar control.
- *value1*—The maximum scroll value. The default value is 32,767.
- *value2*—The variable that will receive the current maximum scroll value.

Example

The following line sets a vertical scroll bar's `Max` property. In this example, the `vsbVScroll1` object is a VScrollBar control that the programmer added to the application's form at design time.

```
vsbVScroll1.Max = 1000
```

 CROSS-REFERENCE
See also VScrollBar and Min.

MaxFileSize

Property

The `MaxFileSize` property represents the maximum number of characters available in which to store the name of the selected file in a CommonDialog control.

Objects with a MaxFileSize Property

CommonDialog

Syntax

```
CommonDialog.MaxFileSize = value1
```

or

```
value2 = CommonDialog.MaxFileSize
```

- *CommonDialog*—A reference to a CommonDialog control.

- *value1* — The maximum number of characters for a file name. The default is 260.
- *value2* — The variable that will receive the property's current setting.

Example

The following line sets a CommonDialog box so that it can accommodate file names of no more than 128 characters. The `dlgCommonDialog1` object is a CommonDialog control that the programmer added to the application's form at design time.

```
dlgCommonDialog1.MaxFileSize = 128
```

 CROSS-REFERENCE
See also CommonDialog and FileName.

MaxLength

Property

The `MaxLength` property represents the maximum number of characters that a control can hold. A value of 0 in this property means that there is no maximum.

Objects with a MaxLength Property

TextBox

RichTextBox

Syntax

object.MaxLength = *value1*

or

value2 = *object*.MaxLength

- *object* — A reference to a TextBox or RichTextBox control.
- *value1* — The maximum number of characters. The default is 0, which means there is no maximum.
- *value2* — The variable that will receive the property's current setting.

Example

The following lines set a TextBox control's maximum capacity to 100 characters. The `txtText1` object is a TextBox control that the programmer added to
the application's form at design time.

```
txtText1.MaxLength = 100
```

 CROSS-REFERENCE
See also TextBox, RichTextBox, and Text.

MDIChild

Property

The `MDIChild` property represents whether a form will be a child window to
an MDIForm object.

Objects with an MDIChild Property

Form

Syntax

```
Form.MDIChild = value1
```

or

```
value2 = Form.MDIChild
```

- *Form* — A reference to a Form object.
- *value1* — The value `True` or `False`. The default is `False`.
- *value2* — The variable that will receive the property's current
  setting.

Example

The following program demonstrates the `MDIChild` property. The first listing
is the program's main window, which is an MDIForm object. The second
part of the listing shows the code for the MDI child-window form. Notice
that its `MDIChild` property is set to `True`, which tells Visual Basic to display
the window as a child of the MDIForm object, as shown in Figure M-8.

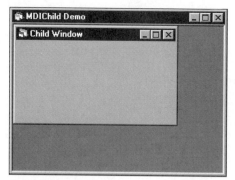

Figure M-8 This program's main window holds an MDI child window.

```
VERSION 5.00
Begin VB.MDIForm MDIForm1
   BackColor       =   &H8000000C&
   Caption         =   "MDIChild Demo"
   ClientHeight    =   3195
   ClientLeft      =   60
   ClientTop       =   345
   ClientWidth     =   4680
   LinkTopic       =   "MDIForm1"
   StartUpPosition =   3  'Windows Default
End
Attribute VB_Name = "MDIForm1"
Attribute VB_GlobalNameSpace = False
Attribute VB_Creatable = False
Attribute VB_PredeclaredId = True
Attribute VB_Exposed = False
VERSION 5.00
Begin VB.Form Form1
   Caption         =   "Child Window"
   ClientHeight    =   3195
   ClientLeft      =   60
   ClientTop       =   345
   ClientWidth     =   4680
   LinkTopic       =   "Form1"
   MDIChild        =   -1  'True
   ScaleHeight     =   3195
   ScaleWidth      =   4680
End
Attribute VB_Name = "Form1"
Attribute VB_GlobalNameSpace = False
Attribute VB_Creatable = False
```

```
Attribute VB_PredeclaredId = True
Attribute VB_Exposed = False
```

 CROSS-REFERENCE
See also Form and MDIForm.

MDIForm

Object

The MDIForm object represents the main window of an MDI (Multiple Document Interface) application. An MDIForm object usually displays one or more MDI child windows, which are Form objects with their MDIChild property set to True.

Properties

The MDIForm object has 33 properties, which are listed as follows. Because many Visual Basic objects have similar properties, the properties' descriptions are listed under their own names, provided alphabetically in this book.

```
ActiveControl
ActiveForm
Appearance
AutoShowChildren
BackColor
Caption
Controls
Count
Enabled
Height
HelpContextID
hWnd
Icon
Left
LinkMode
LinkTopic
MouseIcon
MousePointer
Movable
Name
OLEDropMode
Picture
RightToLeft
```

```
ScaleHeight
ScaleWidth
ScrollBars
StartUpPosition
Tag
Top
Visible
WhatsThisHelp
Width
WindowState
```

Methods

The MDIForm object has ten methods, which are listed as follows. Because many Visual Basic objects have similar methods, the methods' descriptions are listed under their own names, provided alphabetically in this book.

```
Arrange
Hide
Move
OLEDrag
PopupMenu
SetFocus
Show
ValidateControls
WhatsThisMode
ZOrder
```

Events

The MDIForm object responds to 25 events, which are listed below. Because many Visual Basic objects respond to similar events, the events' descriptions are listed under their own names, provided alphabetically in this book.

```
Activate
Click
DblClick
Deactivate
DragDrop
DragOver
Initialize
LinkClose
LinkError
LinkExecute
LinkOpen
```

```
Load
MouseDown
MouseMove
MouseUp
OLECompleteDrag
OLEDragDrop
OLEDragOver
OLEGiveFeedback
OLESetData
OLEStartDrag
QueryUnload
Resize
Terminate
Unload
```

Me

Keyword

The Me keyword provides a reference to the instance of the class in which the keyword appears. For example, in the following lines, the Me keyword refers to the Form object in which the Load method appears.

```
Private Sub Form_Load()
    Me.Caption = "Main Window"
End Sub
```

Of course, in the previous example, the Me keyword isn't needed. The Load method's single line could have been written as

```
frmForm1.Caption = "Main Window"
```

where frmForm1 is the form's name. Or, the line could even have been written using an implicit reference to the form, like this:

```
Caption = "Main Window"
```

Usually, you use the Me keyword to pass an object reference to another object. The Me demo program demonstrates this programming technique. The first part of the following program that follows displays the source code for the program's main window. When you run this program, you see the window shown in Figure M-9. Click the Show Form 2 button to display the program's second form (Figure M-10), whose source code is shown in the second part of the following listing. Type some text into the form's text box, and then click the Set Form1 Caption button. When you do, the second form changes the first form's window caption.

The program works because, when you click the Show Form 2 button, not only does the first form show the second form, but it also passes a reference to itself using the `Me` keyword. You can see this happening in the `btnShowForm_Click()` event procedure, where the program calls the second form's `SetReference` procedure. The `SetReference` procedure stores the reference to the first form, and then uses that reference in the `btnSetCaption_Click()` event procedure to change the first form's caption.

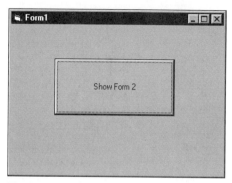

Figure M-9 This is the demo program's first form.

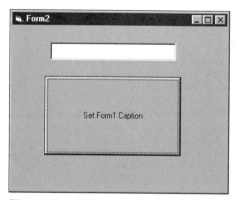

Figure M-10 This is the program's second form, which can change the first form's caption.

```
VERSION 5.00
Begin VB.Form frmForm1
    Caption         =   "Form1"
    ClientHeight    =   3195
    ClientLeft      =   60
```

```
        ClientTop        =    345
        ClientWidth      =    4680
        LinkTopic        =    "Form1"
        ScaleHeight      =    3195
        ScaleWidth       =    4680
        StartUpPosition  =    3   'Windows Default
        Begin VB.CommandButton btnShowForm
           Caption       =    "Show Form 2"
           Height        =    1215
           Left          =    960
           TabIndex      =    0
           Top           =    720
           Width         =    2655
        End
     End
  End
  Attribute VB_Name = "frmForm1"
  Attribute VB_GlobalNameSpace = False
  Attribute VB_Creatable = False
  Attribute VB_PredeclaredId = True
  Attribute VB_Exposed = False

  Private Sub btnShowForm_Click()
      Load frmForm2
      frmForm2.Show
      frmForm2.SetReference Me
  End Sub

  Private Sub Form_Load()
      Load frmForm2
  End Sub
  VERSION 5.00
  Begin VB.Form frmForm2
     Caption          =    "Form2"
     ClientHeight     =    3195
     ClientLeft       =    60
     ClientTop        =    345
     ClientWidth      =    4680
     LinkTopic        =    "Form1"
     ScaleHeight      =    3195
     ScaleWidth       =    4680
     StartUpPosition  =    3   'Windows Default
     Begin VB.TextBox txtNewCaption
        Height        =    375
        Left          =    840
```

```
         TabIndex       =    1
         Top            =    360
         Width          =    2775
      End
      Begin VB.CommandButton btnSetCaption
         Caption        =    "Set Form1 Caption"
         Height         =    1695
         Left           =    720
         TabIndex       =    0
         Top            =    1080
         Width          =    3015
      End
   End
End
Attribute VB_Name = "frmForm2"
Attribute VB_GlobalNameSpace = False
Attribute VB_Creatable = False
Attribute VB_PredeclaredId = True
Attribute VB_Exposed = False

Dim ref As Object

Public Sub SetReference(objRef As Object)
    Set ref = objRef
End Sub

Private Sub btnSetCaption_Click()
    Dim cap As String
    cap = txtNewCaption.Text
    ref.Caption = cap
End Sub
```

Menu

Control

A Menu control represents an application's menu bar and menus. To create a
Menu control, use Visual Basic's menu editor, as shown in Figure M-11. You can
access the menu editor from the Tools menu when a form in your application is
selected.

Figure M-11 Menu controls are unusual in that they must be created with an editor.

Properties

The Menu control has ten properties, which are listed as follows. Because many Visual Basic controls have similar properties, the properties' descriptions are listed under their own names, provided alphabetically in this book.

```
Caption
Checked
Enabled
HelpContextID
Index
Name
Parent
Tag
Visible
WindowList
```

Methods

The Menu control has no methods.

Events

The Menu control responds to one event, Click, which occurs when the user selects a menu item. A program responds to the menu's Click event in the

Click event procedure. For example, a menu called mnuSaveAs will have a Click event procedure called mnuSaveAs_Click, which follows:

```
Private Sub mnuSaveAs_Click()
    ' Handle Click event here.
End Sub
```

Method

Concept

A method is a procedure that's associated with an object. To execute an object's method, you must preface the method's name with the name of the object that owns the method. For example, the following line calls a Form object's Cls method, which clears the form's display area. Note the dot between the object and method names.

```
frmForm1.Cls
```

Mid

Function

The Mid function extracts the specified characters from a source string.

Syntax

```
value = Mid(str, first, num)
```

- *first* — The index of the first character to return.
- *num* (*) — The number of characters to return, starting with *first*. If this argument is not specified, or the specified value is larger than the number of available characters, the function returns all characters from the starting character to the end of the string.
- *str* — The string from which the characters will be extracted.
- *value* — The variable that will receive the returned substring.

(*) = Optional

Example 1

After the following lines execute, the variable `subString` will contain the string "is a test." By specifying only the starting character, the call to `Mid` returns all characters from the starting character to the end of the source string.

```
Dim srcString As String
Dim subString As String
srcString = "This is a test"
subString = Mid(srcString, 6)
```

Example 2

Here, after the following lines execute, the variable `subString` will contain the string "is a." By specifying both a starting character and a length of four characters, the call to `Mid` returns four characters from the starting character.

```
Dim srcString As String
Dim subString As String
srcString = "This is a test"
subString = Mid(srcString, 6, 4)
```

Example 3

Finally, after the following lines execute, the variable `subString` will contain an empty string, because the specified starting character doesn't exist.

```
Dim srcString As String
Dim subString As String
srcString = "This is a test"
subString = Mid(srcString, 15, 4)
```

 CROSS-REFERENCE
See also MidB, Left, and Right.

Mid

Statement

The `Mid` statement replaces specified characters in a string with new characters.

Syntax

```
Mid(str1, first, num) = str2
```

- *first*—The index of the first character to replace.
- *num* (*) —The number of characters to replace, starting with *first*. If this argument is not specified, or the specified value is larger than the number of available characters, the function replaces all characters from the starting character to the end of the string.
- *str1* —The string in which the characters will be replaced.
- *str2*—The replacement string.

(*) = Optional

Example 1

After the following lines execute, the variable str1 will contain the string "This XXXX test." By specifying only the starting character, the call to Mid transfers all characters in str2 to str1.

```
Dim str1 As String
Dim str2 As String
str1 = "This is a test"
str2 = "XXXX"
Mid(str1, 6) = str2
```

Example 2

Here, after the following lines execute, the variable str1 will contain the string "This XX a test." By specifying 6 as a starting character and a length of two characters, the call to Mid replaces two characters in str1, starting with the sixth character in str1.

```
Dim str1 As String
Dim str2 As String
str1 = "This is a test"
str2 = "XXXX"
Mid(str1, 6, 2) = str2
```

Example 3

Finally, after the following lines execute, the variable str1 will contain the string "This XXXX test," demonstrating that, if the specified character count is greater than the number of available characters in the replacement string, Mid uses the entire replacement string.

```
Dim str1 As String
Dim str2 As String
str1 = "This is a test"
```

```
str2 = "XXXX"
Mid(str1, 6, 10) = str2
```

 CROSS-REFERENCE
See also MidB, Left, and Right.

MidB

Function

The MidB function extracts the specified number of bytes from a source string.

Syntax

```
value = MidB(str, first, num)
```

- *first* — The index of the first byte to return.
- *num* (*) — The number of bytes to return, starting with *first*. If this argument is not specified, or the specified value is larger than the number of available bytes, the function returns all bytes from the starting byte to the end of the string.
- *str* — The string from which the bytes will be extracted.
- *value* — The variable that will receive the returned substring.

(*) = Optional

Example 1

After the following lines execute, the variable subString will contain the string "is a test." By specifying only the starting byte, the call to MidB returns all bytes from the starting byte to the end of the source string.

```
Dim srcString As String
Dim subString As String
srcString = "This is a test"
subString = MidB(srcString, 11)
```

Example 2

Here, after the following lines execute, the variable subString will contain the string "is a." By specifying both a starting byte and a length of eight bytes, the call to MidB returns eight bytes from the starting byte.

```
Dim srcString As String
```

```
Dim subString As String
srcString = "This is a test"
subString = MidB(srcString, 11, 8)
```

Example 3

Finally, after the following lines execute, the variable subString will contain an empty string, because the specified starting byte doesn't exist.

```
Dim srcString As String
Dim subString As String
srcString = "This is a test"
subString = MidB(srcString, 29, 8)
```

 CROSS-REFERENCE
See also Mid, Left, and Right.

MidB

Statement

The MidB statement replaces specified bytes in a string with new bytes.

Syntax

```
MidB(str1, first, num) = str2
```

- *first*—The index of the first byte to replace.
- *num* (*) —The number of bytes to replace, starting with *first*. If this argument is not specified, or the specified value is larger than the number of available bytes, the function replaces all bytes from the starting byte to the end of the string.
- *str1*—The string in which the bytes will be replaced.
- *str2*—The replacement string.

(*) = Optional

Example 1

After the following lines execute, the variable str1 will contain the string "This XXXX test." By specifying only the starting byte, the call to MidB transfers all bytes in str2 to str1.

```
Dim str1 As String
```

```
Dim str2 As String
str1 = "This is a test"
str2 = "XXXX"
MidB(str1, 11) = str2
```

Example 2

Here, after the following lines execute, the variable str1 will contain the string "This XX a test." By specifying 11 as the starting byte and a length of four bytes, the call to MidB replaces four bytes in str1, starting with the eleventh byte in str1.

```
Dim str1 As String
Dim str2 As String
str1 = "This is a test"
str2 = "XXXX"
MidB(str1, 11, 4) = str2
```

Example 3

Finally, after the following lines execute, the variable str1 will contain the string "This XXXX test," demonstrating that, if the specified byte count is greater than the number of available bytes in the replacement string, MidB uses the entire replacement string.

```
Dim str1 As String
Dim str2 As String
str1 = "This is a test"
str2 = "XXXX"
MidB(str1, 11, 24) = str2
```

 CROSS-REFERENCE
See also Mid, Left, and Right.

MinButton

Property

The MinButton property represents whether a form has a minimize button with which the user can reduce the window to an icon on the Taskbar. A minimize button can be added only to a form whose BorderStyle property is set to fixed-single, sizable, or fixed-double. Moreover, the MinButton property can be set only at design time. That is, the property is read-only at runtime.

Objects with a MinButton Property

Form

Syntax

```
value = Form.MinButton
```

- *Form* — A reference to a Form object.
- *value* — The variable that will receive the property's current setting of True or False.

Example

The following lines retrieve the current value of a form's MinButton property.

```
Dim minBut As Boolean
minBut = frmForm1.MinButton
```

CROSS-REFERENCE
See also Form, MaxButton, BorderStyle, and WindowState.

Min — CommonDialog Font

Property

The Min property in a Font dialog box represents the minimum font size (in points) included on the dialog's Size box. This property affects the dialog box only when the dialog's cdlCLLimitSize flag is set.

Syntax

```
CommonDialog.Min = value1
```

or

```
value2 = CommonDialog.Min
```

- *CommonDialog* — A reference to a CommonDialog control.
- *value1* — The minimum font size. The default is 0.
- *value2* — The variable that will receive the current minimum font size.

Example

The following lines display a font dialog box with a minimum font size of 8 points. Figure M-12 shows the resultant dialog box with its minimum font size highlighted in the Size box. In this example, the `btnCommand1` and `dlgCommonDialog1` objects are a CommandButton control and a Common-Dialog control that the programmer added to the application's form at design time.

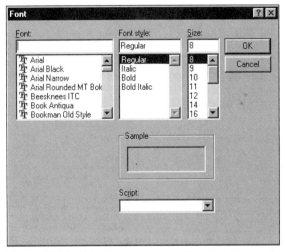

Figure M-12 This Font dialog box lists 8 points as the smallest font size selectable in the Size box.

```
Private Sub btnCommand1_Click()
    dlgCommonDialog1.Flags = cdlCFBoth Or cdlCFLimitSize
    dlgCommonDialog1.Min = 8
    dlgCommonDialog1.Max = 72
    dlgCommonDialog1.ShowFont
End Sub
```

 CROSS-REFERENCE
See also CommonDialog, Max, and Flags.

Min — CommonDialog Print

Property

The `Min` property in a Print dialog box represents the value used for the minimum page number in the dialog's Print Range section. Specifically, the `Min` property determines the lowest acceptable value for the From box, as well as the value displayed in the All option.

Syntax

```
CommonDialog.Min = value1
```

or

```
value2 = CommonDialog.Min
```

- *CommonDialog* — A reference to a CommonDialog control.
- *value1* — The minimum page number. The default is 0.
- *value2* — The variable that will receive the current minimum page number.

Example

The following lines display a Print dialog box with a minimum page number of 2. Figure M-13 shows the resultant dialog box with its minimum page number shown in the To box. Notice also the dialog's All 19 Pages option, the value for which was determined by the `Max` and `Min` properties. In this example, the `btnCommand1` and `dlgCommonDialog1` objects are a CommandButton control and a CommonDialog control that the programmer added to the application's form at design time.

l
m
n

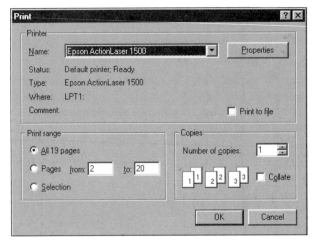

Figure M-13 This Print dialog box lists 2 as the lowest page number to print.

```
Private Sub btnCommand1_Click()
    dlgCommonDialog1.Min = 2
    dlgCommonDialog1.Max = 20
    dlgCommonDialog1.FromPage = 2
    dlgCommonDialog1.ToPage = 20
    dlgCommonDialog1.ShowPrinter
End Sub
```

 CROSS-REFERENCE
See also CommonDialog and Max.

Min — HScrollBar

Property

The Min property represents the lowest value returned by a scroll bar. That is, Min is the horizontal scroll bar's value when the scroll bar's thumb is in its far left position.

Syntax

HScrollBar.Min = *value1*

or

value2 = *HScrollBar*.Min

- *HScrollBar* — A reference to an HScrollBar control.
- *value1* — The minimum scroll value. The default value is 0.
- *value2* — The variable that will receive the current minimum scroll value.

Example

The following line sets a horizontal scroll bar's Min property. In this example, the hsbHScroll1 object is an HScrollBar control that the programmer added to the application's form at design time.

```
hsbHScroll1.Min = 1
```

 CROSS-REFERENCE
See also HScrollBar and Max.

Min — ProgressBar

Property

The Min property represents the progress bar's lowest value. That is, when the progress bar's value is equal to Min, the progress bar's display is empty.

Syntax

```
ProgressBar.Min = value1
```

or

```
value2 = ProgressBar.Min
```

- *ProgressBar* — A reference to a ProgressBar control.
- *value1* — The minimum value. The default is 0.
- *value2* — The variable that will receive the current minimum value.

Example

The following line sets a progress bar's Min property. In this example, the prgProgressBar1 object is a ProgressBar control that the programmer added to the application's form at design time.

```
prgProgressBar1.Min = 10
```

CROSS-REFERENCE
See also ProgressBar and Max.

Min — Slider

Property

The `Min` property represents the Slider control's lowest value. That is, when the user has moved the slider fully to the left, the slider's value is equal to `Min`.

Syntax

```
Slider.Min = value1
```

or

```
value2 = Slider.Min
```

- *Slider* — A reference to a Slider control.
- *value1* — The minimum value. The default is 0.
- *value2* — The variable that will receive the current minimum value.

Example

The following line sets a Slider control's `Min` property. In this example, the `sldSlider1` object is a Slider control that the programmer added to the application's form at design time.

```
sldSlider1.Min = 10
```

CROSS-REFERENCE
See also Slider and Max.

Min — UpDown

Property

The `Min` property represents the UpDown control's lowest value. That is, when the user has clicked the control's down arrow button until the control can go no lower, the control's value is `Min`.

Syntax

```
UpDown.Min = value1
```

or

```
value2 = UpDown.Min
```

- *UpDown* — A reference to an UpDown control.
- *value1* — The minimum value. The default is 0.
- *value2* — The variable that will receive the current minimum value.

Example

The following line sets an UpDown control's `Min` property. In this example, the `updUpDown1` object is an UpDown control that the programmer added to the application's form at design time.

```
updUpDown1.Min = 10
```

CROSS-REFERENCE
See also UpDown and Max.

Min — VScrollBar

Property

The `Min` property represents the lowest value returned by a scroll bar. That is, `Min` is the vertical scroll bar's value when the scroll bar's thumb is in its top-most position.

Syntax

```
VScrollBar.Max = value1
```

or
```
value2 = VScrollBar.Max
```

- *VScrollBar* — A reference to a VScrollBar control.
- *value1* — The minimum scroll value. The default value is 0.
- *value2* — The variable that will receive the current minimum scroll value.

Example

The following line sets a vertical scroll bar's `Min` property. In this example, the `vsbVScroll1` object is a VScrollBar control that the programmer added to the application's form at design time.

```
vsbVScroll1.Max = 1
```

 CROSS-REFERENCE
See also VScrollBar and Max.

MinHeight

Property

The `MinHeight` property represents the minimum height of a Band object in a CoolBar control.

Objects with a MinHeight Property

Band

Syntax

```
Band.MinHeight = value1
```

or

```
value2 = Band.MinHeight
```

- *Band* — A reference to a Band object.
- *value1* — The minimum height.
- *value2* — The variable that will receive the property's current setting.

Example

The following line sets the first band on a CoolBar control to a minimum height of 500. The `CoolBar1` object is a CoolBar control that the programmer added to the application's form at design time.

```
CoolBar1.Bands(1).MinHeight = 500
```

 CROSS-REFERENCE
See also CoolBar and MinWidth.

Minor

Property

The `Minor` property represents the application's minor version number. You can set this property in the Project Properties property sheet, as shown in Figure M-14.

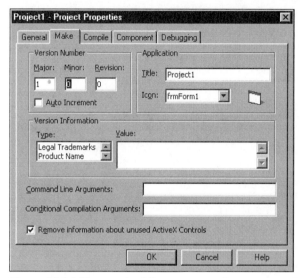

Figure M-14 You set the Minor property from your project's Project Properties property sheet.

Objects with a Minor Property

App

Syntax

```
value = App.Minor
```

- *App* — A reference to the App object.
- *value* — The variable that will receive the minor version number.

Example

In this example, the program retrieves an application's minor version number. Note that the App object is a global Visual Basic object that you don't need to add to your programs.

```
Dim minVersion As Integer
minVersion = App.Minor
```

 CROSS-REFERENCE
See also App, Major, and Revision.

Minus (–)

Operator

The minus (–) operator performs subtraction or indicates a negative value.

Syntax

```
value = exp1 - exp2
```

or

```
-exp3
```

- *exp1* — The expression from which to subtract *exp2*.
- *exp2* — The expression to subtract from *exp1*.
- *exp3* — The expression to negate.
- *value* — The result of the operation.

Example 1

After the following lines execute, result will contain the value 4.

```
Dim exp1, exp2 As Integer
Dim result As Integer
exp1 = 10
exp2 = 6
result = exp1 - exp2
```

Example 2

Here, after the following lines execute, `result` will contain the value −16. Notice that, in this example, `exp1` is a negative number.

```
Dim exp1, exp2 As Integer
Dim result As Integer
exp1 = 10
exp2 = 6
result = -exp1 - exp2
```

Minute

Function

The `Minute` function extracts the minute portion of a time.

Syntax

```
value = Minute(time)
```

- *time* — The time value from which to extract the minutes.
- *value* — The variable that will receive the returned minutes.

Example

After the following lines execute, `intMinute` will contain the value 20.

```
Dim vntTime As Variant
Dim intMinute As Integer
vntTime = #6:20:15 AM#
intMinute = Minute(vntTime)
```

 CROSS-REFERENCE
See also Hour and Second.

MinWidth

Property

The `MinWidth` property represents the minimum width of a Band object in a CoolBar control.

Objects with a MinWidth Property
Band

Syntax

```
Band.MinWidth = value1
```

or

```
value2 = Band.MinWidth
```

- *Band* — A reference to a Band object.
- *value1* — The minimum width.
- *value2* — The variable that will receive the property's current setting.

Example

The following line sets the first band on a CoolBar control to a minimum width of 1000. The `CoolBar1` object is a CoolBar control that the programmer added to the application's form at design time.

```
CoolBar1.Bands(1).MinWidth = 1000
```

 CROSS-REFERENCE
See also CoolBar and MinHeight.

MIRR

Function

The `MIRR` function calculates the modified rate of return on a series of payments and receipts.

Syntax

```
value = MIRR(input(), finance, reinvest)
```

- *finance* — The interest rate paid.
- *input* — An array of positive and negative values, with positive values representing receipts and negative values representing payments. Transactions should be ordered in the array in the order they occurred.

- *reinvest* — The interest rate received on reinvestment.
- *value* — The variable that will receive the calculation's result.

Example

The following lines calculate the rate of return on a series of transactions containing one payment of $1,000 and two receipts of $750.

```
Dim result As Double
Dim inVals(3) As Double
inVals(0) = -1000
inVals(1) = 750
inVals(2) = 750
result = MIRR(inVals(), 0.15, 0.18)
```

MiscFlags

Property

The `MiscFlags` property enables the advanced features of an OLE Container control.

Objects with a MiscFlags Property

OLE Container

Syntax

`OLEContainer.MiscFlags = value1`

or

`value2 = OLEContainer.MiscFlags`

- *OLEContainer* — A reference to an OLE Container control.
- *value1* — One or both of the values `vbOLEMiscFlagMemStorage` and `vbOLEMiscFlagDisableInPlace`. The former flag causes an object's data to be stored in memory rather than in a temporary disk file, whereas the latter flag forces object editing to take place in a separate window rather than in-place. These flags can be combined with the `Or` operator.
- *value2* — The variable that will receive the property's current setting.

Example

The following line sets an OLE Container control's `MiscFlags` property to both of the available options. The `oleContainer` object is an OLE container control that the programmer added to the application's form at design time.

```
oleContainer.MiscFlags = _
    vbOLEMiscFlagMemStorage Or vbOLEMiscFlagDisableInPlace
```

 CROSS-REFERENCE
See also OLE Container.

MixedState

Property

The `MixedState` property represents the indeterminate state of a button in a Toolbar control. An indeterminate state is usually caused when the user selects a number of items with differing states. For example, selected text that contains both italic and normal text would make a button representing the italic attribute indeterminate. A value of `True` for this property dims the button's image, indicating the indeterminate state.

Objects with a MixedState Property

Button

Syntax

```
Button.MixedState = value1
```

or

```
value2 = Button.MixedState
```

- *Button* — A reference to a Button object.
- *value1* — The value `True` or `False`. The default is `False`.
- *value2* — The variable that will receive the property's current setting.

Example

The following line sets the first button in a Toolbar control to its indeterminate state. The `tlbToolbar1` object is a Toolbar control that the programmer added to the application's form at design time.

```
tlbToolbar1.Buttons(1).MixedState = True
```

CROSS-REFERENCE
See also Button and Toolbar.

MkDir

Statement

The MkDir statement creates a new directory.

Syntax

```
MkDir dir
```

- *dir*—The path of the new directory to create. If the path doesn't include a drive specification, the current directory is used.

Example

The following line creates a directory called MyNewDir on the root of drive C.

```
MkDir "c:\MyNewDir"
```

CROSS-REFERENCE
See also ChDir, CurDir, and RmDir.

Mod

Operator

The Mod operator returns the remainder of a division operation.

Syntax

```
result = exp1 Mod exp2
```

- *exp1*—Any valid numerical expression.
- *exp2*—Any valid numerical expression.
- *result*—The remainder of *exp1* divided by *exp2*.

Example

After the following lines execute, `remainder` will contain the value 2.

```
Dim remainder As Integer
Dim exp1, exp2 As Integer
exp1 = 27
exp2 = 5
remainder = exp1 Mod exp2
```

Mode — Multimedia

Property

The `Mode` property represents the mode of an open MCI device. This read-only property returns one of the values in Table M-1.

Table M-1 Settings for the Mode Property

Value	Description
mciModeNotOpen	The MCI device is not open.
mciModePause	The MCI device is paused.
mciModePlay	The MCI device is playing.
mciModeReady	The MCI device is ready.
mciModeRecord	The MCI device is recording.
mciModeSeek	The MCI device is seeking.
mciModeStop	The MCI device is stopped.

Objects with a Mode Property

Multimedia MCI

Syntax

```
value = MultimediaMCI.Mode
```

- *MultimediaMCI* — A reference to a Multimedia MCI control.
- *value* — The variable that will receive the device's current mode.

Example

The following lines retrieve the mode of the current MCI device. The `mciMMControl1` object is a Multimedia MCI control that the programmer added to the application's form at design time.

```
Dim mciMode As Long
mciMode = MMControl1.Mode
```

CROSS-REFERENCE
See also Multimedia MCI.

Month

Function

The `Month` function returns the month part of a date. The valid return values are 1 through 12, inclusive.

Syntax

```
value = Month(date)
```

- *date* — The date from which to get the month.
- *value* — The variable that will receive the month.

Example

The following lines display the message "Month #3" in a message box.

```
Dim dtmDate As Date
Dim monthPart As Integer
dtmDate = DateValue("March 17, 1998")
monthPart = Month(dtmDate)
MsgBox "Month #" & monthPart
```

CROSS-REFERENCE
See also Date (statement), Date (function), Date (keyword), DateAdd, DateDiff, DatePart, DateSerial, DateValue, Day, and Year.

MonthName

Function

The `MonthName` function returns the name of a month given the month's number.

Syntax

```
value = MonthName(num, abbrName)
```

- *abbrName* (*) — A value of `True` or `False` indicating whether the month name should be abbreviated.
- *num* — The number of the month for which to get the name. Must be a value from 1 to 12.
- *value* — The string variable that will receive the month name.

(*) = Optional

Example 1

The following lines load a string array with the names of all the months. For example, 1 is returned as "January."

```
Dim strMonth(12) As String
Dim m As Integer
For m = 1 To 12
    strMonth(m) = MonthName(m)
Next
```

Example 2

Here, the example also loads a string array with the names of all the months, but in this case, the names are abbreviated. For example, 1 is returned as "Jan."

```
Dim strMonth(12) As String
Dim m As Integer
For m = 1 To 12
    strMonth(m) = MonthName(m, True)
Next
```

MouseDown

Event

Visual Basic sends a control a `MouseDown` event when the user clicks the mouse over the control. Use this event when you need information about the mouse click, including the mouse coordinates at the time of the click, the mouse button that was pressed, or the status of the Shift, Ctrl, and Alt keys at the time of the click.

Objects That Receive MouseDown Events

Animation

CheckBox

CommandButton

CoolBar

DirListBox

DriveListBox

FileListBox

Form

Frame

Image

Label

ListBox

ListView

MDIForm

OLE Container

OptionButton

PictureBox

ProgressBar

PropertyPage

RichTextBox

Slider

StatusBar

TabStrip

TextBox

Toolbar

TreeView

UpDown

UserControl

Example

A program can respond to a MouseDown event by implementing the target object's MouseDown event procedure. The following code segment shows how a PictureBox object defines a MouseDown event procedure. In this case, the program displays the mouse coordinates in a message box each time the user clicks the control. The picPicture1 object is a PictureBox control that the programmer added to the form at design time.

```
Private Sub picPicture1_MouseDown(Button As Integer, _
  Shift As Integer, X As Single, Y As Single)
    MsgBox "MouseDown: " & X & "," & Y
End Sub
```

Here, the event procedure's four parameters are the status of the mouse buttons, the status of the keyboard, and the coordinates of the mouse at the time of the event. The Button parameter will be vbLeftButton for the left button, vbRightButton for the right button, and vbMiddleButton for the middle button. The Shift parameter will have bit 0 set if the Shift key was down, bit 1 set if the Ctrl key was down, and bit 2 set if the Alt key was down. The Visual Basic constants that represent these values are vbShiftMask, vbCtrlMask, and vbAltMask, respectively.

 CROSS-REFERENCE
See also MouseUp, MouseMove, and Click.

MouseIcon

Property

The MouseIcon property represents the image the mouse pointer will use when a control's MousePointer property is set to vbCustom.

Objects with a MouseIcon Property

CheckBox

ComboBox

CommandButton

CoolBar

DirListBox

DriveListBox

FileListBox

Form

Frame

HScrollBar

Image

Label

ListBox

ListView

MDIForm

Multimedia MCI

OLE Container

OptionButton

PictureBox

ProgressBar

PropertyPage

RichTextBox

Screen

Slider

StatusBar

TabStrip

TextBox

Toolbar

TreeView

UserControl

VScrollBar

Syntax

```
object.MouseIcon = image1
```

or

```
image2 = object.MouseIcon
```

- *image1*—A reference to the picture object containing the icon. Can be a reference to a `Picture` property or can be loaded with the `LoadPicture` function.

- *image2*—The variable that will receive the reference to the icon.

■ *object* — A reference to a control with a MouseIcon property.

Example

The following lines set the mouse pointer for a form to the icon in the icon1.ico file.

```
frmForm1.MouseIcon = LoadPicture("icon1.ico")
frmForm1.MousePointer = vbCustom
```

 CROSS-REFERENCE
See also MousePointer.

MouseMove

Event

Visual Basic sends a control a MouseMove event when the user moves the mouse over the control. Use this event when you need to track the position of the mouse continually and when you need to get the status of the mouse buttons and the keyboard's Shift, Ctrl, and Alt keys as the mouse moves.

Objects That Receive MouseDown Events

Animation

CheckBox

CommandButton

CoolBar

DirListBox

DriveListBox

FileListBox

Form

Frame

Image

Label

ListBox

ListView

MDIForm

OLE Container

OptionButton

PictureBox

ProgressBar

PropertyPage

RichTextBox

Slider

StatusBar

TabStrip

TextBox

Toolbar

TreeView

UpDown

UserControl

Example

A program can respond to a MouseMove event by implementing the target object's MouseMove event procedure. The following code segment shows how a PictureBox object defines a MouseMove event procedure. In this case, as you move the mouse over the control, the program displays the mouse coordinates in Visual Basic's Immediate window. The picPicture1 object is a PictureBox control that the programmer added to the form at design time.

```
Private Sub picPicture1_MouseDown(Button As Integer, _
  Shift As Integer, X As Single, Y As Single)
    MsgBox "MouseDown: " & X & "," & Y
End Sub
```

Here, the event procedure's four parameters are the status of the mouse buttons, the status of the keyboard, and the coordinates of the mouse at the time of the event. The Button parameter will be vbLeftButton for the left button, vbRightButton for the right button, and vbMiddleButton for the middle button. The Shift parameter will have bit 0 set if the Shift key was down, bit 1 set if the Ctrl key was down, and bit 2 set if the Alt key was down. The Visual Basic constants that represent these values are vbShiftMask, vbCtrlMask, and vbAltMask, respectively.

CROSS-REFERENCE

See also MouseDown, MouseUp, and Click.

MousePointer

Property

The `MousePointer` property represents the appearance of the mouse pointer. The property can be one of these values: `vbDefault`, `vbArrow`, `vbCrosshair`, `vbIbeam`, `vbIconPointer`, `vbSizePointer`, `vbSizeNESW`, `vbSizeNS`, `vbSizeNWSE`, `vbSizeWE`, `vbUpArrow`, `vbHourglass`, `vbNoDrop`, `vbArrowHourglass`, `vbArrowQuestion`, `vbSizeAll`, **and** `vbCustom`. For more information on the `vbCustom` style, see the `MouseIcon` property.

Objects with a MousePointer Property

CheckBox

ComboBox

CommandButton

CoolBar

DirListBox

DriveListBox

FileListBox

Form

Frame

HScrollBar

Image

Label

ListBox

ListView

MDIForm

Multimedia MCI

OLE Container

OptionButton

PictureBox

ProgressBar

PropertyPage

RichTextBox

Screen

Slider

StatusBar

TabStrip
TextBox
Toolbar
TreeView
UserControl
VScrollBar

Syntax

```
object.MousePointer = value1
```

or

```
value2 = object.MousePointer
```

- *object* — A reference to a control with a `MousePointer` property.
- *value1* — The mouse-pointer value.
- *value2* — The variable that will receive the property's current setting.

Example

The following program demonstrates how the `MousePointer` property works. When you run the program, a window appears with 16 black rectangles. As you move the mouse from one rectangle to another, the mouse pointer changes to different forms, as shown in Figure M-15.

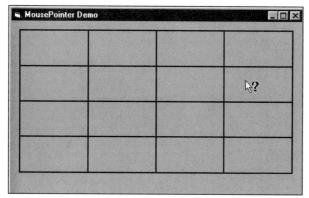

Figure M-15 Each box in this window causes the mouse pointer to change shape.

```
ERSION 5.00
Begin VB.Form frmForm1
   Caption         =    "MousePointer Demo"
   ClientHeight    =    3870
   ClientLeft      =    60
   ClientTop       =    345
   ClientWidth     =    6735
   LinkTopic       =    "Form1"
   ScaleHeight     =    3870
   ScaleWidth      =    6735
   StartUpPosition =    3    'Windows Default
End
Attribute VB_Name = "frmForm1"
Attribute VB_GlobalNameSpace = False
Attribute VB_Creatable = False
Attribute VB_PredeclaredId = True
Attribute VB_Exposed = False

Private Sub Form_Load()
    frmForm1.DrawWidth = 2
    frmForm1.MouseIcon = LoadPicture("icon1.ico")
End Sub

Private Sub Form_MouseMove(Button As Integer, _
  Shift As Integer, X As Single, Y As Single)
    Debug.Print X & "-" & Y
    If X > 200 And X < 1770 Then
        If Y > 200 And Y < 990 Then
            frmForm1.MousePointer = vbArrow
        ElseIf Y > 990 And Y < 1800 Then
            frmForm1.MousePointer = vbCrosshair
        ElseIf Y > 1800 And Y < 2595 Then
            frmForm1.MousePointer = vbIbeam
        ElseIf Y > 2595 And Y < 3390 Then
            frmForm1.MousePointer = vbIconPointer
        End If
    ElseIf X > 1770 And X < 3360 Then
        If Y > 200 And Y < 990 Then
            frmForm1.MousePointer = vbSizePointer
        ElseIf Y > 990 And Y < 1800 Then
            frmForm1.MousePointer = vbSizeNESW
        ElseIf Y > 1800 And Y < 2595 Then
            frmForm1.MousePointer = vbSizeNS
        ElseIf Y > 2595 And Y < 3390 Then
```

```
                    frmForm1.MousePointer = vbSizeNWSE
                End If
            ElseIf X > 3360 And X < 4950 Then
                If Y > 200 And Y < 990 Then
                    frmForm1.MousePointer = vbSizeWE
                ElseIf Y > 990 And Y < 1800 Then
                    frmForm1.MousePointer = vbUpArrow
                ElseIf Y > 1800 And Y < 2595 Then
                    frmForm1.MousePointer = vbHourglass
                ElseIf Y > 2595 And Y < 3390 Then
                    frmForm1.MousePointer = vbNoDrop
                End If
            ElseIf X > 4950 And X < 7120 Then
                If Y > 200 And Y < 990 Then
                    frmForm1.MousePointer = vbArrowHourglass
                ElseIf Y > 990 And Y < 1800 Then
                    frmForm1.MousePointer = vbArrowQuestion
                ElseIf Y > 1800 And Y < 2595 Then
                    frmForm1.MousePointer = vbSizeAll
                ElseIf Y > 2595 And Y < 3390 Then
                    frmForm1.MousePointer = vbCustom
                End If
            End If

End Sub

Private Sub Form_Paint()
    Dim X As Integer
    For X = 0 To 4
        Line (200, X * 800 + 200)-(6500, X * 800 + 200)
    Next
    For X = 0 To 4
        Line (X * 1580 + 200, 200)-(X * 1580 + 200, 3400)
    Next
End Sub
```

CROSS-REFERENCE

See also MouseIcon.

MouseUp

Event

Visual Basic sends a control a `MouseUp` event when the user releases a mouse button over the control. Use this event when you need information about the mouse click, including the mouse coordinates at the time of the click, the mouse button that was pressed, or the status of the Shift, Ctrl, and Alt keys.

Objects That Receive MouseUp Events

Animation

CheckBox

CommandButton

CoolBar

DirListBox

DriveListBox

FileListBox

Form

Frame

Image

Label

ListBox

ListView

MDIForm

OLE Container

OptionButton

PictureBox

ProgressBar

PropertyPage

RichTextBox

Slider

StatusBar

TabStrip

TextBox

Toolbar

TreeView

UpDown

UserControl

Example

A program can respond to a MouseUp event by implementing the target object's MouseUp event procedure. The following code segment shows how a PictureBox object defines a MouseUp event procedure. In this case, the program displays the mouse coordinates in a message box each time the user clicks the control. The picPicture1 object is a PictureBox control that the programmer added to the form at design time.

```
Private Sub picPicture1_MouseUp(Button As Integer, _
    Shift As Integer, X As Single, Y As Single)
      MsgBox "MouseUp: " & X & "," & Y
End Sub
```

Here, the event procedure's four parameters are the status of the mouse buttons, the status of the keyboard, and the coordinates of the mouse at the time of the event. The Button parameter will be vbLeftButton for the left button, vbRightButton for the right button, and vbMiddleButton for the middle button. The Shift parameter will have bit 0 set if the Shift key was down, bit 1 set if the Ctrl key was down, and bit 2 set if the Alt key was down. The Visual Basic constants that represent these values are vbShiftMask, vbCtrlMask, and vbAltMask, respectively.

CROSS-REFERENCE
See also MouseDown, MouseMove, and Click.

Moveable

Property

The Moveable property represents whether a form can be moved.

Objects with a Moveable Property

Form

MDIForm

Syntax

object.Moveable = *value1*

or

value2 = *object*.Moveable

- *object*—A reference to a Form or MDIForm object.

- *value1* — The value `True` or `False`.
- *value2* — The variable that will receive the property's current setting.

Example

The following lines retrieve the current value of a form's `Moveable` property.

```
Dim canMove As Boolean
canMove = frmForm1.Moveable
```

 CROSS-REFERENCE
See also Form and MDIForm.

MoveFile

Method

The `MoveFile` method moves a disk file from one location to another.

Objects with a MoveFile Method

FileSystemObject

Syntax

```
FileSystemObject.MoveFile src, dest
```

- *FileSystemObject* — A reference to a FileSystemObject object.
- *src* — The path to the file or files to move. Wildcard characters can be used with this argument.
- *dest* — The path to which to move the file or files.

Example 1

The following lines move a file called `MyFile.dat` to the Temp directory on the same drive.

```
Dim fileSystem As Object
Set fileSystem = CreateObject("Scripting.FileSystemObject")
fileSystem.MoveFile "c:\MyFile.dat", "c:\Temp\MyFile.dat"
```

Example 2

Here, the following lines move all files with a .bmp extension to the Temp directory on the same drive.

```
Dim fileSystem As Object
Set fileSystem = CreateObject("Scripting.FileSystemObject")
fileSystem.MoveFile "c:\*.bmp", "c:\Temp\"
```

 CROSS-REFERENCE
See also FileSystemObject, Move, and MoveFolder.

Move — File or Folder Object

Method

The `Move` method moves a disk file or folder from one location to another.

Syntax

object`.Move` *dest*

- *object* — A reference to a File or Folder object.
- *dest* — The path to which to move the file or folder.

Example

The following lines move a file called `MyFile.dat` to the Temp directory on the same drive.

```
Dim fileSystem As Object
Dim file As Object
Set fileSystem = CreateObject("Scripting.FileSystemObject")
Set file = fileSystem.GetFile("c:\MyFile.dat")
file.Move "c:\Temp\"
```

 CROSS-REFERENCE
See also FileSystemObject, MoveFile, and MoveFolder.

Move — General Controls

Method

The Move method repositions and resizes a form or control.

Objects with a Move Method

Animation

CheckBox

ComboBox

CommandButton

CoolBar

DirListBox

DriveListBox

FileListBox

Form

Frame

HScrollBar

Image

Label

ListBox

ListView

MDIForm

Multimedia MCI

OLE Container

OptionButton

PictureBox

ProgressBar

RichTextBox

Shape

Slider

StatusBar

TabStrip

TextBox

Toolbar

TreeView

UpDown

VScrollBar

Syntax

```
object.Move x, y, w, h
```

- *h* (*) — The control's new height.
- *object* — A reference to a control with the `Move` method.
- *w* (*) — The control's new width.
- *x* — The control's new horizontal position.
- *y* (*) — The control's new vertical position.

(*) = Optional

Example

The following line moves and resizes a CommandButton control. The `btnCommand11` object is a CommandButton control the programmer added to the application's form at design time.

```
btnCommand1.Move 2000, 2000, 1000, 1000
```

CROSS-REFERENCE
See also Height, Width, Left, and Top.

MoveFolder

Method

The `MoveFolder` method moves a folder and all its contents from one location to another.

Objects with a MoveFolder Method

FileSystemObject

Syntax

```
FileSystemObject.MoveFolder src, dest
```

- *FileSystemObject* — A reference to a FileSystemObject object.

- *src* — The path to the folder or folders to move. Wildcard characters can be used with this argument.
- *dest* — The path to which to move the folder or folders.

Example 1

The following lines move a folder called MyFolder to the Temp directory on the same drive.

```
Dim fileSystem As Object
Set fileSystem = CreateObject("Scripting.FileSystemObject")
fileSystem.MoveFolder "c:\MyFolder", "c:\Temp\"
```

Example 2

Here, the following lines move all folders whose names begin with My to the Temp directory on the same drive.

```
Dim fileSystem As Object
Set fileSystem = CreateObject("Scripting.FileSystemObject")
fileSystem.MoveFolder "c:\My*", "c:\Temp\"
```

 CROSS-REFERENCE
See also FileSystemObject, Move, and MoveFile.

MsgBox

Function

The MsgBox function displays a message box containing a text message, a descriptive icon, and buttons for accepting the user's response.

Syntax

```
value = MsgBox(msg, controls, title, help, helpContext)
```

- *controls* (*) — A value that specifies the type of message box to display. This argument can be a combination of values from Tables M-2, M-3, M-4, M-5, and M-6. (Only one value from each table.) The default is vbOKOnly.
- *help* (*) — A string holding the name of the help file to use for context-sensitive help.
- *helpContext* (*) — The help context ID for the help topic.

- *msg* — The message to display in the message box.
- *title* (*) — The title to display in the message box. The default is the project name.
- *value* — The variable that will receive a value indicating which button the user clicked to exit the message box. This can be a value from Table M-7.

(*) = Optional

Table M-2 Button Settings for the *controls* Argument

Value	Description
vbAbortRetryIgnore	Show Abort, Retry, and Fail buttons.
vbMsgBoxHelpButton	Show a Help button.
vbOKCancel	Show OK and Cancel buttons.
vbOKOnly	Show only the OK button (default).
vbRetryCancel	Show Retry and Cancel.
vbYesNo	Show Yes and No buttons.
vbYesNoCancel	Show Yes, No, and Cancel buttons.

Table M-3 Icon Settings for the *controls* Argument

Value	Description
vbCritical	Shows the critical icon, which is a red circle containing an *X*.
vbExclamation	Shows the exclamation-point icon.
vbInformation	Shows the information icon, which is a dialog bubble containing a lowercase *i*.
vbQuestion	Shows the question-mark icon.

Table M-4 Default Button Settings for the *controls* Argument

Value	Description
vbDefaultButton1	Makes the first button the default.
vbDefaultButton2	Makes the second button the default.
vbDefaultButton3	Makes the third button the default.
vbDefaultButton4	Makes the fourth button the default.

Table M-5 Mode Settings for the *controls* Argument

Value	Description
vbApplicationModal	The user must dismiss the message box before returning to the application.
vbSystemModal	The user must dismiss the message box before returning to any application.

Table M-6 Format Settings for the *controls* Argument

Value	Description
vbMsgBoxRight	The message box displays right-aligned text.
vbMsgBoxRtlReading	The message displays right-to-left text on Arabic and Hebrew systems.
vbMsgBoxSetForeground	Message box becomes the foreground window.

Table M-7 Return Values for the MsgBox Function

Value	Description
vbAbort	User clicked the Abort button.
vbCancel	User clicked the Cancel button.
vbIgnore	User clicked the Ignore button.
vbNo	User clicked the No button.
vbOK	User clicked the OK button.
vbRetry	User clicked the Retry button.
vbYes	User clicked the Yes button.

Example 1

The following lines display a simple message box (see Figure M-16) when the user clicks a button. The programmer added the CommandButton object, btnCommand1, to the form at design time.

Figure M-16 You can display a message box by providing as little as the message text.

```
Private Sub btnCommand1_Click()
    MsgBox "This is a message box test."
End Sub
```

Example 2

Here, the example displays a message box with a title, a question-mark icon, and Yes and No buttons (see Figure M-17). The programmer added the CommandButton object, btnCommand1, to the form at design time.

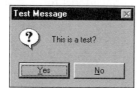

Figure M-17 You can display various icons and buttons in a message box.

```
Private Sub btnCommand1_Click()
    Dim response As Integer
    response = MsgBox("This is a test?", _
        vbYesNo Or vbQuestion, "Test Message")
    If response = vbYes Then
        ' Handle the Yes button here.
    Else
        ' Handle No button here.
    End If
End Sub
```

MsgConversationID

Property

The MsgConversationID property represents the ID of all messages in a thread starting with the indexed message. That is, all messages in a thread have the same value in their MsgConversationID property. A *thread* comprises a message and all the replies associated with the message.

Objects with a MsgConversationID Property

MAPIMessages

Syntax

```
value = MAPIMessages.MsgConversationID
```

- *MAPIMessages* — A reference to a MAPIMessages control.
- *value* — The variable that will receive the property's current value.

Example

In this example, the program retrieves the message conversation ID for the currently indexed message. The mpmMAPIMessages1 object is a MAPIMessages control that the programmer added to the application's form at design time.

```
Dim strConvID As String
strConvID = mpmMAPIMessages1.MsgConversationID
```

CROSS-REFERENCE
See also MAPIMessages, MsgCount, MsgDateReceived, MsgID, MsgIndex, MsgNoteText, MsgOrigAddress, MsgOrigDisplayName, MsgRead, MsgReceiptRequested, MsgSent, MsgSubject, and MsgType.

MsgCount

Property

The MsgCount property represents the number of messages in the current MAPIMessages message series.

Objects with a MsgCount Property

MAPIMessages

Syntax

```
value = MAPIMessages.MsgCount
```

- *MAPIMessages* — A reference to a MAPIMessages control.
- *value* — The variable that will receive the property's current value.

Example

In this example, the program retrieves the message count for a MAPIMessages control's current message series. The mpmMAPIMessages1 object is a MAPIMessages control that the programmer added to the application's form at design time.

```
Dim lngMsgCount As Long
lngMsgCount = mpmMAPIMessages1.MsgCount
```

CROSS-REFERENCE

See also MAPIMessages, MsgConversationID, MsgDateReceived, MsgID, MsgIndex, MsgNoteText, MsgOrigAddress, MsgOrigDisplayName, MsgRead, MsgReceiptRequested, MsgSent, MsgSubject, and MsgType.

MsgDateReceived

Property

The `MsgDateReceived` property represents the date on which the current message was received. The `MsgIndex` property determines the current message.

Objects with a MsgDateReceived Property

MAPIMessages

Syntax

value = MAPIMessages.MsgDateReceived

- *MAPIMessages* — A reference to a MAPIMessages control.
- *value* — The variable that will receive the property's current value.

Example

In this example, the program retrieves the date of a MAPIMessages control's current message. The `mpmMAPIMessages1` object is a MAPIMessages control that the programmer added to the application's form at design time.

```
Dim strMsgDate As String
strMsgDate = mpmMAPIMessages1.MsgDateReceived
```

CROSS-REFERENCE

See also MAPIMessages, MsgConversationID, MsgCount, MsgID, MsgIndex, MsgNoteText, MsgOrigAddress, MsgOrigDisplayName, MsgRead, MsgReceiptRequested, MsgSent, MsgSubject, and MsgType.

MsgID

Property

The `MsgID` property represents the current message's string ID. The `MsgIndex` property determines the current message.

Objects with a MsgID Property

MAPIMessages

Syntax

`value = MAPIMessages.MsgID`

- *MAPIMessages* — A reference to a MAPIMessages control.
- *value* — The variable that will receive the property's current value.

Example

In this example, the program retrieves the string ID of a MAPIMessages control's current message. The `mpmMAPIMessages1` object is a MAPIMessages control that the programmer added to the application's form at design time.

```
Dim strID As String
strID = mpmMAPIMessages1.MsgID
```

 CROSS-REFERENCE
See also MAPIMessages, MsgConversationID, MsgCount, MsgDateReceived, MsgIndex, MsgNoteText, MsgOrigAddress, MsgOrigDisplayName, MsgRead, MsgReceiptRequested, MsgSent, MsgSubject, and MsgType.

MsgIndex

Property

The `MsgIndex` property represents the index of the current message in a MAPIMessages control.

Objects with a MsgIndex Property

MAPIMessages

Syntax

```
MAPIMessages.MsgIndex = value1
```

or

```
value2 = MAPIMessages.MsgIndex
```

- *MAPIMessages* — A reference to a MAPIMessages control.
- *value1* — The index to set.
- *value2* — The variable that will receive the property's current value.

Example

In this example, the program retrieves the index of a MAPIMessages control's current message. The `mpmMAPIMessages1` object is a MAPIMessages control that the programmer added to the application's form at design time.

```
Dim msgIndx As Long
msgIndx = mpmMAPIMessages1.MsgIndex
```

CROSS-REFERENCE

See also MAPIMessages, MsgConversationID, MsgCount, MsgDateReceived, MsgID, MsgNoteText, MsgOrigAddress, MsgOrigDisplayName, MsgRead, MsgReceiptRequested, MsgSent, MsgSubject, and MsgType.

MsgNoteText

Property

The `MsgNoteText` property represents the text of the current message in a MAPIMessages control.

Objects with a MsgNoteText Property

MAPIMessages

Syntax

```
value = MAPIMessages.MsgNoteText
```

- *MAPIMessages* — A reference to a MAPIMessages control.
- *value* — The variable that will receive the message text.

Example

In this example, the program retrieves the text of a MAPIMessages control's current message. The `mpmMAPIMessages1` object is a MAPIMessages control that the programmer added to the application's form at design time.

```
Dim msgText As String
msgText = mpmMAPIMessages1.MsgNoteText
```

CROSS-REFERENCE
See also MAPIMessages, MsgConversationID, MsgCount, MsgDateReceived, MsgID, MsgIndex, MsgOrigAddress, MsgOrigDisplayName, MsgRead, MsgReceiptRequested, MsgSent, MsgSubject, and MsgType.

MsgOrigAddress

Property

The `MsgOrigAddress` property represents the email address of the author of the current message in a MAPIMessages control.

Objects with a MsgOrigAddress Property

MAPIMessages

Syntax

```
value = MAPIMessages.MsgOrigAddress
```

- *MAPIMessages* — A reference to a MAPIMessages control.
- *value* — The variable that will receive the email address.

Example

In this example, the program retrieves the email address of the current message's originator. The `mpmMAPIMessages1` object is a MAPIMessages control that the programmer added to the application's form at design time.

```
Dim msgAddr As String
msgAddr = mpmMAPIMessages1.MsgOrigAddress
```

CROSS-REFERENCE
See also MAPIMessages, MsgConversationID, MsgCount, MsgDateReceived, MsgID, MsgIndex, MsgNoteText, MsgOrigDisplayName, MsgRead, MsgReceiptRequested, MsgSent, MsgSubject, and MsgType.

MsgOrigDisplayName

Property

The `MsgOrigDisplayName` property represents the name of the author of the current message in a MAPIMessages control.

Objects with a MsgOrigDisplayName Property

MAPIMessages

Syntax

`value = MAPIMessages.MsgOrigDisplayName`

- *MAPIMessages* — A reference to a MAPIMessages control.
- *value* — The variable that will receive the author's name.

Example

In this example, the program retrieves the name of the current message's originator. The `mpmMAPIMessages1` object is a MAPIMessages control that the programmer added to the application's form at design time.

```
Dim msgName As String
msgName = mpmMAPIMessages1.MsgOrigDisplayName
```

 CROSS-REFERENCE
See also MAPIMessages, MsgConversationID, MsgCount, MsgDateReceived, MsgID, MsgIndex, MsgNoteText, MsgOrigAddress, MsgRead, MsgReceiptRequested, MsgSent, MsgSubject, and MsgType.

MsgRead

Property

The `MsgRead` property represents whether the current message in a MAPIMessages control has been read.

Objects with a MsgRead Property

MAPIMessages

Syntax

```
value = MAPIMessages.MsgRead
```

- *MAPIMessages* — A reference to a MAPIMessages control.
- *value* — The variable that will receive the property's setting.

Example

In this example, the program retrieves the status of the current message. The `mpmMAPIMessages1` object is a MAPIMessages control that the programmer added to the application's form at design time.

```
Dim msgReadStatus As Boolean
msgReadStatus = mpmMAPIMessages1.MsgRead
```

 CROSS-REFERENCE
See also MAPIMessages, MsgConversationID, MsgCount, MsgDateReceived, MsgID, MsgIndex, MsgNoteText, MsgOrigAddress, MsgOrigDisplayName, MsgReceiptRequested, MsgSent, MsgSubject, and MsgType.

MsgReceiptRequested

Property

The `MsgReceiptRequested` property represents whether the current message in a MAPIMessages control requires a return receipt.

Objects with a MsgReceiptRequested Property

MAPIMessages

Syntax

```
value = MAPIMessages.MsgReceiptRequested
```

- *MAPIMessages* — A reference to a MAPIMessages control.
- *value* — The variable that will receive the property's setting.

Example

In this example, the program determines whether the current message requires a return receipt. The `mpmMAPIMessages1` object is a MAPIMessages control that the programmer added to the application's form at design time.

```
Dim msgReceipt As Boolean
msgReceipt = mpmMAPIMessages1.MsgReceiptRequested
```

 CROSS-REFERENCE
See also MAPIMessages, MsgConversationID, MsgCount, MsgDateReceived, MsgID, MsgIndex, MsgNoteText, MsgOrigAddress, MsgOrigDisplayName, MsgRead, MsgSent, MsgSubject, and MsgType.

MsgSent

Property

The `MsgSent` property represents whether the current message in a MAPIMessages control has been sent.

Objects with a MsgSent Property

MAPIMessages

Syntax

value = MAPIMessages.MsgSent

- *MAPIMessages* — A reference to a MAPIMessages control.
- *value* — The variable that will receive the property's setting.

Example

In this example, the program retrieves the send status of the current message. The mpmMAPIMessages1 object is a MAPIMessages control that the programmer added to the application's form at design time.

```
Dim msgSendStatus As Boolean
msgSendStatus = mpmMAPIMessages1.MsgSent
```

 CROSS-REFERENCE
See also MAPIMessages, MsgConversationID, MsgCount, MsgDateReceived, MsgID, MsgIndex, MsgNoteText, MsgOrigAddress, MsgOrigDisplayName, MsgReceiptRequested, MsgRead, MsgSubject, and MsgType.

MsgSubject

Property

The `MsgSubject` property represents the subject text for the current message in a MAPIMessages control.

Objects with a MsgSubject Property

MAPIMessages

Syntax

```
value = MAPIMessages.MsgSubject
```

- *MAPIMessages* — A reference to a MAPIMessages control.
- *value* — The variable that will receive the property's setting.

Example

In this example, the program retrieves the current message's subject text. The `mpmMAPIMessages1` object is a MAPIMessages control that the programmer added to the application's form at design time.

```
Dim msgSubjectText As String
msgSubjectText = mpmMAPIMessages1.MsgSubject
```

CROSS-REFERENCE
See also MAPIMessages, MsgConversationID, MsgCount, MsgDateReceived, MsgID, MsgIndex, MsgNoteText, MsgOrigAddress, MsgOrigDisplayName, MsgRead, MsgSent, MsgReceiptRequested, and MsgType.

MsgType

Property

The `MsgType` property represents the message type for the current message in a MAPIMessages control.

Objects with a MsgType Property

MAPIMessages

Syntax

```
value = MAPIMessages.MsgType
```

- *MAPIMessages* — A reference to a MAPIMessages control.
- *value* — The variable that will receive the property's setting.

Example

In this example, the program retrieves the current message's type. The `mpmMAPIMessages1` object is a MAPIMessages control that the programmer added to the application's form at design time.

```
Dim strMsgType As String
strMsgType = mpmMAPIMessages1.MsgType
```

CROSS-REFERENCE
See also MAPIMessages, MsgConversationID, MsgCount, MsgDateReceived, MsgID, MsgIndex, MsgNoteText, MsgOrigAddress, MsgOrigDisplayName, MsgRead, MsgSent, MsgReceiptRequested, and MsgSubject.

MultiLine

Property

The `MultiLine` property represents whether a control can display multiple lines of text (Figure M-18) rather than just a single line. This property, which is read-only at runtime, has a default setting of `False`.

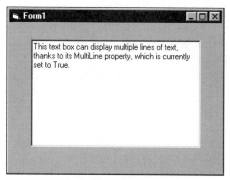

Figure M-18 Simple TextBox controls are capable of displaying multiple lines of text.

Objects with a MultiLine Property

RichTextBox

TextBox

Syntax

```
value = object.MultiLine
```

- *object* — A reference to a RichTextBox or TextBox control.
- *value* — The variable that will receive the property's current setting.

Example

The following lines get the current setting of a TextBox control's `MultiLine` property. The `txtTextBox1` object is a TextBox control that the programmer added to the application's form at design time.

```
Dim multiLineText As Boolean
multiLineText = txtTextbox1.MultiLine
```

CROSS-REFERENCE
See also RichTextBox and TextBox.

Multimedia MCI

Control

A Multimedia control manages multimedia devices, such as CD players, video discs, VCRs, and more. Figure M-19 shows a Multimedia MCI control in a form. Notice that the control looks similar to the controls you might have on a piece of electronic equipment, enabling the user to perform such functions as play, rewind, pause, and fast forward. Use the Components property sheet to add the Multimedia MCI control to your project's toolbox, as shown in Figure M-20.

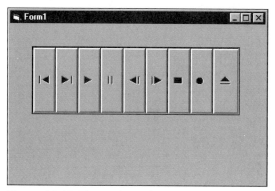

Figure M-19 The Multimedia MCI control resembles the mechanical buttons you might see on a device like a CD player.

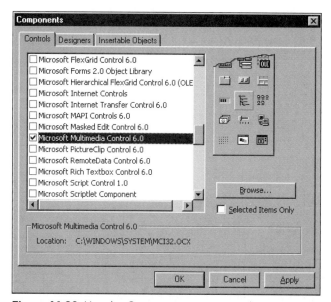

Figure M-20 Use the Components property sheet to add the Multimedia MCI control to your Visual Basic project.

Properties

The Multimedia MCI control has 78 properties, which are listed as follows. Because many Visual Basic controls have similar properties, the properties' descriptions are listed under their own names, provided alphabetically in this book.

```
AutoEnable
BackEnable
BackVisible
BorderStyle
CanEject
CanPlay
CanRecord
CanStep
CausesValidation
Command
Container
DeviceID
DeviceType
DragIcon
DragMode
EjectEnabled
EjectVisible
Enabled
Error
ErrorMessage
FileName
Frames
From
Height
HelpContextID
hWnd
hWndDisplay
Index
Left
Length
Mode
MouseIcon
MousePointer
Name
NextEnabled
NextVisible
Notify
NotifyMessage
NotifyValue
Object
OLEDropMode
Orientation
Parent
```

```
PauseEnabled
PauseVisible
PlayEnabled
PlayVisible
Position
PrevEnabled
PrevVisible
Picture
RecordEnabled
RecordMode
RecordVisible
Sharable
Silent
Start
StepEnabled
StepVisible
StopEnabled
StopVisible
TabIndex
TabStop
Tag
TimeFormat
To
ToolTipText
Top
Track
TrackLength
TrackPosition
Tracks
UpdateInterval
UsesWindows
Visible
Wait
WhatsThisHelpID
Width
```

Methods

The Multimedia MCI control has seven methods, which are listed below. Because many Visual Basic controls have similar methods, the methods' descriptions are listed under their own names, provided alphabetically in this book.

```
Drag
Move
OLEDrag
Refresh
SetFocus
ShowWhatsThis
ZOrder
```

Events

The Multimedia MCI control responds to 49 events, which are listed below. Because many Visual Basic controls respond to similar events, the events' descriptions are listed under their own names, provided alphabetically in this book.

```
BackClick
BackCompleted
BackGotFocus
BackLostFocus
Done
DragDrop
DragOver
EjectClick
EjectCompleted
EjectGotFocus
EjectLostFocus
GotFocus
LostFocus
NextClick
NextCompleted
NextGotFocus
NextLostFocus
OLECompleteDrag
OLEDragDrop
OLEDragOver
OLEGiveFeedback
OLESetData
OLEStartDrag
PauseClick
PauseCompleted
PauseGotFocus
PauseLostFocus
PlayClick
PlayCompleted
PlayGotFocus
```

```
PlayLostFocus
PrevClick
PrevCompleted
PrevGotFocus
PrevLostFocus
RecordClick
RecordCompleted
RecordGotFocus
RecordLostFocus
StatusUpdate
StepClick
StepCompleted
StepGotFocus
StepLostFocus
StopClick
StopCompleted
StopGotFocus
StopLostFocus
Validate
```

The Multimedia MCI control's most commonly used events are probably the click events for each of the buttons. For example, the control generates a PlayClick event when the user clicks the Play button with the mouse. A program responds to the button's click event in the appropriate event procedure. The Play button, for example, on a control named mciMultimedia1 will have a PlayClick event procedure called mciMultimedia1_PlayClick, which is where the program should handle the event, as follows:

```
Private Sub MMControl1_PlayClick(Cancel As Integer)
    ' Handle the PlayClick event here.
End Sub
```

Here, this event procedure's single argument determines whether the Multimedia MCI control performs its default function for the button. Specifically, if the procedure sets Cancel to True, the control will not perform the default function.

MultiRow

Property

The MultiRow property represents whether a TabStrip control can display multiple rows of tabs. Figure M-21 shows a multirow TabStrip control.

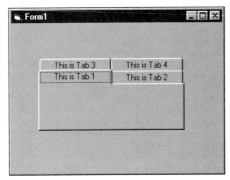

Figure M-21 This TabStrip control sports two rows of tabs.

Objects with a MultiRow Property

TabStrip

Syntax

```
TabStrip.MultiRow = value1
```

or

```
value2 = TabStrip.MultiRow
```

- *TabStrip*—A reference to a TabStrip control.
- *value1*—The value True or False. False is the default.
- *value2*—The variable that will receive the property's current setting.

Example

The following line sets a TabStrip control's MultiRow property so that the control can display more than one row of tabs. The tabTabStrip1 object is a TabStrip control that the programmer added to the application's form at design time.

```
tabTabStrip1.MultiRow = True
```

 **CROSS-REFERENCE**
See also TabStrip.

MultiSelect — FileListBox and ListBox

Property

The MultiSelect property represents whether the user can select multiple items in a control. Figure M-22, for example, shows a ListBox control in which the user has selected several items. The MultiSelect property is read-only at runtime.

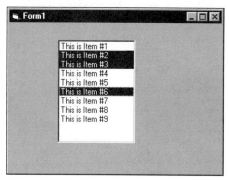

Figure M-22 A ListBox is one type of control that can manage multiple selections.

Syntax

value = *object*.MultiSelect

- *object* — A reference to a ListBox or FileListBox control.
- *value* — The variable that will receive the property's current setting.

Example

The following lines get the multiselect status for a ListBox control and display the result in a message box. The lstList1 object is a ListBox control that the programmer added to the application's form at design time.

```
Dim multiSelectStatus As Integer
multiSelectStatus = lstList1.MultiSelect
If multiSelectStatus = 0 Then
    MsgBox "No multiple selection"
ElseIf multiSelectStatus = 1 Then
    MsgBox "Simple multiple selection"
ElseIf multiSelectStatus = 2 Then
    MsgBox "Extended multiple selection"
End If
```

CROSS-REFERENCE
See also ListBox, FileListBox, and Selected.

MultiSelect — ListView and TabStrip

Property

The MultiSelect property represents whether the user can select multiple items in a control. Figure M-23, for example, shows a ListView control in which the user has selected several items. The MultiSelect property can be set to True or False.

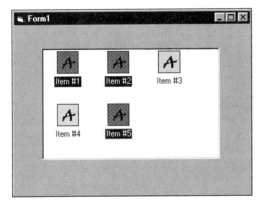

Figure M-23 A ListView control can manage multiple selections.

Syntax

```
object.MultiSelect = value1
```

or

```
value2 = object.MultiSelect
```

- *object* — A reference to a ListView or TabStrip control.
- *value1* — The value True or False.
- *value2* — The variable that will receive the property's current setting.

Example

The following lines get the multiselect status for a ListView control and display the result in a message box. The `lvwListView1` object is a ListView control that the programmer added to the application's form at design time.

```
Dim multiSelectStatus As Boolean
multiSelectStatus = lvwListView1.MultiSelect
If multiSelectStatus = False Then
    MsgBox "No multiple selection"
ElseIf multiSelectStatus = True Then
    MsgBox "Multiple selection enabled"
End If
```

CROSS-REFERENCE

See also ListView, TabStrip, and DeselectAll.

l
m
n

Name

Property

The `Name` property represents the name of an object. This name is used in program code to access the object. For example, you can reference the `Caption` property of a CommandButton object named `btnCommand1` with the code `btnCommand1.Caption`. The `Name` property can be set only at design time. That is, the property is read-only at runtime.

Objects with a Name Property

Animation

CheckBox

Class

ComboBox

CommandButton

CommonDialog

CoolBar

DirListBox

DriveListBox

Extender

FileListBox

Font

Form

Frame

HScrollBar

Image

ImageList

Label

Line

ListBox

ListView

MAPIMessages

MAPISession

MDIForm

Menu

OLE Container

OptionButton

PictureBox

ProgressBar

PropertyPage

RichTextBox

Shape

Slider

StatusBar

SysInfo

TabStrip

TextBox

Timer

Toolbar

TreeView

UpDown

UserControl

VScrollBar

Syntax

```
value = object.Name
```

- *object* — A reference to an object with the Name property.
- *value* — The variable that will receive the object's name.

Example

The following lines retrieve the text that was entered into a TextBox control named txtText1. The programmer added the txtText1 control to the form, and named it, at design time.

```
Dim txt as String
txt = txtText1.Text
```

Name

Statement

The Name statement renames a file or folder. The Name statement can also be used to move a file.

Syntax

```
Name oldName As newName
```

- *newName* — The file or folder's new name.
- *oldName* — The file or folder's old name.

Example 1

The following line renames the MyFile.dat file to MyNewFile.dat.

```
Name "c:\MyFile.dat" As "c:\MyNewFile.dat"
```

Example 2

Here, the example moves the MyFile.dat file from the root of drive C to the Temp folder on drive D.

```
Name "c:\MyFile.dat" As "d:\Temp\MyFile.dat"
```

 CROSS-REFERENCE
See also Kill.

Name — File and Folder

Property

The Name property represents the name of a file or folder. Changing the Name property changes the name of the disk file or folder.

Objects with a Name Property

File
Folder

Syntax

```
object.Name = value1
```

or

```
value2 = object.Name
```

- *object* — A reference to a File or Folder object.
- *value1* — A string containing the new file or folder name.
- *value2* — The variable that will receive the file or folder name.

Example 1

The following lines create a File object and copy the file's name into a string variable named fileName.

```
Dim fileSystem, file As Object
Dim fileName As String
Set fileSystem = CreateObject("Scripting.FileSystemObject")
Set file = fileSystem.GetFile("c:\MyFile.dat")
fileName = file.Name
```

Example 2

Here, the following lines create a File object and change the file's name to MyNewFile.dat.

```
Dim fileSystem, file As Object
Set fileSystem = CreateObject("Scripting.FileSystemObject")
Set file = fileSystem.GetFile("c:\MyFile.dat")
file.Name = "MyNewFile.dat"
```

CROSS-REFERENCE
See also FileSystemObject, File, ShortName, and ShortPath.

Negotiate

Property

The Negotiate property represents whether a control with an Align property is visible when an active object on an MDI child form displays a toolbar. For this property to have an effect, the MDIForm's NegotiateToolbars property must be set to True and the control's Align property must be set to a nonzero value. This property can be set only at design time.

Objects with a Negotiate Property

CoolBar

Extender

PictureBox

ProgressBar

StatusBar

Toolbar

Syntax

This property cannot be accessed at runtime.

Example

Figure N-1 shows a CoolBar control's `Negotiate` property in the control's Properties window, which is where the `Negotiate` property must be set.

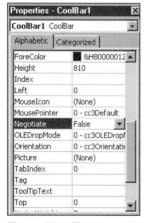

Figure N-1 The Negotiate property must be set at design time.

CROSS-REFERENCE
See also MDIForm, NegotiateToolbars, and Align.

NegotiateMenus

Property

The NegotiateMenus property represents whether a form's menu bar will display an active object's menu bar when that object is selected for editing.

Objects with a NegotiateMenus Property

Form

Syntax

This property is not accessible at runtime.

Example

Figure N-2 shows a Form object's NegotiateMenus property in the object's Properties window, which is where the NegotiateMenus property must be set.

Figure N-2 The NegotiateMenus property must be set at design time.

CROSS-REFERENCE
See also NegotiatePosition.

NegotiatePosition

Property

The `NegotiatePosition` property represents whether a Form's menu will appear in the menu bar when an embedded object's menu bar is being displayed.

Objects with a NegotiatePosition Property

Menu

Syntax

This property is not accessible at runtime.

Example

Figure N-3 shows a Menu object's `NegotiatePosition` property in the menu editor, which is where the `NegotiateMenus` property must be set.

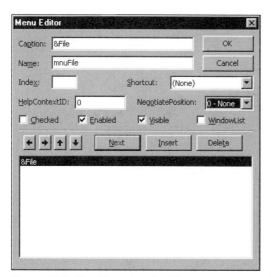

Figure N-3 The NegotiatePosition property must be set at design time using the menu editor.

CROSS-REFERENCE
See also NegotiateMenus.

NegotiateToolbars

Property

The `NegotiateToolbars` property represents whether an active embedded object can display its toolbars in an MDIForm window.

Objects with a NegotiateToolbars Property

MDIForm

Syntax

This property cannot be accessed at runtime.

Example

Figure N-4 shows a MDIForm object's `NegotiateToolbars` property in the object's Properties window, which is where the `NegotiateToolbars` property must be set.

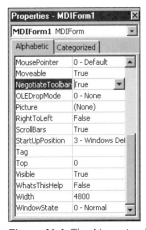

Figure N-4 The NegotiateToolbars property must be set at design time.

CROSS-REFERENCE
See also MDIForm, Negotiate, and Align.

New

Keyword

The New keyword is used to create objects, setting the object's name and allocating storage for the object. The New keyword can be used in the context of a variable declaration and as part of a Set assignment statement. The following example declares an instance of the MyObject object. Note that the New keyword cannot be used to create instances of basic data types, such as Integer, Boolean, String, and so on.

```
Dim objInstance As New MyObject
```

 CROSS-REFERENCE
See also Dim, Private, Public, Set, and Static.

NewIndex

Property

The NewIndex property represents the index of the last item added to a control. This property is useful in a control with a sorted list, because the program may not know ahead of time where the item will end up in the list.

Objects with a NewIndex Property

ComboBox

ListBox

Syntax

value = control.NewIndex

- *control*—A reference to a ComboBox or ListBox control.
- *value*—The variable that will receive the property's current setting.

Example

The following lines add an item to a ListBox control and then retrieve that new item's index. The lstList1 object is a ListBox control that the programmer added to the form at design time.

```
Dim nwIndex As Integer
lstList1.AddItem "Test Item"
```

```
nwIndex = lstList1.NewIndex
```

CROSS-REFERENCE

For more information, see ComboBox, ListBox, List, ListCount, and AddItem.

NewPage

Method

The `NewPage` method ends the current page, sends a form feed to the printer associated with the Printer object, and advances the Printer object's `Page` property by 1.

Objects with a NewPage Method

Printer

Syntax

```
Printer.NewPage
```

- *Printer*—A reference to the Printer object.

Example

The following line starts a new page on the current printer. Note that the Printer object is a global Visual Basic object that you don't need to create explicitly in your programs.

```
Printer.NewPage
```

CROSS-REFERENCE

See also Printer.

NewRow

Property

The `NewRow` property represents whether a band in a CoolBar control will be displayed on a new row of bands.

Objects with a NewRow Property

Band

Syntax

```
Band.NewRow = value1
```

or

```
value2 = Band.NewRow
```

- *Band*—A reference to a Band object.
- *value1*—The value `True` or `False`. The default is `False`.
- *value2*—The variable that will receive the property's current setting.

Example

The following sample program gives you a chance to see the `NewRow` property in action. When you run the program, you see the window shown in Figure N-5. Notice how the CoolBar control has three bands in two rows. Click the Toggle NewRow Property button, and the program sets the third band's `NewRow` property to `True`. This action causes the band to begin a row of its own, as shown in Figure N-6.

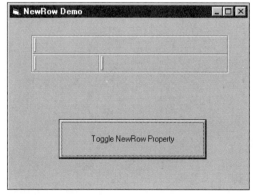

Figure N-5 When the NewRow program runs, the CoolBar's third band is at the end of the second row.

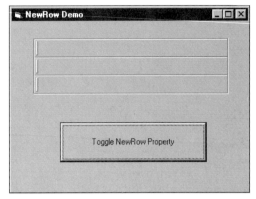

Figure N-6 After the program changes the NewRow property to True, the CoolBar's third band starts a third row.

```
VERSION 5.00
Object = "{38911DA0-E448-11D0-84A3-00DD01104159} _
    #1.1#0"; "COMCT332.OCX"
Begin VB.Form Form1
    Caption         =   "NewRow Demo"
    ClientHeight    =   3630
    ClientLeft      =   165
    ClientTop       =   450
    ClientWidth     =   5235
    LinkTopic       =   "Form1"
    ScaleHeight     =   3630
    ScaleWidth      =   5235
    StartUpPosition =   3   'Windows Default
    Begin ComCtl3.CoolBar CoolBar1
        Height      =   810
        Left        =   480
        TabIndex    =   1
        Top         =   360
        Width       =   4335
        _ExtentX    =   7646
        _ExtentY    =   1429
        _CBWidth    =   4335
        _CBHeight   =   810
        _Version    =   "6.0.8141"
        MinHeight1  =   360
        Width1      =   2880
        NewRow1     =   0   'False
        MinHeight2  =   360
```

```
        Width2          =    1440
        NewRow2         =    -1   'True
        MinHeight3      =    360
        Width3          =    1440
        NewRow3         =    0    'False
     End
     Begin VB.CommandButton btnToggleRow
        Caption         =    "Toggle NewRow Property"
        Height          =    855
        Left            =    1080
        TabIndex        =    0
        Top             =    2160
        Width           =    3255
     End
  End
End
Attribute VB_Name = "Form1"
Attribute VB_GlobalNameSpace = False
Attribute VB_Creatable = False
Attribute VB_PredeclaredId = True
Attribute VB_Exposed = False

Private Sub btnToggleRow_Click()
    Dim nwRow As Boolean
    nwRow = CoolBar1.Bands(3).NewRow
    If nwRow Then
        CoolBar1.Bands(3).NewRow = False
    Else
        CoolBar1.Bands(3).NewRow = True
    End If
End Sub
```

CROSS-REFERENCE
For more information, see CoolBar and Band.

NewSession

Property

The NewSession property represents whether a MAPISession object creates a new session, even if there's already an active session, or uses the currently active session.

Objects with a NewSession Property
MAPISession

Syntax

```
MAPISession.NewSession = value1
```

or

```
value2 = MAPISession.NewSession
```

- *MAPISession* — A reference to a MAPISession control.
- *value1* — The value `True` or `False`. The default is `False`.
- *value2* — The variable that will receive the property's current setting.

Example

The following line instructs a MAPISession object to start a new session. The `mpsMAPISession1` object is a MAPISession control that the programmer added to the form at design time.

```
mpsMAPISession1.NewSession = True
```

CROSS-REFERENCE
See also MAPISession and MAPIMessages.

Next

Keyword

The `Next` keyword is part of the `For/Next`, `For Each`, `On Error`, and `Resume` statements. For example, the following lines add the numbers 1 through 10 using a For/Next loop.

```
Dim x, sum As Integer
sum = 0
For x = 1 To 10
    sum = sum + x
Next x
```

CROSS-REFERENCE
For more information, see For/Next, For Each, On Error, and Resume.

Next

Property

The Next property represents the next sibling node in a TreeView control.

Objects with a Next Property

Node

Syntax

```
value = Node.Next
```

- *Node* — A reference to a Node object.
- *value* — The variable that will receive the node reference.

Example

The following program demonstrates how the Next property works. When you run the program, you see the main window, which holds TreeView, CommandButton, and TextBox controls. Select a node in the TreeView control, and then click the Next Node button. When you do, the name of the current node's next sibling appears in the TextBox control (see Figure N-7). If the currently selected node has no next sibling, the text box displays the message "No next sibling."

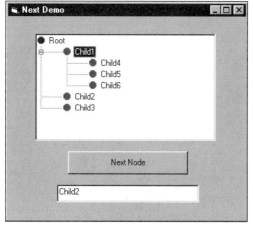

Figure N-7 Here the user has retrieved the name of the Child1 node's next sibling.

```
VERSION 5.00
Object = "{6B7E6392-850A-101B-AFC0-4210102A8DA7} _
    #2.0#0"; "MSCOMCTL.OCX"
Begin VB.Form Form1
   Caption         =   "Next Demo"
   ClientHeight    =   4335
   ClientLeft      =   165
   ClientTop       =   450
   ClientWidth     =   5235
   LinkTopic       =   "Form1"
   ScaleHeight     =   4335
   ScaleWidth      =   5235
   StartUpPosition =   3  'Windows Default
   Begin VB.TextBox txtNextSibling
      Height       =   375
      Left         =   1080
      TabIndex     =   2
      Top          =   3600
      Width        =   3135
   End
   Begin VB.CommandButton btnNextNode
      Caption      =   "Next Node"
      Height       =   495
      Left         =   1320
      TabIndex     =   1
      Top          =   2880
      Width        =   2655
   End
   Begin MSComctlLib.ImageList ilsImageList1
      Left         =   3600
      Top          =   1920
      _ExtentX     =   1005
      _ExtentY     =   1005
      BackColor    =   -2147483643
      MaskColor    =   12632256
      _Version     =   393216
   End
   Begin MSComctlLib.TreeView treTreeView1
      Height       =   2295
      Left         =   600
      TabIndex     =   0
      Top          =   360
      Width        =   3975
      _ExtentX     =   7011
      _ExtentY     =   4048
```

```
        _Version        =    393217
        Style           =    7
        Appearance      =    1
    End
End
Attribute VB_Name = "Form1"
Attribute VB_GlobalNameSpace = False
Attribute VB_Creatable = False
Attribute VB_PredeclaredId = True
Attribute VB_Exposed = False

Private Sub btnNextNode_Click()
    Dim curNode As Node
    Dim nextNode As Node
    Set curNode = treTreeView1.SelectedItem
    Set nextNode = curNode.Next

    On Error GoTo ErrorHandler
    txtNextSibling.Text = nextNode.Text
    Exit Sub

ErrorHandler:
    txtNextSibling.Text = "No next sibling."
End Sub

Private Sub Form_Load()
    ilsImageList1.ListImages.Add , , _
        LoadPicture("circle1.bmp")
    ilsImageList1.ListImages.Add , , _
        LoadPicture("circle2.bmp")

    treTreeView1.ImageList = ilsImageList1

    With treTreeView1.Nodes
        .Add , , "Root", "Root", 1
        .Add "Root", tvwChild, "Child1", "Child1", 2
        .Add "Root", tvwChild, "Child2", "Child2", 2
        .Add "Root", tvwChild, "Child3", "Child3", 2
        .Add "Child1", tvwChild, "Child4", "Child4", 2
        .Add "Child1", tvwChild, "Child5", "Child5", 2
        .Add "Child1", tvwChild, "Child6", "Child6", 2
    End With

    treTreeView1.Nodes(5).EnsureVisible
End Sub
```

CROSS-REFERENCE
See also Node, Child, FirstSibling, LastSibling, Previous, Parent, and Root.

NextClick

Event

Visual Basic sends a Multimedia MCI control a `NextClick` event when the user clicks the control's Next button. By responding to this event, a program can stop the default action of the Next button from occurring.

Objects with a NextClick Event

Multimedia MCI

Example

A program can respond to a `NextClick` event by implementing the Multimedia MCI control's `NextClick` event procedure. By setting the procedure's `Cancel` parameter to `True`, the program can halt the Next button's default action.

```
Private Sub mciMMControl1_NextClick(Cancel As Integer)
    If something Then Cancel = True
End Sub
```

CROSS-REFERENCE
For more information, see NextCompleted and Multimedia MCI.

NextCompleted

Event

Visual Basic sends a Multimedia MCI control a `NextCompleted` event after the Next button's action has been executed. By responding to this event, a program can determine whether any errors occurred.

Objects with a NextCompleted Event

Multimedia MCI

Example

A program can respond to a `NextCompleted` event by implementing the Multimedia MCI control's `NextCompleted` event procedure, which receives an error value as its single parameter.

```
Private Sub mciMMControl1_NextCompleted(Errorcode As Long)
    ' Handle the event here.
End Sub
```

 CROSS-REFERENCE
For more information, see NextClick and Multimedia MCI.

NextEnabled

Property

The `NextEnabled` property represents the enabled status of a Multimedia MCI control's Next button. This property is `True` when the control's Next button is enabled and is `False` when the button is disabled.

Objects with a NextEnabled Property

Multimedia MCI

Syntax

```
Multimedia.NextEnabled = value1
```

or

```
value2 = Multimedia.NextEnabled
```

- *Multimedia* — A reference to a Multimedia MCI control.
- *value1* — The value `True` or `False`.
- *value2* — The variable that will receive the value returned by the property.

Example

The following lines show how to get and set the enabled status of a Multimedia control's Next button. The `mciMMControl` object is a Multimedia MCI control that the programmer added to the form at design time.

```
Dim enable
enable = mciMMControl1.NextEnabled
mciMMControl1.NextEnabled = True
```

 CROSS-REFERENCE
See also Multimedia MCI.

NextGotFocus

Event

Visual Basic sends a Multimedia MCI control a `NextGotFocus` event when the control's Next button receives the focus.

Objects with a NextGotFocus Event

Multimedia MCI

Example

A program can respond to a `NextGotFocus` event by implementing the Multimedia MCI control's `NextGotFocus` event procedure, which receives no parameters, as shown here.

```
Private Sub mciMMControl1_NextGotFocus()
    ' Handle the NextGotFocus event here.
End Sub
```

 CROSS-REFERENCE
For more information, see NextLostFocus and Multimedia MCI.

NextLostFocus

Event

Visual Basic sends a Multimedia MCI control a `NextLostFocus` event when the control's Next button loses the focus.

Objects with a NextLostFocus Event

Multimedia MCI

Example

A program can respond to a `NextLostFocus` event by implementing the Multimedia MCI control's `NextLostFocus` event procedure, which receives no parameters, as shown here.

```
Private Sub mciMMControl1_NextLostFocus()
    ' Handle the event here.
End Sub
```

 CROSS-REFERENCE
For more information, see NextGotFocus and Multimedia MCI.

NextVisible

Property

The `NextVisible` property represents the visible status of a Multimedia MCI control's Next button. This property is `True` when the control's Next button is visible and is `False` when the button is not visible.

Objects with a NextVisible Property

Multimedia MCI

Syntax

Multimedia.NextVisible = *value1*

or

value2 = *Multimedia*.NextVisible

- *Multimedia* — A reference to a Multimedia MCI control.
- *value1* — The value `True` or `False`.
- *value2* — The variable that will receive the value returned by the property.

Example

The following lines show how to get and set the visible status of a Multimedia control's Next button. The `mciMMControl1` object is a Multimedia MCI control that the programmer added to the form at design time.

```
Dim visible
visible = mciMMControl1.NextVisible
mciMMControl1.NextVisible = True
```

 CROSS-REFERENCE
See also Multimedia MCI.

Node

Object

A Node object represents an item in a TreeView control. The *root node* is the node under which the control organizes all the other nodes in the tree. *Child nodes* are arranged under a *parent node* in the tree hierarchy, whereas *sibling nodes* are on the same level of the tree. Figure N-8 illustrates these concepts.

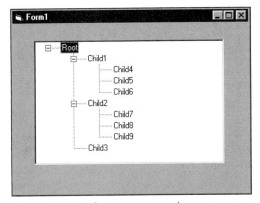

Figure N-8 Nodes in a tree can be root, parent, child, and sibling nodes.

Properties

The Node object has 24 properties. For more information on using a property shown in the following list, look up the individual property's entry, provided alphabetically in this book.

```
BackColor
Bold
Checked
Child
Children
Expanded
```

```
ExpandedImage
FirstSibling
ForeColor
FullPath
Image
Index
Key
LastSibling
Next
Parent
Previous
Root
Selected
SelectedImage
Sorted
Tag
Text
Visible
```

Methods

The Node object has two methods. For more information on using one of the following methods, look up the individual method's entry, provided alphabetically in this book.

```
CreateDragImage
EnsureVisible
```

Events

The Node object does not respond to events.

 CROSS-REFERENCE
For more information, see Nodes and TreeView.

NodeCheck

Event

Visual Basic sends a TreeView control a `NodeCheck` event when the user checks or unchecks a node in the tree. For this event to occur, the TreeView control's `Checkboxes` property must be set to `True`.

Objects with a NodeCheck Event

TreeView

Example

A program can respond to a NodeCheck event by implementing a TreeView control's NodeCheck event procedure. The event procedure's single parameter is a reference to the node that the user checked or unchecked. The following program demonstrates the NodeCheck event. When you run the program, you see a window with TreeView and TextBox controls. Check or uncheck a node in the tree, and the node's name appears in the text box (see Figure N-9), thanks to the NodeCheck event procedure.

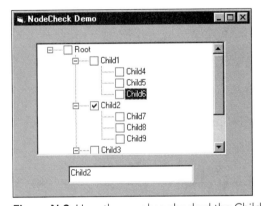

Figure N-9 Here the user has checked the Child2 node.

```
VERSION 5.00
Object = "{6B7E6392-850A-101B-AFC0-4210102A8DA7} _
    #2.0#0"; "MSCOMCTL.OCX"
Begin VB.Form Form1
    Caption         =   "NodeCheck Demo"
    ClientHeight    =   3630
    ClientLeft      =   165
    ClientTop       =   450
    ClientWidth     =   5235
    LinkTopic       =   "Form1"
    ScaleHeight     =   3630
    ScaleWidth      =   5235
    StartUpPosition =   3  'Windows Default
    Begin VB.TextBox txtCheckedNode
        Height          =      375
```

```
        Left            =   1200
        TabIndex        =   1
        Top             =   3000
        Width           =   2775
     End
     Begin MSComctlLib.TreeView treTreeView1
        Height          =   2415
        Left            =   480
        TabIndex        =   0
        Top             =   360
        Width           =   4215
        _ExtentX        =   7435
        _ExtentY        =   4260
        _Version        =   393217
        Style           =   7
        Checkboxes      =   -1   'True
        Appearance      =   1
     End
  End
End
Attribute VB_Name = "Form1"
Attribute VB_GlobalNameSpace = False
Attribute VB_Creatable = False
Attribute VB_PredeclaredId = True
Attribute VB_Exposed = False

Private Sub Form_Load()
    With treTreeView1.Nodes
        .Add , , "Root", "Root"
        .Add "Root", tvwChild, "Child1", "Child1"
        .Add "Root", tvwChild, "Child2", "Child2"
        .Add "Root", tvwChild, "Child3", "Child3"
        .Add "Child1", tvwChild, "Child4", "Child4"
        .Add "Child1", tvwChild, "Child5", "Child5"
        .Add "Child1", tvwChild, "Child6", "Child6"
        .Add "Child2", tvwChild, "Child7", "Child7"
        .Add "Child2", tvwChild, "Child8", "Child8"
        .Add "Child2", tvwChild, "Child9", "Child9"
        .Add "Child3", tvwChild, "Child10", "Child10"
        .Add "Child3", tvwChild, "Child11", "Child11"
        .Add "Child3", tvwChild, "Child12", "Child12"
    End With
    treTreeView1.Nodes(5).EnsureVisible
    treTreeView1.Nodes(8).EnsureVisible
    treTreeView1.Nodes(11).EnsureVisible
```

```
      treTreeView1.LineStyle = tvwRootLines
End Sub

Private Sub treTreeView1_NodeCheck(ByVal Node As
MSComctlLib.Node)
    Dim msg As String
    msg = Node.Text
    txtCheckedNode.Text = msg
End Sub
```

CROSS-REFERENCE
For more information, see Node, NodeClick, and TreeView.

NodeClick

Event

Visual Basic sends a TreeView control a NodeClick event when the user clicks a node in the tree.

Objects with a NodeClick Event

TreeView

Example

A program can respond to a NodeClick event by implementing the TreeView control's NodeClick event procedure. The procedure's single parameter is a reference to the node the user clicked. For example, the following lines display the clicked node's text in a message box. In this case, the treTreeView1 object is a TreeView control that the programmer added to the form at design time.

```
Private Sub treTreeView1_NodeClick _
(ByVal Node As MSComctlLib.Node)
    ' Handle the NodeClick event here.
    Dim msg As String
    msg = Node.Text
    MsgBox msg
End Sub
```

CROSS-REFERENCE
See also Node, TreeView, and NodeCheck.

Nodes

Collection

A Nodes collection holds the Node objects that are associated with the items in a TreeView control.

Properties

A Nodes collection has one property, called `Count`, which represents the number of nodes in the collection.

Methods

The Nodes collection has four methods. For more information on using one of these methods, look up the individual method's entry, provided alphabetically in this book.

```
Add
Clear
Item
Remove
```

 CROSS-REFERENCE
See also Nodes (property), Node, and TreeView.

Nodes

Property

The `Nodes` property represents a reference to a TreeView control's Nodes collection. Each of the TreeView control's Node objects is stored in this collection.

Objects with a Nodes Property

TreeView

Syntax

```
value = TreeView.Nodes
```

- *TreeView* — A reference to a TreeView control.

- *value*—The variable that will receive the Nodes collection reference.

Example

The following lines add nodes to a TreeView control by calling the Nodes collection's `Add` method. The `treTreeView1` object is a TreeView control that the programmer added to the form at design time.

```
With treTreeView1.Nodes
    .Add , , "Root", "Root"
    .Add "Root", tvwChild, "Child1", "Child1"
    .Add "Root", tvwChild, "Child2", "Child2"
    .Add "Root", tvwChild, "Child3", "Child3"
    .Add "Child1", tvwChild, "Child4", "Child4"
    .Add "Child1", tvwChild, "Child5", "Child5"
    .Add "Child1", tvwChild, "Child6", "Child6"
    .Add "Child2", tvwChild, "Child7", "Child7"
    .Add "Child2", tvwChild, "Child8", "Child8"
    .Add "Child2", tvwChild, "Child9", "Child9"
    .Add "Child3", tvwChild, "Child10", "Child10"
    .Add "Child3", tvwChild, "Child11", "Child11"
    .Add "Child3", tvwChild, "Child12", "Child12"
End With
```

CROSS-REFERENCE
See also Nodes (collection), Node, and TreeView.

NonModalAllowed

Property

The `NonModalAllowed` property represents whether a form can be displayed modeless. A *modeless* form enables the user to switch to a different window, whereas a *modal* form must be dismissed before the user can switch to a different window. Dialog boxes and message boxes, for example, are usually modal.

Objects with a NonModalAllowed Property

App

Syntax

```
value = App.NonModalAllowed
```

- *App*—A reference to the App object.
- *value*—The variable that will receive the property's current value, usually `True`.

Example

The following lines get the setting of the `NonModalAllowed` property. Note that the App object is a global Visual Basic object that you don't need to create explicitly in your programs.

```
Dim modeless As Boolean
modeless = App.NonModalAllowed
```

 CROSS-REFERENCE
See also App.

Nothing

Keyword

The `Nothing` keyword kills a variable's reference to an object, leaving the variable holding no reference. For example, the following line disconnects the `objReference` variable from the object it referenced.

```
Set objReference = Nothing
```

 CROSS-REFERENCE
See also Set.

Notify

Property

The `Notify` property represents whether an MCI command executed through a Multimedia MCI control results in a callback, which generates a `Done` event itself. The property affects only the next MCI command executed, being reset after the callback is complete. This property is available only at runtime.

Objects with a Notify Property

Multimedia MCI

Syntax

```
Multimedia.Notify = value1
```

or

```
value2 = Multimedia.Notify
```

- *Multimedia*—A reference to a Multimedia MCI control.
- *value1*—The value True or False.
- *value2*—The variable that will receive the property's current setting.

Example

The following lines open a wave file through a Multimedia MCI control. Because the Notify property is set to False, the open command does not generate a Done event when the command completes. In this example, the mciMMControl1 object is a Multimedia MCI control that the programmer added to the form at design time.

```
mciMMControl1.DeviceType = "WaveAudio"
mciMMControl1.Notify = False
mciMMControl1.Shareable = False
mciMMControl1.Wait = True
mciMMControl1.fileName = fileName
mciMMControl1.Command = "Open"
```

CROSS-REFERENCE
See also Multimedia MCI, Done, NotifyMessage, and NotifyValue.

NotifyMessage

Property

The NotifyMessage property represents the notification string returned with the Done event. This property is available only at runtime, when it is read-only.

Objects with a NotifyMessage Property

Multimedia MCI

Syntax

```
value = Multimedia.NotifyMessage
```

- *Multimedia*—A reference to a Multimedia MCI control.
- *value*—The variable that will receive the property's current setting.

Example

The following lines retrieve the notification message from a Multimedia MCI control. In this example, the mciMMControl1 object is a Multimedia MCI control that the programmer added to the form at design time.

```
Dim msg As String
msg = mciMMControl1.NotifyMessage
```

CROSS-REFERENCE
See also Multimedia MCI, Done, Notify, and NotifyValue.

NotifyValue

Property

The NotifyValue property represents the completion code returned with a notification. This property, which can be set to one of the values in Table N-1, is available only at runtime, when it is read-only.

Table N-1 Values for the NotifyValue Property

Value	Description
mciNotifyAborted	The user aborted the command.
mciNotifyFailure	The MCI command failed to execute.
mciNotifySuccessful	The MCI command executed successfully.
mciNotifySuperseded	The MCI command was superseded by another command.

Objects with a NotifyValue Property

Multimedia MCI

Syntax

```
value = Multimedia.NotifyValue
```

- *Multimedia*—A reference to a Multimedia MCI control.
- *value*—The variable that will receive the property's current setting.

Example

The following lines display a message box that describes the last MCI command's completion code. In this example, the `mciMMControl1` object is a Multimedia MCI control that the programmer added to the form at design time.

```
Dim notCode As Integer
notCode = mciMMControl1.NotifyValue
If notCode = mciNotifySuccessful Then
    MsgBox "Notify Successful"
ElseIf notCode = mciNotifyAborted Then
    MsgBox "Notify Aborted"
ElseIf notCode = mciNotifyFailure Then
    MsgBox "Notify Failure"
ElseIf notCode = mciNotifySuperseded Then
    MsgBox "Notify Superceded"
End If
```

CROSS-REFERENCE
See also Multimedia MCI, Done, Notify, and NotifyMessage.

Now

Function

The Now function returns the current date and time.

Syntax

```
value = Now
```

- *value*—The variable that will receive the date and time string.

Example

The following lines get the current date and time and display them in a message box. Figure N-10 shows the resultant message box.

```
Dim curDate As String
curDate = Now
MsgBox curDate
```

Figure N-10 This message box displays the
value returned by the Now function.

CROSS-REFERENCE
See also Date, Time, Year, Day, Hour, Minute, Second, and Weekday.

NPer

Function

The NPer function returns the number of periods for an annuity.

Syntax

```
value = NPer(intRate, payment, presValue, futValue, payDue)
```

- *futValue* (*) — The desired future value of the annuity. The default is 0.
- *intRate* — The interest rate per period.
- *payDue* (*) — The value 0 if payments are made at the end of the period and 1 if payments are made at the start of the period. The default is 0.
- *payment* — The amount of each period's payment.
- *presValue* — The present value of the annuity.
- *value* — The variable that will receive the number of periods.

(*) = Optional

Example 1

The following lines calculate how many $100 payments are required in order to save $1000 when no interest is applied to the account. After the following lines execute, numPeriods will contain the value 10.

```
Dim numPeriods As Double
numPeriods = NPer(0, -100, 0, 1000, 0)
```

Example 2

The following lines calculate how many $100 payments are required in order to save $1000 when the account gathers interest at 2.5% a month. After the following lines execute, numPeriods will be about 9.04 (rounded to the nearest hundredths).

```
Dim numPeriods As Double
numPeriods = NPer(0.025, -100, 0, 1000, 0)
```

NPV

Function

The NPV function returns an investment's net present value.

Syntax

```
value = NPV(disRate, transactions())
```

- *disRate* — The discount rate per period.
- *transactions()* — An array containing the payment and receipt transactions.
- *value* — The variable that will receive the net present value.

Example

The following lines calculate the net present value for a series of transactions beginning with a $10,000 outlay and including five receipts of $3,000 each. The applied discount rate is 1.5%.

```
Dim transactions(6) As Double
Dim netPV As Double
transactions(0) = -10000
transactions(1) = 3000
transactions(2) = 3000
transactions(3) = 3000
transactions(4) = 3000
transactions(5) = 3000
netPV = NPV(0.015, transactions())
```

Null

Keyword

The `Null` keyword represents the value of a variable that has not yet been assigned a valid value. For example, the following lines check the variable `msg` for a `Null` value.

```
If msg = Null Then
    MsgBox "Value is Null"
End If
```

Number

Property

The `Number` property represents an error-code number.

Objects with a Number Property

Err

Syntax

```
Err.Number = value1
```

or

```
value2 = Err.Number
```

- *Err*—A reference to the Err object.
- *value1*—The error number.
- *value2*—The variable that will receive the error number.

Example

The following lines get the current error number from the Err object. Note that the Err object is a global Visual Basic object that you don't need to create in your programs.

```
Dim errNumber As Integer
errNumber = Err.Number
```

CROSS-REFERENCE
See also Err.

Object

Property

The `Object` property provides access to an object, as well as to the object's properties and methods, for use with OLE automation.

Objects with an Object Property

Animation

CoolBar

ImageList

ListView

MAPIMessages

MAPISession

Multimedia MCI

OLE Container

ProgressBar

RichTextBox

Slider

StatusBar

SysInfo

TabStrip

Toolbar

TreeView

UpDown

Syntax

object.Object

- *object* — A reference to a control with an `Object` property.

Example

The following lines retrieve a reference to a RichTextBox control's object. The `rtfRichTextBox1` object is a RichTextBox control that the programmer added to the form at design time.

```
Dim obj As Object
Set obj = RichTextBox1.object
```

ObjectAcceptFormats

Property

The `ObjectAcceptFormats` property represents a string array that contains the data formats that a linked or embedded object can accept.

Objects with an ObjectAcceptFormats Property

OLE Container

Syntax

value = OLEContainer.ObjectAcceptFormats(index)

- *OLEContainer* — A reference to an OLE Container control.
- *index* — The index of the format to retrieve.
- *value* — The string variable that will receive the format.

Example

The following program demonstrates the `ObjectAcceptFormats` property. When you run the program, a window that contains an OLE container control and two CommandButton controls appears. Click the Insert Object button to display the Insert Object dialog box from which you can select the type of object to embed into the OLE Container control. Then click the Show Formats button to display a message box that shows the data formats that the object can hold. Figure O-1, for example, shows the formats accepted by an embedded Microsoft Word document. If the embedded object reports no formats, or if the object causes an error, a message box appears reporting the problem.

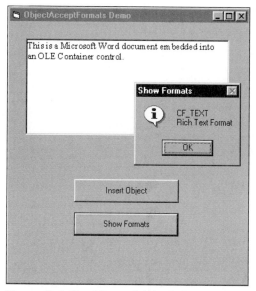

Figure O-1 The Microsoft Word object accepts CF_TEXT and rich-text data.

```
VERSION 5.00
Begin VB.Form Form1
    Caption         =   "ObjectAcceptFormats Demo"
    ClientHeight    =   5565
    ClientLeft      =   165
    ClientTop       =   450
    ClientWidth     =   5235
    LinkTopic       =   "Form1"
    ScaleHeight     =   5565
    ScaleWidth      =   5235
    StartUpPosition =   3   'Windows Default
    Begin VB.CommandButton btnShowFormats
        Caption     =   "Show Formats"
        Height      =   495
        Left        =   1440
        TabIndex    =   1
        Top         =   4080
        Width       =   2295
    End
```

```
        Begin VB.CommandButton btnInsertObject
           Caption         =    "Insert Object"
           Height          =    495
           Left            =    1440
           TabIndex        =    0
           Top             =    3360
           Width           =    2295
        End
        Begin VB.OLE OLE1
           Height          =    2055
           Left            =    360
           TabIndex        =    2
           Top             =    360
           Width           =    4455
        End
     End
Attribute VB_Name = "Form1"
Attribute VB_GlobalNameSpace = False
Attribute VB_Creatable = False
Attribute VB_PredeclaredId = True
Attribute VB_Exposed = False

Private Sub btnInsertObject_Click()
    OLE1.InsertObjDlg
    If OLE1.AppIsRunning Then
        btnShowFormats.Enabled = True
    End If
End Sub

Private Sub btnShowFormats_Click()
    Dim count, index As Integer
    Dim strFormats As String

    On Error GoTo ErrorHandler

    count = OLE1.ObjectAcceptFormatsCount
    If count = 0 Then
        MsgBox "No formats for this object.", _
            vbExclamation, "Show Formats"
    Else
        For index = 0 To count - 1
            strFormats = strFormats & _
                OLE1.ObjectAcceptFormats(index) & vbCrLf
        Next index
```

```
                MsgBox strFormats, vbInformation, "Show Formats"
        End If

        Exit Sub

    ErrorHandler:
        MsgBox "Cannot display formats for this object.", _
            vbExclamation, "Show Formats"
    End Sub

    Private Sub Form_Load()
        btnShowFormats.Enabled = False
    End Sub
```

CROSS-REFERENCE

See also OLE Container, Format, ObjectAcceptFormatsCount, ObjectGetFormats, and ObjectGetFormatsCount.

ObjectAcceptFormatsCount

Property

The `ObjectAcceptFormatsCount` property represents the number of data formats that a linked or embedded object can accept.

Objects with an ObjectAcceptFormatsCount Property

OLE Container

Syntax

`value = OLEContainer.ObjectAcceptFormatsCount`

- *OLEContainer*—A reference to an OLE Container control.
- *value*—The variable that will receive the number of formats.

Example

The following lines get the number of formats accepted by the currently embedded object in an OLE Container control. The `OLE1` object is an OLE Container control that the programmer added to the form at design time.

```
    Dim count As Integer
    count = OLE1.ObjectAcceptFormatsCount
```

CROSS-REFERENCE
See also OLE Container, Format, ObjectAcceptFormats, ObjectGetFormats, and ObjectGetFormatsCount.

ObjectEvent

Event

Visual Basic sends an ObjectEvent event when an object created as a VBControlExtender object generates an event.

Objects That Receive ObjectEvent Events

Extender

Example

A program can respond to an ObjectEvent event by implementing the object's ObjectEvent event procedure. As you can see in the following lines, the procedure's single parameter is an EventInfo object that holds information about the event.

```
Private WithEvents MyObject As VBControlExtender

Private Sub MyObject_ObjectEvent(Info As EventInfo)
    ' Handle the event here.
End Sub
```

ObjectGetFormats

Property

The ObjectGetFormats property represents a string array that contains the data formats that a linked or embedded object can provide.

Objects with an ObjectGetFormats Property

OLE Container

Syntax

```
value = OLEContainer.ObjectGetFormats(index)
```

- *OLEContainer*—A reference to an OLE Container control.
- *index*—The index of the format to retrieve.
- *value*—The string variable that will receive the format.

Example

The following program demonstrates the ObjectGetFormats property. When you run the program, a window that contains an OLE container control and two CommandButton controls appears. Click the Insert Object button to display the Insert Object dialog box from which you can select the type of object to embed into the OLE Container control. Then click the Get Formats button to display a message box that shows the data formats that the object can provide. Figure O-2, for example, shows the formats provided by an embedded Microsoft Paint (Bitmap Image object) document. If the embedded object reports no formats, or if the object causes an error, a message box appears reporting the problem.

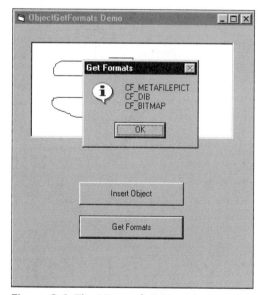

Figure O-2 The Microsoft Paint object provides data in the CF_METAFILEPICT, CF_DIB, and CF_BITMAP formats.

```
VERSION 5.00
Begin VB.Form Form1
    Caption         =   "ObjectGetFormats Demo"
    ClientHeight    =   5565
    ClientLeft      =   165
```

```
ClientTop       =    450
ClientWidth     =    5235
LinkTopic       =    "Form1"
ScaleHeight     =    5565
ScaleWidth      =    5235
StartUpPosition =    3  'Windows Default
Begin VB.CommandButton btnGetFormats
   Caption      =    "Get Formats"
   Height       =    495
   Left         =    1440
   TabIndex     =    1
   Top          =    4080
   Width        =    2295
End
Begin VB.CommandButton btnInsertObject
   Caption      =    "Insert Object"
   Height       =    495
   Left         =    1440
   TabIndex     =    0
   Top          =    3360
   Width        =    2295
End
Begin VB.OLE OLE1
   Height       =    2055
   Left         =    360
   TabIndex     =    2
   Top          =    360
   Width        =    4455
End
End
Attribute VB_Name = "Form1"
Attribute VB_GlobalNameSpace = False
Attribute VB_Creatable = False
Attribute VB_PredeclaredId = True
Attribute VB_Exposed = False

Private Sub btnInsertObject_Click()
   OLE1.InsertObjDlg
   If OLE1.AppIsRunning Then
      btnGetFormats.Enabled = True
   End If
End Sub

Private Sub btnGetFormats_Click()
```

```
        Dim count, index As Integer
        Dim strFormats As String

        On Error GoTo ErrorHandler

        count = OLE1.ObjectGetFormatsCount
        If count = 0 Then
            MsgBox "No formats for this object.", _
                vbExclamation, "Get Formats"
        Else
            For index = 0 To count - 1
                strFormats = strFormats & _
                    OLE1.ObjectGetFormats(index) & vbCrLf
            Next index
                MsgBox strFormats, vbInformation, "Get Formats"
        End If

        Exit Sub

    ErrorHandler:
        MsgBox "Cannot display formats for this object.", _
            vbExclamation, "Get Formats"
    End Sub

    Private Sub Form_Load()
        btnGetFormats.Enabled = False
    End Sub
```

 CROSS-REFERENCE
See also OLE Container, Format, ObjectAcceptFormatsCount, ObjectAccept
Formats, and ObjectGetFormatsCount.

ObjectGetFormatsCount

Property

The ObjectGetFormatsCount property represents the number of data formats
that a linked or embedded object can provide.

Objects with an ObjectGetFormatsCount Property

OLE Container

Syntax

```
value = OLEContainer.ObjectGetFormatsCount
```

- *OLEContainer*—A reference to an OLE Container control.
- *value*—The variable that will receive the number of formats.

Example

The following lines get the number of formats provided by the currently embedded object in an OLE Container control. The OLE1 object is an OLE Container control that the programmer added to the form at design time.

```
Dim count As Integer
count = OLE1.ObjectGetFormatsCount
```

CROSS-REFERENCE
See also OLE Container, Format, ObjectAcceptFormats, ObjectGetFormats, and ObjectAcceptFormatsCount.

ObjectMove

Event

Visual Basic sends an OLE Container control an ObjectMove event when the user moves or resizes a linked or embedded object in the control.

Objects with an ObjectMove Event

OLE Container

Example

A program can respond to an ObjectMove event by implementing the OLE Container control's ObjectMove event procedure. The following code segment shows how an OLE Container control defines an ObjectMove event procedure. As you can see in the procedure's declaration, the procedure's four parameters provide the object's new position (relative to the form's upper-left corner) and size. In this example, the OLE1 object is an OLE Container control that the programmer added to the form at design time.

```
Private Sub OLE1_ObjectMove(Left As Single, _
    Top As Single, Width As Single, Height As Single)
      ' Handle the ObjectMove event here.
End Sub
```

CROSS-REFERENCE
See also OLE Container, Resize, and Move.

ObjectVerbFlags

Property

The `ObjectVerbFlags` property represents the state of menu items associated with verbs in an object's `ObjectVerbs` property. This property returns one of the values from Table O-1. Like the `ObjectVerbs` property, the `ObjectVerbFlags` property is an array, except that it holds integers rather than strings.

Table O-1 Values of an ObjectVerbFlags Element

Value	Description
vbOLEFlagChecked	The menu item associated with the verb is checked.
vbOLEFlagDisabled	The menu item associated with the verb is disabled.
vbOLEFlagEnabled	The menu item associated with the verb is enabled.
vbOLEFlagGrayed	The menu item associated with the verb is grayed.
vbOLEFlagSeparator	The menu item is a menu separator.

Objects with an ObjectVerbFlags Property

OLE Container

OLEObject

Syntax

```
value = object.ObjectVerbFlags
```

- *object*—A reference to an OLE Container or OLEObject object.
- *value*—The variable that will receive the property's current setting.

Example

The following lines retrieve the menu-item state for an embedded object's first verb. A message box then displays the menu state. In this example, the `OLE1` object is an OLE Container control that the programmer added to the form at design time.

```
Dim verbFlag As Integer
```

```
verbFlag = OLE1.ObjectVerbFlags(0)
If verbFlag = vbOLEFlagChecked Then
    MsgBox "Menu item checked.", vbInformation
ElseIf verbFlag = vbOLEFlagDisabled Then
    MsgBox "Menu item disabled.", vbInformation
ElseIf verbFlag = vbOLEFlagEnabled Then
    MsgBox "Menu item enabled.", vbInformation
ElseIf verbFlag = vbOLEFlagGrayed Then
    MsgBox "Menu item grayed.", vbInformation
ElseIf verbFlag = vbOLEFlagSeparator Then
    MsgBox "Menu item is separator", vbInformation
End If
```

CROSS-REFERENCE
See also OLE Container, OLEObject, Verb, and ObjectVerbs.

ObjectVerbs

Property

The ObjectVerbs property represents a string array that contains the OLE verbs that a linked or embedded object supports.

Objects with an ObjectVerbs Property

OLE Container

Syntax

```
value = OLEContainer.ObjectVerbs(index)
```

- *OLEContainer* — A reference to an OLE Container control.
- *index* — The index of the verb to retrieve.
- *value* — The string variable that will receive the verb.

Example

The following program demonstrates the ObjectVerbs property. When you run the program, a window that contains an OLE container control and two CommandButton controls appears. Click the Insert Object button to display the Insert Object dialog box from which you can select the type of object to embed into the OLE Container control. Then click the Get Verbs button to display a message box that shows the verbs the object supports. Figure O-3, for example, shows the verbs supported by an embedded MIDI Sequence object. If the embedded object reports no verbs, or if the object causes an error, a message box appears reporting the problem.

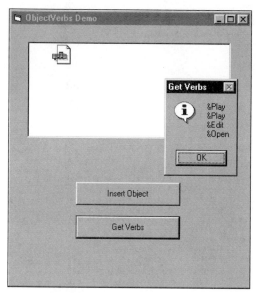

Figure O-3 The MIDI Sequence object supports the Play, Edit, and Open OLE verbs.

```
VERSION 5.00
Begin VB.Form Form1
   Caption         =   "ObjectVerbs Demo"
   ClientHeight    =   5565
   ClientLeft      =   165
   ClientTop       =   450
   ClientWidth     =   5235
   LinkTopic       =   "Form1"
   ScaleHeight     =   5565
   ScaleWidth      =   5235
   StartUpPosition =   3   'Windows Default
   Begin VB.CommandButton btnGetVerbs
      Caption      =   "Get Verbs"
      Height       =   495
      Left         =   1440
      TabIndex     =   1
      Top          =   4080
      Width        =   2295
```

```
        End
        Begin VB.CommandButton btnInsertObject
            Caption          =    "Insert Object"
            Height           =    495
            Left             =    1440
            TabIndex         =    0
            Top              =    3360
            Width            =    2295
        End
        Begin VB.OLE OLE1
            Height           =    2055
            Left             =    360
            TabIndex         =    2
            Top              =    360
            Width            =    4455
        End
    End
Attribute VB_Name = "Form1"
Attribute VB_GlobalNameSpace = False
Attribute VB_Creatable = False
Attribute VB_PredeclaredId = True
Attribute VB_Exposed = False

Private Sub btnInsertObject_Click()
    OLE1.InsertObjDlg
    If OLE1.AppIsRunning Then
        btnGetVerbs.Enabled = True
    End If
End Sub

Private Sub btnGetVerbs_Click()
    Dim count, index As Integer
    Dim strVerbs As String

    On Error GoTo ErrorHandler

    count = OLE1.ObjectVerbsCount
    If count = 0 Then
        MsgBox "No verbs for this object.", _
            vbExclamation, "Get Verbs"
    Else
        For index = 0 To count - 1
            strVerbs = strVerbs & _
                OLE1.ObjectVerbs(index) & vbCrLf
```

```
        Next index
            MsgBox strVerbs, vbInformation, "Get Verbs"
        End If

        Exit Sub

    ErrorHandler:
        MsgBox "Cannot display verbs for this object.", _
            vbExclamation, "Get Verbs"
    End Sub

    Private Sub Form_Load()
        btnGetVerbs.Enabled = False
    End Sub
```

CROSS-REFERENCE
See also OLE Container, Verb, ObjectVerbsCount, DoVerb, FetchVerb, and ObjectVerbFlags.

ObjectVerbsCount

Property

The ObjectVerbsCount property represents the number of verbs that a linked or embedded object supports.

Objects with an ObjectVerbsCount Property

OLE Container

Syntax

```
value = OLEContainer.ObjectVerbsCount
```

- *OLEContainer*—A reference to an OLE Container control.
- *value*—The variable that will receive the number of verbs.

Example

The following lines get the number of verbs supported by the currently embedded object in an OLE Container control. The OLE1 object is an OLE Container control that the programmer added to the form at design time.

```
Dim count As Integer
count = OLE1.ObjectVerbsCount
```

CROSS-REFERENCE
See also OLE Container, Verb, ObjectVerbs, DoVerb, FetchVerb, and
ObjectVerbFlags.

Oct

Function

The Oct function returns the octal representation of a specified number.

Syntax

value = Oct(*num*)

- *num* — The number for which to get the octal representation.
- *value* — The string variable that will receive the octal representation.

Example

After the following lines execute, the variable named octal will contain the
string "20," which is the octal representation of the decimal number 16.

```
Dim octal As String
octal = Oct(16)
```

OLECompleteDrag

Event

Visual Basic sends a control an OLECompleteDrag event when the user drops
the control at the end of a drag-and-drop action. By responding to this event,
the program can determine the appropriate action to take with regards to the
dropped control.

Objects with an OLECompleteDrag Event

Animation
CheckBox
ComboBox

CommandButton

CoolBar

DirListBox

DriveListBox

FileListBox

Form

Frame

Image

Label

ListBox

ListView

MDIForm

Multimedia MCI

OptionButton

PictureBox

ProgressBar

PropertyPage

RichTextBox

Slider

StatusBar

TabStrip

TextBox

Toolbar

TreeView

UpDown

UserControl

Example

A program can respond to an `OLECompleteDrag` event by implementing the control's `OLECompleteDrag` event procedure. The following code segment shows how a CommandButton control might define an `OLECompleteDrag` event procedure. As you can see in the procedure's declaration, the procedure receives a single parameter, which is the action that the program needs to handle. This value can be `vbDropEffectNone` (the drop operation was canceled or the target object cannot receive data from the source object), `vbDropEffectCopy` (the data is copied from the source object to the target), or `vbDropEffectMove` (the data is moved from the source object to the target). In this example, the `btnCommand1` object is a CommandButton control that the programmer added to the form at design time.

```
Private Sub Command1_OLECompleteDrag(Effect As Long)
    ' Handle the OLECompleteDrag event here.
    If Effect = vbDropEffectNone Then
        ' Do something here.
    ElseIf Effect = vbDropEffectCopy Then
        ' Do something here.
    ElseIf Effect = vbDropEffectMove Then
        ' Do something here.
    End If
End Sub
```

CROSS-REFERENCE
See also OLEDrag, OLEDragDrop, OLEDragOver, OLEDragMode, OLEDropMode, OLEDropAllowed, OLEGiveFeedback, and OLEStartDrag.

OLE Container

Control

An OLE Container control enables the program to link or embed objects into the program's window. For example, the program could display and edit a Microsoft Word document, complete with Word's menus and toolbars. Figure O-4 shows an OLE Container control in a form. Notice that the control displays a Microsoft Word document. The OLE Container control is available on Visual Basic's standard toolbox.

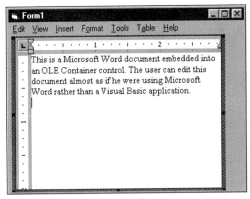

Figure O-4 The OLE Container control can link or embed objects that can be edited in place using the OLE server's menus and toolbars.

Properties

The OLE Container control has 54 properties, which are listed below. Because many Visual Basic controls have similar properties, the following list does not include the properties' descriptions. For information on using a property, look up the individual property's entry, provided alphabetically in this book.

```
Action
Appearance
AppIsRunning
AutoActivate
AutoVerbMenu
BackColor
BackStyle
BorderStyle
CausesValidation
Class
Container
DisplayType
DragIcon
DragMode
Enabled
FileNumber
Format
Height
HelpContextID
HostName
hWnd
Index
Left
lpOleObject
MiscFlags
MouseIcon
MousePointer
Name
Object
ObjectAcceptFormats
ObjectAcceptFormatsCount
ObjectGetFormats
ObjectGetFormatsCount
ObjectVerbFlags
ObjectVerbs
ObjectVerbsCount
OLEDropAllowed
```

```
OLEType
OLETypeAllowed
Parent
PasteOK
Picture
SizeMode
SourceDoc
SourceItem
TabIndex
TabStop
Tag
Top
UpdateOptions
Verb
Visible
WhatsThisHelpID
Width
```

Methods

The OLE Container control has 20 methods, which are listed below. Because many Visual Basic controls have similar methods, the following list does not include the methods' descriptions. For information on using a method, look up the individual method's entry, provided alphabetically in this book.

```
Close
Copy
CreateEmbed
CreateLink
Delete
DoVerb
Drag
FetchVerbs
InsertObjDlg
Move
Paste
PasteSpecialDlg
ReadFromFile
Refresh
SaveToFile
SaveToOle1File
SetFocus
ShowWhatsThis
Update
ZOrder
```

Events

The OLE Container control responds to 16 events, which are listed below. Because many Visual Basic controls respond to similar events, the following list does not include the events' descriptions. For information on using an event, look up the individual event's entry, provided alphabetically in this book.

```
Click
DblClick
DragDrop
DragOver
GotFocus
KeyDown
KeyPress
KeyUp
LostFocus
MouseDown
MouseMove
MouseUp
ObjectMove
Resize
Updated
Validate
```

OLEDrag

Method

The `OLEDrag` method begins a drag-and-drop operation.

Objects with an OLEDrag Method

Animation

CheckBox

ComboBox

CommandButton

CoolBar

DirListBox

DriveListBox

FileListBox

Form

Frame

Image

Label

ListBox

ListView

MDIForm

Multimedia MCI

OptionButton

PictureBox

PropertyPage

RichTextBox

Slider

StatusBar

TabStrip

TextBox

Toolbar

TreeView

UpDown

UserControl

Syntax

```
object.OLEDrag
```

- *object* — A reference to an object with the OLEDrag method.

Example

The following line begins a drag-and-drop operation on a CommandButton control. The `Command1` object is a CommandButton control that the programmer added to the form at design time.

```
Command1.OLEDrag
```

 CROSS-REFERENCE
See also OLECompleteDrag, OLEDragDrop, OLEDragOver, OLEDragMode, OLEDropMode, OLEDropAllowed, OLEGiveFeedback, and OLEStartDrag.

OLEDragDrop

Event

Visual Basic sends a control an OLEDragDrop event when the user drops a control on a drag-and-drop target, but only if the OLEDropMode property is set to manual (1).

Objects with an OLEDragDrop Event

Animation

CheckBox

ComboBox

CommandButton

CoolBar

DirListBox

DriveListBox

FileListBox

Form

Frame

Image

Label

ListBox

ListView

MDIForm

Multimedia MCI

OptionButton

PictureBox

PropertyPage

RichTextBox

Slider

StatusBar

TabStrip

TextBox

Toolbar

n

o

p

TreeView

UpDown

UserControl

Example

A program can respond to an OLEDragDrop event by implementing the control's OLEDragDrop event procedure. The following code segment shows how a CommandButton control might define an OLEDragDrop event procedure. In the example, the btnCommand1 object is a CommandButton control that the programmer added to the form at design time.

```
Private Sub btnCommand1_OLEDragDrop(Data As DataObject, _
   Effect As Long, Button As Integer, Shift As Integer, _
   X As Single, Y As Single)
      ' Handle the OLEDragDrop event here.
End Sub
```

As you can see in the procedure's declaration, the procedure receives six parameters, which are described in Table O-2.

Table O-2 OLEDragDrop Procedure's Parameters

Parameter	Description
Button	A set of bit flags that indicate which mouse buttons were pressed, with bit 0 meaning the left button, bit 1 meaning the right button, and bit 2 meaning the middle button.
DataObject	The data formats that the source can provide and possibly the data itself.
Effect	The action that the program needs to handle. This value can be vbDropEffectNone (the target object cannot receive data from the source object), vbDropEffectCopy (the data is copied from the source object to the target), vbDropEffectMove (the data is moved from the source object to the target), or vbDropEffectScroll (the target window will scroll).
Shift	A set of bit flags that indicate which keys were pressed, with bit 0 meaning the Shift key, bit 1 meaning the Ctrl key, and bit 2 meaning the Alt key.
X	The X coordinate of the mouse pointer, the value of which depends on the settings of the ScaleHeight, ScaleLeft, ScaleTop, and ScaleWidth properties.
Y	The Y coordinate of the mouse pointer, the value of which depends on the settings of the ScaleHeight, ScaleLeft, ScaleTop, and ScaleWidth properties.

CROSS-REFERENCE
See also OLECompleteDrag, OLEDrag, OLEDragOver, OLEDropMode, OLEDragMode, OLEDropAllowed, OLEGiveFeedback, and OLEStartDrag.

OLEDragMode

Property

The OLEDragMode property represents whether Visual Basic handles a drag-and-drop operation automatically or the program handles the operation itself. This property can be the value vbOLEDragAutomatic or vbOLEDragManual.

Objects with an OLEDragMode Property

ComboBox

DirListBox

DriveListBox

FileListBox

Image

ListBox

ListView

PictureBox

RichTextBox

TextBox

TreeView

Syntax

object.OLEDragMode = value1

or

value2 = object.OLEDragMode

- *object* — A reference to a control with an OLEDragMode property.
- *value1* — The OLE drag mode.
- *value2* — The variable that will receive the property's current setting.

Example

The following line sets a PictureBox control to automatic drag-and-drop operations. The `picPicture1` object is a PictureBox control the programmer added to the form at design time.

```
picPicture1.OLEDragMode = vbOLEDragAutomatic
```

 CROSS-REFERENCE
See also OLECompleteDrag, OLEDrag, OLEDragOver, OLEDropMode, OLEDragDrop, OLEDropAllowed, OLEGiveFeedback, and OLEStartDrag.

OLEDragOver

Event

Visual Basic sends a control an `OLEDragOver` event when the user drags an object over the control.

Objects with an OLEDragOver Event

Animation

CheckBox

ComboBox

CommandButton

CoolBar

DirListBox

DriveListBox

FileListBox

Form

Frame

Image

Label

ListBox

ListView

MDIForm

Multimedia MCI

OptionButton

PictureBox

PropertyPage

RichTextBox

Slider

StatusBar

TabStrip

TextBox

Toolbar

TreeView

UpDown

UserControl

Example

A program can respond to an OLEDragOver event by implementing the control's OLEDragOver event procedure. The following code segment shows how a CommandButton control defines an OLEDragOver event procedure. In the example, the Command1 object is a CommandButton control that the programmer added to the form at design time.

```
Private Sub Command1_OLEDragOver(Data As DataObject, _
   Effect As Long, Button As Integer, Shift As Integer, _
   X As Single, Y As Single, State As Integer)
   ' Handle the OLEDragOver event here.
End Sub
```

As you can see in the procedure's declaration, the procedure receives seven parameters, which are described in Table O-3.

Table O-3 OLEDragOver Procedure's Parameters

Parameter	Description
Button	A set of bit flags that indicate which mouse buttons were pressed, with bit 0 meaning the left button, bit 1 meaning the right button, and bit 2 meaning the middle button.
DataObject	The data formats that the source can provide and possibly the data itself.
Effect	The action that the program needs to handle. This value can be vbDropEffectNone (the target object cannot receive data from the source object), vbDropEffectCopy (the data is copied from the source object to the target), vbDropEffectMove (the data is moved from the source object to the target), or vbDropEffectScroll (the target window will scroll).
Shift	A set of bit flags that indicate which keys were pressed, with bit 0 meaning the Shift key, bit 1 meaning the Ctrl key, and bit 2 meaning the Alt key.

Continued

Table O-3 *Continued*

Parameter	Description
State	The state of the dragged control. This can be vbEnter (the control just entered the area containing another control), vbOver (the control is over another control), or vbLeave (the control is leaving the area containing another control).
X	The X coordinate of the mouse pointer, the value of which depends on the settings of the ScaleHeight, ScaleLeft, ScaleTop, and ScaleWidth properties.
Y	The Y coordinate of the mouse pointer, the value of which depends on the settings of the ScaleHeight, ScaleLeft, ScaleTop, and ScaleWidth properties.

CROSS-REFERENCE
See also OLECompleteDrag, OLEDrag, OLEDragDrop, OLEDropMode, OLEDropAllowed, OLEGiveFeedback, and OLEStartDrag.

OLEDropAllowed

Property

The OLEDropAllowed property represents whether an OLE Container control can act as a drag-and-drop target.

Objects with an OLEDropAllowed Property

OLE Container

Syntax

OLEContainer.OLEDropAllowed = *value1*

or

value2 = *OLEContainer*.OLEDropAllowed

- *OLEContainer*—A reference to an OLE Container control.
- *value1*—The value True or False.
- *value2*—The variable that will receive the property's current setting.

Example

The following line sets an OLE Container control to accept OLE drop operations. The `OLE1` object is an OLE Container control that the programmer added to the form at design time.

```
OLE1.OLEDropAllowed = True
```

 CROSS-REFERENCE
See also OLECompleteDrag, OLEDrag, OLEDragOver, OLEDragMode, OLEDragDrop, OLEDropMode, OLEGiveFeedback, and OLEStartDrag.

OLEDropMode

Property

The `OLEDropMode` property represents whether the target object handles a drop operation automatically or the program handles the operation itself. This property can be the value `vbOLEDropAutomatic`, `vbOLEDropManual`, or `vbDropNone`. In the last case, the target object doesn't allow itself to be a drop target.

Objects with an OLEDropMode Property

Animation

CheckBox

ComboBox

CommandButton

CoolBar

DirListBox

DriveListBox

FileListBox

Form

Frame

Image

Label

ListBox

ListView

> MDIForm
>
> Multimedia MCI
>
> OptionButton
>
> PictureBox
>
> PropertyPage
>
> RichTextBox
>
> Slider
>
> StatusBar
>
> TabStrip
>
> TextBox
>
> Toolbar
>
> TreeView
>
> UpDown
>
> UserControl

Syntax

```
object.OLEDropMode = value1
```

or

```
value2 = object.OLEDropMode
```

- *object* — A reference to a control with an `OLEDragMode` property.
- *value1* — The OLE drag mode.
- *value2* — The variable that will receive the property's current setting.

Example

The following line sets a PictureBox control to handle an OLE drop operation automatically. The `picPicture1` object is a PictureBox control the programmer added to the form at design time.

```
picPicture1.OLEDropMode = vbOLEDropAutomatic
```

CROSS-REFERENCE

See also OLECompleteDrag, OLEDrag, OLEDragOver, OLEDragMode, OLEDragDrop, OLEDropAllowed, OLEGiveFeedback, and OLEStartDrag.

OLEGiveFeedback

Event

Visual Basic sends a control an `OLEGiveFeedback` event right after the `OLEDragOver` event, providing a place for the program to change mouse cursors or provide some other type of graphical feedback.

Objects with an OLEGiveFeedback Event

Animation

CheckBox

ComboBox

CommandButton

CoolBar

DirListBox

DriveListBox

FileListBox

Form

Frame

Image

Label

ListBox

ListView

MDIForm

Multimedia MCI

OptionButton

PictureBox

PropertyPage

RichTextBox

Slider

StatusBar

TabStrip

TextBox

Toolbar

TreeView

UpDown

UserControl

Example

A program can respond to an OLEGiveFeedback event by implementing the control's OLEGiveFeedback event procedure. The following code segment shows how a CommandButton control defines an OLEGiveFeedback event procedure. In the example, the btnCommand1 object is a CommandButton control that the programmer added to the form at design time.

```
Private Sub btnCommand1_OLEGiveFeedback _
   (Effect As Long, DefaultCursors As Boolean)
      ' Handle the OLEGiveFeedback event here.
End Sub
```

As you can see in the procedure's declaration, the procedure receives two parameters, which are described in Table O-4.

Table O-4 OLEGiveFeedback Procedure's Parameters

Parameter	Description
DefaultCursors	A value that determines whether the default mouse cursor (True) or a user-defined mouse cursor (False) is displayed.
Effect	The drop action that the program needs to perform. This value can be vbDropEffectNone (the target object cannot receive data from the source object), vbDropEffectCopy (the data is copied from the source object to the target), vbDropEffectMove (the data is moved from the source object to the target), or vbDropEffectScroll (the target window will scroll).

CROSS-REFERENCE

See also OLECompleteDrag, OLEDrag, OLEDragDrop, OLEDropMode, OLEDropAllowed, OLEDragOver, and OLEStartDrag.

OLEObject

Object

An OLEObject object represents a linked or embedded object in a RichTextBox control.

Properties

The OLEObject object has nine properties. For more information on using one of these properties, look up the individual property's entry, provided alphabetically in this book.

```
Class
DisplayType
Enabled
Index
Key
Object
ObjectVerbFlags
ObjectVerbs
ObjectVerbsCount
```

Methods

The OLEObject object has three methods. For more information on using these methods, look up the individual method's entry, provided alphabetically in this book.

```
Clear
DoVerb
FetchVerbs
```

Events

The OLEObject object does not respond to any events.

 CROSS-REFERENCE

See also RichTextBox, OLEObjects (collection), and OLEObjects (property).

OLEObjects

Collection

An OLEObjects collection holds the objects linked or embedded into a RichTextBox control. You can access a RichTextBox's OLEObjects collection through the control's `OLEObjects` property.

Syntax

```
value = RichTextBox.OLEObjects
```

- *RichTextBox* — A reference to a RichTextBox control.
- *value* — A variable that will receive a reference to the OLEObjects collection.

Properties

An OLEObjects collection has one property, Count, which represents the number of objects in the collection. For more information on using this property, look up the individual property's entry, provided alphabetically in this book.

Methods

An OLEObjects collection has four methods. For more information on these methods, look up the individual method's name, provided alphabetically in this book.

```
Add
Clear
Item
Remove
```

Example

In this example, the program retrieves the class name of the first embedded object in a RichTextBox control. The rtfRichTextBox1 object is a RichTextBox control that the programmer added to the form at design time.

```
Dim objClass As String
objClass = rtfRichTextBox1.OLEObjects(0).Class
```

 CROSS-REFERENCE
See also RichTextBox, OLEObject, and OLEObjects (property).

OLEObjects

Property

The OLEObjects property represents a RichTextBox control's OLEObjects collection, which holds the linked or embedded objects in the control.

Objects with an OLEObjects Property

RichTextBox

Syntax

```
value = RichTextBox.OLEObjects
```

- *RichTextBox* — A reference to a RichTextBox control.
- *value* — The variable that will receive a reference to the OLEObjects collection.

Example

In this example, the program retrieves the index of the first embedded object in a RichTextBox control. The `rtfRichTextBox1` object is a RichTextBox control that the programmer added to the form at design time.

```
Dim objIndex As Integer
objIndex = rtfRichTextBox1.OLEObjects(0).Index
```

 CROSS-REFERENCE
See also RichTextBox, OLEObject, and OLEObjects (collection).

OLERequestPendingMsgText

Property

The `OLERequestPendingMsgText` property represents the text that's displayed in a message box in place of the Component Request Pending dialog box. This message box will appear when the user triggers mouse or keyboard input during a pending automation request. If the `OLERequestPendingMsgText` property is not set, the default Component Request Pending dialog box appears instead.

Objects with an OLERequestPendingMsgText Property

App

Syntax

```
App.OLERequestPendingMsgText = value1
```

or

```
value2 = App.OLERequestPendingMsgText
```

- *App* — A reference to the global App object.

- *value1* — The new message string.
- *value2* — The variable that will receive the property's current setting.

Example

The following lines retrieve the current message text from the `OLERequestPendingMsgText` property. Note that the App object is a global Visual Basic object that you don't need to create explicitly in your program.

```
Dim msg As String
msg = App.OLERequestPendingMsgText
```

CROSS-REFERENCE
See also OLERequestPendingMsgTitle, OLERequestPendingTimeout, OLEServerBusyMsgText, OLEServerBusyMsgTitle, OLEServerBusyRaiseError, and OLEServerBusyTimeout.

OLERequestPendingMsgTitle

Property

The `OLERequestPendingMsgTitle` property represents the title that's displayed in a message box in place of the Component Request Pending dialog box. This message box will appear when the user triggers mouse or keyboard input during a pending automation request. If the `OLERequestPendingMsgText` property is not set, the default Component Request Pending dialog box appears instead.

Objects with an OLERequestPendingMsgTitle Property

App

Syntax

```
App.OLERequestPendingMsgTitle = value1
```

or

```
value2 = App.OLERequestPendingMsgTitle
```

- *App* — A reference to the global App object.
- *value1* — The new title string.
- *value2* — The variable that will receive the property's current setting.

Example

The following lines retrieve the current message title from the
OLERequestPendingMsgTitle property. Note that the App object is a global
Visual Basic object that you don't need to create explicitly in your program.

```
Dim msgTitle As String
msgTitle = App.OLERequestPendingMsgTitle
```

 CROSS-REFERENCE
See also OLERequestPendingMsgText, OLERequestPendingTimeout,
OLEServerBusyMsgText, OLEServerBusyMsgTitle, OLEServerBusyRaiseError,
and OLEServerBusyTimeout.

OLERequestPendingTimeout

Property

The OLERequestPendingTimeout property represents the amount of time (in
milliseconds) that must pass before mouse or keyboard input can cause the
Component Request Pending dialog box (or the custom message box) to
appear.

Objects with an OLERequestPendingTimeout Property

App

Syntax

```
App.OLERequestPendingTimeout = value1
```

or

```
value2 = App.OLERequestPendingTimeout
```

- *App* — A reference to the global App object.
- *value1* — The new timeout value. The default is 5000.
- *value2* — The variable that will receive the property's current
  setting.

Example

The following lines retrieve the current pending-timeout value from the
OLERequestPendingTimeout property. Note that the App object is a global
Visual Basic object that you don't need to create explicitly in your program.

```
Dim oleTimeout As Integer
oleTimeout = App.OLERequestPendingTimeout
```

CROSS-REFERENCE
See also OLERequestPendingMsgText, OLERequestPendingMsgTitle,
OLEServerBusyMsgText, OLEServerBusyMsgTitle, OLEServerBusyRaiseError,
and OLEServerBusyTimeout.

OLEServerBusyMsgText

Property

The OLEServerBusyMsgText property represents the message that will appear
in place of the Component Busy dialog box if an automation request receives
no response. If the OLEServerBusyMsgText property is not set, the default
Component Busy dialog box appears instead.

Objects with an OLEServerBusyMsgText Property

App

Syntax

```
App.OLEServerBusyMsgText = value1
```

or

```
value2 = App.OLEServerBusyMsgText
```

- *App* — A reference to the global App object.
- *value1* — The new message text.
- *value2* — The variable that will receive the property's current
  setting.

Example

The following lines retrieve the current message text from the
OLEServerBusyMsgText property. Note that the App object is a global Visual
Basic object that you don't need to create explicitly in your program.

```
Dim msgText As String
msgText = App.OLEServerBusyMsgText
```

CROSS-REFERENCE
See also OLERequestPendingMsgText, OLERequestPendingMsgTitle,
OLERequestPendingTimeout, OLEServerBusyMsgTitle,
OLEServerBusyRaiseError, and OLEServerBusyTimeout.

OLEServerBusyMsgTitle

Property

The `OLEServerBusyMsgTitle` property represents the title that will appear in the message box that takes the place of the Component Busy dialog box. This message box will appear if an automation request receives no response before its timeout. If the `OLEServerBusyMsgText` property is not set, the default Component Busy dialog box appears instead.

Objects with an OLEServerBusyMsgTitle Property

App

Syntax

```
App.OLEServerBusyMsgTitle = value1
```

or

```
value2 = App.OLEServerBusyMsgTitle
```

- *App* — A reference to the global App object.
- *value1* — The new title.
- *value2* — The variable that will receive the property's current setting.

Example

The following lines retrieve the current title from the `OLEServerBusyMsgTitle` property. Note that the App object is a global Visual Basic object that you don't need to create explicitly in your program.

```
Dim msgTitle As String
msgTitle = App.OLEServerBusyMsgTitle
```

 CROSS-REFERENCE
See also OLERequestPendingMsgText, OLERequestPendingMsgTitle,
OLERequestPendingTimeout, OLEServerBusyMsgText,
OLEServerBusyRaiseError, and OLEServerBusyTimeout.

OLEServerBusyRaiseError

Property

The OLEServerBusyRaiseError property represents whether the Component Busy dialog box (or the custom message box) appears when an automation request receives no response or whether the rejected request causes an error.

Objects with an OLEServerBusyRaiseError Property

App

Syntax

App.OLEServerBusyRaiseError = *value1*

or

value2 = App.OLEServerBusyRaiseError

- *App* — A reference to the global App object.
- *value1* — The value True or False. The default is True.
- *value2* — The variable that will receive the property's current setting.

Example

The following line sets an application to display the Component Busy dialog box in the event of an automation-request timeout. Note that the App object is a global Visual Basic object that you don't need to create explicitly in your program.

App.OLEServerBusyRaiseError = False

 CROSS-REFERENCE
See also OLERequestPendingMsgText, OLERequestPendingMsgTitle, OLERequestPendingTimeout, OLEServerBusyMsgText, OLEServerBusyMsgTitle, and OLEServerBusyTimeout.

OLEServerBusyTimeout

Property

The OLEServerBusyTimeout property represents the amount of time (in milliseconds) that must pass before the Component Busy dialog box (or the custom message box) appears.

Objects with an OLEServerBusyTimeout Property

App

Syntax

```
App.OLEServerBusyTimeout = value1
```

or

```
value2 = App.OLEServerBusyTimeout
```

- *App* — A reference to the global App object.
- *value1* — The new timeout value. The default is 10,000.
- *value2* — The variable that will receive the property's current setting.

Example

The following lines retrieve the current timeout value from the OLEServerBusyTimeout property. Note that the App object is a global Visual Basic object that you don't need to create explicitly in your program.

```
Dim oleTimeout As Integer
oleTimeout = App.OLEServerBusyTimeout
```

CROSS-REFERENCE
See also OLERequestPendingMsgText, OLERequestPendingMsgTitle, OLEServerBusyMsgText, OLEServerBusyMsgTitle, OLEServerBusyRaiseError, and OLERequestPendingTimeout.

OLESetData

Event

Visual Basic sends a control an OLESetData event right after the target object calls the GetData method to retrieve data from the source object.

Objects with an OLESetData Event

Animation

CheckBox

ComboBox

CommandButton

CoolBar

DirListBox

DriveListBox

FileListBox

Form

Frame

Image

Label

ListBox

ListView

MDIForm

Multimedia MCI

OptionButton

PictureBox

PropertyPage

RichTextBox

Slider

StatusBar

TabStrip

TextBox

Toolbar

TreeView

UpDown

UserControl

Example

A program can respond to an OLESetData event by implementing the control's OLESetData event procedure. The following code segment shows how a CommandButton control defines an OLESetData event procedure. In the example, the btnCommand1 object is a CommandButton control that the programmer added to the form at design time.

```
Private Sub btnCommand1_OLESetData _
  (Data As DataObject, DataFormat As Integer)
    ' Handle the OLESetData event here.
End Sub
```

As you can see in the procedure's declaration, the procedure receives two parameters, which are described in Table O-5.

Table O-5 OLESetData Procedure's Parameters

Parameter	Description
Data	The DataObject object that will hold the data.
DataFormat	An integer representing the data format.

CROSS-REFERENCE
See also GetData.

OLEStartDrag

Event

Visual Basic sends a control an `OLEStartDrag` event when an OLE drag-and-drop operation begins on the control, either by calling the control's `OLEDrag` method or by an automatic drag-and-drop operation (the `OLEDragMode` property is set to automatic).

Objects with an OLEStartDrag Event

Animation
CheckBox
ComboBox
CommandButton
CoolBar
DirListBox
DriveListBox
FileListBox
Form
Frame
Image
Label
ListBox
ListView

MDIForm

Multimedia MCI

OptionButton

PictureBox

PropertyPage

RichTextBox

Slider

StatusBar

TabStrip

TextBox

Toolbar

TreeView

UpDown

UserControl

Example

A program can respond to an `OLEStartDrag` event by implementing the control's `OLEStartDrag` event procedure. The following code segment shows how a CommandButton control defines an `OLEStartDrag` event procedure. In the example, the `Command1` object is a CommandButton control that the programmer added to the form at design time.

```
Private Sub Command1_OLEStartDrag(Data As DataObject, _
    AllowedEffects As Long)
        ' Handle OLEStartDrag event here.
End Sub
```

As you can see in the procedure's declaration, the procedure receives two parameters, which are described in Table O-6.

Table O-6 OLEStartDrag Procedure's Parameters

Parameter	Description
AllowedEffects	The OLE effects that the dragged control supports. This value can be `vbDropEffectNone` (the target object cannot receive data from the source object), `vbDropEffectCopy` (the data is copied from the source object to the target), or `vbDropEffectMove` (the data is moved from the source object to the target).
DataObject	The data formats that the source can provide and possibly the data itself.

CROSS-REFERENCE

See also OLECompleteDrag, OLEDrag, OLEDragDrop, OLEDropMode, OLEDropAllowed, OLEGiveFeedback, and OLEDragOver.

OLEType

Property

The OLEType property represents whether an OLE Container control contains a linked or embedded object. This property can be one of the values from Table O-7.

Table O-7 Settings for the OLEType Property

Value	Description
vbOLEEmbedded	The object is embedded.
vbOLELinked	The object is linked.
vbOLENone	The control contains no linked or embedded object.

Objects with an OLEType Property

OLE Container

Syntax

```
value = OLEContainer.OLEType
```

- *OLEContainer*—A reference to an OLE Container control.
- *value*—The variable that will receive the property's current setting.

Example

The following program demonstrates the OLEType property. When you run the program, you see in the form an OLE Container control, a CommandButton control, and a TextBox control. Click the Insert Object button to display the Insert Object dialog box, from which you can select an object to link or embed into the OLE Container control. After you insert the object, the object type appears in the text box. Figure O-5, for example, shows an embedded Calendar control.

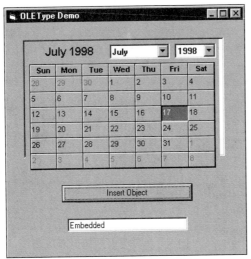

Figure O-5 This Calendar control is embedded into the OLE Container control, as you can tell by the message in the text box.

```
VERSION 5.00
Begin VB.Form Form1
   Caption         =   "OLEType Demo"
   ClientHeight    =   4980
   ClientLeft      =   165
   ClientTop       =   450
   ClientWidth     =   5235
   LinkTopic       =   "Form1"
   ScaleHeight     =   4980
   ScaleWidth      =   5235
   StartUpPosition =   3  'Windows Default
   Begin VB.TextBox txtObjectType
      Height       =   285
      Left         =   1320
      TabIndex     =   2
      Top          =   4200
      Width        =   2655
   End
   Begin VB.CommandButton btnInsertObject
      Caption      =   "Insert Object"
      Height       =   375
      Left         =   1200
      TabIndex     =   1
      Top          =   3480
      Width        =   2895
```

```
        End
        Begin VB.OLE OLE1
            Height          =    2535
            Left            =    360
            TabIndex        =    0
            Top             =    360
            Width           =    4455
        End
    End
    Attribute VB_Name = "Form1"
    Attribute VB_GlobalNameSpace = False
    Attribute VB_Creatable = False
    Attribute VB_PredeclaredId = True
    Attribute VB_Exposed = False

    Private Sub btnInsertObject_Click()
        Dim objType As Integer
        OLE1.InsertObjDlg
        If OLE1.AppIsRunning Then
            objType = OLE1.OLEType
            If objType = vbOLENone Then
                txtObjectType.Text = "None"
            ElseIf objType = vbOLELinked Then
                txtObjectType.Text = "Linked"
            ElseIf objType = vbOLEEmbedded Then
                txtObjectType.Text = "Embedded"
            End If
        End If
    End Sub

    Private Sub Form_Load()
        txtObjectType.Text = "None"
    End Sub
```

CROSS-REFERENCE
See also OLETypeAllowed.

OLETypeAllowed

Property

The OLETypeAllowed property represents the type of object an OLE Container control can hold. This property can be one of the values shown in Table O-8.

Table O-8 Settings for the OLETypeAllowed Property

Value	Description
vbOLEEither	The container can hold both linked and embedded objects.
vbOLEEmbedded	The container can hold only embedded objects.
vbOLELinked	The container can hold only linked objects.

Objects with an OLETypeAllowed Property

OLE Container

Syntax

```
OLEContainer.OLETypeAllowed = value1
```

or

```
value2 = OLEContainer.OLETypeAllowed
```

- *OLEContainer* — A reference to an OLE Container control.
- *value1* — A value from Table O-8.
- *value2* — The variable that will receive the property's current setting.

Example

The following lines retrieve the allowed OLE type from an OLE Container control and display the type in a message box. The OLE1 object is an OLE Container control that the programmer added to the form at design time.

```
Dim typeAllowed As Integer
typeAllowed = OLE1.OLETypeAllowed
If typeAllowed = vbOLEEither Then
    MsgBox "Either linked or embedded.", _
        vbInformation, "Allowed Type"
ElseIf typeAllowed = vbOLELinked Then
    MsgBox "Linked only.", _
        vbInformation, "Allowed Type"
ElseIf typeAllowed = vbOLEEmbedded Then
    MsgBox "Embedded only.", _
        vbInformation, "Allowed Type"
End If
```

CROSS-REFERENCE
See also OLEType.

On

Keyword

The On keyword is used with the On Error, On GoSub, and On GoTo statements, which enable various types of branching in a program. For example, the following lines use the On Error statement to create error-handling code in a procedure. If an error occurs anywhere after the On Error statement, program execution branches to the ErrorHandler label.

```
Private Sub btnGetVerbs_Click()
    Dim count, index As Integer
    Dim strVerbs As String

    On Error GoTo ErrorHandler

    count = OLE1.ObjectVerbsCount
    If count = 0 Then
        MsgBox "No verbs for this object.", _
            vbExclamation, "Get Verbs"
    Else
        For index = 0 To count - 1
            strVerbs = strVerbs & _
                OLE1.ObjectVerbs(index) & vbCrLf
        Next index
        MsgBox strVerbs, vbInformation, "Get Verbs"
    End If

    Exit Sub

ErrorHandler:
    MsgBox "Cannot display verbs for this object.", _
        vbExclamation, "Get Verbs"
End Sub
```

CROSS-REFERENCE
For more information, see On Error, On GoSub, and On GoTo.

On Error

Statement

In the case of a runtime error, the `On Error` statement causes program execution to jump to a specified line.

Syntax

```
On Error Resume Next
```

or

```
On Error GoTo dest
```

- *dest* — A line number or label.

Example 1

The following lines demonstrate how to add an error-handling routine to a procedure. In this case, if the Animation control's `Open` method fails, program execution branches to the `ErrorHandler` label. The programmer added the `dlgCommonDialog1` CommonDialog and `Animation1` Animation controls to the form at design time.

```
Private Sub btnLoad_Click()
    dlgCommonDialog1.Action = 1
    On Error GoTo ErrorHandler
    Animation1.Open dlgCommonDialog1.FileName
    Exit Sub
ErrorHandler:
    MsgBox "Couldn't Open the File"
End Sub
```

Example 2

Here, this example demonstrates how to add an error-handling routine to a procedure using the `On Error Resume Next` statement, which causes program execution to continue on the line after the line that caused the error. In this example, the division by zero causes runtime error #1, which causes program execution to continue with the `If` statement. Note that the `Err` object is a Visual Basic global object that you don't need to create explicitly in your programs.

```
Dim var1, var2 As Integer
Dim result As Double
var1 = 10
var2 = 0

On Error Resume Next
result = var1 / var2

If Err.Number = 11 Then
    MsgBox "Cannot divide by zero.", vbExclamation
Else
    MsgBox result, vbInformation
End If
```

Example 3

Finally, this example demonstrates how to shut off error-handling. The following lines are exactly like those in Example 2, except the programmer added the line On Error GoTo 0, which shuts off all error handling. That is, if a run-time error occurs after the On Error GoTo 0 line, the program will crash, displaying a standard Visual Basic error message, as shown in Figure O-6. In the following lines, the divide-by-zero error gets caught because error-handling is on when the division takes place, so the user sees the message box rather than the system error box.

```
Dim var1, var2 As Integer
Dim result As Double
var1 = 10
var2 = 0

On Error Resume Next
result = var1 / var2

If Err.Number = 11 Then
    MsgBox "Cannot divide by zero.", vbExclamation
Else
    On Error GoTo 0
    MsgBox result, vbInformation
End If
```

n
o
p

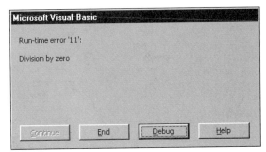

Figure O-6 This is the divide-by-zero runtime error that occurs if the program has turned off error handling.

CROSS-REFERENCE
See also On Error, On GoSub, and On GoTo.

On GoSub

Statement

The On GoSub statement enables program execution to jump to one of a list of destinations depending upon the evaluation of a numeric expression. The matching Return statement causes program execution to jump back to the line after the On GoSub statement.

Syntax

```
On numExp GoSub dest
```

- *dest* — A list of line numbers and/or labels.
- *numExp* — A numeric expression that evaluates to a number between 0 and 255 inclusive.

Example 1

After the following lines execute, the variable intResult will contain the value 2. Because branchExp equals 2 when the program gets to the On GoSub line, the program branches to the second destination in the list, which is Sub2. This action results in intResult being set to 2, after which the Return statement sends program execution back to the line following the On GoSub statement.

```
Private Sub Command1_Click()
    Dim branchExp As Integer
```

```
        Dim intResult As Integer

        intResult = 0
        branchExp = 2
        On branchExp GoSub Sub1, Sub2, Sub3
        Exit Sub

    Sub1:
        intResult = 1
        Return
    Sub2:
        intResult = 2
        Return
    Sub3:
        intResult = 3
        Return
    End Sub
```

Example 2

In this case, after the following lines execute, the variable intResult will contain the value 0. Because branchExp equals 0 when the program gets to the On GoSub line, the program doesn't branch at all, instead going to the first line after the On GoSub statement.

```
    Private Sub Command1_Click()
        Dim branchExp As Integer
        Dim intResult As Integer

        intResult = 0
        branchExp = 0
        On branchExp GoSub Sub1, Sub2, Sub3
        Exit Sub

    Sub1:
        intResult = 1
        Return
    Sub2:
        intResult = 2
        Return
    Sub3:
        intResult = 3
        Return
    End Sub
```

CROSS-REFERENCE
See also On Error and On GoTo.

On GoTo

Statement

The On GoTo statement enables program execution to jump to one of a list of destinations depending upon the evaluation of a numeric expression. Unlike the On GoSub statement, On GoTo does not have a Return statement that returns program execution to the line after the line that caused the branch.

Syntax

On *numExp* GoTo *dest*

- *dest* — A list of line numbers and/or labels.
- *numExp* — A numeric expression that evaluates to a number between 0 and 255 inclusive.

Example 1

After the following lines execute (and before the Exit Sub statement is executed), the variable intResult will contain the value 3. Because branchExp equals 3 when the program gets to the On GoTo line, the program branches to the third destination in the list, which is Sub3. This action results in intResult being set to 3, after which the Exit Sub statement ends the Command1_Click1 procedure.

```
Private Sub Command1_Click()
    Dim branchExp As Integer
    Dim intResult As Integer

    intResult = 0
    branchExp = 3
    On branchExp GoTo Sub1, Sub2, Sub3
    Exit Sub

Sub1:
    intResult = 1
    Exit Sub
Sub2:
    intResult = 2
    Exit Sub
```

```
Sub3:
    intResult = 3
    Exit Sub
End Sub
```

Example 2

In this case, after the following lines execute, the variable intResult will contain the value 0. Because branchExp equals 0 when the program gets to the On GoTo line, the program doesn't branch at all, and instead goes to the first line after the On GoTo statement.

```
Private Sub Command1_Click()
    Dim branchExp As Integer
    Dim intResult As Integer

    intResult = 0
    branchExp = 0
    On branchExp GoSub Sub1, Sub2, Sub3
    Exit Sub

Sub1:
    intResult = 1
    Return
Sub2:
    intResult = 2
    Return
Sub3:
    intResult = 3
    Return
End Sub
```

CROSS-REFERENCE
See also On Error and On GoSub.

Open — Animation

Method

The Open method opens an animation file for display.

Syntax

```
Animation.Open fileName
```

- *Animation*—A reference to an Animation control.
- *fileName*—The path to the file to open.

Example

The following program demonstrates how to open and play an animation file with the Animation control. When you run the program, you see in the form an Animation control and three button controls. Use the Load Animation button to load an .avi file, and then click the Play button to play the animation. Notice the call to the Animation control's Open method in the btnLoad_Click event procedure.

```
VERSION 5.00
Object = "{F9043C88-F6F2-101A-A3C9-08002B2F49FB} _
    #1.2#0"; "COMDLG32.OCX"
Object = "{FE0065C0-1B7B-11CF-9D53-00AA003C9CB6} _
    #2.0#0"; "MSCOMCT2.OCX"
Begin VB.Form frmForm1
    Caption         =   "Open Animation Demo"
    ClientHeight    =   3225
    ClientLeft      =   60
    ClientTop       =   345
    ClientWidth     =   4680
    LinkTopic       =   "Form1"
    ScaleHeight     =   3225
    ScaleWidth      =   4680
    StartUpPosition =   3  'Windows Default
    Begin MSComCtl2.Animation Animation1
        Height      =   975
        Left        =   360
        TabIndex    =   3
        Top         =   360
        Width       =   3975
        _ExtentX    =   7011
        _ExtentY    =   1720
        _Version    =   393216
        FullWidth   =   265
        FullHeight  =   65
    End
    Begin MSComDlg.CommonDialog dlgCommonDialog1
        Left        =   0
        Top         =   1800
        _ExtentX    =   847
        _ExtentY    =   847
```

```
               _Version           =      393216
           End
           Begin VB.CommandButton btnStop
               Caption            =      "Stop"
               Height             =      375
               Left               =      2520
               TabIndex           =      2
               Top                =      2520
               Width              =      1815
           End
           Begin VB.CommandButton btnPlay
               Caption            =      "Play"
               Height             =      375
               Left               =      480
               TabIndex           =      1
               Top                =      2520
               Width              =      1815
           End
           Begin VB.CommandButton btnLoad
               Caption            =      "Load Animation"
               Height             =      615
               Left               =      600
               TabIndex           =      0
               Top                =      1680
               Width              =      3615
           End
           Begin VB.Shape Shape1
               BorderWidth        =      2
               Height             =      1215
               Left               =      240
               Top                =      240
               Width              =      4215
           End
       End
   Attribute VB_Name = "frmForm1"
   Attribute VB_GlobalNameSpace = False
   Attribute VB_Creatable = False
   Attribute VB_PredeclaredId = True
   Attribute VB_Exposed = False

   Private Sub btnLoad_Click()
       dlgCommonDialog1.CancelError = True
       dlgCommonDialog1.Filter = _
           "Video (.avi)|*.avi|All Files (*.*)|*.*"
```

n
o
p

```
              dlgCommonDialog1.FileName = "*.avi"
              dlgCommonDialog1.DialogTitle = "Open Animation"

              On Error GoTo ErrorHandler2
              dlgCommonDialog1.ShowOpen
              On Error GoTo ErrorHandler1
              Animation1.Open dlgCommonDialog1.FileName
              Exit Sub

          ErrorHandler1:
              MsgBox "Cannot play that file.", vbExclamation

          ErrorHandler2:

          End Sub

          Private Sub btnPlay_Click()
              On Error Resume Next
              Animation1.Play
          End Sub

          Private Sub btnStop_Click()
              Animation1.Stop
          End Sub
```

CROSS-REFERENCE
See also Animation.

Open—Files

Statement

The Open statement opens a disk file for a specified type of operation.

Syntax

```
Open name For fileMode fileAccess shareLock _
    As fileNum recLength
```

- *fileAccess* (*)—The keyword Access followed by the keyword Read, Write, or Read Write.

- *shareLock* (*) — The keywords `Lock Read`, `Lock Write`, `Lock Read Write`, or `Shared`.
- *fileMode* — The keyword `Append`, `Input`, `Output`, `Binary`, or `Random`.
- *fileNum* — The file number to be assigned to the file. If the file number is given as a literal, it must be preceded by the # symbol.
- *name* — The path to the file.
- *recLength* (*) — The length of records in a random-access file or the size of the buffer for a sequential file. The value must be preceded by the symbols `Len=`.

(*) = Optional

Example 1

The following lines open a file for binary input and read an integer from the file.

```
Dim intInput As Integer
Open "c:\MyFile.dat" For Binary As #1
Get #1, , intInput
Close #1
```

Example 2

Here, the example opens a binary file for write operations and writes an integer to the file.

```
Dim intOutput As Integer
intOutput = 10
Open "c:\MyFile.dat" For Binary Access Write As #1
Put #1, , intOutput
Close #1
```

Example 3

Finally, the following lines open a random-access file and read five records from the file. The program formats the five records into a message string that's later displayed in a message box.

```
Private Type RecordType
    FirstName As String * 15
    LastName As String * 15
End Type
```

```
Private Sub Command1_Click()
    Dim recData As RecordType
    Dim recNum As Integer
    Dim strMsg, strFName, strLName As String

    strMsg = ""
    Open "c:\MyFile.dat" For Random As #1 Len = 30
    For recNum = 1 To 5
        Get #1, recNum, recData
        strFName = RTrim(recData.FirstName)
        strLName = RTrim(recData.LastName)
        strMsg = strMsg & strLName & ", " _
            & strFName & vbCrLf
    Next
    Close #1
    MsgBox strMsg
End Sub
```

CROSS-REFERENCE
See also Close, FreeFile, Get, Put, Input, and Line Input.

OpenAsTextStream

Method

The OpenAsTextStream method opens a file and creates a TextStream object with which the associated file can be accessed.

Objects with an OpenAsTextStream Method

File

Syntax

txtStream = File.OpenAsTextStream(access, type)

- *access* (*) — One of these values: 1 (for read operations), 2 (for write operations), and 8 (for appending to the file).
- *File* — A reference to a File object.

- *txtStream* — The variable that will receive the TextStream object.
- *type* (*) — One of these values: 0 (opens an ASCII file), –1 (opens a Unicode file), or –2 (opens as the system default).

(*) = Optional

Example 1

The following lines create a FileSystemObject, get a File object, and then open the associated file as a text file. After opening the file, the program reads a line of text and closes the file.

```
Dim fileSystem As Object, file As Object
Dim txtStream As Object
Dim strData As String

Set fileSystem = _
    CreateObject("Scripting.FileSystemObject")
Set file = fileSystem.GetFile("c:\MyFile.txt")
Set txtStream = file.OpenAsTextStream()
strData = txtStream.ReadLine
txtStream.Close
```

Example 2

Here, the example creates a FileSystemObject and opens a text file as a TextStream object. This file is opened for updating in the system default character mode. After opening the file, the program writes a line of text and closes the file.

```
Dim fileSystem As Object, file As Object
Dim txtStream As Object
Set fileSystem = _
    CreateObject("Scripting.FileSystemObject")
Set file = fileSystem.GetFile("c:\MyFile.txt")
Set txtStream = file.OpenAsTextStream(8, -2)
txtStream.WriteLine ("This is a test")
txtStream.Close
```

CROSS-REFERENCE

See also File, FileSystemObject, and OpenTextFile.

OpenTextFile

Method

The `OpenTextFile` method opens a file and creates a TextStream object with which the associated file can be accessed.

Objects with an OpenTextFile Method

FileSystemObject

Syntax

```
txtStream = FileSystemObject.OpenTextFile(name, _
    access, create, type)
```

- *FileSystemObject* — A reference to a FileSystemObject object.
- *type* (*) — One of these values: 0 (opens an ASCII file), –1 (opens a Unicode file), or –2 (opens as the system default).
- *access* (*) — One of these values: 1 (for read operations) or 8 (for appending to the file).
- *name* — The path to the file to open.
- *create* (*) — The value `True` or `False`, which specifies whether the file should be created if it doesn't exist.
- *txtStream* — The variable that will receive the TextStream object.

(*) = Optional

Example 1

The following lines create a FileSystemObject and open a text file as a TextStream object. After opening the file, the program reads a line of text and closes the file.

```
Dim fileSystem As Object
Dim txtStream As Object
Dim strData As String

Set fileSystem = _
    CreateObject("Scripting.FileSystemObject")
Set txtStream = fileSystem.OpenTextFile("c:\MyFile.txt")
strData = txtStream.ReadLine
txtStream.Close
```

Example 2

Here, the example creates a FileSystemObject and opens a text file as a TextStream object. This file is opened for updating in ASCII mode. If the file doesn't exist, it'll be created. After opening the file, the program writes a line of text and closes the file.

```
Dim fileSystem As Object
Dim txtStream As Object

Set fileSystem = _
    CreateObject("Scripting.FileSystemObject")
Set txtStream = fileSystem.OpenTextFile _
  ("c:\MyFile.txt", 8, True, 0)
txtStream.WriteLine ("This is a test.")
txtStream.Close
```

CROSS-REFERENCE

See also File, FileSystemObject, and OpenAsTextStream.

Option

Keyword

The Option keyword is used with the Option Base, Option Compare, Option Explicit, and Option Private statements. For example, the following line specifies that the first element in arrays will be at index 1.

```
Option Base 1
```

CROSS-REFERENCE

For more information, see Option Base, Option Compare, and Option Explicit.

Optional

Keyword

The Optional keyword is used in argument lists to specify that a particular argument is optional. For example, the following procedure definition's single argument need not be supplied when the procedure is called.

```
Private Sub MyProcedure(Optional arg As Integer)
    If arg = Empty Then arg = 0

    ' The rest of the procedure goes here.
End Sub
```

Option Base

Statement

The Option Base statement determines the lowest possible index in an array. The default value is 0, which means that the first element of an array is at index 0. A program can change the lowest index to 1 by using the Option Base statement.

Syntax

```
Option Base lowIndex
```

- *lowIndex* — The value 0 or 1.

Example

The following line sets the lowest index used by arrays to 1.

```
Option Base 1
```

OptionButton

Control

An OptionButton control enables the user to select program options by clicking with the mouse. Programs often use OptionButton controls as *radio buttons*, a set of options only one of which can be selected at a time. Figure O-7 shows several OptionButton controls in a form. The OptionButton control is available on Visual Basic's standard toolbox.

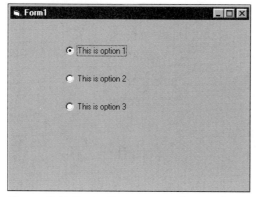

Figure O-7 OptionButton controls provide an easy way for the user to make option
selections.

Properties

The OptionButton control has 42 properties, which are listed below. Because
many Visual Basic controls have similar properties, the following list does not
include the properties' descriptions. For information on using a property, look
up the individual property's entry, provided alphabetically in this book.

```
Alignment
Appearance
BackColor
Caption
CausesValidation
Container
DisabledPicture
DownPicture
DragIcon
DragMode
Enabled
Font
FontBold
FontItalic
FontName
FontSize
FontStrikethru
FontUnderline
ForeColor
Height
HelpContextID
```

n

o

p

```
hWnd
Index
Left
MaskColor
MouseIcon
Name
OLEDropMode
Parent
Picture
RightToLeft
Style
TabIndex
TabStop
Tag
ToolTipText
Top
UseMaskColor
Value
Visible
WhatsThisHelpID
Width
```

Methods

The OptionButton control has seven methods, which are listed below. Because many Visual Basic controls have similar methods, the following list does not include the methods' descriptions. For information on using a method, look up the individual method's entry, provided alphabetically in this book.

```
Drag
Move
OLEDrag
Refresh
SetFocus
ShowWhatsThis
ZOrder
```

Events

The OptionButton control responds to 19 events, which are listed below. Because many Visual Basic controls respond to similar events, the following list does not include the events' descriptions. For information on using an event, look up the individual event's entry, provided alphabetically in this book.

```
Click
DblClick
DragDrop
DragOver
GotFocus
KeyDown
KeyPress
KeyUp
LostFocus
MouseDown
MouseMove
MouseUp
OLECompleteDrag
OLEDragDrop
OLEDragOver
OLEGiveFeedback
OLESetData
OLEStartDrag
Validate
```

The OptionButton control's most commonly used event is Click, which the button generates when the user clicks the button with the mouse. A program responds to the button's Click event in the Click event procedure. An option button called optOption1 will have a Click event procedure called optOption1_Click, which is where the program should handle the event, as shown in the following lines:

```
Private Sub optOption1_Click()
    ' Handle the Click event here.
End Sub
```

Option Compare

Statement

The Option Compare statement determines how string information is compared. Table O-9 shows the values that can be used with this statement.

	Table O-9 Values for the Option Compare Statement
Value	**Description**
Binary	Characters are sorted based on their binary values (default). This is a case-sensitive sort.
Text	Characters are sorted on their text order as specified by the system locale. This is a case-insensitive sort.
Database	Characters are sorted based on the database's locale ID. Used only with Microsoft Access.

Syntax

```
Option Compare type
```

- *type* — A value from Table O-9.

Example

The following line sets the string sorting to case-insensitive text.

```
Option Base Text
```

Option — Explicit

Statement

The `Option Explicit` statement determines whether all variables in a module must be declared before they are referenced. Setting this option helps you avoid typing mistakes when entering variable names.

Syntax

```
Option Explicit
```

Example

The following line specifies that all variables in the module must be declared before they are accessed.

```
Option Explicit
```

CROSS-REFERENCE
For more information, see Dim, ReDim, Static, Public, and Private.

Or

Operator

The Or operator performs a Boolean comparison between two expressions. The result of this comparison is True if one or both of the expressions is True, and is False if neither of the expressions evaluates to True. The Or operator can also be used to perform bit comparisons.

Syntax

```
result = exp1 Or exp2
```

- *exp1* — Any valid expression.
- *exp2* — Any valid expression.
- *result* — The Boolean result of the operation.

Example 1

After the following lines execute, result will contain the value True.

```
Dim expr1, expr2 As Integer
Dim result As Boolean
expr1 = 10
expr2 = 25
result = (expr1 = 10) Or (expr2 = 10)
```

Example 2

Here, after the following lines execute, result will contain the value False.

```
Dim expr1, expr2 As Integer
Dim result As Boolean
expr1 = 10
expr2 = 25
result = (expr1 = 30) Or (expr2 = 10)
```

Example 3

In this example, the program uses the Or operator as part of an If statement. Here, the body of the If statement will not execute because the Or operation results in a value of False.

```
Dim expr1, expr2 As Integer
Dim result As Boolean
expr1 = 10
expr2 = 25
If (expr1 = 30) Or (expr2 = 10) Then
    ' Do something here.
End If
```

CROSS-REFERENCE
See also And.

Orientation — CommonDialog

Property

The Orientation property represents the orientation of paper for a print job. This property can be cdlPortrait (default) for portrait orientation or cdlLandScape for landscape orientation.

Syntax

```
CommonDialog.Orientation = value1
```

or

```
value2 = CommonDialog.Orientation
```

- *CommonDialog* — A reference to a Print CommonDialog control.
- *value1* — The orientation value.
- *value2* — The variable that will receive the property's current setting.

Example

The following line sets a print job to the landscape orientation. In the case of an Epson ActionLaser 1500, this setting results in a printer property sheet shown in Figure O-8. Notice how the Orientation box is set to Landscape. In this example, the dlgCommonDialog1 object is a CommonDialog control that the programmer added to the form at design time.

```
dlgCommonDialog1.Orientation = cdlLandscape
```

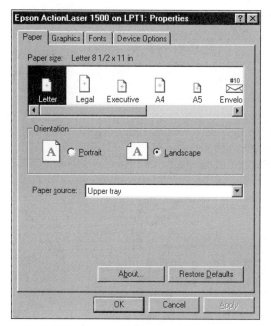

Figure O-8 This print job's orientation was set to landscape by the CommonDialog control's Orientation property.

CROSS-REFERENCE
See also CommonDialog.

Orientation — CoolBar

Property

The Orientation property represents the orientation of a CoolBar control, enabling the control to be positioned horizontally or vertically. This property can be cc30rientationHorizontal or cc30rientationVertical.

Syntax

```
CoolBar.Orientation = value1
```

or

```
value2 = CoolBar.Orientation
```

- *CoolBar*—A reference to a CoolBar control.

- *value1* — The orientation value.
- *value2* — The variable that will receive the property's current setting.

Example

The following program demonstrates the CoolBar control's `Orientation` property. When you first run the program, the CoolBar control appears in its horizontal orientation, as shown in Figure O-9. Click the Orientation button to change the CoolBar to its vertical orientation, as shown in Figure O-10. By clicking the button, you can continue to toggle the CoolBar between its two orientations.

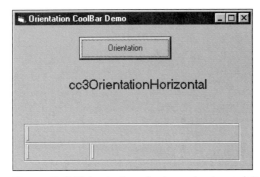

Figure O-9 This window displays a horizontal CoolBar control.

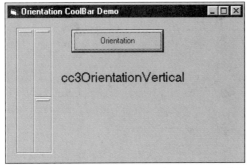

Figure O-10 This window displays a vertical CoolBar control.

```
VERSION 5.00
Object = "{38911DA0-E448-11D0-84A3-00DD01104159} _
    #1.1#0"; "COMCT332.OCX"
Begin VB.Form Form1
   Caption         =   "Orientation CoolBar Demo"
   ClientHeight    =   3060
   ClientLeft      =   165
   ClientTop       =   450
   ClientWidth     =   5235
   LinkTopic       =   "Form1"
   ScaleHeight     =   3060
   ScaleWidth      =   5235
   StartUpPosition =   3   'Windows Default
   Begin VB.CommandButton btnOrientation
      Caption      =   "Orientation"
      Height       =   495
      Left         =   1440
      TabIndex     =   1
      Top          =   240
      Width        =   2055
   End
   Begin ComCtl3.CoolBar CoolBar1
      Height       =   810
      Left         =   195
      TabIndex     =   0
      Top          =   2040
      Width        =   4815
      _ExtentX     =   8493
      _ExtentY     =   1429
      _CBWidth     =   4815
      _CBHeight    =   810
      _Version     =   "6.0.8141"
      MinHeight1   =   360
      Width1       =   2880
      NewRow1      =   0   'False
      MinHeight2   =   360
      Width2       =   1440
      NewRow2      =   -1  'True
      MinHeight3   =   360
      Width3       =   1440
      NewRow3      =   0   'False
   End
```

```
Begin VB.Label lblOrientation
    Caption         =   "Label1"
    BeginProperty Font
        Name            =   "MS Sans Serif"
        Size            =   13.5
        Charset         =   0
        Weight          =   400
        Underline       =   0   'False
        Italic          =   0   'False
        Strikethrough   =   0   'False
    EndProperty
    Height          =   615
    Left            =   1200
    TabIndex        =   2
    Top             =   1080
    Width           =   3735
End
End
Attribute VB_Name = "Form1"
Attribute VB_GlobalNameSpace = False
Attribute VB_Creatable = False
Attribute VB_PredeclaredId = True
Attribute VB_Exposed = False

Private Sub btnOrientation_Click()
    If CoolBar1.Orientation = cc3OrientationVertical Then
        CoolBar1.Orientation = cc3OrientationHorizontal
        CoolBar1.Move 200, 2100, 4800, 1000
        lblOrientation.Caption = "cc3OrientationHorizontal"
    Else
        CoolBar1.Orientation = cc3OrientationVertical
        CoolBar1.Move 200, 200, 1000, 2700
        lblOrientation.Caption = "cc3OrientationVertical"
    End If
End Sub

Private Sub Form_Load()
    CoolBar1.Move 200, 2100, 4800, 1000
    lblOrientation.Caption = "cc3OrientationHorizontal"
End Sub
```

CROSS-REFERENCE
See also CoolBar.

Orientation — Multimedia

Property

The Orientation property represents the orientation of a Multimedia MCI control, enabling the control to be positioned horizontally or vertically. This property can be mciOrientHorz or mciOrientVert.

Syntax

```
Multimedia.Orientation = value1
```

or

```
value2 = Multimedia.Orientation
```

- *Multimedia* — A reference to a Multimedia MCI control.
- *value1* — The orientation value.
- *value2* — The variable that will receive the property's current setting.

Example

The following program demonstrates the Multimedia MCI control's Orientation property. When you first run the program, the multimedia control appears it its horizontal orientation, as shown in Figure O-11. Click the Orientation button to change the multimedia control to its vertical orientation, as shown in Figure O-12. By clicking the button, you can continue to toggle the multimedia control between its two orientations.

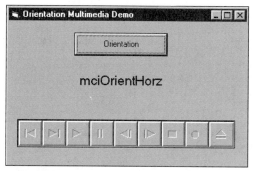

Figure O-11 This window displays a horizontal Multimedia MCI control.

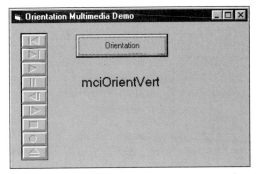

Figure O-12 This window displays a vertical Multimedia MCI control.

```
VERSION 5.00
Object = "{C1A8AF28-1257-101B-8FB0-0020AF039CA3} _
    #1.1#0"; "MCI32.OCX"
Begin VB.Form Form1
    Caption         =   "Orientation Multimedia Demo"
    ClientHeight    =   3060
    ClientLeft      =   165
    ClientTop       =   450
    ClientWidth     =   5235
    LinkTopic       =   "Form1"
    ScaleHeight     =   3060
    ScaleWidth      =   5235
    StartUpPosition =   3  'Windows Default
    Begin MCI.MMControl mciMMControl1
        Height      =    615
        Left        =    240
        TabIndex    =    2
        Top         =    2280
        Width       =    4815
        _ExtentX    =    8493
        _ExtentY    =    1085
        _Version    =    393216
        DeviceType  =    ""
        FileName    =    ""
    End
    Begin VB.CommandButton btnOrientation
        Caption     =    "Orientation"
        Height      =    495
        Left        =    1440
        TabIndex    =    0
```

```
        Top             =    240
        Width           =    2055
    End
    Begin VB.Label lblOrientation
        Caption         =    "Label1"
        BeginProperty Font
            Name        =    "MS Sans Serif"
            Size        =    13.5
            Charset     =    0
            Weight      =    400
            Underline   =    0    'False
            Italic      =    0    'False
            Strikethrough =  0    'False
        EndProperty
        Height          =    615
        Left            =    1560
        TabIndex        =    1
        Top             =    1080
        Width           =    3375
    End
End
Attribute VB_Name = "Form1"
Attribute VB_GlobalNameSpace = False
Attribute VB_Creatable = False
Attribute VB_PredeclaredId = True
Attribute VB_Exposed = False

Private Sub btnOrientation_Click()
    If mciMMControl1.Orientation = mciOrientVert Then
        mciMMControl1.Orientation = mciOrientHorz
        mciMMControl1.Move 200, 2100, 4800, 600
        lblOrientation.Caption = "mciOrientHorz"
    Else
        mciMMControl1.Orientation = mciOrientVert
        mciMMControl1.Move 200, 200, 600, 2100
        lblOrientation.Caption = "mciOrientVert"
    End If
End Sub

Private Sub Form_Load()
    mciMMControl1.Move 200, 2100, 4800, 600
    lblOrientation.Caption = "mciOrientHorz"
End Sub
```

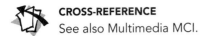

CROSS-REFERENCE
See also Multimedia MCI.

Orientation — Printer

Property

The Orientation property represents the orientation of paper for a print job. This property can be vbPRORPortrait (default) for portrait orientation or vbPRORLandscape for landscape orientation.

Syntax

```
Printer.Orientation = value1
```

or

```
value2 = Printer.Orientation
```

- *Printer* — A reference to the Printer object.
- *value1* — The orientation value.
- *value2* — The variable that will receive the property's current setting.

Example

The following line sets a print job to the landscape orientation. Note that the Printer object is a Visual Basic global object that you don't need to create in your programs.

```
Printer.Orientation = vbPRORLandscape
```

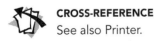

CROSS-REFERENCE
See also Printer.

Orientation — ProgressBar

Property

The Orientation property represents the orientation of a ProgressBar control, enabling the control to be positioned horizontally or vertically. This property can be ccOrientationHorizontal or ccOrientationVertical.

Syntax

```
ProgressBar.Orientation = value1
```

or

```
value2 = ProgressBar.Orientation
```

- *ProgressBar* — A reference to a ProgressBar control.
- *value1* — The orientation value.
- *value2* — The variable that will receive the property's current setting.

Example

The following program demonstrates the ProgressBar control's `Orientation` property. When you first run the program, the control appears in its horizontal orientation, as shown in Figure O-13. Click the Orientation button to change the control to its vertical orientation, as shown in Figure O-14. By clicking the button, you can continue to toggle the control between its two orientations.

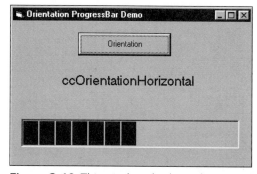

Figure O-13 This window displays a horizontal ProgressBar control.

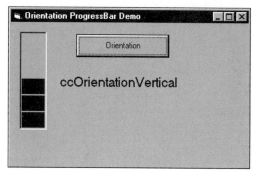

Figure O-14 This window displays a vertical ProgressBar control.

```
VERSION 5.00
Object = "{6B7E6392-850A-101B-AFC0-4210102A8DA7} _
    #2.0#0"; "MSCOMCTL.OCX"
Begin VB.Form Form1
    Caption         =   "Orientation ProgressBar Demo"
    ClientHeight    =   3060
    ClientLeft      =   165
    ClientTop       =   450
    ClientWidth     =   5235
    LinkTopic       =   "Form1"
    ScaleHeight     =   3060
    ScaleWidth      =   5235
    StartUpPosition =   3  'Windows Default
    Begin MSComctlLib.ProgressBar prgProgressBar1
        Height          =   615
        Left            =   240
        TabIndex        =   2
        Top             =   2280
        Width           =   4695
        _ExtentX        =   8281
        _ExtentY        =   1085
        _Version        =   393216
        Appearance      =   1
    End
    Begin VB.CommandButton btnOrientation
        Caption         =   "Orientation"
        Height          =   495
        Left            =   1440
        TabIndex        =   0
        Top             =   240
        Width           =   2055
    End
    Begin VB.Label lblOrientation
        Caption         =   "Label1"
        BeginProperty Font
            Name            =   "MS Sans Serif"
            Size            =   13.5
            Charset         =   0
            Weight          =   400
            Underline       =   0  'False
            Italic          =   0  'False
            Strikethrough   =   0  'False
        EndProperty
```

```
                Height          =    615
                Left            =    1080
                TabIndex        =    1
                Top             =    1080
                Width           =    3375
          End
     End
Attribute VB_Name = "Form1"
Attribute VB_GlobalNameSpace = False
Attribute VB_Creatable = False
Attribute VB_PredeclaredId = True
Attribute VB_Exposed = False

Private Sub btnOrientation_Click()
     If prgProgressBar1.Orientation = _
        ccOrientationVertical Then
          prgProgressBar1.Orientation = ccOrientationHorizontal
          prgProgressBar1.Move 200, 2100, 4800, 600
          lblOrientation.Caption = "ccOrientationHorizontal"
     Else
          prgProgressBar1.Orientation = ccOrientationVertical
          prgProgressBar1.Move 200, 200, 600, 2100
          lblOrientation.Caption = "ccOrientationVertical"
     End If
End Sub

Private Sub Form_Load()
     prgProgressBar1.Value = 50
     prgProgressBar1.Move 200, 2100, 4800, 600
     lblOrientation.Caption = "ccOrientationHorizontal"
End Sub
```

CROSS-REFERENCE
See also ProgressBar.

Orientation — Slider

Property

The Orientation property represents the orientation of a Slider control, enabling the control to be positioned horizontally or vertically. This property can be 0 for horizontal or 1 for vertical.

Syntax

```
Slider.Orientation = value1
```

or

```
value2 = Slider.Orientation
```

- *Slider*—A reference to a Slider control.
- *value1*—The orientation value.
- *value2*—The variable that will receive the property's current setting.

Example

The following program demonstrates the Slider control's `Orientation` property. When you first run the program, the control appears in its horizontal orientation, as shown in Figure O-15. Click the Orientation button to change the control to its vertical orientation, as shown in Figure O-16. By clicking the button, you can continue to toggle the control between its two orientations.

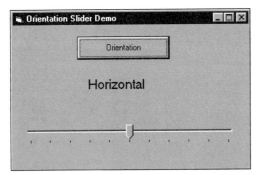

Figure O-15 This window displays a horizontal Slider control.

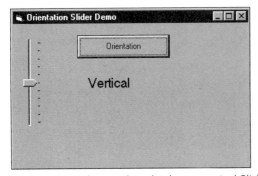

Figure O-16 This window displays a vertical Slider control.

```
VERSION 5.00
Object = "{6B7E6392-850A-101B-AFC0-4210102A8DA7} _
    #2.0#0"; "MSCOMCTL.OCX"
Begin VB.Form Form1
    Caption         =   "Orientation Slider Demo"
    ClientHeight    =   3060
    ClientLeft      =   165
    ClientTop       =   450
    ClientWidth     =   5235
    LinkTopic       =   "Form1"
    ScaleHeight     =   3060
    ScaleWidth      =   5235
    StartUpPosition =   3  'Windows Default
    Begin MSComctlLib.Slider sldSlider1
        Height      =   495
        Left        =   240
        TabIndex    =   2
        Top         =   2280
        Width       =   4695
        _ExtentX    =   8281
        _ExtentY    =   873
        _Version    =   393216
    End
    Begin VB.CommandButton btnOrientation
        Caption     =   "Orientation"
        Height      =   495
        Left        =   1440
        TabIndex    =   0
        Top         =   240
        Width       =   2055
    End
    Begin VB.Label lblOrientation
        Caption     =   "Label1"
        BeginProperty Font
            Name          =   "MS Sans Serif"
            Size          =   13.5
            Charset       =   0
            Weight        =   400
            Underline     =   0    'False
            Italic        =   0    'False
            Strikethrough =   0    'False
        EndProperty
        Height      =   615
        Left        =   1680
```

```
        TabIndex      =   1
        Top           =   1080
        Width         =   2295
    End
End
Attribute VB_Name = "Form1"
Attribute VB_GlobalNameSpace = False
Attribute VB_Creatable = False
Attribute VB_PredeclaredId = True
Attribute VB_Exposed = False

Private Sub btnOrientation_Click()
    If sldSlider1.Orientation = 1 Then
        sldSlider1.Orientation = 0
        sldSlider1.Move 200, 2100, 4800, 600
        lblOrientation.Caption = "Horizontal"
    Else
        sldSlider1.Orientation = 1
        sldSlider1.Move 200, 200, 600, 2100
        lblOrientation.Caption = "Vertical"
    End If
End Sub

Private Sub Form_Load()
    sldSlider1.Value = 5
    sldSlider1.Move 200, 2100, 4800, 600
    lblOrientation.Caption = "Horizontal"
End Sub
```

CROSS-REFERENCE
See also Slider.

Orientation — UpDown

Property

The Orientation property represents the orientation of an UpDown control, enabling the control to be positioned horizontally or vertically. This property can be cc2orientationHorizontal (see **Figure O-17**) or cc2orientationVertical (see Figure O-18).

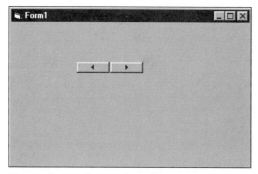

Figure O-17 This window displays a horizontal UpDown control.

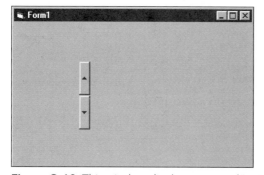

Figure O-18 This window displays a vertical UpDown control.

Syntax

```
UpDown.Orientation = value1
```

or

```
value2 = UpDown.Orientation
```

- *UpDown* — A reference to an UpDown control.
- *value1* — The orientation value.
- *value2* — The variable that will receive the property's current setting.

Example

The following lines retrieve the current value of an UpDown control's Orientation property. The updUpDown1 object is an UpDown control that the programmer added to the form at design time.

```
Dim updOrientation As Integer
updOrientation = updUpDown1.Orientation
```

CROSS-REFERENCE
See also UpDown.

OSBuild

Property

The OSBuild property represents build information about the installed operating system. This property is accessible only at runtime.

Objects with an OSBuild Property

SysInfo

Syntax

```
value = SysInfo.OSBuild
```

- *SysInfo* — A reference to a SysInfo control.
- *value* — The variable that will receive the property's current setting.

Example

The following lines show how to retrieve the value of the SysInfo control's OSBuild property. When running under the first version of Windows 98, after the following lines execute, the buildInfo variable will contain the value "1998." In this example, the SysInfo1 object is a reference to a SysInfo control that the programmer added to the form at design time.

```
Dim buildInfo As String
buildInfo = SysInfo1.OSBuild
```

CROSS-REFERENCE
See also OSPlatform, OSVersion, and SysInfo.

OSPlatform

Property

The OSPlatform property represents platform information about the installed operating system. This property is accessible only at runtime.

Objects with an OSPlatform Property

SysInfo

Syntax

`value = SysInfo.OSPlatform`

- *SysInfo* — A reference to a SysInfo control.
- *value* — The variable that will receive the property's current setting.

Example

The following lines show how to retrieve the value of the SysInfo control's `OSPlatform` property. When running under the first version of Windows 98, after the following lines execute, the `platformInfo` variable will contain the value "1." In this example, the `SysInfo1` object is a reference to a SysInfo control that the programmer added to the form at design time.

```
Dim platformInfo As String
platformInfo = SysInfo1.OSPlatform
```

 CROSS-REFERENCE
See also OSBuild, OSVersion, and SysInfo.

OSVersion

Property

The `OSVersion` property represents version information about the installed operating system. This property is accessible only at runtime.

Objects with an OSVersion Property

SysInfo

Syntax

`value = SysInfo.OSVersion`

- *SysInfo* — A reference to a SysInfo control.
- *value* — The variable that will receive the property's current setting.

n
o
p

Example

The following lines show how to retrieve the value of the SysInfo control's OSVersion property. When running under the first version of Windows 98, after the following lines execute, the versionInfo variable will contain the value "4.1." In this example, the SysInfo1 object is a reference to a SysInfo control that the programmer added to the form at design time.

```
Dim versionInfo As String
versionInfo = SysInfo1.OSVersion
```

 CROSS-REFERENCE
See also OSBuild, OSVersion, and SysInfo.

Overlay

Method

The Overlay method draws, one on top of the other, two images in an ImageList control.

Objects with an Overlay Method

ImageList

Syntax

ImageList.Overlay(*image1*, *image2*)

- *ImageList* — A reference to an ImageList control.
- *image1* — The index or key of the first image to be drawn.
- *image2* — The index or key of the second image to be drawn.

Example

The following program demonstrates the Overlay method. When you first run the program you see a window with two images and two buttons (Figure O-19). Click the Overlay button to draw a third image made up of the first and second image (Figure O-20). As you can see, the Overlay method overlays the circle in the second image over the letter A in the first image. What happened to the red in the second image? Because the program sets the ImageList control's MaskColor property to RGB(255, 0, 0), which is red, the red in the second image becomes transparent when the image is overlaid on the first image. If you want to see the overlay process again, click the Clear button to erase the combined image. Then you can click the Overlay button again.

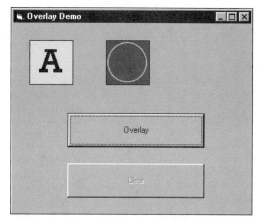

Figure O-19 Here's the program before you click the Overlay button.

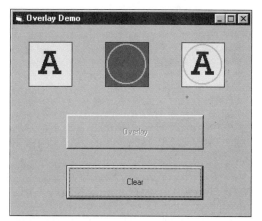

Figure O-20 After you click the Overlay button, the combined image appears on the right.

```
VERSION 5.00
Object = "{6B7E6392-850A-101B-AFC0-4210102A8DA7} _
    #2.0#0"; "MSCOMCTL.OCX"
Begin VB.Form frmForm1
   Caption       =   "Overlay Demo"
   ClientHeight  =   4050
   ClientLeft    =   165
```

```
ClientTop        =    450
ClientWidth      =    5235
LinkTopic        =    "Form1"
ScaleHeight      =    4050
ScaleWidth       =    5235
StartUpPosition  =    3   'Windows Default
Begin VB.CommandButton btnClear
   Caption       =    "Clear"
   Height        =    735
   Left          =    1200
   TabIndex      =    1
   Top           =    3000
   Width         =    3015
End
Begin VB.CommandButton btnOverlay
   Caption       =    "Overlay"
   Height        =    735
   Left          =    1200
   TabIndex      =    0
   Top           =    1920
   Width         =    3015
End
Begin MSComctlLib.ImageList ilsImageList1
   Left          =    4440
   Top           =    2160
   _ExtentX      =    1005
   _ExtentY      =    1005
   BackColor     =    -2147483643
   MaskColor     =    12632256
   _Version      =    393216
End
Begin VB.Image imgImage3
   Height        =    1095
   Left          =    3720
   Top           =    360
   Width         =    1215
End
Begin VB.Image imgImage2
   Height        =    1095
   Left          =    2040
   Top           =    360
   Width         =    1215
End
```

```
        Begin VB.Image imgImage1
            Height          =    1095
            Left            =    360
            Top             =    360
            Width           =    1215
        End
    End
Attribute VB_Name = "frmForm1"
Attribute VB_GlobalNameSpace = False
Attribute VB_Creatable = False
Attribute VB_PredeclaredId = True
Attribute VB_Exposed = False

Private Sub btnOverlay_Click()
    imgImage3.Picture = ilsImageList1.Overlay(1, 2)
    btnOverlay.Enabled = False
    btnClear.Enabled = True
End Sub

Private Sub btnClear_Click()
    imgImage3.Picture = frmForm1.Picture
    btnOverlay.Enabled = True
    btnClear.Enabled = False
End Sub

Private Sub Form_Load()
    ilsImageList1.ListImages.Add , , _
        LoadPicture("image1.gif")
    ilsImageList1.ListImages.Add , , _
        LoadPicture("image2.gif")
    ilsImageList1.MaskColor = RGB(255, 0, 0)
    imgImage1.Picture = _
        ilsImageList1.ListImages(1).Picture
    imgImage2.Picture = _
        ilsImageList1.ListImages(2).Picture
    btnClear.Enabled = False
End Sub
```

CROSS-REFERENCE
See also ImageList, ListImage, and ListImages.

Page

Property

The `Page` property represents the number of the page currently being printed.

Objects with a Page Property

Printer

Syntax

```
value = Printer.Page
```

- *Printer* — A reference to the Printer object.
- *value* — The variable that will receive the page number.

Example

The following lines retrieve the current page number from the Printer object. Note that the Printer object is a global Visual Basic object that you don't need to create explicitly in your programs.

```
Dim pageNum As Integer
pageNum = Printer.Page
```

CROSS-REFERENCE
See also Printer, NewPage, EndDoc, and Print.

Paint

Event

Visual Basic sends an object a `Paint` event when the object's display needs to be updated. This situation could happen, for example, when a control is uncovered from under another window.

Objects with a Paint Event

Form
PictureBox
PropertyPage
UserControl

Example

A program can respond to a `Paint` event by implementing the object's `Paint` event procedure. The following program demonstrates the use of the `Paint` event procedure in a PictureBox control. When you run the program, you see a window with a PictureBox control and two buttons. Click the Draw Display button to draw an image in the PictureBox control (see Figure P-1). Then cover the application with another window so that a part of the PictureBox control's image is under the other window. Uncover the Paint demo application's window. When you do, the program automatically redraws its display. Now click the Paint Event Off button to disable the `Paint` event procedure. Try covering and uncovering the PictureBox control's image again. This time, the program doesn't update the display (see Figure P-2) unless you click the Draw Display button.

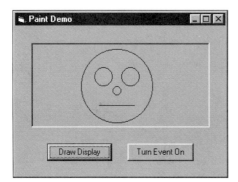

Figure P-1 The Paint Demo application displays a simple drawing in its PictureBox control.

Figure P-2 When the Paint event is off, the program doesn't properly update its display.

```
VERSION 5.00
Begin VB.Form Form1
   Caption         =    "Paint Demo"
   ClientHeight    =    3195
   ClientLeft      =    60
   ClientTop       =    345
   ClientWidth     =    4680
   LinkTopic       =    "Form1"
   ScaleHeight     =    3195
   ScaleWidth      =    4680
   StartUpPosition =    3    'Windows Default
   Begin VB.CommandButton btnTurnOffEvent
      Caption         =    "Paint Event Off"
      Height          =    375
      Left            =    2520
      TabIndex        =    2
      Top             =    2520
      Width           =    1455
   End
   Begin VB.CommandButton btnDrawDisplay
      Caption         =    "Draw Display"
      Height          =    375
      Left            =    720
      TabIndex        =    1
      Top             =    2520
      Width           =    1455
   End
   Begin VB.PictureBox picPicture1
      Height          =    1815
      Left            =    360
```

```
            ScaleHeight      =    1755
            ScaleWidth       =    3915
            TabIndex         =    0
            Top              =    360
            Width            =    3975
        End
    End
End
Attribute VB_Name = "Form1"
Attribute VB_GlobalNameSpace = False
Attribute VB_Creatable = False
Attribute VB_PredeclaredId = True
Attribute VB_Exposed = False


Private eventOn As Boolean

Private Sub btnDrawDisplay_Click()
    picPicture1.Circle (1900, 900), 800
    picPicture1.Circle (2200, 700), 200
    picPicture1.Circle (1600, 700), 200
    picPicture1.Circle (1900, 1000), 100
    picPicture1.Line (1500, 1300)-(2300, 1300)
End Sub

Private Sub btnTurnOffEvent_Click()
    If eventOn Then
        eventOn = False
        btnTurnOffEvent.Caption = "Paint Event On"
    Else
        eventOn = True
        btnTurnOffEvent.Caption = "Paint Event Off"
    End If
End Sub

Private Sub Form_Load()
    eventOn = True
End Sub

Private Sub picPicture1_Paint()
    If eventOn Then btnDrawDisplay_Click
End Sub
```

CROSS-REFERENCE
See also AutoRedraw.

PaintPicture

Method

The `PaintPicture` method draws an image in the display area of an object or control.

Objects with a PaintPicture Method

Form

PictureBox

Printer

PropertyPage

UserControl

Syntax

`object.PaintPicture pic, x1, y1, w1, h1, x2, y2, w2, h2, op`

- *object* — A reference to an object with a PaintPicture method.
- *pic* — A reference to the picture to draw.
- *x1* — The horizontal coordinate at which to draw the image.
- *y1* — The vertical coordinate at which to draw the image.
- *w1* (*) — The width of the image. Larger or smaller values than the image's actual width causes the image to be enlarged or reduced.
- *h1* (*) — The height of the image. Larger or smaller values than the image's actual height causes the image to be enlarged or reduced.
- *x2* (*) — The horizontal coordinate of the image's clipping region.
- *y2* (*) — The vertical coordinate of the image's clipping region.
- *w2* (*) — The width of the image's clipping region.
- *h2* (*) — The height of the image's clipping region.
- *op* (*) — The raster operation to use, which can be one of the values from Table P-1.

(*) = Optional

Table P-1 Raster Operations

Value	Description
vbDstInvert	Inverts the destination pixels
vbMergeCopy	Combines a pattern with the source pixels.
vbMergePaint	Inverts the source pixels and Or's them with the destination pixels.
vbNotSrcCopy	Inverts the source pixels and copies them to the destination pixels.
vbNotSrcErase	Or's the destination and source pixels and then inverts the result.
vbPatCopy	Copies a pattern to the destination pixels.
vbPatInvert	Xor's a pattern with the destination pixels.
vbPatPaint	Inverts the source pixels and Or's them with a pattern, and then Or's the result with the destination pixels.
vbSrcAnd	And's the source and destination pixels.
vbSrcCopy	Copies the source pixels to the destination pixels.
vbSrcErase	Inverts the destination pixels and And's them with the source pixels.
vbSrcInvert	Xor's the source and destination pixels.
vbSrcPaint	Or's the source and destination pixels.

Example

The following program demonstrates the `PaintPicture` method. When you run the program, you see a window with a PictureBox control and three buttons. Click any of the three buttons to draw an image in the PictureBox control's display (see Figure P-3).

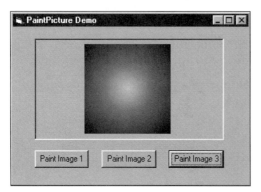

Figure P-3 The PaintPicture Demo application displays one of three images.

```
VERSION 5.00
Begin VB.Form Form1
   Caption         =    "PaintPicture Demo"
   ClientHeight    =    3345
   ClientLeft      =    165
   ClientTop       =    450
   ClientWidth     =    5235
   LinkTopic       =    "Form1"
   ScaleHeight     =    3345
   ScaleWidth      =    5235
   StartUpPosition =    3   'Windows Default
   Begin VB.CommandButton btnPaintImage3
      Caption         =    "Paint Image 3"
      Height          =    375
      Left            =    3480
      TabIndex        =    3
      Top             =    2640
      Width           =    1215
   End
   Begin VB.CommandButton btnPaintImage2
      Caption         =    "Paint Image 2"
      Height          =    375
      Left            =    1995
      TabIndex        =    2
      Top             =    2640
      Width           =    1215
   End
   Begin VB.CommandButton btnPaintImage1
      Caption         =    "Paint Image 1"
      Height          =    375
      Left            =    480
      TabIndex        =    1
      Top             =    2640
      Width           =    1215
   End
   Begin VB.PictureBox picPicture1
      Height          =    2175
      Left            =    480
      ScaleHeight     =    2115
      ScaleWidth      =    4155
      TabIndex        =    0
      Top             =    240
      Width           =    4215
   End
```

```
End
Attribute VB_Name = "Form1"
Attribute VB_GlobalNameSpace = False
Attribute VB_Creatable = False
Attribute VB_PredeclaredId = True
Attribute VB_Exposed = False
Private pic1, pic2, pic3 As Object

Private Sub btnPaintImage1_Click()
    picPicture1.PaintPicture pic1, 1100, 90
End Sub

Private Sub btnPaintImage2_Click()
    picPicture1.PaintPicture pic2, 1100, 90
End Sub

Private Sub btnPaintImage3_Click()
    picPicture1.PaintPicture pic3, 1100, 90
End Sub

Private Sub Form_Load()
    Set pic1 = LoadPicture("pic1.jpg")
    Set pic2 = LoadPicture("pic2.jpg")
    Set pic3 = LoadPicture("pic3.jpg")
End Sub
```

CROSS-REFERENCE
See also Scale, ScaleX, ScaleY, and ScaleMode.

Palette

Property

The Palette property represents an image that the program uses to create a color palette.

Objects with a Palette Property

AmbientProperties

Form

PropertyPage

UserControl

Syntax

```
object.Palette = value1
```

or

```
value2 = object.Palette
```

- *object* — A reference to an object with a `Palette` property.
- *value1* — The path and file name of the image from which to create the palette. The image can be in the .bmp, .dib, or .gif format.
- *value2* — The variable that will receive the property's current setting.

Example

The following line sets a form's palette to the colors contained in the `image.bmp` bitmap.

```
Form1.Palette = LoadPicture("image.bmp")
```

CROSS-REFERENCE
See also PaletteMode.

PaletteMode

Property

The `PaletteMode` property represents the type of palette used with an object. This property can be one of the values shown in Table P-2.

Table P-2 Settings for the PaletteMode Property

Value	Description
vbPaletteModeContainer	The object (a UserControl control) will use the container's ambient Palette property.
vbPaletteModeCustom	The object will use the palette given in the Palette property.
vbPaletteModeHalfTone	The object will use a half-tone palette (default).
vbPaletteModeNone	The object (a UserControl control) will use no palette.
vbPaletteModeObject	The object will use the ActiveX designer application's palette, if the palette exists.
vbPaletteModeUseZOrder	The object will use the palette of the first control that has a palette.

Objects with a PaletteMode Property

Form
PropertyPage
UserControl

Syntax

```
object.PaletteMode = value1
```

or

```
value2 = object.PaletteMode
```

- *object*—A reference to an object with a `PaletteMode` property.
- *value1*—A value from Table P-2.
- *value2*—The variable that will receive the property's current setting.

Example

The following line sets a form's palette mode such that the form uses its `Palette` property to generate its palette.

```
Form1.PaletteMode = vbPaletteModeCustom
```

CROSS-REFERENCE
See also Palette.

Panel

Object

A Panel object represents a panel in a StatusBar control, as shown in Figure P-4. The panels can display text strings, or have special contents, such as the time, the date, and the status of the Caps key.

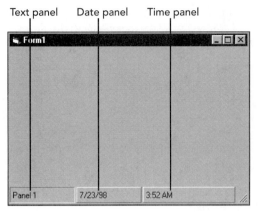

Text panel Date panel Time panel

Figure P-4 A StatusBar control can display one or more panels.

Properties

The Panel object has 15 properties. For more information on using a property shown in the following table, look up the individual property's entry, provided alphabetically in this book.

```
Alignment
AutoSize
Bevel
Enabled
Index
Key
Left
MinWidth
Picture
Style
Tag
Text
ToolTipText
Visible
Width
```

Methods

The Panel object has no methods.

Events

The Panel object does not respond to events.

CROSS-REFERENCE

For more information, Panels (property), Panels (collection), and StatusBar.

PanelClick

Event

Visual Basic sends a StatusBar control a `PanelClick` event when the user clicks a panel in the status bar.

Objects with a PanelClick Event

StatusBar

Example

A program can respond to a `PanelClick` event by implementing the control's `PanelClick` event procedure. The following program shows how a StatusBar control might define a `PanelClick` event procedure. Notice that the `PanelClick` event procedure receives a single parameter, which is a reference to the clicked panel. When you run the program, you see a window with a status bar. The status bar has four panels on which you can click. If you click one of the first three panels, its text changes to "I've been clicked!", as shown in Figure P-5. If you click the fourth panel, the program resets the text in the first three panels.

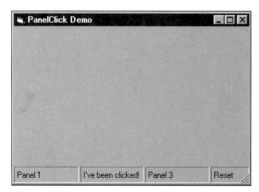

Figure P-5 When you click a panel in this application's status bar, the panel's text changes.

```
VERSION 5.00
Object = "{6B7E6392-850A-101B-AFC0-4210102A8DA7} _
    #2.0#0"; "MSCOMCTL.OCX"
Begin VB.Form Form1
   Caption         =   "PanelClick Demo"
   ClientHeight    =   3345
   ClientLeft      =   165
   ClientTop       =   450
   ClientWidth     =   5235
   LinkTopic       =   "Form1"
   ScaleHeight     =   3345
   ScaleWidth      =   5235
   StartUpPosition =   3  'Windows Default
   Begin MSComctlLib.StatusBar staStatusBar1
      Align        =   2  'Align Bottom
      Height       =   375
      Left         =   0
      TabIndex     =   0
      Top          =   2970
      Width        =   5235
      _ExtentX     =   9234
      _ExtentY     =   661
      _Version     =   393216
      BeginProperty Panels _
        {8E3867A5-8586-11D1-B16A-00C0F0283628}
         NumPanels  =   1
         BeginProperty Panel1 _
           {8E3867AB-8586-11D1-B16A-00C0F0283628}
         EndProperty
      EndProperty
   End
End
Attribute VB_Name = "Form1"
Attribute VB_GlobalNameSpace = False
Attribute VB_Creatable = False
Attribute VB_PredeclaredId = True
Attribute VB_Exposed = False

Private Sub Form_Load()
    staStatusBar1.Panels(1).Text = "Panel 1"
    staStatusBar1.Panels.Add , , "Panel 2"
    staStatusBar1.Panels.Add , , "Panel 3"
    staStatusBar1.Panels.Add , , "Reset"
End Sub
```

```
Private Sub staStatusBar1_PanelClick _
  (ByVal Panel As MSComctlLib.Panel)
    If Panel.Index = 4 Then
        staStatusBar1.Panels(1).Text = "Panel 1"
        staStatusBar1.Panels(2).Text = "Panel 2"
        staStatusBar1.Panels(3).Text = "Panel 3"
    Else
        Panel.Text = "I've been clicked!"
    End If
End Sub
```

 CROSS-REFERENCE
For more information, see StatusBar, Panel, Panels, and PanelDblClick.

PanelDblClick

Event

Visual Basic sends a StatusBar control a `PanelDblClick` event when the user double-clicks a panel in the status bar.

Objects with a PanelDblClick Event

StatusBar

Example

A program can respond to a `PanelDblClick` event by implementing the control's `PanelDblClick` event procedure. The following program shows how a StatusBar control might define a `PanelDblClick` event procedure. Notice that the `PanelDblClick` event procedure receives a single parameter, which is a reference to the clicked panel. When you run the program, you see a window with a status bar. The status bar has three panels, each of which displays an image (Figure P-6). Double-click any panel to change the image it displays.

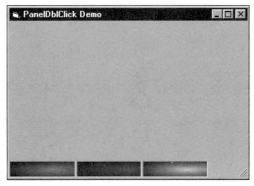

Figure P-6 When you double-click a panel in this application's status bar, the
panel's image changes.

```
VERSION 5.00
Object = "{6B7E6392-850A-101B-AFC0-4210102A8DA7} _
    #2.0#0"; "MSCOMCTL.OCX"
Begin VB.Form Form1
    Caption         =   "PanelDblClick Demo"
    ClientHeight    =   3345
    ClientLeft      =   165
    ClientTop       =   450
    ClientWidth     =   5235
    LinkTopic       =   "Form1"
    ScaleHeight     =   3345
    ScaleWidth      =   5235
    StartUpPosition =   3   'Windows Default
    Begin MSComctlLib.StatusBar staStatusBar1
        Align       =   2   'Align Bottom
        Height      =.  375
        Left        =   0
        TabIndex    =   0
        Top         =   2970
        Width       =   5235
        _ExtentX    =   9234
        _ExtentY    =   661
        _Version    =   393216
        BeginProperty Panels _
          {8E3867A5-8586-11D1-B16A-00C0F0283628}
            NumPanels       =   1
            BeginProperty Panel1 _
              {8E3867AB-8586-11D1-B16A-00C0F0283628}
            EndProperty
```

```
        EndProperty
    End
End
Attribute VB_Name = "Form1"
Attribute VB_GlobalNameSpace = False
Attribute VB_Creatable = False
Attribute VB_PredeclaredId = True
Attribute VB_Exposed = False

Private pic1, pic2, pic3 As Object

Private Sub Form_Load()
    Set pic1 = LoadPicture("c:\pic1.jpg")
    Set pic2 = LoadPicture("c:\pic2.jpg")
    Set pic3 = LoadPicture("c:\pic3.jpg")
    staStatusBar1.Panels.Add
    staStatusBar1.Panels.Add
    staStatusBar1.Panels(1).Picture = pic1
    staStatusBar1.Panels(2).Picture = pic2
    staStatusBar1.Panels(3).Picture = pic3
End Sub

Private Sub staStatusBar1_PanelDblClick(ByVal Panel As
MSComctlLib.Panel)
    If Panel.Picture = pic1 Then
        Panel.Picture = pic2
    ElseIf Panel.Picture = pic2 Then
        Panel.Picture = pic3
    Else
        Panel.Picture = pic1
    End If
End Sub
```

 CROSS-REFERENCE
For more information, see StatusBar, Panel, Panels, and PanelClick.

Panels

Collection

A Panels collection holds the Panel objects that are associated with a StatusBar control.

Properties

A Panels collection has one property, called `Count`, that represents the number of panels in the collection.

Methods

The Panels collection has four methods. For more information on using one of these methods, look up the individual method's entry, provided alphabetically in this book.

```
Add
Clear
Item
Remove
```

 CROSS-REFERENCE
See also Panels (property) and StatusBar.

Panels

Property

The `Panels` property represents a reference to a StatusBar control's Panels collection. Each of the StatusBar control's Panel objects is stored in this collection.

Objects with a Panels Property

StatusBar

Syntax

```
value = StatusBar.Panels
```

- *StatusBar*—A reference to a StatusBar control.
- *value*—The variable that will receive the Panels collection reference.

Example

The following lines add panels to a StatusBar control by calling the Panels collection's `Add` method. The `staStatusBar1` object is a StatusBar control that the programmer added to the form at design time.

```
With staStatusBar1.Panels
    .Add 1, "P1", "Panel 1", sbrText
    .Add 2, "P2", "", sbrCaps
    .Add 3, "P3", "", sbrNum
    .Add 4, "P4", "", sbrScrl
    .Add 5, "P5", "", sbrDate
    .Add 6, "P6", "", sbrTime
End With
```

CROSS-REFERENCE
See also Panels (collection), Panel, and StatusBar.

PaperBin

Property

The `PaperBin` property represents the bin from which the printer will get paper for a print job. This property can be one of the values shown in Table P-3.

Table P-3 Values for the PaperBin Property

Value	Description
vbPRBNAuto	The printer will get paper from the default bin (default).
vbPRBNCassette	The printer will get paper from the cassette.
vbPRBNEnvelope	The printer will get envelopes from the envelope feeder.
vbPRBNEnvManual	The printer will wait for manual insertion of envelopes.
vbPRBNLargeCapacity	The printer will get paper from the large capacity feeder.
vbPRBNLargeFmt	The printer will get paper from the large paper feeder.
vbPRBNLower	The printer will get paper from the bottom bin.
vbPRBNManual	The printer will wait for each sheet to be inserted manually.

Value	Description
vbPRBNMiddle	The printer will get paper from the middle bin.
vbPRBNSmallFmt	The printer will get paper from the small paper feeder.
vbPRBNTractor	The printer will get paper from the tractor feeder.
vbPRBNUpper	The printer will get paper from the top bin.

Objects with a PaperBin Property

Printer

Syntax

```
Printer.PaperBin = value1
```

or

```
value2 = Printer.PaperBin
```

- *Printer* — A reference to the Printer object.
- *value1* — A value from Table P-3.
- *value2* — The variable that will receive the property's current setting.

Example

The following lines show how to get and set the PaperBin property. Note that the Printer object is a global Visual Basic object that you don't need to create in your programs.

```
Dim bin As Integer
bin = Printer.PaperBin
Printer.PaperBin = vbPRBNLower
```

CROSS-REFERENCE
See also Printer and PaperSize.

PaperSize

Property

The `PaperSize` property represents the size of paper that the printer will use for a print job. This property can be one of the values shown in Table P-4.

Table P-4 Values for the PaperSize Property

Value	Description
vbPRPS10x14	10" × 14" sheet
vbPRPS11x17	11" × 17" sheet
vbPRPSA3	297 × 420 mm (A3)
vbPRPSA4	210 × 297 mm (A4)
vbPRPSA4Small	210 × 297 mm (Small A4)
vbPRPSA5	148 × 210 mm (A5)
vbPRPSB4	250 × 354 mm (B4)
vbPRPSB5	182 × 257 mm (B5)
vbPRPSCSheet	C sheet
vbPRPSDSheet	D sheet
vbPRPSEnv10	4-1/8" × 9-1/2" (#10 envelope)
vbPRPSEnv11	4-1/2" × 10-3/8" (#11 envelope)
vbPRPSEnv12	4-1/2" × 11" (#12 envelope)
vbPRPSEnv14	5" × 11-1/2" (#14 envelope)
vbPRPSEnv9	3-7/8" × 8-7/8" (#9 envelope)
vbPRPSEnvB4	250 × 353 mm (B4 envelope)
vbPRPSEnvB5	176 × 250 mm (B5 envelope)
vbPRPSEnvB6	176 × 125 mm (B6 envelope)
vbPRPSEnvC3	324 × 458 mm (C3 envelope)
vbPRPSEnvC4	229 × 324 mm (C4 envelope)
vbPRPSEnvC5	162 × 229 mm (C5 envelope)
vbPRPSEnvC6	114 × 162 mm (C6 envelope)
vbPRPSEnvC65	114 × 229 mm (C65 envelope)
vbPRPSEnvDL	110 × 220 mm (DL envelope)
vbPRPSEnvItaly	110 × 230 mm envelope
vbPRPSEnvMonarch	3-7/8" × 7-1/2" envelope
vbPRPSEnvPersonal	3-5/8" × 6-1/2" envelope
vbPRPSESheet	E sheet
vbPRPSExecutive	7-1/2" × 10-1/2" (executive)
vbPRPSFanfoldLglGerman	8-1/2" × 13" German legal fanfold
vbPRPSFanfoldStdGerman	8-1/2" × 12" German fanfold

Value	Description
vbPRPSFanfoldUS	14-7/8" × 11" fanfold
vbPRPSFolio	8-1/2" × 13" (folio)
vbPRPSLedger	17" × 11" (ledger)
vbPRPSLegal	8-1/2" × 14" (legal)
vbPRPSLetter	8-1/2" × 11" (letter)
vbPRPSLetterSmall	8-1/2" × 11" (small letter)
vbPRPSNote	8-1/2" × 11" (note)
vbPRPSQuarto	215 × 275 mm (quarto)
vbPRPSStatement	5-1/2" × 8-1/2" (statement)
vbPRPSTabloid	11" × 17" (tabloid)
vbPRPSUser	User-defined size

Objects with a PaperSize Property

Printer

Syntax

```
Printer.PaperSize = value1
```

or

```
value2 = Printer.PaperSize
```

- *Printer* — A reference to the Printer object.
- *value1* — A value from Table P-4.
- *value2* — The variable that will receive the property's current setting.

Example

The following lines show how to get and set the PaperSize property. Note that the Printer object is a global Visual Basic object that you don't need to create in your programs.

```
Dim size As Integer
size = Printer.PaperSize
Printer.PaperSize = vbPRPSLegal
```

CROSS-REFERENCE

See also Printer and PaperBin.

ParamArray

Keyword

The `ParamArray` keyword is used in argument lists to specify an optional variable-number of parameters. (The `ParamArray` keyword can be used only as the last parameter in an argument list.) In the following example, `MyProcedure` receives two parameters: an integer and an array of any number of values. In the procedure, the program uses the `UBound` function to determine how many values were passed in the array, displaying each value in a `For` loop. `CallingProc` can call `MyProcedure` with any number of arguments, as long as there's at least the value for `arg1`, which is not optional.

```
Private Sub CallingProc()
    MyProcedure 10, 20, 30, 40, 50, 60
End Sub

Private Sub MyProcedure(arg1 As Integer, _
  ParamArray arg2() As Variant)
    Dim size As Integer
    Dim x As Integer
    MsgBox arg1
    size = UBound(arg2)
    For Index = 0 To size
        MsgBox arg2(Index)
    Next Index
End Sub
```

Parent

Property

The `Parent` property represents an object's parent object. A *parent* is an object that contains other objects.

Objects with a Parent Property

Animation

ButtonMenu

CheckBox

ComboBox

CommandButton

CommonDialog
CoolBar
DirListBox
DriveListBox
Extender
FileListBox
Frame
HScrollBar
Image
ImageList
Label
Line
ListBox
ListView
MAPIMessages
MAPISession
Menu
Node
OLE Container
OptionButton
PictureBox
ProgressBar
RichTextBox
Shape
Slider
StatusBar
TabStrip
TextBox
Timer
Toolbar
TreeView
UpDown
UserControl
VScrollBar

Syntax

```
value = object.Parent
```

- *object* — A reference to an object with a `Parent` property.
- *value* — The variable that will receive the reference to the object's parent object.

Example

The following lines show how to access a control's parent object. Here, the `staStatusBar1` object is a status bar in a form. Because the form is the status bar's parent object, the reference to the parent returned by the `Parent` property can be used to change the form's caption.

```
Dim p As Object
Set p = staStatusBar1.Parent
p.Caption = "Parent"
```

ParentFolder

Property

The `ParentFolder` property represents a reference to a folder that contains other files or folders.

Objects with a ParentFolder Property

File

Folder

Syntax

```
value = object.ParentFolder
```

- *object* — A reference to a File or Folder object.
- *value* — The variable that will receive the parent-folder reference.

Example

The following lines open a file and get the file's parent folder, which in this case is c:\Temp.

```
Dim fileSystem, file As Object
Dim parFolder As String
Set fileSystem = _
    CreateObject("Scripting.FileSystemObject")
Set file = fileSystem.GetFile("c:\Temp\MyFile.dat")
parFolder = file.ParentFolder
```

 CROSS-REFERENCE
See also File, Folder, and FileSystemObject.

Password

Property

The `Password` property represents the password for the current user in a MAPISession control.

Objects with a Password Property

MAPISession

Syntax

```
MAPISession.Password = value1
```

or

```
value2 = MAPISession.Password
```

- *MAPISession* — A reference to a MAPISession control.
- *value1* — The password string.
- *value2* — The variable that will receive the property's current setting.

Example

The following lines show how to get and set a MAPISession control's `Password` property:

```
Dim pWord As String
MAPISession1.Password = "mypassword"
pWord = MAPISession1.Password
```

CROSS-REFERENCE
See also MAPISession.

PasswordChar

Property

The PasswordChar property represents the character used to display text entries in a TextBox control when the password mode is active. If this property is set to a character, then every character the user types will display as the password character. To turn off the password entry mode, set this property to an empty string.

Objects with a PasswordChar Property

TextBox

Syntax

```
TextBox.PasswordChar = value1
```

or

```
value2 = TextBox.PasswordChar
```

- *TextBox* — A reference to a TextBox control.
- *value1* — The password character or "".
- *value2* — The variable that will receive the property's current setting.

Example

The following program demonstrates the PasswordChar property. When you run the program, type some text into the upper text box. The text appears normally. Now, click the Toggle Password Mode button. When you do, the text changes to the password character, which is, in this case, an asterisk. To see that the contents of the text box's Text property haven't changed, click the Show Text button to display the unchanged text in the lower text box (see Figure P-7).

Figure P-7 The PasswordChar Demo application displays text both as the password character and as the text that normally appears.

```
VERSION 5.00
Begin VB.Form Form1
    Caption         =   "PasswordChar Demo"
    ClientHeight    =   3345
    ClientLeft      =   165
    ClientTop       =   450
    ClientWidth     =   5235
    LinkTopic       =   "Form1"
    ScaleHeight     =   3345
    ScaleWidth      =   5235
    StartUpPosition =   3   'Windows Default
    Begin VB.TextBox txtText2
        Height      =   375
        Left        =   840
        TabIndex    =   4
        Top         =   2640
        Width       =   3375
    End
    Begin VB.CommandButton btnShowText
        Caption     =   "Show Text"
        Height      =   375
        Left        =   1560
        TabIndex    =   3
        Top         =   2040
        Width       =   2055
    End
    Begin VB.CommandButton btnToggle
        Caption     =   "Toggle Password Mode"
        Height      =   375
```

```
            Left            =    1560
            TabIndex        =    1
            Top             =    1200
            Width           =    2055
         End
         Begin VB.TextBox txtText1
            Height          =    375
            Left            =    840
            TabIndex        =    0
            Top             =    240
            Width           =    3375
         End
         Begin VB.Label lblLabel1
            Caption         =    "Password Mode Off"
            BeginProperty Font
               Name         =    "MS Sans Serif"
               Size         =    13.5
               Charset      =    0
               Weight       =    400
               Underline    =    0    'False
               Italic       =    0    'False
               Strikethrough =   0    'False
            EndProperty
            Height          =    375
            Left            =    1320
            TabIndex        =    2
            Top             =    720
            Width           =    2535
         End
      End
Attribute VB_Name = "Form1"
Attribute VB_GlobalNameSpace = False
Attribute VB_Creatable = False
Attribute VB_PredeclaredId = True
Attribute VB_Exposed = False

Private Sub btnShowText_Click()
    txtText2.Text = txtText1.Text
End Sub

Private Sub btnToggle_Click()
    If txtText1.PasswordChar = "" Then
        txtText1.PasswordChar = "*"
        lblLabel1 = "Password Mode On"
```

```
        Else
            txtText1.PasswordChar = ""
            lblLabel1 = "Password Mode Off"
        End If
    End Sub

    Private Sub txtText1_Change()
        txtText2.Text = ""
    End Sub
```

CROSS-REFERENCE
See also TextBox and Text.

Paste

Method

The Paste method copies data from the Clipboard to an OLE Container control.

Objects with a Paste Method

OLE Container

Syntax

OLEContainer.Paste

- *OLEContainer*—A reference to an OLE Container control.

Example

The following program demonstrates the Paste method. When you run the program, click the Paste button to paste the contents of the Clipboard into the OLE Container control. If the control cannot accept the Clipboard's contents, a message box informs you of the problem. In that case, use another application to cut or copy new data into the Clipboard and try pasting that data into the OLE Container control. For example, Figure P-8 shows a bitmap pasted into the control.

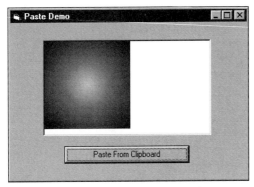

Figure P-8 An OLE Container control can accept many types of data directly from the Clipboard.

```
VERSION 5.00
Begin VB.Form Form1
   Caption         =    "Paste Demo"
   ClientHeight    =    3345
   ClientLeft      =    165
   ClientTop       =    450
   ClientWidth     =    5235
   LinkTopic       =    "Form1"
   ScaleHeight     =    3345
   ScaleWidth      =    5235
   StartUpPosition =    3   'Windows Default
   Begin VB.CommandButton btnPaste
      Caption      =    "Paste From Clipboard"
      Height       =    375
      Left         =    1200
      TabIndex     =    1
      Top          =    2640
      Width        =    2775
   End
   Begin VB.OLE OLE1
      Height       =    2055
      Left         =    720
      TabIndex     =    0
      Top          =    360
      Width        =    3735
   End
End
Attribute VB_Name = "Form1"
Attribute VB_GlobalNameSpace = False
```

```
    Attribute VB_Creatable = False
    Attribute VB_PredeclaredId = True
    Attribute VB_Exposed = False

    Private Sub btnPaste_Click()
        If OLE1.PasteOK Then
            OLE1.Paste
        Else
            MsgBox "Can't paste the current Clipboard Contents", _
                vbExclamation, "Paste"
        End If
    End Sub
```

CROSS-REFERENCE

See also OLE Container, PasteOK, and OLETypeAllowed.

PasteOK

Property

The `PasteOK` property represents whether an OLE Container Control can accept the date currently in the Clipboard. A value of `True` in this property means that the contents of the Clipboard can be pasted into the OLE Container control.

Objects with a PasteOK Property

OLE Container

Syntax

```
value = OLEContainer.PasteOK
```

- *OLEContainer*—A reference to an OLE Container control.
- *value*—The variable that will receive the property's current setting.

Example

The following lines show how to retrieve the value of an OLE Container control's `PasteOK` property. Note that the `OLE1` object is an OLE Container control that the programmer added to the form at design time.

```
Dim paste As Boolean
paste = OLE1.PasteOK
```

CROSS-REFERENCE
See also OLE Container, Paste, and OLETypeAllowed.

PasteSpecialDlg

Method

The `PasteSpecialDlg` method shows the Paste Special dialog box (Figure P-9), with which the user can paste an object into an OLE Container control. The dialog box not only describes the currently available data, but also gives the user a choice between linking or embedding the object. After pasting the object, the user can then edit the object by calling up the server application, which is usually done by double-clicking the embedded or linked object.

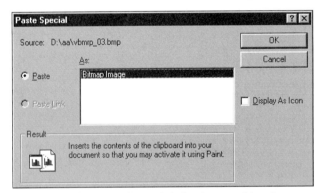

Figure P-9 The Paste Special dialog box enables the user to paste data into an OLE Container control.

Objects with a PasteSpecialDlg Method

OLE Container

Syntax

OLEContainer.PasteSpecialDlg

- *OLEContainer*—A reference to an OLE Container control.

Example

The following line displays the Paste Special dialog box. Note that the OLE1 object is an OLE Container control that the programmer added to the form at design time.

```
OLE1.PasteSpecialDlg
```

 CROSS-REFERENCE
See also OLE Container, Paste, PasteOK, and OLETypeAllowed.

Path—App

Property

The Path property represents the current path, which is the path from which the program was run. This property is read-only at runtime and not available at design time.

Syntax

```
value = App.Path
```

- *App*—A reference to the App object.
- *value*—The variable that will receive the current path string.

Example

The following lines show how to get the current path. Note that the App object is a global Visual Basic object that you don't need to create in your program.

```
Dim strPath As String
strPath = App.Path
```

 CROSS-REFERENCE
See also App.

Path — DirListBox and FileListBox

Property

The Path property represents the currently set path in the control.

Syntax

```
object.Path = value1
```

or

```
value2 = object.Path
```

- *object* — A reference to a DirListBox or FileListBox control.
- *value1* — The new path string.
- *value2* — The variable that will receive the property's current setting.

Example

The following lines show how to get and set the current path for a DirListBox control. Note that the Dir1 object is a DirListBox that the programmer added to the form at design time.

```
Dim strPath As String
strPath = Dir1.Path
Dir1.Path = "C:\MyDirectory"
```

 CROSS-REFERENCE
See also FileName and PathChange.

Path — Drive, File, and Folder

Property

The Path property represents the path for a drive, file, or folder.

Syntax

```
value = object.Path
```

- *object* — A reference to a Drive, File, or Folder object.
- *value* — The variable that will receive the path string.

Example

The following lines show how to get the path for a File object.

```
Dim fileSystem, file As Object
Dim strPath As String
Set fileSystem = _
    CreateObject("Scripting.FileSystemObject")
Set file = fileSystem.GetFile("c:\Temp\MyFile.dat")
strPath = file.Path
```

CROSS-REFERENCE
See also Drive, File, Folder, and FileSystemObject.

PathChange

Event

Visual Basic sends a FileListBox control a `PathChange` event when the program changes the control's path, usually by setting the `Path` property to a new value.

Objects with a PathChange Event

FileListBox

Example

A program can respond to a `PathChange` event by implementing the control's `PathChange` event procedure. The following code segment shows how a FileListBox control defines a `PathChange` event procedure. In this example, the `File1` object is a FileListBox control that the programmer added to the form at design time.

```
Private Sub File1_PathChange()
    ' Handle the PathChange event here.
End Sub
```

CROSS-REFERENCE
For more information, see FileListBox, FileName, and Path.

PathSeparator

Property

The `PathSeparator` property represents the character used in a TreeView control to separate one element of a path to a node from another. For example, in the path RootNode\Child1\Child2, the path separator is the backslash character, which is the default.

Objects with a PathSeparator Property

TreeView

Syntax

```
TreeView.PathSeparator = value1
```

or

```
value2 = TreeView.PathSeparator
```

- *TreeView* — A reference to a TreeView control.
- *value1* — The new separator character.
- *value2* — The variable that will receive the separator character.

Example

The following lines show how to get and set a TreeView control's path separator character. The `treTreeView1` object is a TreeView control that the programmer added to the form at design time.

```
Dim strPathSep As String
strPathSep = treTreeView1.PathSeparator
treTreeView1.PathSeparator = "^"
```

CROSS-REFERENCE
See also Multimedia MCI.

Pattern

Property

The `Pattern` property represents the filters used by the FileListBox control to determine which file names to display. The default setting is "*.*", which displays all files. You can specify multiple filters by separating them with a semicolon.

Syntax

`FileListBox.Pattern = value1`

or

`value2 = FileListBox.Pattern`

- *FileListBox* — A reference to a FileListBox control.
- *value1* — The new file pattern string.
- *value2* — The variable that will receive the path string.

Example

The following program demonstrates the `Pattern` property, as well as the use of the DriveListBox, DirListBox, and FileListBox controls. When you run the program, you see a window with DriveListBox, DirListBox, and FileListBox controls. You can use the DriveListBox and DirListBox controls to change the current path and show different files in the FileListBox. You can also filter which files are shown by typing a file pattern into the text box and clicking the Set Pattern button. Remember that you can set multiple patterns by separating them with semicolons. For example, to see only .exe and .dll files, you type "*.EXE;*.DLL", as shown in Figure P-10.

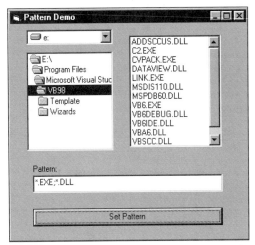

Figure P-10 Change the patterns in the text box to see the way the file list is affected.

```
VERSION 5.00
Begin VB.Form Form1
    Caption         =   "Pattern Demo"
    ClientHeight    =   4605
    ClientLeft      =   165
    ClientTop       =   450
    ClientWidth     =   5235
    LinkTopic       =   "Form1"
    ScaleHeight     =   4605
    ScaleWidth      =   5235
    StartUpPosition =   3   'Windows Default
    Begin VB.CommandButton btnSetPattern
        Caption     =   "Set Pattern"
        Height      =   375
        Left        =   480
        TabIndex    =   5
        Top         =   3960
        Width       =   4215
    End
    Begin VB.TextBox txtPattern
        Height      =   375
        Left        =   480
        TabIndex    =   4
        Text        =   "*.*"
        Top         =   3240
```

```
        Width           =      4215
     End
     Begin VB.FileListBox File1
        Height          =      2430
        Left            =      2640
        TabIndex        =      2
        Top             =      240
        Width           =      2055
     End
     Begin VB.DriveListBox Drive1
        Height          =      315
        Left            =      360
        TabIndex        =      1
        Top             =      120
        Width           =      1935
     End
     Begin VB.DirListBox Dir1
        Height          =      2115
        Left            =      360
        TabIndex        =      0
        Top             =      600
        Width           =      1935
     End
     Begin VB.Label Label1
        Caption         =      "Pattern:"
        Height          =      255
        Left            =      480
        TabIndex        =      3
        Top             =      3000
        Width           =      1935
     End
  End
Attribute VB_Name = "Form1"
Attribute VB_GlobalNameSpace = False
Attribute VB_Creatable = False
Attribute VB_PredeclaredId = True
Attribute VB_Exposed = False

Private Sub btnSetPattern_Click()
    File1.Pattern = txtPattern.Text
End Sub

Private Sub Dir1_Change()
```

o
▶p
q

```
        File1.Path = Dir1.Path
    End Sub

    Private Sub Drive1_Change()
        Dir1.Path = Drive1.Drive
    End Sub
```

CROSS-REFERENCE

See also DriveListBox, FileListBox, DirListBox, and PatternChange.

PatternChange

Event

Visual Basic sends a FileListBox control a `PatternChange` event when the control's file pattern changes. The `Pattern` property, which holds the file patterns, determines which files the control displays.

Objects with a PatternChange Event

FileListBox

Example

A program can respond to a `PatternChange` event by implementing the control's `PatternChange` event procedure. The following code segment shows how a FileListBox control defines a `PatternChange` event procedure. In this example, the `File1` object is a FileListBox control that the programmer added to the form at design time.

```
    Private Sub File1_PatternChange()
        ' Handle the PatternChange event here.
    End Sub
```

CROSS-REFERENCE

For more information, see FileListBox and Pattern.

PauseClick

Event

Visual Basic sends a Multimedia MCI control a `PauseClick` event when the user clicks the control's Pause button. By responding to this event, a program can stop the default action of the Pause button from occurring.

Objects with a PauseClick Event

Multimedia MCI

Example

A program can respond to a `PauseClick` event by implementing the Multimedia MCI control's `PauseClick` event procedure. By setting the procedure's `Cancel` parameter to `True`, the program can halt the Pause button's default action.

```
Private Sub mciMMControl1_PauseClick(Cancel As Integer)
    If something Then Cancel = True
End Sub
```

 CROSS-REFERENCE
For more information, see PauseCompleted and Multimedia MCI.

PauseCompleted

Event

Visual Basic sends a Multimedia MCI control a `PauseCompleted` event after the Pause button's action has been executed. By responding to this event, a program can determine whether any errors occurred.

Objects with a PauseCompleted Event

Multimedia MCI

Example

A program can respond to a `PauseCompleted` event by implementing the Multimedia MCI control's `PauseCompleted` event procedure, which receives an error value as its single parameter. The `mciMMControl1` object is a Multimedia MCI control that the programmer added to the form at design time.

```
Private Sub mciMMControl1_PauseCompleted(Errorcode As Long)
    ' Handle the event here.
End Sub
```

 CROSS-REFERENCE
For more information, see PauseClick and Multimedia MCI.

PauseEnabled

Property

The `PauseEnabled` property represents the enabled status of a Multimedia MCI control's Pause button. This property is `True` when the control's Pause button is enabled and is `False` when the button is disabled.

Objects with a PauseEnabled Property

Multimedia MCI

Syntax

```
Multimedia.PauseEnabled = value1
```

or

```
value2 = Multimedia.PauseEnabled
```

- *Multimedia* — A reference to a Multimedia MCI control.
- *value1* — The value `True` or `False`.
- *value2* — The variable that will receive the value returned by the property.

Example

The following lines show how to get and set the enabled status of a Multimedia control's Pause button. The `mciMMControl1` object is a Multimedia MCI control that the programmer added to the form at design time.

```
Dim enable
enable = mciMMControl1.PauseEnabled
mciMMControl1.PauseEnabled = True
```

CROSS-REFERENCE
See also Multimedia MCI.

PauseGotFocus

Event

Visual Basic sends a Multimedia MCI control a PauseGotFocus event when the control's Pause button receives the focus.

Objects with a PauseGotFocus Event

Multimedia MCI

Example

A program can respond to a PauseGotFocus event by implementing the Multimedia MCI control's PauseGotFocus event procedure, which receives no parameters, as shown here. The mciMMControl1 object is a Multimedia MCI control that the programmer added to the form at design time.

```
Private Sub mciMMControl1_PauseGotFocus()
    ' Handle the PauseGotFocus event here.
End Sub
```

CROSS-REFERENCE
For more information, see PauseLostFocus and Multimedia MCI.

PauseLostFocus

Event

Visual Basic sends a Multimedia MCI control a PauseLostFocus event when the control's Pause button loses the focus.

Objects with a PauseLostFocus Event

Multimedia MCI

Example

A program can respond to a `PauseLostFocus` event by implementing the Multimedia MCI control's `PauseLostFocus` event procedure, which receives no parameters, as shown here. The `mciMMControl1` object is a Multimedia MCI control that the programmer added to the form at design time.

```
Private Sub mciMMControl1_PauseLostFocus()
    ' Handle the event here.
End Sub
```

CROSS-REFERENCE

For more information, see PauseGotFocus and Multimedia MCI.

PauseVisible

Property

The `PauseVisible` property represents the visible status of a Multimedia MCI control's Pause button. This property is `True` when the control's Pause button is visible, and is `False` when the button is not visible.

Objects with a PauseVisible Property

Multimedia MCI

Syntax

Multimedia.PauseVisible = *value1*

or

value2 = *Multimedia*.PauseVisible

- *Multimedia* — A reference to a Multimedia MCI control.
- *value1* — The value `True` or `False`.

■ *value2*—The variable that will receive the value returned by the
property.

Example

The following lines show how to get and set the visible status of a Multimedia
control's Pause button. The `mciMMControl1` object is a Multimedia MCI control
that the programmer added to the form at design time.

```
Dim visible
visible = mciMMControl1.PauseVisible
mciMMControl1.PauseVisible = True
```

CROSS-REFERENCE
See also Multimedia MCI.

Picture

Object

A Picture object represents an image loaded from one of various types of
image files. After loading, this object can be used to set the Picture property
of many kinds of controls and objects. Figure P-11, for example, shows a form
displaying a bitmap that was assigned to its Picture property.

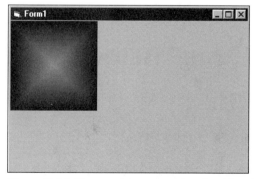

Figure P-11 Picture objects enable other Visual Basic objects and controls to
display images.

Properties

The Picture object has five properties. For more information on using one of these properties, look up the individual property's entry, provided alphabetically in this book.

```
Handle
Height
HPal
Type
Width
```

Methods

The Picture object has one method, Render, which draws all of, or a portion of, the image. For more information on using this method, look up the individual method's entry, provided alphabetically in this book.

Events

The Picture object does not respond to events.

 CROSS-REFERENCE
See also Picture (property).

Picture

Property

The Picture property represents the image that appears on a control.

Objects with a Picture Property

CheckBox
CommandButton
CoolBar
Form
Image
ListImage
ListView

MDI Form

OLE Container

OptionButton

Panel

PictureBox

PropertyPage

UserControl

Syntax

```
object.Picture = value1
```

or

```
value2 = object.Picture
```

- *object*—A reference to a control with a `Picture` property.
- *value1*—A reference to the picture object that will be the control's picture.
- *value2*—The variable that will receive a reference to the control's picture.

Example

In this example, the program loads and sets images for a graphical pushbutton. The `btnCommand1` object is a CommandButton control that the programmer added to the application's form at design time.

```
btnCommand1.Picture = LoadPicture("but1.bmp")
btnCommand1.DownPicture = LoadPicture("but1dn.bmp")
btnCommand1.DisabledPicture = LoadPicture("but1d.bmp")
```

PictureAlignment

Property

The `PictureAlignment` property represents how a picture is aligned in a ListView control. This property can be `lvwBottomLeft`, `lvwBottomRight`, `lvwCenter`, `lvwTile`, `lvwTopLeft`, or `lvwTopRight`. Figure P-12, for example, shows a ListView control's picture with the `lvwCenter` setting, whereas Figure P-13 shows the picture with the `lvwTile` setting.

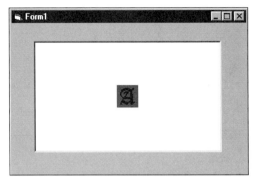

Figure P-12 The picture in this ListView control is centered.

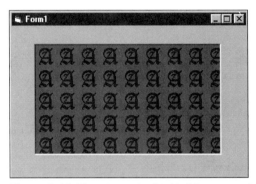

Figure P-13 The picture in this ListView control is tiled.

Objects with a PictureAlignment Property

ListView

Syntax

```
ListView.PictureAlignment = value1
```

or

```
value2 = ListView.PictureAlignment
```

- *ListView* — A reference to a ListView control.
- *value1* — The alignment setting.
- *value2* — The variable that will receive the property's current setting.

Example

The following lines show how to get and set the picture alignment of a ListView control. The `lvwListView1` object is a ListView control that the programmer added to the form at design time.

```
Dim picAlign As Integer
picAlign = lvwListView1.PictureAlignment
lvwListView1.PictureAlignment = lvwBottomRight
```

 CROSS-REFERENCE
See also ListView and Picture.

PictureBox

Control

A PictureBox control enables a program to display various types of images, including bitmaps, icons, GIF, metafile, and JPEG files. Figure P-14 shows several PictureBox controls in a form. The PictureBox control can also be used as a container that can hold other objects. The PictureBox control is available on Visual Basic's standard toolbox.

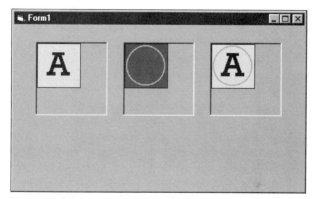

Figure P-14 PictureBox controls display many types of images.

Properties

The PictureBox control has 61 properties, which are listed below. Because many Visual Basic controls have similar properties, the following list does not include the properties' descriptions. For information on using a property, look up the individual property's entry, provided alphabetically in this book.

```
Align
Appearance
AutoRedraw
AutoSize
BackColor
BorderStyle
CausesValidation
ClipControls
Container
CurrentX
CurrentY
DragIcon
DragMode
DrawMode
DrawStyle
DrawWidth
Enabled
FillColor
FillStyle
Font
FontBold
FontItalic
FontName
FontSize
FontStrikethru
FontTransparent
FontUnderline
ForeColor
HasDC
hDC
Height
HelpContextID
hWnd
Image
Index
Left
LinkItem
LinkMode
LinkTimeout
LinkTopic
MouseIcon
MousePointer
Name
OLEDragMode
```

```
OLEDropMode
Parent
Picture
RightToLeft
ScaleHeight
ScaleLeft
ScaleMode
ScaleTop
ScaleWidth
TabIndex
TabStop
Tag
ToolTipText
Top
Visible
WhatsThisHelpID
Width
```

Methods

The PictureBox control has 22 methods, which are listed below. Because many Visual Basic controls have similar methods, the following list does not include the methods' descriptions. For information on using a method, look up the individual method's entry, provided alphabetically in this book.

```
Circle
Cls
Drag
Line
LinkExecute
LinkPoke
LinkRequest
LinkSend
Move
OLEDrag
PaintPicture
Point
PSet
Refresh
Scale
ScaleX
ScaleY
SetFocus
ShowWhatsThis
```

```
TextHeight
TextWidth
ZOrder
```

Events

The PictureBox control responds to 26 events, which are listed below. Because many Visual Basic controls respond to similar events, the following list does not include the events' descriptions. For information on using an event, look up the individual event's entry, provided alphabetically in this book.

```
Change
Click
DblClick
DragDrop
DragOver
GotFocus
KeyDown
KeyPress
KeyUp
LinkClose
LinkError
LinkNotify
LinkOpen
LostFocus
MouseDown
MouseMove
MouseUp
OLECompleteDrag
OLEDragDrop
OLEDragOver
OLEGiveFeedback
OLESetData
OLEStartDrag
Paint
Resize
Validate
```

One of the PictureBox control's most commonly used events is `Click`, which the control generates when the user clicks the control with the mouse. A program responds to the control's `Click` event in the `Click` event procedure. A PictureBox called `picPicture1` will have a `Click` event procedure called `picPicture1_Click`, which is where the program should handle the event, as shown in the following lines:

```
Private Sub picPicture1_Click()
    ' Handle the Click event here.
End Sub
```

CROSS-REFERENCE
See also Image (control).

Placement

Property

The Placement property represents the position of tabs in a TabStrip control. This property can be tabPlacementTop (default), tabPlacementBottom, tabPlacementLeft, or tabPlacementRight. Figure P-15, for example, shows a TabStrip with the tabPlacementTop setting, whereas Figure P-16 shows the same TabStrip control with the tabPlacementBottom setting.

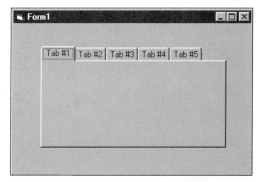

Figure P-15 The tabs in this TabStrip control are positioned on top.

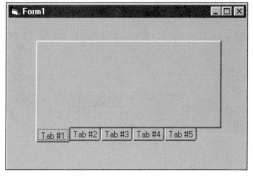

Figure P-16 The tabs in this TabStrip control are positioned on the bottom.

Objects with a Placement Property

TabStrip

Syntax

```
TabStrip.Placement = value1
```

or

```
value2 = TabStrip.Placement
```

- *TabStrip*—A reference to a TabStrip control.
- *value1*—The new placement setting.
- *value2*—The variable that will receive the property's current setting.

Example

The following program demonstrates the Placement property. When you run the program, you see the window shown in Figure P-17. Click the Change Placement button to change the placement of the tabs on the TabStrip control. You can cycle through all four placements by repeatedly clicking the button.

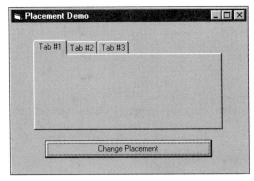

Figure P-17 This is the Placement Demo program when it first appears.

```
VERSION 5.00
Object = "{6B7E6392-850A-101B-AFC0-4210102A8DA7} _
    #2.0#0"; "MSCOMCTL.OCX"
Begin VB.Form Form1
```

```
Caption          =    "Placement Demo"
ClientHeight     =    3210
ClientLeft       =    165
ClientTop        =    450
ClientWidth      =    5235
LinkTopic        =    "Form1"
ScaleHeight      =    3210
ScaleWidth       =    5235
StartUpPosition  =    3   'Windows Default
Begin MSComctlLib.TabStrip TabStrip1
    Height         =    1935
    Left           =    480
    TabIndex       =    1
    Top            =    360
    Width          =    4215
    _ExtentX       =    7435
    _ExtentY       =    3413
    _Version       =    393216
    BeginProperty Tabs _
       {1EFB6598-857C-11D1-B16A-00C0F0283628}
       NumTabs         =    1
       BeginProperty Tab1 _
          {1EFB659A-857C-11D1-B16A-00C0F0283628}
          ImageVarType    =    2
       EndProperty
    EndProperty
End
Begin VB.CommandButton btnChangePlacement
    Caption        =    "Change Placement"
    Height         =    375
    Left           =    720
    TabIndex       =    0
    Top            =    2520
    Width          =    3735
End
End
Attribute VB_Name = "Form1"
Attribute VB_GlobalNameSpace = False
Attribute VB_Creatable = False
Attribute VB_PredeclaredId = True
Attribute VB_Exposed = False
```

```
Private Sub btnChangePlacement_Click()
    If TabStrip1.Placement = tabPlacementTop Then
        TabStrip1.Placement = tabPlacementRight
    ElseIf TabStrip1.Placement = tabPlacementRight Then
        TabStrip1.Placement = tabPlacementBottom
    ElseIf TabStrip1.Placement = tabPlacementBottom Then
        TabStrip1.Placement = tabPlacementLeft
    Else
        TabStrip1.Placement = tabPlacementTop
    End If
End Sub

Private Sub Form_Load()
    TabStrip1.Tabs(1).Caption = "Tab #1"
    TabStrip1.Tabs.Add , , "Tab #2"
    TabStrip1.Tabs.Add , , "Tab #3"
End Sub
```

CROSS-REFERENCE
See also TabStrip, Tab, and Tabs.

Play

Method

The Play method plays an animation sequence.

Objects with a Play Method

Animation

Syntax

Animation.Play *loop, begin, end*

- *Animation* — A reference to an Animation control.
- *loop* (*) — The number of times to play the animation. The default value of −1 plays the animation until explicitly stopped, usually by a call to the control's Stop method.

- *begin* (*) — The number of the first frame to display. The default value of 0 starts the animation sequence at its first frame.

- *end* (*) — The number of the last frame to display. The default value of –1 plays the animation sequence to its last frame.

(*) = Optional

Example

The following program demonstrates the Animation control's Open method. When you run the program, you see the window shown in Figure P-18. Click the Load Animation button to find and load an .avi file (one comes with the program). Then, click the Play button to view the animation sequence. The sequence plays once and stops. Click the Turn On Looping button, and play the animation again. This time, the animation continues playing until you click the Stop or Turn Off Looping button.

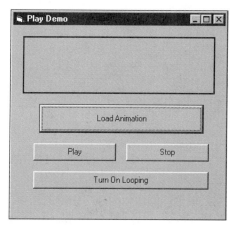

Figure P-18 This animation program can play a sequence once or play it continuously in a loop.

```
VERSION 5.00
Object = "{F9043C88-F6F2-101A-A3C9-08002B2F49FB} _
    #1.2#0"; "COMDLG32.OCX"
Object = "{FE0065C0-1B7B-11CF-9D53-00AA003C9CB6} _
    #2.0#0"; "MSCOMCT2.OCX"
```

```
Begin VB.Form frmForm1
   Caption         =   "Play Demo"
   ClientHeight    =   4110
   ClientLeft      =   60
   ClientTop       =   345
   ClientWidth     =   4680
   LinkTopic       =   "Form1"
   ScaleHeight     =   4110
   ScaleWidth      =   4680
   StartUpPosition =   3   'Windows Default
   Begin VB.CommandButton btnLoop
      Caption      =   "Turn On Looping"
      Height       =   375
      Left         =   480
      TabIndex     =   4
      Top          =   3120
      Width        =   3855
   End
   Begin MSComCtl2.Animation Animation1
      Height       =   975
      Left         =   360
      TabIndex     =   3
      Top          =   360
      Width        =   3975
      _ExtentX     =   7011
      _ExtentY     =   1720
      _Version     =   393216
      FullWidth    =   265
      FullHeight   =   65
   End
   Begin MSComDlg.CommonDialog dlgCommonDialog1
      Left         =   0
      Top          =   1800
      _ExtentX     =   847
      _ExtentY     =   847
      _Version     =   393216
   End
   Begin VB.CommandButton btnStop
      Caption      =   "Stop"
      Height       =   375
      Left         =   2520
      TabIndex     =   2
```

```
            Top           =    2520
            Width         =    1815
         End
         Begin VB.CommandButton btnPlay
            Caption       =    "Play"
            Height        =    375
            Left          =    480
            TabIndex      =    1
            Top           =    2520
            Width         =    1815
         End
         Begin VB.CommandButton btnLoad
            Caption       =    "Load Animation"
            Height        =    615
            Left          =    600
            TabIndex      =    0
            Top           =    1680
            Width         =    3615
         End
         Begin VB.Shape Shape1
            BorderWidth   =    2
            Height        =    1215
            Left          =    240
            Top           =    240
            Width         =    4215
         End
      End
Attribute VB_Name = "frmForm1"
Attribute VB_GlobalNameSpace = False
Attribute VB_Creatable = False
Attribute VB_PredeclaredId = True
Attribute VB_Exposed = False

Private loopAnimation As Boolean

Private Sub btnLoad_Click()
    dlgCommonDialog1.CancelError = True
    dlgCommonDialog1.Filter = _
        "Video (.avi)|*.avi|All Files (*.*)|*.*"
    dlgCommonDialog1.FileName = "*.avi"
    dlgCommonDialog1.DialogTitle = "Open Animation"
```

```
        On Error GoTo ErrorHandler2
        dlgCommonDialog1.ShowOpen
        On Error GoTo ErrorHandler1
        Animation1.Open dlgCommonDialog1.FileName
        Exit Sub

ErrorHandler1:
    MsgBox "Cannot play that file.", vbExclamation

ErrorHandler2:

End Sub

Private Sub btnLoop_Click()
    Animation1.Stop
    If loopAnimation Then
        loopAnimation = False
        btnLoop.Caption = "Turn On Looping"
    Else
        loopAnimation = True
        btnLoop.Caption = "Turn Off Looping"
    End If
End Sub

Private Sub btnPlay_Click()
    On Error Resume Next
    If loopAnimation Then
        Animation1.Play
    Else
        Animation1.Play 1
    End If
End Sub

Private Sub btnStop_Click()
    Animation1.Stop
End Sub

Private Sub Form_Load()
    loopAnimation = False
End Sub
```

 **CROSS-REFERENCE**
See also Animation and Stop.

PlayClick

Event

Visual Basic sends a Multimedia MCI control a `PlayClick` event when the user clicks the control's Play button. By responding to this event, a program can stop the default action of the Play button from occurring.

Objects with a PlayClick Event

Multimedia MCI

Example

A program can respond to a `PlayClick` event by implementing the Multimedia MCI control's `PlayClick` event procedure. By setting the procedure's `Cancel` parameter to `True`, the program can halt the Play button's default action. Here, the `mciMMControl1` object is a Multimedia MCI control that the programmer added to the form at design time.

```
Private Sub mciMMControl1_PlayClick(Cancel As Integer)
    If something Then Cancel = True
End Sub
```

 CROSS-REFERENCE
For more information, see PlayCompleted and Multimedia MCI.

PlayCompleted

Event

Visual Basic sends a Multimedia MCI control a `PlayCompleted` event after the Play button's action has been executed. By responding to this event, a program can determine whether any errors occurred.

Objects with a PlayCompleted Event

Multimedia MCI

o

p

q

Example

A program can respond to a `PlayCompleted` event by implementing the Multimedia MCI control's `PlayCompleted` event procedure, which receives an error value as its single parameter. Here, the `mciMMControl1` object is a Multimedia MCI control that the programmer added to the form at design time.

```
Private Sub mciMMControl1_PlayCompleted(Errorcode As Long)
    ' Handle the event here.
End Sub
```

 CROSS-REFERENCE
For more information, see PlayClick and Multimedia MCI.

PlayEnabled

Property

The `PlayEnabled` property represents the enabled status of a Multimedia MCI control's Play button. This property is `True` when the control's Play button is enabled and is `False` when the button is disabled.

Objects with a PlayEnabled Property

Multimedia MCI

Syntax

Multimedia.PlayEnabled = *value1*

or

value2 = *Multimedia*.PlayEnabled

- *Multimedia* — A reference to a Multimedia MCI control.
- *value1* — The value `True` or `False`.
- *value2* — The variable that will receive the value returned by the property.

Example

The following lines show how to get and set the enabled status of a Multimedia control's Play button. The `mciMMControl1` object is a Multimedia MCI control that the programmer added to the form at design time.

```
Dim enable
enable = mciMMControl1.PlayEnabled
mciMMControl1.PlayEnabled = True
```

 CROSS-REFERENCE
See also Multimedia MCI.

PlayGotFocus

Event

Visual Basic sends a Multimedia MCI control a `PlayGotFocus` event when the control's Play button receives the focus.

Objects with a PlayGotFocus Event

Multimedia MCI

Example

A program can respond to a `PlayGotFocus` event by implementing the Multimedia MCI control's `PlayGotFocus` event procedure, which receives no parameters, as shown here.

```
Private Sub mciMMControl1_PlayGotFocus()
    ' Handle the PlayGotFocus event here.
End Sub
```

 CROSS-REFERENCE
For more information, see PlayLostFocus and Multimedia MCI.

PlayLostFocus

Event

Visual Basic sends a Multimedia MCI control a `PlayLostFocus` event when the control's Play button loses the focus.

Objects with a PlayLostFocus Event

Multimedia MCI

Example

A program can respond to a `PlayLostFocus` event by implementing the Multimedia MCI control's `PlayLostFocus` event procedure, which receives no parameters, as shown here.

```
Private Sub mciMMControl1_PlayLostFocus()
    ' Handle the event here.
End Sub
```

 CROSS-REFERENCE
For more information, see PlayGotFocus and Multimedia MCI.

PlayVisible

Property

The `PlayVisible` property represents the visible status of a Multimedia MCI control's Play button. This property is `True` when the control's Play button is visible, and is `False` when the button is not visible.

Objects with a PlayVisible Property

Multimedia MCI

Syntax

```
Multimedia.PlayVisible = value1
```

or

```
value2 = Multimedia.PlayVisible
```

- *Multimedia* — A reference to a Multimedia MCI control.
- *value1* — The value `True` or `False`.
- *value2* — The variable that will receive the value returned by the property.

Example

The following lines show how to get and set the visible status of a Multimedia control's Play button. The `mciMMControl1` object is a Multimedia MCI control that the programmer added to the form at design time.

```
Dim visible
visible = mciMMControl1.PlayVisible
mciMMControl1.PlayVisible = True
```

CROSS-REFERENCE
See also Multimedia MCI.

Plus (+)

Operator

The plus (+) operator performs addition.

Syntax

```
value = exp1 + exp2
```

- *exp1* — The expression to add to exp2.
- *exp2* — The expression to add to exp1.
- *value* — The result of the operation.

Example

After the following lines execute, `result` will contain the value 16.

```
Dim exp1, exp2 As Integer
Dim result As Integer
exp1 = 10
exp2 = 6
result = exp1 + exp2
```

Pmt

Function

The Pmt function returns a payment for an annuity.

Syntax

```
value = Pmt(intRate, numPayments, presValue,
    futValue, payDue)
```

- *futValue* (★) — The desired future value of the annuity. The default is 0.
- *intRate* — The interest rate per period.
- *numPayments* — The number of payments.
- *payDue* (★) — The value 0 if payments are made at the end of the period and 1 if payments are made at the start of the period. The default is 0.
- *presValue* — The present value of the annuity.
- *value* — The variable that will receive the payment amount.

(★) = Optional

Example

The following program is a loan calculator that demonstrates the Pmt function. When you run the program, enter the required values into the text boxes and click the Calculate button. Your loan payments then appear at the bottom of the window. For example, Figure P-19 shows the monthly payment for a $10,000 loan at 15% interest with 48 payments.

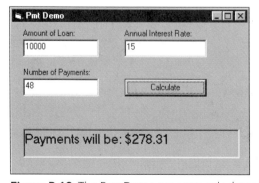

Figure P-19 The Pmt Demo program calculates loan payments for any loan.

```
VERSION 5.00
Begin VB.Form Form1
    Caption         =   "Pmt Demo"
    ClientHeight    =   3210
    ClientLeft      =   165
    ClientTop       =   450
    ClientWidth     =   5235
    LinkTopic       =   "Form1"
    ScaleHeight     =   3210
    ScaleWidth      =   5235
    StartUpPosition =   3   'Windows Default
    Begin VB.CommandButton btnCalculate
        Caption     =   "Calculate"
        Height      =   375
        Left        =   2520
        TabIndex    =   6
        Top         =   1200
        Width       =   1815
    End
    Begin VB.TextBox txtNumPayments
        Height      =   375
        Left        =   240
        TabIndex    =   5
        Top         =   1200
        Width       =   1695
    End
    Begin VB.TextBox txtIntRate
        Height      =   375
        Left        =   2520
        TabIndex    =   3
        Top         =   360
        Width       =   1815
    End
    Begin VB.TextBox txtLoanAmt
        Height      =   375
        Left        =   240
        TabIndex    =   1
        Top         =   360
        Width       =   1695
    End
    Begin VB.Label lblPayment
        BorderStyle =   1   'Fixed Single
        Caption     =   "Payments will be: "
        BeginProperty Font
```

```
                    Name            =    "MS Sans Serif"
                    Size            =    13.5
                    Charset         =    0
                    Weight          =    400
                    Underline       =    0    'False
                    Italic          =    0    'False
                    Strikethrough   =    0    'False
                 EndProperty
                 Height        =    615
                 Left          =    240
                 TabIndex      =    7
                 Top           =    2280
                 Width         =    4815
              End
              Begin VB.Label Label3
                 Caption       =    "Number of Payments:"
                 Height        =    255
                 Left          =    240
                 TabIndex      =    4
                 Top           =    960
                 Width         =    1575
              End
              Begin VB.Label Label2
                 Caption       =    "Annual Interest Rate:"
                 Height        =    255
                 Left          =    2520
                 TabIndex      =    2
                 Top           =    120
                 Width         =    1575
              End
              Begin VB.Label Label1
                 Caption       =    "Amount of Loan:"
                 Height        =    255
                 Left          =    240
                 TabIndex      =    0
                 Top           =    120
                 Width         =    1335
              End
           End
        End
        Attribute VB_Name = "Form1"
        Attribute VB_GlobalNameSpace = False
        Attribute VB_Creatable = False
        Attribute VB_PredeclaredId = True
```

```
Attribute VB_Exposed = False

Private Sub btnCalculate_Click()
    Dim loanAmount As Double
    Dim intRate As Double
    Dim result As Double
    Dim numPayments As Integer
    Dim strResult As String

    On Error GoTo ErrorHandler

    loanAmount = txtLoanAmt.Text
    intRate = txtIntRate.Text
    intRate = intRate / 100 / 12
    numPayments = txtNumPayments.Text
    result = Pmt(intRate, numPayments, -loanAmount)
    result = result + 0.005
    strResult = "$" & Format(result, "###,###,##0.00")

    lblPayment.Caption = "Payments will be: " & strResult

ErrorHandler:
End Sub
```

Point

Method

The Point method gets the RGB value of a pixel.

Objects with a Point Method

PropertyPage

UserControl

Form

PictureBox

Syntax

value = *object*.Point(*xCoord*, *yCoord*)

- *object*—A reference to an object with a Point method.
- *xCoord*—The X coordinate of the pixel to examine.

- *yCoord* — The Y coordinate of the pixel to examine.
- *value* — The returned RGB value.

Example

The following lines get the RGB value of a pixel in a form.

```
Dim rgbVal As Long
Dim xCoord As Single
Dim yCoord As Single
xCoord = 100
yCoord = 145
rgbVal = Form1.Point(xCoord, yCoord)
```

PopupMenu

Method

The PopupMenu method draws a pop-up menu at the mouse pointer's location or at specified coordinates.

Objects with a PopupMenu Method

Form

MDIForm

PropertyPage

UserControl

Syntax

```
object.PopupMenu menu, options, xCoord, yCoord, bold
```

- *bold* (*) — The name of the menu item, if any, to display in bold.
- *menu* — The name of the menu to display.
- *object* — A reference to an object with a PopupMenu method.
- *options* (*) — One alignment value and one button value from Table P-5.
- *xCoord* (*) — The X coordinate at which to display the menu.
- *yCoord* (*) — The Y coordinate at which to display the menu.

(*) = Optional

Table P-5 Values for the Options Argument

Value	Description
vbPopupMenuCenterAlign	Position the menu's center at the X coordinate
vbPopupMenuLeftAlign	Position the menu's left edge at the X coordinate.
vbPopupMenuLeftButton	Respond only to left-button mouse clicks.
vbPopupMenuRightAlign	Position the menu's right edge at the X coordinate.
vbPopupMenuRightButton	Respond to both left- and right-button mouse clicks.

Example 1

The following lines display a pop-up menu at the current mouse coordinates. This menu is left-aligned, responds only to the left mouse button, and shows its third menu item in bold, as shown in Figure P-20. The menu appears at the mouse coordinates because the option X and Y coordinates were left out.

```
PopupMenu mnuTestMenu, vbPopupMenuLeftAlign Or _
    vbPopupMenuLeftButton, , , mnuItem3
```

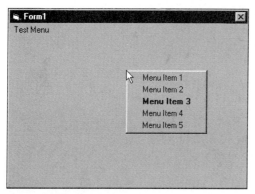

Figure P-20 Visual Basic programs can display pop-up menus anywhere in a window.

Example 2

The following lines display the same pop-up menu as in Example 1. However, now the menu is displayed at the specified coordinates of 1500,1000.

```
PopupMenu mnuTestMenu, vbPopupMenuLeftAlign Or _
    vbPopupMenuLeftButton, 1500, 1000, mnuItem3
```

Port

Property

The Port property represents the port that's connected to the printer.

Objects with a Port Property
Printer

Syntax
```
value = Printer.Port
```

- *Printer*—A reference to the Printer object.
- *value*—The variable that will receive the string containing the printer's port.

Example
The following lines retrieve the printer port string from the Printer object. Note that the Printer object is a Visual Basic global object that you don't need to create in your programs.

```
Dim printPort As String
printPort = Printer.Port
```

 CROSS-REFERENCE
See also Printer.

Position — Band

Property

The Position property represents the position of a band in a CoolBar control. Note that the position is not necessarily the same as the index.

Syntax
```
value = CoolBar.Position
```

- *CoolBar*—A reference to a CoolBar control.
- *value*—The variable that will receive the band's position.

Example

The following lines retrieve the position of the band with the index of 3. The `CoolBar1` object is a CoolBar control that the programmer added to the form at design time.

```
Dim strPosition As String
strPosition = CoolBar1.Bands(3).Position
```

 **CROSS-REFERENCE**
See also CoolBar.

Position — ColumnHeader

Property

The `Position` property represents the position of column header in a ListView control. Note that the position is not necessarily the same as the index.

Syntax

```
ColumnHeader.Position = value1
```

or

```
value2 = ColumnHeader.Position
```

- *ColumnHeader* — A reference to a ColumnHeader object.
- *value1* — The new position.
- *value2* — The variable that will receive the position.

Example

The following program demonstrates getting and setting the `Position` property. When you run the program, click a column in the ListView control, and the column's position and index appear in the window. At first, the two values are the same because the column headers have not been repositioned. For example, Figure P-21 shows the result when you click on the third column header. Now, click the Reposition Columns button, and the program moves the column headers. When you click a column header, as shown in Figure P-22, you'll see that the position and index are different where the user has clicked the "Column 3" header again, which is now in the second position.

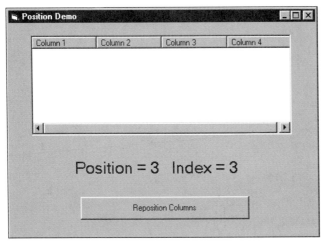

Figure P-21 At first, a column header's position and index are the same value.

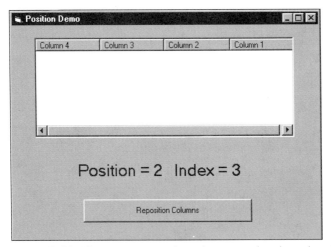

Figure P-22 After rearranging the columns, each column header has different positions, but retains its original index value.

```
VERSION 5.00
Object = "{831FDD16-0C5C-11D2-A9FC-0000F8754DA1} _
    #2.0#0"; "MSCOMCTL.OCX"
Begin VB.Form Form1
    Caption         =   "Position Demo"
    ClientHeight    =   4560
    ClientLeft      =   60
    ClientTop       =   345
```

```
ClientWidth      =   6780
LinkTopic        =   "Form1"
ScaleHeight      =   4560
ScaleWidth       =   6780
StartUpPosition  =   3   'Windows Default
Begin VB.CommandButton btnReposition
   Caption       =   "Reposition Columns"
   Height        =   495
   Left          =   1560
   TabIndex      =   2
   Top           =   3720
   Width         =   3735
End
Begin MSComctlLib.ListView lvwListView1
   Height        =   2175
   Left          =   480
   TabIndex      =   1
   Top           =   240
   Width         =   5775
   _ExtentX      =   10186
   _ExtentY      =   3836
   LabelWrap     =   -1  'True
   HideSelection =   -1  'True
   _Version      =   393217
   ForeColor     =   -2147483640
   BackColor     =   -2147483643
   BorderStyle   =   1
   Appearance    =   1
   NumItems      =   0
End
Begin VB.Label lblPosition
   BeginProperty Font
      Name             =   "MS Sans Serif"
      Size             =   18
      Charset          =   0
      Weight           =   400
      Underline        =   0   'False
      Italic           =   0   'False
      Strikethrough    =   0   'False
   EndProperty
   Height           =   495
   Left             =   1440
   TabIndex         =   0
   Top              =   2880
```

```
        Width          =    4455
    End
End
Attribute VB_Name = "Form1"
Attribute VB_GlobalNameSpace = False
Attribute VB_Creatable = False
Attribute VB_PredeclaredId = True
Attribute VB_Exposed = False
Private repositioned As Boolean

Private Sub btnReposition_Click()
    If Not repositioned Then
        lvwListView1.ColumnHeaders(4).Position = 1
        lvwListView1.ColumnHeaders(3).Position = 2
        lvwListView1.ColumnHeaders(2).Position = 3
        lvwListView1.ColumnHeaders(1).Position = 4
    Else
        lvwListView1.ColumnHeaders(1).Position = 1
        lvwListView1.ColumnHeaders(2).Position = 2
        lvwListView1.ColumnHeaders(3).Position = 3
        lvwListView1.ColumnHeaders(4).Position = 4
    End If
    repositioned = Not repositioned
End Sub

Private Sub Form_Load()
    lvwListView1.ColumnHeaders.Add 1, , "Column 1"
    lvwListView1.ColumnHeaders.Add 2, , "Column 2"
    lvwListView1.ColumnHeaders.Add 3, , "Column 3"
    lvwListView1.ColumnHeaders.Add 4, , "Column 4"
    lvwListView1.View = lvwReport
    repositioned = False
End Sub

Private Sub lvwListView1_ColumnClick _
  (ByVal ColumnHeader As MSComctlLib.ColumnHeader)
    Dim strPosition As String
    strPosition = "Position = " & ColumnHeader.Position
    strPosition = strPosition & _
        "   Index = " & ColumnHeader.Index
    lblPosition.Caption = strPosition
End Sub
```

CROSS-REFERENCE
See also CoolBar.

Position — Multimedia

Property

The `Position` property represents the position within the media of the currently open device. Note that the position value depends upon the type of media. The `TimeFormat` property holds the type of time information associated with a device. For example, the value of the `Position` property could represent milliseconds, bytes, or frames.

Syntax

```
value = Multimedia.Position
```

- *Multimedia* — A reference to a Multimedia MCI control.
- *value* — The variable that will receive the position.

Example

The following lines retrieve the position of the current multimedia device. The `mciMMControl1` object is a Multimedia MCI control that the programmer added to the form at design time.

```
Dim lngPosition As Long
lngPosition = mciMMControl1.Position
```

CROSS-REFERENCE
See also Multimedia MCI and TimeFormat.

PowerQuerySuspend

Event

Visual Basic sends a SysInfo control a `PowerQuerySuspend` event just before the system's power is suspended.

Objects with a PowerQuerySuspend Event

SysInfo

Example

A program can respond to a `PowerQuerySuspend` event by implementing the SysInfo control's `PowerQuerySuspend` event procedure. The following code segment shows how a SysInfo control defines a `PowerQuerySuspend` event procedure. As you can see in the procedure's declaration, the procedure receives one parameter. If the event procedure changes the `Cancel` parameter to True, the system's power suspension is canceled. In this example, the `SysInfo1` object is a SysInfo control that the programmer added to the form at design time.

```
Private Sub SysInfo1_PowerQuerySuspend(Cancel As Boolean)
    ' Handle the PowerQuerySuspend event here.
End Sub
```

 CROSS-REFERENCE
See also SysInfo, PowerResume, PowerStatusChanged, and PowerSuspend.

PowerResume

Event

Visual Basic sends a SysInfo control a `PowerResume` event when the system resumes normal operation after a power suspension.

Objects with a PowerResume Event

SysInfo

Example

A program can respond to a `PowerResume` event by implementing the SysInfo control's `PowerResume` event procedure. The following code segment shows how a SysInfo control defines a `PowerResume` event procedure. In this example, the `SysInfo1` object is a SysInfo control that the programmer added to the form at design time.

```
Private Sub SysInfo1_PowerResume()
    ' Handle the PowerResume event here.
End Sub
```

CROSS-REFERENCE
See also SysInfo, PowerQuerySuspend, PowerStatusChanged, and PowerSuspend.

PowerStatusChanged

Event

Visual Basic sends a SysInfo control a `PowerStatusChanged` event when the system's battery is running low, the user switches between battery and AC power, or the system's battery is finished charging.

Objects with a PowerStatusChanged Event

SysInfo

Example

A program can respond to a `PowerStatusChanged` event by implementing the SysInfo control's `PowerStatusChanged` event procedure. The following code segment shows how a SysInfo control defines a `PowerStatusChanged` event procedure. In this example, the `SysInfo1` object is a SysInfo control that the programmer added to the form at design time.

```
Private Sub SysInfo1_PowerStatusChanged()
    ' Handle the PowerStatusChanged event here.
End Sub
```

CROSS-REFERENCE
See also SysInfo, PowerQuerySuspend, PowerResume, and PowerSuspend.

PowerSuspend

Event

Visual Basic sends a SysInfo control a `PowerSuspend` event right before the system power suspends.

Objects with a PowerSuspend Event

SysInfo

Example

A program can respond to a `PowerSuspend` event by implementing the SysInfo control's `PowerSuspend` event procedure. The following code segment shows how a SysInfo control defines a `PowerSuspend` event procedure. In this example, the `SysInfo1` object is a SysInfo control that the programmer added to the form at design time.

```
Private Sub SysInfo1_PowerSuspend()
    ' Handle the PowerSuspend event here.
End Sub
```

 CROSS-REFERENCE
See also SysInfo, PowerQuerySuspend, PowerResume, and PowerStatusChanged.

PPmt

Function

The `PPmt` function returns the portion of a payment that's applied to an annuity's principal.

Syntax

```
value = PPmt(intRate, period, numPayments,
    presValue, futValue, payDue)
```

- *futValue* (*) — The desired future value of the annuity. The default is 0.
- *intRate* — The interest rate per period.
- *numPayments* — The number of payments.
- *period* — The period for which to calculate the principal.
- *payDue* (*) — The value 0 if payments are made at the end of the period and 1 if payments are made at the start of the period. The default is 0.
- *presValue* — The present value of the annuity.
- *value* — The variable that will receive the payment amount.

(*) = Optional

Example

The following program is a loan calculator that demonstrates the PPmt function. When you run the program, enter the required values into the text boxes (the "Period to calculate" box is the number of the payment period for which you want to calculate the principal and interest) and click the Calculate button. Your loan payment then appears at the bottom of the window, along with a breakdown of how much principal and interest comprise the payment. For example, Figure P-23 shows the monthly payment for a $25,000 loan at 12% interest with 60 payments. Because the selected period is 12, the principal and interest values show how much of the twelfth payment goes toward the loan's principal and how much toward the interest.

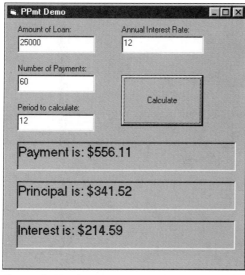

Figure P-23 The PPmt Demo program calculates loan payments along with the amount of principal and interest for a specified payment.

```
VERSION 5.00
Begin VB.Form Form1
    Caption       =   "PPmt Demo"
    ClientHeight  =   5325
    ClientLeft    =   165
    ClientTop     =   450
    ClientWidth   =   5235
    LinkTopic     =   "Form1"
    ScaleHeight   =   5325
    ScaleWidth    =   5235
```

```
StartUpPosition =   3  'Windows Default
Begin VB.TextBox txtPeriod
   Height         =   375
   Left           =   240
   TabIndex       =   7
   Top            =   2040
   Width          =   1695
End
Begin VB.CommandButton btnCalculate
   Caption        =   "Calculate"
   Height         =   1095
   Left           =   2520
   TabIndex       =   6
   Top            =   1200
   Width          =   1815
End
Begin VB.TextBox txtNumPayments
   Height         =   375
   Left           =   240
   TabIndex       =   5
   Top            =   1200
   Width          =   1695
End
Begin VB.TextBox txtIntRate
   Height         =   375
   Left           =   2520
   TabIndex       =   3
   Top            =   360
   Width          =   1815
End
Begin VB.TextBox txtLoanAmt
   Height         =   375
   Left           =   240
   TabIndex       =   1
   Top            =   360
   Width          =   1695
End
Begin VB.Label lblPayment
   BorderStyle    =   1  'Fixed Single
   Caption        =   "Payment is:"
   BeginProperty Font
      Name        =   "MS Sans Serif"
      Size        =   13.5
      Charset     =   0
```

```
         Weight          =    400
         Underline       =    0    'False
         Italic          =    0    'False
         Strikethrough   =    0    'False
      EndProperty
      Height             =    615
      Left               =    240
      TabIndex           =    11
      Top                =    2640
      Width              =    4815
   End
   Begin VB.Label lblInterest
      BorderStyle        =    1  'Fixed Single
      Caption            =    "Interest is: "
      BeginProperty Font
         Name            =    "MS Sans Serif"
         Size            =    13.5
         Charset         =    0
         Weight          =    400
         Underline       =    0    'False
         Italic          =    0    'False
         Strikethrough   =    0    'False
      EndProperty
      Height             =    615
      Left               =    240
      TabIndex           =    10
      Top                =    4320
      Width              =    4815
   End
   Begin VB.Label lblPrincipal
      BorderStyle        =    1  'Fixed Single
      Caption            =    "Principal is: "
      BeginProperty Font
         Name            =    "MS Sans Serif"
         Size            =    13.5
         Charset         =    0
         Weight          =    400
         Underline       =    0    'False
         Italic          =    0    'False
         Strikethrough   =    0    'False
      EndProperty
      Height             =    615
      Left               =    240
      TabIndex           =    9
```

o p q

```
            Top             =    3480
            Width           =    4815
         End
         Begin VB.Label Label4
            Caption         =    "Period to calculate:"
            Height          =    255
            Left            =    240
            TabIndex        =    8
            Top             =    1800
            Width           =    1575
         End
         Begin VB.Label Label3
            Caption         =    "Number of Payments:"
            Height          =    255
            Left            =    240
            TabIndex        =    4
            Top             =    960
            Width           =    1575
         End
         Begin VB.Label Label2
            Caption         =    "Annual Interest Rate:"
            Height          =    255
            Left            =    2520
            TabIndex        =    2
            Top             =    120
            Width           =    1575
         End
         Begin VB.Label Label1
            Caption         =    "Amount of Loan:"
            Height          =    255
            Left            =    240
            TabIndex        =    0
            Top             =    120
            Width           =    1335
         End
      End
Attribute VB_Name = "Form1"
Attribute VB_GlobalNameSpace = False
Attribute VB_Creatable = False
Attribute VB_PredeclaredId = True
```

```
Attribute VB_Exposed = False

Private Sub btnCalculate_Click()
    Dim loanAmount As Double
    Dim intRate As Double
    Dim periodPayment As Double
    Dim periodPrincipal As Double
    Dim periodInterest As Double
    Dim desiredPeriod As Integer
    Dim numPayments As Integer
    Dim strPayment As String
    Dim strPrincipal As String
    Dim strInterest As String

    On Error GoTo ErrorHandler

    loanAmount = txtLoanAmt.Text
    intRate = txtIntRate.Text
    intRate = intRate / 100 / 12
    numPayments = txtNumPayments.Text
    periodPayment = Pmt(intRate, numPayments, -loanAmount)
    strPayment = "$" & Format(periodPayment, _
        "###,###,##0.00")
    desiredPeriod = txtPeriod.Text
    periodPrincipal = PPmt(intRate, desiredPeriod, _
        numPayments, -loanAmount)
    periodPrincipal = periodPrincipal + 0.005
    strPrincipal = "$" & Format(periodPrincipal, _
        "###,###,##0.00")
    periodInterest = periodPayment - periodPrincipal
    periodInterest = periodInterest + 0.005
    strInterest = "$" & Format(periodInterest, _
        "###,###,##0.00")

    lblPayment.Caption = "Payment is: " & strPayment
    lblPrincipal.Caption = "Principal is: " & strPrincipal
    lblInterest.Caption = "Interest is: " & strInterest

ErrorHandler:
End Sub
```

PrevClick

Event

Visual Basic sends a Multimedia MCI control a `PrevClick` event when the user clicks the control's Previous button. By responding to this event, a program can stop the default action of the Previous button from occurring.

Objects with a PrevClick Event

Multimedia MCI

Example

A program can respond to a `PrevClick` event by implementing the Multimedia MCI control's `PrevClick` event procedure. By setting the procedure's `Cancel` parameter to `True`, the program can halt the Previous button's default action.

```
Private Sub mciMMControl1_PrevClick(Cancel As Integer)
    If something Then Cancel = True
End Sub
```

 CROSS-REFERENCE
For more information, see PrevCompleted and Multimedia MCI.

PrevCompleted

Event

Visual Basic sends a Multimedia MCI control a `PrevCompleted` event after the Previous button's action has been executed. By responding to this event, a program can determine whether any errors occurred.

Objects with a PrevCompleted Event

Multimedia MCI

Example

A program can respond to a `PrevCompleted` event by implementing the Multimedia MCI control's `PrevCompleted` event procedure, which receives an error value as its single parameter.

```
Private Sub mciMMControl1_PrevCompleted(Errorcode As Long)
    ' Handle the event here.
End Sub
```

CROSS-REFERENCE
For more information, see PrevClick and Multimedia MCI.

PrevEnabled

Property

The `PrevEnabled` property represents the enabled status of a Multimedia MCI control's Previous button. This property is `True` when the control's Previous button is enabled, and is `False` when the button is disabled.

Objects with a PrevEnabled Property
Multimedia MCI

Syntax

```
Multimedia.PrevEnabled = value1
```

or

```
value2 = Multimedia.PrevEnabled
```

- *Multimedia* — A reference to a Multimedia MCI control.
- *value1* — The value `True` or `False`.
- *value2* — The variable that will receive the value returned by the property.

Example

The following lines show how to get and set the enabled status of a Multimedia control's Previous button. The `mciMMControl` object is a Multimedia MCI control that the programmer added to the form at design time.

```
Dim enable
enable = mciMMControl1.PrevEnabled
mciMMControl1.PrevEnabled = True
```

o
p
q

CROSS-REFERENCE
See also Multimedia MCI.

PrevGotFocus

Event

Visual Basic sends a Multimedia MCI control a `PrevGotFocus` event when the control's Previous button receives the focus.

Objects with a PrevGotFocus Event

Multimedia MCI

Example

A program can respond to a `PrevGotFocus` event by implementing the Multimedia MCI control's `PrevGotFocus` event procedure, which receives no parameters, as shown here.

```
Private Sub mciMMControl1_PrevGotFocus()
    ' Handle the PrevGotFocus event here.
End Sub
```

CROSS-REFERENCE
For more information, see PrevLostFocus and Multimedia MCI.

PrevInstance

Property

The `PrevInstance` property represents whether another instance of the application is already running. A value of `True` means that there is a previous instance of the application.

Objects with a PrevInstance Property

App

Syntax

```
value = App.PrevInstance
```

- *App* — A reference to the App object.
- *value* — The variable that will receive the property's current setting.

Example

The following lines show how to retrieve the value of the `PrevInstance` property. Note that the App object is a Visual Basic global object that you don't need to create in your programs.

```
Dim previous As Boolean
previous = App.PrevInstance
```

 CROSS-REFERENCE
See also App.

Previous

Property

The `Previous` property represents a node's previous sibling in a TreeView control.

Objects with a Previous Property

Node

Syntax

```
value = Node.Previous
```

- *Node* — A reference to a Node object.
- *value* — The variable that will receive the node reference.

Example

The following program demonstrates how the `Previous` property works. When you run the program, you see the main window, which holds TreeView,

CommandButton, and TextBox controls. Select a node in the TreeView control, and then click the Previous Node button. The name of the current node's previous sibling appears in the TextBox control (see Figure P-24). If the currently selected node has no next sibling, the text box displays the message "No next sibling."

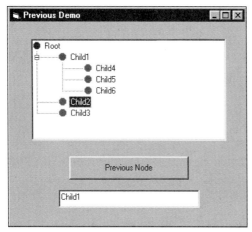

Figure P-24 Here the user has retrieved the name of the Child2 node's previous sibling.

```
VERSION 5.00
Object = "{831FDD16-0C5C-11D2-A9FC-0000F8754DA1} _
    #2.0#0"; "MSCOMCTL.OCX"
Begin VB.Form Form1
   Caption        =   "Previous Demo"
   ClientHeight   =   4335
   ClientLeft     =   165
   ClientTop      =   450
   ClientWidth    =   5235
   LinkTopic      =   "Form1"
   ScaleHeight    =   4335
   ScaleWidth     =   5235
   StartUpPosition =  3   'Windows Default
   Begin MSComctlLib.ImageList ilsImageList1
      Left        =   3960
      Top         =   1680
      _ExtentX    =   1005
      _ExtentY    =   1005
```

```
            BackColor       =    -2147483643
            MaskColor       =    12632256
            _Version        =    393216
         End
         Begin MSComctlLib.TreeView treTreeView1
            Height          =    2175
            Left            =    480
            TabIndex        =    2
            Top             =    360
            Width           =    4335
            _ExtentX        =    7646
            _ExtentY        =    3836
            _Version        =    393217
            Style           =    7
            Appearance      =    1
         End
         Begin VB.TextBox txtPrevSibling
            Height          =    375
            Left            =    1080
            TabIndex        =    1
            Top             =    3600
            Width           =    3135
         End
         Begin VB.CommandButton btnPrevNode
            Caption         =    "Previous Node"
            Height          =    495
            Left            =    1320
            TabIndex        =    0
            Top             =    2880
            Width           =    2655
         End
      End
   End
Attribute VB_Name = "Form1"
Attribute VB_GlobalNameSpace = False
Attribute VB_Creatable = False
Attribute VB_PredeclaredId = True
Attribute VB_Exposed = False

Private Sub btnPrevNode_Click()
    Dim curNode As Node
    Dim previousNode As Node
    Set curNode = treTreeView1.SelectedItem
    Set previousNode = curNode.Previous
```

```
            On Error GoTo ErrorHandler
            txtPrevSibling.Text = previousNode.Text
            Exit Sub

        ErrorHandler:
            txtPrevSibling.Text = "No previous sibling."
        End Sub

        Private Sub Form_Load()
            ilsImageList1.ListImages.Add , , _
                LoadPicture("circle1.bmp")
            ilsImageList1.ListImages.Add , , _
                LoadPicture("circle2.bmp")
            treTreeView1.ImageList = ilsImageList1

            With treTreeView1.Nodes
                .Add , , "Root", "Root", 1
                .Add "Root", tvwChild, "Child1", "Child1", 2
                .Add "Root", tvwChild, "Child2", "Child2", 2
                .Add "Root", tvwChild, "Child3", "Child3", 2
                .Add "Child1", tvwChild, "Child4", "Child4", 2
                .Add "Child1", tvwChild, "Child5", "Child5", 2
                .Add "Child1", tvwChild, "Child6", "Child6", 2
            End With

            treTreeView1.Nodes(5).EnsureVisible
        End Sub
```

 CROSS-REFERENCE
See also Node, Child, FirstSibling, LastSibling, Next, Parent, and Root.

PrevLostFocus

Event

Visual Basic sends a Multimedia MCI control a `PrevLostFocus` event when the control's Previous button loses the focus.

Objects with a PrevLostFocus Event
Multimedia MCI

Example

A program can respond to a `PrevLostFocus` event by implementing the Multimedia MCI control's `PrevLostFocus` event procedure, which receives no parameters, as shown here.

```
Private Sub mciMMControl1_PrevLostFocus()
    ' Handle the event here.
End Sub
```

 CROSS-REFERENCE
For more information, see PrevGotFocus and Multimedia MCI.

PrevVisible

Property

The `PrevVisible` property represents the visible status of a Multimedia MCI control's Previous button. This property is `True` when the control's Previous button is visible, and is `False` when the button is not visible.

Objects with a PrevVisible Property

Multimedia MCI

Syntax

```
Multimedia.PrevVisible = value1
```

or

```
value2 = Multimedia.PrevVisible
```

- *Multimedia* — A reference to a Multimedia MCI control.
- *value1* — The value `True` or `False`.
- *value2* — The variable that will receive the value returned by the property.

Example

The following lines show how to get and set the visible status of a Multimedia control's Previous button. The `mciMMControl1` object is a Multimedia MCI control that the programmer added to the form at design time.

```
Dim visible
visible = mciMMControl1.BackVisible
mciMMControl1.BackVisible = True
```

CROSS-REFERENCE
See also Multimedia MCI.

Print

Method

The `Print` method prints data in Visual Basic's Immediate window or in an object's display area.

Objects with a Print Method

Debug

Form

UserControl

Syntax

`object.Print output`

- *object* — A reference to an object with a `Print` method.
- *output* — The list of items to display in the Immediate window.

Example 1

The following line displays text in a form's window.

```
frmForm1.Print "This is a test"
```

Example 2

This example displays text in the Immediate window. Note that the Debug object is a Visual Basic global object that you don't need to create in your programs.

```
Debug.Print "This is a test"
```

Example 3

This example displays two lines of text, separated by spaces, in a form's window. The `Spc(10)` part of the line places 10 spaces between the two lines.

```
frmForm1.Print "This is a test."; Spc(10); "Another test."
```

Example 4

This example also displays two lines of text in a form's window, but this time separated by tabs. The `Tab(2)` part of the line places two tabs between the text lines.

```
frmForm1.Print "This is a test."; Tab(2); "Another test."
```

Print

Statement

The `Print` statement prints data to a file that was opened with the `Open` statement.

Syntax .

```
Print #num, output
```

- *num* — The file number given to the file in the `Open` statement.
- *output* — The list of items to print to the file.

Example 1

The following lines write a text line to a file.

```
Open "MyFile.txt" For Output As #1
Print #1, "This is a test."
Close #1
```

Example 2

This example writes two lines of text, separated by spaces, to a file. The `Spc(10)` part of the line places 10 spaces between the two lines.

```
Open "MyFile.txt" For Output As #1
Print #1, "This is a test."; Spc(10); "Another test."
Close #1
```

Example 3

This example also writes two lines of text to a file, but separates the lines by tabs. The `Tab(2)` part of the line places two tabs between the text lines.

```
Open "MyFile.txt" For Output As #1
Print #1, "This is a test."; Tab(2); "Another test."
Close #1
```

CROSS-REFERENCE
See also Open, Close, Print, and Write.

Printer

Object

The Printer object represents the current printer on the system. Printer is a global Visual Basic object. That is, you don't need to create the object in your programs in order to use it.

Properties

The Printer object has 41 properties, which are listed below. Because many Visual Basic objects have similar properties, the following list does not include the properties' descriptions. For information on using a property, look up the individual property's entry, provided alphabetically in this book.

```
ColorMode
Copies
CurrentX
CurrentY
DeviceName
DrawMode
DrawStyle
DrawWidth
DriverName
Duplex
FillColor
FillStyle
Font
FontBold
FontCount
FontItalic
Fonts
```

```
FontSize
FontStrikethru
FontTransparent
FontUnderline
ForeColor
hDC
Height
Orientation
Page
PaperBin
PaperSize
Port
PrintQuality
RightToLeft
ScaleHeight
ScaleLeft
ScaleMode
ScaleTop
ScaleWidth
TrackDefault
TwipsPerPixelX
TwipsPerPixelY
Width
Zoom
```

Methods

The Printer object has 12 methods, which are listed below. Because many Visual Basic objects have similar methods, the following list does not include the methods' descriptions. For information on using a method, look up the individual method's entry, provided alphabetically in this book.

```
Circle
EndDoc
KillDoc
Line
NewPage
PaintPicture
PSet
Scale
ScaleX
ScaleY
TextHeight
TextWidth
```

o
p
q

Events

The Printer object does not respond to events.

CROSS-REFERENCE
See also Printers.

PrinterDefault

Property

The `PrinterDefault` property represents whether the user can change the default system printer and its settings from a Print dialog box.

Objects with a PrinterDefault Property

CommonDialog

Syntax

```
CommonDialog.PrinterDefault = value1
```

or

```
value2 = CommonDialog.PrinterDefault
```

- *CommonDialog* — A reference to a CommonDialog control.
- *value1* — The value `True` or `False`.
- *value2* — The variable that will receive the property's current setting.

Example

The following lines show how to get and set a CommonDialog control's `PrinterDefault` property. In the last line of this example, the property value of `True` enables the user to change the printer and its settings based on her selections in the Printer dialog box. Here, the `dlgCommonDialog1` object is a CommonDialog control the programmer added to the form at design time.

```
Dim change As Boolean
change = dlgCommonDialog1.PrinterDefault
dlgCommonDialog1.PrinterDefault = True
```

CROSS-REFERENCE
See also CommonDialog.

Printers

Collection

The Printers collection holds Printer objects that reference all the printers currently available on the system. Note that the Printers collection is a Visual Basic global object that you don't need to create in your programs.

Syntax

```
Printers(index)
```

- *index* — The index of the Printer object to access.

Properties

The Printers collection has one property, Count, which represents the number of printers in the collection. For more information on using this property, look up the individual property's entry, provided alphabetically in this book.

Methods

A Printers collection has one method, Item, which you can use to access a printer in the collection. This method, however, is unnecessary, because you can access a printer in the collection just by adding an index to the collection name.

Example

The following lines get the device name of the first printer in the Printers collection.

```
Dim strDeviceName As String
strDeviceName = Printers(0).DeviceName
```

CROSS-REFERENCE
For more information, see Printer and Printers (property).

PrintForm

Method

The `PrintForm` method prints the contents of a form on a printer.

Objects with a PrintForm Method

Form

Syntax

`Form.PrintForm`

- *Form* — A reference to a Form object.

Example

The following line prints the contents of the form on the current default printer.

`frmForm1.PrintForm`

 **CROSS-REFERENCE**
See also Form.

PrintQuality

Property

The `PrintQuality` property represents the print quality to be used on a printer. This property can be `vbPRPQDraft`, `vbPRPQHigh`, `vbPRPQLow`, or `vbPRPQMedium`.

Objects with a PrintQuality Property

Printer

Syntax

```
Printer.PrintQuality = value1
```

or

```
value2 = Printer.PrintQuality
```

- *Printer* — A reference to the Printer object.
- *value1* — The new print-quality value.
- *value2* — The variable that will receive the property's current setting.

Example

The following line sets the current printer to high-resolution print quality. The Printer object is a global Visual Basic object that you don't need to create in your programs.

```
Printer.PrintQuality = vbPRPQHigh
```

CROSS-REFERENCE
See also Printer.

Private

Keyword

The `Private` keyword is used as part of various types of variable, function, and procedure declarations, as well as in the `Option Private` statement. For example, the following lines declare a procedure that is private to the module in which it is located.

```
Private Sub MyProc()
    ' Body of procedure goes here.
End Sub
```

CROSS-REFERENCE
See also Private (statement), Public, Static, Option Private, Const, Declare, Function, Sub, Enum, Property Get, Property Let, Property Set, and Type.

Private

Statement

The `Private` statement enables you to declare variables that are accessible only from within the module in which the variable is declared. The `Private` statement also allocates space for the declared variable.

Syntax

```
Private events name type
```

- *events* (*) — The keyword `WithEvents`, which specifies that the variable is used with an ActiveX object's events.
- *name* — The variable's name, which can include subscripts for declaring an array.
- *type* (*) — The keyword `As` followed by the variable type. The `New` keyword can also be used (for example, `As New object`) to create a new object with which to associate the variable. If you leave off the type, the variable's data type defaults to `Variant`.

(*) = Optional

 NOTE
You can define several variables with one `Private` statement by separating the declarations with commas.

Example 1

The following lines declare the variables `var1` and `var2` as private variables of the `Variant` type.

```
Private var1
Private var2 As Variant
```

Example 2

Here, the following line uses a single `Private` statement to declare two variables of differing types.

```
Private var1 As Integer, var2 As Variant
```

Example 3

Finally, the following lines declare two private arrays.

```
Private var1(10) As Integer
Private var2(5, 10) As Integer
```

CROSS-REFERENCE
See also Dim, Public, and Static.

Procedure

Concept

A procedure is a block of code that performs a specific task. Procedures don't directly return values (that's what a function does), but can be used to set the values of variables passed into the procedure. Procedures can be assigned user-defined names, which should be descriptive enough to hint at the tasks accomplished by the code. For example, the following procedure draws a simple face in the form's window.

```
Private Sub DrawFace()
    Form1.Circle (1900, 900), 800
    Form1.Circle (2200, 700), 200
    Form1.Circle (1600, 700), 200
    Form1.Circle (1900, 1000), 100
    Form1.Line (1500, 1300)-(2300, 1300)
End Sub
```

CROSS-REFERENCE
See also Function and Event Procedure.

ProductName

Property

The ProductName property represents the application's product name. You can set this property in the Project Properties property sheet, as shown in Figure P-25.

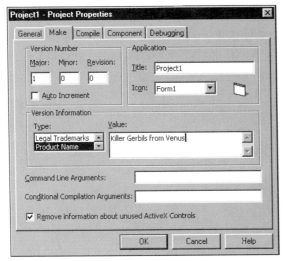

Figure P-25 You set the ProductName property from your project's Project
Properties property sheet.

Objects with a ProductName Property

App

Syntax

```
value = App.ProductName
```

- *App* — A reference to the App object.
- *value* — The variable that will receive the product name.

Example

In this example, the program retrieves an application's product name. Note
that the App object is a global Visual Basic object that you don't need to add
to your programs.

```
Dim strProductName As String
strProductName = App.ProductName
```

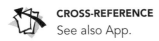

CROSS-REFERENCE
See also App.

ProgressBar

Control

A ProgressBar control enables a program to display the status of an on-going operation graphically. Figure P-26, for example, shows a ProgressBar control in a form. The ProgressBar control is part of the Microsoft Windows Common Controls 6.0 component package, which you can load into your project from the Components dialog box (see Figure P-27). To display the Components dialog box, select the Components command from the Project menu, or press Ctrl+T on your keyboard.

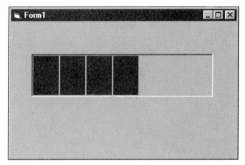

Figure P-26 ProgressBar controls shows the completion status of an ongoing task.

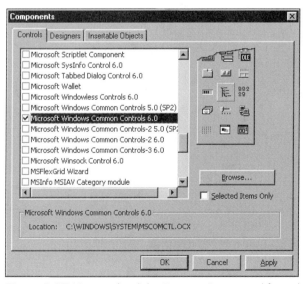

Figure P-27 You can load the ProgressBar control from the Components dialog box.

Properties

The ProgressBar control has 30 properties, which are listed below. Because many Visual Basic controls have similar properties, the following list does not include the properties' descriptions. For information on using a property, look up the individual property's entry, provided alphabetically in this book.

```
Align
Appearance
BorderStyle
Container
DragIcon
DragMode
Enabled
Height
hWnd
Index
Left
Max
Min
MouseIcon
MousePointer
Name
Object
OLEDropMode
Orientation
Parent
Scrolling
RightToLeft
TabIndex
Tag
ToolTipText
Top
Value
Visible
WhatsThisHelpID
Width
```

Methods

The ProgressBar control has six methods, which are listed below. Because many Visual Basic controls have similar methods, the following list does not include the methods' descriptions. For information on using a method, look up the individual method's entry, provided alphabetically in this book.

```
Drag
Move
OLEDrag
Refresh
ShowWhatsThis
ZOrder
```

Events

The ProgressBar control responds to 12 events, which are listed below. Because many Visual Basic controls respond to similar events, the following list does not include the events' descriptions. For information on using an event, look up the individual event's entry, provided alphabetically in this book.

```
Click
DragDrop
DragOver
MouseDown
MouseMove
MouseUp
OLECompleteDrag
OLEDragDrop
OLEDragOver
OLEGiveFeedback
OLESetData
OLEStartDrag
```

In most cases, you won't need to respond to an event on behalf of a ProgressBar control—if you do, the event will probably be Click, which the control generates when the user clicks the control with the mouse. A program responds to the control's Click event in the Click event procedure. A ProgressBar control called Progress1 will have a Click event procedure called Progress1_Click, which is where the program should handle the event, as shown in the following lines:

```
Private Sub Progress1_Click()
    ' Handle the Click event here.
End Sub
```

Property

Concept

A property is a value that represents one of an object's attributes. For example, the TextBox control's `Text` property represents the text that the user has entered into the control, whereas a form's `Caption` property represents the text shown in the window's title bar. The following line sets a form's `Caption` property:

```
Form1.Caption = "SuperWord — MyLetter.spw"
```

 CROSS-REFERENCE
See also Method.

Property

Keyword

The `Property` keyword is used when defining `Property Get`, `Property Let`, and `Property Set` procedure declarations. For example, the following lines show a `Property Get` procedure that returns the value of a property called `TextColor`.

```
Public Property Get TextColor() As Integer
    TextColor = UserControl.TextColor
End Property
```

 CROSS-REFERENCE
For more information, see Property Get, Property Set, and Property Let.

PropertyBag

Object

A PropertyBag object holds the data needed to save and restore an object's properties.

Properties

The PropertyBag object has no properties.

Methods

The PropertyBag object has two methods, which are listed below. For more information on using one of these methods, look up the individual method's entry, provided alphabetically in this book.

```
ReadProperty
WriteProperty
```

Events

The PropertyBag object does not respond to events.

 CROSS-REFERENCE
For more information, see ReadProperty and WriteProperty.

PropertyChanged

Method

The `PropertyChanged` method informs a control's container that a property value has changed, ensuring that the property's value is updated in the Properties window and that property is properly saved when the object is closed.

Objects with a PropertyChanged Method

UserControl

Syntax

`UserControl.PropertyChanged name`

- *UserControl* — A reference to a UserControl object.
- *name* — The name of the property that changed.

Example

The following lines define a `Property Let` procedure that sets a property called `CustomerID` to a new value and calls the `PropertyChanged` method on behalf of the property.

```
Public Property Let CustomerID(ByVal strID As String)
    custID = strID
    PropertyChanged "CustomerID"
End Property
```

CROSS-REFERENCE
See also UserControl, ReadProperty, and WriteProperty.

Property Get Procedure

Concept

The `Property Get` procedure returns a specific property's value from an object. For example, the following example returns the current value of an object's `CustomerID` property, which is stored in a variable of the object called `custID`. The `CustomerID` symbol represents the property's name, whereas the `custID` symbol represents the value's storage. Visual Basic automatically calls a property's `Property Get` procedure when a program statement requests a property's value. For example, the line `currentID = object.CustomerID` causes Visual Basic to call the `CustomerID Property Get` procedure. (In this case, `object` is the object that defines the `CustomerID` property.)

```
Property Get CustomerID() As String
    CustomerID = custID
End Property
```

CROSS-REFERENCE
See also Property Let and Property Set.

Property Let Procedure

Concept

The `Property Let` procedure assigns a value to a specific property. For example, the following example sets the current value of an object's `CustomerID` property, which is stored in a variable of the object called `custID`. The `CustomerID` symbol represents the property's name, whereas the `custID` symbol represents the value's storage. Visual Basic automatically calls a property's `Property Let` procedure when a program statement sets a property's value.

For example, the line `object.CustomerID = currentID` will cause Visual Basic to call the `CustomerID Property Let` procedure. (In this case, `object` is the object that defines the `CustomerID` property.)

```
Property Let CustomerID(strID As String)
    custID = strID
    PropertyChanged "CustomerID"
End Property
```

CROSS-REFERENCE
See also Property Get, Property Set, and PropertyChanged.

PropertyPage

Object

A PropertyPage object represents a page in an object's Property Pages dialog box. Figure P-28, for example, shows the Property Pages dialog box for the ListView control. Notice that the dialog box contains seven separate PropertyPage objects, each of which is represented by a tab.

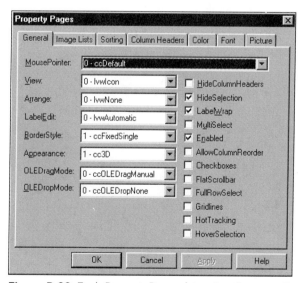

Figure P-28 Each PropertyPage object in a Property Pages dialog box gets its own tab.

Properties

The PropertyPage object has 47 properties, which are listed below. Because many Visual Basic objects and controls have similar properties, the following list does not include the properties' descriptions. For information on using a property, look up the individual property's entry, provided alphabetically in this book.

```
ActiveControl
Appearance
AutoRedraw
BackColor
Caption
Changed
ClipControls
Controls
CurrentX
CurrentY
DrawMode
DrawStyle
DrawWidth
FillColor
FillStyle
Font
FontBold
FontItalic
FontName
FontSize
FontStrikethru
FontTransparent
FontUnderline
ForeColor
hDC
Height
HelpContextID
hWnd
Image
KeyPreview
MouseIcon
MousePointer
Name
OLEDropMode
Palette
PaletteMode
Picture
```

```
RightToLeft
ScaleHeight
ScaleLeft
ScaleMode
ScaleTop
ScaleWidth
SelectedControls
StandardSize
Tag
Width
```

Methods

The PropertyPage object has 15 methods, which are listed below. Because many Visual Basic objects and controls have similar methods, the following list does not include the methods' descriptions. For information on using a method, look up the individual method's entry, provided alphabetically in this book.

```
Circle
Cls
Line
OLEDrag
PaintPicture
Point
PopupMenu
PSet
Refresh
Scale
ScaleX
ScaleY
SetFocus
TextHeight
TextWidth
```

Events

The PropertyPage object responds to 27 events, which are listed below. Because many Visual Basic objects and controls respond to similar events, the following list does not include the events' descriptions. For information on using an event, look up the individual event's entry, provided alphabetically in this book.

```
Activate
ApplyChanges
```

```
Click
DblClick
Deactivate
DragDrop
DragOver
EditProperty
GotFocus
Initialize
KeyDown
KeyPress
KeyUp
Load
LostFocus
MouseDown
MouseMove
MouseUp
OLECompleteDrag
OLEDragOver
OLEGiveFeedback
OLESetData
OLEStartDrag
Paint
SelectionChanged
Terminate
Unload
```

PropertyPages

Property

The PropertyPages property represents the names of property pages for a UserControl object.

Objects with a PropertyPages Property

UserControl

Syntax

```
UserControl.PropertyPages(index) = value1
```

or

```
value2 = UserControl.PropertyPages(index)
```

- *UserControl* — A reference to a UserControl control.
- *index* — The property page's index.
- *value1* — The property page's name.
- *value2* — The variable that will receive the property page's name.

Example

The following lines show how to get a property page's name.

```
Dim pageName As String
pageName = UserControl1.PropertyPages(1)
```

CROSS-REFERENCE
See also UserControl.

Property Set Procedure

Concept

The `Property Set` procedure assigns an object to a specific property. For example, the following example sets the current value of an object's `Customer` property, which is stored in a variable of the object called `custObj`. The `Customer` symbol represents the property's name, whereas the `custObj` symbol represents the value's storage. Visual Basic automatically calls a property's `Property Set` procedure when a program statement sets a property's value to an object. For example, the line `object.Customer = currentCustomer` causes Visual Basic to call the `Customer Property Set` procedure. (In this case, `object` is the object that defines the `Customer` property.)

```
Property Set CustomerID(newCustomer As Object)
    custObj = newCustomer
    PropertyChanged "Customer"
End Property
```

CROSS-REFERENCE
See also Property Get, Property Let, and PropertyChanged.

PSet

Method

The PSet method draws a point in an object's display area.

Objects with a PSet Method

Form

PictureBox

Printer

PropertyPage

UserControl

Syntax

`object.PSet (x,y), color`

- *color* (*) — The point color, which can be set with the RGB or QBColor functions. The default is the color specified in the object's ForeColor property.
- *object* — A reference to an object with a PSet method.
- *x* — The horizontal coordinate for the point. The coordinates can be preceded by the optional Step keyword, which indicates that the coordinates are relative to the CurrentX and CurrentY coordinates.
- *y* — The vertical coordinate for the point. The coordinates can be preceded by the optional Step keyword, which indicates that the coordinates are relative to the CurrentX and CurrentY coordinates.

(*) = Optional

Example

The following program demonstrates the PSet method. When you run the program, enter X and Y point coordinates into the text boxes, and select a color from the Color list box. Then, when you click the Draw Point button, your selected point appears in the PictureBox control. Figure P-29, for example, shows several points drawn in the application's display area. Note that each dot is 16 pixels wide because the program sets the DrawWidth property to 16.

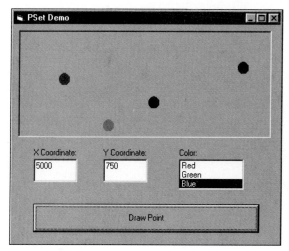

Figure P-29 Draw points anywhere in this application's PictureBox control.

```
VERSION 5.00
Begin VB.Form Form1
   Caption        =    "PSet Demo"
   ClientHeight   =    4680
   ClientLeft     =    60
   ClientTop      =    345
   ClientWidth    =    5970
   LinkTopic      =    "Form1"
   ScaleHeight    =    4680
   ScaleWidth     =    5970
   StartUpPosition =   3   'Windows Default
   Begin VB.ListBox lstColors
      Height       =    645
      ItemData     =    "Form1.frx":0000
      Left         =    3720
      List         =    "Form1.frx":0002
      TabIndex     =    6
      Top          =    2880
      Width        =    1455
   End
   Begin VB.TextBox txtYCoord
      Height       =    495
      Left         =    2040
```

```
           TabIndex       =    3
           Top            =    2880
           Width          =    975
        End
        Begin VB.TextBox txtXCoord
           Height         =    495
           Left           =    480
           TabIndex       =    2
           Top            =    2880
           Width          =    975
        End
        Begin VB.PictureBox picPicture1
           Height         =    2295
           Left           =    120
           ScaleHeight    =    2235
           ScaleWidth     =    5595
           TabIndex       =    1
           Top            =    120
           Width          =    5655
        End
        Begin VB.CommandButton btnDrawPoint
           Caption        =    "Draw Point"
           Height         =    615
           Left           =    480
           TabIndex       =    0
           Top            =    3840
           Width          =    5055
        End
        Begin VB.Label Label3
           Caption        =    "Color:"
           Height         =    255
           Left           =    3720
           TabIndex       =    7
           Top            =    2640
           Width          =    1215
        End
        Begin VB.Label Label2
           Caption        =    "Y Coordinate:"
           Height         =    255
           Left           =    2040
           TabIndex       =    5
           Top            =    2640
```

```
        Width           =    1215
     End
     Begin VB.Label Label1
        Caption         =    "X Coordinate:"
        Height          =    255
        Left            =    480
        TabIndex        =    4
        Top             =    2640
        Width           =    1335
     End
  End
End
Attribute VB_Name = "Form1"
Attribute VB_GlobalNameSpace = False
Attribute VB_Creatable = False
Attribute VB_PredeclaredId = True
Attribute VB_Exposed = False

Private Sub btnDrawPoint_Click()
    Dim colorNum As Integer
    Dim x As Integer, y As Integer

    colorNum = lstColors.ListIndex

    On Error GoTo ErrorHandlerX
    x = txtXCoord.Text
    On Error GoTo ErrorHandlerY
    y = txtYCoord.Text

    If colorNum = 0 Then
        picPicture1.PSet (x, y), RGB(255, 0, 0)
    ElseIf colorNum = 1 Then
        picPicture1.PSet (x, y), RGB(0, 255, 0)
    Else
        picPicture1.PSet (x, y), RGB(0, 0, 255)
    End If
    Exit Sub

ErrorHandlerX:
    MsgBox "X coordinate no good", vbExclamation
    Exit Sub
ErrorHandlerY:
    MsgBox "Y coordinate no good", vbExclamation
```

```
        Exit Sub
    End Sub

    Private Sub Form_Load()
        lstColors.AddItem "Red"
        lstColors.AddItem "Green"
        lstColors.AddItem "Blue"
        lstColors.Selected(0) = True
        picPicture1.DrawWidth = 16
        picPicture1.AutoRedraw = True
    End Sub
```

CROSS-REFERENCE
See also FileSystemObject.

Public

Keyword

The Public keyword is used as part of various types of variable, function, and procedure declarations. For example, the following lines declare a public procedure, which is a procedure that can be called from other modules.

```
Public Sub MyProc()
    ' Body of procedure goes here.
End Sub
```

CROSS-REFERENCE
See also Public (statement), Private, Static, Const, Declare, Function, Sub, Enum, Property Get, Property Let, Property Set, and Type.

Public

Property

The Public property represents whether a control can be used with other applications. This property is available only at design time.

Objects with a Public Property

UserControl

Syntax

This property can be set only in a UserControl object's Properties window at design time.

CROSS-REFERENCE
See also UserControl.

Public

Statement

The Public statement enables you to declare variables that are accessible from other modules. The Public statement also allocates space for the declared variable.

Syntax

```
Public events name type
```

- *events* (★) — The keyword WithEvents, which specifies that the variable is used with an ActiveX object's events.
- *name* — The variable's name, which can include subscripts for declaring an array.
- *type* (★) — The keyword As followed by the variable type. The New keyword can also be used (for example, As New *object*) to create a new object with which to associate the variable. If you leave off the type, the variable's data type defaults to Variant.

(★) = Optional

NOTE
You can define several variables with one Public statement by separating the declarations with commas.

Example 1

The following lines declare the variables var1 and var2 as public variables of the Variant type.

```
Public var1
Public var2 As Variant
```

Example 2

Here, the following line uses a single Public statement to declare two variables of differing types.

```
Public var1 As Integer, var2 As Variant
```

Example 3

Finally, the following lines declare two public arrays.

```
Public var1(10) As Integer
Public var2(5, 10) As Integer
```

 CROSS-REFERENCE
See also Private, Dim, and Static.

Put

Statement

The Put statement writes data to a disk file.

Syntax

```
Get #num, offset, buf
```

- *buf* — The variable from which the data will be written.
- *num* — The file number as assigned to the file with the Open statement.
- *offset* (*) — The offset at which to start writing data. This is the byte number or record number at which to start writing.

(*) = Optional

Example

The following lines open a file and write an integer value using the Put statement.

```
Dim intData As Integer
intData = 25
Open "c:\MyFile.dat" For Binary As #1
Put #1, , intData
Close #1
```

CROSS-REFERENCE
See also Get, Open, and Close.

PV

Function

The PV function calculates the present value of an annuity.

Syntax

```
value = PV(intRate, numPayments, payment, futValue, payDue)
```

- *futValue* (★) — The desired future value of the annuity. The default is 0.
- *intRate* — The interest rate per period.
- *numPayments* — The number of payments.
- *payDue* (★) — The value 0 if payments are made at the end of the period and 1 if payments are made at the start of the period. The default is 0.
- *payment* — The amount of a payment.
- *value* — The variable that will receive the present value.

(★) = Optional

Example

The following program is a present-value calculator that demonstrates the PV function. When you run the program, follow these steps:

1. Enter the yearly payment supplied by the annuity into the Amount of Payment box.
2. Enter the annuity's yearly interest rate into the Annual Interest Rate box.
3. Enter the number of yearly payments into the Number of Payments box.
4. Enter the annuity's future value into the Future Value box.

After entering the data, click the Calculate button. The annuity's present value then appears at the bottom of the window. Figure P-30, for example, shows the present value of an annuity that will supply 10 annual payments of $20,000 each, with a 6.5% annual interest rate and a future value of $200,000.

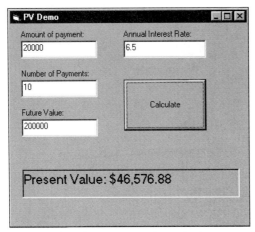

Figure P-30 The present-value calculator can show you the present worth of future investments.

```
VERSION 5.00
Begin VB.Form Form1
    Caption         =   "PV Demo"
    ClientHeight    =   4305
    ClientLeft      =   165
    ClientTop       =   450
    ClientWidth     =   5235
    LinkTopic       =   "Form1"
    ScaleHeight     =   4305
    ScaleWidth      =   5235
    StartUpPosition =   3   'Windows Default
    Begin VB.TextBox txtFutValue
        Height      =   375
        Left        =   240
        TabIndex    =   8
        Top         =   2040
        Width       =   1695
    End
    Begin VB.CommandButton btnCalculate
        Caption     =   "Calculate"
        Height      =   1095
        Left        =   2520
        TabIndex    =   6
        Top         =   1200
        Width       =   1815
    End
```

```
Begin VB.TextBox txtNumPayments
   Height          =    375
   Left            =    240
   TabIndex        =    5
   Top             =    1200
   Width           =    1695
End
Begin VB.TextBox txtIntRate
   Height          =    375
   Left            =    2520
   TabIndex        =    3
   Top             =    360
   Width           =    1815
End
Begin VB.TextBox txtPayment
   Height          =    375
   Left            =    240
   TabIndex        =    1
   Top             =    360
   Width           =    1695
End
Begin VB.Label Label4
   Caption         =    "Future Value:"
   Height          =    255
   Left            =    240
   TabIndex        =    9
   Top             =    1800
   Width           =    1575
End
Begin VB.Label lblPresValue
   BorderStyle     =    1   'Fixed Single
   Caption         =    "Present Value:"
   BeginProperty Font
      Name            =    "MS Sans Serif"
      Size            =    13.5
      Charset         =    0
      Weight          =    400
      Underline       =    0    'False
      Italic          =    0    'False
      Strikethrough   =    0    'False
   EndProperty
   Height          =    615
   Left            =    240
   TabIndex        =    7
```

```
            Top             =    3120
            Width           =    4815
         End
         Begin VB.Label Label3
            Caption         =    "Number of Payments:"
            Height          =    255
            Left            =    240
            TabIndex        =    4
            Top             =    960
            Width           =    1575
         End
         Begin VB.Label Label2
            Caption         =    "Annual Interest Rate:"
            Height          =    255
            Left            =    2520
            TabIndex        =    2
            Top             =    120
            Width           =    1575
         End
         Begin VB.Label Label1
            Caption         =    "Amount of payment:"
            Height          =    255
            Left            =    240
            TabIndex        =    0
            Top             =    120
            Width           =    1695
         End
      End
Attribute VB_Name = "Form1"
Attribute VB_GlobalNameSpace = False
Attribute VB_Creatable = False
Attribute VB_PredeclaredId = True
Attribute VB_Exposed = False

Private Sub btnCalculate_Click()
    Dim intRate As Double
    Dim numPayments As Integer
    Dim paymentAmt As Double
    Dim futValue As Double
    Dim presValue As Double
    Dim strResult As String

    On Error GoTo ErrorHandler
```

```
    intRate = txtIntRate.Text
    intRate = intRate / 100
    paymentAmt = txtPayment.Text
    numPayments = txtNumPayments.Text
    futValue = txtFutValue

    presValue = PV(intRate, numPayments, _
        -paymentAmt, futValue, 1)
    presValue = presValue + 0.005
    strResult = "$" & Format(presValue, "###,###,##0.00")
    lblPresValue.Caption = "Present Value: " & strResult
    Exit Sub

ErrorHandler:
    MsgBox "An error occurred.", vbExclamation
End Sub
```

QBColor

Function

The QBColor function returns the RGB color value of one of Visual Basic's 16 predefined colors. Table Q-1 lists the values you can use with this function.

Table Q-1 Color Values for the QBColor Function

Value	Description
0	Black
1	Blue
2	Green
3	Cyan
4	Red
5	Magenta
6	Yellow
7	White
8	Gray
9	Light Blue
10	Light Green
11	Light Cyan
12	Light Red
13	Light Magenta
14	Light Yellow
15	Bright White

Syntax

```
value = QBColor(colorNum)
```

- *colorNum* — The number of the color to retrieve.
- *value* — The variable that will receive the RGB color value.

Example

The following lines set a form's background color to cyan.

```
Dim rgbValue As Long
rgbValue = QBColor(3)
Form1.BackColor = rgbValue
```

QueryChangeConfig

Event

Visual Basic sends a SysInfo control a `QueryChangeConfig` event when the system's hardware profile is about to be changed. By responding to this event, a program can control whether the change takes place.

Objects with a QueryChangeConfig Event

SysInfo

Example

A program can respond to a `QueryChangeConfig` event by implementing the SysInfo control's `QueryChangeConfig` event procedure. The following code segment shows how a SysInfo control defines a `QueryChangeConfig` event procedure. As you can see in the procedure's declaration, the procedure receives one parameter. If the event procedure changes the `Cancel` parameter to `True`, the system's power suspension is canceled. In this example, the `SysInfo1` object is a SysInfo control that the programmer added to the form at design time.

```
Private Sub SysInfo1_QueryChangeConfig(Cancel As Boolean)
    ' Handle the QueryChangeConfig event here.
End Sub
```

CROSS-REFERENCE
See also SysInfo.

QueryUnload

Event

Visual Basic sends an object a `QueryUnload` event right before a form closes, enabling the program to determine whether it's okay for the form to close.

Objects with a QueryUnload Event

Form

MDIForm

Example

A program can respond to a `QueryUnload` event by implementing the form's `QueryUnload` event procedure. The following code segment shows how a form defines a `QueryUnload` event procedure. As you can see in the procedure's declaration, the procedure receives two parameters. If the event procedure changes the `Cancel` parameter to `True`, the unload event is canceled. The second parameter, `UnloadMode`, specifies the type of action that triggered the unload event and can be one of the values in Table Q-2.

```
Private Sub Form_QueryUnload(Cancel As Integer, _
  UnloadMode As Integer)
    If something Then Cancel = True
End Sub
```

Table Q-2 Values for the UnloadMode Parameter

Value	Description
vbFormControlMenu	The Control menu's Close command was selected.
vbFormCode	The program called the `Unload` statement.
vbAppWindows	Windows is shutting down.
vbAppTaskManager	Task Manager is closing the application.
vbFormMDIForm	A child MDI window's parent MDI form is closing.
vbFormOwner	A form's owner is closing.

CROSS-REFERENCE

See also Form, MDIForm, Load, and Unload.

R

Raise

Method

The Raise method triggers a runtime error.

Objects with a Raise Method

Err

Syntax

Err.Raise *errNum, object, errDescr, helpFile, helpID*

- *errDescr* (*) — The error's description.
- *errNum* — The error number.
- *helpFile* (*) — The path to the Help file that contains information about the error.
- *helpID* (*) — The context ID for the help topic.
- *object* (*) — The name of the object that sent the error.

(*) = Optional

Example 1

The following line generates the overflow runtime error, which is error number 6.

Err.Raise 6

NOTE
Note that the Err object is a global Visual Basic object that you don't need to create in your programs.

Example 2

Here, the following line generates a user-defined error on behalf of an object called MyObject. Notice how the vbObjectError constant is used to define an error number that is guaranteed not to conflict with system-defined errors.

```
Err.Raise vbObjectError + 100, "MyObject", _
    "Invalid value for the Color property", _
    "MyHelp.Hlp", 1145300
```

CROSS-REFERENCE
See also Err, Error, and On Error.

RaiseEvent

Statement

The RaiseEvent statement generates an event on behalf of an object. The object that fires the event is called the *event source*, whereas the object that implements the event code (receives the event) is called the *event sink*.

Syntax

```
RaiseEvent name, args
```

- *args* (*) — The event's argument list, enclosed in parentheses.
- *name* — The name of the event to fire.

(*) = Optional

Example

The following program demonstrates how to define an event source and an event sink, as well as how to fire an event. When you run the program, type text into the Event Text box, and then click the Fire Event button. The event source module adds asterisks to the start and end of the text you entered and sends it back to the event sink module via the SendText event. The SendText event procedure then pastes the text into the Received From Event box, as shown in Figure R-1.

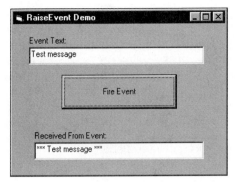

Figure R-1 The text is pasted into the Received From Event box.

The first listing is the code for the event source, called `EventSource`, which is a class module that you create by selecting the Project menu's Add Class Module command. After you create the module and add the source code, Visual Basic generates the listing that follows:

```
VERSION 1.0 CLASS
BEGIN
  MultiUse = -1  'True
  Persistable = 0  'NotPersistable
  DataBindingBehavior = 0  'vbNone
  DataSourceBehavior  = 0  'vbNone
  MTSTransactionMode  = 0  'NotAnMTSObject
END
Attribute VB_Name = "EventSource"
Attribute VB_GlobalNameSpace = False
Attribute VB_Creatable = True
Attribute VB_PredeclaredId = False
Attribute VB_Exposed = False

Public Event SendText(ByVal eventStr As String)

Public Sub initEventText(ByVal eventStr As String)
    Dim msg As String

    msg = "*** " & eventStr & " ***"
    RaiseEvent SendText(msg)
End Sub
```

As you can see by the `Public Event` line, this module defines an event called `SendText`, which gets fired from the `initEventText` method.

The event sink module, which is the main module, creates an `EventSource` object and implements its `SendText` event procedure, which is called when the `EventSource` object fires the event. The event gets fired when the user clicks the Fire Event button, whose `btnFireEvent_Click` procedure calls the `EventSource` object's `initEventText` method. The event sink module looks like this:

```
VERSION 5.00
Begin VB.Form Form1
   Caption          =   "RaiseEvent Demo"
   ClientHeight     =   3195
   ClientLeft       =   60
   ClientTop        =   345
   ClientWidth      =   4680
   LinkTopic        =   "Form1"
   ScaleHeight      =   3195
   ScaleWidth       =   4680
   StartUpPosition  =   3  'Windows Default
   Begin VB.TextBox txtReceivedText
      Height        =   375
      Left          =   480
      TabIndex      =   3
      Top           =   2520
      Width         =   3735
   End
   Begin VB.TextBox txtEventText
      Height        =   375
      Left          =   360
      TabIndex      =   1
      Top           =   480
      Width         =   3855
   End
   Begin VB.CommandButton btnFireEvent
      Caption       =   "Fire Event"
      Height        =   735
      Left          =   1080
      TabIndex      =   0
      Top           =   1080
      Width         =   2535
   End
   Begin VB.Label Label2
      Caption       =   "Received From Event:"
      Height        =   255
      Left          =   480
      TabIndex      =   4
```

```
          Top            =    2280
          Width          =    2055
      End
      Begin VB.Label Label1
          Caption        =    "Event Text:"
          Height         =    255
          Left           =    360
          TabIndex       =    2
          Top            =    240
          Width          =    2055
      End
  End
  Attribute VB_Name = "Form1"
  Attribute VB_GlobalNameSpace = False
  Attribute VB_Creatable = False
  Attribute VB_PredeclaredId = True
  Attribute VB_Exposed = False
  Private WithEvents eventSrc As EventSource

  Private Sub btnFireEvent_Click()
      Dim eventStr As String
      eventStr = txtEventText.Text
      eventSrc.initEventText eventStr
  End Sub

  Private Sub Form_Load()
      Set eventSrc = New EventSource
  End Sub

  Private Sub eventSrc_SendText(ByVal eventStr As String)
      txtReceivedText.Text = eventStr
  End Sub
```

CROSS-REFERENCE
See also Event.

Randomize

Statement

The Randomize statement initializes the random-number generator with a seed value. You can supply an explicit seed number or omit the seed number, which causes Visual Basic to use the system timer's current value as the seed value.

Syntax

```
Randomize seedNum
```

- *seedNum* (*) — The seed number for the random-number generator.

(*) = Optional

Example 1

The following line initializes the random-number generator with the seed value obtained from the system timer.

```
Randomize
```

Example 2

Here, the following line initializes the random-number generator with an explicit seed value.

```
Randomize 1234
```

CROSS-REFERENCE
See also Rnd.

Rate

Function

The Rate function calculates the interest rate for an annuity.

Syntax

```
value = PV(numPayments, payment, presValue,
    futValue, payDue, rateEstimate)
```

- *futValue* (*) — The desired future value of the annuity. The default is 0.
- *numPayments* — The number of payments.
- *payDue* (*) — The value 0 if payments are made at the end of the period and 1 if payments are made at the start of the period. The default is 0.

- *payment* — The amount of a payment.
- *presValue* — The annuity's present value.
- *rateEstimate* (✭) — The value 0 if payments are made at the end of the period and 1 if payments are made at the start of the period. The default is 0.
- *value* — The variable that will receive the interest rate.

(✭) = Optional

Example

The following program is an interest-rate calculator that demonstrates the Rate function. When you run the program, enter the following values into the text boxes:

- Enter the amount of the loan into the Amount of Loan box.
- Enter the amount of a single payment into the Amount of Payment box.
- Enter the number of payments into the Number of Payments box.

After entering the data, click the Calculate button. The loan's interest rate then appears at the bottom of the window. Figure R-2, for example, shows the interest rate of a $10,000 loan with 60 monthly payments of $250 each.

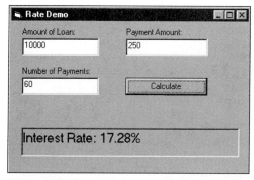

Figure R-2 The interest-rate calculator can show you the interest rate you're paying on a loan.

```
VERSION 5.00
Begin VB.Form Form1
    Caption        =   "Rate Demo"
    ClientHeight   =   3210
    ClientLeft     =   165
```

```
ClientTop        =    450
ClientWidth      =    5235
LinkTopic        =    "Form1"
ScaleHeight      =    3210
ScaleWidth       =    5235
StartUpPosition  =    3   'Windows Default
Begin VB.CommandButton btnCalculate
    Caption      =    "Calculate"
    Height       =    375
    Left         =    2520
    TabIndex     =    6
    Top          =    1200
    Width        =    1815
End
Begin VB.TextBox txtNumPayments
    Height       =    375
    Left         =    240
    TabIndex     =    5
    Top          =    1200
    Width        =    1695
End
Begin VB.TextBox txtPayment
    Height       =    375
    Left         =    2520
    TabIndex     =    3
    Top          =    360
    Width        =    1815
End
Begin VB.TextBox txtLoanAmt
    Height       =    375
    Left         =    240
    TabIndex     =    1
    Top          =    360
    Width        =    1695
End
Begin VB.Label lblInterest
    BorderStyle  =    1   'Fixed Single
    Caption      =    "Interest Rate: "
    BeginProperty Font
        Name         =    "MS Sans Serif"
        Size         =    13.5
        Charset      =    0
        Weight       =    400
        Underline    =    0    'False
```

```
                Italic           =    0    'False
                Strikethrough    =    0    'False
            EndProperty
            Height           =    615
            Left             =    240
            TabIndex         =    7
            Top              =    2280
            Width            =    4815
        End
        Begin VB.Label Label3
            Caption          =    "Number of Payments:"
            Height           =    255
            Left             =    240
            TabIndex         =    4
            Top              =    960
            Width            =    1575
        End
        Begin VB.Label Label2
            Caption          =    "Payment Amount:"
            Height           =    255
            Left             =    2520
            TabIndex         =    2
            Top              =    120
            Width            =    1575
        End
        Begin VB.Label Label1
            Caption          =    "Amount of Loan:"
            Height           =    255
            Left             =    240
            TabIndex         =    0
            Top              =    120
            Width            =    1335
        End
    End
End
Attribute VB_Name = "Form1"
Attribute VB_GlobalNameSpace = False
Attribute VB_Creatable = False
Attribute VB_PredeclaredId = True
Attribute VB_Exposed = False

Private Sub btnCalculate_Click()
    Dim loanAmount As Double
    Dim payAmount As Double
    Dim result As Double
```

```
        Dim numPayments As Integer
        Dim strPayment As String
        Dim strResult As String

        On Error GoTo ErrorHandler

        loanAmount = txtLoanAmt.Text
        payAmount = txtPayment.Text
        numPayments = txtNumPayments.Text
        result = Rate(numPayments, -payAmount, loanAmount)
        result = (result * 12 * 100) + 0.005
        strResult = Format(result, "##0.00") & "%"

        lblInterest.Caption = "Interest Rate: " & strResult

    ErrorHandler:
    End Sub
```

Read

Method

The Read method reads characters from a file associated with a TextStream object.

Objects with a Read Method

TextStream

Syntax

```
string = TextStream.Read(numChars)
```

- *numChars* — The number of characters to read from the file.
- *string* — The string containing the characters read by the method.
- *TextStream* — A reference to a TextStream object.

Example

The following lines create a FileSystemObject, open a text file as a TextStream object, and read ten (10) characters from the file.

```
Dim fileSystem As Object
```

```
Dim textFile As Object
Dim chars As String

Set fileSystem = CreateObject("Scripting.FileSystemObject")
Set textFile = fileSystem.OpenTextFile("c:\MyFile.txt")
chars = textFile.Read(10)
textFile.Close
```

 CROSS-REFERENCE
See also FileSystemObject, ReadAll, ReadLine, Write, and WriteLine.

ReadAll

Method

The `ReadAll` method reads the entire contents of a file associated with a TextStream object.

Objects with a ReadAll Method

TextStream

Syntax

string = *TextStream*.ReadAll

- *string* — The string containing the characters read by the method.
- *TextStream* — A reference to a TextStream object.

Example

The following lines create a FileSystemObject, open a text file as a TextStream object, and read all text from the file.

```
Dim fileSystem As Object
Dim textFile As Object
Dim chars As String

Set fileSystem = CreateObject("Scripting.FileSystemObject")
Set textFile = fileSystem.OpenTextFile("c:\MyFile.txt")
chars = textFile.ReadAll
textFile.Close
```

 **CROSS-REFERENCE**
See also FileSystemObject, Read, ReadLine, Write, and WriteLine.

ReadFromFile

Method

The ReadFromFile method reads an OLE file into an OLE Container control.

Objects with a ReadFromFile Method

OLE Container

Syntax

OLEContainer.ReadFromFile fileNum

- *fileNum* — The file number given to the binary file in the Open statement.
- *OLEContainer* — A reference to an OLE Container control.

Example

The following program demonstrates the ReadFromFile method. When you run the program, double-click on the OLE Container control. You can then edit the bitmap document embedded into the control. After drawing something in the bitmap, click the Save File button to save your work. Finally, close and rerun the program, and click the Load File button. The file you previously saved appears in the OLE Container control. Figure R-3 shows a bitmap being edited in the OLE Container control.

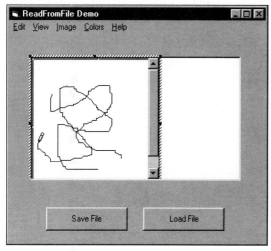

Figure R-3 After editing a bitmap, you can save and reload your work.

```
VERSION 5.00
Begin VB.Form Form1
    Caption         =   "ReadFromFile Demo"
    ClientHeight    =   4755
    ClientLeft      =   60
    ClientTop       =   345
    ClientWidth     =   5730
    LinkTopic       =   "Form1"
    ScaleHeight     =   4755
    ScaleWidth      =   5730
    StartUpPosition =   3   'Windows Default
    Begin VB.CommandButton btnLoadFile
        Caption         =   "Load File"
        Height          =   495
        Left            =   3000
        TabIndex        =   2
        Top             =   3720
        Width           =   1815
    End
    Begin VB.CommandButton btnSaveFile
        Caption         =   "Save File"
        Height          =   495
        Left            =   840
        TabIndex        =   1
        Top             =   3720
        Width           =   1815
```

q

r

s

```
            End
            Begin VB.OLE OLE1
                Class           =       "Paint.Picture"
                Height          =       2655
                Left            =       480
                OleObjectBlob   =       "Form1.frx":0000
                TabIndex        =       0
                Top             =       480
                Width           =       4695
            End
        End
        Attribute VB_Name = "Form1"
        Attribute VB_GlobalNameSpace = False
        Attribute VB_Creatable = False
        Attribute VB_PredeclaredId = True
        Attribute VB_Exposed = False

        Private Sub btnLoadFile_Click()
            On Error GoTo LoadError
            Open "Demo.rff" For Binary As #1
            OLE1.ReadFromFile 1
            Close #1
            Exit Sub

        LoadError:
            MsgBox "File load error.", vbExclamation, "Load File"
        End Sub

        Private Sub btnSaveFile_Click()
            On Error GoTo SaveError
            Open "Demo.rff" For Binary As #1
            OLE1.SaveToFile 1
            Close #1
            MsgBox "File Saved.", vbInformation, "Save File"
            Exit Sub

        SaveError:
            MsgBox "File save error.", vbExclamation, "Save File"
        End Sub
```

 CROSS-REFERENCE

See also OLE Container, SaveToFile, and SaveToOle1File.

ReadLine

Method

The `ReadLine` method reads a line of text from a file associated with a TextStream object.

Objects with a ReadLine Method

TextStream

Syntax

`string = TextStream.ReadLine`

- *string* — The string containing the characters read by the method.
- *TextStream* — A reference to a TextStream object.

Example

The following lines create a FileSystemObject, open a text file as a TextStream object, and read a line of text from the file.

```
Dim fileSystem As Object
Dim textFile As Object
Dim chars As String

Set fileSystem = CreateObject("Scripting.FileSystemObject")
Set textFile = fileSystem.OpenTextFile("c:\MyFile.txt")
chars = textFile.ReadLine
textFile.Close
```

 CROSS-REFERENCE
See also FileSystemObject, Read, ReadAll, Write, and WriteLine.

ReadOnly

Property

The `ReadOnly` property represents whether a FileListBox control can show read-only files. A value of `True` specifies that the control can show read-only files, whereas a value of False indicates that the control will not display read-only files.

Objects with a ReadOnly Property

FileListBox

Syntax

```
FileListBox.ReadOnly = value1
```

or

```
value2 = FileListBox.ReadOnly
```

- *FileListBox* — A reference to a FileListBox control.
- *value1* — The value True or False.
- *value2* — The variable that will receive the property's current setting.

Example

The following lines show how to get and set a FileListBox control's ReadOnly property. The File1 object is a FileListBox control that the programmer added to the form at design time.

```
Dim showReadOnly As Boolean
showReadOnly = File1.ReadOnly
File1.ReadOnly = True
```

CROSS-REFERENCE
See also FileListBox.

ReadProperties

Event

Visual Basic sends an object a ReadProperties event when the object must load its saved properties. This occurs during the reloading of an object that has previously saved its state.

Objects with a ReadProperties Event

Class

UserControl

Example

A program can respond to a `ReadProperties` event by implementing the object's `ReadProperties` event procedure. The following code segment shows how a UserControl control defines a `ReadProperties` event procedure. As you can see in the procedure's declaration, the procedure receives one parameter, which is a `PropertyBag` object that provides access to the saved property values. The program reads the property values by calling the `PropertyBag` object's `ReadProperty` method.

```
Private Sub UserControl_ReadProperties _
   (PropBag As PropertyBag)
     On Error Resume Next
     MyPropertyStorage = _
        PropBag.ReadProperty("MyProperty", "Default Value")
End Sub
```

 CROSS-REFERENCE

See also ReadProperty, UserControl, WriteProperties, and WriteProperty.

ReadProperty

Method

The `ReadProperty` method reads the value of a saved property.

Objects with a ReadProperty Method

PropertyBag

Syntax

value = PropertyBag.ReadProperty(name, default)

- *default* (*) — The default value for the property, which will be used if no saved value exists.

- *name* — The name of the property for which to retrieve the saved value.

- *PropertyBag*—A reference to a `PropertyBag` object.
- *value*—The variable that will receive the value for the property.

(*) = Optional

Example

The following code segment shows how a UserControl control defines a `ReadProperties` event procedure, which uses the `ReadProperty` method to retrieve the value of several properties.

```
Private Sub UserControl_ReadProperties _
  (PropBag As PropertyBag)
    On Error Resume Next
    MyStrPropertyStorage = _
        PropBag.ReadProperty("MyStrProperty", _
          "Default Value")
    MyIntPropertyStorage = _
        PropBag.ReadProperty("MyIntProperty", 0)
    MyColorStorage = _
        PropBag.ReadProperty("MyColorProperty", _
          RGB(255, 255, 255))
End Sub
```

CROSS-REFERENCE
See also ReadProperties, UserControl, WriteProperties, and WriteProperty.

RecipAddress

Property

The `RecipAddress` property represents the email address of the current message recipient.

Objects with a RecipAddress Property

MAPIMessages

Syntax

```
MAPIMessages.RecipAddress = value1
```

or

```
value2 = MAPIMessages.RecipAddress
```

- *MAPIMessages* — A reference to a MAPIMessages control.
- *value1* — The recipient's address.
- *value2* — The variable that will receive the property's current value.

Example

In this example, the program retrieves the recipient address of a MAPIMessages control's current message. The mpmMAPIMessages1 object is a MAPIMessages control that the programmer added to the application's form at design time.

```
Dim strRecipAddress As String
strRecipAddress = mpmMAPIMessages1.RecipAddress
```

CROSS-REFERENCE
See also MAPIMessages, RecipCount, RecipDisplayName, RecipIndex, and RecipType.

RecipCount

Property

The RecipCount property represents the number of recipients to whom the current message is addressed.

Objects with a RecipCount Property

MAPIMessages

Syntax

```
value = MAPIMessages.RecipCount
```

- *MAPIMessages* — A reference to a MAPIMessages control.
- *value* — The variable that will receive the property's current value.

Example

In this example, the program retrieves the number of recipients for a MAPIMessages control's current message. The mpmMAPIMessages1 object is a MAPIMessages control that the programmer added to the application's form at design time.

```
Dim lngRecipCount As Long
lngRecipCount = mpmMAPIMessages1.RecipCount
```

 CROSS-REFERENCE
See also MAPIMessages, RecipAddress, RecipDisplayName, RecipIndex, and RecipType.

RecipDisplayName

Property

The `RecipDisplayName` property represents the name of the recipient to whom the current message is addressed.

Objects with a RecipDisplayName Property

MAPIMessages

Syntax

```
MAPIMessages.RecipDisplayName = value1
```

or

```
value2 = MAPIMessages.RecipDisplayName
```

- *MAPIMessages* — A reference to a MAPIMessages control.
- *value1* — The recipient's display name.
- *value2* — The variable that will receive the property's current value.

Example

In this example, the program retrieves the name of the recipient for a MAPIMessages control's current message. The `mpmMAPIMessages1` object is a MAPIMessages control that the programmer added to the application's form at design time.

```
Dim strRecipName As String
strRecipName = mpmMAPIMessages1.RecipDisplayName
```

CROSS-REFERENCE

See also MAPIMessages, RecipAddress, RecipCount, RecipIndex, and RecipType.

RecipIndex

Property

The `RecipIndex` property sets the index of the recipient to whom the current message is addressed.

Objects with a RecipIndex Property

MAPIMessages

Syntax

```
MAPIMessages.RecipIndex = value1
```

or

```
value2 = MAPIMessages.RecipIndex
```

- *MAPIMessages* — A reference to a MAPIMessages control.
- *value1* — The index of the recipient.
- *value2* — The variable that will receive the property's current value.

Example

In this example, the program retrieves the index of the recipient for a MAPIMessages control's current message. The `mpmMAPIMessages1` object is a MAPIMessages control that the programmer added to the application's form at design time.

```
Dim lngRecipIndex As Long
lngRecipIndex = mpmMAPIMessages1.RecipIndex
```

CROSS-REFERENCE

See also MAPIMessages, RecipAddress, RecipCount, RecipDisplayName, and RecipType.

RecipType

Property

The RecipType property represents the type of recipient to whom the current message is addressed. This property can be one of the values from Table R-1.

Table R-1 Values for the RecipType Property

Value	Description
MapBccList	Specifies that the recipient is an invisible recipient of a message copy.
MapCcList	Specifies that the recipient is to receive a copy of the message.
MapOrigList	Specifies that the recipient is the message's originator.
MapToList	Specifies that the recipient is the recipient in the To field.

Objects with a RecipType Property

MAPIMessages

Syntax

```
MAPIMessages.RecipType = value1
```

or

```
value2 = MAPIMessages.RecipType
```

- *MAPIMessages* — A reference to a MAPIMessages control.
- *value1* — The recipient type from Table R-1.
- *value2* — The variable that will receive the property's current value.

Example

In this example, the program retrieves the type of recipient for a MAPIMessages control's current message. The mpmMAPIMessages1 object is a MAPIMessages control that the programmer added to the application's form at design time.

```
Dim intRecipType As Integer
intRecipType = mpmMAPIMessages1.RecipType
```

CROSS-REFERENCE
See also MAPIMessages, RecipAddress, RecipCount, RecipDisplayName, and RecipIndex.

RecordClick

Event

Visual Basic sends a Multimedia MCI control a `RecordClick` event when the user clicks the control's Record button. By responding to this event, a program can stop the default action of the Record button from occurring.

Objects with a RecordClick Event

Multimedia MCI

Example

A program can respond to a `RecordClick` event by implementing the Multimedia MCI control's `RecordClick` event procedure. By setting the procedure's `Cancel` parameter to `True`, the program can halt the Record button's default action.

```
Private Sub mciMMControl1_RecordClick(Cancel As Integer)
    If something Then Cancel = True
End Sub
```

CROSS-REFERENCE
See also Multimedia MCI and RecordCompleted.

RecordCompleted

Event

Visual Basic sends a Multimedia MCI control a `RecordCompleted` event after the Record button's action has been executed. By responding to this event, a program can determine whether any errors occurred.

Objects with a RecordCompleted Event

Multimedia MCI

Example

A program can respond to a `RecordCompleted` event by implementing the Multimedia MCI control's `RecordCompleted` event procedure, which receives an error value as its single parameter.

```
Private Sub mciMMControl1_RecordCompleted(Errorcode As Long)
    ' Handle the event here.
End Sub
```

 CROSS-REFERENCE
See also Multimedia MCI and RecordClick.

RecordEnabled

Property

The `RecordEnabled` property represents the enabled status of a Multimedia MCI control's Record button. This property is `True` when the control's Record button is enabled and is `False` when the button is disabled.

Objects with a RecordEnabled Property

Multimedia MCI

Syntax

Multimedia.RecordEnabled = *value1*

or

value2 = *Multimedia*.RecordEnabled

- *Multimedia* — A reference to a Multimedia MCI control.
- *value1* — The value `True` or `False`.
- *value2* — The variable that will receive the value returned by the property.

Example

The following lines show how to get and set the enabled status of a Multimedia control's Record button.

```
Dim enable
enable = mciMMControl1.RecordEnabled
mciMMControl1.RecordEnabled = True
```

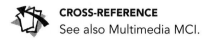 **CROSS-REFERENCE**
See also Multimedia MCI.

RecordGotFocus

Event

Visual Basic sends a Multimedia MCI control a `RecordGotFocus` event when the control's Record button receives the focus.

Objects with a RecordGotFocus Event

Multimedia MCI

Example

A program can respond to a `RecordGotFocus` event by implementing the Multimedia MCI control's `RecordGotFocus` event procedure, which receives no parameters, as shown here.

```
Private Sub mciMMControl1_RecordGotFocus()
    ' Handle the RecordGotFocus event here.
End Sub
```

 CROSS-REFERENCE
See also Multimedia MCI and RecordLostFocus.

RecordLostFocus

Event

Visual Basic sends a Multimedia MCI control a `RecordLostFocus` event when the control's Record button loses the focus.

Objects with a RecordLostFocus Event

Multimedia MCI

Example

A program can respond to a `RecordLostFocus` event by implementing the Multimedia MCI control's `RecordLostFocus` event procedure, which receives no parameters, as shown here.

```
Private Sub mciMMControl1_RecordLostFocus()
    ' Handle the RecordLostFocus event here.
End Sub
```

CROSS-REFERENCE
See also Multimedia MCI and RecordGotFocus.

RecordMode

Property

The `RecordMode` property represents the recording mode for an MCI device. The property can be set to `mciRecordInsert` or `mciRecordOverwrite`.

NOTE
Not all recording devices support both the insert and overwrite modes.

Objects with a RecordMode Property

Multimedia MCI

Syntax

```
Multimedia.RecordMode = value1
```

or

```
value2 = Multimedia.RecordMode
```

- *Multimedia* — A reference to a Multimedia MCI control.
- *value1* — The value `mciRecordInsert` or `mciRecordOverwrite`.
- *value2* — The variable that will receive the property's current setting.

Example

The following lines show how to get and set the insert mode of a Multimedia control's `RecordMode` property. The `mciMMControl1` object is a Multimedia MCI control that the programmer added to the form at design time.

```
Dim mode As Integer
mode = mciMMControl1.RecordMode
mciMMControl1.RecordMode = mciRecordInsert
```

CROSS-REFERENCE
See also Multimedia MCI.

RecordVisible

Property

The `RecordVisible` property represents the visible status of a Multimedia MCI control's Record button. This property is `True` when the control's Play button is visible and is `False` when the button is not visible.

Objects with a RecordVisible Property

Multimedia MCI

Syntax

Multimedia.RecordVisible = *value1*

or

value2 = *Multimedia*.RecordVisible

- *Multimedia* — A reference to an Multimedia MCI control.
- *value1* — The value `True` or `False`.
- *value2* — The variable that will receive the value returned by the property.

Example

The following lines show how to get and set the visible status of a Multimedia control's Record button.

```
Dim visible
visible = mciMMControl1.RecordVisible
mciMMControl1.RecordVisible = True
```

CROSS-REFERENCE
See also Multimedia MCI.

ReDim

Statement

The ReDim statement enables you to redimension the size of a dynamic array. A *dynamic array* is an array that's been declared with no dimension. For example, the following line declares a dynamic array called MyArray:

```
Dim MyArray() As Integer
```

You can't access the dynamic array until you've used the ReDim statement to set the dynamic array's size. However, you can use ReDim multiple times.

Syntax

ReDim *preserve name(indexes) type*

- *preserve* (*) — The keyword Preserve, which will preserve the contents of the dynamic array when it's resized. However, when using Preserve, you can change only the upper bound of the last array dimension.
- *name* — The dynamic array's name.
- *indexes* — The subscripts for the dynamic array. For a single dimension array, this can be just the upper bound, or it can be the lower and upper bound separated by the keyword To. Multiple-dimension arrays can be created by listing each dimension separated with commas.
- *type* (*) — The keyword As followed by the variable type. If you leave off the type, the variable's data type defaults to Variant.

    (*) = Optional

NOTE
You can redimension several dynamic arrays with one ReDim statement by separating the declarations with commas.

Example 1

The following lines declare the variable `var1` as a dynamic array of `Variant`. The `ReDim` statement then sets the array's size. The array will have valid indexes from 0 to 10.

```
Dim var1() As Variant
ReDim var1(10)
```

Example 2

Here, the following line uses a single `ReDim` statement to redimension two dynamic arrays of differing data types.

```
Dim var1() As Integer
Dim var2() As Variant
ReDim var1(10), var2(15)
```

Example 3

In this example, the following lines declare a dynamic array and redimension it as a two-dimensional array with valid indexes from 5 to 20.

```
Dim var1() As Integer
ReDim var1(5 To 20, 5 To 20)
```

Example 4

Finally, the following lines declare a dynamic array, redimension it as a two-dimensional array with valid indexes from 5 to 7, set the array's contents, and then redimension the array to make it larger while retaining its contents.

```
Dim var1() As Integer
ReDim var1(5 To 7, 5 To 7)
var1(5, 5) = 0
var1(5, 6) = 1
var1(5, 7) = 2
var1(6, 5) = 3
var1(6, 6) = 4
var1(6, 7) = 5
ReDim Preserve var1(5 To 7, 5 To 10)
```

CROSS-REFERENCE

See also Dim, Private, Public, and Static.

Refresh

Method

The `Refresh` method completely redraws an object.

Objects with a Refresh Method

CheckBox

ComboBox

CommandButton

CoolBar

DirListBox

DriveListBox

FileListBox

Form

Frame

HScrollBar

Image

Label

Line

ListBox

ListView

Multimedia MCI

OLE Container

OptionButton

PictureBox

PropertyPage

RichTextBox

Shape

Slider

StatusBar

TabStrip

TextBox

Toolbar

TreeView

UserControl

VscrollBar

Syntax

object.Refresh

- *object*—A reference to an object with a Refresh method.

Example

The following program demonstrates the Refresh method. When you run the program, use the controls to navigate to any folder on your hard drive, preferably one that contains only a few files. When you do, the files in the folder appear in the FileListBox on the right-hand side of the window (Figure R-4). Now, using Windows Explorer, add a file to the folder you're viewing with the Refresh Demo program. When you switch back to the demo program, you'll see that the new file doesn't yet appear in the list. Click the Refresh File List button, which causes the program to call the FileListBox control's Refresh method. The new file then appears in the file list.

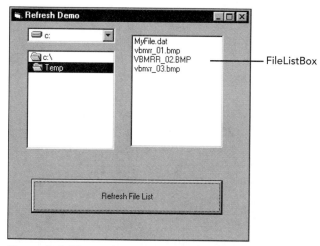

Figure R-4 Files in the currently selected folder appear in the FileListBox control.

```
VERSION 5.00
Begin VB.Form Form1
   Caption         =    "Refresh Demo"
   ClientHeight    =    4605
```

```
              ClientLeft      =    165
              ClientTop       =    450
              ClientWidth     =    5235
              LinkTopic       =    "Form1"
              ScaleHeight     =    4605
              ScaleWidth      =    5235
              StartUpPosition =    3  'Windows Default
              Begin VB.CommandButton btnRefresh
                 Caption        =    "Refresh File List"
                 Height         =    735
                 Left           =    480
                 TabIndex       =    3
                 Top            =    3360
                 Width          =    4215
              End
              Begin VB.FileListBox File1
                 Height         =    2430
                 Left           =    2640
                 TabIndex       =    2
                 Top            =    240
                 Width          =    2055
              End
              Begin VB.DriveListBox Drive1
                 Height         =    315
                 Left           =    360
                 TabIndex       =    1
                 Top            =    120
                 Width          =    1935
              End
              Begin VB.DirListBox Dir1
                 Height         =    2115
                 Left           =    360
                 TabIndex       =    0
                 Top            =    600
                 Width          =    1935
              End
           End
           Attribute VB_Name = "Form1"
           Attribute VB_GlobalNameSpace = False
           Attribute VB_Creatable = False
           Attribute VB_PredeclaredId = True
           Attribute VB_Exposed = False

           Private Sub btnRefresh_Click()
```

```
        Dir1.Refresh
        File1.Refresh
    End Sub

    Private Sub Dir1_Change()
        File1.Path = Dir1.Path
    End Sub

    Private Sub Drive1_Change()
        Dir1.Path = Drive1.Drive
    End Sub
```

CROSS-REFERENCE
See also FileSystemObject.

Rem

Statement

The Rem statement enables a programmer to place comments in a program's source code. The Visual Basic compiler ignores all comments when checking syntax or compiling program lines.

Syntax

```
Rem comment
```

- *comment* (*) — The comment's text.

(*) = Optional

Example 1

In this example, the Rem line describes the procedure's action.

```
    Private Sub btnCommand1_Click()
        Rem Beep the system speaker.
        Beep
    End Sub
```

Example 2

Here, the Rem keyword is replaced with the apostrophe character ('), which is a short-cut, and more common, method of specifying a comment.

```
Private Sub btnCommand1_Click()
    ' Beep the system speaker.
    Beep
End Sub
```

Remove

Method

The Remove method deletes an object from an object collection.

Objects with a Remove Method

Bands

Buttons

Collection

ColumnHeaders

ListImages

Nodes

OLEObjects

Panels

Tabs

Syntax

```
collection.Remove index
```

- *collection* — A reference to a collection-type object.
- *index* — The index of the object to remove from the collection.

Example

The following line removes the ListItem object at index 4 in a ListView control. The lvwListView1 object is a ListView control that the programmer added to the form at design time.

```
lvwListView1.ListItems.Remove 4
```

CROSS-REFERENCE
See also Add and Clear.

RemoveItem

Method

The `RemoveItem` method deletes an item from a ComboBox or ListBox control.

Objects with a RemoveItem Method

ComboBox

ListBox

Syntax

object.RemoveItem *index*

- *object* — A reference to a ComboBox or ListBox control.
- *index* — The index of the item to remove from the control.

Example

The following line removes the item at index 2 in a ListBox control. The `lstList1` object is a ListBox control that the programmer added to the form at design time.

```
lstList1.RemoveItem 2
```

CROSS-REFERENCE
See also AddItem and Clear.

Render

Method

The `Render` method draws an image, or part of an image, stored in a `Picture` object. A better method to use to perform this task is `PaintPicture`.

Objects with a Render Method

Picture

Syntax

```
Picture.Render(hDC, x1, y1, w1, h1, _
    x2, y2, w2, h2, worldBounds)
```

- *h1*—The height of the destination area in the object's scale units.
- *h2*—The height of the source image in HIMETRIC units.
- *hDC*—The destination object's device-context handle.
- *Picture*—A reference to a `Picture` object.
- *w1*—The width of the destination area in the object's scale units.
- *w2*—The width of the source image in HIMETRIC units.
- *worldBounds*—Should be `Null` except when targeting output to a metafile, in which case this is a reference to a RECTL structure.
- *x1*—The X coordinate of the destination area's upper-left corner in the object's scale units.
- *x2*—The X coordinate of the source image's upper-left corner in HIMETRIC units.
- *y1*—The Y coordinate of the destination area's upper-left corner in the object's scale units.
- *y2*—The Y coordinate of the source image's upper-left corner in HIMETRIC units.

 CROSS-REFERENCE
See also PaintPicture and Picture.

Replace

Function

The `Replace` function replaces a substring with another substring.

Syntax

```
value = Replace(sourceStr, searchStr, replacementStr, _
    begin, number, type)
```

- *begin* (*) — The character in *sourceStr* at which to start the search. The default is 1.
- *number* (*) — The number of replacements to make. The default is –1 to make all replacements.
- *replacementStr* — The substring with which to replace *searchStr*.
- *searchStr* — The substring for which to search.
- *sourceStr* — The string to search.
- *type* (*) — The type of comparison to make, which can be a value from Table R-2.
- *value* — The variable that will receive the resultant string.

(*) = Optional

Table R-2 Settings for the *type* Argument

Setting	Description
vbBinaryCompare	Performs a binary comparison.
vbDatabaseCompare	Performs a comparison using Access database information.
vbTextCompare	Compares values as text.
vbUseCompareOption	Compares values based on the program's Option Compare setting.

Example 1

In this example, after the following lines execute, the variable str4 will contain the string "111XXX333XXX444." The Replace function in this case replaces all occurrences of "222" in str1 with "XXX."

```
Dim str1 As String
Dim str2 As String
Dim str3 As String
Dim str4 As String

str1 = "111222333222444"
str2 = "222"
str3 = "XXX"
str4 = Replace(str1, str2, str3)
```

Example 2

In this example, the variable `str4` will contain the string "111XXX333222444." The `Replace` function in this case replaces only the first occurrence of "222" in `str1` with "XXX," because the fifth parameter instructs the function to make only one replacement.

```
Dim str1 As String
Dim str2 As String
Dim str3 As String
Dim str4 As String

str1 = "111222333222444"
str2 = "222"
str3 = "XXX"
str4 = Replace(str1, str2, str3, 1, 1)
```

Example 3

Finally, in this example, the variable `str4` will contain the string "333XXX444." The `Replace` function starts building the resultant string at the seventh character of `str1`, replacing the second occurrence of "222" in `str1` with "XXX."

```
Dim str1 As String
Dim str2 As String
Dim str3 As String
Dim str4 As String

str1 = "111222333222444"
str2 = "222"
str3 = "XXX"
str4 = Replace(str1, str2, str3, 7, 1)
```

CROSS-REFERENCE
See also Filter.

Reply

Method

The `Reply` method sets up a reply to the currently indexed message in a MAPIMessages control.

Objects with a Reply Method

MAPIMessages

Syntax

`MAPIMessages.Reply`

- *MAPIMessages* — A reference to a MAPIMessages control.

Example

The following line starts a reply to the current message. The `mpmMAPIMessages1` object is a MAPIMessages control that the programmer added to the form at design time.

`mpmMAPIMessages1.Reply`

 CROSS-REFERENCE
See also MAPIMessages and ReplyAll.

ReplyAll

Method

The `ReplyAll` method sets up a reply to all recipients associated with the currently indexed message in a MAPIMessages control. These recipients include the message's author and those recipients listed in the To and CC fields.

Objects with a ReplyAll Method

MAPIMessages

Syntax

`MAPIMessages.ReplyAll`

- *MAPIMessages* — A reference to a MAPIMessages control.

Example

The following line starts a reply to all recipients associated with the current message. The `mpmMAPIMessages1` object is a MAPIMessages control that the programmer added to the form at design time.

```
mpmMAPIMessages1.ReplyAll
```

CROSS-REFERENCE
See also MAPIMessages and Reply.

ReportIcon

Property

The `ReportIcon` property represents the image shown next to a ListView control's subitems when the control is in report view.

Objects with a ReportIcon Property

ListSubItem

Syntax

```
ListSubItem.ReportIcon = value1
```

or

```
value2 = ListSubItem.ReportIcon
```

- *ListSubItem* — A reference to a ListSubItem control.
- *value1* — The index or key of an image in an ImageList control. The ImageList control assigned to the ListView control's `SmallIcons` property holds the images for the `ReportIcon` property.
- *value2* — The variable that will receive the property's current setting.

Example

The following lines initialize ImageList and ListView controls, populating the ListView with items and subitems and displaying those items in the report view, as shown in Figure R-5. Notice the icons that appear next to each subitem. These icons appear because of the setting of each subitem's `ReportIcon` property.

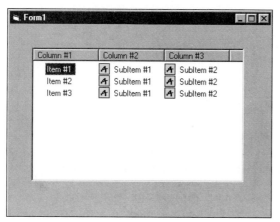

Figure R-5 This ListView control displays icons next to its subitems.

```
Dim lstItem As ListItem

ilsImageList1.ListImages.Add , , LoadPicture("c:\icon2.ico")
lvwListView1.SmallIcons = ilsImageList1

lvwListView1.ColumnHeaders.Add , , "Column #1"
lvwListView1.ColumnHeaders.Add , , "Column #2"
lvwListView1.ColumnHeaders.Add , , "Column #3"

Set lstItem = lvwListView1.ListItems.Add(, , "Item #1")
lstItem.ListSubItems.Add , , "SubItem #1"
lstItem.ListSubItems.Add , , "SubItem #2"
lstItem.ListSubItems(1).ReportIcon = 1
lstItem.ListSubItems(2).ReportIcon = 1

Set lstItem = lvwListView1.ListItems.Add(, , "Item #2")
lstItem.ListSubItems.Add , , "SubItem #1"
lstItem.ListSubItems.Add , , "SubItem #2"
lstItem.ListSubItems(1).ReportIcon = 1
lstItem.ListSubItems(2).ReportIcon = 1

Set lstItem = lvwListView1.ListItems.Add(, , "Item #3")
lstItem.ListSubItems.Add , , "SubItem #1"
lstItem.ListSubItems.Add , , "SubItem #2"
lstItem.ListSubItems(1).ReportIcon = 1
lstItem.ListSubItems(2).ReportIcon = 1

lvwListView1.View = lvwReport
```

q
r
s

CROSS-REFERENCE
See also Multimedia MCI.

Reset

Statement

The Reset statement closes any and all files that were opened with the Open statement, as well as writes any buffered data to the files.

Syntax

```
Reset
```

Example

The following lines open three files and write a line of text to each file. The final line, which is the Reset statement, writes all data from the file buffers and then closes the files.

```
Open "c:\MyFile1.txt" For Output As #1
Open "c:\MyFile2.txt" For Output As #2
Open "c:\MyFile3.txt" For Output As #3
Print #1, "This is a test"
Print #2, "This is another test"
Print #3, "Still another test"
Reset
```

CROSS-REFERENCE
See also Close.

Resize — General Controls

Event

Visual Basic sends an object a Resize event when the object first appears or is resized in some way.

Objects with a Resize Event
CoolBar

UserControl

Form

MDIForm

PictureBox

Example

A program can respond to a Resize event by implementing the object's Resize event procedure. The following code segment shows how a PictureBox control defines a Resize event procedure. In this example, the picPicture1 object is a PictureBox control that the programmer added to the form at design time.

```
Private Sub picPicture1_Resize()
    ' Handle the Resize event here.
End Sub
```

Resize — OLE Container

Event

Visual Basic sends an OLE Container control a Resize event when the control first appears or is resized in some way.

Example

A program can respond to a Resize event by implementing the OLE Container control's Resize event procedure. The following code segment shows how an OLE Container control defines a Resize event procedure. As you can see, the procedure receives two parameters, which are the control's new height and width. In this example, the OLE1 object is an OLE Container control that the programmer added to the form at design time.

```
Private Sub OLE1_Resize(HeightNew As Single, _
    WidthNew As Single)
    ' Handle the Resize event here.
End Sub
```

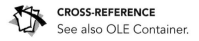

CROSS-REFERENCE

See also OLE Container.

ResolveName

Method

The ResolveName method matches the current message recipient's name with an email address in the address book.

Objects with a ResolveName Method

MAPIMessages

Syntax

MAPIMessages.ResolveName

- *MAPIMessages* — A reference to a MAPIMessages control.

Example

The following line resolves a recipient's name with its email address. The mpmMAPIMessages1 object is a MAPIMessages control that the programmer added to the form at design time.

mpmMAPIMessages1.ResolveName

CROSS-REFERENCE
See also AddressResolveUI and MAPIMessages.

RestoreToolbar

Method

The RestoreToolbar method restores the configuration of a customized toolbar that was saved with the SaveToolbar method. The user can customize the toolbar by double-clicking it, which brings up the Customize Toolbar dialog box, as shown in Figure R-6.

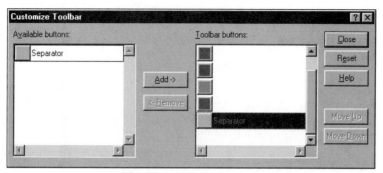

Figure R-6 The Customize Toolbar Dialog box enables the modification of a toolbar's buttons.

Objects with a RestoreToolbar Method

Toolbar

Syntax

`Toolbar.RestoreToolbar appName, subkeyName, keyName`

- *Toolbar* — A reference to a Toolbar control.
- *appName* — The application's name, which is the main key in the HKEY_CURRENT_USER section of the Registry. This key must have been added to the Registry by the `SaveToolbar` method.
- *subkeyName* — The subkey under which the toolbar configuration was saved. This key must have been added to the Registry by the `SaveToolbar` method.
- *keyName* — The name of the key with which the toolbar configuration is associated. This key must have been added to the Registry by the `SaveToolbar` method.

Example

The following program demonstrates how to save and restore a custom toolbar configuration. When you first run the program (Figure R-7), double-click the toolbar (in an area without buttons) to display the Customize Toolbar dialog box. Use the dialog box's controls to remove one or two buttons from the toolbar, and then close the dialog box. Closing the dialog box triggers the toolbar's `Change` event. In the `tlbToolbar1_Change` event procedure, the program calls `SaveToolbar` method to save the toolbar's new settings to the Registry. Now, exit the application and rerun it. Click the Restore Toolbar button, and the toolbar reloads your custom configuration.

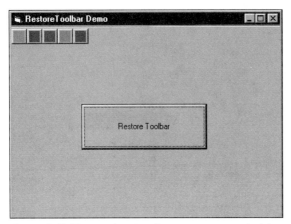

Figure R-7 This application features a customizable toolbar.

NOTE

The toolbar restoration will fail if, in the Customize Toolbar dialog box, you added separators to the buttons or if you tried to move a button more than one position up or down. Also, the restoration won't work if your toolbar contains buttons that are not associated with an image in an ImageList control. You can, however, always restore the original toolbar by clicking the Customize Toolbar dialog box's Reset button.

```
VERSION 5.00
Object = "{831FDD16-0C5C-11D2-A9FC-0000F8754DA1} _
    #2.0#0"; "MSCOMCTL.OCX"
Begin VB.Form Form1
    Caption         =   "RestoreToolbar Demo"
    ClientHeight    =   4080
    ClientLeft      =   60
    ClientTop       =   345
    ClientWidth     =   5940
    LinkTopic       =   "Form1"
    ScaleHeight     =   272
    ScaleMode       =   3   'Pixel
    ScaleWidth      =   396
    StartUpPosition =   3   'Windows Default
    Begin VB.CommandButton btnRestore
        Caption     =   "Restore Toolbar"
        Height      =   975
        Left        =   1560
        TabIndex    =   1
        Top         =   1680
```

```
          Width            =    2775
       End
       Begin MSComctlLib.ImageList ilsImageList1
          Left             =    5160
          Top              =    3240
          _ExtentX         =    1005
          _ExtentY         =    1005
          BackColor        =    -2147483643
          MaskColor        =    12632256
          _Version         =    393216
       End
       Begin MSComctlLib.Toolbar tlbToolbar1
          Align            =    1    'Align Top
          Height           =    630
          Left             =    0
          TabIndex         =    0
          Top              =    0
          Width            =    5940
          _ExtentX         =    10478
          _ExtentY         =    1111
          ButtonWidth      =    609
          ButtonHeight     =    953
          Appearance       =    1
          _Version         =    393216
       End
    End
    Attribute VB_Name = "Form1"
    Attribute VB_GlobalNameSpace = False
    Attribute VB_Creatable = False
    Attribute VB_PredeclaredId = True
    Attribute VB_Exposed = False

    Private Sub Form_Load()
        ilsImageList1.ListImages.Add , , _
            LoadPicture("button1.bmp")
        ilsImageList1.ListImages.Add , , _
            LoadPicture("button2.bmp")
        ilsImageList1.ListImages.Add , , _
            LoadPicture("button3.bmp")
        ilsImageList1.ListImages.Add , , _
            LoadPicture("button4.bmp")
        ilsImageList1.ListImages.Add , , _
            LoadPicture("button5.bmp")
        tlbToolbar1.ImageList = ilsImageList1
```

```
        tlbToolbar1.Buttons.Add , , , , 1
        tlbToolbar1.Buttons.Add , , , , 2
        tlbToolbar1.Buttons.Add , , , , 3
        tlbToolbar1.Buttons.Add , , , , 4
        tlbToolbar1.Buttons.Add , , , , 5
    End Sub

    Private Sub tlbToolbar1_Change()
        tlbToolbar1.SaveToolbar "RestoreToolbarDemo", _
            "UserSettings", "tlbToolbar1"
    End Sub

    Private Sub btnRestore_Click()
        tlbToolbar1.RestoreToolbar "RestoreToolbarDemo", _
            "UserSettings", "tlbToolbar1"
    End Sub
```

CROSS-REFERENCE
See also Customize, SaveToolbar, and Toolbar.

Resume

Keyword

The Resume keyword is part of the On Error and Resume statements, which determine where program execution will continue after a runtime error. For example, the following line tells Visual Basic to continue program execution right after the line that caused the error:

```
On Error Resume Next
```

CROSS-REFERENCE
See also On Error and Resume (statement).

Resume

Statement

The Resume statement causes program execution to jump back to a specified line after a runtime error.

Syntax

```
Resume dest
```

- *dest* (*) — The keyword Next, or the line number or line label where program execution should continue. If Next is used, program execution continues at the line following the line that caused the error. If the *dest* argument is left off completely, program execution continues on the line that caused the error.

(*) = Optional

Example 1

When the following lines execute, an out-of-bounds runtime error will occur on the line that tries to set element 6 of the array. Because of the On Error statement, program execution then jumps to the ErrorHandler label, where the program displays a "Bad array index" message. The Resume Next statement then sends program execution back to the line after the line that caused the error. This line displays the "Resumed" message.

```
Private Sub Command1_Click()
    Dim intArray(5) As Integer
    On Error GoTo ErrorHandler
    intArray(6) = 0
    MsgBox "Resumed", vbInformation
    Exit Sub

ErrorHandler:
    MsgBox "Bad array index.", vbExclamation
    Resume Next
End Sub
```

Example 2

Here, when the following lines execute, just as in the previous example, an out-of-bounds runtime error will occur on the line that tries to set element 6 of the array. Because of the On Error statement, program execution then jumps to the ErrorHandler label, where the program displays an "Enlarging the array" message and uses the ReDim statement to increase the size of the array to 10 elements. The Resume statement then sends program execution back to the line that caused the error, which can now execute successfully, setting the array's element 6 to 0.

```
Private Sub Command1_Click()
    Dim intArray() As Integer
```

```
          ReDim intArray(5)
          On Error GoTo ErrorHandler
          intArray(6) = 0
          MsgBox "Resumed", vbInformation
          Exit Sub

      ErrorHandler:
          MsgBox "Enlarging the array", vbExclamation
          ReDim intArray(10)
          Resume
      End Sub
```

Example 3

Finally, when the following lines execute, just as in the previous examples, an out-of-bounds runtime error will occur on the line that tries to set element 6 of the array. Because of the On Error statement, program execution then jumps to the ErrorHandler label, where the program displays a "Bad array index" message. The Resume ResumeHere statement then sends program execution back to the ResumeHere label.

```
      Private Sub Command1_Click()
          Dim intArray(5) As Integer
          On Error GoTo ErrorHandler
          intArray(6) = 0
      ResumeHere:
          MsgBox "Resumed", vbInformation
          Exit Sub

      ErrorHandler:
          MsgBox "Bad array index.", vbExclamation
          Resume ResumeHere
      End Sub
```

CROSS-REFERENCE
See also On Error and Resume (keyword).

Revision

Property

The `Revision` property represents the application's major revision number. You can set this property in the Project Properties property sheet, as shown in Figure R-8.

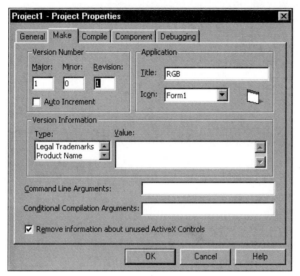

Figure R-8 You set the Revision property from your project's Project Properties property sheet.

Objects with a Revision Property

App

Syntax

```
value = App.Revision
```

- *App*—A reference to the App object.
- *value*—The variable that will receive the revision number.

Example

In this example, the program retrieves an application's revision number. Note that the App object is a global Visual Basic object that you don't need to add to your programs.

```
Dim revNum As Integer
revNum = App.Revision
```

CROSS-REFERENCE
See also App, Minor, and Major.

RGB

Function

The RGB function generates a color value from the specified red, green, and blue elements.

Syntax

```
value = RGB(red, green, blue)
```

- *red* — The value for red, which can be from 0 to 255. The higher the value, the brighter the red color component.
- *green* — The value for green, which can be from 0 to 255. The higher the value, the brighter the green color component.
- *blue* — The value for blue, which can be from 0 to 255. The higher the value, the brighter the blue color component.
- *value* — The variable that will receive the color value.

Example

The following program demonstrates how the RGB function works. When you run the program, the main window appears with four color bars (Figure R-9). The first three bars show the current intensity of the red, green, and blue color components, and the fourth bar shows the final RGB color when the three components are combined. To change the colors, type new values into the Red, Green, and Blue text boxes.

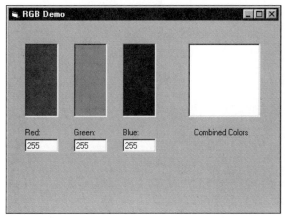

Figure R-9 The RGB Demo application shows how easy the RGB function is to use.

```
VERSION 5.00
Begin VB.Form Form1
   Caption          =    "RGB Demo"
   ClientHeight     =    4080
   ClientLeft       =    60
   ClientTop        =    345
   ClientWidth      =    5940
   LinkTopic        =    "Form1"
   ScaleHeight      =    272
   ScaleMode        =    3    'Pixel
   ScaleWidth       =    396
   StartUpPosition  =    3    'Windows Default
   Begin VB.TextBox txtBlue
      Height        =    285
      Left          =    2520
      TabIndex      =    9
      Text          =    "255"
      Top           =    2520
      Width         =    735
   End
   Begin VB.TextBox txtGreen
      Height        =    285
      Left          =    1440
      TabIndex      =    7
      Text          =    "255"
      Top           =    2520
      Width         =    735
   End
```

```
Begin VB.TextBox txtRed
   Height           =    285
   Left             =    360
   TabIndex         =    5
   Text             =    "255"
   Top              =    2520
   Width            =    735
End
Begin VB.PictureBox picColor
   Height           =    1575
   Left             =    3960
   ScaleHeight      =    1515
   ScaleWidth       =    1515
   TabIndex         =    3
   Top              =    480
   Width            =    1575
End
Begin VB.PictureBox picBlue
   Height           =    1575
   Left             =    2520
   ScaleHeight      =    1515
   ScaleWidth       =    675
   TabIndex         =    2
   Top              =    480
   Width            =    735
End
Begin VB.PictureBox picGreen
   Height           =    1575
   Left             =    1440
   ScaleHeight      =    1515
   ScaleWidth       =    675
   TabIndex         =    1
   Top              =    480
   Width            =    735
End
Begin VB.PictureBox picRed
   Height           =    1575
   Left             =    360
   ScaleHeight      =    1515
   ScaleWidth       =    675
   TabIndex         =    0
   Top              =    480
   Width            =    735
End
```

```
         Begin VB.Label Label4
            Caption         =    "Combined Colors"
            Height          =    375
            Left            =    4080
            TabIndex        =    10
            Top             =    2280
            Width           =    1455
         End
         Begin VB.Label Label3
            Caption         =    "Blue:"
            Height          =    255
            Left            =    2520
            TabIndex        =    8
            Top             =    2280
            Width           =    735
         End
         Begin VB.Label Label2
            Caption         =    "Green:"
            Height          =    255
            Left            =    1440
            TabIndex        =    6
            Top             =    2280
            Width           =    735
         End
         Begin VB.Label Label1
            Caption         =    "Red:"
            Height          =    255
            Left            =    360
            TabIndex        =    4
            Top             =    2280
            Width           =    735
         End
End
Attribute VB_Name = "Form1"
Attribute VB_GlobalNameSpace = False
Attribute VB_Creatable = False
Attribute VB_PredeclaredId = True
Attribute VB_Exposed = False
Private Sub Form_Load()
    picRed.BackColor = RGB(255, 0, 0)
    picGreen.BackColor = RGB(0, 255, 0)
    picBlue.BackColor = RGB(0, 0, 255)
    picColor.BackColor = RGB(255, 255, 255)
End Sub
```

q

r

s

```
Private Sub txtRed_Change()
    ChangeColor
End Sub

Private Sub txtGreen_Change()
    ChangeColor
End Sub

Private Sub txtBlue_Change()
    ChangeColor
End Sub

Private Sub ChangeColor()
    Dim red As Integer
    Dim green As Integer
    Dim blue As Integer

    On Error Resume Next
    red = txtRed.Text
    green = txtGreen.Text
    blue = txtBlue.Text
    picRed.BackColor = RGB(red, 0, 0)
    picGreen.BackColor = RGB(0, green, 0)
    picBlue.BackColor = RGB(0, 0, blue)
    picColor.BackColor = RGB(red, green, blue)
End Sub
```

RichTextBox

Control

A RichTextBox control is like a mini word processor that can be embedded in an application's window. A RichTextBox control enables a user not only to type text, but also to format the text in various ways. Figure R-10, for example, shows a RichTextBox control in a form. The RichTextBox control is found in the Microsoft Rich TextBox Control 6.0 component, which you can load into your project from the Components dialog box (Figure R-11). To display the Components dialog box, select the Components command from the Project menu, or press Ctrl+T on your keyboard.

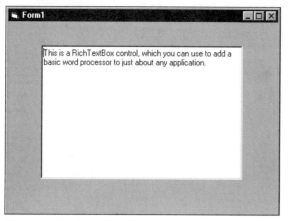

Figure R-10 A RichTextBox control gives an application the power to edit text in various ways.

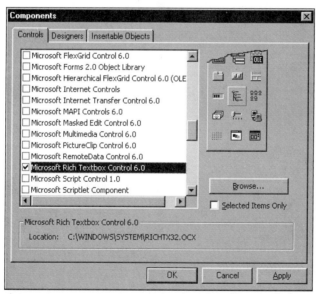

Figure R-11 You can load the RichTextBox control from the Components dialog box.

Properties

The RichTextBox control has 63 properties, which are listed below. Because many Visual Basic controls have similar properties, the following list does not include the properties' descriptions. For information on using a property, look up the individual property's entry, provided alphabetically in this book.

```
Appearance
AutoVerbMenu
BackColor
BorderStyle
BulletIndent
CausesValidation
Container
DisableNoScroll
DragIcon
DragMode
Enabled
FileName
Font
Height
HelpContextID
HideSelection
hWnd
Index
Left
Locked
MaxLength
MouseIcon
MousePointer
MultiLine
Name
Object
OLEDragMode
OLEDropMode
OLEObjects
Parent
RightMargin
ScrollBars
SelAlignment
SelBold
SelBullet
SelCharOffset
SelColor
SelFontName
SelFontSize
SelHangingIndent
SelIndent
SelItalic
SelLength
SelPrint
```

```
SelProtected
SelRightIndent
SelRTF
SelStart
SelStrikethru
SelTabCount
SelTabs
SelText
SelUnderline
TabIndex
TabStop
Tag
Text
TextRTF
ToolTipText
Top
Visible
WhatsThisHelpID
Width
```

Methods

The RichTextBox control has 14 methods, which are listed below. Because many Visual Basic controls have similar methods, the following list does not include the methods' descriptions. For information on using a method, look up the individual method's entry, provided alphabetically in this book.

```
Drag
Find
GetLineFromChar
LoadFile
Move
OLEDrag
Refresh
SaveFile
SelPrint
SetFocus
ShowWhatsThis
Span
UpTo
ZOrder
```

q

▶ r

s

Events

The RichTextBox control responds to 21 events, which are listed below. Because many Visual Basic controls respond to similar events, the following list does not include the events' descriptions. For information on using an event, look up the individual event's entry, provided alphabetically in this book.

```
Change
Click
DblClick
DragDrop
DragOver
GotFocus
KeyDown
KeyPress
KeyUp
LostFocus
MouseDown
MouseMove
MouseUp
OLECompleteDrag
OLEDragDrop
OLEDragOver
OLEGiveFeedback
OLESetData
OLEStartDrag
SelChange
Validate
```

One of the RichTextBox control's most commonly used events is `Change`, which the control generates when the text in the control changes. A program responds to the button's `Change` event in the `Change` event procedure. A RichTextBox control called `rtfRichTextBox1` will have a `Change` event procedure called `rtfRichTextBox1_Change`, which is where the program should handle the event, as shown in the following lines:

```
Private Sub rtfRichTextBox1_Change()
    ' Handle the Change event here.
End Sub
```

Another handy RichTextBox event is `SelChange`, which the control generates whenever the user changes the selected text in the control or moves the text cursor (which marks the current insertion point). A RichTextBox defines the `SelChange` event procedure like this:

```
Private Sub rtfRichTextBox1_SelChange()
    ' Handle the SelChange event here.
End Sub
```

 **CROSS-REFERENCE**
See also TextBox.

Right

Function

The Right function returns characters from the right portion of a string.

Syntax

```
value = Right(str, numChars)
```

- *str* — The string from which to get the characters.
- *numChars* — The number of characters to extract from the right portion of the string.
- *value* — The variable that will receive the returned characters.

Example

After the following lines execute, the strChars variable will contain the text "A Test."

```
Dim strMsg As String
Dim strChars As String
strMsg = "This Is A Test"
strChars = Right(strMsg, 6)
```

 CROSS-REFERENCE
See also Left and Mid.

RightB

Function

The RightB function returns bytes from the right portion of a string.

Syntax

```
value = RightB(str, numBytes)
```

- *str*—The string from which to get the bytes.
- *numBytes*—The number of bytes to extract from the right portion of the string.
- *value*—The variable that will receive the returned bytes.

Example

After the following lines execute, the `strBytes` variable will contain the text "Test," because four characters normally are represented with eight bytes of data.

```
Dim strMsg As String
Dim strBytes As String
strMsg = "This Is A Test"
strBytes = RightB(strMsg, 8)
```

CROSS-REFERENCE
See also Left, Right, and Mid.

RightMargin

Property

The `RightMargin` property represents a RichTextBox control's right margin.

Objects with a RightMargin Property

RichTextBox

Syntax

```
RichTextBox.RightMargin = value1
```

or

```
value2 = RichTextBox.RightMargin
```

- *RichTextBox*—A reference to a RichTextBox control.
- *value1*—The new right margin in twips.

- *value2*—The variable that will receive the property's current setting.

Example

The following lines show how to get and set a RichTextBox control's right margin.

```
Dim margin As Integer
margin = rtfRichTextBox1.RightMargin
rtfRichTextBox1.RightMargin = 500
```

 CROSS-REFERENCE
See also RichTextBox.

RightToLeft

Property

The RightToLeft property represents how text is displayed in an object. If this property is True, text is arranged to be read from right to left, such as in Hebrew. If the property is False, text is arranged to be read from left to right, as in English.

Objects with a RightToLeft Property

AmbientProperties

CheckBox

ComboBox

CommandButton

Form

HScrollBar

Label

ListBox

MDIForm

OptionButton

PictureBox

Printer

PropertyPage

> TextBox
>
> UserControl
>
> VScrollBar

Syntax

`object.RightToLeft = value1`

or

`value2 = object.RightToLeft`

- *object* — A reference to an object with a `RightToLeft` property.
- *value1* — The value `True` or `False`. The default is `False`.
- *value2* — The variable that will receive the property's current setting.

Example

The following lines show how to get and set a TextBox control's `RightToLeft` property. The `txtTextBox1` object is a TextBox control that the programmer added to the form at design time.

```
Dim rtl As Boolean
rtl = txtTextBox1.RightToLeft
txtTextBox1.RightToLeft = True
```

RmDir

Statement

The `RmDir` statement deletes an empty directory. An error occurs if the specified directory contains files.

Syntax

`RmDir dir`

- *dir* — The path of the directory to remove. If the path doesn't include a drive specification, the current directory is used.

Example

The following line removes a directory called `MyNewDir` on the root of drive C.

```
RmDir "c:\MyNewDir"
```

 CROSS-REFERENCE
See also ChDir, CurDir, and MkDir.

Rnd

Function

The `Rnd` function returns a random number between 0 and 1.

Syntax

```
value = Rnd(seed)
```

- *seed* (★) — A value from Table R-3.
- *value* — The variable that will receive the random number.

(★) = Optional

Table R-3 Settings for the *seed* Argument

Setting	Description
Value omitted	Function returns the next random number.
Negative number	Function returns the same value every time. The supplied value is used as a seed.
0	Function returns the previously generated random number.
Positive number	Function returns the next random number.

Example 1

The following lines generate a random number between 0 and 1.

```
Dim rndNum As Single
Randomize
rndNum = Rnd
```

Example 2

Here, the following lines generate the same random number, using –10 as the seed. Changing the seed value changes the generated random number.

```
Dim rndNum1 As Single
Dim rndNum2 As Single
Randomize
rndNum1 = Rnd(-10)
rndNum2 = Rnd(-10)
```

Example 3

In this example, the lines generate a random number between 0 and 8.

```
Dim rndNum As Integer
Randomize
rndNum = Int(Rnd * 9)
```

Example 4

Finally, in this example, the lines generate 20 random numbers between 5 and 15 and store the numbers in an Integer array.

```
Dim low As Integer
Dim high As Integer
Dim rndNums(20) As Integer

low = 5
high = 15
Randomize
For x = 0 To 19
    rndNums(x) = Int(Rnd * (high - low + 1) + low)
Next
```

CROSS-REFERENCE
See also Randomize.

Root

Property

The Root property represents a Node object's root node in a TreeView control.

Objects with a Root Property

Node

Syntax

`value = Node.Root`

- *Node* — A reference to a Node object.
- *value* — The variable that will receive the reference to the root node.

Example

The following lines retrieve the root node of the tenth Node object in a TreeView control. The `treTreeView1` object is a TreeView control that the programmer added to the form at design time.

```
Dim rootNode As Node
Set rootNode = treTreeView1.Nodes(10).Root
```

 CROSS-REFERENCE
See also Child, FirstSibling, LastSibling, Next, Parent, and Previous.

RootFolder

Property

The `RootFolder` property represents a reference to the Folder object associated with the drive's root folder.

Objects with a RootFolder Property

Drive

Syntax

`value = Drive.RootFolder`

- *Drive* — A reference to a Drive object.
- *value* — The variable that will receive the reference to the root Folder object.

Example

The following lines show how to get a reference to a Folder object that represents a drive's root folder.

```
Dim fileSystem As Object
Dim drive As Object
Dim rFolder As Object

Set fileSystem = CreateObject("Scripting.FileSystemObject")
Set drive = fileSystem.GetDrive("c:")
Set rFolder = drive.RootFolder
```

 **CROSS-REFERENCE**
See also Drive.

Round

Function

The Round function returns a value that's been rounded to a given number of decimal places.

Syntax

```
value = Round(num, numPlaces)
```

- *num* — The value to be rounded.
- *numPlaces* (*) — The number of decimal places to which to round. If this argument is left off, the function rounds the given number to an Integer value.
- *value* — The variable that will receive the rounded number.

(*) = Optional

Example 1

After the following lines execute, the variable newValue will contain the result 12.346.

```
Dim value As Single
Dim newValue As Single
value = 12.345678
newValue = Round(value, 3)
```

Example 2

Here, after the following lines execute, the variable `newValue` will contain the result 12.

```
Dim value As Single
Dim newValue As Integer
value = 12.345678
newValue = Round(value)
```

RowCount

Property

The `RowCount` property represents the number of rows of bands displayed in a CoolBar control.

Objects with a RowCount Property

CoolBar

Syntax

```
value = CoolBar.RowCount
```

- *CoolBar* — A reference to a CoolBar control.
- *value* — The variable that will receive the row count.

Example

The following lines show how to get the number of rows of bands in a CoolBar control. The `CoolBar1` object is a CoolBar control that the programmer added to the form at design time.

```
Dim numRows As Integer
numRows = CoolBar1.RowCount
```

CROSS-REFERENCE
See also CoolBar, Panel, and Panels.

RSet

Statement

The RSet statement copies a string into the right portion of a string variable, filling any remaining characters with spaces.

Syntax

```
RSet var1 = str
```

- *var1* — The string variable to which to copy *str*.
- *str* — The string to copy.

Example 1

After the following lines execute, msg will contain the string " XXXX" (ten spaces followed by four *X*s).

```
Dim msg As String
msg = "This is a test"
RSet msg = "XXXX"
```

Example 2

Here, after the following lines execute, msg will contain the string "12345678901234." Note that the source string gets truncated if the destination string isn't big enough to hold all the characters.

```
Dim msg As String
msg = "This is a test"
RSet msg = "12345678901234567890"
```

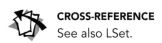

CROSS-REFERENCE
See also LSet.

RTrim

Function

The RTrim function removes trailing spaces from a string.

Syntax

```
value = RTrim(str)
```

- *str* — The string from which to remove trailing spaces.
- *value* — The variable that will receive the new string.

Example

After the following lines execute, the `newMsg` variable will contain the string "This is a test."

```
Dim msg As String
Dim newMsg As String
msg = "This is a test            "
newMsg = RTrim(msg)
```

CROSS-REFERENCE
See also LTrim and Trim.

q

r

s

Save

Method

The Save method saves the current message in the compose buffer.

Objects with a Save Method

MAPIMessages

Syntax

MAPIMessages.Save

- *MAPIMessages* — A reference to a MAPIMessages control.

Example

The following line saves the message in the compose buffer of a MAPIMessages control. The mpmMAPIMessages1 object is a MAPIMessages control that the programmer added to the form at design time.

mpmMAPIMessages1.Save

 CROSS-REFERENCE
See also MAPIMessages.

SaveFile

Method

The SaveFile method saves a file from a RichTextBox control. The file can be in the .rtf or plain text format.

Objects with a SaveFile Method

RichTextBox

Syntax

```
RichTextBox.SaveFile fileName, type
```

- *fileName* — The path of the file to save.
- *RichTextBox* — A reference to a RichTextBox control.
- *type* (*) — Can be `rtfRTF` to save an RTF file or `rtfText` to save a plain text file. The default is `rtfRTF`.

(*) = Optional

Example

The following program demonstrates how to save and load files with a RichTextBox control. When you run the program, type some text into the RichTextBox control (see Figure S-1), and then click the Save File button to save your work. The Save dialog box then appears, enabling you to choose to save an RTF or text file. After saving a file, you can reload it at any time by clicking the Load File button.

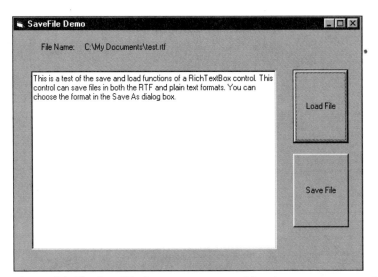

Figure S-1 The SaveFile Demo program enables the user to save and load files in two formats, RTF or plain text.

```
VERSION 5.00
Object = "{F9043C88-F6F2-101A-A3C9-08002B2F49FB} _
   #1.2#0"; "COMDLG32.OCX"
Object = "{3B7C8863-D78F-101B-B9B5-04021C009402} _
   #1.2#0"; "RICHTX32.OCX"
Begin VB.Form frmForm1
   Caption         =   "SaveFile Demo"
   ClientHeight    =   5100
   ClientLeft      =   60
   ClientTop       =   345
   ClientWidth     =   7590
   ScaleHeight     =   5100
   ScaleWidth      =   7590
   StartUpPosition =   3  'Windows Default
   Begin VB.CommandButton btnSaveFile
      Caption      =   "Save File"
      Height       =   1575
      Left         =   6120
      TabIndex     =   4
      Top          =   2640
      Width        =   1215
   End
   Begin RichTextLib.RichTextBox rtfRichTextBox1
      Height       =   3855
      Left         =   360
      TabIndex     =   3
      Top          =   840
      Width        =   5415
      _ExtentX     =   9551
      _ExtentY     =   6800
      _Version     =   393217
      Enabled      =   -1  'True
      TextRTF      =   $"form1.frx":0000
   End
   Begin MSComDlg.CommonDialog dlgCommonDialog1
      Left         =   6960
      Top          =   4440
      _ExtentX     =   847
      _ExtentY     =   847
      _Version     =   393216
   End
   Begin VB.CommandButton btnLoadFile
      Caption      =   "Load File"
      Height       =   1575
```

```
                 Left            =    6120
                 TabIndex        =    0
                 Top             =    840
                 Width           =    1215
              End
              Begin VB.Label lblLabel2
                 Height          =    255
                 Left            =    1560
                 TabIndex        =    2
                 Top             =    240
                 Width           =    4095
              End
              Begin VB.Label Label1
                 Caption         =    "File Name:"
                 Height          =    255
                 Left            =    600
                 TabIndex        =    1
                 Top             =    240
                 Width           =    855
              End
           End
        End
        Attribute VB_Name = "frmForm1"
        Attribute VB_GlobalNameSpace = False
        Attribute VB_Creatable = False
        Attribute VB_PredeclaredId = True
        Attribute VB_Exposed = False

        Private Sub btnLoadFile_Click()
            Dim strFileName As String

            dlgCommonDialog1.Filter = _
                "RTF (*.rtf)|*.rtf|Text (*.txt)|*.txt"
            dlgCommonDialog1.FileName = "*.rtf"
            dlgCommonDialog1.CancelError = True
            On Error GoTo CancelHandler
            dlgCommonDialog1.ShowOpen
            strFileName = dlgCommonDialog1.FileName
            On Error GoTo ErrorHandler
            rtfRichTextBox1.LoadFile strFileName
            lblLabel2 = strFileName
            Exit Sub
        ErrorHandler:
            MsgBox "Couldn't Open the File"
        CancelHandler:
```

```
    End Sub

    Private Sub btnSaveFile_Click()
        Dim strFileName As String

        dlgCommonDialog1.Filter = _
            "RTF (*.rtf)|*.rtf|Text (*.txt)|*.txt"
        dlgCommonDialog1.CancelError = True
        On Error GoTo CancelHandler
        dlgCommonDialog1.ShowSave
        strFileName = dlgCommonDialog1.FileName
        On Error GoTo ErrorHandler
        If dlgCommonDialog1.FilterIndex = 1 Then
            rtfRichTextBox1.SaveFile strFileName, rtfRTF
        Else
            rtfRichTextBox1.SaveFile strFileName, rtfText
        End If
        lblLabel2 = strFileName
        Exit Sub

    ErrorHandler:
        MsgBox "Couldn't Open the File"
    CancelHandler:
    End Sub
```

CROSS-REFERENCE

See also LoadFile and RichTextBox.

SavePicture

Statement

The SavePicture statement saves an image to disk. If the image was originally loaded from disk, it is saved to disk in the same format. Image graphics are always saved as bitmaps.

Syntax

SavePicture *picture*, *fileName*

- *fileName*—The name of the file to which to save the image.
- *picture*—The Picture or Image object from which to save the image.

Example

The following line saves an image from a Form object to a bitmap file named `testpic.bmp`.

```
SavePicture Form1.Image, "testpic.bmp"
```

 CROSS-REFERENCE
See also Image, LoadPicture, LoadResPicture, and Picture.

SaveSetting

Statement

The `SaveSetting` statement saves a key setting to the Registry.

Syntax

```
SaveSetting app, regSection, regKey, keyVal
```

- *app* — The application's name.
- *keyVal* — The value of the key to be saved.
- *regSection* — The name of the Registry section.
- *regKey* — The name of the Registry key.

Example

The following lines save the value of the Width key to the Init section of the PicMachine application's Registry entry. (PicMachine is the name of a fictional application.)

```
SaveSetting "PicMachine", "Init", "Width", 50
```

 CROSS-REFERENCE
See also DeleteSetting, GetAllSettings, and GetSetting.

SaveToFile

Method

The `SaveToFile` method saves a file from an OLE Container control.

Objects with a SaveToFile Method

OLE Container

Syntax

```
OLEContainer.SaveToFile fileNum
```

- *fileNum* — The file number given to the binary file in the `Open` statement.
- *OLEContainer* — A reference to an OLE Container control.

Example

The following program demonstrates the `SaveToFile` method. When you run the program, double-click the OLE Container control. You can then edit the bitmap document embedded into the control. After drawing something in the bitmap, click the Save File button to save your work. Finally, close and rerun the program, and click the Load File button. The file you previously saved appears in the OLE Container control. Figure S-2 shows a bitmap being edited in the OLE Container control.

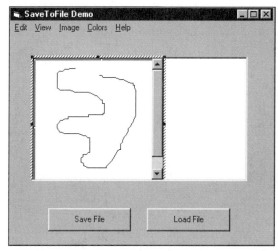

Figure S-2 After editing a bitmap, you can save and reload your work.

```
VERSION 5.00
Begin VB.Form Form1
   Caption        =     "SaveToFile Demo"
   ClientHeight   =     4755
```

```
        ClientLeft      =    60
        ClientTop       =    345
        ClientWidth     =    5730
        LinkTopic       =    "Form1"
        ScaleHeight     =    4755
        ScaleWidth      =    5730
        StartUpPosition =    3   'Windows Default
        Begin VB.CommandButton btnLoadFile
            Caption         =    "Load File"
            Height          =    495
            Left            =    3000
            TabIndex        =    2
            Top             =    3720
            Width           =    1815
        End
        Begin VB.CommandButton btnSaveFile
            Caption         =    "Save File"
            Height          =    495
            Left            =    840
            TabIndex        =    1
            Top             =    3720
            Width           =    1815
        End
        Begin VB.OLE OLE1
            Class           =    "Paint.Picture"
            Height          =    2655
            Left            =    480
            OleObjectBlob   =    "Form1.frx":0000
            TabIndex        =    0
            Top             =    480
            Width           =    4695
        End
    End
Attribute VB_Name = "Form1"
Attribute VB_GlobalNameSpace = False
Attribute VB_Creatable = False
Attribute VB_PredeclaredId = True
Attribute VB_Exposed = False

Private Sub btnLoadFile_Click()
    On Error GoTo LoadError
    Open "Demo.rff" For Binary As #1
    OLE1.ReadFromFile 1
    Close #1
```

```
        Exit Sub

LoadError:
    MsgBox "File load error.", vbExclamation, "Load File"
End Sub

Private Sub btnSaveFile_Click()
    On Error GoTo SaveError
    Open "Demo.rff" For Binary As #1
    OLE1.SaveToFile 1
    Close #1
    MsgBox "File Saved.", vbInformation, "Save File"
    Exit Sub

SaveError:
    MsgBox "File save error.", vbExclamation, "Save File"
End Sub
```

CROSS-REFERENCE
See also OLE Container, ReadFromFile, and SaveToOle1File.

SaveToolbar

Method

The SaveToolbar method saves the configuration of a customized toolbar to the system Registry. The user can customize the toolbar by double-clicking it, which brings up the Customize Toolbar dialog box, as shown in Figure S-3.

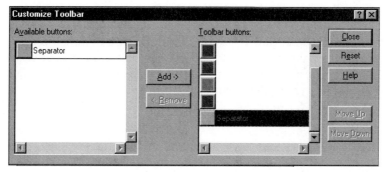

Figure S-3 The Customize Toolbar dialog box enables the user to modify a toolbar's buttons.

Objects with a SaveToolbar Method

Toolbar

Syntax

`Toolbar.SaveToolbar(appName, subkeyName, keyName)`

- *appName* — The application's name, which is the main key in the HKEY_CURRENT_USER section of the Registry. This key must have been added to the Registry by the `SaveToolbar` method.
- *keyName* — The name of the key with which the toolbar configuration is associated.
- *subkeyName* — The subkey under which the toolbar configuration was saved. This key must have been added to the Registry by the `SaveToolbar` method.
- *Toolbar* — A reference to a Toolbar control.

Example

The following program demonstrates how to save and restore a custom toolbar configuration. When you first run the program (Figure S-4), double-click the toolbar (in an area without buttons) to display the Customize Toolbar dialog box. Use the dialog box's controls to remove one or two buttons from the toolbar, and then close the dialog box. Closing the dialog box triggers the toolbar's `Change` event. In the `tlbToolbar1_Change` event procedure, the program calls the `SaveToolbar` method to save the toolbar's new settings to the Registry. Now, exit the application and rerun it. Click the Restore Toolbar button, and the toolbar reloads your custom configuration.

 NOTE
The toolbar restoration will fail if, in the Customize Toolbar dialog box, you added separators to the buttons or if you tried to move a button more than one position up or down. Also, the restoration won't work if your toolbar contains buttons that are not associated with an image in an ImageList control. You can, however, always restore the original toolbar by clicking the Customize Toolbar dialog box's Reset button.

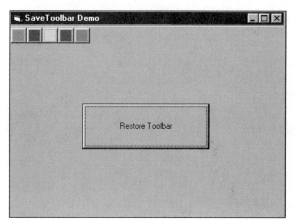

Figure S-4 This application features a customizable toolbar.

```
VERSION 5.00
Object = "{831FDD16-0C5C-11D2-A9FC-0000F8754DA1} _
    #2.0#0"; "MSCOMCTL.OCX"
Begin VB.Form Form1
    Caption         =   "SaveToolbar Demo"
    ClientHeight    =   4080
    ClientLeft      =   60
    ClientTop       =   345
    ClientWidth     =   5940
    LinkTopic       =   "Form1"
    ScaleHeight     =   272
    ScaleMode       =   3  'Pixel
    ScaleWidth      =   396
    StartUpPosition =   3  'Windows Default
    Begin VB.CommandButton btnRestore
        Caption         =   "Restore Toolbar"
        Height          =   975
        Left            =   1560
        TabIndex        =   1
        Top             =   1680
        Width           =   2775
    End
    Begin MSComctlLib.ImageList ilsImageList1
        Left            =   5160
        Top             =   3240
        _ExtentX        =   1005
        _ExtentY        =   1005
        BackColor       =   -2147483643
```

```
          MaskColor        =    12632256
          _Version         =    393216
       End
       Begin MSComctlLib.Toolbar tlbToolbar1
          Align            =    1  'Align Top
          Height           =    630
          Left             =    0
          TabIndex         =    0
          Top              =    0
          Width            =    5940
          _ExtentX         =    10478
          _ExtentY         =    1111
          ButtonWidth      =    609
          ButtonHeight     =    953
          Appearance       =    1
          _Version         =    393216
       End
    End
End
Attribute VB_Name = "Form1"
Attribute VB_GlobalNameSpace = False
Attribute VB_Creatable = False
Attribute VB_PredeclaredId = True
Attribute VB_Exposed = False

Private Sub Form_Load()
    ilsImageList1.ListImages.Add , , _
        LoadPicture("button1.bmp")
    ilsImageList1.ListImages.Add , , _
        LoadPicture("button2.bmp")
    ilsImageList1.ListImages.Add , , _
        LoadPicture("button3.bmp")
    ilsImageList1.ListImages.Add , , _
        LoadPicture("button4.bmp")
    ilsImageList1.ListImages.Add , , _
        LoadPicture("button5.bmp")
    tlbToolbar1.ImageList = ilsImageList1
    tlbToolbar1.Buttons.Add , , , , 1
    tlbToolbar1.Buttons.Add , , , , 2
    tlbToolbar1.Buttons.Add , , , , 3
    tlbToolbar1.Buttons.Add , , , , 4
    tlbToolbar1.Buttons.Add , , , , 5
End Sub
```

```
Private Sub tlbToolbar1_Change()
    tlbToolbar1.SaveToolbar "RestoreToolbarDemo", _
        "UserSettings", "tlbToolbar1"
End Sub

Private Sub btnRestore_Click()
    tlbToolbar1.RestoreToolbar "RestoreToolbarDemo", _
        "UserSettings", "tlbToolbar1"
End Sub
```

CROSS-REFERENCE
See also Customize, RestoreToolbar, and Toolbar.

SaveToOle1File

Method

The SaveToOle1File method saves a file from an OLE Container control to a Version 1.0 OLE file.

Objects with a SaveToOle1File Method

OLE Container

Syntax

OLEContainer.SaveToOle1File *fileNum*

- *fileNum* — The file number given to the binary file in the Open statement.
- *OLEContainer* — A reference to an OLE Container control.

Example

The following lines demonstrate the SaveToOle1File method. The OLE1 object is an OLE Container control that the programmer added to the form at design time.

```
Open "Demo.rff" For Binary As #1
OLE1.SaveToOle1File 1
Close #1
```

CROSS-REFERENCE
See also OLE Container, ReadFromFile, and SaveToFile.

Scale

Method

The Scale method enables a program to set the coordinates used to reference the display area of an object. If the method is called with no arguments, the scaling is set to twips.

Objects with a Scale Method

Form

PictureBox

Printer

PropertyPage

UserControl

Syntax

```
object.Scale(x1, y1)-(x2, y2)
```

- *object* — A reference to an object with a Scale method.
- *x1* (*) — The X coordinate of the upper-left corner.
- *y1* (*) — The Y coordinate of the upper-left corner.
- *x2* (*) — The X coordinate of the lower-right corner.
- *y2* (*) — The Y coordinate of the lower-right corner.

(*) = Optional

Example 1

The following lines set the coordinate system of a form so that the upper-left corner has the coordinates 0,0 and the lower-right corner has the coordinates 100,100. The call to the Line method then draws a line from one corner to the other, as shown in Figure S-5.

```
Form1.Scale (0, 0)-(100, 100)
Form1.Line (0, 0)-(100, 100)
```

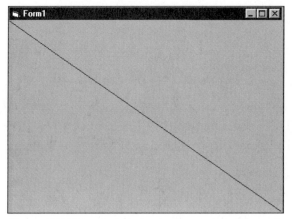

Figure S-5 This window shows the results of the call to the Line method shown in Example 1.

Example 2

The following line sets the coordinate system back to twips.

```
Form1.Scale
```

CROSS-REFERENCE
See also ScaleHeight, ScaleLeft, ScaleMode, ScaleTop, and ScaleWidth.

ScaleHeight

Property

The `ScaleHeight` property enables a program to set the vertical coordinates used to reference the display area of an object.

Objects with a ScaleHeight Property

Form
MDIForm
PictureBox
Printer
PropertyPage
UserControl

Syntax

object.ScaleHeight = *value1*

or

value2 = *object*.ScaleHeight

- *object*—A reference to an object with a ScaleHeight property.
- *value1*—The new scaling value.
- *value2*—The variable that will receive the property's current setting.

Example

The following line shows how to set a Form object's ScaleHeight property.

Form1.ScaleHeight = 100

 CROSS-REFERENCE
See also Scale, ScaleLeft, ScaleMode, ScaleTop, and ScaleWidth.

ScaleLeft

Property

The ScaleLeft property enables a program to set the minimum coordinate for the left edge of an object's display area.

Objects with a ScaleLeft Property

Form

MDIForm

PictureBox

Printer

PropertyPage

UserControl

Syntax

object.ScaleLeft = *value1*

or

value2 = *object*.ScaleLeft

- *object* — A reference to an object with a `ScaleLeft` property.
- *value1* — The new minimum left coordinate.
- *value2* — The variable that will receive the property's current setting.

Example

The following line shows how to set a Form object's `ScaleLeft` property.

```
Form1.ScaleLeft = 100
```

CROSS-REFERENCE
See also Scale, ScaleHeight, ScaleMode, ScaleTop, and ScaleWidth.

ScaleMode

Property

The `ScaleMode` property represents the type of coordinates used for an object's display area. This property can be one of the values shown in Table S-1.

Table S-1 Values for the ScaleMode Property

Value	Description
vbCentimeters	Specifies that coordinates represent centimeters.
vbCharacters	Specifies that coordinates represent characters.
vbContainerPosition	Specifies that a control's position is determined by the container's scale mode.
vbContainerSize	Specifies that a control's size is determined by the container's scale mode.
vbHimetric	Specifies that coordinates are hi-metric.
vbInches	Specifies that coordinates represent inches.
vbMillimeters	Specifies that coordinates represent millimeters.
vbPixels	Specifies that coordinates represent pixels.
vbPoints	Specifies that coordinates represent points.
vbTwips	Specifies that coordinates represent twips. (Default.)
vbUser	Specifies that one or more of the scaling properties (ScaleHeight, ScaleWidth, ScaleLeft, and ScaleTop) have been set to a user-defined value.

r
s
t

Objects with a ScaleMode Property

Form
PictureBox
Printer
PropertyPage
UserControl

Syntax

```
object.ScaleMode = value1
```

or

```
value2 = object.ScaleMode
```

- *object*—A reference to an object with a `ScaleMode` property.
- *value1*—A value from Table S-1.
- *value2*—The variable that will receive the property's current setting.

Example

The following line shows how to set a Form object's `ScaleMode` property.

```
Form1.ScaleMode = vbPixels
```

 CROSS-REFERENCE
See also Scale, ScaleHeight, ScaleLeft, ScaleTop, and ScaleWidth.

ScaleTop

Property

The `ScaleTop` property enables a program to set the minimum coordinate for the top edge of an object's display area.

Objects with a ScaleTop Property

Form
MDIForm
PictureBox

Printer

PropertyPage

UserControl

Syntax

object.ScaleTop = *value1*

or

value2 = *object*.ScaleTop

- *object*—A reference to an object with a ScaleTop property.
- *value1*—The new minimum top edge coordinate.
- *value2*—The variable that will receive the property's current setting.

Example

The following line shows how to set a Form object's ScaleTop property.

Form1.ScaleTop = 100

 CROSS-REFERENCE
See also Scale, ScaleHeight, ScaleLeft, ScaleMode, and ScaleWidth.

ScaleUnits

Property

The ScaleUnits property represents a string value that contains the type of units associated with a container object's coordinates.

Objects with a ScaleUnits Property

AmbientProperties

Syntax

value = *AmbientProperties*.ScaleUnits

- *AmbientProperties*—A reference to an AmbientProperties object.
- *value*—The variable that will receive the scale-units string.

Example

The following lines show how to retrieve the value of the `ScaleUnits` property from within a UserControl object.

```
Dim units As String
units = Ambient.ScaleUnits
```

 CROSS-REFERENCE
See also Scale, ScaleHeight, ScaleLeft, ScaleMode, ScaleTop, and ScaleWidth.

ScaleWidth

Property

The `ScaleWidth` property enables a program to set the horizontal coordinates used to reference the display area of an object.

Objects with a ScaleWidth Property

Form
MDIForm
PictureBox
Printer
PropertyPage
UserControl

Syntax

```
object.ScaleWidth = value1
```

or

```
value2 = object.ScaleWidth
```

- *object* — A reference to an object with a `ScaleWidth` property.
- *value1* — The new scaling value.
- *value2* — The variable that will receive the property's current setting.

Example

The following line shows how to set a Form object's `ScaleWidth` property.

```
Form1.ScaleWidth = 100
```

 CROSS-REFERENCE
See also Scale, ScaleLeft, ScaleMode, and ScaleTop.

ScaleX

Method

The `ScaleX` method converts horizontal coordinates of one unit type to horizontal coordinates of another unit type.

Objects with a ScaleX Method

Form

PictureBox

Printer

PropertyPage

UserControl

Syntax

```
value = object.ScaleX(num, fromType, toType)
```

- *object* — A reference to an object with a ScaleX property.
- *num* — The number of units to convert.
- *fromType* (*) — The type of unit from which to convert. Must be a value from Table S-2.
- *toType* (*) — The type of unit to which to convert. Must be a value from Table S-2.
- *value* — The variable that will receive the converted value.

(*) = Optional

Table S-2 Values for the *fromType* and *toType* Arguments

Value	Description
vbCentimeters	Specifies that coordinates represent centimeters.
vbCharacters	Specifies that coordinates represent characters.
vbContainerPosition	Specifies that a control's position is determined by the container's scale mode.
vbContainerSize	Specifies that a control's size is determined by the container's scale mode.
vbHimetric	Specifies that coordinates are hi-metric. (Default.)
vbInches	Specifies that coordinates represent inches.
vbMillimeters	Specifies that coordinates represent millimeters.
vbPixels	Specifies that coordinates represent pixels.
vbPoints	Specifies that coordinates represent points.
vbTwips	Specifies that coordinates represent twips.
vbUser	Specifies that one or more of the scaling properties (ScaleHeight, ScaleWidth, ScaleLeft, and ScaleTop) have been set to a user-defined value.

Example

The following lines convert 1440 twips to the equivalent inches, which is 1, because there are 1440 twips to a logical inch.

```
Dim pixels As Integer
pixels = Form1.ScaleX(1440, vbTwips, vbInches)
```

 CROSS-REFERENCE
See also Scale, ScaleLeft, ScaleMode, ScaleTop, ScaleWidth, and ScaleY.

ScaleY

Method

The ScaleY method converts vertical coordinates of one unit type to vertical coordinates of another unit type.

Objects with a ScaleY Method

Form

PictureBox

Printer

PropertyPage

UserControl

Syntax

```
value = object.ScaleY(num, fromType, toType)
```

- *object* — A reference to an object with a ScaleY property.
- *num* — The number of units to convert.
- *fromType* (*) — The type of unit from which to convert. Must be a value from Table S-3.
- *toType* (*) — The type of unit to which to convert. Must be a value from Table S-3.
- *value* — The variable that will receive the converted value.

(*) = Optional

Table S-3 Values for the *fromType* and *toType* Arguments

Value	Description
vbCentimeters	Specifies that coordinates represent centimeters.
vbCharacters	Specifies that coordinates represent characters.
vbContainerPosition	Specifies that a control's position is determined by the container's scale mode.
vbContainerSize	Specifies that a control's size is determined by the container's scale mode.
vbHimetric	Specifies that coordinates are hi-metric. (Default.)
vbInches	Specifies that coordinates represent inches.
vbMillimeters	Specifies that coordinates represent millimeters.
vbPixels	Specifies that coordinates represent pixels.
vbPoints	Specifies that coordinates represent points.
vbTwips	Specifies that coordinates represent twips.
vbUser	Specifies that one or more of the scaling properties (ScaleHeight, ScaleWidth, ScaleLeft, and ScaleTop) have been set to a user-defined value.

Example

The following lines convert 1440 vertical twips to the equivalent inches, which is 1, because there are 1440 twips to a logical inch.

```
Dim pixels As Integer
pixels = Form1.ScaleY(1440, vbTwips, vbInches)
```

CROSS-REFERENCE
See also Scale, ScaleLeft, ScaleMode, ScaleTop, ScaleWidth, and ScaleX.

Screen

Object

The Screen object represents various system properties such as the current screen and printer fonts, the size of the screen, the displayed mouse pointer, and so on.

Properties

The Screen object has 10 properties, which are listed below. For more information on using the following properties, look up the individual property's entry, provided alphabetically in this book.

```
ActiveControl
ActiveForm
FontCount
Fonts
Height
MouseIcon
MousePointer
TwipsPerPixelX
TwipsPerPixelY
Width
```

Methods

The Screen object has no methods.

Events

The Screen object does not respond to events.

CROSS-REFERENCE
See also Global and Screen (property).

Screen

Property

The Screen property represents a reference to the current Screen object, which is a global Visual Basic object.

Objects with a Screen Property

Global

Syntax

```
value = Screen
```

- *value* — The variable that will receive the reference to the Screen object.

Example

The following lines show how to get the width of the screen.

```
Dim scrWidth As Integer
scrWidth = Screen.Width
```

CROSS-REFERENCE
See also Global and Screen (object).

Scroll

Property

The Scroll property represents whether a TreeView control displays scroll bars.

Objects with a Scroll Property
TreeView

Syntax

```
TreeView.Scroll = value1
```

or

```
value2 = TreeView.Scroll
```

- *TreeView*—A reference to a TreeView control.
- *value1*—The value True or False.
- *value2*—The variable that will receive the property's current setting.

Example

The following lines show how to get and set a TreeView control's Scroll property. The treTreeView1 object is a TreeView control that the programmer added to the form at design time.

```
Dim boolScroll As Boolean
boolScroll = treTreeView1.Scroll
treTreeView1.Scroll = True
```

CROSS-REFERENCE
See also TreeView.

ScrollBars—MDIForm

Property

The ScrollBars property represents whether an object displays scroll bars. This property is read-only at runtime. You set this property in the object's Properties window at design time, as shown in Figure S-6.

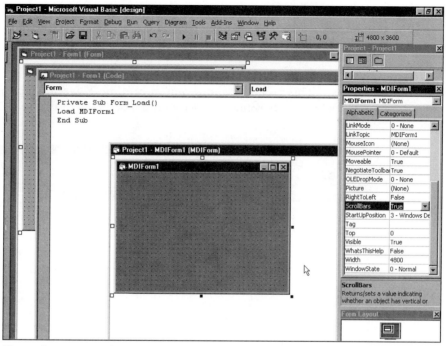

Figure S-6 You set the ScrollBars property in the object's Properties window.

Syntax

```
value = MDIForm.ScrollBars
```

- *MDIForm* — A reference to a MDIForm object.
- *value* — The variable that will receive the property's current setting, which can be True or False.

Example

The following lines show how to retrieve the setting of a MDIForm object's ScrollBars property.

```
Dim boolScroll As Boolean
boolScroll = MDIForm1.ScrollBars
```

CROSS-REFERENCE
See also MDIForm.

ScrollBars — RichTextBox

Property

The `ScrollBars` property represents whether a RichTextBox control displays scroll bars. This property is read-only at runtime. You set this property in the control's Properties window at design time, as shown in Figure S-7.

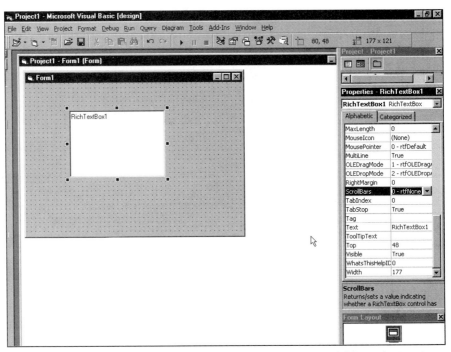

Figure S-7 The RichTextBox control's ScrollBars property is available at design time in the control's Properties window.

Syntax

```
value = RichTextBox.ScrollBars
```

- *RichTextBox* — A reference to a RichTextBox control.
- *value* — The variable that will receive the property's current setting, which can be `rtfBoth`, `rtfHorizontal`, `rtfNone`, or `rtfVertical`.

Example

The following lines show how to retrieve the setting of a RichTextBox control's `ScrollBars` property. The `rtfRichTextBox1` object is a RichTextBox control that the programmer added to the form at design time.

```
Dim intScroll As Integer
intScroll = rtfRichTextBox1.ScrollBars
If intScroll = rtfNone Then
    MsgBox "Has no scroll bars."
ElseIf intScroll = rtfBoth Then
    MsgBox "Has both scroll bars."
ElseIf intScroll = rtfHorizontal Then
    MsgBox "Has a horizontal scroll bar."
ElseIf intScroll = rtfVertical Then
    MsgBox "Has a vertical scroll bar."
End If
```

CROSS-REFERENCE
See also RichTextBox.

ScrollBars — TextBox

Property

The `ScrollBars` property represents whether a TextBox control displays scroll bars. This property is read-only at runtime. You set this property in the control's Properties window at design time, as shown in Figure S-8.

Syntax

value = *TextBox*.ScrollBars

- *TextBox* — A reference to a TextBox control.
- *value* — The variable that will receive the property's current setting, which can be `vbBoth`, `vbHorizontal`, `vbSBNone`, or `vbVertical`.

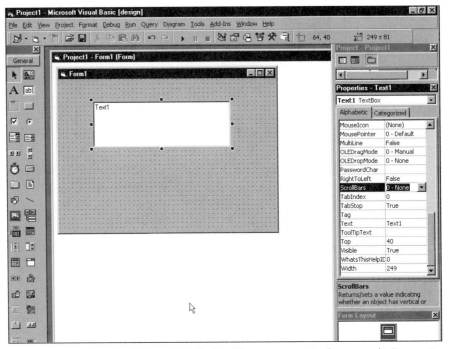

Figure S-8 You set a TextBox control's ScrollBars property in the control's Properties window at design time.

Example

The following lines show how to retrieve the setting of a TextBox control's ScrollBars property. The txtText1 object is a TextBox control that the programmer added to the form at design time.

```
Dim intScroll As Integer
intScroll = txtText1.ScrollBars
If intScroll = vbSBNone Then
    MsgBox "Has no scroll bars."
ElseIf intScroll = vbBoth Then
    MsgBox "Has both scroll bars."
ElseIf intScroll = vbHorizontal Then
    MsgBox "Has a horizontal scroll bar."
ElseIf intScroll = vbVertical Then
    MsgBox "Has a vertical scroll bar."
End If
```

CROSS-REFERENCE
See also TextBox.

ScrollBarSize

Property

The ScrollBarSize property represents the width in twips of a scroll bar.

Objects with a ScrollBarSize Property
SysInfo

Syntax

value = SysInfo.ScrollBarSize

- *SysInfo* — A reference to a SysInfo control.
- *value* — The variable that will receive a scroll bar's width.

Example

The following lines show how to retrieve the width of a scroll bar. The SysInfo1 object is a SysInfo control that the programmer added to the form at design time.

```
Dim intScrollWidth As Integer
intScrollWidth = SysInfo1.ScrollBarSize
```

CROSS-REFERENCE
See also SysInfo.

Scroll — General Controls

Event

Visual Basic sends an object a Scroll event when the user changes the setting of the object's horizontal or vertical scroll bars.

Objects with a Scroll Event
ComboBox

DirListBox

DriveListBox

FileListBox

> HScrollBar
>
> VScrollBar
>
> ListBox

Example

A program can respond to a `Scroll` event by implementing the object's `Scroll` event procedure. The following code segment shows how an HScrollBar control defines an `Scroll` event procedure. In this example, the `hsbHScroll1` object is an HScrollBar control that the programmer added to the form at design time.

```
Private Sub hsbHScroll1_Scroll()
    ' Handle the Scroll event here.
End Sub
```

 CROSS-REFERENCE
See also Change and Value.

Scroll — Slider

Event

Visual Basic sends a Slider control a `Scroll` event when the user or the program moves the control's slider.

Example

A program can respond to a `Scroll` event by implementing the Slider control's `Scroll` event procedure. The following code segment shows how a Slider control defines a `Scroll` event procedure. In this example, the `sldSlider1` object is a Slider control that the programmer added to the form at design time.

```
Private Sub sldSlider1_Scroll()
    ' Handle the Scroll event here.
End Sub
```

CROSS-REFERENCE
See also LargeChange, SmallChange, and Value.

Scrolling

Property

The `Scrolling` property represents the way a ProgressBar control displays its bar. The two possible values for this property are `ccScrollingStandard` (the bar increments by blocks) or `ccScrollingSmooth` (the bar increments smoothly rather than in blocks).

Objects with a Scrolling Property

ProgressBar

Syntax

`ProgressBar.Scrolling = value1`

or

`value2 = ProgressBar.Scrolling`

- *ProgressBar*—A reference to a ProgressBar control.
- *value1*—The value `ccScrollingStandard` or `ccScrollingSmooth`.
- *value2*—The variable that will receive the property's current setting.

Example

The following program demonstrates a ProgressBar control's `Scrolling` property. When you run the program, you see a window with a progress bar and a button. The progress bar continually updates its display, filling its bar with color blocks, as shown in Figure S-9. Click the Toggle Scrolling button to switch the progress bar to smooth scrolling (see Figure S-10).

r
s
t

Figure S-9 This progress bar uses color blocks to display its bar.

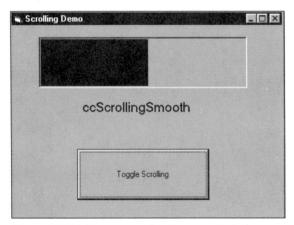

Figure S-10 This progress bar increments its bar smoothly.

```
VERSION 5.00
Object = "{831FDD16-0C5C-11D2-A9FC-0000F8754DA1} _
   #2.0#0"; "MSCOMCTL.OCX"
Begin VB.Form Form1
   Caption         =    "Scrolling Demo"
   ClientHeight    =    4080
   ClientLeft      =    60
   ClientTop       =    345
   ClientWidth     =    5940
   LinkTopic       =    "Form1"
   ScaleHeight     =    272
   ScaleMode       =    3   'Pixel
   ScaleWidth      =    396
```

```
        StartUpPosition =   3   'Windows Default
        Begin VB.Timer Timer1
           Left            =   4920
           Top             =   2520
        End
        Begin VB.CommandButton btnToggleScrolling
           Caption         =   "Toggle Scrolling"
           Height          =   1095
           Left            =   1440
           TabIndex        =   1
           Top             =   2640
           Width           =   2895
        End
        Begin MSComctlLib.ProgressBar ProgressBar1
           Height          =   1095
           Left            =   600
           TabIndex        =   0
           Top             =   240
           Width           =   4575
           _ExtentX        =   8070
           _ExtentY        =   1931
           _Version        =   393216
           Appearance      =   1
        End
        Begin VB.Label lblScrollingType
           Caption         =   "Label1"
           BeginProperty Font
              Name            =   "MS Sans Serif"
              Size            =   13.5
              Charset         =   0
              Weight          =   400
              Underline       =   0   'False
              Italic          =   0   'False
              Strikethrough   =   0   'False
           EndProperty
           Height          =   495
           Left            =   1560
           TabIndex        =   2
           Top             =   1560
           Width           =   3255
        End
     End
     Attribute VB_Name = "Form1"
     Attribute VB_GlobalNameSpace = False
```

```
Attribute VB_Creatable = False
Attribute VB_PredeclaredId = True
Attribute VB_Exposed = False

Private Sub btnToggleScrolling_Click()
    Dim scrollType As Integer
    scrollType = ProgressBar1.Scrolling
    If scrollType = ccScrollingSmooth Then
        ProgressBar1.Scrolling = ccScrollingStandard
        lblScrollingType.Caption = "ccScrollingStandard"
    Else
        ProgressBar1.Scrolling = ccScrollingSmooth
        lblScrollingType.Caption = "ccScrollingSmooth"
    End If
End Sub

Private Sub Form_Load()
    lblScrollingType.Caption = "ccScrollingStandard"
    Timer1.Interval = 50
End Sub

Private Sub Timer1_Timer()
    Dim val As Integer
    val = ProgressBar1.Value + 1
    If val > 100 Then val = 0
    ProgressBar1.Value = val
End Sub
```

CROSS-REFERENCE
See also ProgressBar.

Second

Function

The Second function extracts the second portion of a time.

Syntax

value = Second(*time*)

- *time* — The time value from which to extract the seconds.
- *value* — The variable that will receive the returned seconds.

Example

After the following lines execute, `intSeconds` will contain the value 15.

```
Dim vntTime As Variant
Dim intSeconds As Integer
vntTime = #6:20:15 AM#
intSeconds = Second(vntTime)
```

CROSS-REFERENCE
See also Hour and Minute.

Seek

Function

The `Seek` function returns the position of the file pointer in a file that was opened with the `Open` statement. In most files, the position returned is the off-set of the next byte to be read or written. In a random-access file, the returned value is the record number, rather than the byte number.

Syntax

```
value = Seek(fileNum)
```

- *fileNum* — The file number assigned to the file in the `Open` statement.
- *value* — The variable that will receive the file position.

Example

After the following lines execute, the variable `filePointer` will contain the value 19, meaning that the next byte to get written will be offset 19 bytes from the start of the file. This value results from writing 16 text characters (the quotes and the string) plus a carriage-return/linefeed pair: 18 characters in all.

```
Dim filePointer As Long
Open "c:\MyFile.txt" For Output As #1
Write #1, "This is a test"
filePointer = Seek(1)
Close #1
```

r
s
t

CROSS-REFERENCE
See also Loc and Seek (statement).

Seek

Statement

The Seek statement sets the position of the file pointer in a file that was opened with the Open statement. In most files, the set position is the offset of the next byte to be read or written. In a random-access file, the set position is the record number, rather than the byte number.

Syntax

```
Seek fileNum, offset
```

- *fileNum* — The file number assigned to the file in the Open statement. If using a literal, you must preface the file number with the # symbol. If referencing the file number with a variable, no # symbol is needed.
- *offset* — The position at which to set the file pointer.

Example

The following lines write a line of text to a file, reposition the file pointer at the start of the file, and write over the first string of characters with a string of *X*s.

```
Dim filePointer As Long
Open "c:\MyFile.txt" For Output As #1
Write #1, "This is a test"
Seek #1, 1
Write #1, "XXXXXXXXXXXXXX"
Close #1
```

CROSS-REFERENCE
See also Loc and Seek (function).

SelAlignment

Property

The `SelAlignment` property represents the alignment of text in a RichTextBox control. This property can be set to `rtfLeft` (default), `rtfCenter`, or `rtfRight`.

Objects with a SelAlignment Property

RichTextBox

Syntax

```
RichTextBox.SelAlignment = value1
```

or

```
value2 = RichTextBox.SelAlignment
```

- *RichTextBox* — A reference to a RichTextBox control.
- *value1* — The value `rtfLeft`, `rtfCenter`, or `rtfRight`.
- *value2* — The variable that will receive the property's current setting.

Example

The following lines show how to get and set a RichTextBox control's `SelAlignment` property. The `rtfRichTextBox1` object is a RichTextBox control that the programmer added to the form at design time.

```
Dim align As Integer
align = rtfRichTextBox1.SelAlignment
rtfRichTextBox1.SelAlignment = vbCenter
```

CROSS-REFERENCE
See also RichTextBox.

r
s
t

SelBold

Property

The SelBold property represents the bold text attribute for selected text in a RichTextBox. This property can be set to Null, True, or False. A return value of Null indicates that the selected text contains a mix of bold and nonbold characters.

Objects with a SelBold Property

RichTextBox

Syntax

```
RichTextBox.SelBold = value1
```

or

```
value2 = RichTextBox.SelBold
```

- *RichTextBox* — A reference to a RichTextBox control.
- *value1* — The value True or False.
- *value2* — The variable that will receive the property's current setting.

Example

The following lines show how to get and set a RichTextBox control's SelBold property. The rtfRichTextBox1 object is a RichTextBox control that the programmer added to the form at design time.

```
Dim fontBold
fontBold = rtfRichTextBox1.SelBold
rtfRichTextBox1.SelBold = True
```

 **CROSS-REFERENCE**
See also RichTextBox.

SelBullet

Property

The `SelBullet` property represents whether text in a RichTextBox will be formatted as a bulleted list. This property can be set to `Null`, `True`, or `False`. A return value of `Null` indicates that the selected text contains a mix of bulleted and nonbulleted text.

Objects with a SelBullet Property

RichTextBox

Syntax

```
RichTextBox.SelBullet = value1
```

or

```
value2 = RichTextBox.SelBullet
```

- *RichTextBox* — A reference to a RichTextBox control.
- *value1* — The value `True` or `False`.
- *value2* — The variable that will receive the property's current setting.

Example

The following lines show how to get and set a RichTextBox control's `SelBullet` property. The `rtfRichTextBox1` object is a RichTextBox control that the programmer added to the form at design time.

```
Dim bullet
bullet = rtfRichTextBox1.SelBullet
rtfRichTextBox1.SelBullet = True
```

CROSS-REFERENCE

See also RichTextBox.

SelChange

Event

Visual Basic sends a Multimedia MCI control a SelChange event when the user moves the text cursor or changes the selected text in a RichTextBox control.

Objects with a SelChange Event

RichTextBox

Example

A program can respond to a SelChange event by implementing the RichTextBox control's SelChange event procedure. The following code segment shows how a RichTextBox control defines a SelChange event procedure. In this example, the rtfRichTextBox1 object is a RichTextBox control that the programmer added to the form at design time.

```
Private Sub rtfRichTextBox1_SelChange()
    ' Handle the SelChange event here.
End Sub
```

CROSS-REFERENCE
See also RichTextBox.

SelCharOffset

Property

The SelCharOffset property represents whether text in a RichTextBox is drawn normally or drawn as subscript or superscript text. This property can be set to Null (selected text has a mixed offset), 0 (normal text), a positive number (superscript), or a negative number (subscript).

Objects with a SelCharOffset Property

RichTextBox

Syntax

```
RichTextBox.SelCharOffset = value1
```

or

```
value2 = RichTextBox.SelCharOffset
```

- *RichTextBox* — A reference to a RichTextBox control.
- *value1* — The character offset value.
- *value2* — The variable that will receive the property's current setting.

Example

The following lines show how to get and set a RichTextBox control's `SelCharOffset` property. In this case, the selected text, or the next text typed into the control, will be subscripted by 50 twips. The `rtfRichTextBox1` object is a RichTextBox control that the programmer added to the form at design time.

```
Dim offset As Integer
offset = rtfRichTextBox1.SelCharOffset
rtfRichTextBox1.SelCharOffset = -50
```

 CROSS-REFERENCE
See also RichTextBox.

SelColor

Property

The `SelColor` property represents the color of text in a RichTextBox control. This property can be set to `Null` (selected text has mixed colors) or a color supplied by the `RGB` function, the `QBColor` function, or the Visual Basic system color constants.

Objects with a SelColor Property

RichTextBox

Syntax

```
RichTextBox.SelColor = value1
```

or

```
value2 = RichTextBox.SelColor
```

- *RichTextBox* — A reference to a RichTextBox control.
- *value1* — The new color value.
- *value2* — The variable that will receive the property's current setting.

Example

The following lines show how to get and set a RichTextBox control's `SelColor` property. In this case, the selected text, or the next text typed into the control, will be red. The `rtfRichTextBox1` object is a RichTextBox control that the programmer added to the form at design time.

```
Dim txtColor As Long
txtColor = rtfRichTextBox1.SelColor
rtfRichTextBox1.SelColor = RGB(255, 0, 0)
```

 CROSS-REFERENCE
See also RichTextBox.

SelCount

Property

The `SelCount` property represents the number of selected items in a ListBox control.

Objects with a SelCount Property

ListBox

Syntax

```
value = ListBox.SelCount
```

- *ListBox* — A reference to a ListBox control.
- *value* — The variable that will receive the number of selected items.

Example

The following lines show how to retrieve the value of a ListBox control's `SelCount` property. The `lstList1` object is a ListBox control that the programmer added to the form at design time.

```
Dim numSelected As Integer
numSelected = lstList1.SelCount
```

CROSS-REFERENCE
See also ListBox, MultiSelect, and Selected (FileListBox and ListBox).

Select Case

Statement

The `Select Case` statement enables a program to perform a specific block of code based on the value of an expression.

Syntax

```
Select Case exp
Case expList
    codeBlock
...
End Select
```

or

```
Select Case exp
Case expList
    codeBlock
...
Case Else
    elseBlock
End Select
```

- ... — Any number of additional Case clauses.
- *codeBlock* — The code lines that the program will execute if one of the associated expressions matches the value of *exp*.
- *elseBlock* — The code lines that the program will execute if none of the Case expressions matches the value of *exp*.
- *exp* — The expression to be evaluated by the Select Case statement.
- *expList* — One or more expressions that determine whether the associated code block will execute. To cause the code block to execute, one of the expressions must evaluate to the same value as *exp*. The expression list can include single expressions, multiple expressions separated by commas, or a range of expressions using the To keyword.

Example 1

The following lines will cause the message "num = 3" to appear in a message box.

```
Dim num As Integer
num = 3
Select Case num
Case 1
    MsgBox "num = 1"
Case 2
    MsgBox "num = 2"
Case 3
    MsgBox "num = 3"
Case 4
    MsgBox "num = 4"
End Select
```

Example 2

Here, the following lines will cause the message "num not between 1 and 3" to appear in a message box.

```
Dim num As Integer
num = 5
Select Case num
Case 1
```

```
    MsgBox "num = 1"
Case 2
    MsgBox "num = 2"
Case 3
    MsgBox "num = 3"
Case Else
    MsgBox "num not between 1 and 3"
End Select
```

Example 3

In this example, the following lines will cause the message "num between 1 and 3" to appear in a message box.

```
Dim num As Integer
num = 3
Select Case num
Case 1 To 3
    MsgBox "num between 1 and 3"
Case 4
    MsgBox "num = 4"
Case 5, 6
    MsgBox "num is 5 or 6"
Case Else
    MsgBox "num not between 1 and 6"
End Select
```

Example 4

Here, the following lines will cause the message "num2 = 10" to appear in a message box. Notice that Select Case statements can be nested.

```
Dim num As Integer
Dim num2 As Integer
num = 2
num2 = 10
Select Case num
Case 1 To 3
    Select Case num2
    Case 10
        MsgBox "num2 = 10"
    Case 11
```

r
s
t

```
            MsgBox "num2 = 11"
        Case 12
            MsgBox "num2 = 12"
        End Select
    Case Else
        MsgBox "num not between 1 and 3"
    End Select
```

Example 5

Finally, the following lines will cause the message "a to h" to appear in a message box. Notice that when using string expressions, Visual Basic evaluates the expressions by alphabetical order.

```
Dim msg As String
msg = "apple"
Select Case msg
Case "a" To "h"
    MsgBox "a to h"
Case "i" To "p"
    MsgBox "i to p"
Case "q" To "z"
    MsgBox "q to z"
End Select
```

SelectedControls

Collection

A SelectedControls collection holds all the selected controls in an object.

Syntax

value = *PropertyPage*.SelectedControls

- *PropertyPage* — A reference to a PropertyPage object.
- *value* — The variable that will receive a reference to a collection.

Properties

A `SelectedControls` collection has one property, `Count`, which represents the number of bands in the collection. For more information on using this property, look up the property's entry, provided alphabetically in this book.

Methods

A SelectedControls collection has one method, Item, which returns an object from the collection. For more information on using this method, look up the method's entry, provided alphabetically in this book.

 CROSS-REFERENCE
See also PropertyPage and SelectedControls (property).

SelectedControls

Property

The `SelectedControls` property represents a reference to a PropertyPage object's SelectedControls collection.

Objects with a SelectedControls Property

PropertyPage

Syntax

```
value = PropertyPage.SelectedControls
```

- *PropertyPage* — A reference to a PropertyPage object.
- *value* — The variable that will receive the reference to the SelectedControls collection.

Example

The following lines show how to get a reference to a selected control from a SelectedControls collection. In this case, the property returns the second control in the collection (the first control has an index of 0).

```
Dim cntrl As Object
cntrl = PropertyPage1.SelectedControls(1)
```

CROSS-REFERENCE
See also PropertyPage and SelectedControls (collection).

Selected—FileListBox and ListBox

Property

The Selected property represents whether an item is selected in a FileListBox
or ListBox control. A program can use the Selected property to select an item
programmatically or to check an item's current selected state.

Syntax

object.Selected = *value1*

or

value2 = *object*.Selected

- *object*—A reference to a FileListBox or ListBox control.
- *value1*—The value True or False.
- *value2*—The variable that will receive the property's current
setting.

Example

The following lines show how to get and set the selected status of an item in a
ListBox control. Figure S-11 shows the list box after the item at index 3 (the
first item has an index of 0) has been selected. The lstList1 object is a
ListBox control that the user added to the form at design time.

```
Dim itemSelected As Boolean
lstList1.Selected(3) = True
itemSelected = lstList1.Selected(3)
```

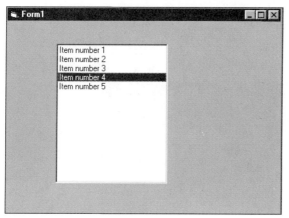

Figure S-11 The program has selected the fourth item in this ListBox control.

 CROSS-REFERENCE
See also ListBox, ListCount, and ListIndex.

Selected — ListView

Property

The Selected property represents whether an object in a control is selected. However, for a ListView control's objects, the SelectedItem property determines which item is selected, with the Selected property only returning an object's selected state.

Syntax

value = ListView.Selected

- *ListView* — A reference to a ListView control.
- *value* — The variable that will receive the property's current setting of True or False.

Example

The following lines show how to set the selected item in a ListView control, as well as how to get the item's selected state. Figure S-12 shows the ListView control with the third item selected. The lvwListView1 object is a ListView control that the user added to the form at design time.

```
Dim itemSelected As Boolean
Set lvwListView1.SelectedItem = lvwListView1.ListItems(3)
itemSelected = lvwListView1.ListItems(3).Selected
```

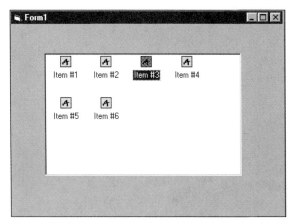

Figure S-12 The program has selected the third item in this ListView control.

 CROSS-REFERENCE
See also ListView and SelectedItem.

Selected—TabStrip and TreeView

Property

The Selected property represents whether an object in a control is selected. A program can use the Selected property to select a Node or Tab object programmatically or to check an object's current selected state.

Syntax

```
object.Selected = value1
```

or

```
value2 = object.Selected
```

- *object*—A reference to a TabStrip or TreeView control.
- *value1*—The value True or False.
- *value2*—The variable that will receive the property's current setting.

Example

The following lines show how to get and set the selected status of a Tab object in a TabStrip control. Figure S-13 shows the tab strip after the third tab has been selected. The `tabTabStrip1` object is a TabStrip control that the user added to the form at design time.

```
Dim selectedStatus As Boolean
selectedStatus = tabTabStrip1.Tabs(3).Selected
tabTabStrip1.Tabs(3).Selected = True
```

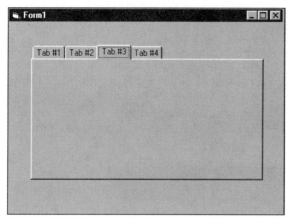

Figure S-13 The program has selected the third tab in this TabStrip control.

CROSS-REFERENCE
See also TabStrip and TreeView.

SelectedImage

Property

The `SelectedImage` property represents the index of an ImageList image to use as a Node object's icon when the node is selected.

Objects with a SelectedImage Property

TreeView

Syntax

```
TreeView.SelectedImage = value1
```

or

```
value2 = TreeView.SelectedImage
```

- *TreeView* — A reference to a TreeView control.
- *value1* — The index or key of the image to use as the selected image.
- *value2* — The variable that will receive the property's current setting.

Example

The following program demonstrates the SelectedImage property. When you run the program, select any node in the TreeView control, and the node's icon will change from yellow to red. Figure S-14 shows the program with one of its nodes selected. Notice in the source code how the red icon (circle2.bmp), whose index in its ImageList control is 2, gets set as each node's selected icon.

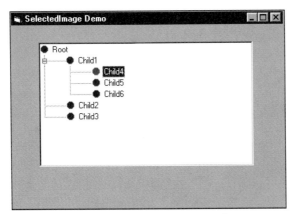

Figure S-14 When you select a node in this program, the node's icon changes color.

```
VERSION 5.00
Object = "{831FDD16-0C5C-11D2-A9FC-0000F8754DA1} _
    #2.0#0"; "MSCOMCTL.OCX"
Begin VB.Form Form1
    Caption        =    "SelectedImage Demo"
    ClientHeight    =    3885
    ClientLeft      =    60
```

```
        ClientTop        =    345
        ClientWidth      =    5955
        LinkTopic        =    "Form1"
        ScaleHeight      =    3885
        ScaleWidth       =    5955
        StartUpPosition  =    3  'Windows Default
        Begin MSComctlLib.ImageList ilsImageList1
            Left         =    4680
            Top          =    3240
            _ExtentX     =    1005
            _ExtentY     =    1005
            BackColor    =    -2147483643
            MaskColor    =    12632256
            _Version     =    393216
        End
        Begin MSComctlLib.TreeView treTreeView1
            Height       =    2655
            Left         =    600
            TabIndex     =    0
            Top          =    360
            Width        =    4695
            _ExtentX     =    8281
            _ExtentY     =    4683
            _Version     =    393217
            Style        =    7
            Appearance   =    1
        End
    End
Attribute VB_Name = "Form1"
Attribute VB_GlobalNameSpace = False
Attribute VB_Creatable = False
Attribute VB_PredeclaredId = True
Attribute VB_Exposed = False

Private Sub Form_Load()
    Dim x As Integer

    ilsImageList1.ListImages.Add , , _
        LoadPicture("circle1.bmp")
    ilsImageList1.ListImages.Add , , _
        LoadPicture("circle2.bmp")

    treTreeView1.ImageList = ilsImageList1

    With treTreeView1.Nodes
```

```
                  .Add , , "Root", "Root", 1
                  .Add "Root", tvwChild, "Child1", "Child1", 1
                  .Add "Root", tvwChild, "Child2", "Child2", 1
                  .Add "Root", tvwChild, "Child3", "Child3", 1
                  .Add "Child1", tvwChild, "Child4", "Child4", 1
                  .Add "Child1", tvwChild, "Child5", "Child5", 1
                  .Add "Child1", tvwChild, "Child6", "Child6", 1
              End With

              For x = 1 To 7
                  treTreeView1.Nodes(x).SelectedImage = 2
              Next

              treTreeView1.Nodes(7).EnsureVisible
          End Sub
```

 CROSS-REFERENCE
See also ListView, Node, Nodes, and TreeView.

SelectedItem

Property

The `SelectedItem` property represents a reference to the currently selected item in a control.

Objects with a SelectedItem Property

ListView

TabStrip

TreeView

Syntax

object.SelectedItem = *value1*

or

value2 = *object*.SelectedItem

- *object* — A reference to a control with a `SelectedItem` property.
- *value1* — A reference to the item to set to the selected state.

- *value2* — The variable that will receive the reference to the selected item.

Example

The following lines show how to set the selected item in a ListView control, as well as how to get the item's selected state. The `lvwListView1` object is a ListView control that the user added to the form at design time.

```
Dim itemSelected As Boolean
Set lvwListView1.SelectedItem = lvwListView1.ListItems(3)
itemSelected = lvwListView1.ListItems(3).Selected
```

CROSS-REFERENCE
See also Selected (ListView) and Selected (TabStrip and TreeView).

SelectionChanged

Event

Visual Basic sends a PropertyPage object a `SelectionChanged` event when the user changes the selected controls, which means some properties may need to be updated to new values the user entered.

Objects with a SelectionChanged Event

PropertyPage

Example

A program can respond to a `SelectionChanged` event by implementing the PropertyPage object's `SelectionChanged` event procedure. The following code segment shows how a PropertyPage object defines a `SelectionChanged` event procedure.

```
Private Sub PropertyPage_SelectionChanged()
    ' Handle the SelectionChanged event here.
End Sub
```

CROSS-REFERENCE
See also PropertyPage, SelectedControls (collection), and SelectedControls (property).

SelectRange

Property

The `SelectRange` property represents whether a Slider control can display a range selection.

Objects with a SelectRange Property

Slider

Syntax

```
Slider.SelectRange = value1
```

or

```
value2 = Slider.SelectRange
```

- *Slider* — A reference to a Slider control.
- *value1* — The value `True` or `False`.
- *value2* — The variable that will receive the property's current setting.

Example

The following lines show how to get and set a Slider control's `SelectRange` property. The `sldSlider1` object is a Slider control that the programmer added to the form at design time.

```
Dim range As Boolean
range = sldSlider1.SelectRange
sldSlider1.SelectRange = True
```

 CROSS-REFERENCE
See also ClearSel, SelLength (Slider), SelStart (Slider), and Slider.

SelFontName

Property

The SelFontName property represents the font that will be used to display selected text in a RichTextBox control. Setting this property will also affect how newly typed text will appear.

Objects with a SelFontName Property

RichTextBox

Syntax

```
RichTextBox.SelFontName = value1
```

or

```
value2 = RichTextBox.SelFontName
```

- *RichTextBox* — A reference to a RichTextBox control.
- *value1* — The new font name.
- *value2* — The variable that will receive the property's current setting.

Example

The following lines show how to get and set a RichTextBox control's SelFontName property. In this case, the selected text, or the next text typed into the control, will be displayed in the Arial font. The rtfRichTextBox1 object is a RichTextBox control that the programmer added to the form at design time.

```
Dim txtFont As String
txtFont = rtfRichTextBox1.SelFontName
rtfRichTextBox1.SelFontName = "Arial"
```

CROSS-REFERENCE
See also RichTextBox.

SelFontSize

Property

The SelFontSize property represents the font size that will be used to display selected text in a RichTextBox control. Setting this property will also affect how newly typed text will appear.

Objects with a SelFontSize Property

RichTextBox

Syntax

RichTextBox.SelFontSize = *value1*

or

value2 = *RichTextBox*.SelFontSize

- *RichTextBox* — A reference to a RichTextBox control.
- *value1* — The new font size.
- *value2* — The variable that will receive the property's current setting.

Example

The following lines show how to get and set a RichTextBox control's SelFontSize property. In this case, the selected text, or the next text typed into the control, will be displayed with a size of 18 points. The rtfRichTextBox1 object is a RichTextBox control that the programmer added to the form at design time.

```
Dim txtSize As Integer
txtSize = rtfRichTextBox1.SelFontSize
rtfRichTextBox1.SelFontSize = 18
```

CROSS-REFERENCE
See also RichTextBox.

SelHangingIndent

Property

The `SelHangingIndent` property represents the amount that all but the first line of a paragraph should be indented in a RichTextBox control.

Objects with a SelHangingIndent Property

RichTextBox

Syntax

```
RichTextBox.SelHangingIndent = value1
```

or

```
value2 = RichTextBox.SelHangingIndent
```

- *RichTextBox* — A reference to a RichTextBox control.
- *value1* — The amount to indent text.
- *value2* — The variable that will receive the property's current setting.

Example

The following lines show how to get and set a RichTextBox control's `SelHangingIndent` property. The `rtfRichTextBox1` object is a RichTextBox control that the programmer added to the form at design time.

```
Dim hangingIndent As Integer
hangingIndent = rtfRichTextBox1.SelHangingIndent
rtfRichTextBox1.SelHangingIndent = 10
```

CROSS-REFERENCE
See also RichTextBox.

SelIndent

Property

The `SelIndent` property represents the left margin for text in a RichTextBox control.

Objects with a SelIndent Property

RichTextBox

Syntax

```
RichTextBox.SelIndent = value1
```

or

```
value2 = RichTextBox.SelIndent
```

- *RichTextBox* — A reference to a RichTextBox control.
- *value1* — The amount to indent text on the left.
- *value2* — The variable that will receive the property's current setting.

Example

The following lines show how to get and set a RichTextBox control's SelIndent property. The rtfRichTextBox1 object is a RichTextBox control that the programmer added to the form at design time.

```
Dim textIndent As Integer
textIndent = rtfRichTextBox1.SelIndent
rtfRichTextBox1.SelIndent = 10
```

 **CROSS-REFERENCE**
See also RichTextBox.

SelItalic

Property

The SelItalic property represents the italic text attribute for selected text in a RichTextBox control. This property can be set to Null, True, or False. A return value of Null indicates that the selected text contains a mix of italic and nonitalic characters.

Objects with a SelItalic Property

RichTextBox

Syntax

```
RichTextBox.SelItalic = value1
```

or

```
value2 = RichTextBox.SelItalic
```

- *RichTextBox* — A reference to a RichTextBox control.
- *value1* — The value `True` or `False`.
- *value2* — The variable that will receive the property's current setting.

Example

The following lines show how to get and set a RichTextBox control's `SelItalic` property. The `rtfRichTextBox1` object is a RichTextBox control that the programmer added to the form at design time.

```
Dim fontItalic
fontItalic = rtfRichTextBox1.SelItalic
rtfRichTextBox1.SelItalic = True
```

CROSS-REFERENCE
See also RichTextBox.

SelLength — General Controls

Property

The `SelLength` property represents the number of characters that have been selected in a control.

Objects with a SelLength Property

ComboBox
RichTextBox
TextBox

Syntax

```
object.SelLength = value1
```

or

```
value2 = object.SelLength
```

- *object* — A reference to a control with a SelLength property.
- *value1* — The new selection length.
- *value2* — The variable that will receive the property's current setting.

Example

The following program demonstrates a RichTextBox control's SelLength property. When you run the program, type the first character to select into the Start box, type the number of characters to select into the Length box, and then click the Set Selection button to select the specified portion of the text. You can also use your mouse or keyboard to select text right in the RichTextBox control, in which case the Start and Length boxes automatically update themselves with your selection values. Figure S-15 shows the program after the user has selected a block of text.

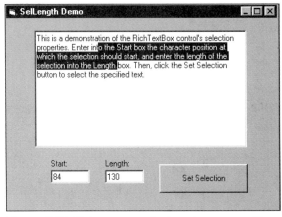

Figure S-15 This program displays the start and length of a text selection.

```
VERSION 5.00
Object = "{3B7C8863-D78F-101B-B9B5-04021C009402} _
   #1.2#0"; "RICHTX32.OCX"
Begin VB.Form Form1
   Caption        =   "SelLength Demo"
   ClientHeight   =   4080
   ClientLeft     =   60
   ClientTop      =   345
```

```
ClientWidth      =    5940
LinkTopic        =    "Form1"
ScaleHeight      =    272
ScaleMode        =    3  'Pixel
ScaleWidth       =    396
StartUpPosition  =    3  'Windows Default
Begin VB.CommandButton btnSetSelection
   Caption       =    "Set Selection"
   Height        =    615
   Left          =    3360
   TabIndex      =    5
   Top           =    3120
   Width         =    1935
End
Begin VB.TextBox txtLength
   Height        =    285
   Left          =    2160
   TabIndex      =    4
   Top           =    3240
   Width         =    855
End
Begin VB.TextBox txtStart
   Height        =    285
   Left          =    960
   TabIndex      =    2
   Top           =    3240
   Width         =    855
End
Begin RichTextLib.RichTextBox rtfRichTextBox1
   Height        =    2535
   Left          =    600
   TabIndex      =    0
   Top           =    240
   Width         =    4695
   _ExtentX      =    8281
   _ExtentY      =    4471
   _Version      =    393217
   Enabled       =    -1  'True
   TextRTF       =    $"Form1.frx":0000
End
Begin VB.Label Label2
   Caption       =    "Length:"
   Height        =    255
```

```
            Left          =    2160
            TabIndex      =    3
            Top           =    3000
            Width         =    735
         End
         Begin VB.Label Label1
            Caption       =    "Start:"
            Height        =    255
            Left          =    960
            TabIndex      =    1
            Top           =    3000
            Width         =    735
         End
      End
   End
Attribute VB_Name = "Form1"
Attribute VB_GlobalNameSpace = False
Attribute VB_Creatable = False
Attribute VB_PredeclaredId = True
Attribute VB_Exposed = False
Private Sub btnSetSelection_Click()
    Dim start As Integer
    Dim length As Integer

    On Error GoTo ErrorHandler
    start = txtStart.Text
    length = txtLength.Text
    rtfRichTextBox1.SelStart = start
    rtfRichTextBox1.SelLength = length
    rtfRichTextBox1.SetFocus
    Exit Sub

ErrorHandler:
    MsgBox "Please enter valid values.", _
        vbExclamation, "SelLength Demo"
End Sub

Private Sub Form_Load()
    Dim msg As String
    msg = "This is a demonstration of the RichTextBox "
    msg = msg & "control's selection properties. Enter "
    msg = msg & "into the Start box the character position "
    msg = msg & "at which the selection should start, "
    msg = msg & "and enter the length of the selection "
    msg = msg & "into the Length box. Then, click the "
```

```
        msg = msg & "Set Selection button to select the "
        msg = msg & "specified text."
        rtfRichTextBox1.Text = msg
        rtfRichTextBox1.HideSelection = False

        txtStart.Text = "0"
        txtLength.Text = "0"

    End Sub

    Private Sub rtfRichTextBox1_SelChange()
        txtStart.Text = rtfRichTextBox1.SelStart
        txtLength.Text = rtfRichTextBox1.SelLength
    End Sub
```

CROSS-REFERENCE

See also SelectRange, SelStart (General Controls), and Slider.

SelLength — Slider

Property

The SelLength property represents the length of a selected range in a Slider control.

Syntax

Slider.SelLength = *value1*

or

value2 = *Slider*.SelLength

- *Slider* — A reference to a Slider control.
- *value1* — The new selection length.
- *value2* — The variable that will receive the property's current setting.

Example

The following lines show how to get and set a Slider control's SelLength property. Figure S-16 shows what a Slider looks like when the user has selected a range of values. The `sldSlider1` object is a Slider control that the programmer added to the form at design time.

```
Dim length As Integer
sldSlider1.SelectRange = True
sldSlider1.SelStart = 2
length = sldSlider1.SelLength
sldSlider1.SelLength = 4
```

CROSS-REFERENCE
See also SelStart, SelectRange, and Slider.

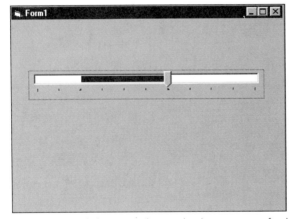

Figure S-16 Slider controls can display a range of selections.

SelPrint

Method

The `SelPrint` method sends text from a RichTextBox control to a device context that can print the text.

Objects with a SelPrint Method

RichTextBox

Syntax

`RichTextBox.SelPrint(hDC)`

- *RichTextBox* — A reference to a RichTextBox control.
- *hDC* — The device context of the device that will print the text.

Example

The following line prints text from a RichTextBox control to the current default printer, represented by the Printer object. The `rtfRichTextBox1` object is a RichTextBox control that the programmer added to the form at design time.

```
rtfRichTextBox1.SelPrint(Printer.hDC)
```

CROSS-REFERENCE
See also RichTextBox.

SelProtected

Property

The `SelProtected` property represents whether the user can edit text in a RichTextBox control. A value of `True` disables all editing on the selected text, whereas a value of `False` enables editing. A return value of `Null` indicates that the current text selection contains both protected and unprotected text.

Objects with a SelProtected Property

RichTextBox

Syntax

RichTextBox`.SelProtected = `*value1*

or

value2` = `*RichTextBox*`.SelProtected`

- *RichTextBox* — A reference to a RichTextBox control.
- *value1* — The value `True` or `False`.
- *value2* — The variable that will receive the property's current setting.

r
s
t

Example

The following lines show how to get and set the value of the `SelProtected` property of a RichTextBox control. The `rtfRichTextBox1` object is a RichTextBox control that the programmer added to the form at design time.

```
Dim protected
protected = rtfRichTextBox1.SelProtected
rtfRichTextBox1.SelProtected = True
```

CROSS-REFERENCE
See also RichTextBox.

SelRightIndent

Property

The `SelRightIndent` property represents the right margin for text in a RichTextBox control.

Objects with a SelRightIndent Property

RichTextBox

Syntax

```
RichTextBox.SelRightIndent = value1
```

or

```
value2 = RichTextBox.SelRightIndent
```

- *RichTextBox* — A reference to a RichTextBox control.
- *value1* — The amount to indent text on the right.
- *value2* — The variable that will receive the property's current setting.

Example

The following lines show how to get and set a RichTextBox control's `SelRightIndent` property. The `rtfRichTextBox1` object is a RichTextBox control that the programmer added to the form at design time.

```
Dim textIndent As Integer
textIndent = rtfRichTextBox1.SelRightIndent
rtfRichTextBox1.SelRightIndent = 10
```

 **CROSS-REFERENCE**
See also RichTextBox.

SelRTF

Property

The SelRTF property represents a block of selected text in RTF format. The property returns the selected text as RTF text or sets the current selection to the given string.

Objects with a SelRTF Property

RichTextBox

Syntax

```
RichTextBox.SelRTF = value1
```

or

```
value2 = RichTextBox.SelRTF
```

- *RichTextBox* — A reference to a RichTextBox control.
- *value1* — The string to paste into the text at the current insertion point or to replace the current text selection.
- *value2* — The variable that will receive the RTF formatted text.

Example

The following lines show how to get and set the value of the SelRTF property of a RichTextBox control. The rtfRichTextBox1 object is a RichTextBox control that the programmer added to the form at design time.

```
Dim txt As String
txt = rtfRichTextBox1.SelRTF
rtfRichTextBox1.SelRTF = "This is a test."
```

r
s
t

CROSS-REFERENCE
See also RichTextBox and SelText.

SelStart — General Controls

Property

The SelStart property represents the index of the first selected character in a control.

Objects with a SelStart Property

ComboBox

RichTextBox

TextBox

Syntax

```
object.SelStart = value1
```

or

```
value2 = object.SelStart
```

- *object* — A reference to a control with a SelStart property.
- *value1* — The new character index.
- *value2* — The variable that will receive the property's current setting.

Example

The following lines show how to get and set a TextBox control's SelStart property. The txtText1 object is a TextBox control that the programmer added to the form at design time.

```
Dim start As Integer
start = txtText1.SelStart
txtText1.SelStart = 20
```

CROSS-REFERENCE
See also SelLength (General Controls).

SelStart — Slider

Property

The SelStart property represents the starting value of a selected range in a Slider control.

Syntax

```
Slider.SelStart = value1
```

or

```
value2 = Slider.SelStart
```

- *Slider* — A reference to a Slider control.
- *value1* — The new selection start.
- *value2* — The variable that will receive the property's current setting.

Example

The following lines show how to get and set a Slider control's SelStart property. The sldSlider1 object is a Slider control that the programmer added to the form at design time.

```
Dim length As Integer
sldSlider1.SelectRange = True
sldSlider1.SelStart = 2
length = sldSlider1.SelLength
sldSlider1.SelLength = 4
```

CROSS-REFERENCE
See also SelectRange, SelLength (Slider), and Slider.

r
s
t

SelStrikethru

Property

The `SelStrikethru` property represents the strikethrough text attribute for selected text in a RichTextBox control. This property can be set to `Null`, `True`, or `False`. A return value of `Null` indicates that the selected text contains a mix of strikethrough and nonstrikethrough characters.

Objects with a SelStrikethru Property

RichTextBox

Syntax

RichTextBox.SelStrikethru = *value1*

or

value2 = *RichTextBox*.SelStrikethru

- *RichTextBox* — A reference to a RichTextBox control.
- *value1* — The value `True` or `False`.
- *value2* — The variable that will receive the property's current setting.

Example

The following lines show how to get and set a RichTextBox control's `SelStrikethru` property. The `rtfRichTextBox1` object is a RichTextBox control that the programmer added to the form at design time.

```
Dim fontStrikethru
fontStrikethru = rtfRichTextBox1.SelStrikethru
rtfRichTextBox1.SelStrikethru = True
```

 **CROSS-REFERENCE**
See also RichTextBox.

SelTabCount

Property

The SelTabCount property represents the number of tabs set in a RichTextBox control.

Objects with a SelTabCount Property

RichTextBox

Syntax

```
RichTextBox.SelTabCount = value1
```

or

```
value2 = RichTextBox.SelTabCount
```

- *RichTextBox* — A reference to a RichTextBox control.
- *value1* — The number of tabs to place in the RichTextBox control.
- *value2* — The variable that will receive the tab count.

Example

The following lines show how to get and set the value of the SelTabCount property of a RichTextBox control. The rtfRichTextBox1 object is a RichTextBox control that the programmer added to the form at design time.

```
Dim tabCount As Integer
tabCount = rtfRichTextBox1.SelTabCount
rtfRichTextBox1.SelTabCount = 5
```

CROSS-REFERENCE
See also RichTextBox and SelTabs.

r

s

t

SelTabs

Property

The `SelTabs` property represents the position of tabs set in a RichTextBox control.

Objects with a SelTabs Property

RichTextBox

Syntax

`RichTextBox.SelTabs(index) = value1`

or

`value2 = RichTextBox.SelTabs(index)`

- *RichTextBox* — A reference to a RichTextBox control.
- *index* — The number of the tabs to access. The first tab has an index of 0.
- *value1* — The position at which to set the tab.
- *value2* — The variable that will receive the tab position.

Example

The following lines show how to set the positions of tabs in a RichTextBox control. The `rtfRichTextBox1` object is a RichTextBox control that the programmer added to the form at design time.

```
rtfRichTextBox1.SelTabCount = 2
rtfRichTextBox1.SelTabs(0) = 100
rtfRichTextBox1.SelTabs(1) = 200
```

CROSS-REFERENCE
See also RichTextBox and SelTabCount.

SelText

Property

The SelText property represents a block of selected text in text format. The property returns the selected text or sets the current selection to the given string.

Objects with a SelText Property

ComboBox

RichTextBox

TextBox

Syntax

```
object.SelText = value1
```

or

```
value2 = object.SelText
```

- *object* — A reference to a control with a SelText property.
- *value1* — The string to paste into the text at the current insertion point or to replace the current text selection.
- *value2* — The variable that will receive the selected text.

Example

The following lines show how to get and set the value of the SelText property of a RichTextBox control. The rtfRichTextBox1 object is a RichTextBox control that the programmer added to the form at design time.

```
Dim txt As String
txt = rtfRichTextBox1.SelText
rtfRichTextBox1.SelText = "This is a test"
```

CROSS-REFERENCE
See also SelRTF.

SelUnderline

Property

The SelUnderline property represents the underline text attribute for selected text in a RichTextBox control. This property can be set to Null, True, or False. A return value of Null indicates that the selected text contains a mix of underline and nonunderline characters.

Objects with a SelUnderline Property

RichTextBox

Syntax

```
RichTextBox.SelUnderline = value1
```

or

```
value2 = RichTextBox.SelUnderline
```

- *RichTextBox* — A reference to a RichTextBox control.
- *value1* — The value True or False.
- *value2* — The variable that will receive the property's current setting.

Example

The following lines show how to get and set a RichTextBox control's SelUnderline property. The rtfRichTextBox1 object is a RichTextBox control that the programmer added to the form at design time.

```
Dim fontUnderline
fontUnderline = rtfRichTextBox1.SelUnderline
rtfRichTextBox1.SelUnderline = True
```

CROSS-REFERENCE
See also RichTextBox.

Send

Method

The Send method sends a message from a MAPIMessages control.

Objects with a Send Method

MAPIMessages

Syntax

`MAPIMessages.Send(flag)`

- *MAPIMessages* — A reference to a MAPIMessages control.
- *flag* (*) — The value `True` or `False` (default). A value of `True` specifies that the MAPIMessages control should display a dialog box to the user, whereas a value of `False` sends the message without displaying the dialog box.

(*) = Optional

Example

The following line sends a message after displaying a dialog box into which the user can enter the parts of the message. The `mpmMAPIMessages1` object is a MAPIMessages control that the programmer added to the form at design time.

`mpmMAPIMessages1.Send(True)`

 CROSS-REFERENCE
See also MAPIMessages.

SendKeys

Statement

The SendKeys statement sends keystrokes to the window with the input focus.

Syntax

`SendKeys text, mode`

- *text*—A string containing the keystrokes to send. Some characters act as control characters for the SendKeys statement and must be enclosed in braces in order to send the literal characters. For example, to send a percent symbol as a literal character, you would add {%} to your string. Use the codes in Table S-4 to send special keystrokes like Backspace or Enter. You can specify combination keystrokes by using the + symbol for shift, the ^ symbol for Ctrl, and the % symbol for Alt. For example, to specify the keystroke Ctrl+T, you add ^T to the output string. Finally, you can send repeating keystrokes by adding a repeat count to the character. So, the code {DEL 10} means to send ten Delete keystrokes.
- *mode* (*)—The value True or False (default). A value of True specifies that the window that receives the keystrokes must process the input before the system returns control to the sending application. A value of False returns control to the sending application immediately.

(*) = Optional

Table S-4 Special Character Codes for SendKeys

Key	Character Code
Backspace	{BS}, {BKSP}, or {BACKSPACE}
Break	{BREAK}
Caps lock	{CAPSLOCK}
Delete	{DEL} or {DELETE}
Down arrow	{DOWN}
End	{END}
Enter	{ENTER}
Esc	{ESC}
F1 through F16	{F1} through {F16}
Help	{HELP}
Home	{HOME}
Insert	{INS} or {INSERT}
Left arrow	{LEFT}
Num lock	{NUMLOCK}
Page down	{PGDN}
Page up	{PGUP}
Print screen	{PRTSC}
Right arrow	{RIGHT}
Scroll lock	{SCROLLLOCK}
Tab	{TAB}
Up arrow	{UP}

Example

The following lines send the keystrokes A, B, C, and Alt+Z to whatever window currently has the input focus. The application immediately resumes processing after sending the keystrokes.

```
Dim keys As String
keys = "ABC%Z"
SendKeys keys, False
```

Separators

Property

The Separators property represents whether separators appear between buttons in a TabStrip control when the control's style is set to tabButtons or tabFlatButtons.

Objects with a Separators Property

TabStrip

Syntax

```
TabStrip.Separators = value1
```

or

```
value2 = TabStrip.Separators
```

- *TabStrip* — A reference to a TabStrip control.
- *value1* — The value True or False.
- *value2* — The variable that will receive the property's current setting.

Example

The following lines show how to set up a TabStrip control's Separators property. The tabTabStrip1 object is a TabStrip control that the programmer added to the form at design time.

```
tabTabStrip1.Tabs(1).Caption = "Tab #1"
tabTabStrip1.Tabs.Add , , "Tab #2"
tabTabStrip1.Tabs.Add , , "Tab #3"
tabTabStrip1.Tabs.Add , , "Tab #4"
```

```
tabTabStrip1.Tabs.Add , , "Tab #5"
tabTabStrip1.Style = tabButtons
tabTabStrip1.Separators = True
```

CROSS-REFERENCE
See also Style (TabStrip) and TabStrip.

SerialNumber

Property

The SerialNumber property represents the serial number of a disk drive.

Objects with a SerialNumber Property

Drive

Syntax

value = Drive.SerialNumber

- *Drive* — A reference to a Drive object.
- *value* — The variable that will receive the serial number.

Example

The following lines show how to get a serial number for drive C and display the serial number in a message box.

```
Dim fileSystem As Object
Dim drive As Object
Set fileSystem = CreateObject("Scripting.FileSystemObject")
Set drive = fileSystem.GetDrive("c")
MsgBox drive.SerialNumber
```

CROSS-REFERENCE
See also Drive, FileSystemObject, and GetDrive.

SessionID

Property

The SessionID property represents the handle for a messaging session.

Objects with a SessionID Property

MAPIMessages

MAPISession

Syntax

```
value = object.SessionID
```

- *object* — A reference to a MAPISession or MAPIMessages control.
- *value* — The variable that will receive the session ID.

Example

The following lines show how to get a session ID from a MAPISession control. The mpsMAPISession1 object is a MAPISession control that the programmer added to the form at design time.

```
Dim ID As Integer
ID = mpsMAPISession1.SessionID
```

 CROSS-REFERENCE
See also MAPIMessages and MAPISession.

Set

Keyword

The Set keyword is part of the Set and Property Set statements, which set the values of object variables and properties. For example, the following lines define a Property Set procedure.

```
Property Set CustomerID(newCustomer As Object)
    custObj = newCustomer
    PropertyChanged "Customer"
End Property
```

CROSS-REFERENCE
See also Property Set Procedure and Set (statement).

Set

Statement

The Set statement is used to assign an object value to a variable. Unlike the Let keyword, which is optional in an assignment statement, the Set keyword must be supplied when assigning values to objects.

Syntax

```
Set var1 = value
```

- *value* — The object value to assign to the variable.
- *var1* — The name of the variable to which to assign an object value.

Example

The following lines set the variable named objVar to an instance of a MyObject object.

```
Dim objVar As Object
Dim MyObject As Object
Set objVar = MyObject
```

 CROSS-REFERENCE
See also Let and Set (keyword).

SetAttr

Statement

The SetAttr statement sets a file's attributes, such as the file's archive or read-only bits. Constants that represent the file attributes are vbArchive, vbHidden, vbNormal, vbReadOnly, and vbSystem. You can assign multiple attributes by summing the attribute values.

NOTE
You cannot set the attributes of an open file. If you try, an error will result.

Syntax

```
SetAttr file, attr
```

- *attr* — The values for the attributes to assign the file.
- *file* — The path and name of the file.

Example 1

The following lines set a file's system attribute.

```
SetAttr "c:\MyFile.dat", vbSystem
```

Example 2

Here, the following lines simultaneously set a file's archive and read-only attributes.

```
SetAttr "c:\MyFile.dat", vbArchive + vbReadOnly
```

CROSS-REFERENCE
See also FileAttr and GetAttr.

SetData

Method

The SetData method places graphical data into the Clipboard.

Objects with a SetData Method

Clipboard

Syntax

```
Clipboard.SetData graphic, type
```

- *Clipboard*—A reference to a Clipboard object.
- *graphic*—The graphical data to place in the Clipboard.
- *type* (*)—The data format of the graphical data, which can be vbCFBitmap, vbCFDIB, vbCFMetafile, or vbCFPalette.

(*) = Optional

Example

The following lines transfer graphical data from the form to the Clipboard and then from the Clipboard to an Image control. The Clipboard object is a Visual Basic global object that you don't need to create in your programs, whereas the imgImage1 object is an Image control that the programmer added to the form at design time.

```
Form1.Picture = LoadPicture("c:\image1.gif")
Clipboard.SetData Form1.Picture
imgImage1.Picture = Clipboard.GetData
```

CROSS-REFERENCE
See also Clipboard, GetData, GetFormat, GetText, and SetText.

SetFocus

Method

The SetFocus method gives the input focus to a control.

Objects with a SetFocus Method

Animation
CheckBox
ComboBox
CommandButton
DirListBox
DriveListBox
FileListBox
Form
HScrollBar

ListBox

ListView

MDIForm

OLE Container

OptionButton

PictureBox

PropertyPage

RichTextBox

Slider

TabStrip

TextBox

TreeView

UpDown

UserControl

VScrollBar

Syntax

`object.SetFocus`

- *object*—A control with a `SetFocus` method.

Example

The following line gives the input focus to a CommandButton control. The `btnCommand1` object is a CommandButton control that the programmer added to the form at design time.

`btnCommand1.SetFocus`

 CROSS-REFERENCE
See also GotFocus and LostFocus.

SetText

Method

The `SetText` method sends text data to the Clipboard.

Objects with a SetText Method

Clipboard

Syntax

```
Clipboard.SetText txt, dataType
```

- *Clipboard* — A reference to a Clipboard object.
- *dataType* (*) — The type of text data, which can be `vbCFLink`, `vbCFText`, or `vbCFRTF`.
- *txt* — The text to place in the Clipboard.

(*) = Optional

Example

The following line sends text data to the Clipboard, extracts the text from the Clipboard, and displays it in a message box. The Clipboard object is a Visual Basic global object that you don't need to create in your programs.

```
Dim strText As String
Dim strtext2 As String
strText = "This is a test."
Clipboard.SetText strText, vbCFText
strtext2 = Clipboard.GetText(vbCFText)
MsgBox strtext2
```

 CROSS-REFERENCE
See also Clipboard, GetData, GetFormat, GetText, and SetData.

SettingChanged

Event

Visual Basic sends a SysInfo control a `SettingChanged` event when a system setting changes.

Objects with a SettingChanged Event

SysInfo

Example

A program can respond to a `SettingChanged` event by implementing the SysInfo control's `SettingChanged` event procedure. The following code segment shows how a SysInfo control defines a `SettingChanged` event procedure. As you can see in the procedure's declaration, the procedure receives one parameter, which is the information about the setting that was changed. In this example, the `SysInfo1` object is a SysInfo control that the programmer added to the form at design time.

```
Private Sub SysInfo1_SettingChanged(ByVal Item As Integer)
    ' Handle the SettingChanged event here.
End Sub
```

CROSS-REFERENCE
See also SysInfo.

Sgn

Function

The `Sgn` function returns the sign of a number.

Syntax

```
value = Sgn(num)
```

- *num* — The number for which to get the sign.
- *value* — The variable that will receive the value that indicates the sign. A value of –1 means that *num* is negative, a value of 1 means that *num* is positive, and a value of 0 means that *num* is 0.

Example

The following lines determine the sign of a variable named `val1`. After the lines execute, the `result` will contain the value –1.

```
Dim val1 As Integer
Dim result As Integer
val1 = -35
result = Sgn(val1)
```

Shape

Control

A Shape control enables a program to display various types of shapes, including rectangles, circles, rounded squares, and so on. Figure S-17 shows a Shape control in a form. In this case, the control is showing a rounded rectangle shape. The Shape control is available on Visual Basic's standard toolbox.

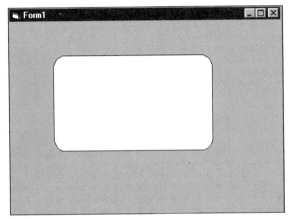

Figure S-17 The Shape control displays various types of shapes.

Properties

The Shape control has 19 properties, which are listed below. Because many Visual Basic controls have similar properties, the following list does not include the properties' descriptions. For information on using a property, look up the individual property's entry, provided alphabetically in this book.

```
BackColor
BackStyle
BorderColor
BorderStyle
BorderWidth
DrawMode
FillColor
FillStyle
Height
Index
Left
```

```
Name
Parent
Shape
Tag
ToolTipText
Top
Visible
Width
```

Methods

The Shape control has three methods, which are listed below. Because many Visual Basic controls have similar methods, the following list does not include the methods' descriptions. For information on using a method, look up the individual method's entry, provided alphabetically in this book.

```
Move
Refresh
ZOrder
```

Events

The Shape control does not respond to events.

Shape

Property

The `Shape` property represents the shape displayed by a Shape control. This property can be set to a value from Table S-5.

Table S-5 Values for the Shape Property

Value	Description
vbShapeCircle	Circle
vbShapeOval	Oval
vbShapeRectangle	Rectangle
vbShapeRoundedRectangle	Rectangle with rounded corners
vbShapeRoundedSquare	Square with rounded corners
vbShapeSquare	Square

Objects with a Shape Property

Shape

Syntax

Shape.Shape = *value1*

or

value2 = *Shape*.Shape

- *Shape*—A reference to a Shape control.
- *value1*—A value from Table S-5.
- *value2*—The variable that will receive the shape setting.

Example

The following program demonstrates the Shape control's Shape property. When you run the program, you see a window that contains a shape control and a button. Click the button to change the type of shape displayed by the control. For example, Figure S-18 shows the Shape control displaying an oval. Each time you click the button, a different shape appears.

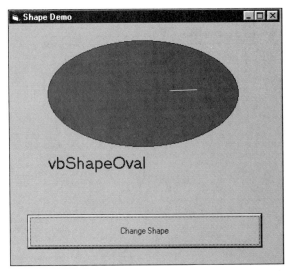

Figure S-18 This Shape control is displaying an oval.

```
VERSION 5.00
Begin VB.Form Form1
   Caption         =     "Shape Demo"
   ClientHeight    =     5130
   ClientLeft      =     60
   ClientTop       =     345
   ClientWidth     =     5940
   LinkTopic       =     "Form1"
   ScaleHeight     =     342
   ScaleMode       =     3   'Pixel
   ScaleWidth      =     396
   StartUpPosition =     3   'Windows Default
   Begin VB.CommandButton btnChangeShape
      Caption      =     "Change Shape"
      Height       =     735
      Left         =     360
      TabIndex     =     0
      Top          =     4080
      Width        =     5175
   End
   Begin VB.Label lblShapeType
      Caption      =     "Label1"
      BeginProperty Font
         Name           =    "MS Sans Serif"
         Size           =    18
         Charset        =    0
         Weight         =    400
         Underline      =    0    'False
         Italic         =    0    'False
         Strikethrough  =    0    'False
      EndProperty
      Height       =     495
      Left         =     840
      TabIndex     =     1
      Top          =     2760
      Width        =     4935
   End
   Begin VB.Shape shpShape1
      Height       =     2295
      Left         =     840
      Top          =     360
```

```
        Width            =    4215
    End
End
Attribute VB_Name = "Form1"
Attribute VB_GlobalNameSpace = False
Attribute VB_Creatable = False
Attribute VB_PredeclaredId = True
Attribute VB_Exposed = False

Private Sub btnChangeShape_Click()
    Select Case shpShape1.Shape
    Case vbShapeRectangle
        shpShape1.Shape = vbShapeSquare
        lblShapeType = "vbShapeSquare"
    Case vbShapeSquare
        shpShape1.Shape = vbShapeOval
        lblShapeType = "vbShapeOval"
    Case vbShapeOval
        shpShape1.Shape = vbShapeCircle
        lblShapeType = "vbShapeCircle"
    Case vbShapeCircle
        shpShape1.Shape = vbShapeRoundedRectangle
        lblShapeType = "vbShapeRoundedRectangle"
    Case vbShapeRoundedRectangle
        shpShape1.Shape = vbShapeRoundedSquare
        lblShapeType = "vbShapeRoundedSquare"
    Case vbShapeRoundedSquare
        shpShape1.Shape = vbShapeRectangle
        lblShapeType = "vbShapeRectangle"
    End Select
End Sub

Private Sub Form_Load()
    shpShape1.FillStyle = vbFSSolid
    shpShape1.FillColor = RGB(255, 0, 0)
    shpShape1.Shape = vbShapeRectangle
    lblShapeType = "vbShapeRectangle"
End Sub
```

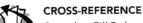

CROSS-REFERENCE
See also FillColor, FillStyle, and Shape (control).

Shareable

Property

The Shareable property represents whether an MCI device can be shared between applications.

Objects with a Shareable Property

Multimedia MCI

Syntax

```
Multimedia.Shareable = value1
```

or

```
value2 = Multimedia.Shareable
```

- *Multimedia* — A reference to a Multimedia MCI control.
- *value1* — The value True or False.
- *value2* — The variable that will receive the property's current setting.

Example

The following lines show how to get and set a Multimedia MCI control's Shareable property. In this example, the mciMMControl1 object is a Multimedia MCI control that the programmer added to the form at design time.

```
Dim share As Boolean
share = mciMMControl1.Shareable
mciMMControl1.Shareable = True
```

CROSS-REFERENCE
See also Multimedia MCI.

ShareName

Property

The ShareName property represents a Drive object's network share name.

Objects with a ShareName Property

Drive

Syntax

```
value = Drive.ShareName
```

- *Drive* — A reference to a Drive object.
- *value* — The variable that will receive the property's current setting.

Example

The following lines show how to get the value of a Drive object's `ShareName` property.

```
Dim fileSystem As Object
Dim drive As Object
Dim driveShareName As String
Set fileSystem = _
    CreateObject("Scripting.FileSystemObject")
Set drive = fileSystem.GetDrive("C")
driveShareName = drive.ShareName
```

 CROSS-REFERENCE
See also Drive, DriveLetter, and DriveType.

Shell

Function

The `Shell` function runs a specified executable file and returns the process's task ID or the value 0 if the command fails.

Syntax

```
value = Shell(fileName, style)
```

- *fileName* — The path and file name of the executable file to run.
- *style* (*) — The window style in which the program will be run. This can be a value from Table S-6.
- *value* — The variable that will receive the process ID or, in the case of failure, the value 0.

(*) = Optional

Table S-6 Values for the *style* Argument

Value	Description
vbHide	Program is displayed in a hidden window that receives the focus.
vbMaximizedFocus	Program window is maximized with the focus.
vbMinimizedFocus	Program window is minimized with the focus.
vbMinimizedNoFocus	Program is displayed in a minimized window, but the currently active window retains the focus.
vbNormalFocus	Program is displayed in a normal window with the focus.
vbNormalNoFocus	Program is displayed in a normal window, but the currently active window retains the focus.

Example

The following lines run the WordPad application in a maximized window and report the results.

```
Dim result As Double
result = Shell("c:\windows\write.exe", vbMaximizedFocus)
If result = 0 Then
    MsgBox "Application failed", vbExclamation
Else
    MsgBox "Task ID is " & result, vbInformation
End If
```

CROSS-REFERENCE
See also AppActivate.

Shortcut

Property

The Shortcut property represents a hotkey for a Menu object. The hotkey enables the user to select the menu command from the keyboard.

Objects with a Shortcut Property

Menu

Example

You use the menu editor to set shortcuts for menu items, as shown in Figure S-19.

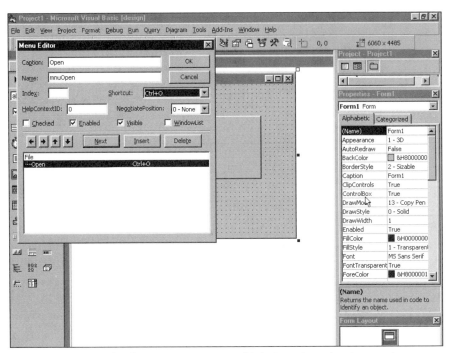

Figure S-19 Here, the Open menu command is being given the shortcut key Ctrl+O.

CROSS-REFERENCE
See also Menu.

ShortName

Property

The ShortName property represents the old DOS 8.3-style (or short) name for a file or folder.

Objects with a ShortName Property

File

Folder

Syntax

```
value = object.ShortName
```

- *object* — A reference to a File or Folder object.
- *value* — The variable that will receive the file or folder short name.

Example

The following lines create a File object and display the file's short name in a message box. In this case, the short name is MYLONG~1.DAT.

```
Dim fileSystem As Object
Dim file As Object
Dim shortFileName As String
Set fileSystem = CreateObject("Scripting.FileSystemObject")
Set file = fileSystem.GetFile("c:\MyLongNamedFile.dat")
shortFileName = file.ShortName
MsgBox shortFileName
```

CROSS-REFERENCE
See also File, FileSystemObject, Name, and ShortPath.

ShortPath

Property

The ShortPath property represents the old DOS 8.3-style (short) path name for a file, folder, or drive.

Syntax

```
value = object.ShortPath
```

- *object* — A reference to a Drive, File, or Folder object.
- *value* — The variable that will receive the short path string.

Example

The following lines create a File object and display the file's short path in a message box. In this case, the short path name is C:\TEMPOR~1\MYFILE.DAT.

```
Dim fileSystem As Object
Dim file As Object
Dim shortPathName As String
Set fileSystem = _
    CreateObject("Scripting.FileSystemObject")
Set file = fileSystem.GetFile("c:\TemporaryFiles\MyFile.dat")
shortPathName = file.ShortPath
MsgBox shortPathName
```

 CROSS-REFERENCE
See also Drive, File, FileSystemObject, Folder, and Path.

Show

Event

Visual Basic sends a UserControl control a Show event when the control's Visible property is set to True.

Objects with a Show Event

UserControl

Example

A program can respond to a Show event by implementing the UserControl control's Show event procedure. The following code segment shows how a UserControl control defines a Show event procedure.

```
Private Sub UserControl_Show()
    ' Handle the Show event here.
End Sub
```

 **CROSS-REFERENCE**
See also UserControl.

ShowColor

Method

The ShowColor method displays the Color common dialog box, as shown in Figure S-20.

Objects with a ShowColor Method

CommonDialog

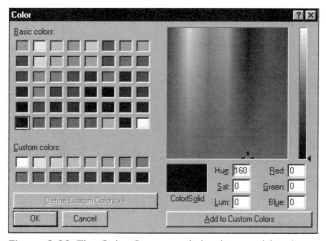

Figure S-20 The Color Common dialog box enables the user to select colors easily.

Syntax

CommonDialog.ShowColor

- *CommonDialog* — A reference to a CommonDialog control.

Example

The following lines show how to display the Color common dialog box and extract the chosen color. In this case, the btnCommand1 and dlgCommonDialog1 objects are a CommandButton control and a CommonDialog control that the programmer added to the form at design time.

```
Private Sub btnCommand1_Click()
    Dim chosenColor As Integer
    dlgCommonDialog1.CancelError = True
```

```
    On Error GoTo ErrorHandler
    dlgCommonDialog1.ShowColor
    chosenColor = dlgCommonDialog1.Color
ErrorHandler:
End Sub
```

CROSS-REFERENCE
See also Color, ShowFont, ShowHelp, ShowOpen, ShowPrinter, and ShowSave.

ShowFont

Method

The `ShowFont` method displays the Font common dialog box, as shown in Figure S-21.

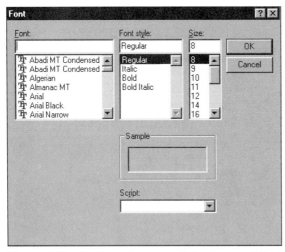

Figure S-21 The Font Common dialog box enables the user to select fonts easily.

Objects with a ShowFont Method

CommonDialog

Syntax

`CommonDialog.ShowFont`

■ *CommonDialog* — A reference to a CommonDialog control.

Example

The following lines show how to display the Font common dialog box and extract the chosen font name. In this case, the `btnCommand1` and `dlgCommonDialog1` objects are a CommandButton control and a CommonDialog control that the programmer added to the form at design time.

```
Private Sub btnCommand1_Click()
    Dim strFontName As String
    dlgCommonDialog1.Flags = cdlCFBoth
    dlgCommonDialog1.CancelError = True
    On Error GoTo ErrorHandler
    dlgCommonDialog1.ShowFont
    strFontName = dlgCommonDialog1.FontName
    MsgBox strFontName
ErrorHandler:
End Sub
```

CROSS-REFERENCE

See also Flags, FontName, ShowColor, ShowHelp, ShowOpen, ShowPrinter, and ShowSave.

Show — Form and MDIForm

Method

The Show method displays a Form or MDIForm object.

Syntax

object.Show *mode, owner*

- *mode* (★) — The value 0 for a modeless form or 1 for a modal form.
- *object* — A reference to a Form or MDIForm object.
- *owner* (★) — A reference to the form's owner.

(★) = Optional

Example

The following line displays a Form object named `frmForm2`.

```
frmForm2.Show
```

CROSS-REFERENCE
See also Form, Load, MDIForm, and Unload.

Show — MAPIMessages

Method

The Show method displays information about email recipients.

Syntax

MAPIMessages.Show *dialog*

- *dialog* (*) — The value True or False. True specifies that information about the current recipient will be displayed in a dialog box, whereas False (the default) specifies that the Address Book should be displayed.

- *MAPIMessages* — A reference to a MAPIMessages control.

(*) = Optional

Example

The following line displays the Address Book on behalf of a MAPIMessages control. The mpmMAPIMessages1 object is a MAPIMessages control that the programmer added to the form at design time.

mpmMAPIMessages.Show

CROSS-REFERENCE
See also MAPIMessages.

ShowGrabHandles

Property

The ShowGrabHandles property represents whether a control displays sizing handles.

Objects with a ShowGrabHandles Property

AmbientProperties

Syntax

`value = Ambient.ShowGrabHandles`

- *Ambient* — A reference to the AmbientProperties object.
- *value* — The variable that will receive the property's current setting of `True` or `False`.

Example

The following lines show how to get the value of the `ShowGrabHandles` property.

```
Dim handles As Boolean
handles = Ambient.ShowGrabHandles
```

CROSS-REFERENCE
See also AmbientProperties.

ShowHatching

Property

The `ShowHatching` property represents whether a control displays hatch marks at design time when the control has the focus.

Objects with a ShowHatching Property

AmbientProperties

Syntax

`value = Ambient.ShowHatching`

- *Ambient* — A reference to the AmbientProperties object.
- *value* — The variable that will receive the property's current setting of `True` or `False`.

Example

The following lines show how to get the value of the ShowHatching property.

```
Dim hatch As Boolean
hatch = Ambient.ShowHatching
```

 **CROSS-REFERENCE**
See also AmbientProperties.

ShowHelp

Method

The ShowHelp method displays the Help common dialog box, as shown in Figure S-22.

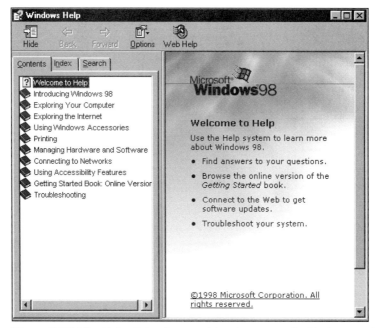

Figure S-22 The Help dialog box enables the user to find help on various topics.

Objects with a ShowHelp Method

CommonDialog

Syntax

CommonDialog.ShowHelp

- *CommonDialog* — A reference to a CommonDialog control.

Example

The following lines show how to display the Windows Help common dialog box set to the help file's index. In this case, the btnCommand1 and dlgCommonDialog1 objects are a CommandButton control and a Common Dialog control that the programmer added to the form at design time.

```
Private Sub btnCommand1_Click()
    dlgCommonDialog1.HelpFile = "c:\windows\windows.hlp"
    dlgCommonDialog1.HelpCommand = cdlHelpIndex
    On Error GoTo ErrorHandler
    dlgCommonDialog1.ShowHelp
ErrorHandler:
End Sub
```

CROSS-REFERENCE

See also HelpCommand, HelpFile, ShowColor, ShowFont, ShowOpen, ShowPrinter, and ShowSave.

ShowInTaskbar

Property

The ShowInTaskbar property represents whether a form displays its icon in the taskbar. This property can be set only at design time, and is read-only at runtime.

Objects with a ShowInTaskbar Property

Form

Syntax

```
value = Form.ShowInTaskbar
```

- *Form* — A reference to a Form object.
- *value* — The variable that will receive the property's current setting of True or False.

Example

The following lines show how to get the value of a Form object's ShowInTaskbar property.

```
Dim showInBar As Boolean
showInBar = frmForm1.ShowInTaskbar
```

CROSS-REFERENCE
See also Form

ShowOpen

Method

The ShowOpen method displays the Open common dialog box, as shown in Figure S-23.

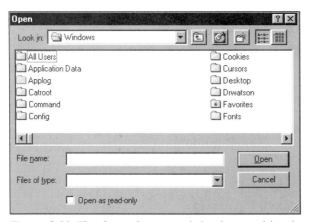

Figure S-23 The Open Common dialog box enables the user to locate the file to open.

Objects with a ShowOpen Method

CommonDialog

Syntax

`CommonDialog.ShowOpen`

- *CommonDialog*—A reference to a CommonDialog control.

Example

The following lines show how to display the Open common dialog box and to get the selected file name. Here, the `btnCommand1` and `dlgCommonDialog1` objects are a CommandButton control and a CommonDialog control that the programmer added to the form at design time.

```
Private Sub btnCommand1_Click()
    Dim chosenFile As String
    dlgCommonDialog1.CancelError = True
    On Error GoTo ErrorHandler
    dlgCommonDialog1.ShowOpen
    chosenFile = dlgCommonDialog1.fileName
    MsgBox chosenFile
ErrorHandler:
End Sub
```

 CROSS-REFERENCE
See also HelpCommand, HelpFile, ShowColor, ShowFont, ShowHelp, ShowPrinter, and ShowSave.

ShowPrinter

Method

The `ShowPrinter` method displays the Print common dialog box, as shown in Figure S-24.

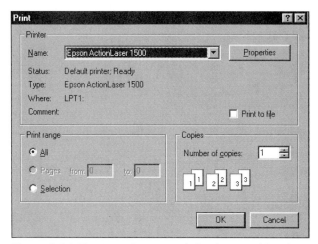

Figure S-24 The Print Common dialog box enables the user to set attributes for a print job.

Objects with a ShowPrinter Method

CommonDialog

Syntax

CommonDialog.ShowPrinter

- *CommonDialog*—A reference to a CommonDialog control.

Example

The following lines show how to display the Print common dialog box. Here, the btnCommand1 and dlgCommonDialog1 objects are a CommandButton control and a CommonDialog control that the programmer added to the form at design time.

```
Private Sub btnCommand1_Click()
    dlgCommonDialog1.CancelError = True
    On Error GoTo ErrorHandler
    dlgCommonDialog1.ShowPrinter
ErrorHandler:
End Sub
```

CROSS-REFERENCE
See also HelpCommand, HelpFile, ShowColor, ShowFont, ShowHelp, ShowOpen, and ShowSave.

ShowSave

Method

The `ShowSave` method displays the Save As common dialog box, as shown in Figure S-25.

Objects with a ShowSave Method

CommonDialog

Syntax

`CommonDialog.ShowSave`

- *CommonDialog* — A reference to a CommonDialog control.

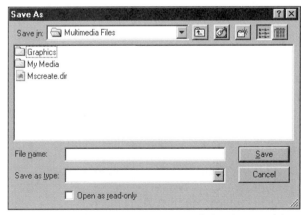

Figure S-25 The Save As Common dialog box enables the user to select a file name under which to save a file.

Example

The following lines show how to display the Save As common dialog box and how to retrieve the selected file name. Here, the `btnCommand1` and `dlgCommonDialog1` objects are a CommandButton control and a CommonDialog control that the programmer added to the form at design time.

```
Private Sub btnCommand1_Click()
    Dim chosenFile As String
    dlgCommonDialog1.CancelError = True
    On Error GoTo ErrorHandler
    dlgCommonDialog1.ShowSave
    chosenFile = dlgCommonDialog1.fileName
    MsgBox chosenFile
ErrorHandler:
End Sub
```

 CROSS-REFERENCE
See also HelpCommand, HelpFile, ShowColor, ShowFont, ShowHelp, ShowOpen, and ShowPrinter.

ShowTips

Property

The `ShowTips` property represents whether an object can display tooltip text. A *tooltip* is a small box that contains text that describes the associated object. For example, a toolbar button may have a tooltip that briefly describes the button's function. This property can be set only at design time, and is read-only at runtime.

Objects with a ShowTips Property

StatusBar

TabStrip

Toolbar

Syntax

```
value = object.ShowTips
```

- *object* — A reference to a control with a ShowTips property.
- *value* — The variable that will receive the property's current setting of True or False.

Example

The following lines show how to get the value of a Toolbar control's ShowTips property. The tlbToolbar1 object is a Toolbar control that the programmer added to the form at design time.

```
Dim tips As Boolean
tips = tlbToolbar1.ShowTips
```

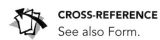

CROSS-REFERENCE
See also Form.

ShowWhatsThis

Method

The ShowWhatsThis method displays context-sensitive help associated with an object.

Objects with a ShowWhatsThis Method

Animation

CheckBox

ComboBox

CommandButton

DirListBox

DriveListBox

FileListBox

Frame

HScrollBar

Image

Label

ListBox
ListView
OLE Container
OptionButton
PictureBox
ProgressBar
RichTextBox
Slider
StatusBar
TabStrip
TextBox
Toolbar
TreeView
UpDown
VScrollBar

Syntax

object.ShowWhatsThis

- *object* — A reference to a control with a ShowWhatsThis method.

Example

The following line displays a help topic for a CommandButton control named btnChangeColor.

btnChangeColor.ShowWhatsThis

 CROSS-REFERENCE
See also WhatsThisHelp and WhatsThisHelpID.

SignOff

Method

The SignOff method ends a message session with a MAPISession control.

Objects with a SignOff Method

MAPISession

Syntax

MAPISession.SignOff

- *MAPISession* — A reference to a MAPISession control.

Example

The following line signs off the user from a message session. The mpsMAPISession1 object is a MAPISession control that the programmer added to the form at design time.

mpsMAPISession1.SignOff

CROSS-REFERENCE

See also MAPIMessages, MAPISession, and SignOn.

SignOn

Method

The SignOn method starts a message session with a MAPISession control.

Objects with a SignOn Method

MAPISession

Syntax

MAPISession.SignOn

- *MAPISession* — A reference to a MAPISession control.

Example

The following line signs the user on to a message session. The mpsMAPISession1 object is a MAPISession control that the programmer added to the form at design time.

mpsMAPISession1.SignOn

CROSS-REFERENCE
See also MAPIMessages, MAPISession, and SignOff.

Silent

Property

The Silent property represents whether a Multimedia MCI control will play sound or be silent.

Objects with a Silent Property

Multimedia MCI

Syntax

Multimedia.Silent = *value1*

or

value2 = *Multimedia*.Silent

- *Multimedia* — A reference to a Multimedia MCI control.
- *value1* — The value True or False.
- *value2* — The variable that will receive the property's current setting.

Example

The following lines show how to get and set a Multimedia control's Silent property. The mciMMControl1 object is a Multimedia MCI control that the programmer added to the form at design time.

```
Dim quiet As Boolean
quiet = mciMMControl1.Silent
mciMMControl1.Silent = True
```

CROSS-REFERENCE
See also Multimedia MCI.

SimpleText

Property

The `SimpleText` property represents the text displayed in a StatusBar control whose `Style` property is set to `sbrSimple`.

Objects with a SimpleText Property

StatusBar

Syntax

```
StatusBar.SimpleText = value1
```

or

```
value2 = StatusBar.SimpleText
```

- *StatusBar*—A reference to a StatusBar control.
- *value1* — The text to display in the StatusBar control.
- *value2* — The variable that will receive the property's current setting.

Example

The following lines show how to get and set a StatusBar control's `SimpleText` property.

```
Dim txt As String
staStatusBar1.Style = sbrSimple
txt = staStatusBar1.SimpleText
staStatusBar1.SimpleText = "This is a test"
```

 CROSS-REFERENCE
See also StatusBar and Style (StatusBar).

Sin

Function

The `Sin` function calculates the sine of an angle.

Syntax

```
value = Sin(angle)
```

- *angle* — The angle in radians.
- *value* — The variable that will receive the sine of the angle.

Example

The following lines calculate the sine of an angle that measures 2.3 radians.

```
Dim result As Double
result = Sin(2.3)
```

 CROSS-REFERENCE
See also Atn, Cos, and Tan.

SingleSel

Property

The SingleSel property represents whether a TreeView control expands selected Node objects.

Objects with a SingleSel Property

TreeView

Syntax

```
TreeView.SingleSel = value1
```

or

```
value2 = TreeView.SingleSel
```

- *TreeView* — A reference to a TreeView control.
- *value1* — The value True (selected Node objects expand) or False (selected Node objects do not expand). The default is False.
- *value2* — The variable that will receive the property's current setting.

Example

The following lines show how to get and set a TreeView control's `SingleSel` property. The `treTreeView1` object is a TreeView control that the programmer added to the form at design time.

```
Dim selExpand As Boolean
selExpand = treTreeView1.SingleSel
treTreeView1.SingleSel = True
```

CROSS-REFERENCE
See also TreeView.

Size

Method

The `Size` method resizes a UserControl control.

Objects with a Size Method

UserControl

Syntax

`UserControl.Size width, height`

- *UserControl*—A reference to a UserControl control.
- *height*—The control's new height in twips.
- *width*—The control's new width in twips.

Example

The following line resizes a UserControl control.

`UserControl1.Resize 500, 500`

CROSS-REFERENCE
See also Height, UserControl, and Width.

Size—File and Folder

Property

The Size property represents the size of a file or the total size of all files and subfolders in a folder.

Syntax

```
value = object.Size
```

- *object* — A reference to a File or Folder object.
- *value* — The variable that will receive the file or folder's size in bytes.

Example

The following lines show how to get the size of a file using the Size property.

```
Dim fileSystem As Object
Dim file As Object
Dim fileSize As Long
Set fileSystem = _
    CreateObject("Scripting.FileSystemObject")
Set file = fileSystem.GetFile("c:\MyFile.dat")
fileSize = file.Size
MsgBox fileSize
```

 CROSS-REFERENCE
See also File and Folder.

Size—Font

Property

The Size property represents the size of a font associated with a Font object.

Syntax

```
Font.Size = value1
```

or

```
value2 = Font.Size
```

- *Font*—A reference to a Font object.
- *value1*—The font's new size in points.
- *value2*—The variable that will receive the font's size.

Example

The following program demonstrates the Font object's Size property. When you run the program, click the Change Font Size button. Each time you do, a line of text appears with a different font size. Figure S-26, for example, shows a 24-point font.

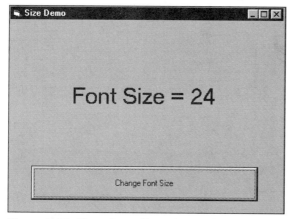

Figure S-26 Changing a Font object's Size property changes the size of the text that's displayed with that font.

```
VERSION 5.00
Begin VB.Form Form1
    Caption         =   "Size Demo"
    ClientHeight    =   4080
    ClientLeft      =   60
```

```
        ClientTop       =    345
        ClientWidth     =    5940
        LinkTopic       =    "Form1"
        ScaleHeight     =    272
        ScaleMode       =    3   'Pixel
        ScaleWidth      =    396
        StartUpPosition =    3   'Windows Default
        Begin VB.CommandButton btnChangeFontSize
            Caption     =    "Change Font Size"
            Height      =    735
            Left        =    480
            TabIndex    =    0
            Top         =    3120
            Width       =    4935
        End
    End
End
Attribute VB_Name = "Form1"
Attribute VB_GlobalNameSpace = False
Attribute VB_Creatable = False
Attribute VB_PredeclaredId = True
Attribute VB_Exposed = False

Dim fSize As Integer

Private Sub btnChangeFontSize_Click()
    fSize = fSize + 8
    If fSize > 32 Then fSize = 8
    Form1.Font.Size = fSize
    Form1.Cls
    Form1.CurrentX = 90
    Form1.CurrentY = 90
    Print "Font Size = " & fSize
End Sub
```

CROSS-REFERENCE
See also File and Folder.

SizeMode

Property

The SizeMode property determines how an OLE Container control displays its objects. This property can be set to one of the values shown in Table S-7.

Table S-7 Values for the SizeMode Property

Value	Description
vbOLESizeAutoSize	The OLE Container control resizes itself in order to accommodate the object's size.
vbOLESizeClip	The OLE Container control displays the object at the object's normal size, clipping the object if the object is too large for the container. This is the default setting.
vbOLESizeStretch	The OLE Container control enlarges the object to fit the control, not necessarily retaining the object's proportions.
vbOLESizeZoom	The OLE Container control enlarges the object to fit the control, retaining the object's proportions.

Objects with a SizeMode Property

OLE Container

Syntax

```
OLEContainer.SizeMode = value1
```

or

```
value2 = OLEContainer.SizeMode
```

- *OLEContainer* — A reference to an OLE Container control.
- *value1* — One of the values from Table S-7.
- *value2* — The variable that will receive the property's current setting.

Example

The following lines show how to get and set an OLE Container control's SizeMode property. The oleContainer1 object is an OLE Container control that the programmer added to the form at design time.

```
Dim mode As Integer
mode = oleContainer1.SizeMode
oleContainer1.SizeMode = vbOLESizeZoom
```

 CROSS-REFERENCE
See also OLE Container and Resize.

Skip

Method

The Skip method skips over a specified number of characters in a text file.

Objects with a Skip Method

TextStream

Syntax

```
TextStream.Skip numChars
```

- *TextStream* — A reference to a TextStream object.
- *numChars* — The number of characters to skip.

Example

The following lines create a FileSystemObject, open a TextStream object, skip the first five characters in the file, and then read and display the remaining characters in the first line of the file.

```
Dim fileSystem As Object
Dim textFile As Object
Dim txt As String
Set fileSystem = CreateObject("Scripting.FileSystemObject")
Set textFile = fileSystem.OpenTextFile("c:\MyFile.txt")
textFile.Skip 5
txt = textFile.ReadLine
MsgBox txt
```

 CROSS-REFERENCE
See also SkipLine and TextStream.

SkipLine

Method

The SkipLine method skips over a line of text in a text file.

Objects with a SkipLine Method
TextStream

Syntax

```
TextStream.SkipLine
```

- *TextStream* — A reference to a TextStream object.

Example

The following lines create a FileSystemObject, open a TextStream object, skip the first line in the file, and then read and display the next line of text in the file.

```
Dim fileSystem As Object
Dim textFile As Object
Dim txt As String
Set fileSystem = CreateObject("Scripting.FileSystemObject")
Set textFile = fileSystem.OpenTextFile("c:\MyFile.txt")
textFile.SkipLine
txt = textFile.ReadLine
MsgBox txt
```

CROSS-REFERENCE
See also Skip and TextStream Skip.

Slash (/)

Operator

The slash (/) operator performs normal division.

Syntax

```
result = exp1 / exp2
```

- *exp1* — Any valid numerical expression.
- *exp2* — Any valid numerical expression.
- *result* — The result of the division.

Example 1

After the following lines execute, `result` will contain the value 3.

```
Dim result
result = 12 / 4
```

Example 2

Here, after the following lines execute, `result` will also contain the value 2.4.

```
Dim result
result = 12 / 5
```

Example 3

Finally, after the following lines execute, `result` will contain the value 2.0875.

```
Dim result, num1, num2, num3
num1 = 12.5
num2 = 4.2
num3 = 7
result = (num1 + num2) / (num3 + 1)
```

CROSS-REFERENCE
See also Backslash (\).

Slider

Control

A Slider control enables a user to select a value from a range of values. The Slider control can also be programmed to select a range of values within the control's minimum and maximum values.

The Slider control is part of the Microsoft Windows Common Controls 6.0 component package and can be added to the Visual Basic toolbox from the Components dialog box. To display the Components dialog box, press Ctrl+T on your keyboard, or select the Project menu's Components command.

Properties

The Slider control has 38 properties, which are listed below. Because many Visual Basic controls have similar properties, the following list does not include the properties' descriptions. For information on using a property, look up the individual property's entry, provided alphabetically in this book.

```
BorderStyle
CausesValidation
Container
DragIcon
DragMode
Enabled
Height
HelpContextID
hWnd
Index
LargeChange
Left
Max
Min
MouseIcon
MousePointer
Name
Object
OLEDropMode
Orientation
Parent
SelectRange
SelLength
SelStart
SmallChange
TabIndex
TabStop
Tag
Text
TextPosition
TickFrequency
TickStyle
ToolTipText
Top
Value
```

```
Visible
WhatsThisHelpID
Width
```

Methods

The Slider control has nine methods, which are listed below. Because many Visual Basic controls have similar methods, the following list does not include the methods' descriptions. For information on using a method, look up the individual method's entry, provided alphabetically in this book.

```
ClearSel
Drag
GetNumTicks
Move
OLEDrag
Refresh
SetFocus
ShowWhatsThis
ZOrder
```

Events

The Slider control responds to 20 events, which are listed below. Because many Visual Basic controls respond to similar events, the following list does not include the events' descriptions. For information on using an event, look up the individual event's entry, provided alphabetically in this book.

```
Change
Click
DragDrop
DragOver
GotFocus
KeyDown
KeyPress
KeyUp
LostFocus
MouseDown
MouseMove
MouseUp
OLECompleteDrag
OLEDragDrop
OLEDragOver
OLEGiveFeedback
```

```
OLESetData
OLEStartDrag
Scroll
Validate
```

The Slider control's most commonly used event is Change, which the control generates when the user changes the slider's setting. A program responds to the Change event in the Change event procedure. For example, a slider called sldSlider1 will have a Change event procedure called sldSlider1_Change, which is where the program should handle the event, as shown in the following lines:

```
Private Sub sldSlider1_Change()
    ' Handle the Change event here.
End Sub
```

SLN

Function

The SLN function calculates an asset's straight-line depreciation.

Syntax

```
value = SLN(cost, finalValue, lifetime)
```

- *cost* — The asset's original cost.
- *finalValue* — The asset's value at the end of its lifetime.
- *Lifetime* — The asset's lifetime.
- *value* — The variable that will receive the depreciation for a period.

Example

The following program demonstrates how to use the SLN function. When you run the program, enter the following values:

- Enter the cost of the asset into the Asset cost box.
- Enter the ending value of the asset into the Ending Value box.
- Enter the lifetime of the object in years into the Lifetime in Years box.

After entering the required values, click the Calculate button to calculate and view the amount of depreciation per year. Figure S-27, for example, shows the depreciation per year for a car that cost $15,000 to purchase and will be worth $4,000 after ten years.

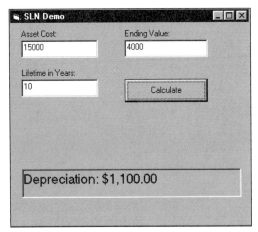

Figure S-27 The SLN function calculates depreciation per period.

```
VERSION 5.00
Begin VB.Form Form1
   Caption         =   "SLN Demo"
   ClientHeight    =   4305
   ClientLeft      =   165
   ClientTop       =   450
   ClientWidth     =   5235
   LinkTopic       =   "Form1"
   ScaleHeight     =   4305
   ScaleWidth      =   5235
   StartUpPosition =   3   'Windows Default
   Begin VB.CommandButton btnCalculate
      Caption      =   "Calculate"
      Height       =   495
      Left         =   2520
      TabIndex     =   6
      Top          =   1200
      Width        =   1815
   End
   Begin VB.TextBox txtLifetime
      Height       =   375
      Left         =   240
```

```
      TabIndex       =    5
      Top            =    1200
      Width          =    1695
   End
   Begin VB.TextBox txtEndingValue
      Height         =    375
      Left           =    2520
      TabIndex       =    3
      Top            =    360
      Width          =    1815
   End
   Begin VB.TextBox txtCost
      Height         =    375
      Left           =    240
      TabIndex       =    1
      Top            =    360
      Width          =    1695
   End
   Begin VB.Label lblDepreciation
      BorderStyle    =    1    'Fixed Single
      Caption        =    "Depreciation:"
      BeginProperty Font
         Name        =    "MS Sans Serif"
         Size        =    13.5
         Charset     =    0
         Weight      =    400
         Underline   =    0    'False
         Italic      =    0    'False
         Strikethrough =  0    'False
      EndProperty
      Height         =    615
      Left           =    240
      TabIndex       =    7
      Top            =    3120
      Width          =    4815
   End
   Begin VB.Label Label3
      Caption        =    "Lifetime in Years:"
      Height         =    255
      Left           =    240
      TabIndex       =    4
      Top            =    960
      Width          =    1575
   End
```

```
            Begin VB.Label Label2
               Caption        =    "Ending Value:"
               Height         =    255
               Left           =    2520
               TabIndex       =    2
               Top            =    120
               Width          =    1575
            End
            Begin VB.Label Label1
               Caption        =    "Asset Cost:"
               Height         =    255
               Left           =    240
               TabIndex       =    0
               Top            =    120
               Width          =    1695
            End
         End
Attribute VB_Name = "Form1"
Attribute VB_GlobalNameSpace = False
Attribute VB_Creatable = False
Attribute VB_PredeclaredId = True
Attribute VB_Exposed = False

Private Sub btnCalculate_Click()
    Dim cost As Double
    Dim endValue As Double
    Dim lifetime As Double
    Dim depreciation As Double
    Dim strResult As String

    On Error GoTo ErrorHandler

    cost = txtCost.Text
    endValue = txtEndingValue.Text
    lifetime = txtLifetime.Text

    depreciation = SLN(cost, endValue, lifetime)
    strResult = "$" & Format(depreciation, "###,###,##0.00")
    lblDepreciation.Caption = "Depreciation: " & strResult
    Exit Sub

ErrorHandler:
    MsgBox "An error occurred.", vbExclamation
End Sub
```

SmallChange — HScrollBar and VScrollBar

Property

The SmallChange property represents how far a scroll bar scrolls when the user clicks the control's arrow buttons. If the program doesn't set this property, the property defaults to 1.

Syntax

```
Scroll.SmallChange = value1
```

or

```
value2 = Scroll.SmallChange
```

- *Scroll* — A reference to an HScrollBar or VScrollBar control.
- *value1* — The amount the scroll bar should change.
- *value2* — The variable that will receive the property's current setting.

Example

In this example, the program sets an HScrollBar control to scroll 10 units each time the user clicks the scroll bar's arrow buttons. The hsbHScroll1 object is an HScrollBar control that the programmer added to the application's form at design time.

```
hsbHScroll1.SmallChange = 10
```

 CROSS-REFERENCE
See also Change, HScrollBar, LargeChange, Max, Min, Value, and VScrollBar.

SmallChange — Slider

Property

The SmallChange property represents how many ticks the slider moves when the user presses the left or right arrows on the keyboard. If the program does not set this property, the property defaults to 1.

Syntax

```
Slider.SmallChange = value1
```

or

```
value2 = Slider.SmallChange
```

- *Slider*—A reference to a Slider control.
- *value1*—The amount the slider should change.
- *value2*—The variable that will receive the property's current setting.

Example

In this example, the program sets a Slider control to change five ticks each time the user presses the left or right arrow keys on the keyboard. The sldSlider1 object is a Slider control that the programmer added to the application's form at design time.

```
sldSlider1.SmallChange = 5
```

CROSS-REFERENCE
See also LargeChange, Max, Min, Slider, and Value.

SmallIcon

Property

The SmallIcon property holds a reference to the small icon that Visual Basic displays next to a ListView control's ListItem object. This small icon appears when the ListView control is in small-icon view.

Objects with a SmallIcon Property

ListItem

Syntax

```
ListItem.SmallIcon = value1
```

or

```
value2 = ListItem.SmallIcon
```

- *ListItem* — A reference to a ListItem object.
- *value1* — A key or index to an image in an ImageList control.
- *value2* — The variable that will receive the icon's key or index.

Example

The following program demonstrates the `Icon` and `SmallIcon` properties in a ListView control. When you run the program, you see the window shown in Figure S-28. At this point, the control is in its small icon view. Click the Toggle View button to switch the control to its icon view, as shown in Figure S-29.

Figure S-28 This ListView control is set to small icon view.

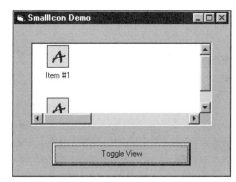

Figure S-29 This ListView control is set to icon view.

```
VERSION 5.00
Object = "{6B7E6392-850A-101B-AFC0-4210102A8DA7} _
    #2.0#0"; "MSCOMCTL.OCX"
Begin VB.Form frmForm1
    Caption         =   "SmallIcon Demo"
```

```
ClientHeight    =    3195
ClientLeft      =    60
ClientTop       =    345
ClientWidth     =    4680
LinkTopic       =    "Form1"
ScaleHeight     =    3195
ScaleWidth      =    4680
StartUpPosition =    3  'Windows Default
Begin MSComctlLib.ImageList ilsImageList2
   Left         =    4080
   Top          =    2520
   _ExtentX     =    1005
   _ExtentY     =    1005
   BackColor    =    -2147483643
   MaskColor    =    12632256
   _Version     =    393216
End
Begin MSComctlLib.ImageList ilsImageList1
   Left         =    120
   Top          =    2520
   _ExtentX     =    1005
   _ExtentY     =    1005
   BackColor    =    -2147483643
   MaskColor    =    12632256
   _Version     =    393216
End
Begin VB.CommandButton btnToggleView
   Caption      =    "Toggle View"
   Height       =    495
   Left         =    840
   TabIndex     =    1
   Top          =    2520
   Width        =    3015
End
Begin MSComctlLib.ListView lvwListView1
   Height       =    1935
   Left         =    480
   TabIndex     =    0
   Top          =    360
   Width        =    3735
   _ExtentX     =    6588
   _ExtentY     =    3413
   LabelWrap    =    -1  'True
```

```
        HideSelection    =    -1   'True
        _Version         =    393217
        ForeColor        =    -2147483640
        BackColor        =    -2147483643
        BorderStyle      =    1
        Appearance       =    1
        NumItems         =    0
    End
End
Attribute VB_Name = "frmForm1"
Attribute VB_GlobalNameSpace = False
Attribute VB_Creatable = False
Attribute VB_PredeclaredId = True
Attribute VB_Exposed = False

Private Sub btnToggleView_Click()
    If lvwListView1.View = lvwIcon Then
        lvwListView1.View = lvwSmallIcon
    Else
        lvwListView1.View = lvwIcon
    End If
End Sub

Private Sub Form_Load()
    Dim x As Integer

    ilsImageList1.ListImages.Add , , LoadPicture("icon1.ico")
    lvwListView1.Icons = ilsImageList1
    ilsImageList2.ListImages.Add , , LoadPicture("icon2.ico")
    lvwListView1.SmallIcons = ilsImageList2
    lvwListView1.View = lvwSmallIcon

    Set Item = lvwListView1.ListItems.Add(, , "Item #1")
    Set Item = lvwListView1.ListItems.Add(, , "Item #2")
    Set Item = lvwListView1.ListItems.Add(, , "Item #3")
    Set Item = lvwListView1.ListItems.Add(, , "Item #4")
    Set Item = lvwListView1.ListItems.Add(, , "Item #5")

    For x = 1 To 5
        lvwListView1.ListItems(x).Icon = 1
        lvwListView1.ListItems(x).SmallIcon = 1
    Next x
End Sub
```

CROSS-REFERENCE
See also Icon, Icons, ListItem, ListView, and SmallIcons.

SmallIcons

Property

The SmallIcons property represents the ImageList control that contains the small images to be displayed with items in a ListView control. These images are displayed when the ListView control is in its small-icon view.

Objects with a SmallIcons Property

ListView

Syntax

```
ListView.SmallIcons = value1
```

or

```
value2 = ListView.SmallIcons
```

- *ListView* — A reference to a ListView control.
- *value1* — A reference to an ImageList control.
- *value2* — The variable that will receive a reference to the ImageList control.

Example

The following lines initialize an ImageList control with a single image and then set a ListView control's SmallIcons property to the ImageList. The ilsImageList1 and lvwListView1 objects are ImageList and ListView controls that the programmer added to the application's form at design time.

```
ilsImageList1.ListImages.Add , , LoadPicture("reddot.ico")
lvwListView1.SmallIcons = ilsImageList1
```

CROSS-REFERENCE
See also Icon, Icons, ListItem, ListView, and SmallIcon.

Sorted — ListBox and ComboBox

Property

The Sorted property represents whether a control displays its items in sorted order. This property is read-only at runtime, so it must be set in the control's Properties window at design time.

Syntax

```
object.Sorted = value1
```

or

```
value2 = object.Sorted
```

- *object* — A reference to a ListBox or ComboBox control.
- *value1* — The value True or False.
- *value2* — The variable that will receive the property's current setting.

Example

The following program demonstrates a ListBox control with its Sorted property set to True. When you run the program, type an item into the text box and click the Add Above Item button. The program adds the item to the list box. Continue adding items and notice how the ListBox control automatically alphabetizes the items as they are added. Figure S-30 shows the program after the user has entered several items.

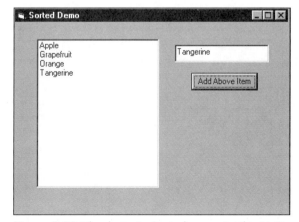

Figure S-30 Thanks to its Sorted property, this ListBox control automatically sorts new items.

```
VERSION 5.00
Begin VB.Form Form1
   Caption          =   "Sorted Demo"
   ClientHeight     =   4080
   ClientLeft       =   60
   ClientTop        =   345
   ClientWidth      =   5940
   LinkTopic        =   "Form1"
   ScaleHeight      =   272
   ScaleMode        =   3  'Pixel
   ScaleWidth       =   396
   StartUpPosition =    3  'Windows Default
   Begin VB.CommandButton btnAddItem
      Caption       =   "Add Above Item"
      Height        =   375
      Left          =   3840
      TabIndex      =   2
      Top           =   1080
      Width         =   1455
   End
   Begin VB.TextBox txtAddItem
      Height        =   375
      Left          =   3480
      TabIndex      =   1
      Top           =   480
      Width         =   2055
   End
   Begin VB.ListBox lstList1
      Height        =   3180
      ItemData      =   "Form1.frx":0000
      Left          =   480
      List          =   "Form1.frx":0002
      Sorted        =   -1   'True
      TabIndex      =   0
      Top           =   360
      Width         =   2655
   End
End
Attribute VB_Name = "Form1"
Attribute VB_GlobalNameSpace = False
Attribute VB_Creatable = False
Attribute VB_PredeclaredId = True
Attribute VB_Exposed = False
```

```
Private Sub btnAddItem_Click()
    lstList1.AddItem txtAddItem.Text
    txtAddItem.SetFocus
End Sub
```

CROSS-REFERENCE
See also ComboBox and ListBox.

Sorted — ListView

Property

The Sorted property represents whether the control sorts its items according to the settings of the SortOrder and SortKey properties.

Syntax

```
ListView.Sorted = value1
```

or

```
value2 = ListView.Sorted
```

- *ListView* — A reference to a ListView control.
- *value1* — The value True or False.
- *value2* — The variable that will receive the property's current setting.

Example

The following lines show how to get and set the value of a ListView control's Sorted property. The lvwListView1 object is a ListView control that the programmer added to the form at design time.

```
Dim sort As Boolean
sort = lvwListView1.Sorted
lvwListView1.SortOrder = lvwAscending
lvwListView1.SortKey = 0
lvwListView1.Sorted = True
```

CROSS-REFERENCE
See also ListView, SortKey, and SortOrder.

Sorted — Node

Property

The Sorted property represents whether a TreeView control alphabetically sorts sibling Node objects.

Syntax

```
Node.Sorted = value1
```

or

```
value2 = Node.Sorted
```

- *Node* — A reference to a Node object.
- *value1* — The value True or False.
- *value2* — The variable that will receive the property's current setting.

Example

The following lines show how to get and set the value of a Node object's Sorted property. The treTreeView1 object is a TreeView control that the programmer added to the form at design time.

```
Dim sort As Boolean
sort = treTreeView1.Nodes(2).Sorted
treTreeView1.Nodes(2).Sorted = True
```

 CROSS-REFERENCE
See also Sorted (TreeView) and TreeView.

Sorted — TreeView

Property

The Sorted property represents whether a TreeView control alphabetically sorts its root-level nodes.

Syntax

```
TreeView.Sorted = value1
```

or

```
value2 = TreeView.Sorted
```

- *TreeView* — A reference to a TreeView control.
- *value1* — The value `True` or `False`.
- *value2* — The variable that will receive the property's current setting.

Example

The following lines show how to get and set the value of a TreeView control's `Sorted` property. The `treTreeView1` object is a TreeView control that the programmer added to the form at design time.

```
Dim sort As Boolean
sort = treTreeView1.Sorted
treTreeView1.Sorted = True
```

 CROSS-REFERENCE
See also TreeView and Sorted (Node).

SortKey

Property

The `SortKey` property represents whether a control sorts its items by the item text or by the subitems with the specified index.

Objects with a SortKey Property

ListView

Syntax

`ListView.SortKey = value1`

or

`value2 = ListView.SortKey`

- *ListView* — A reference to a ListView control.
- *value1* — The value 0 (default) if the control is to sort on item text, or the index of the subitem collection to sort.
- *value2* — The variable that will receive the property's current setting.

Example 1

The following lines set up a ListView control to display several columns in report view. Because the code sets the Sorted property to True and the SortKey property to 0, the ListItem objects will be in the order Item #1, Item #2, and Item #3 (see Figure S-31), regardless of the fact that they are added to the control in reverse order. In this example, the ImageList1 and lvwListView1 objects are an ImageList and ListView control that the programmer added to the form at design time.

```
Dim item As ListItem
ImageList1.ListImages.Add , , LoadPicture("c:\icon2.ico")
lvwListView1.Icons = ImageList1
lvwListView1.View = lvwReport
lvwListView1.Sorted = True
lvwListView1.SortKey = 0
lvwListView1.ColumnHeaders.Add , , "Column #1"
lvwListView1.ColumnHeaders.Add , , "Column #2"
lvwListView1.ColumnHeaders.Add , , "Column #3"
Set item = lvwListView1.ListItems.Add(, , "Item #3")
item.SubItems(1) = "SubItem #1"
item.SubItems(2) = "SubItem #2"
Set item = lvwListView1.ListItems.Add(, , "Item #2")
item.SubItems(1) = "SubItem #1"
item.SubItems(2) = "SubItem #2"
Set item = lvwListView1.ListItems.Add(, , "Item #1")
item.SubItems(1) = "SubItem #1"
item.SubItems(2) = "SubItem #2"
```

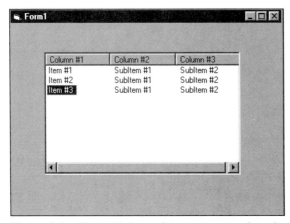

Figure S-31 These ListItem objects are sorted on the item text, which is displayed in the first column.

Example 2

In this example, the following lines also set up a ListView control to display several columns in report view. But now, because the code sets the Sorted property to True and the SortKey property to 1, the ListItem objects will be sorted according to the subitems in the second column, as shown in Figure S-32. Notice in the figure how the first column is out of order, regardless of the fact that they were added to the control in order. In this example, the ImageList1 and lvwListView1 objects are an ImageList and ListView control that the programmer added to the form at design time.

```
Dim item As ListItem
ImageList1.ListImages.Add , , LoadPicture("c:\icon2.ico")
lvwListView1.Icons = ImageList1
lvwListView1.View = lvwReport
lvwListView1.Sorted = True
lvwListView1.ColumnHeaders.Add , , "Column #1"
lvwListView1.ColumnHeaders.Add , , "Column #2"
lvwListView1.ColumnHeaders.Add , , "Column #3"
Set item = lvwListView1.ListItems.Add(, , "Item #1")
item.SubItems(1) = "SubItem #Z"
item.SubItems(2) = "SubItem #2"
Set item = lvwListView1.ListItems.Add(, , "Item #2")
item.SubItems(1) = "SubItem #A"
item.SubItems(2) = "SubItem #2"
Set item = lvwListView1.ListItems.Add(, , "Item #3")
item.SubItems(1) = "SubItem #F"
item.SubItems(2) = "SubItem #2"
lvwListView1.SortKey = 1
```

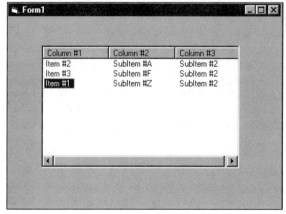

Figure S-32 These ListItem objects are sorted based on the subitems in the second column.

CROSS-REFERENCE
See also ListView, Sorted (ListView), and SortOrder.

SortOrder

Property

The SortOrder property represents whether a control sorts its items in ascending or descending order.

Objects with a SortOrder Property

ListView

Syntax

ListView.SortOrder = value1

or

value2 = ListView.SortOrder

- *ListView* — A reference to a ListView control.
- *value1* — The value lvwAscending or lvwDescending.
- *value2* — The variable that will receive the property's current setting.

Example

The following lines set up a ListView control to display several columns in report view. Because the code sets the Sorted property to True, the SortKey property to 0, and the SortOrder property to lvwAscending, the ListItem objects will be in the order Item #1, Item #2, Item #3, and Item #4 (see Figure S-33). The control sorts them this way, regardless of the fact that the items are added to the control out of order. If the SortOrder key were changed to lvwDescending, the control would look like Figure S-34. In this example, the ImageList1 and lvwListView1 objects are an ImageList and ListView control that the programmer added to the form at design time.

```
Dim item As ListItem
ImageList1.ListImages.Add , , LoadPicture("c:\icon2.ico")
lvwListView1.Icons = ImageList1
lvwListView1.View = lvwReport
lvwListView1.Sorted = True
lvwListView1.SortOrder = lvwAscending
lvwListView1.SortKey = 0
lvwListView1.ColumnHeaders.Add , , "Column #1"
lvwListView1.ColumnHeaders.Add , , "Column #2"
lvwListView1.ColumnHeaders.Add , , "Column #3"
Set item = lvwListView1.ListItems.Add(, , "Item #2")
item.SubItems(1) = "SubItem #1"
item.SubItems(2) = "SubItem #2"
Set item = lvwListView1.ListItems.Add(, , "Item #3")
item.SubItems(1) = "SubItem #1"
item.SubItems(2) = "SubItem #2"
Set item = lvwListView1.ListItems.Add(, , "Item #4")
item.SubItems(1) = "SubItem #1"
item.SubItems(2) = "SubItem #2"
Set item = lvwListView1.ListItems.Add(, , "Item #1")
item.SubItems(1) = "SubItem #1"
item.SubItems(2) = "SubItem #2"
```

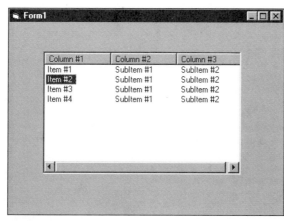

Figure S-33 These ListItem objects are sorted in ascending order.

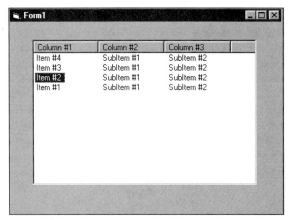

Figure S-34 These ListItem objects are sorted in descending order.

Source

Property

The Source property represents the name of the object that generated an error.

Objects with a Source Property

Err

Syntax

```
Err.Source = value1
```

or

```
value2 = Err.Source
```

- *Err*—A reference to the Err object.
- *value1*—A string containing the name of the error-generating object.
- *value2*—The variable that will receive the name string.

Example

The following lines show how to get and set the Err object's Source property. The Err object is a global Visual Basic object that you don't need to create in your programs.

```
Dim objName As String
objName = Err.Source
Err.Source = "MyApplication"
```

CROSS-REFERENCE
See also Err.

SourceDoc

Property

The SourceDoc property represents the file name used to link or embed an object in an OLE Container control. However, this property is now obsolete. You should use the CreateEmbed and CreateLink methods—which don't require you to set the SourceDoc property—to embed or link objects.

Objects with a SourceDoc Property

OLE Container

Syntax

```
OLEContainer.SourceDoc = value1
```

or

```
value2 = OLEContainer.SourceDoc
```

- *OLEContainer*—A reference to an OLE Container control.
- *value1*—A string that contains the document file name.
- *value2*—The variable that will receive the current file name.

Example

The following lines show how to get and set an OLE Container control's SourceDoc property. The oleContainer1 object is an OLE Container control that the programmer added to the form at design time.

```
Dim docName As String
docName = oleContainer1.SourceDoc
oleContainer1.SourceDoc = "c:\MyDocuments\MyReport.doc"
```

CROSS-REFERENCE
See also Action, CreateEmbed, CreateLink, OLE Container, and SourceItem.

SourceItem

Property

The `SourceItem` property represents the data to include when linking or embedding an object in an OLE Container control.

Objects with a SourceItem Property

OLE Container

Syntax

```
OLEContainer.SourceItem = value1
```

or

```
value2 = OLEContainer.SourceItem
```

- *OLEContainer*—A reference to an OLE Container control.
- *value1*—A string that contains the string describing the data.
- *value2*—The variable that will receive the data string.

Example

The following lines show how to get and set an OLE Container control's `SourceItem` property. The `oleContainer1` object is an OLE Container control that the programmer added to the form at design time.

```
Dim strData As String
strData = oleContainer1.SourceItem
oleContainer1.SourceItem = "A3:C6"
```

 CROSS-REFERENCE
See also Action, CreateEmbed, CreateLink, OLE Container, and SourceDoc.

Space

Function

The `Space` function returns the specified number of space characters.

Syntax

```
value = Space(numSpaces)
```

- *numSpaces*—The number of spaces to return.
- *value*—The variable that will receive the string containing the spaces.

Example 1

After the following lines execute, the variable spcs will contain a string of five space characters.

```
Dim spcs As String
spcs = Space(5)
```

Example 2

The following lines display a message box that shows the strings "0123456789" and "ABCDEFGHIJ" separated by five spaces, as shown in Figure S-35.

```
Dim txt1 As String
Dim txt2 As String
txt1 = "0123456789"
txt2 = "ABCDEFGHIJ"
MsgBox txt1 & Space(5) & txt2, vbInformation
```

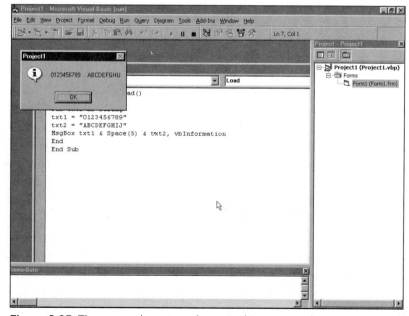

Figure S-35 The space characters shown in this message box were created by the Space function.

CROSS-REFERENCE
See also Spc and String (function).

Span

Method

The Span method selects text in a RichTextBox control based on a specified set of characters.

Objects with a Span Method

RichTextBox

Syntax

`RichTextBox.Span chars, searchForward, notInclude`

- *notInclude* (*) — A Boolean value that determines whether the specified characters are the characters to be selected (False) or the characters at which selection should stop (True). The default value is False.
- *RichTextBox* — A reference to a RichTextBox control.
- *searchForward* (*) — A Boolean value that determines whether the control should search forward (True) from the text cursor or search backward (False). The default is True.

(*) = Optional

Example

The following program demonstrates the Span method. When you run the program, type a character set into the text box, select the desired Span options with the check boxes, and then click the Call Span button to see the results in the RichTextBox control. For example, type **S** into the text box, and click the Call Span button. (Leave the RichTextBox's text cursor at the beginning of the text, and leave the Forward and Not Include options selected.) The control then selects all characters up to the first instance of the character "S," as shown in Figure S-36. On the other hand, if you type " adhisT" (the first character is a space) into the text box, turn off the Not Include option, and click the Call Span button, the control will select the text "This is a d," as shown in Figure S-37.

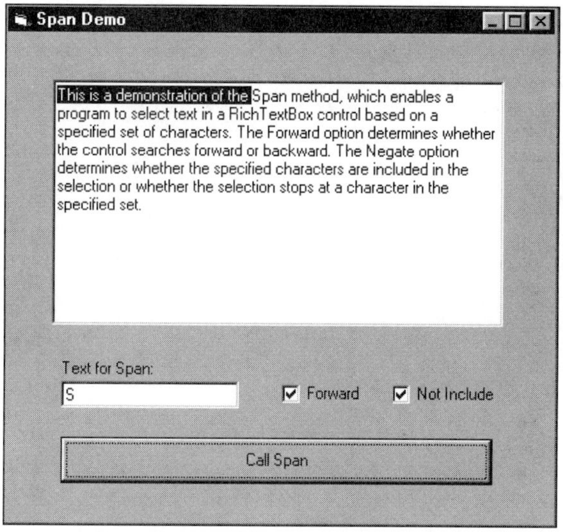

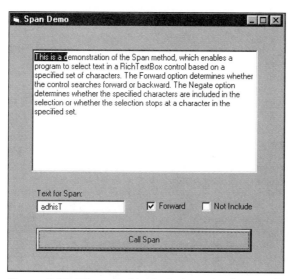

Figure S-36 When the Not Include option is selected, Span stops the text selection at the first occurrence of a character in the specified character set.

Figure S-37 When the Not Include option is not selected, Span stops the text selection at the first occurrence of a character that's not in the specified character set.

```
VERSION 5.00
Object = "{3B7C8863-D78F-101B-B9B5-04021C009402} _
    #1.2#0"; "RICHTX32.OCX"
Begin VB.Form Form1
    Caption         =   "Span Demo"
    ClientHeight    =   5205
    ClientLeft      =   60
    ClientTop       =   345
    ClientWidth     =   5940
    LinkTopic       =   "Form1"
    ScaleHeight     =   347
    ScaleMode       =   3   'Pixel
    ScaleWidth      =   396
    StartUpPosition =   3   'Windows Default
    Begin VB.CheckBox chkForward
        Caption         =   "Forward"
        Height          =   255
        Left            =   3000
        TabIndex        =   5
        Top             =   3720
        Width           =   1215
    End
    Begin VB.CommandButton btnCallSpan
        Caption         =   "Call Span"
        Height          =   495
        Left            =   600
        TabIndex        =   4
        Top             =   4320
        Width           =   4695
    End
    Begin VB.CheckBox chkNotInclude
        Caption         =   "Not Include"
        Height          =   255
        Left            =   4200
        TabIndex        =   3
        Top             =   3720
        Width           =   1215
    End
    Begin VB.TextBox txtSpanText
        Height          =   285
        Left            =   600
```

```
        TabIndex        =    2
        Top             =    3720
        Width           =    1935
     End
     Begin RichTextLib.RichTextBox rtfRichTextBox1
        Height          =    2655
        Left            =    480
        TabIndex        =    0
        Top             =    480
        Width           =    4935
        _ExtentX        =    8705
        _ExtentY        =    4683
        _Version        =    393217
        Enabled         =    -1  'True
        TextRTF         =    $"Form1.frx":0000
     End
     Begin VB.Label Label1
        Caption         =    "Text for Span:"
        Height          =    255
        Left            =    600
        TabIndex        =    1
        Top             =    3480
        Width           =    2055
     End
  End
End
Attribute VB_Name = "Form1"
Attribute VB_GlobalNameSpace = False
Attribute VB_Creatable = False
Attribute VB_PredeclaredId = True
Attribute VB_Exposed = False

Private Sub btnCallSpan_Click()
    Dim spanText As String
    Dim notInclude As Boolean
    Dim forward As Boolean
    spanText = txtSpanText.Text
    notInclude = (chkNotInclude.Value = vbChecked)
    forward = (chkForward.Value = vbChecked)
    rtfRichTextBox1.Span spanText, forward, notInclude
End Sub
```

r
s
t

```
Private Sub Form_Load()
    Dim msg As String
    msg = "This is a demonstration of the Span "
    msg = msg & "method, which enables a program to "
    msg = msg & "select text in a RichTextBox control "
    msg = msg & "based on a specified set of characters. "
    msg = msg & "The Forward option determines whether "
    msg = msg & "the control searches forward or backward. "
    msg = msg & "The Negate option determines whether "
    msg = msg & "the specified characters are included "
    msg = msg & "in the selection or whether the selection "
    msg = msg & "stops at a character in the specified set."
    rtfRichTextBox1.Text = msg
    rtfRichTextBox1.HideSelection = False
    chkForward.Value = vbChecked
    chkNotInclude.Value = vbChecked
End Sub
```

CROSS-REFERENCE
See also RichTextBox.

Spc

Function

The Spc function inserts space characters into the output generated by a Print or Print # statement.

Syntax

Spc(*numSpaces*)

■ *numSpaces*—The number of space characters to insert.

Example 1

The following lines print in a form the strings "0123456789" and "ABCDE-FGHIJ" separated by 10 spaces, as shown in Figure S-38.

```
frmForm1.CurrentX = 30
frmForm1.CurrentY = 50
frmForm1.FontSize = 14
frmForm1.Print "0123456789"; Spc(10); "ABCDEFGHIJ"
```

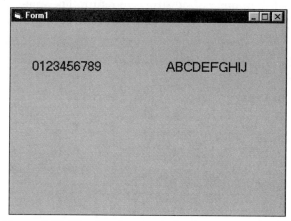

Figure S-38 The Spc function helps format text displayed in a form.

Example 2

The following lines output the strings "0123456789" and "ABCDEFGHIJ" separated by 10 spaces to a file called MyFile.txt.

```
Open "c:\MyFile.txt" For Output As #1
Print #1, "0123456789"; Spc(10); "ABCDEFGHIJ"
Close #1
```

CROSS-REFERENCE
See also Space and String (function).

Split

Function

The Split function returns a set of substrings based on a specified delimiter.

Syntax

```
value = Split(srcString, delimiter, num, type)
```

- *delimiter* (*) — The character that separates one substring from another. The default is a space character.
- *num* (*) — The number of substrings to return. The value –1 (which is the default) specifies that the function should return all substrings.
- *srcString* — The string from which to extract the substrings.
- *type* — The type of string comparison to use. Must be a value from Table S-8.
- *value* — The variable that will receive a reference to the resultant string array.

(*) = Optional

Table S-8 Values for the *type* Argument

Value	Description
vbBinaryCompare	Searches using a binary comparison.
vbDatabaseCompare	Searches based on data in a Microsoft Access database.
vbTextCompare	Searches using a text comparison
vbUseCompareOption	Searches based on the program's Option Compare statement.

Example

The following program demonstrates the Split function. When you run the program, notice that the Source String text box contains a string of words separated by commas, the Delimiter box contains a comma, and the Count box contains –1. If you click the Split String button without changing any of these entries, the program calls Split with the selected parameters and displays a message box containing the five substrings "one," "two," "three," "four," and "five," as shown in Figure S-39. You can experiment with the Split function by changing the values in the program's text boxes. For example, if you change the Count box to 2, the program displays the two substrings "one" and "two,three,four,five."

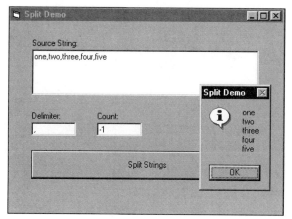

Figure S-39 The Split function can act as a tokenizer, separating individual elements from a text string.

```
VERSION 5.00
Begin VB.Form frmForm1
    Caption         =   "Split Demo"
    ClientHeight    =   4080
    ClientLeft      =   60
    ClientTop       =   345
    ClientWidth     =   5940
    LinkTopic       =   "Form1"
    ScaleHeight     =   272
    ScaleMode       =   3   'Pixel
    ScaleWidth      =   396
    StartUpPosition =   3   'Windows Default
    Begin VB.CommandButton btnSplit
        Caption     =   "Split Strings"
        Height      =   615
        Left        =   480
        TabIndex    =   6
        Top         =   2760
        Width       =   5055
    End
    Begin VB.TextBox txtCount
        Height      =   285
        Left        =   1920
        TabIndex    =   5
        Top         =   2160
        Width       =   975
    End
```

```
Begin VB.TextBox txtDelimiter
   Height          =    285
   Left            =    480
   TabIndex        =    3
   Top             =    2160
   Width           =    975
End
Begin VB.TextBox txtSrcString
   Height          =    975
   Left            =    480
   MultiLine       =    -1   'True
   TabIndex        =    1
   Top             =    600
   Width           =    4935
End
Begin VB.Label Label3
   Caption         =    "Count:"
   Height          =    255
   Left            =    1920
   TabIndex        =    4
   Top             =    1920
   Width           =    1335
End
Begin VB.Label Label2
   Caption         =    "Delimiter:"
   Height          =    255
   Left            =    480
   TabIndex        =    2
   Top             =    1920
   Width           =    1335
End
Begin VB.Label Label1
   Caption         =    "Source String:"
   Height          =    255
   Left            =    480
   TabIndex        =    0
   Top             =    360
   Width           =    1335
   End
End
Attribute VB_Name = "frmForm1"
Attribute VB_GlobalNameSpace = False
Attribute VB_Creatable = False
Attribute VB_PredeclaredId = True
```

```vb
Attribute VB_Exposed = False

Private Sub btnSplit_Click()
    Dim srcString As String
    Dim delimiter As String
    Dim count As Integer
    Dim strngs() As String
    Dim msg As String
    Dim x As Integer

    srcString = txtSrcString.Text
    delimiter = txtDelimiter.Text
    On Error GoTo CountError
    count = txtCount.Text
    On Error GoTo SplitError
    strngs = Split(srcString, delimiter, count)
    On Error GoTo 0
    msg = ""
    For x = 0 To UBound(strngs)
        msg = msg & strngs(x) & vbCrLf
    Next
    MsgBox msg, vbInformation, "Split Demo"

    Exit Sub

CountError:
    MsgBox "Enter a valid value into Count", _
        vbExclamation, "Split Demo"
    txtCount.SetFocus
    Exit Sub

SplitError:
    msg = "Be sure you've entered valid values"
    msg = msg & vbCrLf & "into the Source String and"
    msg = msg & vbCrLf & "Delimiter text boxes"
    MsgBox msg, vbExclamation, "Split Demo"
    txtSrcString.SetFocus
    Exit Sub
End Sub

Private Sub Form_Load()
    txtCount.Text = "-1"
    txtDelimiter.Text = ","
    txtSrcString = "one,two,three,four,five"
End Sub
```

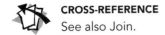 **CROSS-REFERENCE**
See also Join.

Sqr

Function

The Sqr function returns the square root of a number.

Syntax

```
value = Sqr(num)
```

- *num* — The number for which to calculate the square root.
- *value* — The variable that will receive the square root.

Example

The following lines calculate how many $100 payments are required in order to save $1,000 when no interest is applied to the account. After the following lines execute, result will contain the value 10.

```
Dim result As Double
result = Sqr(100)
```

StandardSize

Property

The StandardSize property represents the size of a PropertyPage object. You can set the StandardSize property in the PropertyPage object's Properties window.

Objects with a StandardSize Property

PropertyPage

Syntax

```
PropertyPage.StandardSize = value
```

- *PropertyPage*—A reference to a PropertyPage object.
- *value*—The value 0 (custom size, the default), 1 (small), or 2 (large).

CROSS-REFERENCE
See also PropertyPage.

Start

Property

The Start property represents the starting position of a Multimedia MCI control. The actual position depends upon the setting of the TimeFormat property. This property cannot be accessed at design time and is read-only at runtime.

Objects with a Start Property

Multimedia MCI

Syntax

```
value = Multimedia.Start
```

- *Multimedia*—A reference to a Multimedia MCI control.
- *value*—The variable that will receive the property's current setting.

Example

The following lines show how to get a Multimedia MCI control's starting position. In this example, the mciMMControl1 object is a Multimedia MCI control that the programmer added to the form at design time.

```
Dim startPos As Long
startPos = mciMMControl1.Start
```

CROSS-REFERENCE
See also Multimedia MCI.

StartLabelEdit

Method

The StartLabelEdit method begins the editing process on an item in a control. You usually use this method to initiate editing when the control's LabelEdit property is set to manual. However, the StartLabelEdit method also works fine when the LabelEdit property is set to automatic.

Objects with a StartLabelEdit Method

ListView

TreeView

Syntax

object.StartLabelEdit

- *object* — A reference to a ListView or TreeView control.

Example

The following line starts the editing process on the selected node in a TreeView control. In this example, the treTreeView1 object is a TreeView control that the programmer added to the form at design time.

treTreeView1.StartLabelEdit

 CROSS-REFERENCE
See also AfterLabelEdit, BeforeLabelEdit, and LabelEdit.

StartLogging

Method

The StartLogging method sets the attributes of an application's logging process.

Objects with a StartLogging Method

App

Syntax

```
App.StartLogging path, mode
```

- *App*— A reference to the App object.
- *mode*— The logging mode, which can be a value from Table S-9.
- *path*— The path name to the logging file.

Table S-9 Values for the *mode* Argument

Value	Description
vbLogAuto	Sends log messages to the log file set in the LogPath property or to Windows NT's event log.
vbLogOff	Turns logging off.
vbLogOverwrite	Starts a new log file each time the application runs.
vbLogThreadID	Adds the current thread ID to the log message.
vbLogToFile	Sends log messages to the file set by the LogPath property.
vbLogToNT	Sends log messages to Windows NT's event log.

Example

The following line sets the attributes for an application's logging process. The App object is a global Visual Basic object that you don't need to create in your programs.

```
App.StartLogging "c:\LogFile.txt", vbLogAuto
```

CROSS-REFERENCE
See also LogEvent, LogMode, and LogPath.

StartUpPosition

Property

The StartUpPosition property represents the position at which a form will first appear. This property is accessible only at design time, so must be set in the form's Properties window rather than in code. The possible settings are vbStartUpManual (no position specified), vbStartUpOwner (centered in the UserForm's owner item), vbStartUpScreen (centered on the screen), and vbStartUpWindowsDefault (Windows' default position).

Objects with a StartUpPosition Property
Form

MDIForm

CROSS-REFERENCE
See also Form and MDIForm.

Static

Keyword

The Static keyword is part of the Static statement and can also be used with function and procedure declarations. For example, the following lines define a function whose local variables retain their values as long as the program runs. Specifically, in this example, the variable var1 increments each time the MyFunc function is called. This results in MyFunc returning the value 1 on the first call, 2 on the second call, 3 on the third call, and so on.

```
Private Static Function MyFunc() As Integer
    Dim var1 As Integer
    var1 = var1 + 1
    MyFunc = var1
End Function
```

CROSS-REFERENCE
See also Function, Procedure, and Static (statement).

Static

Statement

The Static statement enables a program to declare variables whose values are retained as long as the program runs.

Syntax

```
Static name type
```

- *name* — The variable's name, which can include subscripts for declaring an array.
- *type* (*) — The keyword As followed by the variable type. The New keyword can also be used (i.e. As New *object*) to create a new object with which to associate the variable. If you leave off the type, the variable's data type defaults to Variant.

(*) = Optional

NOTE
You can define several variables with one Static statement by separating the declarations with commas.

Example

The following lines define a function that declares a static variable called var1, whose value is retained as long as the program runs. Specifically, in this example, the variable var1 increments each time the MyFunc function is called. This results in MyFunc returning the value 1 on the first call, 2 on the second call, 3 on the third call, and so on.

```
Private Function MyFunc() As Integer
    Static var1 As Integer
    var1 = var1 + 1
    MyFunc = var1
End Function
```

StatusBar

Control

A StatusBar control enables a program to display various types of messages in a bar at the bottom of the application's window. Programs often use a status bar to display status information such as the current date and time, as well as the status of the Caps Lock, Insert, and other keys. Figure S-40 shows a status bar in a window.

The StatusBar control is part of the Microsoft Windows Common Controls 6.0 component package and can be added to the Visual Basic toolbox from the Components dialog box, as shown in Figure S-41. To display the Components dialog box, press Ctrl+T on your keyboard, or select the Project menu's Components command.

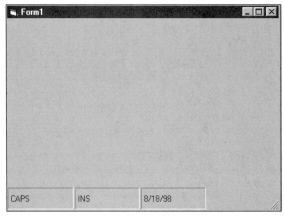

Figure S-40 A status bar control displays an application's status messages.

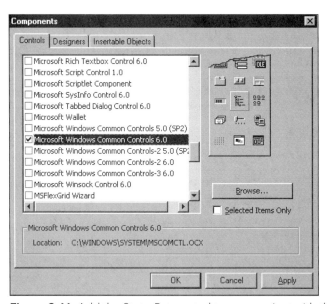

Figure S-41 Add the StatusBar control to your project with the Components dialog box.

Properties

The StatusBar control has 27 properties, which are listed below. Because many Visual Basic controls have similar properties, the following list does not include the properties' descriptions. For information on using a property, look up the individual property's entry, provided alphabetically in this book.

```
Align
Container
DragIcon
DragMode
Enabled
Font
Height
hWnd
Index
Left
MouseIcon
MousePointer
Name
Object
OLEDropMode
Panels
Parent
ShowTips
SimpleText
Style
TabIndex
Tag
ToolTipText
Top
Visible
WhatsThisHelpID
Width
```

Methods

The StatusBar control has six methods, which are listed below. Because many Visual Basic controls have similar methods, the following list does not include the methods' descriptions. For information on using a method, look up the individual method's entry, provided alphabetically in this book.

```
Drag
Move
OLEDrag
Refresh
ShowWhatsThis
ZOrder
```

r
s
t

Events

The StatusBar control responds to 15 events, which are listed below. Because many Visual Basic controls respond to similar events, the following list does not include the events' descriptions. For information on using an event, look up the individual event's entry, provided alphabetically in this book.

```
Click
DblClick
DragDrop
DragOver
MouseDown
MouseMove
MouseUp
OLECompleteDrag
OLEDragDrop
OLEDragOver
OLEGiveFeedback
OLESetData
OLEStartDrag
PanelClick
PanelDblClick
```

The StatusBar control's most commonly used event is `PanelDblClick`, which the control generates when the user double-clicks one of the control's panels. A program responds to the `PanelDblClick` event in the `PanelDblClick` event procedure. A status bar called `staStatusBar1` will have a `PanelDblClick` event procedure called `staStatusBar1_PanelDblClick`, which is where the program should handle the event, as shown in the following lines:

```
Private Sub staStatusBar1_PanelDblClick _
  (ByVal Panel As MSComctlLib.Panel)
    ' Handle the PanelDblClick event here.
End Sub
```

As you can see, the `PanelDblClick` event procedure receives one parameter, which is a reference to the panel that was double-clicked.

StatusUpdate

Event

Visual Basic sends a Multimedia MCI control a `StatusUpdate` event at intervals of time specified in the `UpdateInterval` property. This event enables a program to update the application's display as a multimedia is playing media.

This event might be used, for example, to update the track time for a CD player application.

Objects with a StatusUpdate Event

Multimedia MCI

Example

A program can respond to a StatusUpdate event by implementing the control's StatusUpdate event procedure. The following code segment shows how a Multimedia MCI control defines a StatusUpdate event procedure. In this example, the mciMMControl1 object is a Multimedia MCI control that the programmer added to the form at design time.

```
Private Sub mciMMControl1_StatusUpdate()
    ' Handle the StatusUpdate event here.
End Sub
```

 CROSS-REFERENCE

See also Multimedia MCI and UpdateInterval.

Step

Keyword

The Step keyword is part of the For/Next and For Each/Next statements, which enable a program to perform a loop a specified number of times. The Step portion of the statement determines the value by which the loop-control variable will be incremented. For example, the following For/Next loop increments the loop-control variable indx by 5 each time through the loop. In this case, a message box appears six times, displaying the values 0, 5, 10, 15, 20, and 25.

```
For indx = 0 To 25 Step 5
    MsgBox indx
Next indx
```

 CROSS-REFERENCE

See also For/Next and For Each.

Stop
Method

The Stop method stops the playback of an.avi file in an Animation control. A program can call the Stop method only for an animation sequence that was started with the Play method. If the animation sequence was displayed in autoplay mode, calling the Stop method generates an error.

Objects with a Stop Method

Animation

Syntax

```
Animation.Stop
```

- *Animation* — A reference to an Animation control.

Example

The following program demonstrates the Animation control's Stop method. When you run the program, you see the window shown in Figure S-42. Click the Load Animation button, and choose an.avi file from the dialog box that appears. (The file filecopy.avi is included with the program.) After loading an animation file, click the Play button to start the animation sequence, and click the Stop button to stop the animation sequence.

Figure S-42 Clicking the Stop button invokes the Stop method.

```
VERSION 5.00
Object = "{F9043C88-F6F2-101A-A3C9-08002B2F49FB} _
    #1.2#0"; "COMDLG32.OCX"
Object = "{86CF1D34-0C5F-11D2-A9FC-0000F8754DA1} _
    #2.0#0"; "MSCOMCT2.OCX"
Begin VB.Form frmForm1
    Caption         =   "Stop Demo"
    ClientHeight    =   3225
    ClientLeft      =   60
    ClientTop       =   345
    ClientWidth     =   4680
    LinkTopic       =   "Form1"
    ScaleHeight     =   3225
    ScaleWidth      =   4680
    StartUpPosition =   3  'Windows Default
    Begin MSComCtl2.Animation Animation1
        Height      =   975
        Left        =   360
        TabIndex    =   3
        Top         =   360
        Width       =   3975
        _ExtentX    =   7011
        _ExtentY    =   1720
        _Version    =   393216
        FullWidth   =   265
        FullHeight  =   65
    End
    Begin MSComDlg.CommonDialog dlgCommonDialog1
        Left        =   0
        Top         =   1800
        _ExtentX    =   847
        _ExtentY    =   847
        _Version    =   393216
    End
    Begin VB.CommandButton btnStop
        Caption     =   "Stop"
        Height      =   375
        Left        =   2520
        TabIndex    =   2
        Top         =   2520
        Width       =   1815
    End
```

```
        Begin VB.CommandButton btnPlay
            Caption         =       "Play"
            Height          =       375
            Left            =       480
            TabIndex        =       1
            Top             =       2520
            Width           =       1815
        End
        Begin VB.CommandButton btnLoad
            Caption         =       "Load Animation"
            Height          =       615
            Left            =       600
            TabIndex        =       0
            Top             =       1680
            Width           =       3615
        End
        Begin VB.Shape Shape1
            BorderWidth     =       2
            Height          =       1215
            Left            =       240
            Top             =       240
            Width           =       4215
        End
End
Attribute VB_Name = "frmForm1"
Attribute VB_GlobalNameSpace = False
Attribute VB_Creatable = False
Attribute VB_PredeclaredId = True
Attribute VB_Exposed = False

Private Sub btnLoad_Click()
    dlgCommonDialog1.CancelError = True
    dlgCommonDialog1.DialogTitle = "Open AVI File"
    dlgCommonDialog1.Filter = _
        "AVI Animation (*.avi)|*.avi|All Files (*.*)|*.*"
    dlgCommonDialog1.FileName = "*.avi"
    On Error GoTo CancelError
    dlgCommonDialog1.ShowOpen
    On Error GoTo ErrorHandler
    Animation1.Open dlgCommonDialog1.FileName
    Exit Sub
ErrorHandler:
    MsgBox "Couldn't Open the File"
```

```
CancelError:
End Sub

Private Sub btnPlay_Click()
    Animation1.Play
End Sub

Private Sub btnStop_Click()
    Animation1.Stop
End Sub
```

CROSS-REFERENCE
See also Animation and Play.

Stop

Statement

The Stop statement pauses program execution, leaving the program's state such that it can continue execution where it left off. To continue program execution after using the Stop statement, click Visual Basic's Start button, select the Run menu's Start command, or press F5 on your keyboard.

NOTE
If a compiled program encounters a Stop statement, Stop acts like the End statement, closing any open files and halting program execution.

Syntax

```
Stop
```

Example

The following lines demonstrate the Stop statement. The first line displays a message box right before the Stop statement executes. The Stop statement then pauses program execution. If the programmer then presses F5 to continue program execution, the second message box (in the third code line) appears.

```
MsgBox "Before the Stop statement"
Stop
MsgBox "After the Stop statement"
```

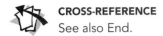

CROSS-REFERENCE
See also End.

Str

Function

The Str function converts a numerical expression to a string.

Syntax

```
value = Str(numExpr)
```

- *numExpr*—Any valid numerical expression.
- *value*—The variable that will receive the string value.

Example 1

After the following lines execute, the variable result will contain the string "125."

```
Dim result As String
Dim num As Integer
num = 125
result = Str(num)
```

Example 2

Here, after the following lines execute, the variable result will contain the string "5."

```
Dim result As String
Dim num1 As Integer
Dim num2 As Integer
num1 = 125
num2 = 25
result = Str(num1 / num2)
```

CROSS-REFERENCE
See also Val.

StrComp

Function

The StrComp function compares two strings.

Syntax

```
value = StrComp(str1, str2, compType)
```

- *compType* (*) — The type of search to perform. Can be a value from Table S-10.
- *str1* — The first string to compare.
- *str2* — The second string to compare.
- *value* — The variable that will receive the result of the comparison, with –1 meaning str1 is less than str2, 0 meaning the strings are equal, and 1 meaning str2 is less than str1.

(*) = Optional

Table S-10 Values for the *compType* Argument

Value	Description
vbBinaryCompare	Searches using a binary comparison.
vbDatabaseCompare	Searches based on data in a Microsoft Access database.
vbTextCompare	Searches using a text comparison.
vbUseCompareOption	Searches based on the program's Option Compare statement.

Example

After the following lines execute, result will contain the value 0, which indicates that the compared strings are equal.

```
Dim result As Integer
Dim str1, str2 As String
str1 = "two"
str2 = "two"
result = StrComp(str1, str2)
```

CROSS-REFERENCE
See also InStr and InStrRev

StrConv

Function

The StrConv function converts a string to a new string with the attributes given as the function's arguments.

Syntax

```
value = StrConv(str, convType, localeID)
```

- *convType* — The type of conversion, which can be a value from Table S-11.
- *localeID* (*) — The locale ID. The default is the system locale ID.
- *str* — A reference to the string to convert.
- *value* — The variable that will receive the converted string.

Table S-11 Values for the *convType* Argument

Value	Description
vbFromUnicode	Converts Unicode characters to the system default.
vbHiragana	Converts katakana characters to hiragana (Japan only).
vbKatakana	Converts hiragana characters to katakana (Japan only).
vbLowerCase	Converts characters to all lowercase.
vbNarrow	Converts wide characters to narrow characters (Far East only).
vbProperCase	Converts the first letter of each word to uppercase.
vbUnicode	Converts characters to Unicode.
vbUpperCase	Converts characters to all uppercase.
vbWide	Converts narrow characters to wide characters (Far East only).

Example 1

The following lines display a message box containing the converted string "THIS IS A TEST." Notice how all characters in the source string "this is a test" have been changed to uppercase.

```
Dim srcString As String
Dim destString As String
srcString = "this is a test"
destString = StrConv(srcString, vbUpperCase)
MsgBox destString
```

Example 2

Here, the following lines display a message box containing the converted string "This Is A Test." Notice how the first letter of each word in the source string "this is a test" has been changed to propercase.

```
Dim srcString As String
Dim destString As String
srcString = "this is a test"
destString = StrConv(srcString, vbProperCase)
MsgBox destString
```

 **CROSS-REFERENCE**
See also Chr.

Stretch

Property

The Stretch property represents whether an image stretches to the size of the Image control that contains the image.

Objects with a Stretch Property

Image

Syntax

```
Image.Stretch = value1
```

or

```
value2 = Image.Stretch
```

- *Image* — A reference to an Image control.
- *value1* — The value True or False.
- *value2* — The variable that will receive the property's current setting.

Example

The following program demonstrates the Image control's Stretch property. When you run the program, you see the window shown in Figure S-43. This window contains an unstretched picture in an Image control. Click the Stretch button to set the Image control's `Stretch` property to `True`, which results in the window shown in Figure S-44. You can continue to click the button to switch the `Stretch` property between `True` and `False`.

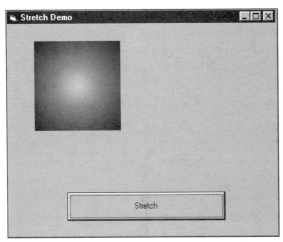

Figure S-43 The Image control's Stretch property starts off with a value of False.

Figure S-44 When the Image control's Stretch property gets set to True, the picture fills the control.

```
VERSION 5.00
Begin VB.Form frmForm1
   Caption         =    "Stretch Demo"
   ClientHeight    =    4515
   ClientLeft      =    60
   ClientTop       =    345
   ClientWidth     =    5940
   LinkTopic       =    "Form1"
   ScaleHeight     =    301
   ScaleMode       =    3  'Pixel
   ScaleWidth      =    396
   StartUpPosition =    3  'Windows Default
   Begin VB.CommandButton btnStretch
      Caption      =    "Stretch"
      Height       =    615
      Left         =    1320
      TabIndex     =    0
      Top          =    3600
      Width        =    3495
   End
   Begin VB.Image imgImage1
      Height       =    2895
      Left         =    600
      Top          =    360
      Width        =    4695
   End
End
Attribute VB_Name = "frmForm1"
Attribute VB_GlobalNameSpace = False
Attribute VB_Creatable = False
Attribute VB_PredeclaredId = True
Attribute VB_Exposed = False


Private Sub btnStretch_Click()
   If imgImage1.Stretch = False Then
      imgImage1.Stretch = True
      btnStretch.Caption = "No Stretching"
   Else
      imgImage1.Stretch = False
      btnStretch.Caption = "Stretch"
      imgImage1.Refresh
   End If
   imgImage1.Move 40, 24, 313, 193
End Sub
```

```
Private Sub Form_Load()
    imgImage1.Picture = LoadPicture("pic3.jpg")
    btnStretch.Caption = "Stretch"
End Sub
```

CROSS-REFERENCE
See also Image and PictureBox.

Strikethrough

Property

The Strikethrough property represents whether a font is strikethrough.

Objects with a Strikethrough Property

Font

Syntax

Font.Strikethrough = *value1*

or

value2 = Font.Strikethrough

- *Font* — A reference to a Font object.
- *value1* — The value True or False.
- *value2* — The variable that will receive the property's current setting.

Example

The following line sets a Form object's font to strikethrough.

```
frmForm1.Font.Strikethrough = True
```

CROSS-REFERENCE
See also Font, Italic, and Underline.

String

Function

The String function returns a string made up of a character repeated a specified number of times.

Syntax

```
value = String(numChars, char)
```

- *numChars*—The number of times to repeat the character in the string.
- *char*—The character to repeat.
- *value*—The variable that will receive the string of repeating characters.

Example

The following lines create the string "$$$$$$$$$$$$$$$."

```
Dim result As String
result = String(15, "$")
```

CROSS-REFERENCE
See also Space.

String

Keyword

The String keyword is used to declare variables of the string data type. The String keyword also represents a call to the String function. As an example of using the String keyword, the following line declares a variable called msg that can contain text data.

```
Dim msg As String
```

CROSS-REFERENCE
See also String (function).

r
s
t

StrReverse

Function

The `StrReverse` function reverses the order of characters in the specified string.

Syntax

```
value = StrReverse(sourceStr)
```

- *sourceStr* — The string to reverse.
- *value* — The variable that will receive the reversed string.

Example

After the following lines execute, the variable `result` will contain the string value "9876543210," which is the reverse of the string `srcString`.

```
Dim result As String
Dim srcString As String
srcString = "0123456789"
result = StrReverse(srcString)
```

 CROSS-REFERENCE
See also StrConv.

Style — Band

Property

The `Style` property represents the way a Band object looks and acts.

Syntax

```
Band.Style = value1
```

or

```
value2 = Band.Style
```

- *Band* — A reference to a Band object.
- *value1* — The Band object's style setting, which can be a value from Table S-12.

■ *value2* — The variable that will receive the property's current setting.

Table S-12 Values for the Style Property

Value	Description
cc3BandFixedSize	The user cannot resize the Band object.
cc3BandNormal	The user can resize the Band object (default).

Example

The following lines show how to get and set the style of a Band object. The CoolBar1 object is a CoolBar control that the programmer added to the form at design time.

```
Dim panelStyle As Integer
panelStyle = CoolBar1.Bands(1).Style
CoolBar1.Bands(1).Style = cc3BandFixedSize
CoolBar1.Bands(1).MinWidth = 200
```

CROSS-REFERENCE
See also Band, Bands, and CoolBar.

Style — Button

Property

The Style property represents the way a Button object looks and acts.

Syntax

Button.Style = *value1*

or

value2 = *Button*.Style

■ *Button* — A reference to a Button object.

■ *value1* — The Button object's style setting, which can be a value from Table S-13.

■ *value2* — The variable that will receive the property's current setting.

Table S-13 Values for the Style Property

Value	Description
tbrButtonGroup	Displays the button as a radio button that stays pressed until another button in the same group is pressed.
tbrCheck	Displays the button as a check button.
tbrDefault	Displays the button in its standard form (default).
tbrDropDown	Displays the button as a menu button.
tbrPlaceholder	Displays the button as a separator whose width can be set.
tbrSeparator	Displays the button as a separator, which is a blank space in the toolbar.

Example

The following lines show how to get and set the style of a Button object. The Toolbar1 object is a Toolbar control that the programmer added to the form at design time.

```
Dim butStyle As Integer
butStyle = Toolbar1.Buttons(1).Style
Toolbar1.Buttons(1).Style = tbrDropdown
```

CROSS-REFERENCE
See also Button, Buttons, and Toolbar.

Style—CheckBox, CommandButton, and OptionButton

Property

The Style property represents the way a CheckBox, CommandButton, or OptionButton control looks and acts.

Syntax

object.Style = *value1*

or

value2 = *object*.Style

- *object*—A reference to a CheckBox, CommandButton, or OptionButton control.

- *value1* — The control's style setting, which can be a value from Table S-14.
- *value2* — The variable that will receive the property's current setting.

Table S-14 Values for the Style Property

Value	Description
vbButtonGraphical	Displays the control with an associated image.
vbButtonStandard	Displays the control in its standard form (default).

Example

The following lines show how to get and set the style of a CommandButton control. The `btnCommand1` object is a CommandButton control that the programmer added to the form at design time.

```
Dim butStyle As Integer
butStyle = btnCommand1.Style
```

CROSS-REFERENCE
See also CheckBox, CommandButton, and OptionButton.

Style — ComboBox

Property

The `Style` property represents the way a ComboBox control looks and acts. This property must be set at design time and is read-only at runtime.

Syntax

```
value = ComboBox.Style
```

- *ComboBox* — A reference to a ComboBox control.
- *value* — The variable that will receive the property's current setting, which can be a value from Table S-15.

Table S-15 Values for the Style Property

Value	Description
vbComboDropDown	Displays a combo box with an edit box and a drop-down list (default).
vbComboDropdownList	Displays a combo box with an edit box and a drop-down list, but the user can select items only from the list.
vbComboSimple	Displays a combo box with an edit box and an always-visible list. That is, the list doesn't drop down.

Example

The following lines show how to get the style of a ComboBox control. The cboCombo1 object is a ComboBox control that the programmer added to the form at design time.

```
Dim comboStyle As Integer
comboStyle = cboCombo1.Style
```

CROSS-REFERENCE
See also ComboBox.

Style — ListBox

Property

The Style property represents the way a ListBox control looks and acts. This property must be set at design time and is read-only at runtime.

Syntax

value = ListBox.Style

- *ListBox* — A reference to a ListBox control.
- *value* — The variable that will receive the property's current setting, which can be a value from Table S-16.

Table S-16 Values for the Style Property

Value	Description
vbListBoxCheckBox	Displays a list box whose items have check boxes.
vbListBoxStandard	Displays a list box in its standard form (default).

Example

The following lines show how to get the style of a ListBox control. The `lstList1` object is a ListBox control that the programmer added to the form at design time.

```
Dim listStyle As Integer
listStyle = lstList1.Style
```

CROSS-REFERENCE
See also ListBox.

Style — Panel

Property

The `Style` property represents the way a Panel object looks and acts.

Syntax

```
Panel.Style = value1
```

or

```
value2 = Panel.Style
```

- *Panel* — A reference to a Panel object.
- *value1* — The Panel object's style setting, which can be a value from Table S-17.
- *value2* — The variable that will receive the property's current setting.

Table S-17 Values for the Style Property

Value	Description
sbrCaps	The panel displays the status of the keyboard's Caps key.
sbrDate	The panel displays the current date.
sbrIns	The panel displays the status of the keyboard's Insert key.
sbrKana	The panel displays the status of the keyboard's Scroll Lock key with the word KANA.
sbrNum	The panel displays the status of the keyboard's Num Lock key.
sbrScrl	The panel displays the status of the keyboard's Scroll Lock key.
sbrText	The panel displays text or a bitmap.
sbrTime	The panel displays the current time.

Example

The following lines show how to get and set the style of a Panel object to display the current date. The `staStatusBar1` object is a StatusBar control that the programmer added to the form at design time.

```
Dim panelStyle As Integer
panelStyle = staStatusBar1.Panels(1).Style
staStatusBar1.Panels(1).Style = sbrDate
```

 CROSS-REFERENCE
See also StatusBar, Panel, and Panels.

Style — StatusBar

Property

The `Style` property represents the way a StatusBar control looks and acts.

Syntax

StatusBar.Style = *value1*

or

value2 = *StatusBar*.Style

- *StatusBar* — A reference to a StatusBar control.
- *value1* — The control's style setting, which can be a value from Table S-18.

- *value2* — The variable that will receive the property's current setting.

Table S-18 Values for the Style Property

Value	Description
sbrNormal	The status bar can display multiple panels (default).
sbrSimple	The status bar displays a single panel.

Example

The following lines show how to get and set the style of a StatusBar control. The `staStatusBar1` object is a StatusBar control that the programmer added to the form at design time.

```
Dim staStyle As Integer
staStyle = staStatusBar1.Style
staStatusBar1.Style = sbrSimple
```

 CROSS-REFERENCE
See also StatusBar.

Style — TabStrip

Property

The `Style` property represents the way a TabStrip control looks and acts.

Syntax

```
TabStrip.Style = value1
```

or

```
value2 = TabStrip.Style
```

- *TabStrip* — A reference to a TabStrip control.
- *value1* — The TabStrip control's style setting, which can be a value from Table S-19.
- *value2* — The variable that will receive the property's current setting.

Table S-19 Values for the Style Property

Value	Description
tabButtons	The tab strip displays the tabs as pushbuttons.
tabFlatButtons	The tab strip displays the tabs as pushbuttons, but the buttons are flat when not selected.
tabTabs	The tab strip displays normal tabs (default).

Example

The following lines show how to get and set the style of a TabStrip control as pushbuttons. The `tabTabStrip1` object is a TabStrip control that the programmer added to the form at design time.

```
Dim tabStyle As Integer
tabStyle = tabTabStrip1.Style
tabTabStrip1.Style = tabButtons
```

CROSS-REFERENCE
See also TabStrip, Tab, and Tabs.

Style — Toolbar

Property

The `Style` property represents the way a Toolbar control looks and acts.

Syntax

```
Toolbar.Style = value1
```

or

```
value2 = Toolbar.Style
```

- *Toolbar* — A reference to a Toolbar control.
- *value1* — The Toolbar control's style setting, which can be a value from Table S-20.
- *value2* — The variable that will receive the property's current setting.

Table S-20 Values for the Style Property

Value	Description
tbrFlat	The toolbar displays flat buttons.
tbrStandard	The toolbar displays normal buttons (default).

Example

The following lines show how to get and set the style of a Toolbar control to display flat buttons. The `tlbToolbar1` object is a Toolbar control that the programmer added to the form at design time.

```
Dim toolStyle As Integer
toolStyle = tlbToolbar1.Style
tlbToolbar1.Style = tbrFlat
```

 CROSS-REFERENCE
See also TabStrip, Tab, and Tabs.

Style — TreeView

Property

The `Style` property represents the way a TreeView control looks and acts.

Syntax

```
TreeView.Style = value1
```

or

```
value2 = TreeView.Style
```

- *TreeView* — A reference to a TreeView control.
- *value1* — The TreeView control's style setting, which can be a value from Table S-21.
- *value2* — The variable that will receive the property's current setting.

Table S-21 Values for the Style Property

Value	Description
tvwPictureText	The TreeView control displays images and text.
tvwPlusMinusText	The TreeView control displays text, as well as plus signs on expandable nodes and minus signs on collapsible nodes.
tvwPlusPictureText	The TreeView control displays images and text, as well as plus signs on expandable nodes.
tvwTextOnly	The TreeView control displays only text.
tvwTreelinesPictureText	The TreeView control displays images, text, and lines between nodes.
tvwTreelinesPlusMinusPictureText	The TreeView control displays images, text, and lines between nodes, as well as plus signs on expandable nodes and minus signs on collapsible nodes. (Default.)
tvwTreelinesPlusMinusText	The TreeView control displays text and lines between nodes, as well as plus signs on expandable nodes and minus signs on collapsible nodes.
tvwTreelinesText	The TreeView control displays text and lines between nodes.

Example

The following lines show how to get and set the style of a TreeView control. The `treTreeView1` object is a TreeView control that the programmer added to the form at design time.

```
Dim treeStyle As Integer
treeStyle = treTreeView1.Style
treTreeView1.Style = tvwPlusMinusText
```

CROSS-REFERENCE
See also Tab, Tabs, and TabStrip.

Sub

Keyword

The Sub keyword is used to declare Visual Basic procedures. The keyword specifies the procedure's starting line and ending line. It can also be used in the `Exit Sub` statement to exit the procedure from anywhere within the procedure's body statements. The following lines illustrate defining a Visual Basic procedure.

```
Private Sub MyProc(val1 As Integer, val2 As Integer)
    ' Procedure body statements go here.
End Sub
```

CROSS-REFERENCE
See also Function.

SubFolders

Property

The `SubFolders` property represents a Folders collection that contains a Folder object for each subfolder within a folder.

Objects with a SubFolders Property

Folder

Syntax

```
value = Folder.SubFolders
```

- *Folder*—A reference to a Folder object.
- *value2*—The variable that will receive the reference to the Folders collection.

Example

The following lines display, one at a time, the names of the subfolders in the root folder of drive C.

```
Dim fileSystem As Object
Dim folder As Object
Dim subFolders As Object
```

```
Set fileSystem = CreateObject("Scripting.FileSystemObject")
Set folder = fileSystem.GetFolder("c:\")
Set subFolders = folder.subFolders
For Each folder In subFolders
    MsgBox folder.Name, vbInformation, "Subfolders"
Next
```

CROSS-REFERENCE
See also FileSystemObject, Folder, Folders, and Name.

SubItemIndex

Property

The `SubItemIndex` property represents the subitem index associated with a ColumnHeader object.

Objects with a SubItemIndex Property

ColumnHeader

Syntax

`value = ColumnHeader.SubItemIndex`

- *ColumnHeader*—A reference to a ColumnHeader object.
- *value*—The variable that will receive the index of the associated subitem.

Example

The following lines show how to get the index of the subitem associated with a ColumnHeader object in a ListView control. In this case, the program gets the index associated with the second column header. The `lvwListView1` object is a ListView control that the programmer added to the form at design time.

```
Dim subIndex As Integer
subIndex = lvwListView1.ColumnHeaders(2).SubItemIndex
```

 CROSS-REFERENCE
See also ListView, ColumnHeader, and ColumnHeaders.

SubItems

Property

The SubItems property represents the strings that make up a ListItem object's subitems.

Objects with a SubItems Property

ListItem

Syntax

ListItem.SubItems(*index*) = *value1*

or

value2 = *ListItem*.SubItems(*index*)

- *index* — The index of the subitem to access.
- *ListItem* — A reference to a ListItem object.
- *value1* — The string value for the subitem.
- *value2* — The variable that will receive the subitem's string value.

Example

The following lines populate a ListView control with list items and subitems and display the ListView control in its report view. Figure S-45 shows the resultant ListView control.

r
s
t

```
Dim item As ListItem
lvwListView1.View = lvwReport
lvwListView1.Sorted = True
lvwListView1.SortOrder = lvwAscending
lvwListView1.SortKey = 0
lvwListView1.ColumnHeaders.Add , , "Column #1"
lvwListView1.ColumnHeaders.Add , , "Column #2"
lvwListView1.ColumnHeaders.Add , , "Column #3"
Set item = lvwListView1.ListItems.Add(, , "Item #2")
item.SubItems(1) = "SubItem #1"
item.SubItems(2) = "SubItem #2"
Set item = lvwListView1.ListItems.Add(, , "Item #3")
item.SubItems(1) = "SubItem #1"
item.SubItems(2) = "SubItem #2"
Set item = lvwListView1.ListItems.Add(, , "Item #4")
item.SubItems(1) = "SubItem #1"
item.SubItems(2) = "SubItem #2"
Set item = lvwListView1.ListItems.Add(, , "Item #1")
item.SubItems(1) = "SubItem #1"
item.SubItems(2) = "SubItem #2"
```

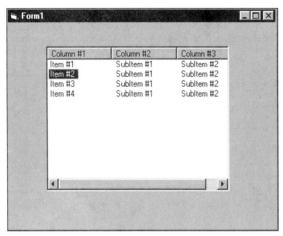

Figure S-45 The subitems appear under all columns except the first, which displays the list items themselves.

CROSS-REFERENCE

See also ListView, ListItem, ListItems, ColumnHeader, ColumnHeaders, and View.

SupportsMnemonics

Property

The SupportsMnemonics property represents whether a container handles its controls' hotkeys. For example, the user may be able to select a button by selecting a hotkey of Ctrl+W on the keyboard. If the control's container can handle this type of key processing, its SupportsMnemonics property will be set to True.

Objects with a SupportsMnemonics Property

AmbientProperties

Syntax

value = Ambient.SupportsMnemonics

- *Ambient* — A reference to an AmbientProperties object.
- *value* — The variable that will receive the property's current setting, which can be True or False.

Example

The following lines show how to get the value of the SupportsMnemonics property.

```
Dim handlesHotKeys As Boolean
handlesHotKeys = Ambient.SupportsMnemonics
```

 CROSS-REFERENCE
See also AmbientProperties.

Switch

Function

The Switch function matches expressions with a series of values and returns the matching value for the first expression that evaluates to True.

Syntax

```
value = Switch(expr, data, ...)
```

- ... — Additional expression and data pairs.
- *expr* — An expression that evaluates to True or False.
- *data* — The value that Switch should return if expr is True.
- *value* — The variable that will receive the result or receive a Null if no expressions evaluate to True.

Example 1

In the following example, a message box will display the string value "Anderson."

```
Dim firstName As String
Dim lastName
firstName = "Greg"
lastName = Switch(firstName = "Mack", "McHenry", _
    firstName = "Greg", "Anderson", _
    firstName = "Felix", "the Cat")
MsgBox lastName
```

Example 2

After the following lines execute, the variable lastName will contain Null. This is because none of the Switch function's expressions evaluate to True.

```
Dim firstName As String
Dim lastName
firstName = "Roger"
lastName = Switch(firstName = "Mack", "McHenry", _
    firstName = "Greg", "Anderson", _
    firstName = "Felix", "the Cat")
```

CROSS-REFERENCE
See also Choose, IIf, and Select Case.

SYD

Function

The SYD function calculates an asset's sum-of-years digits depreciation.

Syntax

```
value = SYD(cost, finalValue, lifetime, period)
```

- *cost* — The asset's original cost.
- *finalValue* — The asset's value at the end of its lifetime.
- *lifetime* — The asset's lifetime.
- *period* — The period for which to calculate the depreciation.
- *value* — The variable that will receive the depreciation for a period.

Example

The following program demonstrates how to use the SYD function. When you run the program, enter the following values:

- Enter the cost of the asset into the Asset cost box.
- Enter the ending value of the asset into the Ending Value box.
- Enter the lifetime of the object in years into the Lifetime in Years box.
- Enter the year (from 1 to the lifetime) for which to calculate the depreciation into the Year to Calculate box.

After entering the required values, click the Calculate button to calculate and view the amount of depreciation per year. Figure S-46, for example, shows the depreciation for the first year for a car that cost $15,000 to purchase and will be worth $4,000 after ten years.

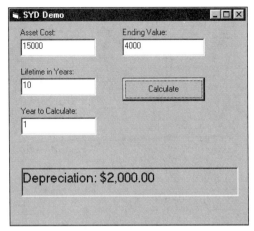

Figure S-46 The SYD function calculates depreciation for a given period.

```
VERSION 5.00
Begin VB.Form Form1
   Caption         =    "SYD Demo"
   ClientHeight    =    4305
   ClientLeft      =    165
   ClientTop       =    450
   ClientWidth     =    5235
   LinkTopic       =    "Form1"
   ScaleHeight     =    4305
   ScaleWidth      =    5235
   StartUpPosition =    3   'Windows Default
   Begin VB.TextBox txtYearToCalculate
      Height       =    375
      Left         =    240
      TabIndex     =    9
      Top          =    2040
      Width        =    1695
   End
   Begin VB.CommandButton btnCalculate
      Caption      =    "Calculate"
      Height       =    495
      Left         =    2520
      TabIndex     =    6
      Top          =    1200
      Width        =    1815
   End
```

```
Begin VB.TextBox txtLifetime
   Height          =     375
   Left            =     240
   TabIndex        =     5
   Top             =     1200
   Width           =     1695
End
Begin VB.TextBox txtEndingValue
   Height          =     375
   Left            =     2520
   TabIndex        =     3
   Top             =     360
   Width           =     1815
End
Begin VB.TextBox txtCost
   Height          =     375
   Left            =     240
   TabIndex        =     1
   Top             =     360
   Width           =     1695
End
Begin VB.Label Label4
   Caption         =     "Year to Calculate:"
   Height          =     255
   Left            =     240
   TabIndex        =     8
   Top             =     1800
   Width           =     1575
End
Begin VB.Label lblDepreciation
   BorderStyle     =     1  'Fixed Single
   Caption         =     "Depreciation:"
   BeginProperty Font
      Name            =     "MS Sans Serif"
      Size            =     13.5
      Charset         =     0
      Weight          =     400
      Underline       =     0     'False
      Italic          =     0     'False
      Strikethrough   =     0     'False
   EndProperty
   Height          =     615
   Left            =     240
```

```
            TabIndex        =    7
            Top             =    3120
            Width           =    4815
         End
         Begin VB.Label Label3
            Caption         =    "Lifetime in Years:"
            Height          =    255
            Left            =    240
            TabIndex        =    4
            Top             =    960
            Width           =    1575
         End
         Begin VB.Label Label2
            Caption         =    "Ending Value:"
            Height          =    255
            Left            =    2520
            TabIndex        =    2
            Top             =    120
            Width           =    1575
         End
         Begin VB.Label Label1
            Caption         =    "Asset Cost:"
            Height          =    255
            Left            =    240
            TabIndex        =    0
            Top             =    120
            Width           =    1695
         End
End
Attribute VB_Name = "Form1"
Attribute VB_GlobalNameSpace = False
Attribute VB_Creatable = False
Attribute VB_PredeclaredId = True
Attribute VB_Exposed = False

Private Sub btnCalculate_Click()
    Dim cost As Double
    Dim endValue As Double
    Dim LifeTime As Double
    Dim depreciation As Double
    Dim yearToCalc As Double
    Dim strResult As String
```

```
      On Error GoTo ErrorHandler

      cost = txtCost.Text
      endValue = txtEndingValue.Text
      LifeTime = txtLifetime.Text
      yearToCalc = txtYearToCalculate.Text

      depreciation = SYD(cost, endValue, LifeTime, yearToCalc)
      strResult = "$" & Format(depreciation, "###,###,##0.00")
      lblDepreciation.Caption = "Depreciation: " & strResult
      Exit Sub

ErrorHandler:
      MsgBox "An error occurred.", vbExclamation
End Sub
```

SyncBuddy

Property

The SyncBuddy property represents whether the contents of an UpDown control's buddy control will be synchronized with the value of the UpDown control.

Objects with a SyncBuddy Property

UpDown

Syntax

UpDown.SyncBuddy = *value1*

or

value2 = *UpDown*.SyncBuddy

- *UpDown*—A reference to an UpDown control.
- *value1*—The value True or False.
- *value2*—The variable that will receive the property's current setting.

Example

The following lines show how to get and set an UpDown control's `SyncBuddy` property. In this example, the `updUpDown1` object is an UpDown control that the programmer added to the form at design time.

```
Dim sync As Boolean
sync = updUpDown1.SyncBuddy
updUpDown1.SyncBuddy = True
```

CROSS-REFERENCE
See also UpDown, BuddyControl, BuddyProperty, and AutoBuddy.

SysColorsChanged

Event

Visual Basic sends a SysInfo control a `SysColorsChanged` event when the system colors are changed.

Objects with a SysColorsChanged Event

SysInfo

Example

A program can respond to a `SysColorsChanged` event by implementing the SysInfo control's `SysColorsChanged` event procedure. The following code segment shows how a SysInfo control defines a `SysColorsChanged` event procedure. In this example, the `SysInfo1` object is a SysInfo control that the programmer added to the form at design time.

```
Private Sub SysInfo1_SysColorsChanged()
    ' Handle the SysColorChanged event here.
End Sub
```

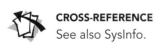

CROSS-REFERENCE
See also SysInfo.

SysInfo

Control

A SysInfo control enables a program to respond to various types of system events, as well as to get information about the system (such as screen work-area size and battery status). The SysInfo control has no user interface and so cannot be seen at runtime. However, the control appears as an icon on the form at design time, as shown in Figure S-47. You can add the SysInfo control to your Visual Basic toolbox from the Components dialog box, as shown in Figure S-48. To display the Components dialog box, press Ctrl+T on your keyboard, or select the Project menu's Components command.

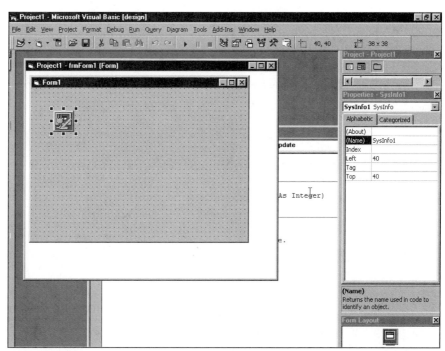

Figure S-47 An icon represents the SysInfo control on a form.

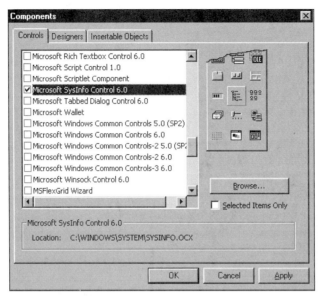

Figure S-48 Add the SysInfo control to your project with the Components dialog box.

Properties

The SysInfo control has 18 properties, which are listed below. Because many Visual Basic controls have similar properties, the following list does not include the properties' descriptions. For information on using a property, look up the individual property's entry, provided alphabetically in this book.

```
ACStatus
BatteryFullTime
BatteryLifePercent
BatteryLifeTime
BatteryStatus
Index
Name
Object
OSBuild
OSPlatform
OSVersion
Parent
ScrollBarSize
Tag
WorkAreaHeight
```

```
WorkAreaLeft
WorkAreaTop
WorkAreaWidth
```

Methods

The SysInfo control has no methods.

Events

The SysInfo control responds to 18 events, which are listed below. Because many Visual Basic controls respond to similar events, the following list does not include the events' descriptions. For information on using an event, look up the individual event's entry, provided alphabetically in this book.

```
ConfigChangeCancelled
ConfigChanged
DeviceArrival
DeviceOtherEvent
DeviceQueryRemove
DeviceQueryRemoveFailed
DeviceRemoveComplete
DeviceRemovePending
DevModeChanged
DisplayChanged
PowerQuerySuspend
PowerResume
PowerStatusChanged
PowerSuspend
QueryChangeConfig
SettingChanged
SysColorsChanged
TimeChanged
```

Tab

Function

The Tab function is used with the Print statement and method to output data to the specified column.

Syntax

```
Tab(col)
```

- *col* (*) — The column at which the output should be placed. The default is the next print zone, which is the next column that begins on a 14-column boundary.

(*) = Optional

Example 1

The following lines print to a file the strings "Word1" and "Word2" separated by four spaces, which places the start of the second word in column 10 of the output.

```
Open "c:\MyFile.txt" For Output As #1
Print #1, "Word1"; Tab(10); "Word2"
Close #1
```

Example 2

Here, the following lines print to a file the strings "Word1" and "Word2" separated by nine spaces, which places the start of the second word in column 15 of the output. Column 15 is the next column after "Word1" that begins on the first 14-column boundary.

```
Open "c:\MyFile.txt" For Output As #1
Print #1, "Word1"; Tab(15); "Word2"
Close #1
```

CROSS-REFERENCE
See also Print, Space, and Spc.

Tab

Object

A Tab object represents a tab in a TabStrip control, as shown in Figure T-1. The TabStrip control can contain multiple Tab objects, which enable the user to switch the form between different pages of options.

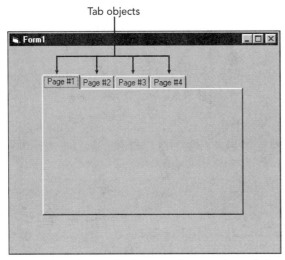

Figure T-1 Tabs are like buttons that switch a Tab Strip from one page to another.

Properties

The Tab object has 12 properties, which are listed below. For more information on using a property shown in the following table, look up the individual property's entry, provided alphabetically in this book.

```
Caption
Height
HighLighted
Image
Index
Key
Left
Selected
Tag
ToolTipText
Top
Width
```

Methods

The Tab object has no methods.

Events

The Tab object does not respond to events.

 CROSS-REFERENCE
See also Tabs (property) and TabStrip.

TabFixedHeight

Property

The `TabFixedHeight` property represents the height of tabs in a TabStrip control when the control's `TabWidthStyle` property is set to `tabFixed`.

Objects with a TabFixedHeight Property

TabStrip

Syntax

```
TabStrip.TabFixedHeight = value1
```

or

```
value2 = TabStrip.TabFixedHeight
```

- *TabStrip* — A reference to a TabStrip control.
- *value1* — The tabs' fixed height, which is based on the setting of the container's `ScaleMode` property.
- *value2* — The variable that will receive the property's current setting.

Example

The following lines show how to get and set the fixed height of a TabStrip control's tabs.

```
Dim fixHeight As Integer
fixHeight = TabStrip1.TabFixedHeight
TabStrip1.TabFixedHeight = 150
```

s
t
u

CROSS-REFERENCE
See also TabFixedWidth, TabMinWidth, TabStrip, TabStyle, and TabWidthStyle.

TabFixedWidth

Property

The `TabFixedWidth` property represents the width of tabs in a TabStrip control when the control's `TabWidthStyle` property is set to `tabFixed`.

Objects with a TabFixedWidth Property

TabStrip

Syntax

```
TabStrip.TabFixedWidth = value1
```

or

```
value2 = TabStrip.TabFixedWidth
```

- *TabStrip* — A reference to a TabStrip control.
- *value1* — The tabs' fixed width, which is based on the setting of the container's `ScaleMode` property.
- *value2* — The variable that will receive the property's current setting.

Example

The following lines show how to get and set the fixed width of a TabStrip control's tabs.

```
Dim fixWidth As Integer
fixWidth = TabStrip1.TabFixedWidth
TabStrip1.TabFixedWidth = 150
```

CROSS-REFERENCE
See also TabFixedHeight, TabMinWidth, TabStrip, and TabStyle.

TabIndex

Property

The `TabIndex` property represents the tab order of a control in a form.

Objects with a TabIndex Property

Animation

CheckBox

ComboBox

CommandButton

CoolBar

DirListBox

DriveListBox

FileListBox

Frame

HScrollBar

Label

ListBox

ListView

OLE Container

OptionButton

PictureBox

ProgressBar

RichTextBox

Slider

StatusBar

TabStrip

TextBox

Toolbar

TreeView

UpDown

VScrollBar

s

t

u

Syntax

```
object.TabIndex = value1
```

or

```
value2 = object.TabIndex
```

- *object* — A reference to an object with a `TabIndex` property.
- *value1* — The new tab-order position, which must be at least 0 and no more than the number of controls on the form minus 1.
- *value2* — The variable that will receive the property's current setting.

Example

The following program demonstrates the use of the `TabIndex` property. When you run the program, the main window appears, with the upper-left button having the input focus (Figure T-2). Press your keyboard's Tab key to tab from one button to another, taking note of the buttons' tab order. Then, click a button. The program makes that button the first control in the tab order. Now, when you tab through the controls, the tab order is different because Visual Basic reorders the controls to accommodate the change in the clicked control's `TabIndex` property.

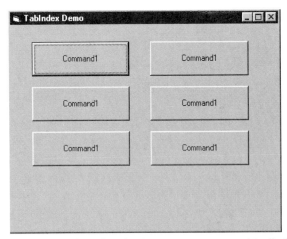

Figure T-2 The TabIndex Demo program graphically illustrates the use of the TabIndex property.

```
VERSION 5.00
Begin VB.Form frmForm1
   Caption         =    "TabIndex Demo"
   ClientHeight    =    4395
   ClientLeft      =    60
   ClientTop       =    345
   ClientWidth     =    5940
   LinkTopic       =    "Form1"
   ScaleHeight     =    293
   ScaleMode       =    3  'Pixel
   ScaleWidth      =    396
   StartUpPosition =    3  'Windows Default
   Begin VB.CommandButton Command1
      Caption      =    "Command1"
      Height       =    735
      Index        =    5
      Left         =    3120
      TabIndex     =    5
      Top          =    2280
      Width        =    2175
   End
   Begin VB.CommandButton Command1
      Caption      =    "Command1"
      Height       =    735
      Index        =    4
      Left         =    480
      TabIndex     =    4
      Top          =    2280
      Width        =    2175
   End
   Begin VB.CommandButton Command1
      Caption      =    "Command1"
      Height       =    735
      Index        =    3
      Left         =    3120
      TabIndex     =    3
      Top          =    1320
      Width        =    2175
   End
   Begin VB.CommandButton Command1
      Caption      =    "Command1"
      Height       =    735
      Index        =    2
      Left         =    480
```

s
t
u

```
                    TabIndex        =    2
                    Top             =    1320
                    Width           =    2175
                End
                Begin VB.CommandButton Command1
                    Caption         =    "Command1"
                    Height          =    735
                    Index           =    1
                    Left            =    3120
                    TabIndex        =    1
                    Top             =    360
                    Width           =    2175
                End
                Begin VB.CommandButton Command1
                    Caption         =    "Command1"
                    Height          =    735
                    Index           =    0
                    Left            =    480
                    TabIndex        =    0
                    Top             =    360
                    Width           =    2175
                End
            End
        End
        Attribute VB_Name = "frmForm1"
        Attribute VB_GlobalNameSpace = False
        Attribute VB_Creatable = False
        Attribute VB_PredeclaredId = True
        Attribute VB_Exposed = False

        Private Sub Command1_Click(Index As Integer)
            Command1(Index).TabIndex = 0
        End Sub
```

CROSS-REFERENCE
See also TabStop.

TabMinWidth

Property

The TabMinWidth property represents the minimum width of tabs in a TabStrip control if the control's TabWidthStyle property is not set to tabFixed.

Objects with a TabMinWidth Property
TabStrip

Syntax

```
TabStrip.TabMinWidth = value1
```

or

```
value2 = TabStrip.TabMinWidth
```

- *TabStrip* — A reference to a TabStrip control.
- *value1* — The tabs' minimum width, which is based on the setting of the container's `ScaleMode` property.
- *value2* — The variable that will receive the property's current setting.

Example

The following lines show how to get and set the minimum width of a TabStrip control's tabs.

```
Dim minWidth As Integer
minWidth = TabStrip1.TabMinWidth
TabStrip1.TabMinWidth = 150
```

CROSS-REFERENCE
See also TabFixedHeight, TabFixedWidth, TabStrip, TabStyle, and TabWidthStyle.

Tabs

Collection

A Tabs collection holds the Tab objects displayed in a TabStrip control. You can access a TabStrip control's Tabs collection through the control's `Tabs` property.

Syntax

```
value = TabStrip.Tabs
```

- *TabStrip* — A reference to a TabStrip control.
- *value* — The variable that will receive a reference to the Tabs collection.

Properties

A Tabs collection has one property, `Count`, which represents the number of Tab objects in the collection. For more information on using this property, look up the individual property's entry, provided alphabetically in this book.

Methods

A Tabs collection has four methods, which are listed below. For more information on a method, look up the individual method's name, provided alphabetically in this book.

```
Add
Clear
Item
Remove
```

Example

In this example, the program uses a Tabs collection's `Item` method to access a tab and set its caption.

```
tabTabStrip1.Tabs.Item(1).Caption = "A new caption"
```

 CROSS-REFERENCE
See also Tab, Tabs (property), and TabStrip.

Tabs

Property

The `Tabs` property represents a TabStrip control's Tabs collection.

Objects with a Tabs Property

TabStrip

Syntax

```
value = TabStrip.Tabs
```

- *TabStrip* — A reference to a TabStrip control.
- *value* — The variable that will receive a reference to the Tabs collection.

Example

The following lines add tabs to a TabStrip control by calling the Tabs collection's Add method. The tabTabStrip1 object is a TabStrip control that the programmer added to the form at design time.

```
With tabTabStrip1.Tabs
    .Add 1, "T1", "Tab #1"
    .Add 2, "T2", "Tab #2"
    .Add 3, "T3", "Tab #3"
    .Add 4, "T4", "Tab #4"
    .Add 5, "T5", "Tab #5"
    .Add 6, "T6", "Tab #6"
End With
```

 CROSS-REFERENCE
See also Tab, Tabs (collection), and TabStrip.

TabStop

Property

The TabStop property represents whether you can give a control the input focus by tabbing to the control.

Objects with a TabStop Property

Animation

CheckBox

ComboBox

CommandButton

DirListBox

DriveListBox

> FileListBox
>
> HScrollBar
>
> ListBox
>
> ListView
>
> OLE Container
>
> OptionButton
>
> PictureBox
>
> RichTextBox
>
> Slider
>
> TabStrip
>
> TextBox
>
> TreeView
>
> UpDown
>
> VScrollBar

Syntax

`object.TabStop = value1`

or

`value2 = object.TabStop`

- *object* — A reference to an object with a `TabStop` property.
- *value1* — The value `True` or `False`.
- *value2* — The variable that will receive the property's current setting.

Example

The following program demonstrates the use of a control's `TabStop` property. When you run the program, the main window appears, containing six TextBox controls (Figure T-3). Press your keyboard's Tab key to tab through the controls in their tab order. Now, double-click any control. When you do, the program changes the control's `TabIndex` property to `False`. Tab through the controls again, and you'll see that the one you double-clicked gets skipped. You can turn off the `TabIndex` property of any or all of the controls in the window. You can also turn the `TabIndex` property for a control back on by double-clicking the control a second time.

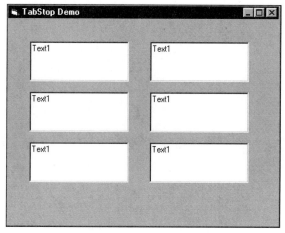

Figure T-3 The TabStop Demo program enables you to remove controls from the application's tab order.

```
VERSION 5.00
Begin VB.Form frmForm1
    Caption         =   "TabStop Demo"
    ClientHeight    =   4395
    ClientLeft      =   60
    ClientTop       =   345
    ClientWidth     =   5940
    LinkTopic       =   "Form1"
    ScaleHeight     =   293
    ScaleMode       =   3  'Pixel
    ScaleWidth      =   396
    StartUpPosition =   3  'Windows Default
    Begin VB.TextBox Text1
        Height      =   855
        Index       =   5
        Left        =   3120
        TabIndex    =   5
        Text        =   "Text1"
        Top         =   2640
        Width       =   2175
    End
```

```
Begin VB.TextBox Text1
   Height          =    855
   Index           =    4
   Left            =    480
   TabIndex        =    4
   Text            =    "Text1"
   Top             =    2640
   Width           =    2175
End
Begin VB.TextBox Text1
   Height          =    855
   Index           =    3
   Left            =    3120
   TabIndex        =    3
   Text            =    "Text1"
   Top             =    1560
   Width           =    2175
End
Begin VB.TextBox Text1
   Height          =    855
   Index           =    2
   Left            =    480
   TabIndex        =    2
   Text            =    "Text1"
   Top             =    1560
   Width           =    2175
End
Begin VB.TextBox Text1
   Height          =    855
   Index           =    1
   Left            =    3120
   TabIndex        =    1
   Text            =    "Text1"
   Top             =    480
   Width           =    2175
End
Begin VB.TextBox Text1
   Height          =    855
   Index           =    0
   Left            =    480
   TabIndex        =    0
```

```
          Text          =    "Text1"
          Top           =    480
          Width         =    2175
       End
End
Attribute VB_Name = "frmForm1"
Attribute VB_GlobalNameSpace = False
Attribute VB_Creatable = False
Attribute VB_PredeclaredId = True
Attribute VB_Exposed = False

Private Sub Text1_DblClick(Index As Integer)
    If Text1(Index).TabStop = True Then
        Text1(Index).TabStop = False
    Else
        Text1(Index).TabStop = True
    End If
End Sub
```

CROSS-REFERENCE
See also TabIndex.

TabStrip

Control

A TabStrip control enables a program to organize multiple pages of information in a single window.

Example

To select the page, you want to click the page's tab. For example, Figure T-4 shows a TabStrip control with five tabs. The TabStrip control is part of the Microsoft Windows Common Controls 6.0 package and must be added to your Visual Basic toolbox from the Components dialog box, as shown in Figure T-5. To display the Components dialog box, press Ctrl+T on your keyboard.

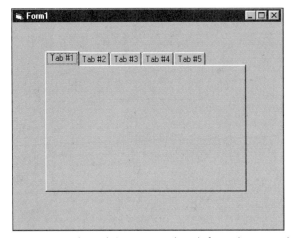

Figure T-4 This TabStrip control, with five tabs, provides an easy way to organize multiple pages of information into a single window.

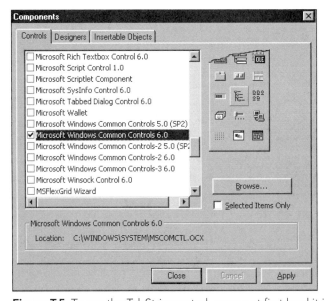

Figure T-5 To use the TabStrip control, you must first load it into your toolbox.

Properties

The TabStrip control has 44 properties, which are listed below. Because many Visual Basic controls have similar properties, the following list does not include the properties' descriptions. For information on using a property, look up the individual property's entry, provided alphabetically in this book.

CausesValidation
ClientHeight
ClientLeft
ClientTop
ClientWidth
Container
DragIcon
DragMode
Enabled
Font
Height
HelpContextID
HotTracking
hWnd
ImageList
Index
Left
MouseIcon
MousePointer
MultiRow
MultiSelect
Name
Object
OLEDropMode
Parent
Placement
SelectedItem
Separators
ShowTips
Style
TabFixedHeight
TabFixedWidth
TabIndex
TabMinWidth
Tabs
TabStop
TabStyle
TabWidthStyle
Tag
ToolTipText
Top
Visible
WhatsThisHelpID
Width

s
t
u

Methods

The TabStrip control has eight methods, which are listed below. Because many Visual Basic controls have similar methods, the following list does not include the methods' descriptions. For information on using a method, look up the individual method's entry, provided alphabetically in this book.

```
DeselectAll
Drag
Move
OLEDrag
Refresh
SetFocus
ShowWhatsThis
ZOrder
```

Events

The TabStrip control responds to 19 events, which are listed below. Because many Visual Basic controls respond to similar events, the following list does not include the events' descriptions. For information on using an event, look up the individual event's entry, provided alphabetically in this book.

```
BeforeClick
Click
DragDrop
DragOver
GotFocus
KeyDown
KeyPress
KeyUp
LostFocus
MouseDown
MouseMove
MouseUp
OLECompleteDrag
OLEDragDrop
OLEDragOver
OLEGiveFeedback
OLESetData
OLEStartDrag
Validate
```

The TabStrip's control's most commonly used event is BeforeClick, which the control generates when you click on one of the tabs. A program responds to the control's BeforeClick event in the BeforeClick event procedure. A

TabStrip called `tabTabStrip1` will have a `BeforeClick` event procedure called `tabTabStrip1_BeforeClick`, which is where the program should handle the event, as shown in the following lines:

```
Private Sub tabTabStrip1_BeforeClick(Cancel As Integer)
    ' Handle the BeforeClick event here.
End Sub
```

The `BeforeClick` event procedure's single parameter, `Cancel`, enables a program to cancel the switch to another page. Setting `Cancel` to `True` causes the TabStrip control to ignore the click. You can use this event to validate the contents of a page before allowing the user to switch to another page.

TabStyle

Property

The `TabStyle` property represents how a TabStrip control positions tabs when the user selects a tab. This property can be set to `tabTabStandard` or `tabTabOpposite`.

Objects with a TabStyle Property

TabStrip

Syntax

```
TabStrip.TabStyle = value1
```

or

```
value2 = TabStrip.TabStyle
```

- *TabStrip* — A reference to a TabStrip control.
- *value1* — The value `tabTabStandard` or `tabTabOpposite`.
- *value2* — The variable that will receive the property's current setting.

Example

The following lines show how to get and set a TabStrip control's `TabStyle` property.

```
Dim tabStyle As Integer
tabStyle = tabTabStrip1.TabStyle
tabTabStrip1.TabStyle = tabTabOpposite
```

CROSS-REFERENCE
See also TabFixedHeight, TabFixedWidth, TabMinWidth, TabStrip, and
TabWidthStyle.

TabWidthStyle

Property

The `TabWidthStyle` property represents how a TabStrip determines the width
of the control's tabs. This property can be a value from Table T-1. Figures T-6
through T-8 show the different types of tab width styles.

Table T-1 Values for the TabWidthStyle Property

Value	Description
tabFixed	Causes all tabs to have the width given in the TabFixedWidth property.
tabJustified	In a multirow TabStrip control, causes the rows of tabs to be justified such that each row spans the full width of the control.
tabNonJustified	Causes tabs to be just wide enough to hold their contents.

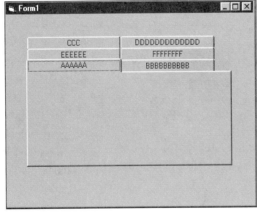

Figure T-6 This TabStrip control's TabWidthStyle property is set to tabFixed.

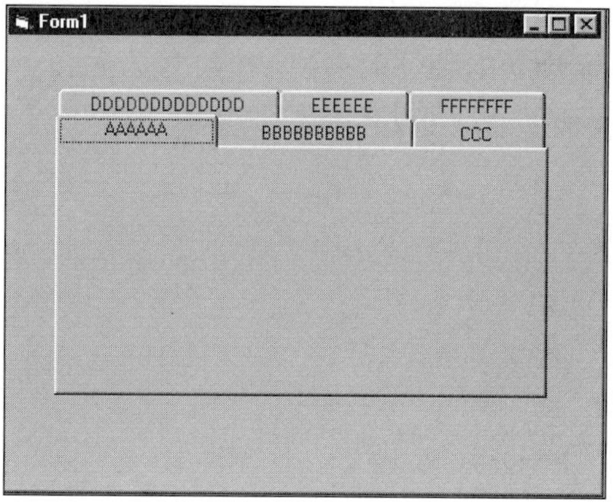

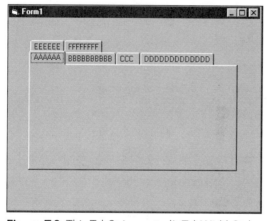

Figure T-7 This TabStrip control's TabWidthStyle property is set to tabJustified.

Figure T-8 This TabStrip control's TabWidthStyle property is set to tabNonJustified.

Objects with a TabWidthStyle Property

TabStrip

Syntax

```
TabStrip.TabWidthStyle = value1
```

or

```
value2 = TabStrip.TabWidthStyle
```

- *TabStrip*—A reference to a TabStrip control.
- *value1*—A value from Table T-1.
- *value2*—The variable that will receive the property's current setting.

Example

The following lines show how to get and set a TabStrip control's TabWidthStyle property.

```
Dim widthStyle As Integer
tabTabStrip1.MultiRow = True
widthStyle = tabTabStrip1.TabWidthStyle
tabTabStrip1.TabWidthStyle = tabJustified
```

 CROSS-REFERENCE
See also TabFixedHeight, TabFixedWidth, TabMinWidth, and TabStrip.

Tag

Property

The Tag property represents a storage place for user-defined data that can be associated with a control or object.

Objects with a Tag Property

Animation

Band

Button

CheckBox

ColumnHeader

ComboBox

CommandButton

CommonDialog

DirListBox

DriveListBox

FileListBox

Form

Frame

HScrollBar

Image
ImageList
Label
Line
ListBox
ListImage
ListItem
ListSubItem
ListView
MAPIMessages
MAPISession
MDIForm
Menu
Multimedia MCI
Node
OLE Container
OptionButton
Panel
PictureBox
ProgressBar
PropertyPage
RichTextBox
Shape
Slider
StatusBar
SysInfo
Tab
TabStrip
TextBox
Timer
Toolbar
TreeView
UpDown
UserControl
VScrollBar

s
t
u

Syntax

```
object.Tag = value1
```

or

```
value2 = object.Tag
```

- *object* — A reference to an object with a `Tag` property.
- *value1* — A string containing the tag data.
- *value2* — The variable that will receive the tag string.

Example

The following lines show how to get and set a TextBox control's `Tag` property. The `txtTextBox1` object is a TextBox control that the programmer added to the form at design time.

```
Dim strTag As String
strTag = txtTextBox1.Tag
txtTextBox1.Tag = "My tag"
```

Tan

Function

The `Tan` function returns the tangent of an angle.

Syntax

```
value = Tan(angle)
```

- *angle* — The angle in radians.
- *value* — The variable that will receive the tangent.

Example

The following lines calculate the tangent of a 60-degree angle.

```
Dim tangent As Double
Dim angle As Double
Dim pi As Double
pi = 3.14159
angle = 60 * (pi / 180)
tangent = Tan(angle)
```

CROSS-REFERENCE
See also Atn, Cos, and Sin.

TaskVisible

Property

The `TaskVisible` property represents whether Windows lists the application in the Windows task list. The `TaskVisible` property can be set to `False` only if the application does not display a window.

Objects with a TaskVisible Property

App

Syntax

```
App.TaskVisible = value1
```

or

```
value2 = App.TaskVisible
```

- *App* — A reference to the App object.
- *value1* — The value `True` or `False`.
- *value2* — The variable that will receive the property's current setting.

Example

The following lines show how to get and set an application's task-visible status. Note that the App object is a global Visual Basic object that you don't need to create in your programs.

```
Dim tskVisible As Boolean
tskVisible = App.TaskVisible
App.TaskVisible = True
```

CROSS-REFERENCE
See also App and ShowInTaskbar.

Terminate

Event

Visual Basic sends an object a `Terminate` event when the object is removed from memory. The exception is when an object terminates abnormally, in which case the object never generates the `Terminate` event.

Objects with a Terminate Event

PropertyPage

UserControl

Form

MDIForm

Example

A program can respond to a `Terminate` event by implementing an object's `Terminate` event procedure. The following code segment shows how a Form object defines a `Terminate` event procedure.

```
Private Sub Form_Terminate()
    ' Handle the Terminate event here.
End Sub
```

 CROSS-REFERENCE
See also Initialize, QueryUnload, and Unload.

TextAlign

Property

The `TextAlign` property represents the preferred text alignment for controls in a form. This property can return a value from 0 to 4, with 0 meaning general alignment, 1 meaning left alignment, 2 meaning center alignment, 3 meaning right alignment, and 4 meaning fully justified alignment.

Objects with a TextAlign Property

AmbientProperties

Syntax

```
value = Ambient.TextAlign
```

- *Ambient*—A reference to the AmbientProperties object.
- *value*—The variable that will receive the property's current setting.

Example

The following lines show how to get the value of the TextAlign property.

```
Dim txtAlign As Integer
txtAlign = UserControl.Ambient.TextAlign
If txtAlign = 0 Then
    MsgBox "General Alignment"
ElseIf txtAlign = 1 Then
    MsgBox "Left Alignment"
ElseIf txtAlign = 2 Then
    MsgBox "Center Alignment"
ElseIf txtAlign = 3 Then
    MsgBox "Right Alignment"
ElseIf txtAlign = 4 Then
    MsgBox "Justified Alignment"
End If
```

CROSS-REFERENCE
See also AmbientProperties and UserControl.

TextAlignment

Property

The TextAlignment property represents how text is displayed in a Toolbar control's buttons. This property can be set to tbrTextAlignBottom (the default) or tbrTextAlignRight. Figure T-9 shows the bottom alignment, whereas Figure T-10 shows the right alignment.

s
t
u

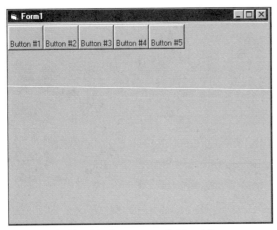

Figure T-9 This Toolbar control's TextAlignment property is set to tbrTextAlignBottom.

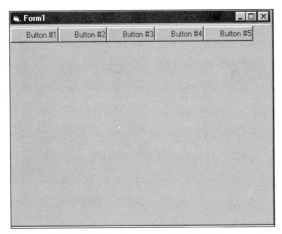

Figure T-10 This Toolbar control's TextAlignment property is set to tbrTextAlignRight.

Objects with a TextAlignment Property

Toolbar

Syntax

```
Toolbar.TextAlignment = value1
```

or

```
value2 = Toolbar.TextAlignment
```

- *Toolbar*— A reference to a Toolbar control.
- *value1*— The value `tbrTextAlignBottom` (the default) or `tbrTextAlignRight`.
- *value2*— The variable that will receive the property's current setting.

Example

The following lines show how to get and set a Toolbar control's `TextAlignment` property. The `tlbToolbar1` object is a Toolbar control that the programmer added to the form at design time.

```
Dim txtAlignment As Integer
txtAlignment = tlbToolbar1.TextAlignment
tlbToolbar1.TextAlignment = tbrTextAlignRight
```

 CROSS-REFERENCE
See also Button, Buttons, and Toolbar.

TextBackground

Property

The `TextBackground` property represents whether a ListView control's ListItem objects have transparent or opaque backgrounds. This property, which can be set to `lvwTransparent` (the default) or `lvwOpaque`, has a noticeable effect only when the ListView control is displaying a background picture.

Objects with a TextBackground Property
ListView

Syntax

`ListView.TextBackground = value1`

or

`value2 = ListView.TextBackground`

- *ListView*— A reference to a ListView control.
- *value1*— The value `lvwTransparent` (the default) or `lvwOpaque`.
- *value2*— The variable that will receive the property's current setting.

Example

The following program illustrates the use of the `TextBackground` property. When you run the program, you see the ListView control shown in Figure T-11. Notice that the list items have transparent backgrounds that allow the background picture to show through. Now, click the Toggle Background button, and the list item backgrounds become opaque, as shown in Figure T-12. You can continue to toggle the background between the two possible settings by clicking the Toggle Background button.

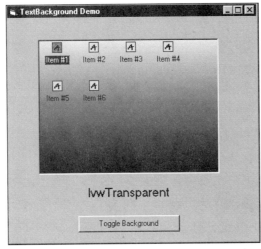

Figure T-11 These list items have transparent backgrounds.

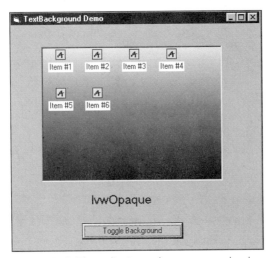

Figure T-12 These list items have opaque backgrounds.

```
VERSION 5.00
Object = "{831FDD16-0C5C-11D2-A9FC-0000F8754DA1}#2.0#0";
"MSCOMCTL.OCX"
Begin VB.Form frmForm1
   AutoRedraw      =   -1  'True
   Caption         =   "Form1"
   ClientHeight    =   5145
   ClientLeft      =   60
   ClientTop       =   345
   ClientWidth     =   5940
   LinkTopic       =   "Form1"
   ScaleHeight     =   343
   ScaleMode       =   3  'Pixel
   ScaleWidth      =   396
   StartUpPosition =   3  'Windows Default
   Begin VB.CommandButton btnToggleBackground
      Caption      =   "Toggle Background"
      Height       =   375
      Left         =   1680
      TabIndex     =   1
      Top          =   4560
      Width        =   2415
   End
   Begin MSComctlLib.ImageList ilsImageList1
      Left         =   3720
      Top          =   2760
      _ExtentX     =   1005
      _ExtentY     =   1005
      BackColor    =   -2147483643
      MaskColor    =   12632256
      _Version     =   393216
   End
   Begin MSComctlLib.ListView lvwListView1
      Height       =   3135
      Left         =   720
      TabIndex     =   0
      Top          =   480
      Width        =   4335
      _ExtentX     =   7646
      _ExtentY     =   5530
      LabelWrap    =   -1  'True
      HideSelection =  -1  'True
      _Version     =   393217
      ForeColor    =   -2147483640
```

```
        BackColor       =    -2147483643
        BorderStyle     =    1
        Appearance      =    1
        NumItems        =    0
     End
     Begin VB.Label lblBackground
        Caption         =    "lvwTransparent"
        BeginProperty Font
           Name              =    "MS Sans Serif"
           Size              =    13.5
           Charset           =    0
           Weight            =    400
           Underline         =    0    'False
           Italic            =    0    'False
           Strikethrough     =    0    'False
        EndProperty
        Height          =    495
        Left            =    1920
        TabIndex        =    2
        Top             =    3840
        Width           =    2175
     End
  End
End
Attribute VB_Name = "frmForm1"
Attribute VB_GlobalNameSpace = False
Attribute VB_Creatable = False
Attribute VB_PredeclaredId = True
Attribute VB_Exposed = False

Private Sub btnToggleBackground_Click()
    If lvwListView1.TextBackground = lvwTransparent Then
        lvwListView1.TextBackground = lvwOpaque
        lblBackground.Caption = "lvwOpaque"
    Else
        lvwListView1.TextBackground = lvwTransparent
        lblBackground.Caption = "lvwTransparent"
    End If
End Sub

Private Sub Form_Load()
    ilsImageList1.ListImages.Add 1, "Image1", _
        LoadPicture("icon2.ico")
```

```
        lvwListView1.Icons = ilsImageList1
        lvwListView1.Picture = LoadPicture("bkimage.jpg")
        lvwListView1.ListItems.Add , , "Item #1", 1
        lvwListView1.ListItems.Add , , "Item #2", 1
        lvwListView1.ListItems.Add , , "Item #3", 1
        lvwListView1.ListItems.Add , , "Item #4", 1
        lvwListView1.ListItems.Add , , "Item #5", 1
        lvwListView1.ListItems.Add , , "Item #6", 1
        lvwListView1.TextBackground = lvwTransparent
        frmForm1.AutoRedraw = True
    End Sub
```

 CROSS-REFERENCE
See also ListItem, ListItems, and ListView.

TextBox

Control

A TextBox control enables the user to enter text into a small box in a window. Programs often use TextBox controls to get data from the user, but the program can also display text in a TextBox control. Figure T-13 shows several TextBox controls in a form. The TextBox control is available on Visual Basic's standard toolbox.

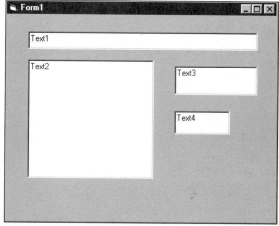

Figure T-13 TextBox controls come in many shapes and sizes.

Properties

The TextBox control has 52 properties, which are listed below. Because many Visual Basic controls have similar properties, the following list does not include the properties' descriptions. For information on using a property, look up the individual property's entry, provided alphabetically in this book.

```
Alignment
Appearance
BackColor
BorderStyle
CausesValidation
Container
DragIcon
DragMode
Enabled
Font
FontBold
FontItalic
FontName
FontSize
FontStrikethru
FontUnderline
ForeColor
Height
HelpContextID
HideSelection
hWnd
Index
Left
LinkItem
LinkMode
LinkTimeout
LinkTopic
Locked
MaxLength
MouseIcon
MousePointer
MultiLine
Name
OLEDragMode
OLEDropMode
Parent
```

```
PasswordChar
RightToLeft
ScrollBars
SelLength
SelStart
SelText
Style
TabIndex
TabStop
Tag
Text
ToolTipText
Top
Visible
WhatsThisHelpID
Width
```

Methods

The TextBox control has 11 methods, which are listed below. Because many Visual Basic controls have similar methods, the following list does not include the methods' descriptions. For information on using a method, look up the individual method's entry, provided alphabetically in this book.

```
Drag
LinkExecute
LinkPoke
LinkRequest
LinkSend
Move
OLEDrag
Refresh
SetFocus
ShowWhatsThis
ZOrder
```

Events

The TextBox control responds to 24 events, which are listed below. Because many Visual Basic controls respond to similar events, the following list does not include the events' descriptions. For information on using an event, look up the individual event's entry, provided alphabetically in this book.

```
Change
Click
```

```
DblClick
DragDrop
DragOver
GotFocus
KeyDown
KeyPress
KeyUp
LinkClose
LinkError
LinkNotify
LinkOpen
LostFocus
MouseDown
MouseMove
MouseUp
OLECompleteDrag
OLEDragDrop
OLEDragOver
OLEGiveFeedback
OLESetData
OLEStartDrag
Validate
```

The TextBox control's most commonly used event is `Change`, which the control generates when the user changes the text in the control. A program responds to the button's `Change` event in the `Change` event procedure. A text box called `txtText1` will have a `Change` event procedure called `txtText1_Change`, which is where the program should handle the event, as shown in the following lines:

```
Private Sub txtText1_Change()
    ' Handle the Change event here.
End Sub
```

Text — ComboBox

Property

The `Text` property represents the text that appears in the ComboBox control's edit box or the text the user has selected. If the control is a drop-down or simple combo box, this property is the text in the edit box. If the control is a drop-down list combo box, the `Text` property represents the text item selected in the list.

Syntax

```
ComboBox.Text = value1
```

or

```
value2 = ComboBox.Text
```

- *ComboBox* — A reference to a ComboBox control.
- *value1* — The string to place into the control's edit box.
- *value2* — The variable that will receive the property's current text.

Example

The following lines show how to get and set a ComboBox control's text. The cboCombo1 object is a ComboBox control that the programmer added to the form at design time.

```
Dim txt As String
txt = cboCombo1.Text
cboCombo1.Text = "ComboBox Text"
```

CROSS-REFERENCE
See also ComboBox.

Text — ListBox

Property

The Text property represents the text that the user has selected in the ListBox control's list.

Syntax

```
ListBox.Text = value1
```

or

```
value2 = ListBox.Text
```

- *ListBox* — A reference to a ListBox control.
- *value1* — The string item to set to the selected state.
- *value2* — The variable that will receive the property's current selected item.

Example

The following lines show how to get and set a ListBox control's text. The lstList1 object is a ListBox control that the programmer added to the form at design time.

```
Dim txt As String
txt = lstList1.Text
lstList1.Text = "Item #3"
```

CROSS-REFERENCE
See also ListBox.

Text—TextBox

Property

The Text property represents the text that appears in the TextBox control or the text that the user has typed into the control.

Syntax

```
TextBox.Text = value1
```

or

```
value2 = TextBox.Text
```

- *TextBox* — A reference to a TextBox control.
- *value1* — The string to display in the control.
- *value2* — The variable that will receive the property's current text.

Example

The following lines show how to get and set a TextBox control's text. The txtText1 object is a TextBox control that the programmer added to the form at design time.

```
Dim txt As String
txt = txtText1.Text
txtText1.Text = "TextBox Text"
```

CROSS-REFERENCE
See also SelLength, SelStart, SelText, and TextBox.

TextHeight

Method

The `TextHeight` method returns the height of a string as it will appear displayed in the current font. The unit of measurement depends on the setting of the container's `ScaleMode` property. That is, if a form's `ScaleMode` property is set to pixels, the text height will be returned as pixels, whereas if the form's `ScaleMode` property is set to twips, the text height will be returned as twips, and so on.

Objects with a TextHeight Method

Form

PictureBox

Printer

PropertyPage

UserControl

Syntax

```
height = object.TextHeight(str)
```

- *height* — The variable that will receive the text height.
- *object* — A reference to an object with a `TextHeight` method.
- *str* — The string for which the method should calculate the height.

Example

The following lines show how to retrieve the height of a text line.

```
Dim txtHeight As Integer
txtHeight = frmForm1.TextHeight("This is a test.")
```

 CROSS-REFERENCE

See also Scale, ScaleMode, and TextWidth.

s
t
u

TextPosition

Property

The TextPosition property represents where tooltip text appears on a Slider control. This property can be set to sldAboveLeft or sldBelowRight. A vertical Slider would position its text to the left or right, rather than above or below.

Objects with a TextPosition Property

Slider

Syntax

```
Slider.TextPosition = value1
```

or

```
value2 = Slider.TextPosition
```

- *Slider*—A reference to a Slider control.
- *value1*—The value sldAboveLeft or sldBelowRight.
- *value2*—The variable that will receive the property's current setting.

Example

The following lines show how to get and set a Slider control's text position.

```
Dim txtPosition As Integer
txtPosition = Slider1.TextPosition
Slider1.TextPosition = sldAboveLeft
```

 **CROSS-REFERENCE**
See also Slider.

TextRTF

Property

The TextRTF property represents, as RTF-formatted text, the text in a RichTextBox control.

Objects with a TextRTF Property
RichTextBox

Syntax

```
RichTextBox.TextRTF = value1
```

or

```
value2 = RichTextBox.TextRTF
```

- *RichTextBox* — A reference to a RichTextBox control.
- *value1* — The text to place into the control.
- *value2* — The variable that will receive the property's current text in RTF format.

Example

The following lines show how to get and set the text type in a RichTextBox control. Figure T-14 shows the type of text returned from the `TextRTF` property. Notice the format codes embedded in the text. In this example, the `rtfRichTextBox1` object is a RichTextBox control that the programmer added to the form at design time.

```
Dim rtfText As String
rtfText = rtfRichTextBox1.TextRTF
rtfRichTextBox1.TextRTF = "RichTextBox Text"
```

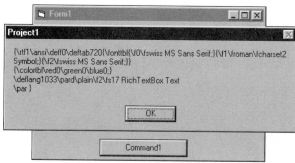

Figure T-14 This is the type of text returned from the TextRTF property.

CROSS-REFERENCE
See also SelRTF.

TextStream

Object

A TextStream object represents a data stream associated with a text file.

Properties

The TextStream object has four properties, which are listed below. For more information on using a property shown here, look up the individual property's entry, provided alphabetically in this book.

```
AtEndOfLine
AtEndOfStream
Column
Line
```

Methods

The TextStream object has nine methods, which are listed below. For more information on using a method shown here, look up the individual method's entry, provided alphabetically in this book.

```
Close
Read
ReadAll
ReadLine
Skip
SkipLine
Write
WriteBlankLines
WriteLine
```

Events

The TextStream object does not respond to events.

Example

The following lines create a FileSystemObject object from which the program creates a TextStream object. This TextStream object represents a file named MyText.txt. After creating the file, the program writes three lines of text to the file, and then closes the file.

```
Dim fileSystem As Object
Dim txtStream As Object
```

```
Set fileSystem = CreateObject("Scripting.FileSystemObject")
Set txtStream = fileSystem.CreateTextFile("c:\MyText.txt")
txtStream.WriteLine ("Line #1")
txtStream.WriteLine ("Line #2")
txtStream.WriteLine ("Line #3")
txtStream.Close
```

CROSS-REFERENCE
See also FileSystemObject.

TextWidth

Method

The TextWidth method returns the width of a string as it will appear displayed in the current font. The unit of measurement depends on the setting of the container's ScaleMode property. That is, if a form's ScaleMode property is set to pixels, the text width will be returned as pixels, whereas if the form's ScaleMode property is set to twips, the text width will be returned as twips, and so on.

Objects with a TextWidth Method

Form

PictureBox

Printer

PropertyPage

UserControl

Syntax

```
width = object.TextWidth(str)
```

- *object* — A reference to an object with a TextWidth method.
- *str* — The string for which the method should calculate the width.
- *width* — The variable that will receive the text width.

Example

The following lines show how to retrieve the width of a text line.

```
Dim txtWidth As Integer
txtWidth = frmForm1.TextWidth("This is a test.")
```

CROSS-REFERENCE
See also Scale, ScaleMode, and TextHeight.

Then

Keyword

The `Then` keyword is part of the `If/Then` statement, which enables a program to route execution based on the value of variables. You can also use the `Then` keyword with the `#If` compiler directive. The following lines show a simple `If/Then` statement.

```
If x = 12 Then Y = 100
```

 CROSS-REFERENCE
See also If/Then.

ThreadID

Property

The `ThreadID` property represents the ID of the currently executing thread.

Objects with a ThreadID Property

App

Syntax

```
value = App.ThreadID
```

- *App*—A reference to the App object.
- *value*—The variable that will receive the thread ID.

Example

The following lines show how to get a program's thread ID. Note that the App object is a global Visual Basic object that you don't need to create in your programs.

```
Dim id As Long
id = App.ThreadID
```

CROSS-REFERENCE
See also App.

TickFrequency

Property

The TickFrequency property determines the number of tick marks that appear on a Slider control. The tick-frequency value is the number of units between tick marks. That is, if a Slider has a range of 10 and the TickFrequency property is set to 1, a tick mark will appear at each of the possible 11 values (including 0) in the control, for a total of 11 tick marks. If the TickFrequency property of the same control were set to 2, there would be six tick marks, one at each value of 0, 2, 4, 6, 8, and 10.

Objects with a TickFrequency Property

Slider

Syntax

Slider.TickFrequency = *value1*

or

value2 = *Slider*.TickFrequency

- *Slider* — A reference to a Slider control.
- *value1* — The tick frequency.
- *value2* — The variable that will receive the property's current setting.

Example

The following program demonstrates the TickFrequency property. When you run the program, you see the window shown in Figure T-15. As you can see, the Slider control starts off with a tick frequency of 5. Enter a tick frequency between 1 and 100 into the text box, and then click the Set Tick Frequency button. The Slider control updates itself with a new set of tick marks. For example, Figure T-16 shows the control with a tick frequency of 20.

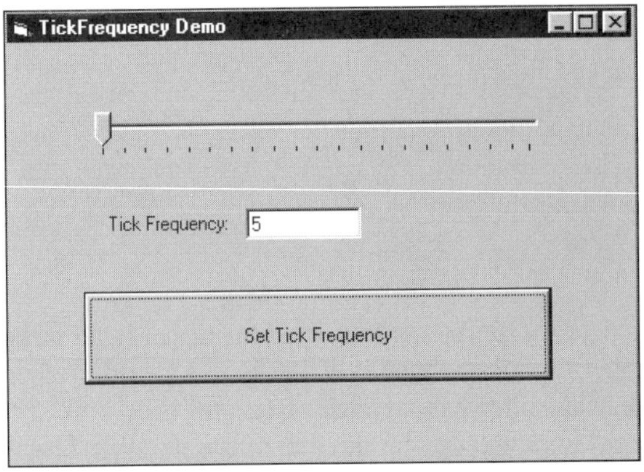

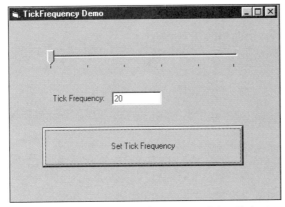

Figure T-15 Here, the tick frequency of the Slider is set to 5.

Figure T-16 Here, the tick frequency of the Slider is set to 20.

```
VERSION 5.00
Object = "{831FDD16-0C5C-11D2-A9FC-0000F8754DA1} _
    #2.0#0"; "MSCOMCTL.OCX"
Begin VB.Form frmForm1
    Caption         =   "TickFrequency Demo"
    ClientHeight    =   3840
    ClientLeft      =   60
    ClientTop       =   345
    ClientWidth     =   5940
    LinkTopic       =   "Form1"
    ScaleHeight     =   256
    ScaleMode       =   3  'Pixel
    ScaleWidth      =   396
    StartUpPosition =   3  'Windows Default
```

```
        Begin VB.CommandButton btnSetFreq
            Caption         =       "Set Tick Frequency"
            Height          =       855
            Left            =       720
            TabIndex        =       3
            Top             =       2280
            Width           =       4455
        End
        Begin VB.TextBox txtFreq
            Height          =       285
            Left            =       2280
            TabIndex        =       1
            Top             =       1530
            Width           =       1095
        End
        Begin MSComctlLib.Slider Slider1
            Height          =       630
            Left            =       720
            TabIndex        =       0
            Top             =       600
            Width           =       4455
            _ExtentX        =       7858
            _ExtentY        =       1111
            _Version        =       393216
        End
        Begin VB.Label Label1
            Caption         =       "Tick Frequency:"
            Height          =       255
            Left            =       960
            TabIndex        =       2
            Top             =       1560
            Width           =       1215
        End
    End
End
Attribute VB_Name = "frmForm1"
Attribute VB_GlobalNameSpace = False
Attribute VB_Creatable = False
Attribute VB_PredeclaredId = True
Attribute VB_Exposed = False

Private Sub btnSetFreq_Click()
    Dim freq As Integer
    On Error GoTo ErrorHandler
    freq = txtFreq.Text
```

```
        Slider1.TickFrequency = freq
        Exit Sub

ErrorHandler:
        MsgBox "Enter a valid value.", vbExclamation
End Sub

Private Sub Form_Load()
        Slider1.Min = 1
        Slider1.Max = 100
        Slider1.TickFrequency = 5
        txtFreq.Text = 5
End Sub
```

 CROSS-REFERENCE
See also GetNumTicks, Max, Min, Slider, and TickStyle.

TickStyle

Property

The TickStyle property determines where tick marks are drawn on a Slider control. This property can be set to sldBoth, sldBottomRight, sldNoTicks, or sldTopLeft. Whether the tick marks appear above, below, right, or left depends not only upon the setting of the TickStyle property, but also upon whether the control is vertical or horizontal.

Objects with a TickStyle Property

Slider

Syntax

Slider.TickStyle = *value1*

or

value2 = *Slider*.TickStyle

- *Slider*—A reference to a Slider control.
- *value1*—The tick style value.
- *value2*—The variable that will receive the property's current setting.

Example

The following program demonstrates the `TickStyle` property. When you run the program, you see the window shown in Figure T-17. As you can see, the Slider control starts off with tick marks both above and below the control. Click the Toggle Tick Style button to see another tick style. For example, Figure T-18 shows the control with the `sldTopLeft` tick style.

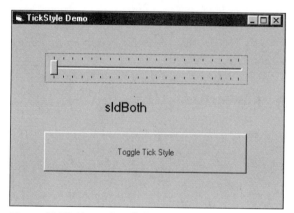

Figure T-17 Here, the Slider's tick style is set to sldBoth.

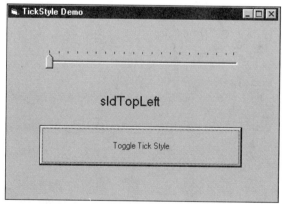

Figure T-18 Here, the Slider's tick style is set to sldTopLeft.

```
VERSION 5.00
Object = "{831FDD16-0C5C-11D2-A9FC-0000F8754DA1} _
    #2.0#0"; "MSCOMCTL.OCX"
Begin VB.Form frmForm1
   Caption         =   "TickStyle Demo"
   ClientHeight    =   3840
```

```
ClientLeft      =    60
ClientTop       =    345
ClientWidth     =    5940
LinkTopic       =    "Form1"
ScaleHeight     =    256
ScaleMode       =    3    'Pixel
ScaleWidth      =    396
StartUpPosition =    3    'Windows Default
Begin VB.CommandButton btnToggle
   Caption         =    "Toggle Tick Style"
   Height          =    855
   Left            =    720
   TabIndex        =    1
   Top             =    2280
   Width           =    4455
End
Begin MSComctlLib.Slider Slider1
   Height          =    630
   Left            =    720
   TabIndex        =    0
   Top             =    600
   Width           =    4455
   _ExtentX        =    7858
   _ExtentY        =    1111
   _Version        =    393216
End
Begin VB.Label lblTickStyle
   Caption         =    "Label1"
   BeginProperty Font
      Name            =    "MS Sans Serif"
      Size            =    13.5
      Charset         =    0
      Weight          =    400
      Underline       =    0    'False
      Italic          =    0    'False
      Strikethrough   =    0    'False
   EndProperty
   Height          =    495
   Left            =    2040
   TabIndex        =    2
   Top             =    1560
   Width           =    3015
End
End
```

```
Attribute VB_Name = "frmForm1"
Attribute VB_GlobalNameSpace = False
Attribute VB_Creatable = False
Attribute VB_PredeclaredId = True
Attribute VB_Exposed = False

Private Sub btnToggle_Click()
    If Slider1.TickStyle = sldBottomRight Then
        Slider1.TickStyle = sldTopLeft
        lblTickStyle.Caption = "sldTopLeft"
    ElseIf Slider1.TickStyle = sldTopLeft Then
        Slider1.TickStyle = sldBoth
        lblTickStyle.Caption = "sldBoth"
    ElseIf Slider1.TickStyle = sldBoth Then
        Slider1.TickStyle = sldNoTicks
        lblTickStyle.Caption = "sldNoTicks"
    ElseIf Slider1.TickStyle = sldNoTicks Then
        Slider1.TickStyle = sldBottomRight
        lblTickStyle.Caption = "sldBottomRight"
    End If
End Sub

Private Sub Form_Load()
    Slider1.Min = 1
    Slider1.Max = 100
    Slider1.TickFrequency = 5
    Slider1.TickStyle = sldBoth
    lblTickStyle.Caption = "sldBoth"
End Sub
```

CROSS-REFERENCE
See also GetNumTicks, Max, Min, Slider, and TickFrequency.

Time

Function

The Time function returns the system time.

Syntax

```
value = Time
```

- *value* — The variable that will receive the current time.

Example

The following lines retrieve the current time in the format hh:mm:ss AM/PM. For example, the returned time might be something like 12:45:15 PM.

```
Dim curTime As Variant
curTime = Time
```

CROSS-REFERENCE
See also Date and Time (statement).

Time

Statement

The Time statement sets the current system time.

Syntax

```
Time(timeVal)
```

- *timeValue* — A value that represents the time.

Example

The following line demonstrates how to set the system time with the Time statement.

```
Time = #12:45:15 PM#
```

CROSS-REFERENCE
See also Date and Time (function).

TimeChanged

Event

Visual Basic sends a SysInfo control a TimeChanged event when the user or an application changes the system time.

Objects with a TimeChanged Event

SysInfo

Example

A program can respond to a `TimeChanged` event by implementing the SysInfo control's `TimeChanged` event procedure. The following code segment shows how a SysInfo control defines a `TimeChanged` event procedure. In this example, the `SysInfo1` object is a SysInfo control that the programmer added to the form at design time.

```
Private Sub SysInfo1_TimeChanged()
    ' Handle the TimeChanged event here.
End Sub
```

 CROSS-REFERENCE
See also SettingChanged and SysInfo.

TimeFormat

Property

The `TimeFormat` property represents the time format used with the current media loaded into a Multimedia MCI control. This property returns one of the values shown in Table T-2.

Table T-2 Values of the TimeFormat Property

Value	Description
mciFormatBytes	Bytes as four-byte integers.
mciFormatFrames	Frames as a four-byte integer.
mciFormatHms	Hours, minutes, and seconds as a four-byte integer, in the order hours (least-significant byte), minutes, and seconds. The most-significant byte is not used.
mciFormatMilliseconds	Milliseconds as a four-byte integer.
mciFormatMsf	Minutes, seconds, and frames as a four-byte integer, in the order minutes (least-significant byte), seconds, and frames. The most-significant byte is not used.
mciFormatSamples	Samples as four-byte integers.
mciFormatSmpte24	24-frame SMPTE hours, minutes, seconds, and frames as a four-byte integer, in the order hours (least-significant byte), minutes, seconds, and frames.
mciFormatSmpte25	25-frame SMPTE hours, minutes, seconds, and frames as a four-byte integer, in the order hours (least-significant byte), minutes, seconds, and frames.

Continued

Table T-2 *Continued*	
Value	**Description**
mciFormatSmpte30	30-frame SMPTE hours, minutes, seconds, and frames as a four-byte integer, in the order hours (least-significant byte), minutes, seconds, and frames.
mciFormatSmpte30Drop	30-drop-frame SMPTE hours, minutes, seconds, and frames as a four-byte integer, in the order hours (least-significant byte), minutes, seconds, and frames.
mciFormatTmsf	Tracks, minutes, seconds, and frames as a four-byte integer, in the order tracks (least-significant byte), minutes, seconds, and frames.

Objects with a TimeFormat Property

Multimedia MCI

Syntax

```
value = Multimedia.TimeFormat
```

- *Multimedia* — A reference to a Multimedia MCI control.
- *value* — The variable that will receive the property's current setting.

Example

The following lines show how to get the value of a Multimedia control's `TimeFormat` property.

```
Dim intTimeFormat As Long
intTimeFormat = MMControl1.TimeFormat
If intTimeFormat = mciFormatBytes Then
    MsgBox "mciFormatBytes"
ElseIf intTimeFormat = mciFormatFrames Then
    MsgBox "mciFormatFrames"
ElseIf intTimeFormat = mciFormatHms Then
    MsgBox "mciFormatHms"
ElseIf intTimeFormat = mciFormatMilliseconds Then
    MsgBox "mciFormatMilliseconds"
ElseIf intTimeFormat = mciFormatMsf Then
    MsgBox "mciFormatMsf"
ElseIf intTimeFormat = mciFormatSamples Then
    MsgBox "mciFormatSamples"
ElseIf intTimeFormat = mciFormatSmpte24 Then
    MsgBox "mciFormatSmpte24"
```

```
ElseIf intTimeFormat = mciFormatSmpte25 Then
    MsgBox "mciFormatSmpte25"
ElseIf intTimeFormat = mciFormatSmpte30 Then
    MsgBox "mciFormatSmpte30"
ElseIf intTimeFormat = mciFormatSmpte30Drop Then
    MsgBox "mciFormatSmpte30Drop"
ElseIf intTimeFormat = mciFormatTmsf Then
    MsgBox "mciFormatTmsf"
End If
```

CROSS-REFERENCE
See also Multimedia MCI.

Timer

Control

A Timer control enables a program to respond to time events that are triggered when the control reaches a specified time interval. A Timer control isn't visible at runtime, but appears as a small clock in the form at design time, as shown in Figure T-19. The Timer control is included in the standard Visual Basic toolbox.

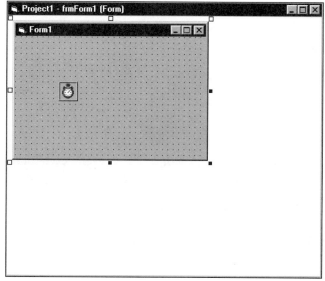

Figure T-19 The Timer control is visible only at design time.

Properties

The Timer control has six properties, which are listed below. Because many Visual Basic controls have similar properties, the following list does not include the properties' descriptions. For information on using a property, look up the individual property's entry, provided alphabetically in this book.

```
Enabled
Index
Interval
Name
Parent
Tag
```

Methods

The Timer control has no methods.

Events

The Timer control responds to one event, Timer, which is triggered each time the control reaches the time interval specified in the Interval property. A program responds to the control's Timer event in the Timer event procedure. An Timer control called Timer1 will have a Timer event procedure called Timer1_Timer, which is where the program should handle the event, as shown in the following lines:

```
Private Sub Timer1_Timer()
    ' Handle the Timer event here.
End Sub
```

Timer

Event

Visual Basic sends a Timer control a Timer event each time the control reaches the time interval set in its Interval property.

Objects with a Timer Event

Timer

Example

A program can respond to a `Timer` event by implementing the Timer control's `Timer` event procedure. The following code segment shows how a Timer control defines a `Timer` event procedure. In this example, the `Timer1` object is a Timer control that the programmer added to the form at design time.

```
Private Sub Timer1_Timer()
    ' Handle the Timer event here.
End Sub
```

 CROSS-REFERENCE
See also Timer (control) and Interval.

Timer

Function

The `Timer` function returns the elapsed seconds since midnight.

Syntax

```
value = Timer
```

- *value* — The variable that will receive the number of seconds since midnight.

Example

The following lines wait 10 seconds before showing a message box.

```
Dim curTime As Single
curTime = Timer
Do
Loop Until Timer > curTime + 10
MsgBox "Time is up!"
```

 CROSS-REFERENCE
See also Timer (control).

s
t
u

TimeSerial

Function

The TimeSerial function converts a set of integer values to a time value.

Syntax

```
value = TimeSerial(hour, minute, second)
```

- *hour* — The hour from 0 to 23.
- *minute* — The minute from 0 to 59.
- *second* — The second from 0 to 59.
- *value* — The variable that will receive the time value.

Example 1

After the following lines execute, the variable vntTime will contain the value "5:15:25 AM."

```
Dim vntTime As Variant
vntTime = TimeSerial(5, 15, 25)
```

Example 2

Here, after the following lines execute, the variable vntTime will contain the value "1:14:05 PM," showing that you can use numerical expressions with the TimeSerial function.

```
Dim vntTime As Variant
Dim intHour As Integer
Dim intMinute As Integer
Dim intSecond As Integer
intHour = 15
intMinute = 24
intSecond = 5
vntTime = TimeSerial(intHour - 2, intMinute - 10, intSecond)
```

CROSS-REFERENCE
See also DateSerial, DateValue, Hour, Minute, Now, Second, and TimeValue.

TimeValue

Function

The `TimeValue` function converts a string value, or other type of expression, into a time value.

Syntax

```
value = TimeValue(time)
```

- *time* — The expression, usually a string, representing the time.
- *value* — The variable that will receive the time value.

Example

After the following lines execute, the variable `vntTime` will contain the value "5:45:00 PM."

```
Dim vntTime As Variant
vntTime = TimeValue("17:45")
```

 CROSS-REFERENCE
See also DateSerial, DateValue, Hour, Minute, Now, Second, and TimeSerial.

Title

Property

The `Title` property represents the application title that's shown in the Windows task list.

Objects with a Title Property
App

Syntax

```
App.Title = value1
```

or

```
value2 = App.Title
```

- *App*—A reference to an App object.
- *value1*—A string containing the application's task name.
- *value2*—The variable that will receive the property's current setting.

Example

The following lines show how to get and set the App object's Title property. Note that the App object is a global Visual Basic object that you don't need to create in your programs. Although you can set the Title property at runtime, you should set its value in the Project Properties property sheet, as shown in Figure T-20.

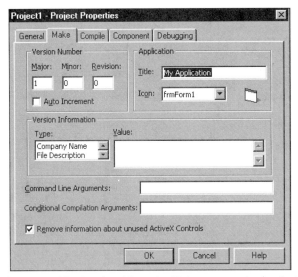

Figure T-20 You should set the Title property in the Project Properties property sheet.

```
Dim strTitle As String
strTitle = App.Title
App.Title = "Application Title"
```

CROSS-REFERENCE
See also App.

To

Property

The To property represents the point at which media loaded into a Multimedia MCI control should stop playing.

Objects with a To Property

Multimedia MCI

Syntax

```
Multimedia.To = value1
```

or

```
value2 = Multimedia.To
```

- *Multimedia* — A reference to a Multimedia MCI control.
- *value1* — The value that represents the stopping point.
- *value2* — The variable that will receive the property's current setting.

Example

The following program demonstrates the use of a Multimedia MCI control's To property. When you run the program, click the Load Wave File button, and then select a wave file to play. (The guitar.wav file comes with the program.) When the program loads the wave file, it displays the start and end of the file in the From and To text boxes (Figure T-21). These values represent milliseconds. Click the Play button to hear the entire file, or you can change the values in the From and To boxes in order to hear only a segment of the file. Don't, however, change the values to anything less than 0 or greater than the value that originally appears in the To box. If you do, you'll hear nothing when you play the file.

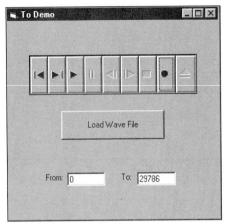

Figure T-21 The To Demo program can play any portion of a wave file.

```
VERSION 5.00
Object = "{C1A8AF28-1257-101B-8FB0-0020AF039CA3} _
    #1.1#0"; "MCI32.OCX"
Object = "{F9043C88-F6F2-101A-A3C9-08002B2F49FB} _
    #1.2#0"; "COMDLG32.OCX"
Begin VB.Form Form1
    Caption         =   "To Demo"
    ClientHeight    =   4215
    ClientLeft      =   60
    ClientTop       =   345
    ClientWidth     =   4680
    LinkTopic       =   "Form1"
    ScaleHeight     =   4215
    ScaleWidth      =   4680
    StartUpPosition =   3   'Windows Default
    Begin VB.TextBox txtTo
        Height      =   285
        Left        =   2880
        TabIndex    =   5
        Top         =   3240
        Width       =   855
    End
    Begin VB.TextBox txtFrom
        Height      =   285
        Left        =   1320
        TabIndex    =   3
```

```
      Top              =     3240
      Width            =     855
   End
   Begin MSComDlg.CommonDialog dlgCommonDialog1
      Left             =     4080
      Top              =     3600
      _ExtentX         =     847
      _ExtentY         =     847
      _Version         =     393216
   End
   Begin MCI.MMControl mciMMControl1
      Height           =     855
      Left             =     480
      TabIndex         =     1
      Top              =     720
      Width            =     3735
      _ExtentX         =     6588
      _ExtentY         =     1508
      _Version         =     393216
      DeviceType       =     ""
      FileName         =     ""
   End
   Begin VB.CommandButton btnLoadWave
      Caption          =     "Load Wave File"
      Height           =     615
      Left             =     1200
      TabIndex         =     0
      Top              =     1920
      Width            =     2295
   End
   Begin VB.Label Label2
      Caption          =     "To:"
      Height           =     255
      Left             =     2520
      TabIndex         =     4
      Top              =     3240
      Width            =     375
   End
   Begin VB.Label Label1
      Caption          =     "From:"
      Height           =     255
      Left             =     840
      TabIndex         =     2
      Top              =     3240
```

```
            Width            =     495
      End
End
Attribute VB_Name = "Form1"
Attribute VB_GlobalNameSpace = False
Attribute VB_Creatable = False
Attribute VB_PredeclaredId = True
Attribute VB_Exposed = False
Private Sub btnLoadWave_Click()
    Dim fileName

    dlgCommonDialog1.CancelError = True
    On Error GoTo CancelErr
    dlgCommonDialog1.DialogTitle = "Choose Wave File"
    dlgCommonDialog1.fileName = "*.wav"
    dlgCommonDialog1.ShowOpen
    fileName = dlgCommonDialog1.fileName

    mciMMControl1.DeviceType = "WaveAudio"
    mciMMControl1.Shareable = False
    mciMMControl1.Wait = True
    mciMMControl1.Notify = False
    mciMMControl1.fileName = fileName
    mciMMControl1.Command = "Open"
    txtTo.Text = mciMMControl1.Length
CancelErr:
End Sub

Private Sub Form_Load()
    txtFrom.Text = 0
    txtTo.Text = 0
End Sub

Private Sub mciMMControl1_PlayClick(Cancel As Integer)
    Dim intFrom As Long
    Dim intTo As Long
    On Error GoTo errorHandler
    intFrom = txtFrom.Text
    intTo = txtTo.Text
```

```
        mciMMControl1.From = intFrom
        mciMMControl1.To = intTo
        Exit Sub

    errorHandler:
        MsgBox "Please enter valid To and From values.", _
            vbExclamation, "To Demo"
        Cancel = True
    End Sub
```

CROSS-REFERENCE
See also Multimedia MCI and From.

Toolbar

Control

A Toolbar control gives the user quick access to frequently required commands. Programs often use Toolbar controls to mirror important commands found in the application's menu bar. Figure T-22 shows a basic toolbar with five buttons. The Toolbar control is part of the Microsoft Windows Common Controls 6.0 package, which you can add to your project from the Components dialog box, as shown in Figure T-23.

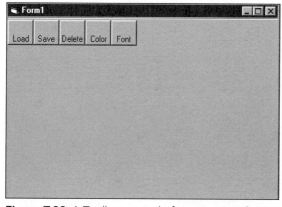

Figure T-22 A Toolbar control often contains shortcut buttons for menu commands.

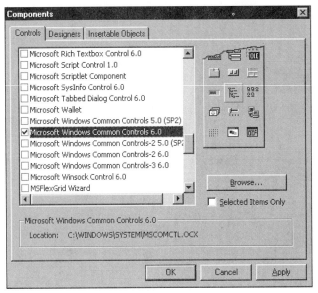

Figure T-23 Use the Components dialog box to add the Toolbar control to your Visual Basic toolbox.

Properties

The Toolbar control has 38 properties, which are listed below. Because many Visual Basic controls have similar properties, the following list does not include the properties' descriptions. For information on using a property, look up the individual property's entry, provided alphabetically in this book.

```
Align
AllowCustomize
Appearance
BorderStyle
ButtonHeight
Buttons
ButtonWidth
Container
Controls
DisabledImageList
DragIcon
DragMode
Enabled
Height
HelpContextID
HelpFile
HotImageList
```

```
hWnd
ImageList
Index
Left
MouseIcon
MousePointer
Name
Object
OLEDropMode
Parent
ShowTips
Style
TabIndex
Tag
TextAlignment
ToolTipText
Top
Visible
WhatsThisHelpID
Width
Wrappable
```

Methods

The Toolbar control has nine methods, which are listed below. Because many Visual Basic controls have similar methods, the following list does not include the methods' descriptions. For information on using a method, look up the individual method's entry, provided alphabetically in this book.

```
Customize
Drag
Move
OLEDrag
Refresh
RestoreToolbar
SaveToolbar
ShowWhatsThis
ZOrder
```

Events

The Toolbar control responds to 17 events, which are listed below. Because many Visual Basic controls respond to similar events, the following list does not include the events' descriptions. For information on using an event, look up the individual event's entry, provided alphabetically in this book.

```
ButtonClick
ButtonDropDown
ButtonMenuClick
Change
Click
DblClick
DragDrop
DragOver
MouseDown
MouseMove
MouseUp
OLECompleteDrag
OLEDragDrop
OLEDragOver
OLEGiveFeedback
OLESetData
OLEStartDrag
```

The Toolbar control's most commonly used event is `ButtonClick`, which the control generates when the user clicks a toolbar button with the mouse. A program responds to the `ButtonClick` event in the `ButtonClick` event procedure. A Toolbar control called `tlbToolbar1` will have a `ButtonClick` event procedure called `tlbToolbar1_ButtonClick`, which is where the program should handle the event, as shown in the following lines:

```
Private Sub tlbToolbar1_ButtonClick _
  (ByVal Button As MSComctlLib.Button)
    ' Handle the ButtonClick event here.
End Sub
```

As you can see, the `ButtonClick` event procedure receives a single parameter, which is a reference to the Button object that represents the button the user clicked.

ToolboxBitmap

Property

The `ToolboxBitmap` property represents the icon that will identify a custom control in the toolbox. You set this bitmap in the control's Properties window.

Objects with a ToolboxBitmap Property

UserControl

CROSS-REFERENCE
See also UserControl.

ToolTipText

Property

The ToolTipText property represents the text that appears when the mouse pointer hovers over a control for a second or two. This text usually gives a brief description of the control's function, which is particularly handy if the control contains only an image and no text. Figure T-24 shows the tooltip text for a CommandButton control.

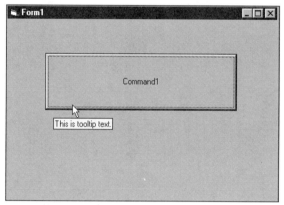

Figure T-24 This tooltip text for a CommandButton control provides you with usage hints.

Objects with a ToolTipText Property

Animation

Button

CheckBox

ComboBox

CommandButton

CoolBar

DirListBox

DriveListBox

FileListBox

Frame

Image

Label

ListBox

ListView

Multimedia MCI

OptionButton

Panel

PictureBox

ProgressBar

RichTextBox

Slider

StatusBar

Tab

TabStrip

TextBox

Toolbar

TreeView

UpDown

Syntax

```
object.ToolTipText = value1
```

or

```
value2 = object.ToolTipText
```

- *object* — A reference to an object with a `ToolTipText` property.
- *value1* — A string containing the tooltip text.
- *value2* — The variable that will receive the property's current setting.

Example

The following lines show how to get and set a CommandButton button's `ToolTipText` property. The `btnCommand1` object is a CommandButton control that the programmer added to the form at design time.

```
Dim strToolTip As String
strToolTip = btnCommand1.ToolTipText
btnCommand1.ToolTipText = "This is tooltip text."
```

CROSS-REFERENCE
See also ShowTips.

Top

Property

The `Top` property represents the vertical position of an object inside its container, with the units of measurement depending on the container's `ScaleMode`. The object's vertical position is measured from the container's top edge.

Objects with a Top Property

Animation
Button
CheckBox
ColumnHeader
ComboBox
CommandButton
CommonDialog
CoolBar
DirListBox
DriveListBox
FileListBox
Form
Frame
HScrollBar
Image
Label
ListBox
ListItem
ListView
MDIForm
Multimedia MCI
OLE Container
OptionButton

Panel

PictureBox

ProgressBar

RichTextBox

Shape

Slider

StatusBar

SysInfo

Tab

TabStrip

TextBox

Timer

Toolbar

TreeView

UpDown

VScrollBar

Syntax

```
object.Top = value1
```

or

```
value2 = object.Top
```

- *object* — A reference to an object with a Top property.
- *value1* — The vertical position of the object from the top of its container.
- *value2* — The variable that will receive the property's current setting.

Example

The following line positions a CommandButton control 500 twips from the top edge of its form. The btnCommand1 object is a CommandButton control that the programmer added to the application's form at design time.

```
btnCommand1.Top = 500
```

CROSS-REFERENCE
See also Height, Left, and Width.

ToPage

Property

The `ToPage` property represents the value that will appear in a Print dialog box's To text box.

Objects with a ToPage Property

CommonDialog

Syntax

```
CommonDialog.ToPage = value1
```

or

```
value2 = CommonDialog.ToPage
```

- *CommonDialog* — A reference to a CommonDialog control.
- *value1* — The ending page number.
- *value2* — The variable that will receive the ending page number.

Example

In this example, the program sets a Print dialog box's To box to 2. The `dlgCommonDialog1` object is a CommonDialog control that the programmer added to the application's form at design time.

```
CommonDialog1.ToPage = 2
```

 CROSS-REFERENCE
See also Flags and FromPage.

TopIndex

Property

The `TopIndex` property represents the index of the item at the top of a list.

Objects with a TopIndex Property

ComboBox

DirListBox

s
t
u

DriveListBox

FileListBox

ListBox

Syntax

object.TopIndex = *value1*

or

value2 = *object*.TopIndex

- *object* — A reference to a control with a TopIndex property.
- *value1* — The new index number for the top item.
- *value2* — The variable that will receive the index number.

Example

The following example program gives you a quick look at how the TopIndex property affects a ListBox control. When you run the program, you see a ListBox loaded with 101 items with indexes from 0 to 100. However, the control can display only six items at a time. By entering an index into the text box and clicking the Set Top Index button, you can scroll to any item without using the ListBox control's scroll bars. Figure T-25, for example, shows the ListBox scrolled to display item #25.

Figure T-25 By setting the TopIndex property, a program can manipulate the scrolling of a list in a control.

```
VERSION 5.00
Begin VB.Form frmForm1
```

```
Caption          =    "TopIndex Demo"
ClientHeight     =    3840
ClientLeft       =    60
ClientTop        =    345
ClientWidth      =    3090
LinkTopic        =    "Form1"
ScaleHeight      =    256
ScaleMode        =    3    'Pixel
ScaleWidth       =    206
StartUpPosition  =    3    'Windows Default
Begin VB.TextBox txtIndex
   Height        =    285
   Left          =    720
   TabIndex      =    3
   Top           =    2040
   Width         =    1215
End
Begin VB.CommandButton btnSetIndex
   Caption       =    "Set Top Index"
   Height        =    615
   Left          =    360
   TabIndex      =    1
   Top           =    2760
   Width         =    2295
End
Begin VB.ListBox lstList1
   Height        =    1230
   Left          =    480
   TabIndex      =    0
   Top           =    360
   Width         =    2055
End
Begin VB.Label Label1
   Caption       =    "Top Index:"
   Height        =    255
   Left          =    720
   TabIndex      =    2
   Top           =    1800
   Width         =    855
End
End
Attribute VB_Name = "frmForm1"
Attribute VB_GlobalNameSpace = False
Attribute VB_Creatable = False
```

```
Attribute VB_PredeclaredId = True
Attribute VB_Exposed = False

Private Sub btnSetIndex_Click()
    Dim indx As Integer
    indx = txtIndex.Text
    lstList1.TopIndex = indx
End Sub

Private Sub Form_Load()
    Dim x As Integer
    Dim itemName As String
    For x = 0 To 100
        itemName = "This is item #" & x
        lstList1.AddItem itemName
    Next
End Sub
```

CROSS-REFERENCE
See also Flags and FromPage.

TotalSize

Property

The TotalSize property represents the size of a drive.

Objects with a TotalSize Property

Drive

Syntax

`value = Drive.TotalSize`

- *Drive*—A reference to a Drive object.
- *value*—The variable that will receive the drive's size in bytes.

Example

The following lines show how to get a drive's size.

```
Dim fileSystem As Object
Dim drive As Object
```

```
Dim drvSize As Long
Set fileSystem = CreateObject("Scripting.FileSystemObject")
Set drive = fileSystem.GetDrive("c")
drvSize = drive.TotalSize
```

CROSS-REFERENCE
See also AvailableSpace, Drive, and FreeSpace.

Track

Property

The Track property represents the track for which the TrackLength and TrackPosition properties contain information.

Objects with a Track Property

Multimedia MCI

Syntax

```
Multimedia.Track = value1
```

or

```
value2 = Multimedia.Track
```

- *Multimedia* — A reference to a Multimedia MCI control.
- *value1* — The track number.
- *value* — The variable that will receive the property's current setting.

Example

The following lines show how to get and set the value of a Multimedia control's Track property. In this example, the mciMMControl1 object is a Multimedia MCI control that the programmer added to the form at design time.

```
Dim trk As Long
trk = mciMMControl1.Track
mciMMControl1.Track = 5
```

CROSS-REFERENCE
See also Multimedia MCI, TrackLength, and TrackPosition.

TrackDefault

Property

The `TrackDefault` property represents whether the Printer object switches to a different printer when the user changes the default printer.

Objects with a TrackDefault Property

Printer

Syntax

```
Printer.TrackDefault = value1
```

or

```
value2 = Printer.TrackDefault
```

- *Printer* — A reference to the Printer object.
- *value1* — The value `True` (default) or `False`.
- *value2* — The variable that will receive the property's current setting.

Example

The following lines show how to get and set the Printer object's `TrackDefault` property. Note that the Printer object is a global Visual Basic object that you don't need to create in your programs.

```
Dim useDfltPrinter As Boolean
useDfltPrinter = Printer.TrackDefault
Printer.TrackDefault = False
```

CROSS-REFERENCE
See also Printer.

TrackLength

Property

The `TrackLength` property represents the length of the track specified in the `Track` property.

Objects with a TrackLength Property

Multimedia MCI

Syntax

```
value = Multimedia.TrackLength
```

- *Multimedia* — A reference to a Multimedia MCI control.
- *value* — The variable that will receive the property's current setting.

Example

The following lines show how to get the value of a Multimedia control's TrackLength property. In this example, the mciMMControl1 object is a Multimedia MCI control that the programmer added to the form at design time.

```
Dim trkLength As Long
trkLength = mciMMControl1.TrackLength
```

CROSS-REFERENCE

See also Multimedia MCI, TimeFormat, and Track.

TrackPosition

Property

The TrackPosition property represents the starting position of the track specified in the Track property.

Objects with a TrackPosition Property

Multimedia MCI

Syntax

```
value = Multimedia.TrackPosition
```

- *Multimedia* — A reference to a Multimedia MCI control.
- *value* — The variable that will receive the property's current setting.

Example

The following lines show how to get the value of a Multimedia control's `TrackPosition` property. In this example, the `mciMMControl1` object is a Multimedia MCI control that the programmer added to the form at design time.

```
Dim trkPosition As Long
trkPosition = mciMMControl1.TrackPosition
```

 CROSS-REFERENCE
See also Multimedia MCI, TimeFormat, and Track.

Tracks

Property

The `Tracks` property represents the number of tracks on the media that are currently open in a Multimedia MCI control.

Objects with a Tracks Property

Multimedia MCI

Syntax

```
value = Multimedia.Tracks
```

- *Multimedia*—A reference to a Multimedia MCI control.
- *value*—The variable that will receive the property's current setting.

Example

The following lines show how to get the value of a Multimedia control's `Tracks` property. In this example, the `mciMMControl1` object is a Multimedia MCI control that the programmer added to the form at design time.

```
Dim trkCount As Long
trkCount = mciMMControl1.Tracks
```

 CROSS-REFERENCE
See also Multimedia MCI, Track, TrackLength, and TrackPosition.

TreeView

Control

A TreeView control enables a program to display various types of data in a hierarchical arrangement. For example, Windows Explorer uses a tree view control to display the contents of a disk. Figure T-26 shows a simple TreeView control in a form. The TreeView control is part of the Microsoft Windows Common Controls 6.0 package, which you can add to your project from the Components dialog box, as shown in Figure T-27.

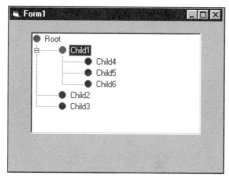

Figure T-26 This simple TreeView control in a form organizes data into a hierarchy.

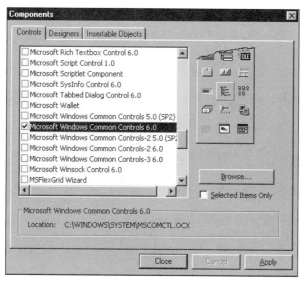

Figure T-27 Use the Components dialog box to add the TreeView control to your Visual Basic toolbox.

Properties

The TreeView control has 45 properties, which are listed below. Because many Visual Basic controls have similar properties, the following list does not include the properties' descriptions. For information on using a property, look up the individual property's entry, provided alphabetically in this book.

```
Appearance
BorderStyle
CausesValidation
CheckBoxes
Container
DragIcon
DragMode
DropHighlight
Enabled
Font
FullRowSelect
Height
HelpContextID
HideSelection
HotTracking
hWnd
ImageList
Indentation
Index
LabelEdit
Left
LineStyle
MouseIcon
MousePointer
Name
Nodes
OLEDragMode
OLEDropMode
Parent
PathSeparator
Picture
Scroll
SelectedItem
Style
SingleSel
Sorted
Style
```

```
TabIndex
TabStop
Tag
ToolTipText
Top
Visible
WhatsThisHelpID
Width
```

Methods

The TreeView control has 10 methods, which are listed below. Because many Visual Basic controls have similar methods, the following list does not include the methods' descriptions. For information on using a method, look up the individual method's entry, provided alphabetically in this book.

```
Drag
GetVisibleCount
HitTest
Move
OLEDrag
Refresh
SetFocus
ShowWhatsThis
StartLabelEdit
ZOrder
```

Events

The TreeView control responds to 25 events, which are listed below. Because many Visual Basic controls respond to similar events, the following list does not include the events' descriptions. For information on using an event, look up the individual event's entry, provided alphabetically in this book.

```
AfterLabelEdit
BeforeLabelEdit
Click
Collapse
DblClick
DragDrop
DragOver
Expand
GotFocus
KeyDown
KeyPress
```

```
KeyUp
LostFocus
MouseDown
MouseMove
MouseUp
NodeCheck
NodeClick
OLECompleteDrag
OLEDragDrop
OLEDragOver
OLEGiveFeedback
OLESetData
OLEStartDrag
Validate
```

The TreeView control's most commonly used event is `NodeClick`, which the control generates when the user clicks a node. A program responds to the `NodeClick` event in the `NodeClick` event procedure. A TreeView control called `treTreeView1` will have a `NodeClick` event procedure called `treTreeView1_NodeClick`, which is where the program should handle the event, as shown in the following lines:

```
Private Sub TreeView1_NodeClick _
  (ByVal Node As MSComctlLib.Node)
    ' Handle the NodeClick event here.
End Sub
```

As you can see, the `NodeClick` event procedure receives a single parameter, which is a reference to the Node object associated with the clicked node.

Trim

Function

The `Trim` function removes leading and trailing spaces from a string.

Syntax

```
value = Trim(str)
```

- *str* — The string from which to remove leading and trailing spaces.
- *value* — The variable that will receive the new string.

Example

After the following lines execute, `newMsg` will contain the string "This is a test."

```
Dim msg As String
Dim newMsg As String
msg = "    This is a test      "
newMsg = Trim(msg)
```

 CROSS-REFERENCE
See also LTrim and RTrim.

True

Keyword

The `True` keyword is used to represent a true Boolean condition, which, in Visual Basic, has a value of –1. The following line uses the `True` keyword in an `If` statement to control program execution based on the value of the Boolean variable `gotName`.

```
If gotName Then
    ' Do something.
Else
    ' Do something else.
End If
```

 CROSS-REFERENCE
See also False.

Twips

Concept

A twip is a unit of measurement used in Visual Basic. A twip equals 1/1,440 of an inch, 1/567 of a centimeter, or 1/20 of a point.

TwipsPerPixelX

Property

The `TwipsPerPixelX` property represents the number of twips per pixel in the horizontal direction. For example, if the Screen object returns 15 for the `TwipsPerPixelX` property, the horizontal measurement of each pixel on the screen is 15 twips.

Objects with a TwipsPerPixelX Property

Printer

Screen

Syntax

value = *object*.TwipsPerPixelX

- *object*—A reference to a Printer or Screen object.
- *value*—The variable that will receive the property's current setting.

Example

The following lines show how to get the horizontal number of twips per pixel for the screen. Note that the Screen object is a global Visual Basic object that you don't need to create in your programs.

```
Dim numTwips As Integer
numTwips = Screen.TwipsPerPixelX
```

CROSS-REFERENCE

See also Printer, ScaleHeight, ScaleLeft, ScaleMode, ScaleTop, ScaleWidth, Screen, and TwipsPerPixelY.

TwipsPerPixelY

Property

The `TwipsPerPixelY` property represents the number of twips per pixel in the vertical direction. For example, if the Screen object returns 15 for the `TwipsPerPixelY` property, the vertical measurement of each pixel on the screen is 15 twips.

Objects with a TwipsPerPixelY Property

Printer

Screen

Syntax

```
value = object.TwipsPerPixelY
```

- *object*—A reference to a Printer or Screen object.
- *value*—The variable that will receive the property's current setting.

Example

The following lines show how to get the vertical number of twips per pixel for the screen. Note that the Screen object is a global Visual Basic object that you don't need to create in your programs.

```
Dim numTwips As Integer
numTwips = Screen.TwipsPerPixelY
```

CROSS-REFERENCE

See also Printer, ScaleHeight, ScaleLeft, ScaleMode, ScaleTop, ScaleWidth, Screen, and TwipsPerPixelX.

Type

Keyword

The Type keyword is used for declaring user-defined data types. For example, the following lines define a data record for a store customer.

```
Private Type CustomerInfo
    FirstName As String * 30
    LastName As String * 30
    Phone As String * 15
    AmountDue As Currency
End Type
```

CROSS-REFERENCE

See also Dim and ReDim.

s
t
u

Type—File and Folder

Property

The Type property represents a string indicating the type of file associated with a File or Folder object.

Syntax

`value = object.Type`

- *object*—A reference to a File or Folder object.
- *value*—The variable that will receive the property's current setting.

Example

After the following lines execute, the string variable strFileType will contain the value "GIF Image."

```
Dim fileSystem As Object
Dim file As Object
Dim strFileType As String
Set fileSystem = CreateObject("Scripting.FileSystemObject")
Set file = fileSystem.GetFile("c:\image1.gif")
strFileType = file.Type
```

CROSS-REFERENCE
See also File, FileSystemObject, and Folder.

Type—Picture

Property

The Type property represents the format of a Picture object. This value can be vbPicTypeBitmap, vbPicTypeEMetafile, vbPicTypeIcon, vbPicTypeMetafile, and vbPicTypeNone.

Syntax

```
value = Picture.Type
```

- *Picture*—A reference to a Picture object.
- *value*—The variable that will receive the property's current setting.

Example

The following lines show how to get the picture type of a form's Picture object. After getting the picture type, the example displays the result in a message box.

```
Dim picType As Integer
picType = frmForm1.Picture.Type
If picType = vbPicTypeBitmap Then
    MsgBox "vbPicTypeBitmap"
ElseIf picType = vbPicTypeEMetafile Then
    MsgBox "vbPicTypeEMetafile"
ElseIf picType = vbPicTypeIcon Then
    MsgBox "vbPicTypeIcon"
ElseIf picType = vbPicTypeMetafile Then
    MsgBox "vbPicTypeMetafile"
ElseIf picType = vbPicTypeNone Then
    MsgBox "vbPicTypeNone"
End If
```

CROSS-REFERENCE
See also File, FileSystemObject, and Folder.

TypeName

Function

The TypeName function returns a string describing the specified variable's data type.

Syntax

```
value = TypeName(variable)
```

- *value*—The variable that will receive the data type string.
- *variable*—The name of the variable for which to return the data type.

Example

After the following lines execute, the `varType` variable will contain the string value "Integer."

```
Dim var1 As Integer
Dim varType As String
varType = TypeName(var1)
```

CROSS-REFERENCE

See also IsArray, IsDate, IsEmpty, IsError, IsMissing, IsNull, IsNumeric, IsObject, and VarType.

UBound

Function

The UBound function gets the highest valid index for a specified dimension of an array. For example, a single-dimension array with three elements with indexes 0, 1, and 2 has an upper bound of 2, which is the value UBound will return for the array.

Syntax

```
value = UBound(array, dim)
```

- *array* — The array for which to return the upper bound.
- *dim* (*) — The array dimension for which to return the upper bound.
- *value* — The variable that will receive the upper bound.

(*) = Optional

Example 1

The following lines get the upper bound of a single-dimension array named intArray(). After the lines execute, hiIndex will be equal to 10.

```
Dim intArray(10) As Integer
Dim hiIndex As Integer
hiIndex = UBound(intArray)
```

Example 2

In this case, the following lines get the upper bound of the second dimension of a two-dimension array named intArray(). After the lines execute, hiIndex will be equal to 25.

```
Dim intArray(10, 25) As Integer
Dim hiIndex As Integer
hiIndex = UBound(intArray, 2)
```

CROSS-REFERENCE
See also LBound and Option Base.

UBound

Property

The UBound property represents the highest index for a control in a control array. For example, an array of three CommandButton controls with indexes of 0, 1, and 2 have a UBound property setting of 2.

Syntax

```
value = ControlArray.UBound
```

- *ControlArray* — A reference to a control array.
- *value* — The variable that will receive the property's current setting.

Example

The following lines get the highest index for an array of TextBox controls. The txtText1() object is a TextBox array that the programmer added to the application's form at design time.

```
Dim hiIndex As Integer
hiIndex = txtText1().UBound
```

CROSS-REFERENCE
See also Index and LBound.

UCase

Function

The UCase function changes the characters in a string to all uppercase.

Syntax

```
value = UCase(str)
```

- *str* — The string to change to uppercase.
- *value* — The variable that will receive the converted string.

Example

After the following lines execute, the `strUCase` variable will contain the text "THIS IS A TEST."

```
Dim strMsg, strUCase As String
strMsg = "This Is A Test"
strUCase = UCase(strMsg)
```

 CROSS-REFERENCE
See also LCase.

UnattendedApp

Property

The `UnattendedApp` property represents whether the application will run without displaying a user interface. A value of `True` indicates that the application displays no user interface, whereas `False` indicates that the application does display a user interface.

Objects with an UnattendedApp Property

App

Syntax

```
value = App.UnattendedApp
```

- *App* — A reference to an App object.
- *value* — The variable that will receive the property's current setting.

Example

The following lines show you how to get the value of an App object's `UnattendedApp` property. Note that the App object is a global Visual Basic object that you don't need to create in your programs.

```
Dim result As Boolean
result = App.UnattendedApp
```

 **CROSS-REFERENCE**
See also App.

Underline

Property

The Underline property represents whether a font is underlined.

Objects with an Underline Property

Font

Syntax

```
Font.Underline = value1
```

or

```
value2 = Font.Underline
```

- *Font*—A reference to a Font object.
- *value1*—The value True or False.
- *value2*—The variable that will receive the property's current setting.

Example

The following line sets a Form object's font to underlined.

```
frmForm1.Font.Underline = True
```

 CROSS-REFERENCE
See also Font, Italic, and Strikethrough.

Unload

Event

Visual Basic sends a form an Unload event when the form is about to be dismissed from the screen. This event is often used to perform last-minute clean-up tasks, such as warning the user to save a document.

Objects with an Unload Event

Form

MDIForm

PropertyPage

Example

A program can respond to an Unload event by implementing the form's Unload event procedure. The following code segment shows how a form defines an Unload event procedure. As you can see in the procedure's declaration, the procedure receives a single parameter, which is a value the procedure can use to cancel the Unload event. That is, setting Cancel to True stops Visual Basic from continuing to process the Unload event, leaving the form on the screen.

```
Private Sub Form_Unload(Cancel As Integer)
    ' Handle the Unload event here.
    If something Then Cancel = True
End Sub
```

CROSS-REFERENCE

See also Load, QueryUnload, Terminate, and Unload (statement).

Unload

Statement

The Unload statement triggers an Unload event, which removes a form from the screen and memory.

Syntax

```
Unload Form
```

- *Form* — A reference to the form to unload.

Example

The following line removes the form frmForm1 from the screen and memory.

```
Unload frmForm1
```

t
u
v

CROSS-REFERENCE
See also Load, QueryUnload, and Unload (event).

UpClick

Event

Visual Basic sends an UpDown control an UpClick event when the user clicks the control's up or right arrow.

Objects with an UpClick Event

UpDown

Example

A program can respond to an UpClick event by implementing the control's UpClick event procedure. The following code segment shows how an UpDown control defines an UpClick event procedure. In this example, the updUpDown1 object is an UpDown control that the programmer added to the form at design time.

```
Private Sub updUpDown1_UpClick()
    ' Handle the UpClick event here.
End Sub
```

CROSS-REFERENCE
See also DownClick.

Update

Method

The Update method gets and displays data from a source application (an application that's supplying an OLE object).

Objects with an Update Method

OLE Container

Syntax

OLEContainer.Update

- *OLEContainer*—A reference to an OLE Container control.

Example

The following line updates an OLE Container control. The `oleContainer1` object is an OLE Container control that the programmer added to the form at design time.

oleContainer1.Update

CROSS-REFERENCE
See also OLE Container and Updated.

Updated

Event

Visual Basic sends an OLE Container control an `Updated` event when the data in the control's embedded or linked object changes.

Objects with an Updated Event

OLE Container

Example

A program can respond to an `Updated` event by implementing the OLE Container control's `Updated` event procedure. The following code segment shows how an OLE Container control defines an `Updated` event procedure. As you can see, the event procedure receives a single parameter, which is a code that indicates the type of change that occurred. This parameter can be the value `vbOLEChanged`, `vbOLESaved`, `vbOLEClosed`, or `vbOLERenamed`. In this example, the `oleContainer1` object is an OLE Container control that the programmer added to the form at design time.

```
Private Sub oleContainer1_Updated(Code As Integer)
    ' Handle the Updated event here.
End Sub
```

t
u
v

CROSS-REFERENCE
See also OLE Container, Update, and UpdateOptions.

UpdateInterval

Property

The UpdateInterval property represents how often a Multimedia MCI control receives StatusUpdate events.

Objects with an UpdateInterval Property

Multimedia MCI

Syntax

```
Multimedia.UpdateInterval = value1
```

or

```
value2 = Multimedia.UpdateInterval
```

- *Multimedia* — A reference to a Multimedia MCI control.
- *value1* — The update interval in milliseconds.
- *value2* — The variable that will receive the property's current setting.

Example

The following program demonstrates how to use the UpdateInterval property. When you run the program, click the Load Wave File button and load a wave file (the guitar.wav file comes with the program). Click the multimedia control's Play button and watch the Location counter update itself at the default interval of 1000 milliseconds, as shown in Figure U-1. (The Location counter shows the current position of the wave file as it plays.) At any time, you can change the interval to another value by typing the value into the Interval box and clicking the Set Interval button.

Play Button

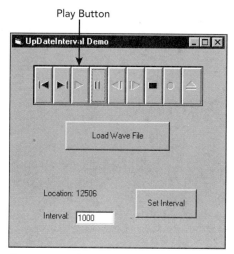

Figure U-1 The Location counter changes at the rate set by the Interval box.

```
VERSION 5.00
Object = "{C1A8AF28-1257-101B-8FB0-0020AF039CA3} _
    #1.1#0"; "MCI32.OCX"
Object = "{F9043C88-F6F2-101A-A3C9-08002B2F49FB} _
    #1.2#0"; "COMDLG32.OCX"
Begin VB.Form Form1
    Caption         =   "UpDateInterval Demo"
    ClientHeight    =   4215
    ClientLeft      =   60
    ClientTop       =   345
    ClientWidth     =   4680
    LinkTopic       =   "Form1"
    ScaleHeight     =   4215
    ScaleWidth      =   4680
    StartUpPosition =   3  'Windows Default
    Begin VB.CommandButton btnSetInterval
        Caption     =   "Set Interval"
        Height      =   615
        Left        =   2760
        TabIndex    =   5
        Top         =   3000
        Width       =   1335
    End
    Begin VB.TextBox txtInterval
        Height      =   285
```

```
      Left              =      1440
      TabIndex          =      3
      Top               =      3480
      Width             =      855
   End
   Begin MSComDlg.CommonDialog dlgCommonDialog1
      Left              =      4080
      Top               =      3600
      _ExtentX          =      847
      _ExtentY          =      847
      _Version          =      393216
   End
   Begin MCI.MMControl mciMMControl1
      Height            =      855
      Left              =      480
      TabIndex          =      1
      Top               =      360
      Width             =      3735
      _ExtentX          =      6588
      _ExtentY          =      1508
      _Version          =      393216
      DeviceType        =      ""
      FileName          =      ""
   End
   Begin VB.CommandButton btnLoadWave
      Caption           =      "Load Wave File"
      Height            =      615
      Left              =      1200
      TabIndex          =      0
      Top               =      1560
      Width             =      2295
   End
   Begin VB.Label lblLocation
      Height            =      255
      Left              =      1440
      TabIndex          =      6
      Top               =      3000
      Width             =      855
   End
   Begin VB.Label Label2
      Caption           =      "Interval:"
      Height            =      255
      Left              =      720
      TabIndex          =      4
```

```
        Top             =    3480
        Width           =    615
    End
    Begin VB.Label Label1
        Caption         =    "Location:"
        Height          =    255
        Left            =    720
        TabIndex        =    2
        Top             =    3000
        Width           =    735
    End
End
End
Attribute VB_Name = "Form1"
Attribute VB_GlobalNameSpace = False
Attribute VB_Creatable = False
Attribute VB_PredeclaredId = True
Attribute VB_Exposed = False

Private Sub btnLoadWave_Click()
    Dim fileName

    dlgCommonDialog1.CancelError = True
    On Error GoTo CancelErr
    dlgCommonDialog1.DialogTitle = "Choose Wave File"
    dlgCommonDialog1.fileName = "*.wav"
    dlgCommonDialog1.ShowOpen
    fileName = dlgCommonDialog1.fileName

    mciMMControl1.DeviceType = "WaveAudio"
    mciMMControl1.Shareable = False
    mciMMControl1.Wait = True
    mciMMControl1.Notify = False
    mciMMControl1.fileName = fileName
    mciMMControl1.Command = "Open"
    txtTo.Text = mciMMControl1.Length
CancelErr:
End Sub

Private Sub btnSetInterval_Click()
    Dim interval As Integer
    interval = txtInterval.Text
    mciMMControl1.UpdateInterval = interval
End Sub
```

```
Private Sub Form_Load()
    lblLocation.Caption = "0"
    txtInterval.Text = "1000"
End Sub

Private Sub mciMMControl1_PlayClick(Cancel As Integer)
    Dim interval As Integer
    On Error GoTo errorHandler
    interval = txtInterval.Text
    mciMMControl1.UpdateInterval = interval
    Exit Sub

errorHandler:
    MsgBox "Please enter a valid interval value.", _
        vbExclamation, "UpdateInterval Demo"
    Cancel = True
End Sub

Private Sub mciMMControl1_StatusUpdate()
    Dim curLocation As Long
    curLocation = mciMMControl1.Position
    lblLocation.Caption = curLocation
End Sub
```

CROSS-REFERENCE
See also Multimedia MCI and StatusUpdate.

UpdateOptions

Property

The UpdateOptions property represents the manner in which a linked or embedded object is updated. This property can be a value listed in Table U-1.

Table U-1 Values for the UpdateOptions Property

Value	Description
vbOLEAutomatic	Updates the object automatically whenever the object's contents change.
vbOLEFrozen	Updates the object when the user saves the data from the source application.
vbOLEManual	Updates the object when the program calls the Update method.

Objects with an UpdateOptions Property
OLE Container

Syntax

```
OLEContainer.UpdateOptions = value1
```

or

```
value2 = OLEContainer.UpdateOptions
```

- *OLEContainer*—A reference to an OLE Container control.
- *value1*—A value from Table U-1.
- *value2*—The variable that will receive the property's current setting.

Example

The following lines show how to get and set the value of an OLE Container control's UpdateOptions property. The object is updated when the program calls the Update method. In this example, the oleContainer1 object is an OLE Container control that the programmer added to the form at design time.

```
Dim options As Integer
options = oleContainer1.UpdateOptions
oleContainer1.UpdateOptions = vbOLEManual
```

CROSS-REFERENCE
See also OLE Container, Update, and Updated.

UpDown

Control

An UpDown control enables the user to select a value from a program-specified range. Figure U-2 shows an UpDown control (along with its buddy control, a text box) in a form. The UpDown control is part of the Microsoft Windows Common Controls-2 6.0 package. You can add this control to your Visual Basic toolbox from the Components dialog box, as shown in Figure U-3.

t
u
v

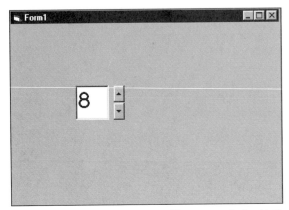

Figure U-2 Like a slider or scrollbar control, the UpDown control provides a way for the user to select specific values.

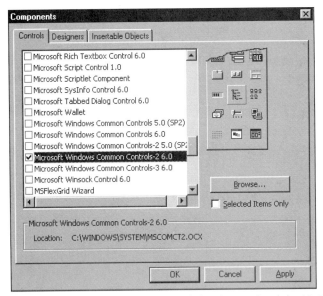

Figure U-3 Use the Components dialog box to load the UpDown control.

Properties

The UpDown control has 33 properties, which are listed below. Because many Visual Basic controls have similar properties, the following list does not include the properties' descriptions. For information on using a property, look up the individual property's entry, provided alphabetically in this book.

```
Alignment
AutoBuddy
BuddyControl
BuddyProperty
CausesValidation
Container
DragIcon
DragMode
Enabled
Height
HelpContextID
hWnd
Increment
Index
Left
Max
Min
Name
Object
OLEDropMode
Orientation
Parent
SyncBuddy
TabIndex
TabStop
Tag
ToolTipText
Top
Value
Visible
WhatsThisHelpID
Width
Wrap
```

Methods

The UpDown control has six methods, which are listed below. Because many Visual Basic controls have similar methods, the following list does not include the methods' descriptions. For information on using a method, look up the individual method's entry, provided alphabetically in this book.

```
Drag
Move
```

```
OLEDrag
SetFocus
ShowWhatsThis
ZOrder
```

Events

The UpDown control responds to 20 events, which are listed below. Because many Visual Basic controls respond to similar events, the following list does not include the events' descriptions. For information on using an event, look up the individual event's entry, provided alphabetically in this book.

```
Change
DownClick
DragDrop
DragOver
GotFocus
KeyDown
KeyPress
KeyUp
LostFocus
MouseDown
MouseMove
MouseUp
OLECompleteDrag
OLEDragDrop
OLEDragOver
OLEGiveFeedback
OLESetData
OLEStartDrag
UpClick
Validate
```

The UpDown control's most commonly used event is Change, which the control generates when the user changes the control's value. A program responds to the control's Change event in the Change event procedure. An UpDown control called updUpDown1 will have a Change event procedure called updUpDown1_Change, which is where the program should handle the event, as shown in the following lines:

```
Private Sub updUpDown1_Change()
    ' Handle the Change event here.
End Sub
```

UpTo

Method

The UpTo method positions the text cursor in a RichTextBox control based on a specified set of characters.

Objects with an UpTo Method

RichTextBox

Syntax

`RichTextBox.UpTo chars, searchForward, notInclude`

- *RichTextBox* — A reference to a RichTextBox control.
- *chars* — The characters for which to search.
- *notInclude* (*) — A Boolean value that determines whether the specified characters are the characters before which to place the cursor (False) or the characters before which the cursor should not be placed. The default value is False.
- *searchForward* (*) — A Boolean value that determines whether the control should search forward (True) from the text cursor or search backward (False). The default is True.

(*) = Optional

Example

The following program demonstrates the UpTo method. When you run the program, type a character set into the text box, select the desired UpTo options with the check boxes, and then click the Call UpTo button to see the results in the RichTextBox control. For example, type U into the text box, and click the Call UpTo button. (Leave the RichTextBox's text cursor at the beginning of the text, and leave the Forward option selected and the Not Include option unselected.) The control then positions its text cursor right before the first instance of the character "U", as shown in Figure U-4. On the other hand, if you type " Thisadem" (the first character is a space) into the text box, turn on the Not Include option, and click the Call UpTo button, the control will move the text cursor right before the "o" in "demonstration", as shown in Figure U-5.

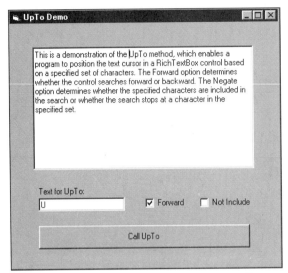

Figure U-4 When the Not Include option is off, UpTo places the cursor at the first occurrence of a character in the specified character set.

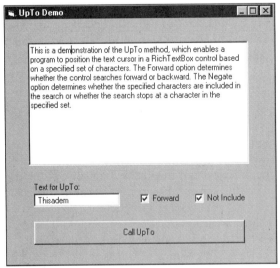

Figure U-5 When the Not Include option is selected, UpTo places the cursor at the first occurrence of a character that's not in the specified character set.

```
VERSION 5.00
Object = "{3B7C8863-D78F-101B-B9B5-04021C009402} _
    #1.2#0"; "RICHTX32.OCX"
Begin VB.Form Form1
   Caption          =   "UpTo Demo"
   ClientHeight     =   5205
   ClientLeft       =   60
   ClientTop        =   345
   ClientWidth      =   5940
   LinkTopic        =   "Form1"
   ScaleHeight      =   347
   ScaleMode        =   3   'Pixel
   ScaleWidth       =   396
   StartUpPosition  =   3   'Windows Default
   Begin VB.CheckBox chkForward
      Caption       =   "Forward"
      Height        =   255
      Left          =   3000
      TabIndex      =   5
      Top           =   3720
      Width         =   1215
   End
   Begin VB.CommandButton btnCallUpTo
      Caption       =   "Call UpTo"
      Height        =   495
      Left          =   600
      TabIndex      =   4
      Top           =   4320
      Width         =   4695
   End
   Begin VB.CheckBox chkNotInclude
      Caption       =   "Not Include"
      Height        =   255
      Left          =   4200
      TabIndex      =   3
      Top           =   3720
      Width         =   1215
   End
   Begin VB.TextBox txtUpToText
      Height        =   285
      Left          =   600
      TabIndex      =   2
      Top           =   3720
      Width         =   1935
   End
```

```
        Begin RichTextLib.RichTextBox rtfRichTextBox1
           Height          =     2655
           Left            =     480
           TabIndex        =     0
           Top             =     480
           Width           =     4935
           _ExtentX        =     8705
           _ExtentY        =     4683
           _Version        =     393217
           TextRTF         =     $"Form1.frx":0000
        End
        Begin VB.Label Label1
           Caption         =     "Text for UpTo:"
           Height          =     255
           Left            =     600
           TabIndex        =     1
           Top             =     3480
           Width           =     2055
        End
     End
  Attribute VB_Name = "Form1"
  Attribute VB_GlobalNameSpace = False
  Attribute VB_Creatable = False
  Attribute VB_PredeclaredId = True
  Attribute VB_Exposed = False

  Private Sub btnCallUpTo_Click()
     Dim uptoText As String
     Dim notInclude As Boolean
     Dim forward As Boolean
     uptoText = txtUpToText.Text
     notInclude = (chkNotInclude.Value = vbChecked)
     forward = (chkForward.Value = vbChecked)
     rtfRichTextBox1.UpTo uptoText, forward, notInclude
     rtfRichTextBox1.SetFocus
  End Sub

  Private Sub Form_Load()
     Dim msg As String
     msg = "This is a demonstration of the UpTo "
     msg = msg & "method, which enables a program to "
     msg = msg & "position the text cursor in a RichTextBox "
     msg = msg & "control based on a specified set of "
     msg = msg & "characters. The Forward option determines "
```

```
    msg = msg & "whether the control searches forward or "
    msg = msg & "backward. The Negate option determines "
    msg = msg & "whether the specified characters are "
    msg = msg & "included in the search or whether the "
    msg = msg & "search stops at a character "
    msg = msg & "in the specified set."
    rtfRichTextBox1.Text = msg
    rtfRichTextBox1.HideSelection = False
    chkForward.Value = vbChecked
    chkNotInclude.Value = vbUnchecked
End Sub
```

CROSS-REFERENCE
See also RichTextBox.

UseCoolbarColors

Property

The UseCoolbarColors property represents whether a Band object in a CoolBar control will use the colors specified in the CoolBar control's ForeColor and BackColor properties.

Objects with a UseCoolbarColors Property

Band

Syntax

Band.UseCoolbarColors = *value1*

or

value2 = *Band*.UseCoolbarColors

- *Band* — A reference to a Band object.
- *value1* — The value True (default) or False.
- *value2* — The variable that will receive the property's current setting.

t
u
v

Example

The following lines show how to get and set the value of a Band object's UseCoolbarColors property. The Coolbar1 object is a CoolBar control that the programmer added to the form at design time.

```
Dim coolbarColors As Boolean
coolbarColors = CoolBar1.Bands(1).UseCoolbarColors
CoolBar1.Bands(1).UseCoolbarColors = True
```

CROSS-REFERENCE
See also Band, Bands, CoolBar, and UseCoolbarPicture.

UseCoolbarPicture

Property

The UseCoolbarPicture property represents whether a Band object in a CoolBar control will use the picture specified in the CoolBar control's Picture property.

Objects with a UseCoolbarPicture Property

Band

Syntax

Band.UseCoolbarPicture = value1

or

value2 = Band.UseCoolbarPicture

- *Band* — A reference to a Band object.
- *value1* — The value True (default) or False.
- *value2* — The variable that will receive the property's current setting.

Example

The following lines show how to get and set the value of a Band object's UseCoolbarPicture property. The Coolbar1 object is a CoolBar control that the programmer added to the form at design time.

```
Dim coolbarPicture As Boolean
coolbarPicture = CoolBar1.Bands(1).UseCoolbarPicture
CoolBar1.Bands(1).UseCoolbarPicture = True
```

CROSS-REFERENCE
See also Band, Bands, CoolBar, and UseCoolbarColors.

UseMaskColor

Property

The `UseMaskColor` property represents whether a control creates transparent image areas using the color specified in the `MaskColor` property.

Objects with a UseMaskColor Property

CheckBox
CommandButton
ImageList
OptionButton

Syntax

```
object.UseMaskColor = value1
```

or

```
value2 = object.UseMaskColor
```

- *object* — A reference to an object with a `UseMaskColor` property.
- *value1* — The value `True` or `False` (default).
- *value2* — The variable that will receive the property's current setting.

Example

The following lines show how to get and set the value of a CommandButton control's `UseMaskColor` property. The `btnCommand1` object is a CommandButton control that the programmer added to the form at design time.

```
Dim useMask As Boolean
useMask = btnCommand1.UseMaskColor
btnCommand1.UseMaskColor = True
```

 CROSS-REFERENCE
See also MaskColor.

t
u
v

UseMnemonic

Property

The UseMnemonic property represents whether a Label control can display and respond to an underlined hotkey. The hotkey is defined using an ampersand in the control's Caption property. For example, defining a CommandButton's Caption property as "&Command1" causes the "C" on the button to be underlined as a hotkey.

Objects with a UseMnemonic Property

Label

Syntax

```
Label.UseMnemonic = value1
```

or

```
value2 = Label.UseMnemonic
```

- *Label*—A reference to a Label control.
- *value1*—The value True (default) or False.
- *value2*—The variable that will receive the property's current setting.

Example

The following lines show how to get and set the value of a Label control's UseMnemonic property. The lblLabel1 object is a Label control that the programmer added to the form at design time.

```
Dim result As Boolean
result = lblLabel1.UseMnemonic
lblLabel1.UseMnemonic = True
```

 CROSS-REFERENCE
See also Caption and Label.

UserControl

Control

A UserControl control enables the programmer to design his or her own custom controls. You can add a UserControl control to your project from the Visual Basic's Project menu.

Properties

At design time, the UserControl control has 62 properties, which are listed below. Because many Visual Basic controls have similar properties, the following list does not include the properties' descriptions. For information on using a property, look up the individual property's entry, provided alphabetically in this book.

```
AccessKeys
ActiveControl
Ambient
Appearance
AutoRedraw
BackColor
BackStyle
BorderStyle
ClipBehavior
ClipControls
ContainedControls
ContainerHWnd
Controls
Count
CurrentX
CurrentY
DrawMode
DrawStyle
DrawWidth
Enabled
EventsFrozen
Extender
FillColor
FillStyle
Font
FontBold
```

t
u
v

```
FontItalic
FontName
FontSize
FontStrikethru
FontTransparent
FontUnderline
ForeColor
HasDC
hDC
Height
HitBehavior
hWnd
Hyperlink
Image
KeyPreview
MaskColor
MaskPicture
MouseIcon
MousePointer
Name
OLEDropMode
Palette
PaletteMode
Parent
ParentControls
Picture
PropertyPages
RightToLeft
ScaleHeight
ScaleLeft
ScaleMode
ScaleTop
ScaleWidth
Style
Tag
Width
```

Methods

The UserControl control has 19 methods, which are listed below. Because many Visual Basic controls have similar methods, the following list does not include the methods' descriptions. For information on using a method, look up the individual method's entry, provided alphabetically in this book.

```
Circle
Cls
Line
OLEDrag
PaintPicture
Point
PopupMenu
PropertyChanged
PSet
Refresh
Scale
ScaleX
ScaleY
SetFocus
Size
TextHeight
TextWidth
ValidateControls
ZOrder
```

Events

The UserControl control responds to 32 events, which are listed below. Because many Visual Basic controls respond to similar events, the following list does not include the events' descriptions. For information on using an event, look up the individual event's entry, provided alphabetically in this book.

```
AccessKeyPress
AmbientChanged
Click
DblClick
DragDrop
DragOver
EnterFocus
ExitFocus
GotFocus
Hide
HitTest
Initialize
InitProperties
KeyDown
KeyPress
KeyUp
```

t

u

v

```
LostFocus
MouseDown
MouseMove
MouseUp
OLECompleteDrag
OLEDragDrop
OLEDragOver
OLEGiveFeedback
OLESetData
OLEStartDrag
Paint
ReadProperties
Resize
Show
Terminate
WriteProperties
```

UserMode

Property

The `UserMode` property represents whether a UserControl control is being used at design time or runtime. A value of `True` means that the control is in run mode, whereas a value of `False` means that the control is in design mode.

Objects with a UserMode Property

AmbientProperties

Syntax

```
value = Ambient.UserMode
```

- *Ambient*—A reference to an AmbientProperties object.
- *value*—The variable that will receive the property's current setting.

Example

The following lines show how to retrieve the user mode of a UserControl control.

```
Dim mode As Boolean
mode = UserControl.Ambient.UserMode
```

```
If mode = True Then
    MsgBox "Run Mode"
Else
    MsgBox "Design Mode"
End If
```

CROSS-REFERENCE
See also Ambient and UserControl.

UserName

Property

The UserName property represents the user name for an email session.

Objects with a UserName Property

MAPISession

Syntax

```
MAPISession.UserName = value1
```

or

```
value2 = MAPISession.UserName
```

- *MAPISession* — A reference to a MAPISession control.
- *value1* — A string that contains the user name.
- *value2* — The variable that will receive the user name.

Example

The following lines show how to retrieve the value of a MAPISession control's UserName property.

```
Dim name As String
name = MAPISession1.UserName
```

CROSS-REFERENCE
See also MAPISession.

UseWindows

Property

The UseWindows property represents whether an MCI device displays output in a window. This property is accessible only at runtime, when it is read-only.

Objects with a UseWindows Property

Multimedia MCI

Syntax

value = Multimedia.UseWindows

- *Multimedia* — A reference to a Multimedia MCI control.
- *value* — The variable that will receive the property's setting of True or False.

Example

The following lines show how to retrieve the value of a Multimedia MCI control's UseWindows property. The mciMMControl1 object is a reference to a Multimedia MCI control.

```
Dim useWindw As Boolean
useWindw = mciMMControl1.UseWindows
```

CROSS-REFERENCE
See also Multimedia MCI.

Val

Function

The Val function converts a string of numerical characters to a numerical value.

Syntax

```
value = Val(str)
```

- *str*—The string to convert.
- *value*—The variable that will receive the numerical result.

Example 1

After the following lines execute, the variable result will contain the integer value 1436.

```
Dim result As Integer
Dim strNumber As String
strNumber = "1436"
result = Val(strNumber)
```

Example 2

Here, after the following lines execute, the variable result will contain the integer value 143. This is because the Val function stops reading the source string as soon as it finds a character that can't be converted to a numerical value.

```
Dim result As Integer
Dim strNumber As String
strNumber = "143def6"
result = Val(strNumber)
```

Example 3

Finally, after the following lines execute, the variable `result` will contain the floating-point value 145.36.

```
Dim result As Single
Dim strNumber As String
strNumber = "145.36"
result = Val(strNumber)
```

CROSS-REFERENCE
See also Str.

Validate

Event

Visual Basic sends a control a `Validate` event when the focus leaves the control and moves to a control whose `CausesValidation` property is set to `True`.

Objects with a Validate Event

Animation
Button
CheckBox
ComboBox
CommandButton
DirListBox
DriveListBox
FileListBox
HScrollBar
ListBox
ListView
Multimedia MCI
OptionButton
PictureBox
RichTextBox
Slider

TabStrip

TextBox

TreeView

UpDown

VScrollBar

Example

A program can respond to a `Validate` event by implementing the control's `Validate` event procedure. The following code segment shows how a TextBox control defines a `Validate` event procedure. In this example, the `txtText1` object is a TextBox control that the programmer added to the form at design time.

```
Private Sub txtText1_Validate(Cancel As Boolean)
    ' Handle the Validate event here.
End Sub
```

 CROSS-REFERENCE
See also CausesValidation.

Value — Button

Property

The `Value` property represents the state of the control, which can be pressed or unpressed.

Syntax

Button.Value = *value1*

or

value2 = *Button*.Value

- *Button* — A reference to a Button object.
- *value1* — The value `tbrUnpressed` or `tbrPressed`.
- *value2* — The variable that will receive the property's current setting.

u

v

w

Example

The following lines show how to get and set the pressed state of a Button object. The `tlbToolbar1` object is a Toolbar control that the programmer added to the form at design time.

```
Dim state As Integer
state = tlbToolbar1.Buttons(1).Value
tlbToolbar1.Buttons(1).Value = tbrPressed
```

 CROSS-REFERENCE
See also Button and Toolbar.

Value—CheckBox and OptionButton

Property

The `Value` property represents the state of the control, which can be checked, unchecked, or grayed.

Syntax

object.Value = *value1*

or

value2 = *object*.Value

- *object*—A reference to a CheckBox or OptionButton control.
- *value1*—The value `vbUnchecked`, `vbChecked`, or `vbGrayed`.
- *value2*—The variable that will receive the property's current setting.

Example

The following lines show how to get and set the checked state of an OptionButton control. The `optOption1` object is an OptionButton control that the programmer added to the form at design time.

```
Dim state As Integer
state = optOption1.Value
optOption1.Value = vbChecked
```

 CROSS-REFERENCE
See also CheckBox and OptionButton.

Value — CommandButton

Property

The Value property represents the state of the control, which can be clicked or not clicked. For example, you can force a CommandButton control to generate a Click event by setting its Value property to True.

Syntax

```
CommandButton.Value = value1
```

or

```
value2 = CommandButton.Value
```

- *CommandButton* — A reference to a CommandButton control.
- *value1* — The value True or False.
- *value2* — The variable that will receive the property's current setting.

Example

The following lines show how to get and set the state of a CommandButton control. The btnCommand1 object is a CommandButton control that the programmer added to the form at design time.

```
Dim state As Boolean
state = btnCommand1.Value
btnCommand1.Value = True
```

 CROSS-REFERENCE
See also CommandButton and OptionButton.

Value — HScrollBar, VScrollBar, and UpDown

Property

The Value property represents the position of the control, which must be a value between the control's Min and Max properties.

Syntax

```
object.Value = value1
```

or

```
value2 = object.Value
```

- *object* — A reference to an HScrollBar, VScrollBar, or UpDown control.
- *value1* — The scroll bar's new position.
- *value2* — The variable that will receive the property's current setting.

Example

The following lines show how to get and set the position of a VScrollBar control. In this case, the position is halfway between the Min and Max settings of 0 and 1000, respectively. The vsbVScroll1 object is a VScrollBar control that the programmer added to the form at design time.

```
Dim position As Integer
vsbVScroll1.Min = 0
vsbVScroll1.Max = 1000
position = vsbVScroll1.Value
vsbVScroll1.Value = 500
```

 CROSS-REFERENCE
See also HScrollBar, Max, Min, and VScrollBar.

Value — ProgressBar

Property

The Value property represents the portion of the control that is filled. This value must be a value between the control's Min and Max properties.

Syntax

```
ProgressBar.Value = value1
```

or

```
value2 = ProgressBar.Value
```

- *ProgressBar* — A reference to a ProgressBar control.

- *value1* — The progress bar's new position.
- *value2* — The variable that will receive the property's current setting.

Example

The following lines show how to get and set the value of a ProgressBar control. In this case, the Value setting is halfway between the Min and Max values of 0 and 100, respectively. The ProgressBar1 object is a Progress control that the programmer added to the form at design time.

```
Dim filled As Integer
ProgressBar1.Min = 0
ProgressBar1.Max = 100
filled = ProgressBar1.Value
ProgressBar1.Value = 50
```

CROSS-REFERENCE
See also Max, Min, and ProgressBar.

Value — Slider

Property

The Value property represents the position of a Slider control. This position must be a value between the control's Min and Max properties.

Syntax

Slider.Value = value1

or

value2 = Slider.Value

- *Slider* — A reference to a Slider control.
- *value1* — The slider's new position.
- *value2* — The variable that will receive the property's current setting.

Example

The following lines show how to get and set the position of a Slider control. In this case, the Value setting is halfway between the Min and Max values of 0 and

100, respectively. The `sldSlider1` object is a Slider control that the programmer added to the form at design time.

```
Dim position As Integer
sldSlider1.Min = 0
sldSlider1.Max = 100
position = sldSlider1.Value
sldSlider1.Value = 50
```

 CROSS-REFERENCE
See also Max, Min, and Slider.

VariantHeight

Property

The `VariantHeight` property represents whether a CoolBar control displays its bands all the same height or can display the bands in various heights.

Objects with a VariantHeight Property

CoolBar

Syntax

```
CoolBar.VariantHeight = value1
```

or

```
value2 = CoolBar.VariantHeight
```

- *CoolBar* — A reference to a CoolBar control.
- *value1* — The value `True` or `False`.
- *value2* — The variable that will receive the property's current setting.

Example

The following lines show how to get and set the value of a CoolBar control's `VariantHeight` property. The `CoolBar1` object is a CoolBar control that the programmer added to the form at design time.

```
Dim varHeight As Boolean
varHeight = CoolBar1.VariantHeight
CoolBar1.VariantHeight = True
```

CROSS-REFERENCE
See also CoolBar and MinHeight.

VarType

Function

The `VarType` function returns a value that indicates a variable's data type. The function can return one of the following values:

```
vbArray
vbBoolean
vbByte
vbCurrency
vbDataObject
vbDate
vbDecimal
vbDouble
vbEmpty
vbError
vbInteger
vbLong
vbNull
vbObject
vbSingle
vbString
vbUserDefinedType
vbVariant
```

Syntax

```
value = VarType(variable)
```

- *value* — The value that indicates the variable's data type.
- *variable* — The variable for which to get the type.

Example

The following lines demonstrate how to use the `VarType` function to get the data type of the `var1` variable. In this case, a message box appears, displaying the text "Boolean Data Type."

```
Dim vType As Integer
Dim var1 As Boolean
```

u

v

w

```
vType = VarType(var1)
If vType = vbBoolean Then
    MsgBox "Boolean Data Type"
End If
```

CROSS-REFERENCE
See also IsArray, IsDate, IsEmpty, IsError, IsMissing, IsNull, IsNumeric, IsObject, and TypeName.

Verb

Property

The `Verb` property represents the operation that an OLE Container control will execute when its `Action` method is called. This property is obsolete; new programs should use the `DoVerb` method instead of the `Action` method.

Objects with a Verb Property

OLE Container

Syntax

```
OLEContainer.Verb = value1
```

or

```
value2 = OLEContainer.Verb
```

- *OLEContainer* — A reference to an OLE Container control.
- *value1* — The number of the verb to execute.
- *value2* — The variable that will receive the property's current setting.

Example

The following lines show how to get and set the value of an OLE Container control's `Verb` property. The `oleContainer1` object is an OLE Container control that the programmer added to the form at design time.

```
Dim verbNum As Integer
verbNum = oleContainer1.Verb
oleContainer1.Verb = 2
```

CROSS-REFERENCE
See also Action, DoVerb, ObjectVerbs, ObjectVerbsCount, and OLE Container.

View

Property

The `View` property represents the data view displayed by a ListView control. This property can be set to `lvwIcon`, `lvwSmallIcon`, `lvwList`, or `lvwReport`.

Objects with a View Property

ListView

Syntax

`ListView.View = value1`

or

`value2 = ListView.View`

- *ListView* — A reference to a ListView control.
- *value1* — The value `lvwIcon`, `lvwSmallIcon`, `lvwList`, or `lvwReport`.
- *value2* — The variable that will receive the property's current setting.

Example

The following lines show how to get and set a ListView control's view. The `lvwListView1` object is a ListView control that the programmer added to the form at design time.

```
Dim view As Integer
view = lvwListView1.view
lvwListView1.view = lvwReport
```

CROSS-REFERENCE
See also ListView.

u
v
w

Visible

Property

The Visible property represents whether a control is visible or hidden.

Objects with a Visible Property

Animation
Band
Button
CheckBox
ComboBox
CommandButton
DirListBox
DriveListBox
FileListBox
Form
Frame
HScrollBar
Image
Label
Line
ListBox
ListView
MDIForm
Menu
Multimedia MCI
Node
OLE Container
OptionButton
Panel
PictureBox
ProgressBar
RichTextBox
Shape
Slider

StatusBar

TabStrip

TextBox

Toolbar

TreeView

UpDown

VScrollBar

Syntax

```
object.Visible = value1
```

or

```
value2 = object.Visible
```

- *object* — A reference to an object with a Visible property.
- *value1* — The value True or False.
- *value2* — The variable that will receive the property's current setting.

Example

The following lines show how to get and set a Multimedia MCI control's visible status. The mciMMControl1 object is a Multimedia MCI control that the programmer added to the form at design time.

```
Dim vis As Boolean
vis = mciMMControl1.Visible
mciMMControl1.Visible = True
```

CROSS-REFERENCE
See also Hide and Show.

VolumeName

Property

The VolumeName property represents a drive's volume name.

Objects with a VolumeName Property

Drive

Syntax

```
value = Drive.VolumeName
```

- *Drive* — A reference to a Drive object.
- *value* — The variable that will receive the volume name.

Example

The following lines show how to get a drive's volume name.

```
Dim fileSystem As Object
Dim volName As String
Dim drive As Object
Set fileSystem = CreateObject("Scripting.FileSystemObject")
Set drive = fileSystem.GetDrive("c")
volName = drive.VolumeName
```

 CROSS-REFERENCE
See also Drive and FileSystemObject.

VScrollBar

Control

A VScrollBar control comprises a sliding button within a vertical track that the user can use to scroll or to select values from a range. The VScrollBar control is available on Visual Basic's standard toolbox.

Properties

The VScrollBar control has 28 properties, which are listed as follows. Because many Visual Basic controls have similar properties, the properties' descriptions are listed under their own names elsewhere in this book.

```
CausesValidation
Container
Default
DragIcon
DragMode
Enabled
Height
HelpContextID
hWnd
```

```
Index
LargeChange
Left
Max
Min
MouseIcon
MousePointer
Name
Parent
RightToLeft
SmallChange
TabIndex
TabStop
Tag
Top
Value
Visible
WhatsThisHelpID
Width
```

Methods

The VScrollBar control has six methods, which are listed below. Because many Visual Basic controls have similar methods, the methods' descriptions are listed under their own names elsewhere in this book.

```
Drag
Move
Refresh
SetFocus
ShowWhatsThis
ZOrder
```

Events

The VScrollBar control responds to 10 events, which are listed below. Because many Visual Basic controls respond to similar events, the events' descriptions are listed under their own names elsewhere in this book.

```
Change
DragDrop
DragOver
GotFocus
KeyDown
```

u
v
w

```
KeyPress
KeyUp
LostFocus
Scroll
Validate
```

The VScrollBar control's most commonly used event is Change, which the control generates when the user sets it to a new value. A program responds to the control's Change event in the Change event procedure. A scroll bar called vsbVScroll1 will have a Change event procedure called vsbVScroll1_Change, which is where the program should handle the event. In the following example, a message box displays the scroll bar's new value whenever the user changes the value.

```
Private Sub vsbVScroll1_Change()
    MsgBox vsbVScroll1.Value
End Sub
```

W

Wait

Property

The Wait property represents whether the Multimedia MCI control waits for a command to complete before performing the next command. This property is accessible only at runtime.

Objects with a Wait Property

Multimedia MCI

Syntax

```
Multimedia.Wait = value1
```

or

```
value2 = Multimedia.Wait
```

- *Multimedia* — A reference to a Multimedia MCI control.
- *value1* — The value True or False (default).
- *value2* — The variable that will receive the property's current setting.

Example

The following lines show how to get and set the value of a Multimedia control's Wait property. The mciMMControl1 object is a Multimedia MCI control that the programmer added to the form at design time.

```
Dim mciWait As Boolean
mciWait = mciMMControl1.Wait
mciMMControl1.Wait = True
```

CROSS-REFERENCE
See also Multimedia MCI.

Weekday

Function

The Weekday function calculates an integer that represents the day of the week given a date.

Syntax

```
value = Weekday(date, firstDay)
```

- *date* — The date for which to calculate the day of the week.
- *firstDay* (*) — A value that specifies the first day of the week. Can be vbUseSystem (use the system setting for the first day of the week), vbSunday (**default**), vbMonday, vbTuesday, vbWednesday, vbThursday, vbFriday, or vbSaturday.
- *value* — The variable that will receive the day of the week, which can be vbSunday, vbMonday, vbTuesday, vbWednesday, vbThursday, vbFriday, or vbSaturday (the values 1 through 7, respectively).

(*) = Optional

Example 1

The following lines show how to use the Weekday function. In this case, the program displays a message box containing the result "Thursday."

```
Dim strDate As String
Dim intWeekDay As Integer
strDate = "January 21, 1999"
intWeekDay = Weekday(strDate)
Select Case intWeekDay
Case vbSunday
    MsgBox "Sunday"
Case vbMonday
    MsgBox "Monday"
Case vbTuesday
    MsgBox "Tuesday"
Case vbWednesday
    MsgBox "Wednesday"
Case vbThursday
    MsgBox "Thursday"
Case vbFriday
    MsgBox "Friday"
```

```
Case vbSaturday
    MsgBox "Saturday"
End Select
```

Example 2

Here, the following lines have the same result as Example 1, but use a different type of date format for the source date, which, in this case, is stored in the variable vntDate.

```
Dim vntDate As Variant
Dim intWeekDay As Integer
vntDate = #1/21/1999#
intWeekDay = Weekday(vntDate)
Select Case intWeekDay
Case vbSunday
    MsgBox "Sunday"
Case vbMonday
    MsgBox "Monday"
Case vbTuesday
    MsgBox "Tuesday"
Case vbWednesday
    MsgBox "Wednesday"
Case vbThursday
    MsgBox "Thursday"
Case vbFriday
    MsgBox "Friday"
Case vbSaturday
    MsgBox "Saturday"
End Select
```

CROSS-REFERENCE
See also Date, Day, Month, Now, WeekdayName, and Year.

WeekdayName

Function

The WeekdayName function returns a string containing the name of the day of the week for a specified day number.

Syntax

value = WeekdayName(*day*, *form*, *firstDay*)

- *day*—The day number for which to get the name. This value depends on the value of the *firstDay* argument.
- *firstDay* (*)—A value that specifies the first day of the week. Can be vbUseSystem (use the system setting for the first day of the week), vbSunday (default), vbMonday, vbTuesday, vbWednesday, vbThursday, vbFriday, or vbSaturday.
- *form* (*)—A value that specifies the form of the string to be returned. A value of True specifies an abbreviated day name, whereas as False specifies a full day name.
- *value*—The variable that will receive the day name.

(*) = Optional

Example 1

The following lines show how to use the WeekdayName function. In this case, the program displays a message box containing the result "Thursday."

```
Dim strDate As String
Dim intWeekDay As Integer
Dim strDayName As String
strDate = "January 21, 1999"
intWeekDay = Weekday(strDate)
strDayName = WeekdayName(intWeekDay, False, vbSunday)
MsgBox strDayName
```

Example 2

Here, the following lines have the same result as Example 1, but use a different type of date format for the source date, which, in this case, is stored in the variable vntDate.

```
Dim vntDate As Variant
Dim intWeekDay As Integer
Dim strDayName As String
vntDate = #1/21/1999#
intWeekDay = Weekday(vntDate)
strDayName = WeekdayName(intWeekDay, False, vbSunday)
MsgBox strDayName
```

Example 3

Finally, this example displays a message box displaying the value "Fri." The day name is abbreviated because the WeekdayName function's second argument has been changed to True, which specifies an abbreviated name. The function is returning "Fri" rather than "Thu" because the third argument, which specifies the first day of the week, has been changed from vbSunday to vbMonday.

```
Dim vntDate As Variant
Dim intWeekDay As Integer
Dim strDayName As String
vntDate = #1/21/1999#
intWeekDay = Weekday(vntDate)
strDayName = WeekdayName(intWeekDay, True, vbMonday)
MsgBox strDayName
```

CROSS-REFERENCE
See also Date, Day, Month, Now, Weekday, and Year.

Weight

Property

The Weight property represents the weight of a Font object. A font's weight determines the boldness of the characters.

Objects with a Weight Property

Font

Syntax

```
Font.Weight = value1
```

or

```
value2 = Font.Weight
```

- *Font* — A reference to a Font object.
- *value1* — The new weight value.
- *value2* — The variable that will receive the property's current setting.

Example

The following program demonstrates a Font object's Weight property. When you run the program, you see the window shown in Figure W-1. By entering a value in the Weight text box and clicking the Set Weight button, you can change the displayed text between normal and bold. Note, however, that

Visual Basic supports only two font weights: 400 and 700. Visual Basic converts other values to one of these weights.

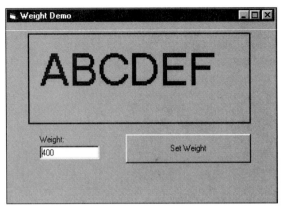

Figure W-1 By entering a weight value, you can change the displayed text between normal and bold.

```
VERSION 5.00
Begin VB.Form frmForm1
   Caption        =   "Weight Demo"
   ClientHeight   =   3840
   ClientLeft     =   60
   ClientTop      =   345
   ClientWidth    =   5940
   LinkTopic      =   "Form1"
   ScaleHeight    =   256
   ScaleMode      =   3  'Pixel
   ScaleWidth     =   396
   StartUpPosition =  3  'Windows Default
   Begin VB.CommandButton btnSetWeight
      Caption        =   "Set Weight"
      Height         =   615
      Left           =   2640
      TabIndex       =   3
      Top            =   2400
      Width          =   2775
   End
   Begin VB.TextBox txtWeight
      Height         =   285
      Left           =   720
      TabIndex       =   2
```

```
                   Top              =    2640
                   Width            =    1335
                End
                Begin VB.Shape shpShape1
                   Height           =    1935
                   Left             =    480
                   Top              =    240
                   Width            =    4935
                End
                Begin VB.Label Label1
                   Caption          =    "Weight:"
                   Height           =    255
                   Left             =    720
                   TabIndex         =    1
                   Top              =    2400
                   Width            =    735
                End
                Begin VB.Label lblSample
                   Caption          =    "Label1"
                   Height           =    1455
                   Left             =    720
                   TabIndex         =    0
                   Top              =    480
                   Width            =    4335
                End
             End
          End
          Attribute VB_Name = "frmForm1"
          Attribute VB_GlobalNameSpace = False
          Attribute VB_Creatable = False
          Attribute VB_PredeclaredId = True
          Attribute VB_Exposed = False

          Private Sub btnSetWeight_Click()
             Dim wght As Integer
             On Error GoTo ErrorHandler
             wght = txtWeight.Text
             lblSample.Font.Weight = wght
             Exit Sub

          ErrorHandler:
             MsgBox "Enter a valid weight.", _
                 vbExclamation, "Weight Demo"
          End Sub
```

```
Private Sub Form_Load()
    shpShape1.BorderWidth = 2
    lblSample.Caption = "ABCDEF"
    lblSample.Font.Size = 48
    txtWeight.Text = lblSample.Font.Weight
End Sub
```

 CROSS-REFERENCE
See also Bold and Font.

Wend

Keyword

The Wend keyword marks the end of a While loop, as shown in this example:

```
While something
    ' Do Something here.
Wend
```

 CROSS-REFERENCE
See also While.

WhatsThisButton

Property

The WhatsThisButton property represents whether a form displays a "What's This?" button, as shown in Figure W-2. A "What's This?" button enables you to get quick help about the objects displayed in some windows. Whether the form actually displays the button depends on the settings of the WhatsThisHelp, BorderStyle, MinButton, and MaxButton properties. Specifically, the WhatsThisHelp property must be True; the BorderStyle property must be vbFixedSingle, vbSizable, or vbFixedDouble; and the MinButton and MaxButton properties must be False. You should set these properties, including the WhatsThisButton property, in the form's Properties window at design time.

"What's This?" button

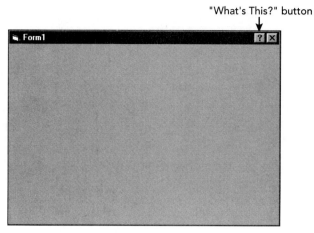

Figure W-2 A "What's This?" button enables you to get quick help on the objects displayed in some kinds of windows.

Objects with a WhatsThisButton Property

Form

Syntax

```
value = Form.WhatsThisButton
```

- *Form* — A reference to a Form object.
- *value* — The variable that will receive the property's current setting.

Example

The following lines show how to get the "What's This?" button status of a Form object.

```
Dim helpButton As Boolean
helpButton = frmForm.WhatsThisButton
```

CROSS-REFERENCE
See also BorderStyle, Form, MaxButton, MinButton, ShowWhatsThis, WhatsThisHelp, WhatsThisHelpID, and WhatsThisMode.

V
▶ W
X

WhatsThisHelp

Property

The `WhatsThisHelp` property represents whether an object supports context-sensitive help. You should set this property in the form's Properties window at design time. If `WhatsThisHelp` is `True`, the form can display help via a "What's This?" button or by calling the `WhatsThisMode` or `ShowWhatsThis` methods.

Objects with a WhatsThisHelp Property

Form

MDIForm

Syntax

```
value = Form.WhatsThisHelp
```

- *Form* — A reference to a Form object.
- *value* — The variable that will receive the property's current setting.

Example

The following lines show how to get the context-sensitive help status of a Form object.

```
Dim helpStatus As Boolean
helpStatus = frmForm.WhatsThisHelp
```

 CROSS-REFERENCE
See also Form, ShowWhatsThis, WhatsThisButton, WhatsThisHelpID, and WhatsThisMode.

WhatsThisHelpID

Property

The `WhatsThisHelpID` property represents an object's context-sensitive help topic ID number.

Objects with a WhatsThisHelpID Property

Animation

CheckBox

ComboBox

CommandButton

CoolBar

DirListBox

DriveListBox

FileListBox

Frame

HScrollBar

Image

Label

ListBox

ListView

OLE Container

OptionButton

PictureBox

ProgressBar

RichTextBox

Slider

StatusBar

TabStrip

TextBox

Toolbar

TreeView

UpDown

VScrollBar

Syntax

```
object.WhatsThisHelpID = value1
```

or

```
value2 = object.WhatsThisHelpID
```

- *object* — A reference to an object with a `WhatsThisHelpID` property.
- *value1* — The help topic ID for the object's context-sensitive help.
- *value2* — The variable that will receive the property's current setting.

Example

The following lines show how to get and set a CommandButton control's context-sensitive help ID (in this case, 1000). In this case, the `btnCommand1` object is a CommandButton control that the programmer added to the form at design time.

```
Dim helpID As Integer
helpID = btnCommand1.WhatsThisHelpID
btnCommand1.WhatsThisHelpID = 1000
```

CROSS-REFERENCE
See also ShowWhatsThis, WhatsThisButton, WhatsThisHelp, and WhatsThisMode.

WhatsThisMode

Method

The `WhatsThisMode` method triggers the same process as when you click on a "What's This?" button. That is, the mouse cursor changes to the "What's This?" cursor, as shown in Figure W-3. This enables you to click on an item to get context-sensitive help.

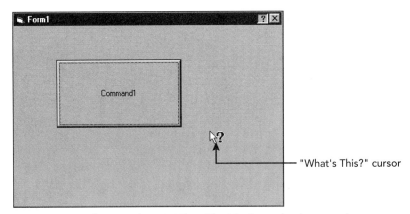

Figure W-3 Calling an object's WhatsThisMode method causes the mouse cursor to change to the "What's This?" cursor.

Objects with a WhatsThisMode Method

Form

MDIForm

Syntax

```
object.WhatsThisMode
```

- *object* — A reference to a Form or MDIForm object.

Example

The following line puts a Form object into the "What's This?" mode.

```
frmForm1.WhatsThisMode
```

 CROSS-REFERENCE
See also Form, MDIForm, ShowWhatsThis, WhatsThisButton, WhatsThisHelp, and WhatsThisHelpID.

While

Statement

A `While` loop repeats a block of statements until the Boolean control expression becomes `False`.

Syntax

```
While control
    bodyStatements
Wend
```

- *bodyStatements* — The statements that are to be executed as long as *control* evaluates to `True`.
- *control* — A Boolean expression whose value determines whether the loop continues. A result of `False` ends the loop.

Example

In this example, the `While` loop displays ten message boxes one at a time. When the variable `counter` reaches the value 10, the loop stops because the result of the loop's control expression is `False`.

```
Dim counter As Integer
counter = 0
While counter < 10
    counter = counter + 1
    MsgBox counter
Wend
```

CROSS-REFERENCE
See also Do.

Width

Property

The Width property represents the width of a control or object. Except for the Form, Printer, Screen, and Picture objects, the value of the Width property depends on the setting of the control container's ScaleMode property. That is, a CommandButton control's width is measured in pixels, for example, if the container's ScaleMode property is set to pixels. The Form, Printer, and Screen objects always return Width values in twips, whereas the Picture object returns HiMetric measurements. The Printer object returns the width of a page, and the Screen object returns the width of the screen.

Objects with a Width Property

CheckBox

ComboBox

CommandButton

DirListBox

DriveListBox

FileListBox

Form

Frame

HScrollBar

Image

Label

ListBox

MDIForm

OLE Container

OptionButton

Picture

PictureBox

Printer

PropertyPage

Screen

Shape
TextBox
UserControl
VScrollBar

Syntax

```
object.Width = value1
```

or

```
value2 = object.Width
```

- *object* — A reference to a control or object with a `Width` property.
- *value1* — The object's new width setting. (Not all objects can be resized.)
- *value2* — The variable that will receive the control or object's current width.

Example

In this example, the program sets the width (which is 1500) of a CommandButton control. The `btnCommand1` object is a CommandButton control that the programmer added to the application's form at design time.

```
btnCommand1.Width = 1500
```

 CROSS-REFERENCE
See also Height, Left, and Top.

Windowless

Property

The `Windowless` property represents whether a UserControl object gets a window handle. A value of `True` yields a UserControl object with no window handle. A value of `False` yields a UserControl object with a window handle. You must set this property in the UserControl object's Properties window at design time. The property is unavailable at runtime.

Objects with a Windowless Property

UserControl

CROSS-REFERENCE
See also UserControl.

WindowList

Property

The WindowList property represents whether a Menu object has a list of MDI child windows. This property can be set only at design time using the Menu editor, as shown in Figure W-4. Note that only one menu can have a WindowList property set to True.

The Window List property

Figure W-4 You set the WindowList property when creating menus with the Menu editor.

Objects with a WindowList Property

Menu

Syntax

```
value = Menu.WindowList
```

- *Menu*—A reference to a Menu object.
- *value*—The variable that will receive the property's current setting of True or False.

Example

The following program demonstrates how the WindowList property enables a menu to track the currently open MDI child window. (The first listing is the main MDI window, and the second listing is the MDI child window.) When you run the program, create a few windows using the File menu's Open command. Then, look at the Windows menu. Each window you created will be listed there. By clicking an entry in the Windows menu, you can jump to any open window. Figure W-5 shows the program with four child windows.

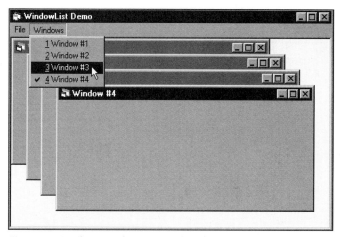

Figure W-5 This Windows menu has four MDI child windows.

```
VERSION 5.00
Begin VB.MDIForm MDIForm1
    BackColor       =   &H80000018&
    Caption         =   "WindowList Demo"
    ClientHeight    =   4380
    ClientLeft      =   165
    ClientTop       =   735
    ClientWidth     =   7080
    LinkTopic       =   "MDIForm1"
    StartUpPosition =   3   'Windows Default
    Begin VB.Menu mnuFile
        Caption         =   "File"
```

```
        Begin VB.Menu mnuOpen
            Caption         =      "Open"
        End
    End
    Begin VB.Menu mnuWindows
        Caption         =      "Windows"
        WindowList      =      -1  'True
    End
End
Attribute VB_Name = "MDIForm1"
Attribute VB_GlobalNameSpace = False
Attribute VB_Creatable = False
Attribute VB_PredeclaredId = True
Attribute VB_Exposed = False

Private wndCount As Integer

Private Sub MDIForm_Load()
    wndCount = 0
End Sub

Private Sub mnuOpen_Click()
    Dim childForm As New Form1
    wndCount = wndCount + 1
    childForm.Caption = "Window #" & wndCount
    childForm.Show
End Sub

VERSION 5.00
Begin VB.Form Form1
    Caption         =      "Form1"
    ClientHeight    =      3195
    ClientLeft      =      60
    ClientTop       =      345
    ClientWidth     =      4680
    LinkTopic       =      "Form1"
    MDIChild        =      -1  'True
    ScaleHeight     =      3195
    ScaleWidth      =      4680
End
Attribute VB_Name = "Form1"
Attribute VB_GlobalNameSpace = False
Attribute VB_Creatable = False
```

```
Attribute VB_PredeclaredId = True
Attribute VB_Exposed = False
```

CROSS-REFERENCE
See also MDI Form.

WindowState

Property

The WindowState property represents the state of a window. Setting this property also sets the window's visible state. For example, setting a window's WindowState property to vbMinimized minimizes the window.

Objects with a WindowState Property

Form

MDIForm

Syntax

object.WindowState = *value1*

or

value2 = *object*.WindowState

- *object* — A reference to a Form or MDIForm object.
- *value1* — The value vbNormal, vbMinimized, or vbMaximized.
- *value2* — The variable that will receive the property's current setting.

Example

The following lines show how to get and set a Form object's WindowState property. In this case, the window is maximized.

```
Dim wndState As Integer
wndState = frmForm1.WindowState
frmForm1.WindowState = vbMaximized
```

CROSS-REFERENCE
See also Form, MDIForm, and Resize.

With

Statement

The With statement enables a program to perform a block of statements on an object without having to specify the object's name continually.

Syntax

```
With object
    bodyStatements
End With
```

- *object* — The object on which to perform the statements.
- *bodyStatements* — The statements to perform on the *object*.

Example

The following lines add five items to a ListView control. The lvwListView1 object is a ListView control that the programmer added to the form at design time.

```
With lvwListView1.ListItems
    .Add , , "Item #1"
    .Add , , "Item #2"
    .Add , , "Item #3"
    .Add , , "Item #4"
    .Add , , "Item #5"
End With
```

WithEvents

Keyword

The WithEvents keyword enables a program to declare objects that respond to events. For example, the following line declares a variable of a custom class called EventSource.

```
Private WithEvents eventSrc As EventSource
```

CROSS-REFERENCE
See also Dim, Private, and Public.

WordWrap

Property

The WordWrap property represents whether a Label control can expand vertically to contain its text. For this property to have an effect, the AutoSize property must be set to True.

Objects with a WordWrap Property

Label

Syntax

```
Label.WordWrap = value1
```

or

```
value2 = Label.WordWrap
```

- *Label*—A reference to a Label control.
- *value1*—The value True or False.
- *value2*—The variable that will receive the property's current setting.

Example

The following lines show how to get and set the value of a Label control's WordWrap property. The lblLabel1 object is a Label control that the programmer added to the form at design time. In this case, the Autosize property is set to True.

```
Dim wrap As Boolean
wrap = lblLabel1.WordWrap
lblLabel1.AutoSize = True
lblLabel1.WordWrap = True
```

CROSS-REFERENCE
See also AutoSize and Label.

V

▶ W

X

WorkAreaHeight

Property

The WorkAreaHeight property represents the height of the screen's work area, which is the height of the screen minus any space consumed by the taskbar. You use the WorkAreaHeight property in conjunction with the WorkAreaWidth, WorkAreaTop, and WorkAreaLeft properties to size and position a window such that the window fills the work area without covering the taskbar.

Objects with a WorkAreaHeight Property

SysInfo

Syntax

```
value = SysInfo.WorkAreaHeight
```

- *SysInfo* — A reference to a SysInfo control.
- *value* — The variable that will receive the work-area height.

Example

The following lines show how to size and position a window so that the taskbar — no matter its size or position — stays uncovered. The SysInfo1 object is a SysInfo control that the programmer added to the form at design time.

```
Private Sub Form_Load()
    frmForm1.Top = SysInfo1.WorkAreaTop
    frmForm1.Left = SysInfo1.WorkAreaLeft
    frmForm1.Height = SysInfo1.WorkAreaHeight
    frmForm1.Width = SysInfo1.WorkAreaWidth
End Sub
```

 CROSS-REFERENCE
See also SysInfo, WorkAreaLeft, WorkAreaTop, and WorkAreaWidth.

WorkAreaLeft

Property

The WorkAreaLeft property represents the left edge of the screen's work area, which depends on the position of the taskbar. You use the WorkAreaLeft property in conjunction with the WorkAreaWidth, WorkAreaHeight, and WorkAreaTop properties to size and position a window such that the window fills the work area without covering the taskbar.

Objects with a WorkAreaLeft Property

SysInfo

Syntax

```
value = SysInfo.WorkAreaLeft
```

- *SysInfo*—A reference to a SysInfo control.
- *value*—The variable that will receive the work-area left edge.

Example

The following lines show how to size and position a window so that the taskbar—no matter its size or position—stays uncovered. The `SysInfo1` object is a SysInfo control that the programmer added to the form at design time.

```
Private Sub Form_Load()
    frmForm1.Top = SysInfo1.WorkAreaTop
    frmForm1.Left = SysInfo1.WorkAreaLeft
    frmForm1.Height = SysInfo1.WorkAreaHeight
    frmForm1.Width = SysInfo1.WorkAreaWidth
End Sub
```

CROSS-REFERENCE
See also SysInfo, WorkAreaHeight, WorkAreaTop, and WorkAreaWidth.

WorkAreaTop

Property

The `WorkAreaTop` property represents the top edge of the screen's work area, which depends on the position of the taskbar. You use the `WorkAreaTop` property in conjunction with the `WorkAreaWidth`, `WorkAreaHeight`, and `WorkAreaLeft` properties to size and position a window such that the window fills the work area without covering the taskbar.

Objects with a WorkAreaTop Property

SysInfo

Syntax

```
value = SysInfo.WorkAreaTop
```

- *SysInfo*—A reference to a SysInfo control.
- *value*—The variable that will receive the work-area top edge.

Example

The following lines show how to size and position a window so that the taskbar—no matter its size or position—stays uncovered. The `SysInfo1` object is a SysInfo control that the programmer added to the form at design time.

```
Private Sub Form_Load()
    frmForm1.Top = SysInfo1.WorkAreaTop
    frmForm1.Left = SysInfo1.WorkAreaLeft
    frmForm1.Height = SysInfo1.WorkAreaHeight
    frmForm1.Width = SysInfo1.WorkAreaWidth
End Sub
```

CROSS-REFERENCE
See also SysInfo, WorkAreaHeight, WorkAreaLeft, and WorkAreaWidth.

WorkAreaWidth

Property

The `WorkAreaWidth` property represents the width of the screen's work area, which is the width of the screen minus any space consumed by the taskbar. You use the `WorkAreaWidth` property in conjunction with the `WorkAreaHeight`, `WorkAreaTop`, and `WorkAreaLeft` properties to size and position a window such that the window fills the work area without covering the taskbar.

Objects with a WorkAreaWidth Property

SysInfo

Syntax

```
value = SysInfo.WorkAreaWidth
```

- *SysInfo* — A reference to a SysInfo control.
- *value* — The variable that will receive the work-area width.

Example

The following lines show how to size and position a window so that the taskbar — no matter its size or position — stays uncovered. The `SysInfo1` object is a SysInfo control that the programmer added to the form at design time.

```
Private Sub Form_Load()
    frmForm1.Top = SysInfo1.WorkAreaTop
    frmForm1.Left = SysInfo1.WorkAreaLeft
    frmForm1.Height = SysInfo1.WorkAreaHeight
    frmForm1.Width = SysInfo1.WorkAreaWidth
End Sub
```

CROSS-REFERENCE
See also SysInfo, WorkAreaHeight, WorkAreaLeft, and WorkAreaTop.

Wrap

Property

The `Wrap` property represents whether the value of an UpDown control wraps around from its maximum value to its minimum value or vice versa.

Objects with a Wrap Property

UpDown

Syntax

```
UpDown.Wrap = value1
```

or

```
value2 = UpDown.Wrap
```

- *UpDown* — A reference to an UpDown control.
- *value1* — The value `True` or `False`.
- *value2* — The variable that will receive the property's current setting.

Example

The following lines show how to get and set the value of an UpDown control's `Wrap` property. The `updUpDown1` object is an UpDown control that the programmer added to the form at design time.

```
Dim boolWrap As Boolean
boolWrap = updUpDown1.Wrap
updUpDown1.Wrap = True
```

CROSS-REFERENCE
See also Max, Min, UpDown, and Value.

Wrappable

Property

The `Wrappable` property represents whether a Toolbar control's buttons wrap around when the user resizes the window and thus the toolbar. Figure W-6 shows an application with a full-width, simple toolbar, whereas Figure W-7 shows what happens to the toolbar's buttons when the Toolbar control's `Wrappable` property is set to `True` (which is the default) and the user reduces the size of the window. If the `Wrappable` property is set to `False`, and the user reduces the width of the window, buttons to the right fall out of view.

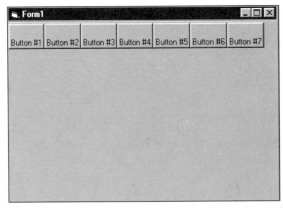

Figure W-6 This application displays a full-width toolbar.

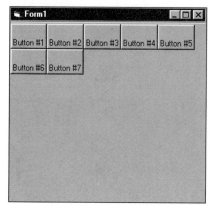

Figure W-7 This application displays a wrapped toolbar.

Objects with a Wrappable Property

Toolbar

Syntax

```
Toolbar.Wrappable = value1
```

or

```
value2 = Toolbar.Wrappable
```

- *Toolbar*—A reference to a Toolbar control.
- *value1*—The value True or False.
- *value2*—The variable that will receive the property's current setting.

Example

The following lines show how to get and set the value of a Toolbar control's Wrappable property. The tlbToolbar1 object is a Toolbar control that the programmer added to the form at design time.

```
Dim boolWrap As Boolean
boolWrap = tlbToolbar1.Wrappable
tlbToolbar1.Wrappable = True
```

CROSS-REFERENCE
See also Toolbar.

Write

Method

The Write method writes text to the file associated with a TextStream object.

Objects with a Write Method

TextStream

Syntax

`TextStream.Write(str)`

- *TextStream* — A reference to a TextStream object.
- *str* — A string containing the text to write to the file.

Example

The following lines create a FileSystemObject, through which the program creates a TextStream object. The program then calls the TextStream object's Write method to write text to the file.

```
Dim fileStream As Object
Dim fileSystem As Object
Set fileSystem = CreateObject("Scripting.FileSystemObject")
Set fileStream = fileSystem.CreateTextFile("c:\MyText.txt")
fileStream.Write ("This is a test")
fileStream.Close
```

CROSS-REFERENCE

See also Close, FileSystemObject, Read, ReadAll, ReadLine, TextStream, WriteBlankLines, and WriteLine.

Write

Statement

The Write statement writes one or more values to a file that was opened with the Open statement. Multiple values can be written, with Write automatically placing delimiters (commas) between the values as written to the file. The Write statement also places string values within quotes.

Syntax

```
Write #fileNum, values
```

- *fileNum* — The file number assigned to the file by the `Open` statement.
- *values* (*) — One or more comma-delimited values to be written to the file. Leaving off this argument causes `Write` to write a blank line to the file.

(*) = Optional

Example 1

The following lines write a text string to a file.

```
Open "c:\MyFile.dat" For Output As #1
Write #1, "This is a test"
Close #1
```

Example 2

Here, the following lines write an integer value, a Boolean value, and a text string to a file. The data that appears in the file looks like this: `156,#TRUE#,"This is a test."`

```
Dim var1 As Integer
Dim var2 As Boolean
Dim var3 As String
var1 = 156
var2 = True
var3 = "This is a test."
Open "c:\MyFile.dat" For Output As #1
Write #1, var1, var2, var3
Close #1
```

 CROSS-REFERENCE
See also Close, Input, Open, and Print.

WriteBlankLines

Method

The `WriteBlankLines` method writes blank lines to the file associated with a TextStream object.

Objects with a WriteBlankLines Method
TextStream

Syntax

TextStream.WriteBlankLines(*numLines*)

- *numLines* — The number of blank lines to write to the file.
- *TextStream* — A reference to a TextStream object.

Example

The following lines create a FileSystemObject, through which the program creates a TextStream object. The program then calls the TextStream object's WriteBlankLines method to write five blank lines to the file.

```
Dim fileStream As Object
Dim fileSystem As Object
Set fileSystem = CreateObject("Scripting.FileSystemObject")
Set fileStream = fileSystem.CreateTextFile("c:\MyText.txt")
fileStream.WriteBlankLines (5)
fileStream.Close
```

CROSS-REFERENCE

See also Close, FileSystemObject, Read, ReadAll, ReadLine, TextStream, Write (method), and WriteLine.

WriteLine

Method

The WriteLine method writes a line of text followed by a newline character to the file associated with a TextStream object.

Objects with a WriteLine Method
TextStream

Syntax

TextStream.WriteLine(*str*)

- *str*—A string containing the text to write to the file. If this argument is not supplied, the method writes a blank line to the file.
- *TextStream*—A reference to a TextStream object.

Example

The following lines create a FileSystemObject, through which the program creates a TextStream object. The program then calls the TextStream object's `WriteLine` method to write text to the file.

```
Dim fileStream As Object
Dim fileSystem As Object
Set fileSystem = CreateObject("Scripting.FileSystemObject")
Set fileStream = fileSystem.CreateTextFile("c:\MyText.txt")
fileStream.WriteLine ("This is a test.")
fileStream.Close
```

CROSS-REFERENCE
See also Close, FileSystemObject, Read, ReadAll, ReadLine, TextStream, Write (method), and WriteBlankLines.

WriteProperties

Event

Visual Basic sends an object a `WriteProperties` event when the object must save its properties.

Objects with a WriteProperties Event

Class
UserControl

Example

A program can respond to a `WriteProperties` event by implementing the object's `WriteProperties` event procedure. The following code segment shows how a UserControl control defines a `WriteProperties` event procedure. As you can see in the procedure's declaration, the procedure receives one parameter, which is a PropertyBag object that provides access to the saved property values. The program reads the property values by calling the PropertyBag object's `ReadProperty` method.

```
Private Sub UserControl_WriteProperties _
  (PropBag As PropertyBag)
    PropBag.WriteProperty "MyProperty", _
        strValue, "Default Value"
End Sub
```

CROSS-REFERENCE
See also ReadProperties, ReadProperty, UserControl, and WriteProperty.

WriteProperty

Method

The `WriteProperty` method saves the value of a changed property.

Objects with a WriteProperty Method

PropertyBag

Syntax

`PropertyBag.WriteProperty name, value, default`

- *default* (*) — The default value for the property. If the value of the property is identical to the default, the method does not save the property.
- *name* — The name of the property to save.
- *PropertyBag* — A reference to a PropertyBag object.
- *value* — The variable that contains the value for the property.

(*) = Optional

Example

The following code segment shows how a UserControl control defines a `WriteProperties` event procedure, which uses the `WriteProperty` method to store the value of several properties.

```
Private Sub UserControl_WriteProperties _
  (PropBag As PropertyBag)
    PropBag.WriteProperty "MyStrProperty", _
```

```
         strValue, "Default Value"
     PropBag.WriteProperty "MyIntProperty", _
         intValue, 0
     PropBag.ReadProperty "MyColorProperty", clrValue, _
         RGB(255, 255, 255)
End Sub
```

 CROSS-REFERENCE
See also ReadProperties, ReadProperty, UserControl, and WriteProperties.

Xor

Operator

The Xor operator performs a Boolean comparison between two expressions, returning True if only one of the compared expressions is True. That is, unlike the Or operator, if both compared expressions are True, Xor returns False.

Syntax

```
result = exp1 Xor exp2
```

- *exp1* — Any valid expression.
- *exp2* — Any valid expression.
- *result* — The Boolean result of the operation.

Example 1

After the following lines execute, result will contain the value True. In this example, only one of the compared expressions is True.

```
Dim expr1, expr2 As Integer
Dim result As Boolean
expr1 = 10
expr2 = 25
result = (expr1 = 10) Xor (expr2 = 10)
```

Example 2

Here, after the following lines execute, result will contain the value False. In this example, neither of the compared expressions is True.

```
Dim expr1, expr2 As Integer
Dim result As Boolean
expr1 = 10
expr2 = 25
result = (expr1 = 30) Xor (expr2 = 10)
```

Example 3

Finally, after the following lines execute, `result` will contain the value `False`. In this example, both of the compared expressions are `True`.

```
Dim expr1, expr2 As Integer
Dim result As Boolean
expr1 = 10
expr2 = 25
result = (expr1 = 10) Xor (expr2 = 25)
```

CROSS-REFERENCE
See also And and Or.

Year

Function

The Year function returns the year part of a date.

Syntax

```
value = Year(date)
```

- *date* — The date from which to get the year.
- *value* — The variable that will receive the year.

Example

The following lines display the message "Year #1998" in a message box.

```
Dim dtmDate As Date
Dim yearPart As Integer
dtmDate = DateValue("March 17, 1998")
yearPart = Year(dtmDate)
MsgBox "Year #" & yearPart
```

CROSS-REFERENCE
See also Date (function), Date (keyword), Date (statement), DateAdd, DateDiff, DatePart, DateSerial, DateValue, and Day.

Zoom

Property

The Zoom property represents the amount of scaling to be performed on printer output.

Objects with a Zoom Property

Printer

Syntax

```
Printer.Zoom = value1
```

or

```
value2 = Printer.Zoom
```

- *Printer* — A reference to the Printer object.
- *value1* — The percentage by which to zoom the output. For example, 50 reduces the size of the output by one half, whereas 200 doubles the size of the output.
- *value2* — The variable that will receive the property's current setting.

Example

The following lines show how to get and set the value of the Printer object's Zoom property. The Printer object is a global Visual Basic object that you don't need to create in your programs.

```
Dim scaleValue As Integer
scaleValue = Printer.Zoom
Printer.Zoom = 75
```

 **CROSS-REFERENCE**
See also Printer.

ZOrder

Method

The ZOrder method sets the z-order (front-to-back arrangement) of objects.

Objects with a ZOrder Method

Animation
CheckBox
ComboBox
CommandButton
DirListBox
DriveListBox
FileListBox
Form
Frame
HScrollBar
Image
Label
ListBox
ListView
MDIForm
OLE Container
OptionButton
PictureBox
ProgressBar
RichTextBox
Shape
Slider
StatusBar
TabStrip
TextBox
Toolbar
TreeView
UpDown
VScrollBar

Syntax

```
object.ZOrder(value)
```

- *object*—A reference to an object with a ZOrder method.
- *value*—The new z-order.

Example

The following program demonstrates the ZOrder method. When you run the program, you see the window shown in Figure Z-1. What you don't see is the TextBox control that's hidden under the Frame control. Click the Toggle Z-Order button to place the Frame control in the bottom of the z-order, and the TextBox control appears, as shown in Figure Z-2.

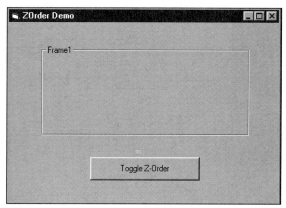

Figure Z-1 A Frame control hides a TextBox control.

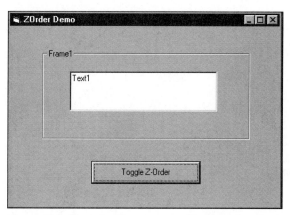

Figure Z-2 Now, the Frame control is placed to the bottom of the z-order, which reveals the TextBox control.

```
VERSION 5.00
Begin VB.Form frmForm1
   Caption         =   "ZOrder Demo"
   ClientHeight    =   3840
   ClientLeft      =   60
   ClientTop       =   345
   ClientWidth     =   5940
   LinkTopic       =   "Form1"
   ScaleHeight     =   256
   ScaleMode       =   3   'Pixel
   ScaleWidth      =   396
   StartUpPosition =   3   'Windows Default
   Begin VB.CommandButton btnToggleZOrder
      Caption         =   "Toggle Z-Order"
      Height          =   495
      Left            =   1800
      TabIndex        =   2
      Top             =   2880
      Width           =   2415
   End
   Begin VB.Frame frmFrame1
      Caption         =   "Frame1"
      Height          =   1935
      Left            =   720
      TabIndex        =   1
      Top             =   480
      Width           =   4575
   End
   Begin VB.TextBox Text1
      Height          =   855
      Left            =   1320
      TabIndex        =   0
      Text            =   "Text1"
      Top             =   960
      Width           =   3255
   End
End
Attribute VB_Name = "frmForm1"
Attribute VB_GlobalNameSpace = False
Attribute VB_Creatable = False
Attribute VB_PredeclaredId = True
Attribute VB_Exposed = False

Private z As Integer
```

```
Private Sub btnToggleZOrder_Click()
    If z = 0 Then
        frmFrame1.ZOrder (1)
        z = 1
    Else
        frmFrame1.ZOrder (0)
        z = 0
    End If
End Sub

Private Sub Form_Load()
    z = 0
End Sub
```

x
y
z

The CD-ROM that accompanies this book contains all the sample programs described in each chapter. These programs are organized into directories that are named after the chapters. That is, you can find the programs mentioned in Chapter A in the A folder, the programs mentioned in Chapter B in the B folder, and so on. (Note that not every chapter contains a sample program.) This appendix lists the CD-ROM's entire contents so you can quickly find the programs you want to study.

Each program on the CD-ROM includes not only the source code but also all the project files generated by Visual Basic. To experiment with any program under Visual Basic, copy the appropriate program directory to your hard drive and then double-click the program's .vbp file to load the project into Visual Basic. You can then modify the source code, compile the program, or do whatever you like with the project.

Please note that after you copy files from the CD-ROM to your hard drive, you'll need to turn off the read-only attribute on any files you plan to modify. (You won't need to do this if you install the entire CD-ROM contents as described in the installation instruction at the very end of this book.) Visual Basic cannot save modified files until you make the files editable. To turn off the read-only attribute on a set of files (after copying them to your hard drive), highlight the files in Windows Explorer and right-click the group. Then, select the Properties command from the context menu, and turn off the Read-Only checkbox in the property sheet that appears.

CD-ROM Contents

The following is a list of all the programs included on this book's CD-ROM. The list includes the chapter directory names, as well as the names of program directories inside each chapter directory. Each program directory contains the source code, project files, and any additional files needed for the specific program.

IDG Books Worldwide, Inc. End-User License Agreement

READ THIS. You should carefully read these terms and conditions before opening the software packet(s) included with this book ("Book"). This is a license agreement ("Agreement") between you and IDG Books Worldwide, Inc. ("IDGB"). By opening the accompanying software packet(s), you acknowledge that you have read and accept the following terms and conditions. If you do not agree and do not want to be bound by such terms and conditions, promptly return the Book and the unopened software packet(s) to the place you obtained them for a full refund.

1. **License Grant.** IDGB grants to you (either an individual or entity) a nonexclusive license to use one copy of the enclosed software program(s) (collectively, the "Software") solely for your own personal or business purposes on a single computer (whether a standard computer or a workstation component of a multiuser network). The Software is in use on a computer when it is loaded into temporary memory (RAM) or installed into permanent memory (hard disk, CD-ROM, or other storage device). IDGB reserves all rights not expressly granted herein.

2. **Ownership.** IDGB is the owner of all right, title, and interest, including copyright, in and to the compilation of the Software recorded on the disk(s) or CD-ROM ("Software Media"). Copyright to the individual programs recorded on the Software Media is owned by the author or other authorized copyright owner of each program. Ownership of the Software and all proprietary rights relating thereto remain with IDGB and its licensers.

3. **Restrictions On Use and Transfer.**

   (a) You may only (i) make one copy of the Software for backup or archival purposes, or (ii) transfer the Software to a single hard disk, provided that you keep the original for backup or archival purposes. You may not (i) rent or lease the Software, (ii) copy or reproduce the Software through a LAN or other network system or through any computer subscriber system or bulletin-board system, or (iii) modify, adapt, or create derivative works based on the Software.

   (b) You may not reverse engineer, decompile, or disassemble the Software. You may transfer the Software and user documentation on a permanent basis, provided that the transferee agrees to accept the terms and conditions of this Agreement and you retain no copies. If the Software is an update or has been updated, any transfer must include the most recent update and all prior versions.

4. **Restrictions On Use of Individual Programs.** You must follow the individual requirements and restrictions detailed for each individual program in the appendix of this Book. These limitations are also contained in the individual license agreements recorded on the Software Media. These limitations may include a requirement that after using the program for a specified period of time, the user must pay a registration fee or discontinue use. By opening the Software packet(s), you will be agreeing to abide by the licenses and restrictions for these individual programs that are detailed in the appendix and on the Software Media. None of the material on this Software Media or listed in this Book may ever be redistributed, in original or modified form, for commercial purposes.

5. **Limited Warranty.**

   (a) IDGB warrants that the Software and Software Media are free from defects in materials and workmanship under normal use for a period of sixty (60) days from the date of purchase of this Book. If IDGB receives notification within the warranty period of defects in materials or workmanship, IDGB will replace the defective Software Media.

   (b) **IDGB AND THE AUTHOR OF THE BOOK DISCLAIM ALL OTHER WARRANTIES, EXPRESS OR IMPLIED, INCLUDING WITHOUT LIMITATION IMPLIED WARRANTIES OF MERCHANTABILITY AND FITNESS FOR A PARTICULAR PURPOSE, WITH RESPECT TO THE SOFTWARE, THE PROGRAMS, THE SOURCE CODE CONTAINED THEREIN, AND/OR THE TECHNIQUES DESCRIBED IN THIS BOOK. IDGB DOES NOT WARRANT THAT THE FUNCTIONS CONTAINED IN THE SOFTWARE WILL MEET YOUR REQUIREMENTS OR THAT THE OPERATION OF THE SOFTWARE WILL BE ERROR FREE.**

   (c) This limited warranty gives you specific legal rights, and you may have other rights that vary from jurisdiction to jurisdiction.

6. **Remedies.**

   (a) IDGB's entire liability and your exclusive remedy for defects in materials and workmanship shall be limited to replacement of the Software Media, which may be returned to IDGB with a copy of your receipt at the following address: Software Media Fulfillment

Department, Attn.: *Visual Basic® 6 Master Reference*, IDG Books Worldwide, Inc., 7260 Shadeland Station, Ste. 100, Indianapolis, IN 46256, or call 1-800-762-2974. Please allow three to four weeks for delivery. This Limited Warranty is void if failure of the Software Media has resulted from accident, abuse, or misapplication. Any replacement Software Media will be warranted for the remainder of the original warranty period or thirty (30) days, whichever is longer.

(b) In no event shall IDGB or the author be liable for any damages whatsoever (including without limitation damages for loss of business profits, business interruption, loss of business information, or any other pecuniary loss) arising from the use of or inability to use the Book or the Software, even if IDGB has been advised of the possibility of such damages.

(c) Because some jurisdictions do not allow the exclusion or limitation of liability for consequential or incidental damages, the above limitation or exclusion may not apply to you.

7. **U.S. Government Restricted Rights.** Use, duplication, or disclosure of the Software by the U.S. Government is subject to restrictions stated in paragraph (c)(1)(ii) of the Rights in Technical Data and Computer Software clause of DFARS 252.227-7013, and in subparagraphs (a) through (d) of the Commercial Computer— Restricted Rights clause at FAR 52.227-19, and in similar clauses in the NASA FAR supplement, when applicable.

8. **General.** This Agreement constitutes the entire understanding of the parties and revokes and supersedes all prior agreements, oral or written, between them and may not be modified or amended except in a writing signed by both parties hereto that specifically refers to this Agreement. This Agreement shall take precedence over any other documents that may be in conflict herewith. If any one or more provisions contained in this Agreement are held by any court or tribunal to be invalid, illegal, or otherwise unenforceable, each and every other provision shall remain in full force and effect.

CD-ROM Installation Instructions

The CD-ROM that accompanies this book includes a batch file for transferring all the files on the CD-ROM to your hard drive. To transfer the files, perform the following steps:

1. Place the CD-ROM in your CD-ROM drive.
2. In Windows, select Start and then the Run command. The Run dialog box appears.
3. In the dialog box's Open box, type **x:\install x y**, where **x** is the letter for your CD-ROM drive and **y** is the destination drive. (Don't add colons to the drive letters.) For example, if your CD-ROM drive is drive D, and you want to copy the CD-ROM's files to drive C, you would type **d:\install d c** into the Run dialog box's Open box.
4. A DOS window appears, in which you can watch the batch file copy the CD-ROM's files to your destination drive.

After the file copying is complete, the book's program files will be available in the VBMRef directory on your destination drive.